Delights from the Garden of Eden

A Cookbook and a History of the Iraqi Cuisine

Nawal Nasrallah

ISBN: 1-4033-4792-1 (e-book)
ISBN: 1-4033-4793-X (Paperback)

This book is printed on acid free paper.

Photography: Nawal Nasrallah, unless otherwise credited.
Arabic Calligraphy: Shakir Mustafa

1stBooks — rev. 10/18/04

*In loving memory of
my son Bilal,
who has been the inspiration
behind this project all along.*

Apology

Considering the hardships that Iraq has been going through for more than a decade, some might think that this is not be the right time to write about food. But as a wife, a mother, a woman, and a human being, I find in food and in memories of food my refuge, my comfort and consolation when things are not looking good, as they say here. My sympathies go to Naomi Shihab Nye, an Arab American writer, who wrote,

> Nor can I forget the journalist in Dubai who called me a donkey for talking about vegetables when there was injustice in the world.
>
> *I can talk about sumac too.* When a friend asks what's that purple spice in the little shake-up jar at the Persian restaurant, tears cloud my eyes.
>
> *Is it good for you?*
>
> Are vegetables, in some indelible way, smarter than we are? Are animals?
>
> ("Long Overdue")

Maybe it would make Naomi feel a little bit better if she knows that the donkey is the most patient and most sensitive creature in the world. The sight of a bereaved mother donkey banging her head hard against the wall is the most touching sight that man can ever see.

Acknowledgments

I am deeply indebted to my family for their unwavering support. The encouragement and advice my husband, Shakir Mustafa, has always provided were indispensable. My daughter and son, Iba and Shamam, and my daughter-in-law, Andrea, obliged me with their readiness to taste and comment on the dishes. I appreciate their tactfulness when in my enthusiasm I sometimes went overboard.

My friends, both in Indiana and Boston, showed sustained interest in the project the past six years. They opened their hearts and homes for me, and their invaluable suggestions are very much appreciated.

I would like to thank Carol Christiansen, Permission Manager of Random house, Charles Kline of the Photographic Archives at the University of Pennsylvania Museum, Ali Zayni of iraqiart.com, Jim Eisenbraun, publisher, and my friends Amal and Salih Altoma for their support.

My deepest sympathies are with all the Iraqi mothers who must find it hard these days to put food on the table. Innovative as they are, they will nonetheless come up with a treat to cheer up their families, simple yet delicious.

Last but not least, my deepest gratitude is to the creators of this wonderful cuisine through the centuries, especially those who started it--the ancient Mesopotamian *nuhatimmus* (Akkadian for "cooks").

بالعافيه

Contents

List of Boxes

INTRODUCTION
IRAQI COOKING IN PERSPECTIVE

INTRODUCTION

Iraqi Cooking in Perspective

He who eats too much will not (be able to) sleep.

A Sumerian Proverb, ca 3500 BC (Gordon, 97)

That Little Street in Baghdad

As a crossroad for several eastern and western cultures, Iraq had the ingredients for a multiracial society. Nowhere this pluralistic culture is more evident than in the little street in Baghdad where I grew up. It was a middle-class neighborhood, with eucalyptus trees lining both sides of the street, and in the springtime the whole neighborhood would be infused with the intoxicating aroma of the blossoms of citrus trees planted all along the fences. Those shady places were like magnets for the neighborhood kids, where we used to play, fight, reconcile, tell stories, and chatter about everything and anything. As lunchtime approached, the time for the main meal of the day, we started playing our guessing game as the pleasant and most welcome aromas of food sneaked out of the simmering pots, and meandered along our street. We would sniff these floating aromas and guess whose mom is cooking what for that day. Although the dominant aroma would be that of stew and rice, cooked practically everyday, the guessing would still be intriguing for there were so many kinds of stews to guess at. And almost always there would be a single distinctive aroma of a special dish, and we knew that one of us would soon be called by his or her mom to distribute samplings of that dish for the neighbors. As the custom had always been, it was not fit to return the neighbor's dish empty, so it would be returned with a comparable dish that is equally if not more delicious. Thus our guessing game was kept alive by this exchange of hospitality, and from those little dishes coming and going we came to learn a lot about people coming from all walks of life, and of diverse ethnic and religious backgrounds. Such diversity was not a unique situation in the city of Baghdad, which across the centuries became a melting pot of sorts for all these groups.

My maternal grandparents owned some date palm groves in southern Iraq, and my mother and her siblings, as she always liked to reminisce, led a carefree childhood in the midst of these date groves, chasing the sheep and goats, and stealing a sip or two of milk right from the dugs of the goats when grown ups were not watching. She was brought up to be married to a *sheikh*, but this was not meant to be. Instead she got married to a schoolteacher from Basrah, and with him and with a growing family they moved to different cities south and north. With these travels my mother inevitably widened her culinary repertoire, and when we settled in that little street in Baghdad we were exposed to even more diversity.

I remember the best shrimp with rice came from a *Basrawi* woman (from Basrah, the port city in the south), whom everybody called *Um Sahira* ("mother of Sahira"), as the custom was to call the parent after his or her eldest child. Whenever the occasion arose, she would boast of the excellence of the *baharat* (mixed spices) her relatives brought her from Basrah. She would laugh, and her gilded side tooth would gleam and glitter, and tell us how when she cooked the shrimp with rice the exciting aroma of her spices was everywhere. Her back yard neighbor would tell her that as the

1

aroma was sucked by the air cooler into their living room, the kids would jokingly open up pieces of bread in front of the air cooler as if they were filling their sandwiches with the aroma of *Um Sahira's* spices.

Although we used to buy *kubbat Mosul* (flat discs of bulgar dough) readymade, the best ever made was by our Mosuli neighbor (from Mosul, a big city in the north), *Um Yunis*. They were so huge and yet so thin, as thin as the onion's skin as people used to say describing the perfect *kubba*. Our first encounter with a Kurdish specialty called *parda palau* (rice pies) was on a very sad occasion when my brother passed away. As the custom was, neighbors were to help out people in bereavement by cooking food for them. That was the only time we ever received a dish from that Kurdish neighbor, of whom we knew almost nothing. We knew her name was Mary, but we were not sure that was her real name. She was a middle-aged retired belly dancer, and mingling with her was almost tabooed due to her profession. Apparently she was even abandoned by her family, and she kept to herself all the time. One thing we came to know about her was her excellent cooking. It was sad though how her life of isolation was ended. Apparently her youngest brother, who was a soldier on leave then, visited her, asked for money, she refused, they argued, and he stabbed her with kebab skewers. It was only after days that the murder was discovered, when the smell in the street that time was not of food but of a decaying body. For a long time after that the sight of kebab skewers freaked us out, and we lost appetite for all skewered foods. But life went on, although it took us a while until we resumed our street games routine.

Three or four doors down from where we lived, there lived a nice quiet Jewish family. The father was a physician and the mother, *Um Naseem,* was a housewife. They didn't have children our age. On Saturdays she used to ask us kids to light the stove for her, and we didn't understand the reason behind this, neither was she ready to explain it to us. But she would, on occasions, send our families a delicious dish that she called *tibeet.* It was chicken with rice that comes with an exquisite crunchy crust due to the prolonged time of simmering. Our Armenian neighbor was, without dispute, the best pastry maker. The simple sponge cakes with jelly and custard she made on her daughter's birthday were very tasty. She volunteered once to teach my eldest sisters how to make her famous jam pies. During Christmas time our *Athuri* neighbors (Christians who claim descent from the Assyrians) would send slices of delicious aromatic fruitcake. When their daughter divulged the secret that they soaked the dried fruits in brandy, we started to act like drunk whenever we ate of the cake. My grandma (*bibi*), who was staying with us at the time, also liked that cake, but when she heard about the brandy part, she hurried to the water tap, and amidst our laughter, started washing her mouth frantically asking for God's forgiveness.

Around the house where we lived, there grew *rarinj* trees (orange of Seville). This cheap variety of orange was sweet and sour and had a very thick and bitter peel. My mother mainly used it with salads as a substitute for lemon juice, that is, until our Christian Mosuli next door neighbor once told us that she could show us how to make delicious jam from the peel, and thirst quenching *sherbet* syrup from the juice.

First hand experience of a foreign cuisine came with the arrival of a small Indian family who stayed for some time in one of the apartments in our street. Their daughter was our age and her mom, whom we started calling *Um Nilo,* used to visit us sometimes, which was a chance for us to practice the little English we knew at the time. My grandma, who was not a sociable person on regular basis, always looked forward to these visitations, and I am not sure whether it was because of *Um Nilo's* "chapaties," those delicious small spicy flat Indian breads, or to brush up her "English." I remember the times when *Um Nilo* used to ask grandma a question, of course expecting us to translate for her. Grandma would immediately switch to the Egyptian dialect she must have picked up from watching Egyptian movies, and answer the question abruptly. We would all laugh and ask why she was doing this, and she would say, "Well, the woman doesn't know Arabic."

We also had a Palestinian neighbor who was my mom's friend-- her kids were too young for us. She used to tell us of the fruits in her homeland, especially the beautiful and succulent cherries, of which we didn't know anything at the time. She would never get tired of telling us how once she bought two pounds of cherries that mysteriously disappeared. Upon "investigation" her youngest son confessed, and here she would mimic her son's small quivering voice, *"Akaltu an w'khayyi* (my brother and I ate it)." It was fun listening to a dialect other than our own being spoken live. Of the dishes she made I particularly remember her tahini, it was creamy in texture, and always came garnished with lots of olive oil, and whole chickpeas in the middle.

As to what we used to put in the neighbors' dishes in return, it was almost always *mutabbag samak* (browned slices of fish layered with aromatic rice and raisins), for my mom, as a true southerner, was a devout lover of fish. And while these dainty dishes kept on coming and going from one house to the other, stew with rice and bread were destined for the family table to be enjoyed on almost daily basis. Variety came from using different kinds of vegetables, and different cuts of meat, to be had with lots of fresh greens, salad and condiments. Occasionally, especially when entertaining guests, special dishes would be prepared such as dolma, *kubba, sheikh mahshi* (stuffed vegetables), or an array of *nawashif* dishes (dishes that have no sauce in them). But after that, back to the stew.

Back to the Roots

Iraq now shares with the rest of the Near Eastern countries culinary traditions based on balanced dietary trends that emphasize grains and vegetables, moderate intake of meat, and the use of varieties of spices. Such trends would no doubt appeal to health conscious consumers everywhere. However, the Iraqi cuisine has an undeniably distinctive character of its own that testifies to the diversity of its roots, and the refinement it developed over years of trial and improvement.

The Iraqi cuisine evolved over several thousands of years during which the land became the scene for cultural exchanges through migration, invasion, counter-invasion, and colonization. It has its origins in civilizations that preceded and interacted with western cultures. The Sumerians, Babylonians, and Assyrians, collectively referred to as ancient Mesopotamians, played a significant role in shaping the Near East for three thousand years before Christianity. As the *Epic of Gilgamesh* and the codes of Hamourabi may testify, the cultural sophistication the Mesopotamians achieved naturally extended to its cuisine. Archaeological records, for instance, show that the ancient Mesopotamians made about twenty kinds of cheese, flavored, sweetened, and sharp. They knew over a hundred kinds of soup, and their records list about three hundred varieties of bread, some spiced and some sweetened with date syrup and honey. In fact, the first documented "cookbook" in human history was written in Akkadian on clay tablets, on the land of Babylon, about 3700 years ago. Here is how it all began.

The Old Testament tells us that once upon a time great empires flourished on the land of Mesopotamia, the land between the two rivers, Tigris and Euphrates. The inhabitants of this region were known as the Babylonians and Assyrians. Biblical allusions, along with references in Greek and Roman histories, are generally vague or even contradictory. For instance, an older people who lived in Iraq, the Sumerians, were never mentioned. The Bible tells us that the descendants of Noah lived on the land of Shinar (Genesis II: 2), which in all probability was a distorted form of the southern Iraqi ancient name of S(h)umer. Mesopotamia is also believed to be the land where the Great Flood took place. This major incident was first described in the *Epic of Gilgamesh*, a work that preceded Homer's *Iliad* and the *Odyssey* by more than 1300 years.

There was also the belief that the Garden of Eden was located in Mesopotamia, which points to another historical significance. While excavating in Ur in 1949, archaeologists found the platform of the temple ziggurat, built around 2000 BC. Beneath that ziggurat they excavated nineteen levels at the bottom of which was a little sand mound surrounded by a reed fence with a tiny chapel. This was believed to be the city of Eridu, the first shrine in human history and the mythical mound of creation. According to Sumerian mythology, that was the first land that rose from the great sea of fresh water at the beginning of time. Out of this primeval ocean of sweet water all human and natural life came.

The Sumerians also thought of Ur as the location for the walled garden that enclosed the sacred Kiskanu tree (Wood 21). This Mythical tree might well have been the prototype of the Tree of Life in the Biblical Garden of Eden, and the Qur'anic Tree in *Janat Adan*. Undoubtedly the names of both gardens can be traced back to the Sumerian "Edin." This mythical Sumerian "Edinic" place was probably the natural landscape of the wild uncultivated grassland of southern Mesopotamia. To this day Iraqi folk stories tell of a tree in the southern region reputed to be Adam's and Eve's Tree of Knowledge. In the city of Basrah there still is an ancient tree known as "Adam's tree." People visit it for blessings, and those who have a wish to be fulfilled would tie to its branches, strips of cloth of all colors and material.

The Book of Genesis makes references to ancient cities, such as Babylon, Akkad and Erech. According to the bible, Abraham began his wanderings with Sarah from Ur, capital of the Chaldeans, in the southern part of the region (Genesis II: 31). In the northern modern city of Mosul, built on the site of ancient Nineveh, tradition has it that the shrine of the prophet Jonah is located there. On the summit of an archaeological mound in the heart of the city of modern Mosul, the Mosque of *Nabi Younis* (Prophet Jonah) was constructed after the traditional design with the characteristic narrow labyrinthine streets. In the first half of the fourteenth century AD, the famous traveler Ibn Battuta of Tangier visited this place, admired the Mosque and said that about a mile from it there was a spring called by his name. This mosque and the buildings surrounding it have defied all serious attempts at excavation, due to the sanctity of the holy shrine. Locals have reported, though, that when houses in the shrine's proximity happened to fall or were repaired, people would stumble upon some bricks with cuneiform inscriptions, and they would usually put them to such domestic use as rebuilding their kitchen and living room walls. It has even been reported that while an inhabitant was digging in the *sirdab* (basement) of his house he came across the head of a winged bull (Fagan 156).

It was only relatively recently that the world knew of the ancient Mesopotamia. The main reason why such an old civilization has been overlooked is that the available building material the ancients used was largely mud brick, which was not as durable as stone. Annual floods, rain and shifting sands slowly leveled and buried the towers and palaces, and all that was left were the irregular mounds of land known as *tilal* (hills). During the second half of the nineteenth century and the twentieth century, however, archaeological excavations revealed the hidden history of the land to the entire world. To the locals, these mounds are not just a source of pride but also favorite picnic spots, particularly in springtime. My family's favorite spot was the mounds near the remains of the ancient wall of Nineveh, across the street from where we lived, and the ancient city of Namrud, a mere twenty-minute drive south of Mosul. In those ancient sites, it was not uncommon to come across broken pieces of jars or bits of bricks with cuneiform inscriptions on them, lying there on the grassy mounds.

**Me and the kids flying a kite on the archaeological mounds of Nineveh
(Photo Shakir Mustafa)**

The Hanging Gardens of Babylon: Labor of Love

The Hanging Gardens of Babylon were roof-like gardens built within the walls of the royal palace in Babylon. It is believed that Nebuchadnezzar II (604-562 BC) built them for his homesick Median wife, Amytus, who was originally from the mountainous northern region. This labor of love became one of the seven wonders of the world of antiquity, and was described by Greek historians such as Berossus, Strabo, Philo, and Siculus. They told how the gardens sloped like a hillside, and rose tier upon tier to the roof of the king's palace, thus raising the level of the plantations above the heads of spectators about 75 feet above ground level. Earth was piled on these tiers, which were thickly planted with trees and flowers, brought from every corner of the vast empire. The size and charm of these plants were a pleasure to the beholders.

The gardens were said to be quadrangular consisting of arched vaults located on checkered cube-like foundations. A stairway leads to the uppermost terrace roofs. They were kept green by an ingenious irrigation and water supply system. Through a hidden network of pipes, water was pumped from the nearby Euphrates river, and by means of some hydraulic engines concealed in columns and operated by shifts of slaves, water was pumped up to the highest tier of the gardens and flowed down to the sloping channels.

It was there in those luscious gardens that the queen and the royal ladies strolled under the rich shade of huge trees, surrounded by exotic and fragrant shrubs and flowers. Some believe those gardens were accessible to the public, as well.

CHRONOLOGY

This brief sketch of the historical development of the region is meant to provide contexts for later references to historical periods, monarchs and influences.

6,000 BC: Herdsmen and farmers in the north of Mesopotamia migrated south to the basin between the Tigris and the Euphrates, a plain that stretches from present day Baghdad to the Gulf. Villages and towns were built, and grains, basically barley, were cultivated. Irrigation evolved forming the agricultural basis of the prehistoric Ubaid culture (From the name of the mound Tell Ubaid). Those people gave their settlements names like Lagash, Ur, Eridu, Kish, and Nippur.

Ca 4,000 BC: Semitic nomads inhabiting the Syrian Desert and the Arabian Peninsula were attracted to the area. Some came as invaders, others as immigrants, and the mingling of the Ubaidian and Semitic cultures laid the foundation for the world's first true civilization.

3500 BC: The Sumerians, whose origin is still an unsolved mystery, arrived on the scene and their ethnic and cultural fusion with the indigenous people helped the rise of an impressive civilization. They developed the irrigation systems, creating food surplus, needed in the development of the world's first cities. They traded with the neighboring countries, exporting barley and textiles and importing stone, timber and metals.

Sumeria became powerful and rich with art, architecture and education. The Sumerians invented writing, most probably driven by the need to keep trading records. The writing characters they produced were known as cuneiform, meaning wedge-shaped, since the stylus used for writing left an imprint in the form of a wedge. Besides, a powerful priesthood emerged to serve local deities at temples that had to be tended and cared for daily. Although Sumer was a small country, it was composed of no fewer than 13 politico-religious units known as "city-states," and the bitter struggle for supremacy among the rulers led to Sumer's decline.

2300 BC: Sargon, the Akkadian, took hold of power and established a new city, called Akkad, as a capital, and from the Sargonic period onwards, the central region of Mesopotamia was known as Akkad. Sargon started the first Mesopotamian Empire. The Akkadians were an ethnic group of Semitic origin, and they shared the life and religion and culture of the Sumerians. The only difference between them was a linguistic one. In all other aspects those two ethnic groups were indistinguishable.

1792-1595 BC: Babylonia gained control under Hammurabi, famous for his legal codes. Commerce, astrology, and the arts flourished.

1600 BC: The Babylonians were invaded by the Indo-European Hittites of Anatolia (Asia Minor) who plundered and destroyed, then withdrew to their homeland, leaving Babylon weak and drained.

1595-1170 BC: The Kassites, a non-Semitic people, swooped down to the south from the Zagros Mountains in the north, and seized control of Babylonia. Then the Elamites of Persia overthrew the last of the Kassite kings. They plundered Babylonia, and took with them spoils of war, including the stone inscribed with Hamurabi's code of laws and a gigantic statue of Marduk, the Babylonian chief god. Shamed and dishonored, the Babylonians, led by Nabuchadnezzar I, attacked Elam, and returned the statue of the god. In the north, Assyria gained control.

10th-9th centuries BC: A period of floods, famine, wars and invasions. Babylonia was prey to the Assyrians, who then gained power and became the masters of the entire Fertile Crescent.

612-539 BC: The Assyrians were ousted by the Medes of the Persian plateau, and the Chaldeans of Babylon. The Neo-Babylonian Empire emerged. Though it lasted only 75 years, it was the most brilliant and glorious era in the history of Mesopotamia, under the reign of Nabuchadnezzar II, who took the Israelites captives. Babylonia was rebuilt. The hanging gardens, one of the world's seven wonders, was built.

539 BC: Babylonia was conquered by the Persians.

331 BC: Alexander the Great defeated Persia and entered Babylon, beginning the Hellenistic rule.

Ca 223 BC: The Mesopotamian region was taken from the Greeks by the Parthians, a Persian tribe of nomads. During this period city of Hatra was established in the north. Hatra controlled the trade routes of the west-northern desert, and held a strategic position between the opposing states of Rome in the West and Parthia in the East. The region was occupied by the Sassanides, also from Persia, from 227 BC-636 AD.

637-1285 AD: Five years after the death of the prophet Muhammad, the Arabs defeated the Sassanides, and gained control of Iraq. In 750 AD the Abbasid Caliphs ruled the area. Caliph al-Mansur founded the round city of Baghdad in 762 AD, soon to become one of the greatest cultural centers in the world. This era was the golden age in the arts and science, during which scholars and artisans became the custodians of Europe's ancient heritage. The Caliph Harun al-Rasheed and his Baghdad were mythologized in the *Arabian Nights*, along with other fictitious Baghdadi characters such as Sindbad the sailor, Aladdin, and Ali Baba.

1258 AD: The Mongols destroyed Baghdad, a city of 800,000 people, and ended the Abbasid caliphate. Baghdad was almost totally destroyed, its irrigation system was ruined, and libraries plundered.

1534-1932 AD: Iraq became the battle ground between the Ottomans and Persians. In 1534 the Turks entered Baghdad. The Turkish domination lasted about 400 years. After the break up of the Ottoman Empire, the British colonization began in 1917. The discovery of oil changed the course of the country's history. In 1932, Iraq was admitted to the League of Nations as an independent country.

The Mesopotamian Diet

The dietary knowledge available today of the ancient Mesopotamian period is largely deduced from countless archaeological findings, excavated artifacts, artistic presentations on bas reliefs, cylinder seals, and a big number of cuneiform clay tablets. Cylinder seals, plaques, and reliefs depict scenes of people engaged in eating, drinking, and feasting. The cuneiform tablets give details on crops, cattle, and foods offered to the gods, the king and his household, in addition to food ratios of the general public. The most interesting of these documents are the official, economic and personal letters immortalized in the baked cuneiform letters. They all attest to the fact that apart from occasional famines due to wars and natural disasters, the Mesopotamians enjoyed a rich and varied diet, basically composed of cereals, legumes, garden products, milk, cheese, fish, and white and red meat. One can safely assume the majority of the population took advantage of the resources available.

Ancient Wives in Ancient Kitchens

Beneath some 7,500 years of detritus, excavators at Tell [mound] Hassuna, in Iraq, uncovered a farming village whose kitchens consisted of two cooking areas. In the hot, dry months, women prepared and cooked food in airy courtyards equipped with hearths and, in some cases, ovens. But in variable weather they worked comfortably around indoor hearths, perhaps venturing out to bake loaves of unleavened bread.

Such kitchens were in many ways the focal point of the agricultural revolution. The foods processed in them represented a radical change in diet, with wheat and barley replacing game and other wild foods as the mainstay. Fired vessels of pottery--too cumbersome and fragile for hunter-gatherers to carry in their wanderings--served as durable containers for cooking or storing foods and liquids. Such wares enabled cooks to prepare or preserve the harvested grains by boiling, parching, germinating or fermenting them (Leonard 42).

Interestingly, in his *Chemistry and Chemical Technology in Ancient Mesopotamia*, M. Levey contends that it was in ancient kitchens that the early tools and chemical processes originated. No wonder the names of the earliest known chemists and perfumeresses were those of women (44).

Agricultural Products

At the center of life in ancient Mesopotamia was agriculture. When the first farmers in upper Mesopotamia migrated to the south well before 4,000 BC, they had to adapt their skills to the special conditions of the southern plain where rain was scarce, and crops had to be irrigated.

Field products

Grains such as wheat, barley and millet were planted in autumn and harvested in April. Barley was cultivated more than wheat, because it proved to be more resilient and thus could thrive in poor and alkaline soil. Wheat, on the other hand, prospered in upper Mesopotamia, where soil was more fertile, and grains were irrigated by rainwater. They cultivated a variety of barley and wheat to meet the different demands of their cooking.

Once harvested, grains were threshed, winnowed, washed, dried and stored. For consumption, the kernels were husked. They were sometimes toasted to make the task of grinding them a little easier. For immediate use, barley flour was made into unleavened bread by cooking it on hot surfaces. This kind of bread is still made in rural areas in modern Iraq. However, a good percentage of the cultivated barley was made into beer, a staple drink at the time. It was consumed by both men and women, and was believed to bring joy to the heart and happiness to the liver. In a Sumerian proverb, pleasure and distress were epitomized by the following:

Pleasure--it is beer!
Discomfort--it is an expedition! (Gordon 264)

When a new building was built, the first brick used was made of clay mixed with honey, wine and beer.

From wheat flour they made fermented bread and baked it in domed clay ovens, known in Sumerian as "tanuru"(cf. Arabic, *tannour*. For more on bread, see Chapter 1). These cultivated cereals were also made into porridges. The last to reach the agricultural scene was rice. It was introduced around 1,000 BC and was planted in the marshes, sprout by sprout, in shallow paddies, harvested by hand, then carried in flat-bottomed canoes to the neighboring villages.

Sesame (Akkadian "samsamu") was cultivated mainly for its oil. As revealed in an Assyrian law code, oil was an important staple of life. This law dealt with the husband who deserted his wife and "left her neither oil, nor wool, nor clothes" (Levey 85). Legumes and beans, such as lentils, peas, mung beans, and chickpeas (Akk. "amusu," cf. Arabic *hummus*) were grown in abundance. When the epic hero Gilgamesh set out on his journey for immortality he carried chickpeas with him as part of his provision. There is also evidence that dried white beans were also cooked (Levey 51). Stew of dried white beans (*margat fasoulya yabsa*) is still one of our favorite food dishes.

Such legumes were valuable sources of protein and an affordable substitute for meat. They were used widely in cooking porridges, soups and stews, as the Iraqis still do to this day. It is believed also that the ancients cooked rice with lentils, which is one of our staple dishes now. (Recent studies have shown that the combination of rice and lentils consolidates the received wisdom about them.) Flax was cultivated for the production of linen as well as oil.

Vegetable Gardens

As a general rule, Mesopotamians had small vegetable gardens attached to their houses, in addition to the fields where they worked for a living. Those gardens grew a lot of greens ("nibatu" or "arqu" in the Akkadian). They grew cucumbers, root vegetables, such as beets and turnips (Akk."laptu," cf. Arabic. *lift*), lettuce (Akk. "khassu," cf. Arabic. *khas*), Swiss chard (Akk. "silki," cf. Arabic *siliq*), watercress, and cabbages. Herbs also grew in plenty, such as mint, dill, and "erishtu" (an unidentified herb that sounds so much like the *rishad* herb that now grows exclusively in Iraq). The vegetables most frequently mentioned in their records were different kinds of onion, garlic, and "karasu" (leeks, cf. Arabic *kurrath*). Apparently these vegetables and greens were affordable and so much in use that when Mesopotamians went poor and hungry they said, "in their stomachs, the greens are too little" (Levey 50).

They used a lot of spices and aromatics in their cooking such as cassia, anise, fennel, nigella seeds, coriander (Akk. "kisibaru," cf. Arabic *kizbara*), marjoram, turmeric, juniper berries, ginger, thyme, and cardamom. Cumin (Akk. "kamunu") was sprinkled on bread or mixed into it, as is still done today. Saffron ("azupiranu" in Akkadian, cf. Arabic *za'faran*) was known but was used mainly for medicinal purposes. To season their dishes they used mustard and salt which they mixed together as is done commercially these days. In their homes, they usually kept a mustard box and a salt box on their tables. Besides, mustard and salt were used as a weapon of vengeance and destruction. An

Assyrian text tells how one of the kings scattered salt and mustard on the land of Elam to lay it waste. Mustard was added to flavor wheat bread and beer. Of all these; however, salt was the staple ingredient. In the Akkadian it was called "tabti." In an incantation, salt was addressed thus:
     You salt, who are born in a bright spot,
     Without you no meal in the temple is prepared.

Salt also developed an ethically symbolic significance. If an Assyrian said about a person "he is the man of my salt," he meant, "he is my friend"(Joannes 32). Salt to this day connotes such a meaning, as loyalty is associated with sharing bread and salt. Interestingly, the symbolic linkage of salt and bread was established thousands of years ago. A Sumerian proverb on lack of resources goes like this:

     If you have bread, you have no salt,
     If you have salt, you have no bread.

To protect the low-lying vegetables and greens, higher trees were planted. These in turn were planted in the shade of date palms. This way of cultivating vegetables and arranging trees for maximum shade and protection proved successful enough that it is in use to this day. It also explains why in ancient texts and *Qur'anic* verses fruit trees in general, but figs, pomegranates, and grape vines in particular, were often mentioned in conjunction with date palms. We also know that kings were directly involved in laying out gardens and parks and orchards, and that they introduced exotic trees and plants. The Hanging Gardens of Babylon are a good example.

Of all the fruits, date palms perhaps were the first to be domesticated in the area. They were mentioned in texts from the middle third millenium BC, and appeared in seals, plaques and paintings. Hot and humid climate in the south, and the availability of water created favorable conditions for growing date palms. They grew along the riverbanks and canals, as they still do today. The southern city of Basrah has one of the most extensive date palm groves in the world. There, they are automatically fed with fresh water when the water level of *shat-al-Arab* (the conjunction of the two rivers) rises twice a day, due to the back up effect of the Gulf tide. It was also the date palm that was chosen to represent the mythical Tree of Life. It came to stand for fertility and plentitude. Virtually every part of it was broken up and used in one way or another. Likewise, pomegranates were valued as a symbol of fecundity and were served in feasts and weddings.

Irrigation was mainly conducted by means of very simple bucket-like water lifting instruments called "dalu," which is also the Arabic word used for "bucket."

Animal Products

Fresh milk from sheep, goats, and cows was not popular as a drink by itself, probably because it spoiled fast in warm climates. It was rather used with other ingredients to make their favorite "mirsu," for instance, which was dessert of mashed dates, mixed with fine oil, yellow milk (rich, full fat milk), and other ingredients, or the "pappasu," which was a combination of cream and honey (Levey 54).

Milk was more commonly made into yogurt, cheese and butter. Clarified butter ("samnu" in the Akkadian, cf. Arabic, *samn*) and sour milk (yogurt) were often mentioned in offering lists prepared by temple officials. The cows were brought to yield milk not only when their calves needed it but all year round. They were treated as family members. In their letters the Babylonians asked about the health of the cow along with the rest of the family members. The goats, sheep and pigs were easily domesticated to ensure a ready supply of fresh meat. Cattle destined for sacrifice were fattened and usually ended on the tables for gods and kings. Animal fat was made from the fat tail of sheep, which up until recently was one of the important sources of fat in cooking. Mesopotamians also valued pork. According to a Sumerian proverb it was too good for a slave girl who had to make do with the lean ham:

> Meat with fat is too good! Meat with suet is too good!
> What shall we give the slave-girl to eat?
> Let her eat ham of the pig! (Gordon 143)

Pork later incurred taboos from Judaism and Islam. Geese and ducks were domesticated from early times, but the chicken did not reach the region until the first millenium B.C. The fowlers or bird keepers were mentioned in records frequently, and the practice of fattening birds with dough was known.

The two major rivers, the Tigris and the Euphrates, were abundant sources for fish, and the southern marshes teemed with animal life. Textual and archaeological evidence show that the ancient inhabitants consumed fish, wild fowl, and turtles long before agriculture was established in the area. Full use was made of these assets in the third millenium. Fish was dried or salted and even smoked, as well as eaten fresh. The roes were preserved separately and eaten as a delicacy. Up until the middle of the second millenium B.C. texts containing lists of fish names and references to fish were abundant. In his history, Herodotus (484-425 B.C.) mentions the "three tribes in Babylon who eat nothing but fish. They were caught and dried in the sun, after which they were brayed in a mortar, and strained through a linen sieve. Some prefer to make cakes of this material, while others bake it into a kind of bread" (75). However, late Babylonian and Assyrian texts rarely mentioned fish and fishing. The word "fisherman," in the Neo-Babylonian era even came to denote a "lawless person." The reason behind this taboo might well be that people escaping justice used to find refuge in the southern marshes, which at the same time was the homeland of fishermen (Kramer, *Cradle of Civilization* 94). This by no means indicates that people stopped fishing or eating fish. Assyrian bas-reliefs of the first millenium depict the netting of fish in a fishpond, and fishing was certainly carried on in the new Babylonian period.

Babylon and Assyria through the Eyes of Herodotus, the Historian (484-425 BC)

Little rain falls in Assyria, enough, however, to make the corn begin to sprout, after which the plant is nourished and the ears formed by means of irrigation from the river. For the river does not, as in Egypt, overflow the corn-lands of its own accord, but is spread over them by the hand, or by the help of engines. The whole of Babylonia is, like Egypt, intersected with canals. The largest of them all, which runs towards the winter sun, and is impassable except in boats, is carried from the Euphrates into another stream, called the Tigris, the river upon which the town Nineveh formerly stood. Of all the countries that we knew there is none which is so fruitful in grain…. The blade of the wheat-plant and barley-plant is often four fingers in breadth. As for the millet and the sesame, I shall not say to what height they grow, though within my own knowledge; for I am not ignorant that what I have already written concerning the fruitfulness of Babylonia must seem incredible to those who have never visited the country. The only oil they use is made from the sesame-plant. Palm-trees grow in great numbers over the whole of the flat country, mostly of the kind which bears fruit, and this fruit supplies them with bread, wine, and honey…. The natives tie the fruit of the male-palms… to the branches of the date-bearing palm, to let the gall-fly enter the dates and ripen them, and to prevent the fruit from falling off (72-3).

On navigation in the river Tigris, Herodotus has the following to say:

The boats which come down the river to Babylon are circular, and made of skins. The frames, which are of willow, are cut in the country of the Armenians above Assyria, and on these, which serve for hulls, a covering of skins is stretched outside…. They are then entirely filled with straw and their cargo is put on board, after which they are suffered to float down the stream. Their chief freight is wine, stored in casks made of the wood of the palm-tree. They are managed by two men who stand upright in them, each plying an oar, one pulling and the other pushing…. Each vessel has a live ass on board; those of larger size have more than one. When they reach Babylon, the cargo is landed and offered for sale; after which the men break up their boats, sell the straw and the frames, and loading their asses with the skins, set off on their way back to Armenia. The current is too strong to allow a boat to return upstream, for which reason they make their boats of skins rather than wood (73).

Villagers transporting water melon using a coracle (guffa), which is made of reeds, covered with skins and plastered inside and out with bitumen for waterproofing. The guffa is peculiar to Mesopotamia and has been in use ever since ancient times. Photo, Kerim and Hasso Bros, Baghdad.

Pioneers of the Gourmet Cuisine

Considering all the options available, ordinary people in ancient Mesopotamia must have had the opportunity to consume healthy food. However, it was the "gods," the kings, and the affluent who enjoyed the gourmet cuisine. The gods, for sure, were given credit for abundant crops, and famine was interpreted as an expression of their wrath. The public's offerings of agricultural products and sacrifices of poultry, fish, and cattle were made all the time to mollify the gods. An ancient Sumerian clay tablet written around 3000B.C. listed items to be included in meals prepared for the gods, which in all probability was meant as kitchen memorandum for training priests. It included a main course of meat, such as ducks, doves, lamb, beef, and fish. Olive oil or sesame oil were listed as a dressing, and the garnishes were dates, figs, cucumber, pistachio, and other nuts, apricots, prunes, and dried raisins. For the sweet-toothed gads, sweet fruitcakes were served at the end of the meal. For beverages, wine was offered.

The society of the Mesopotamian gods was curiously a duplicate of the human one. The temple idols were fed with the best food money could buy. They had a lot of people in their services such as bakers, brewers, butchers, and dairymen. The gods' effigies were served two meals a day, one in the morning and another at night. As the menu suggests, each meal contained two courses, a main and a secondary. The procedure was to start by bringing a table before the images and offering bowls of water for the gods to wash their fingers before eating. All the "eating" activities were to be accompanied by music, and when the meal was over, the place would be fumigated to dispel the odors of food. The tables would be cleared and bowls of water were brought again for the gods to wash their fingers. Interestingly, all the eating procedures of the gods, from washing the hands to eating, were hidden from the human eyes. To prevent any contact between the gods and the physical world, a linen curtain would be drawn while the gods were supposedly engaged in washing, eating and drinking. The blessed "leftovers" of the gods, so to speak, were then taken to the king. When a god paid a visit to a city, a welcome meal was served. For instance when Innana (Ishtar) was invited to Eridu, she was served fresh water, cream and beer (Joannes 33).

A modern impression of a Sumerian cylinder seal, 3rd millennium BC, depicting a group of men and women feasting together. Tables are laden with breads.
University of Pennsylvania Museum of Archaeology and Anthropology.

According to an Assyrian text, the protocol for a great royal feast held in winter was as follows: After servants bring royal furniture into the room, the king takes his place, followed by his high officials, one at a time, then the crown prince and the rest of the king's sons. Servants would tend to the incense, burners, heating braziers, water for washing hands, torches, and fans. It was the custom also to sprinkle the king with the water in which the gods washed their hands, a ritual which brings to mind a custom still practiced in the Arab world. When the visit is over, the host or hostess sprinkles the guests with rose water as they leave the house so that they have lingering fragrant memories of the visit.

The general public did on occasions join the deities and the kings in feasting on well-prepared, lavish menus. The ninth century B.C. Assyrian ruler Ashurnasripal II boasted of having entertained around 70,000 people on the occasion of the inauguration of his palace in the city of Kalhu. His chroniclers gave a detailed account of the huge amounts his multinational party consumed (see p.). Broadly speaking, it included meat dishes, side dishes, desserts, and perfumed oils for anointing their bodies. Such grand feasts were normally accompanied with entertainment such as music, singing, dancing, acting and juggling. It is not certain whether the women of the royal family were invited to such festivities. In all probability the queens' households had parties of their own (Joannes 35).

On private levels, meals were shared to seal formal agreements, or to strengthen friendships. Merchants would seal bargains by sharing a drink. A document dating back to the second millenium B.C., recorded that "Bread was eaten, beer was drunk, and bodies were anointed with perfumed oil." Even larger feasts were held for weddings. It was considered a mark of disgrace to reject an invitation to a meal. In all these activities, sharing a meal mattered more than the components of the meals themselves (Joannes 33).

As to eating utensils, people used spoons made of wood or metal and, occasionally, ivory, or their fingers. The earliest spoons known from ancient Mesopotamia were made of bitumen. Indeed, such utensils never vanished from the scene. Ladles made of bitumen used for scooping water out of earthen clay water vessels, known as *hib,* can still be seen in rural areas. Knives had blades of bronze, iron or flint. Their eating bowls were mostly made of clay and tamarisk wood. Glass was known in the Assyrian times but was still a rarity, and earthenware goblets, jugs, cups, handled vases, and narrow-necked jars were used instead. For preservation, the vessels would be sealed with linen and clay stoppers. Evidently people used tablecloths and table napkins, which were held by servants for diners to wipe their hands when they washed them after the meals.

Regarding the eating habits of ordinary people, two meals a day were served, one in the morning and another in the evening. Mention of three meals a day was rarely made in their records. The meals themselves were divided into major and minor servings, to be washed down with beer. In their texts they also included "the sweet water of the Tigris and Euphrates, the well and canal" as part of the meal. No special rooms were set aside for dining. There is evidence that the upper classes ate seated on chairs, whereas the commoners squatted or sat cross-legged, and had their meals from a tray placed on the ground or a low stool. Some people still like to do this, on occasion, even though they have dining tables and chairs.

Sumerian Codes of hospitality

Let it be plentiful--lest there be too little!
Let it be more than enough--lest it have to be added to!
Let it be boiling hot--lest it get cold!

(ca 3500 BC, Gordon 465)

The Mesopotamian Menu

The Mesopotamian cuisine was varied, rich and sophisticated. We know this from a great number of written documents and artifacts, recovered from many archaeological cites in Iraq. There is, for instance, the bilingual (Sumerian/Akkadian) document written on twenty-four cuneiform tablets in which over eight- hundred food and drink items were classified into four hundred headings. From this glossary we learn they made twenty varieties of cheese, such as the basic cream cheese, similar to the soft cheese we made today from drained yogurt, fresh cheese, both flavored and sweetened, and sharp cheese. From this record we also learn they knew about one hundred kinds of soup, thick and nourishing enough to stick to the ribs, using lentils, chickpeas, turnip, bulgar, and fish.

From the ancient documents we also learn they knew how to make sausages from intestine casings. They preserved foods by salting, drying, pickling and preserving in honey. Pickled grasshoppers were a delicacy at that time. They made the fermented sauce, "siqqu," from fish, shellfish and grasshoppers. It was meant for both, kitchen and table use, more or less like Worcestershire sauce or fish sauce are used nowadays. They made vinegar from grapes, and referred to it as "grape water." A lot of aromatics such as onion, leeks, and garlic were incorporated into the dishes, as well as seasonings like mint, juniper berries, mustard, coriander, cumin, salt and ashes. Interestingly social class was defined by what kind of spices people used. "Naga" was for the poor, and "gazi" was for the rich. According to a Sumerian proverb poverty was when you had meat but you had no "gazi," and when you had "gazi," you had no meat (Limet 138). Stews were thickened and flavored with grains, breadcrumbs, flour, milk, beer and even blood. (Judaism and Islam later prohibited the use of blood in cooking.)

Apparently they baked a lot of bread. Around three hundred kinds of bread were made, and in Sumerian records they were categorized as leavened, unleavened, excellent, ordinary, fresh and dry. They ranged in size from large to tiny. Different kinds of grains were used, and were spiced differently. The most basic kind of these breads was the flat bread baked in the clay oven, called "tinuru," in Sumerian, from which the Arabic *tannour* was derived. Other breads were improved by adding milk, oil and butter and these were called "ninda" bread. More fancy pastries were baked which were beyond the means of the ordinary people. These were the "gug" and "kuku" cakes (as called in Sumerian, and the Akkadian, respectively) from which our cakes and ka'aks were derived. They were made with top quality flour and clarified butter, and were flavored with cream cheese, raisins and dates. The other kind was the "girilam" cakes, which were more like the fruitcakes we make nowadays. They were sweetened with honey, dried fruits such as dates and figs, and bound with flour. Their cookies were sometimes shaped like hearts, heads, hands, ears and even breasts.

17

Others were shaped like rings, crescents, and turbans. Their "gulupu" cookies were made of dough of flour and oil, were filled with raisins and dates, and baked. Most of these pastries were perfumed with rose water and the spirit of almond and were baked in the *tannour* oven, which, when covered, created an interior humid enough for baking pastries. Some of these pastries, such as the "gulupu" cookies, bear a striking resemblance to today's traditional date-stuffed *kleicha* cookies

Although most people had the *tannour* ovens in their houses, in big cities, bread and pastry making was a flourishing business. Apprentices were to serve for sixteen months to learn the tricks of the trade. It was the custom to consume a lot of pastries during their religious festivals, something with which we are quite familiar today. Their popular halwa was made of dates, which were cooked and mashed with clarified butter and honey. This was, perhaps, the mother of all the date *halwas* of the region. In Akkadian it was called "mirsu," from which the Arabic *marasa* (to mash) was derived.

In short, Mesopotamians had a large repertoire to draw on. No wonder the Sumerians took pride in the superiority of their cuisine. The Bedouins, they proudly argued, "did not know what civilized life was. They ate their food raw, and if you were to give them flour, eggs, and honey for a cake they would not know what to do with them" (Limet 137).

Cooks Beware!
A Sumerian Caveat

I am going to pour off the fat from the meat,
I am sliding the roasted barley off (the roasting pan)
Who(ever) may hold the bowl (to receive it), watch out for your feet!"
(Gordon 472)

Cooking Techniques and Kitchen Utensils

Masopotamians made skillful use of fire. To broil or roast meat, they put it on open flames. To control heat they put ashes or potsherds on the coals. They even used certain terms to describe grilling. Fish, for instance, was "placed on the fire," (probably glowing coals), or was "touched with fire" (Limet, 139). For those of us who grew up in Baghdad, such grilling options are quite familiar. Fresh *shabout* or *bunni* fish are grilled *masgouf* way, along the bank of the river Tigris, suspended on sticks around the flames to be "touched by fire," and afterwards they are "placed on the fire." Skewered meat including locusts were grilled shish kebab way using braziers. The Akkadian word for grilling was "kababu," which means to "char" food on fire (*The American Heritage Dictionary*, Appendix II, Semitic Roots), from which stemmed all manifestations of kebab across the world for centuries.

As for baking, the exterior hot walls of clay cylinder ovens were used for baking unleavened bread. The domed clay ovens, known in the Akkadian as "tinuru, were fueled with bramble or desert bushes, and generated less intense interior heat. When the top opening was closed, enough humidity was created to bake fermented leavened breads, cakes and other dishes (Limet 139). These ovens were never allowed to extinguish since it would have been interpreted as a premonition of death or a catastrophe to befall the family (Levey 45).

The Sumerians and Akkadians refined the practice of making stew by cooking meat and vegetables in liquid such as water and oil or animal fat, thickened with milk or bread crumbs, and enhanced with spices, herbs, and garnishes. As the Babylonian recipes I'll comment on shortly reveal, making stew was a common culinary technique at the time.

The recipes suggest all kinds of elaborate and time-consuming activities, such as mixing, sprinkling, squeezing using a cloth, pounding (Akk. "maraqu"), steeping, shredding, grating, crumbling, mashing (Akk. "harasu"), filtering, and so on. Cooking in liquid also required the use of metal cauldrons, known as "ruqqu" (thin? from which Arabic *raqeeq*, was derived?), used for the initial stages of quick boiling. For simmering they used fired clay pots with lids on them, called "diqaru" (cf. Arabic *qidr*) which were put on the opening of the clay oven to cook gently over a long period of time (Bottèro, "The Culinary Tablets at Yale" 14). The Babylonian recipes described below called for the use of an "assalu"-platter for slow cooking of porridge, and a "sabiltu" vessel. They also called for a pan called "maqaltu," which might well have been used as a frying pan, for it is curiously similar to the Arabic *miqlat* (frying pan).

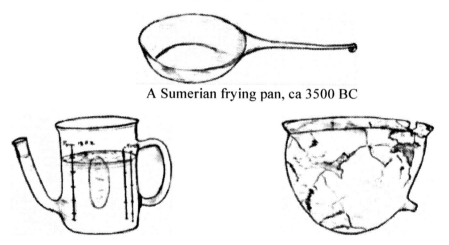

A Sumerian frying pan, ca 3500 BC

Right: The ancient Mesopotamians used this utensil to separate oil from water (ca 3500 BC).
Left: A 21st-century AD oil separator, based on the same ancient principle.

**The reverse of the Babylonian culinary tablet, 4644, ca 1700 BC.
Total number of stew recipes on both sides is 25.
On this side we see the dividing line after which were given the last 5 recipes
containing vegetables. Yale Babylonian Collection.**

Babylonian Recipes
The First Documented Recipes in Human History

In 1933 Yale University acquired three Akkadian cuneiform tablets believed at first to be pharmaceutical formulas. A closer examination by the French Assyriologist Jean Bottèro revealed the oldest cooking recipes. Bottèro thinks they were written around 1700 B.C. in Babylonia. His discovery was made known in the early1980's. Despite some damage in the recipes, Bottèro finds enough text to reveal a cuisine of "striking richness, refinements, sophistication, and artistry," and concludes that "previously we would not have dared to think a cuisine four thousand years old was so advanced" ("The Cuisine of Ancient Mesopotamia" 39-40). We should know that these tablets are by no means inclusive of what constituted the entire ancient Mesopotamian cuisine. Bottèro assumes they are just "strays from a huge collection," and speculates on "the possibility that a whole library of similar texts was devoted to the 'science of cooking'" (*Mesopotamian Culinary Texts* 7).

The shortest of these three tablets (# 4648) contains fifty-three lines of text, but it is badly preserved. Despite some breaks in the other two, there is enough in them to give us an idea on what the ancient Mesopotamian cooking was.

Tablet 4644

This tablet is the best preserved. In its seventy-five lines there are twenty-five briefly described recipes of stews. Of these, twenty-one are meat stews, and they are:
Meat stew, Assyrian style stew, red stew, clear or glistening stew, venison stew, gazelle stew, goat's kid stew, bitter stew, stew with crumbs, "zamzaganu" (?) stew, dodder stew, lamb stew, ram stew, "bidsud" (?) stew, spleen stew, Elamite stew, "amursanu"-pigeon stew, leg of mutton stew, "halazu" (?) stew, salted stew, and francolin stew.

The last four stews are cooked with vegetables, and they are:
"Tuh'u"- beet stew, "kanasu" (?) stew, "hirsu" (?) stew. The last one is a vegetarian stew of turnips.

One common feature these recipes share is that they were all cooked in liquid, which, according to Bottèro, was indisputably a step forward in the history of culinary techniques, in comparison to roasting and grilling. The sauce can indefinitely be varied and enriched by adding a number of ingredients, which made possible the creation of a genuine cuisine with all its complexities, namely the Mesopotamian cuisine (*Mesopotamian Culinary Texts* 17).

In the Akkadian, the name of each dish is preceded by the generic term "mei," which means water. The French translator is a little unhappy with this nomenclature because "mei" does not give an idea on the consistency of the resulting liquid. However, to people familiar with Iraqi food and cooking this poses no problem whatsoever. The Akkadian word for water is the same as the word for water in Arabic. In the modern Iraqi dialect "mei" refers to water, but the same word is also commonly used to refer to the "liquid in which food is cooked regardless of consistency. In our cooking vocabulary, *mei dijaaj* or *laham,* for instance, means the "liquid in which chicken or meat is cooked" i.e. broth or stalk, respectively. On the other hand, *mei marag*, means liquid of stew, which is normally thicker in consistency than broth or stalk.

Like our modern recipes, each Babylonian recipe was named after the main ingredient in the dish, such as Turnip Stew; the main cut of meat, such as Leg of Mutton Stew; or appearance of the prepared dish such as Red Stew, or Glistening Stew. Two stews were named after the source of their origin: the ethnic Assuriatu Stew was derived from Assur; and the foreign Elamite Stew from Elam, south-east Persia.

The dish name is followed by a brief account of the recipe. Neither precise amounts nor time are given. Their terse style was obviously less to teach than to remind the cook of the necessary ingredients and steps. Obviously they did not need the details, they already knew them. It is worth mentioning, though, that laconic as they were, the recipes did not neglect to include pieces of information or details rendered important by the writer. For instance, the original name given to the Elamite stew was "Zukanda." In the Dodder Stew, which called for cured rather than fresh meat, cooking duration was given, "when the pot has barely sat on the stove, carve and serve" (*Mesopotamian Culinary Texts* 9) because the meat was already cooked.

Characteristics of the Babylonian Stew Dishes

The main components of these stews were meat, dissolved fat from the sheep tail, and water. Fat was important not only for flavor but because it helped raise the boiling temperature, which allowed for a more tenderizing cooking process for tough cuts of meat (*Mesopotamian Culinary Texts* 17). Variety was achieved by adding different kinds of meat, sometimes in big chunks, sometimes chopped. In several recipes two kinds of meat were combined in one dish, such as in the Francolin Stew, where a fresh leg of mutton was added to the bird. The extremities along with the heads of the slaughtered animals were prepared into a dish amazingly similar to the modern Iraqi traditional *pacha* dish. The recipe is "Goat's Kid Stew" which calls for the head, legs and tail to be singed first on a direct source of heat before cooking, exactly as we still do today.

Vegetables such as beets and turnips, along with still unidentified vegetables were used. Lots of spices, the most important of which being aromatic wood (cassia?), cumin and coriander, were added at different stages of the cooking, and were given in combinations to ensure the utmost flavor. Herbs were also added, such as mint, dill, and an unidentified herb referred to in the recipes as "halazzu" for which Bottèro gives another name, "erishtu." The recipe specified that "four sprigs or stems are used to spice up the taste" (*Mesopotamian Culinary Texts* 5). Bottèro could not identify the herb, but it sounds like *rishshad*, the exclusively Iraqi herb with small leaves, and a refreshing but slightly sharp peppery taste.

Supplementary ingredients such as onion and garlic make their presence literally in every single recipe, sometimes mashed and added. As for the herb known in Akkadian as "karasu," judging from the *kurrath* herb available in the region nowadays, it was more like garlic chives, or table leeks, in which the interest is in the green tender stalks rather than the bulbous root. Salt "as required" was enlisted in most of the recipes.

To thicken and enrich the sauces they used breadcrumbs. In fact one of the stews was called "Stew with Crumbs," after the last stage of cooking, which instructed the cook to "crush and sift spiced grain cakes, and sprinkle in the pot before removing it from the fire" (*Mesopotamian Culinary Texts* 9). This sounds so much like one type of *thareed* dishes known since pre-Islamic and medieval times that used breadcrumbs to sop up the broth. There is a recipe in a tenth-century A.D. Baghdadi cookbook that describes a *thareed* dish similar to this stew. It is called *al-thareeda al-Iraqiyya* (al-Warraq 208-9, more on this in the medieval section, below).

Milk and "kisimmu" were also added as sauce thickeners. The latter was a sour milk product similar to the *kishk* (dough made of grain and yogurt, dried, and crushed when needed) still used in northern Iraq and the adjoining countries. As instructed in the recipes, it was crushed with garlic and used as people do to this day. The Turkmans in northern Iraq call it, *kisham*, and the resemblance to the Akkadian "kisimmu" is telling. In the Lamb Stew, they combined breadcrumbs and milk along with fat, onion, mashed garlic and leeks, creating what would have been similar to our modern bèchamel sauce (white sauce). In the "Spleen Stew" recipe, besides milk and breadcrumbs, bits of toasted "qaiatu"-dough were added. Although the dough is still unidentified, I find this mention most intriguing. Adding those small pieces of dough might well have been man's first attempts at making pasta, more specifically, thin noodles, similar to what later began to be called *sha'riya* (as thin as hair) in the Arab cuisine. Bottèro's rendering was "bits of roasted qaiatu-dough" (10). I suspect it is related to the Akkadian "qatanu," which means "to become thin or fine," from which Arabic *qitan* (thin strip or cord) was derived. In Iraq today, *qayateen* and *qitan* are still used with relation to cords, such as shoelaces.

Beer and blood were mentioned in some of the recipes, but these occur less frequently. Blood in particular was mostly used as a marinating agent for meat. For garnish raw condiments, such chopped fresh mint, coriander (cilantro) and leeks were added, and the instruction, to add "after cooking," was quite clear on that.

Tablet 8958

Tablet 8958 is much longer than the previous one, and in its approximately 200 lines of text, only seven recipes were given. They all dealt with preparations of various types of birds, both domestic and game, that were presented in an extensively detailed manner. The writer of the tablet, for instance, felt the need to specify that bird should be put on the platter "lying on its back." He also gave substitutes, such as using "baru" if "kisimmu" was not available. He further gave instructions to serve the dish before it cools, and suggested that "garlic, greens, and vinegar" were to be served with the dish. As to what to do with leftovers of the broth, "it can be eaten later, by itself," he suggests.

In all these recipes great care was given to thorough cleaning of the birds before simmering them. A slaughtered bird was soaked in hot water, and plucked, and then washed in cold water. The neck was left attached to the body. Then it was cut open, gizzard and pluck removed, and washed again with cold water. The gizzard was split open, and membrane peeled off. This was exactly the way I have seen chickens plucked and cleaned when hens destined for the table were bought alive.

All the recipes include a preliminary step in which the birds were put in a cauldron, but due to lack of information and breaks in the tablet, it was not clear whether water was added, or for what purpose they were put in the cauldron. However, judging from a recipe in the previous tablet, namely, Francolin Stew, the directions were not to add the bird to the simmering stew before cooking it first in the cauldron. It is safe to assume, therefore, that the birds were put in the cauldron to parboil, before adding them to the pot.

In the tablet there were also directions to take the birds out of the cauldron, and wipe and clean them well with cold water, sometimes sprinkle them with vinegar, rub them with salt and mint, and then simmer them with a fresh change of water with condiments. It is my assumption that the preliminary stage of parboiling the birds, was to make sure of the cleanliness of the birds, and what's more important, to get rid of any unpleasant "birdie" odors. I know of people who still do this with red meat and chicken to get clean broth that is clear of any scum particles, or any unpleasant "chickeny" smells.

The bird dishes featured in this tablet verged on the sour side in their final taste. "Vinegar as required" was added in addition to "andahsu." Bottèro thought it was some sort of alliaceous plant because it was listed with onion and leeks. However, according to *The Assyrian Herbal*, "andahsu" was a sort of plums (cf. Arabic *'injas*, 129-130). It is my hunch this fruit was similar to the *goaja* plums that are still growing in Iraq. When still unripe and green these plums can be very sour. Actually, in the tenth-century Baghdadi cookbook, this type of plums was used in several dishes, such as the *Bustaniya* (like an orchard) dish. The writer referred to it as "small and sour *ijas*," and was mashed in order to extract its sour juice (al-Warraq 163). The sourness in one of the Babylonian recipes was balanced with honey.

In at least three of the recipes given in this tablet we have man's first attempts at making savory pies, apparently prepared for festive occasions, with an eye on surprising the diners with what lied hidden under the crust. The recipes went through four stages. The first was cleaning the birds, and parboiling and wiping them. The second, was simmering them in white sauce prepared from water, milk, fat, aromatic wood (cassia?), and rue. When it came to a boil, mashed garlic and leeks with onion, but "in moderation" were added to the sauce. The third stage painstakingly described preparing the dough, in which "sasku"-flour was soaked in milk until well saturated, then kneaded with "siqu" brine (similar to fish sauce), and mashed leeks and garlic. Some of this dough was made into "sebetu" small breads. A "makaltu"-platter (with high sides), big enough to accommodate the birds and the sauce, was lined with a thin layer of dough, letting the dough overhang the sides by "four fingers." A top crust was made by first sprinkling another matching size platter with chopped mint, then lining it with a thin layer of dough. Both layers were baked.

Just before serving, the sauce was refreshed with added, pounded leeks, garlic and "andahsu" (sour green plums). The birds were carefully arranged in the pot, lined with the cooked crust, scattering the chopped gizzards and plucks all over. Some of the sauce was poured on the birds. The small "sebetu" breads were arranged on top, and the whole dish was covered with the top crust attractively speckled with the chopped mint. The dish was then taken to the table.

The other one was even more elaborate, with ample suggestions and directions for accompanying porridges. The laborious preparations of the dish clearly aimed at creating a sweet and sour effect. The sauce was prepared much like the previous pie, with extra red meat, beer, and "a carefully measured amount of vinegar," added to it. An "asallu"-platter was lined with a thin layer of dough made from coarsely ground "ziqqu"-flour, with buttermilk and butter, and was baked. Batter from "tiktu"-flour, and aromatic beer was poured on the lined "asallu"-platter. On top of this they spread leek, garlic, honey, butter, and one of the prepared porridges. Then the cooked birds were arranged on top. It is not certain how the rest went due to breaks in the tablet, but Bottèro concludes that we can imagine the whole casserole would be covered with the top crust and then served.

Tablet 4648

This tablet is badly damaged, and Bottèro was able to decipher only three fragmentary parts, two of which dealt with bird recipes, also using vinegar, beer and "andahsu" for flavor. The significance of this tablet for me as an Iraqi cook is that I recognize in it two common cooking practices. There is a reference to preparing "sasku"-flour (ellipses follow), then adding to it meat, which has been chopped first. If it turns out the flour was made into dough before mixing it with the chopped meat, it would have been so much like the *khubuz laham* we still bake in Iraq. It is simply bread dough, mixed with chopped meat, onion, parsley, and spices (see chapter 1, on breads)

In one of the recipes, there is a reference to an ingredient used in making green porridge. In the Akkadian it was referred to as "butumtu," translated in the recipe as "green wheat." Nowadays there are trees in northern Iraq that produce small nuts, the size of a chickpea each, which when broken would reveal nut-meat similar in color and taste to pistachio. We call these nuts *butum*. If the Akkadian "butumtu" were the same as our modern *butum*, then we might just as well see in such a document man's first recorded attempts to incorporate the delicious and nourishing nuts into his diet, a practice that has been characteristic of Middle Eastern cuisine all along.

One last remark. In case you'll be tempted to go to the kitchen and try some of these recipes, let me assure you they have been tried. Jack Sasson, who translated these recipes from French to English, said that during the 1986 meetings of *The American Oriental Society* in New Haven, a banquet was adapted from these recipes. He thought the result was "quite delicious" (*Mesopotamian Culinary Texts* 8, n.8). Besides, the staff of the French magazine *Actuel*, tried the pie dish, took a photo for it, and then ate it. They thought it was "a real treat" (*Aramco World* 8). However, Bottèro, the decipherer of these recipes, said "he would not wish such meals on any save his worst enemies" (*The Culinary Tablets at Yal*e 19, n.40). The Babylonian tablets must have given him a hard time.

They Wrote on Clay

It is unlikely that those recipes were written by a cook, or were meant to be as an instructive manual for the cooks of the temples or palaces, for it is almost certain that the ancient cooks were illiterate. The writing system of ancient Mesopotamia was complicated. It was not alphabetical like most of the modern languages, but was both ideographic and syllabic that took years of constant hard work to master. That's why reading and writing was a profession by itself. A reading public as we know it today was nonexistent. Therefore it is Bottèro's conclusion that these recipes were written for "administrative and normative purposes, so that what was done in cooking might be set down and codified by means of recipes" ("The Cuisine of Mesopotamia" 46).

Obvious is the case that all these luxurious dishes belonged to the haute cuisine of the palace and temple. It was unlikely that the majority of the people had the time or the means to cook such elaborate stews and pies. However, Bottèro rightly concludes that in any given society and culture "imagination and taste are contagious." It is fair to assume with him that "the women who cooked in their modest homes knew how to turn out dishes which were just as tasty and imaginative as those which the "nuhatimmu" [Sumerian for professional chefs] of the palace created, though they were probably simpler and not so varied" ("The Cuisine of Mesopotamia" 46).

Assyrian carved alabaster depicting Elamite prisoners
having a simple meal.

The Question of Consistency and Continuity

Bottèro thinks that the consistency and continuity of this cuisine are manifest in the "mersu" stew, dated earlier than the Babylonian tablets. It was basically a number of vegetables and cumin simmered until sauce was reduced. He also sees consistency in some dishes cooked a thousand years later (i.e. the Middle Ages, *Mesopotamian Culinary Texts* 21). I could not agree more. Judging from the extant medieval Baghdadi cookbooks and from our own present day culinary practices, I see in these ancient recipes the beginnings of a long tradition that is still with us. In them I see the meat and vegetable stew dishes, cooked with different cuts of meat, enriched with fat of sheep tail, thickened with various agents, and flavored with lots of garlic and onion. These stews, along with a side dish of rice, are still a staple dish in modern Iraq.

In the recipes I also see the same flair for combining spices and herbs to produce aromatic dishes. The taste for combining the sweet and sour we find in one of these recipes has evolved into the countless sweet and sour dishes, the trade mark of the medieval era, some remnants of which we still have cooking. I see in them our love for bread and the thoroughly traditional *pacha* and *thareed* dishes that have been simmering in our pots all these centuries. I see in the "bits of toasted 'qaiatu'-

25

dough," thrown into the boiling stew but a stage in the long history of man's attempts to perfect the art of making pasta, particularly the fine noodles we nowadays call *sha'riya*.

Last and not least, I see in them the same knack for culinary showmanship and love for intrigue, that culminated in the *makhfiyat* (hidden) and *maghmoumat* (covered) dishes of the medieval times and the stuffed *kubba* and *mahshiyyat* dishes of modern times. I see this in the Babylonian pie dishes, laboriously contrived of birds simmered to perfection in white sauce, covered with a top crust, only to be uncovered in front of the awe-stricken eaters. Still, I shall let Bottèro, the decipherer of these tablets, have the last word:

> We know nothing of the culinary habits of neighboring ancient cultures. Whatever they may have been, certainly no one, after taking cognizance of the three Yale recipe collections, would deny that ancient Mesopotamia had its own original cuisine, a grand cuisine implying and demanding a subtle taste and an evident concern for real gastronomy.... There is some likelihood that this venerable cuisine may have inspired, from an early time, a whole tradition, whose long course, difficult or impossible to follow at first, has merged into the vast "Arabo-Turkish" culinary complex that still delights us. (*Mesopotamian Culinary Texts* 21)

Medieval Baghdadi Cooking

Our second distinguished culinary period is the rule of the Abbasid caliphs, eighth to thirteenth centuries AD during which a flourishing civilization was established

Navel of the Earth

When the Abbasids came to power they founded for their capital the round city of Baghdad in 762 AD. It was built on the ruined site of the ancient city Bagdadu (also known as Seleucia), which was established around 310 BC. The ancient Bagdadu was an important trade city and was the center of Hellenism in Mesopotamia. But it did not survive for long, it was destroyed in 164 AD after less than five centuries. When the Abbasids came they chose the site for its location, fertility and wholesome air. According to one of the contemporary historians (al-Hamawi) Iraq was the center of the world, and Baghdad was the navel of the earth, and "paradise on earth."

Gardens of Eden

During the Abbasid period Baghdad was legendary for the beauty and lusciousness of its sequestered pleasure gardens, with their soothing gushing streams, pools and fountains. There also were the picturesque public pleasure spots outside the city where people used to picnic. Their orchards brimmed with all kinds of fruit trees and aromatic flowers and herbs, and the bounteous vegetable gardens made it possible for the creative cooks to conjure up the fabulous dishes for which the medieval Baghdadi cuisine was renowned. In their contemporary literature Baghdad was often compared to the celestial gardens of Paradise (*Jannat Adan*). In the verse lines excerpted in al-Tawheedi's tenth-century *Al-Risala Al-Baghdadiya* (Baghdadi tract) the poet says:

I yearn for Baghdad, my homeland,
It was my haven in times of distress.

On the day I took my leave of it,
I was like Adam when from heaven was expelled. (111)

In another passage in the same book, the protagonist Abu al-Qasim sings praises of Baghdad as follows:

I would not even exchange it with the eternal Paradise. Its soil is ambergris, its stones are rubies, its air is gentle, and its water is nectar. It is spacious and aptly situated. It looks as though the beauties of the world are spread all over it. A duplicate of Paradise, the centerpiece of the world and its navel, its face and its luminous forehead. (90)

Such descriptions were clearly inspired by the beautiful verses of the Qur'an in which are given vivid accounts of what awaits the believers in *jannat Adan*, the celestial gardens of Paradise, under which rivers flow. It is a peaceful and densely shaded place, where the believers, clad in green silken gowns, will be sitting on sequestered luxurious recliners, and enjoying God's everlasting bounty. Fruit trees of all kinds such as pomegranate, banana, date, grapevines, are all within easy reach. They will also have whatever they crave of meat and poultry.

Like the Hanging Gardens of Babylon, the fountains gush with water that flows down from above the rooftops of palaces (*tasneem*). There are rivers that flow with never-changing water, rivers that flow with milk that will never sour, rivers of delicious wine, and others of purified honey. The heavenly drinks are pure sealed nectar with a lingering taste of mastic, and wine flavored with ginger, served in containers of silver and glass.

In essence, the Muslim Paradise is a continuation of the Judeo-Christian paradise, which in turn bears telling resemblance to the Mesopotamian paradisiacal narratives that go far back in time to the Akkadians and Sumerians. We knew of this only quite recently when Sumerian texts were translated, revealing an amazing wealth of information on these ancient peoples. Samuel Kramer in his *History Begins at Sumer* asserts that "the very idea of a divine paradise, a garden of the gods, is of Sumerian origin," and its location was a place they called Dulman, the land of the pure, the clean, and the bright." It was the "land of the living," the home of the immortals who "know neither sickness nor death." At first it lacked water, but then the water god, Enki, ordered it to be filled "with water brought up from the earth." Thus it became "a divine garden, green with fruit-laden fields and meadows." It was the land of painless and effortless labor. The nine "months of womanhood" were reduced to nine days, and when labor came to goddess Ninmu, baby goddess Ninkurra painlessly slipped out of her "like good princely cream" (143-5).

Besides such mythical gardens, the ancient Mesopotamian kings were famous for designing their own terrestrial paradises where exotic plants of trees and flowers, brought from far and wide, grew. The most famous of these were definitely the hanging gardens of Babylon. They were irrigated by drawing water from the river Euphrates by pumping it by means of hydraulic engines all the way up to the top level of the gardens that rose tier upon tier.

Baghdad rapidly became the marketplace of the world, an important trading highway and a gateway from which caravans set out to bring back foods from afar. Merchants ventured as far as

China for cinnamon and other spices (*baharat*). Politically and culturally it was a period of tremendous power and luxury. When Islam spread westwards to Spain, with it spread the Baghdadi lifestyle of luxury and culture. In short, Baghdad became a great influential metropolis. It was a great place for agriculture. The land itself was used to the utmost, to the extent that Iraq was called Ardh *al-Sawad*, (the black-land country), because the whole region was cultivated, and was densely populated. We read in history books that a rooster crowing in one village was heard and answered back by the rooster of the neighboring village.

Grocery Shopping in Medieval Baghdad

During the flourishing Abbasid period, Baghdad became an international open market for merchandise from all over the world, in addition to its own vast local repertoire. In *The Arabian Nights* story of "The Porter and the Three Ladies of Baghdad," for instance, the porter was asked by a lady shopper to take his crate and follow her. She first raps on the door of a Nazarene, who sells her strained wine as clear as olive oil. She then goes to the fruits shop and buys Syrian apples, Osmani (Ottoman) quinces, Omani peaches, cucumbers of Nile growth, Egyptian limes, Sultani oranges and citrons. The same shop offers flowers and aromatic herbs, as well. She buys Aleppine jasmine, scented myrtle berries, chamomile, violets, eglantine, narcissus, and pomegranate blooms. She stops at the butcher's booth and buys 10 pounds of mutton. At the grocer's, she stops and buys dried fruits, pistachio, Tihami raisins, and shelled almonds.

From the confectioner's she buys an earthen platter, and piles it with all kinds of sweetmeats, open-worked tarts (*zilabia*), fritters scented with musk (*qata'if*), lemon cakes, melon preserves, Zaynab's combs (puff pastry soaked in syrup?), lady's fingers (cannoli-like pastry), and *qadhi's* tit-bits (judge's morsels dipped in syrup).

Her next stopping place is the perfumer's. She buys ten sorts of scented waters, rose scented with musk, orange flower, water lily, willow-flower, violet and five others. She also buys two loaves of sugar, a bottle for perfume spraying, a lump of incense, aloe wood, ambergris and musk, with candles of Alexandria wax. Her last station is the grocer's, where she buys pickled safflowers and olives, in brine and in oil, with tarragon, cream cheese and hard Syrian cheese (Vol.1, 82-3).

Great Chefs, Great Cities

Location: Ancient Sumer, Ur
Time: 2900-2300 BC

The culinary profession then as it is now, was dominated by the male sex. While within the domain of the household, it was the women who were responsible for preparing the meals, the haute cuisine of the privileged at the temple and the palace was monopolized by the male chefs. Cooking was a profession learnt through apprenticeship. The period of training was sixteen months, during which period the son is loaned to the craftsman. Textual evidence also attests to the fact that cooking was acknowledged as an art--a list of the Sumerian artisans began with "cooks." Other artisans included were jewelers and metal workers who by far were the most important craftsmen of Sumer. In other lists, the cook sometimes was referred to as "the great cook," or "chief cook." Some of them even acquired considerable power and prestige. One of these "great chefs" had his own seal, given to him by the king (Limet 140).

Location: Baghdad.
Time: The Abbasid Caliphate, eighth to thirteenth centuries AD.

The court cuisine of the Abbasid Caliphate was legendary for its lavishness and sophistication. Cooking was definitely not a mere private skill, nor was it looked upon as just a profession. It was by common consent an art worthy of being pursued and perfeced. The caliphs, princes, courtiers, men of learning, boon companions, and entertainers, they were all expected to be well informed in the gastronomical arts. In one of the stories in *The Arabian Nights*, the famous Caliph Haroun al-Rasheed catches fish and prepares a delicious meal for a damsel and her lover. The caliph, in disguise, comes with his catch, "and behold the fishes were still alive and jumping, whereupon the damsel exclaimed, "By Allah! O my lord, these are indeed fine fish: would they were fried!" Behind the scene, al-Rasheed's minister offered to fry them for him but he insisted, "By the tombs of my forbears, none shall fry it but I, with my own hands!" So he went to the gardener's hut, where he searched and found all that he required, even to salt and saffron and wild marjoram and else besides. Then he turned to the brazier and, setting on the frying-pan, fried a right good fish. When it was done, he laid it on a banana-leaf, and gathering from the garden wind-fallen fruits, limes [*leimo*] and lemons [*leimoun*], carried the fish to the pavilion and set the dish before them (Vol. II, 33).

Some of these political personages even wrote cookbooks and manuals. In this field Ibrahim Ibn al-Mahdi, half-brother of Haroun al-Rasheed, looms large. Politically he did not play an important role for he was more inclined towards the arts, poetry, music, singing and gastronomy. Indeed, he was the prince of epicures. Although his actual book perished, so many of his recipes and dishes inspired by them, usually referred to as "*Ibrahimiyat*" were

immortalized in poems, anecdotes and in all the extant medieval cookbooks, east and west of the Arab world.

Gastronomy, apparently, was largely a male dominated field. There were quite few references to female chefs or gastronomes. Of the rare female gourmets mentioned in contemporary chronicles and cookbooks was Buran, the wife of the Abbasid Caliph al-Ma'moun (ninth century). She was accredited with inventing sumptuous eggplant dishes collectively called *Buraniyat*, after her name. Even today her name still resounds in as far a way places from Baghdad as Spain and Afghanistan.

Of the professional female cooks, we know of al-Mahdi's slave girl, Bid'a, about whom poems singing praises of her culinary skills were composed, and whose reputation as an excellent cook went far and wide. In the medieval Andalusian cookbooks, there were several recipes for *al-Badi'iya*, a dish called after her name. She was particularly famous for her *Sikbaj*, a sweet and sour meat and vegetable dish, seasoned with spices and thickened with ground nuts. Al-Warraq, the tenth century cookbook writer, recorded how once she made this dish for the Caliph al-Ameen. It was a festival to the senses. The aromas were incredible, the dish looked like an adorned bride, or an orchard flower (*zahrat'l bustan*), what with all the stuffed foods, the sausages, and small sandwiches. The s*anbousa* pastries alternated with vegetables and herbs. All these foods were artistically arranged on a huge platter in the middle of which was a bowl of white sharp mustard (133-4).

In al-Warraq's cookbook there were several references to professional cooks such as a female cook named Um-Hakeem, renowned for her dish of *Qalya* (dish of fried meat). Of the male cooks he mentioned Abu-Sameen (father of the fat one), who apparently descended from a long line of cooks. He was once referred to as Abdallah Ibn Sameen (son of the fat one), and his brother Abu-Ishaq Ibn Sameen was equally famous. There was also mention of famous confectioners, such as Abu-Mu'ala al-Halawani, and Saleem al-Hallawi.

Gastronomes of the Abbasid Era

When papermaking and stationary became significant businesses in Baghdad in the ninth century AD, literary creativity flourished, and books started to be copied on paper, for sale to interested readers. Of these books were the tales of *The Arabian Nights*, cookbooks and gastronomic guides and manuals. The tradition of composing cookery manuals in Arabic goes back to the second half of the eighth century AD. Ibn al-Nadeem, author of the *Fihrist* (ca. 990), for instance, provided a comprehensive list of cooking guides written by such celebrities as Ibrahim Ibn al-Mahdi, half brother of Haroun al-Rasheed. Others include Yahya al-Mausili, astrologer and musician, Ibn Masawaih, physician of Haroun al-Rasheed and his successors who were reputed to have had their meals only in his presence. Unfortunately none of these books survived. By the end of the tenth century AD, at least 28 titles were acknowledged in Arabic chronicles Again, none survived, lost or perished when the Mongols attacked Baghdad in 1258 AD and ransacked the city. Books were the second casualties after human beings. It was said that the river Tigris turned red the first day and blue the second, from the ink of books thrown into it.

Luckily we are still able to make a vivid picture of what the gastronomic situation was at the time from the countless anecdotes the medieval Arab historians included in their chronicles. From such books we learn of the lavish feasts held by the caliphs and the affluent, and of the public feasts they occasionally provided on certain religious and political occasions. On one such memorable public event registered in history, 1,000 tables were set. On each table were put ten dishes of each of the following: *thareed* (a famous dish of lamb and bread sopped in rich flavorful broth), grilled meat, and fish. The "waiters" went around serving drinks of honeyed water and *laban* (diluted yogurt). Of the caliphs' menus, it was said they were composed of no less than 300 kinds of dishes per meal. Once in a dinner invitation, the caliph Haroun al-Rasheed was offered a small dish, which he thought was made of tiny pieces of fish. It turned out that those tiny pieces were actually tongues of fish, 150 tongues in all. Apparently despite all the food varieties and luxuries available at the time, the basic dietary ingredients of dates, butter, and bread remained all time's favorites for everybody. One of the Abbasid Caliphs was reputed to have said that the beauty of a dinner table was determined by how much bread was put on it.

In addition to anecdotes, many songs and poems were composed on food, and were known as the "poems of the table." Ibn al-Mahdi, the prince of epicures, was its advocate, and Ibn al-Roumi, following his steps, became the most outstanding "table poet" in his own right. The tenth century historian, al-Mas'oudi, narrates in his *Murouj al-Dhahab* (Meadows of Gold) how the caliph Ibn al-Mustakfi, (d. 949) expressed his desire to assemble one day to converse on the different varieties of food, and the poetry composed on the subject. The poems recited on that occasion describe an interesting collection of dishes and recipes, starting with appetizers, and ending with desserts. (Most of these poems are quoted in the following chapters, wherever relevant). It is also said that Al-Mu'tasim, the Abbasid Caliph, was known to have organized cooking contests. Besides, we still have several physicians' dietetic treatises, such as al-Tabari's, Ibn Masawaih's, and al-Razi's. They abound with important information on food in general.

Among the upper classes there was a considerable interest in the culinary arts and in writing and reading about them. The aspiring courtiers and boons, for instance, were expected to talk about food intelligently, and to have full mastery of table manners. Such accomplishments were their sure passports, so to speak, to the world of the sophisticated, affluent, and the powerful. This in fact explains why, in addition to books and manuals on cooking and food, many manuals were composed on table etiquette.

As for food of ordinary people and descriptions of their daily lives, we can go to the non-religious literature written during the period, which provides us a wealth of information. There is al-Jahiz's satire *al-Bukhala'* (the misers), for instance, written in the ninth century AD, in the port city of Basrah. The book is a collection of amusing and humorous anecdotes on miserly people, many of which inevitably revolve around food, and eating and drinking. One of the misers, for instance, explains to his friends why he uncharacteristically distributed a gift of date syrup amongst his friends. Had he sold it, he explains, he would have been shamed. Had he kept it, it would have incurred further expenses such as buying butter and what not, for his wife might have wanted to make puddings and cookies (*'asida, aruziya,* and *bastanud*). Thus it would have ended up being even more costly than raising his kids (63).

Another amusing source on daily life in Baghdad was written by al-Jahiz's disciple Abu Hayyan al-Tawhidi. In his *Al-Risala al-Baghdadiya* (the Baghdadi tract, tenth century) the protagonist is a Baghdadi himself who spends a whole day being hosted by a household in the Persian city, Asfahan. His narrative gives us a realistic account of what life was like in Baghdad at the time, with a list of the foods and dishes prepared by the high and low. From his book we learn how the Baghdadis used to go on joy rides in boats on the river Tigris, and how they used to picnic in the countless pleasure spots outside Baghdad where they spend the day eating, drinking and carousing. Another interesting source of information is the *Maqamat* (the assemblies) of al-Hamadani (tenth century), and of al-Hariri (twelfth century). The roguish protagonists travel in the Islamic world, and food expectedly is one of their pursuits.

Finally, the well-known *Arabian Nights* offers dazzling accounts of the lifestyles of the extravagant and the ordinary alike. It was tremendously popular even at that time, especially amongst the masses. It opened to them gates into a world of fantasy abundant in romance, intrigue, and women and men seeking all kinds of fulfillment. Mouthwatering accounts of exotic and mundane foods and dishes are practically on every page. In the story of the porter and the three ladies, Scheherazade tells of numerous food items available in Baghdad to grocery shoppers at the time. In the story of 'Azeez and 'Azeeza, The lover's devotion was put to the test by making him choose between his heart and stomach. Needless to say the lover failed the test the first two nights.

He was hungry for he had not tasted food for a long time, "by reason of the violence" of his love. He uncovered the table and to his heart's, or stomach's, delight he found:

> four chickens reddened with roasting and seasoned with spices, round which were four saucers, one containing sweetmeats, another conserve of pomegranate-seeds, and a third almond pastry (baklawa) and a fourth honey fritters (*zilabiya*); and the contents of these saucers were part sweet and part sour. So I ate of the fritters and a piece of meat, then went on to the almond-cakes and ate what I could; after which I fell upon the sweetmeats, whereof I swallowed a spoonful or two or three or four, ending with part of chicken and a mouthful of something beside (Burton, vol. 2, 310-1).

After all this who would blame the lover for laying his head on a cushion and surrendering to sleep, thus flunking the test?

There were also stories that told the depraved ordinary there was more in life than just a piece of bread stuffed with cheese. When, in one of the stories, a man, who suddenly got lucky, asked his mother what she wanted for dinner, he laughed when she asked for a simple meal. From now on, and as a rich woman, he boasted, she'd better demand browned chicken and meat, steamed rice, sausages, stuffed gourds, stuffed lamb, *qata'f*, etc, etc.

Cookbooks of the Abbasid Era

Luckily some of the many Arabic cookbooks proper written during this period survived the destruction and wear and tear of time. The earliest of these is the tenth-century *Kitab al-Tabeekh* (the book of cookery) by Ibn Sayyar al-Warraq of Baghdad. It deals mostly with urban ninth century cooking. Only two copies exist, one at the University Library of Helsinki, and the other at the Bodleian Library. The text itself was made accessible to the public only in 1987.

The second medieval Baghdadi cookbook, also entitled *Kitab al-Tabeekh* (book of cookery), was written by Ibn al-Khateeb al-Baghdadi, in 1226. The manuscript was first discovered by the Iraqi scholar Daoud al-Chalabi, and published in 1934 in Mosul. The British scholar A. J. Arberry translated it into English in 1939. This discovery was a breakthrough with regard to knowledge of medieval cooking, for it contained medieval recipes of dishes that were, up until that time, known only in name if not at all. For decades it was the only significant document we had of the Baghdadi cuisine.

Besides these two cookbooks, there also survived copies of others written in several regions of the medieval Arab world over different periods of time. These are *Kitab al-Wusla ila'l Habeeb fi Wasf al-Tayyibat wa'l Teeb* (loosely translated as "the way to the heart is through the stomach") reputedly written by the thirteenth century historian Ibn al-Adeem of Aleppo. Of this we have ten extant copies (Rodinson, 116-21). There is the late medieval Egyptian anonymous *Kanz al-Fawa'id fi Tanwi' al-At'ima* (the treasure of goodness in preparing varied foods). Of this there are three copies in Cairo (Rodinson, 104). There is also the fifteenth-century manual of *Kitab al-Tabeekh* (cookbook) by ibn al-Mubarrid of Damascus, translated into English by Charles Perry in 1985. In Andalusia, Muslim Spain, two cookbooks survived. The first is the thirteenth-century *Kitab Fidhalat al-Khiwan fi Tayyibat al-Ta'am wal Alwan* (the superfluity of the food) by Ibn Razin al-Tujibi, and the second is the thirteenth-century *Anonymous Andalusian Cookbook*, (recently translated into English by Charles Perry). All these books, through their many acknowledged direct borrowings and adaptations of the Baghdadi dishes, throw further light on the Baghdadi cuisine which had a profound impact on other regions that extend as far as Spain and Italy. They are also important in that they give information sometimes overlooked by the Baghdadi writers. For instance, in the anonymous Andalusian cookbook, the writer commends the Abbasid caliphs of the *Mashriq* (Eastern

Abbasid caliphate, the capital of which was Baghdad) for their love of bread. They command their bakers to prepare many kinds of bread and present them on a huge tray, so that they make their pick.

Of these, I am focusing on the two Baghdadi cookbooks principally for their relevance to the development of Iraqi cuisine. Al-Warraq's, in particular, is historically significant for it is the earliest cookbook ever to be preserved from the medieval world. We do not have a single book of medieval Persian cuisine, which only survived in anecdotes and poems. The emergence of the Chinese "world's first cuisine" can only be dated back to the southern Sung period of around twelfth century AD, and the available sources do not provide specific preparations for dishes. With the exception of the fourth century AD compilation of Apicius, the first European fragmentary *Book of Cookery* was written in the fourteenth century (Waines 8).

As for who these two Baghdadi authors were, almost nothing is known. There is the possibility; however, that al-Warraq might have had connections with the printing and book selling business (from *waraq*, paper). As deduced from his Preface, it is almost certain that he had access or connections with the Caliph's palace and the important people at the time. Apparently he was commissioned by an important personage. "You have asked of me, may God lengthen your stay," he says addressing his commissioner, "to compose a book for you in which to include different kinds of dishes that were prepared for kings, caliphs, and the state dignitaries." And this is what he does in the book. He includes recipes of dishes prepared for or by caliphs such as Haroun al-Rasheed, al-Ma'moun, al-Mutawakil, al-Ma'tamid, and al-Wathiq. There are countless dishes by Prince Ibrahim Ibn al-Mahdi, the physician Ibn-Masawaih, and professional palace cooks such as Ibn Dahqana, and Abu-Sameen (father of the fat one), the personal cook of Caliph al-Wathiq.

The book is encyclopedic in scope. In its 132 short chapters, spread over 342 pages, al-Warraq practically covers all kinds of food categories--breads, condiments, dairy products, stews, fish, *tannour*-grilled meats, lots of baked stuffed kids, lambs, and chicken, sausages, cold vegetable dishes, desserts and thirst quenching drinks, and much more. In addition to these, there is a wealth of food related information. He discusses the properties of different foods, how to choose the best ingredients to ensure satisfactory results, kitchen utensils and gadgets, healing properties of foods, choice ingredients for washing the hand, table etiquette, and a of myriad of culinary poems and anecdotes to entertain the reader.

Interesting Tidbits from al-Warraq's Cookbook

- Do not use the same knife to cut meat and vegetables.
- Do not use spices that have been around for a while and "expired."
- To test the cleanliness of a pot, put a stone in one nostril and the washed pot close to the other and sniff. They should smell the same.
- Iron pans are the best for frying fish. This will result in having nicely crisped skins.
- To get rid of the taste of burned food, put a couple of whole walnuts in the pot and let them cook with the food for a while, then discard the walnuts.
- Eat only what you have the appetite for. If you eat what you do not crave, it will eat you.
- Some foods are aphrodisiac and have the power to increase male sperms, such as sweets in general, especially dates and grapes, carrot drink, eggs, onions, coconut, pine nuts, asparagus, and chickpeas.
- Eat cheese after a heavy meal, for it helps with the digestion (much like what the

French do).

- Cumin and cinnamon are gas-repellent and digestive.
- Having too much rose water would cause hair to turn white.
- Juice of pomegranate, apple cider, and quince juice are kidney-stone repellents.
- Cauliflower causes stomach gargles.
- Serve a variety of dishes, and prolong a meal as much as possible, (Another French gastronomical habit)
- Exercise before a meal, but avoid it after a heavy meal.
- A brief snooze after a meal is recommended, provided you lie on your back, and do not use a high pillow.
- How to make yogurt without using milk: peel pieces of coconut. Shred it, then cover it with water, and squeeze it with fingers until it becomes milky in texture. Strain and let it sour as you do with regular milk.
- How to make omelet without eggs: Cook chickpeas until mushy in texture, and mix them with boiled onion, oil and coriander. Then mash mixture and fry it as you do with eggs.

At the approach of the thirteenth century, the Abbasid dynasty was in state of decline. The task of writing cookbooks and preparing manuals during the period was mainly undertaken by less illustrious personages, such as obscure scholars and amateur epicures. Ibn al-Khateeb al-Baghdadi was such a one. Of his personal life practically nothing is known aside from what we deduce from the preface to his cookbook.

About his incentive in writing the book, he mentions in the preface that he is dissatisfied with the several books he has come across. They contain "mention of strange and unfamiliar dishes, in the composition of which unwholesome and unsatisfying ingredients are used" (32). He acknowledges cooking as a noble art, and food as a perfectly acceptable indulgence, and assures the readers that it will do no harm to specialize in it. As for whom he wrote it, he did it for his own use, he says, "and for the use of whoever may wish to employ it" (33). This time we know we are dealing with the middle class Abbasid cuisine, and the choice of the dishes in the book is pretty much determined by the writer's own private taste."I have mentioned in it," he says,"dishes selected by myself, perhaps passing over briefly such as are well-known and in common use" (33). Stylistically it is different from al-Warraq's, who wrote his in a noticeably more leisurely fashion, as his aim was to entertain as much as instruct. Al-Baghdadi's, on the other hand, was of a more pragmatic nature. He declares that his "principle throughout has been brevity and succinctness, and the avoidance of prolixity and long-windedness." And indeed he does just that.

Despite its modest size (42 pages), the book is admirably comprehensive. All the necessary details are there, and in crucial recipes exact amounts or precise instructions are given. In preparing the *Narinjiya*, a stew soured by using a cheap variety of orange, known as orange of Seville, his directions are that the oranges should be peeled by one person and pressed by another. For those who have actually handled these oranges, the reason is quite obvious, the peel is devastatingly bitter and would otherwise ruin the stew. It is such remarks that makes the reader believe that he is dealing with a culinary writer who knows what he is talking about. The Iraqi scholar Daoud al-Chalabi, the discoverer and editor of the manuscript, was all admiration of al-Baghdadi's method. He said in his preface, that he had described the dishes, "in exact language, just as though he was detailing some alchemical operation" (Arberry 30).

The book contains around 158 recipes covering a wide variety of dishes including stuffed foods characteristic of the Iraqi cuisine to this day. It has:

22 sour, and sweet and sour stews

6 milk dishes, such as *labaniya* (yogurt dish)

17 plain (not sour) stews, soups and grain dishes

8 fried and dry dishes

22 simple and sweet dishes, stuffed foods such as *Madfouna* (buried) and *Makhfiya* (hidden) A long paragraph on chicken dishes which are made almost like the red meat dishes

9 *harisa* and *tannour*-baked dishes

10 fried and soused (marinated and simmered in vinegar) dishes, savory pastries, and sandwiches

12 fish dishes

14 sauces, condiments, relishes, and vegetable side dishes

judhab (meat and bread puddings) and *khabees* (condensed vegetarian puddings)

9 *halwas*

13 sweet pastries, such as *khushkanaj* (cookies) and *qata'if* (crepes).

Al-Baghdadi's cookbook must have been quite popular in the Arab and Islamic world, for we now have available several manuscripts under the title *Wasf al-At'ima al-Mu'tada* (description of familiar foods), which were in fact augmented versions of his book. The added recipes came from many sources, and were inserted at different times. The manuscripts date back to the period between fourteenth and eighteenth centuries. One of them, in particular, was handsomely executed for one of the Turkish Sultans (*Wasf al-At'ima* 276-7), and incidentally proves how far reaching al-Baghdadi's fame and influence was.

35

Summaqiya

Al-summaqiyat is a number of medieval stews in which choice chunks of meat were simmered in flavorful sumac juice. They were also knows as *al-Harouniyat* for they were Caliph Haroun al-Rasheed's favorite. Nowadays, in the northern city of Mosul where dried whole berries of sumac are readily available, people still prepare similar dishes which they call S*ummaq*. I know of a playful folkloric Mosuli song which sings its praises, but also bemoans the fact that it is loaded with fat, the opening lines are:
Ya simmaq, ya simmaq.
Akli dhini ma tindhaq.

As prepared in al-Bahgdadi's thirteenth-century cookbook, pieces of fat meat were simmered until almost done. Then chard, carrots, onion, leeks, and peeled eggplant were added. In another pot, the key ingredient sumac was boiled with salt and pith of a loaf, and then strained. Medium-sized meatballs were made from lean meat, and were added to the pot along with seasonings of dried coriander, cumin, pepper, ginger, cinnamon, mastic, and some sprigs of fresh mint. In a final stage, the prepared sumac liquid along with ground walnuts, ground garlic, dry mint, and a few pieces of whole walnut were added. Some people, the recipe goes, would like to garnish the dish with "eyes of eggs" (eggs poached with the heat of the simmering pot, sunny side up, 39). Al-Warraq's tenth-century preparations were much simpler. They were choice cuts of meat simmered in water and oil, with salt, chopped leeks, and strained *ma' al-summaq* (sumac juice). To get this juice Al-Warraq recommends warming up soaked sumac berries under the sun, or letting them steep in hot water, rather than boiling them.

Interestingly, this stew along with other sweet and sour dishes, namely *al-rummaniya* (pomegranate stew), *al-leimouniya* (lemon stew), *al-Ma'mouniya* (stew after the name of the Abbasid Caliph al-Ma'moun), they all feature in a fifteenth-century Italian cookbook (Rodinson, "*Rummaniya*," and "*Ma'mouniya*," and Rosenberger, 222)

Characteristics of the Medieval Baghdadi Cuisine

With the advent of the Abbasids, Mesopotamia regained its past glory, and Baghdad was transformed into the prosperous cosmopolitan capital of the world. In addition to its already vast repertoire of animal stock and agricultural products, new foodstuffs were introduced, such as eggplant, which added to the richness and variety of its cuisine. In his "Studies in Arabic Manuscripts," Maxime Rodinson aptly points out that examining the extant medieval recipes "amply demonstrates how this cuisine had absorbed local traditions, making use of ancient techniques, adopting exotic elements and enriching the whole with greater complexity and refinement" (149). In other words, in discussing the Baghdadi cuisine one has to take into consideration several factors. For instance, the local culinary tradition which, as we have seen in the preceding sections, had its roots in the ancient Mesopotamian culinary practices, in addition to the Abbasids' own heritage. The region's affluence also contributed to making it more pluralistic, and facilitated interactions between different ethnic and religious groups. Moreover, immigrant communities of Persians, Armenians,

Kurds, and foreign "slave girls" (such as the Georgians and Caucasians) brought their native recipes with them. Of these factors, however, the Persian influence seems to get the most attention due to the fact that they, and especially the Barmacides, enjoyed power and prestige during the beginning of the Abbasid rule. It was fashionable to do things the Persian way, and that included cooking. As to how much influence they actually exerted on the cooking scene, a closer examination of the data we have available now would indicate that the influence has been overstated.

True, we cannot help but notice, in the medieval literature and chronicles, the recurrent mention of Persian sounding dish names, such as *sikbaj, zirbaj, nirbaj,* or Arabic words given the medieval Persian suffix --*aj,* such as *lauzeenaj* and *jawzeenaj* (confections with almonds and walnuts, respectively), or even named after a place in Persia, such as *sughdiya.* These dishes were real enough. Recipes for making them were given in the contemporary cookbooks. Al-Baghdadi, himself, (thirteenth century) opens his book with a chapter on sour and sweet and sour dishes, first of which was *sikbaja.* Al-Warraq (tenth century) tells us how famous *sikbaja* was. Once Khosrau Anu-Sherwan lost his appetite and ordered a number of court cooks to cook their best dishes. They all came up with *sikbaj,* a meat dish in which the sauce was thickened with ground almonds, soured with vinegar, sweetened with honey, and seasoned with spices. He called it the queen of dishes, and monopolized it to himself and the closest members of his family. It was only after his fall that others started cooking it (132). This and other dishes might sound like straightforward Persian dishes, but that seems only part of the truth. In the case of *lauzeenaj* (confection with almonds), for instance, it was believed to be an ancient Persian pastry. It was mentioned in the Middle Persian book *The Story of King Khusrau and His Page.* However, if we know that almond in Persian was *badam,* and that in the Akkadian it was called "luzu"(from which the Arabic *louz* was derived (*Assyrian Herbal,* 182), then we certainly have in hand a curious case of ancient culinary borrowing.

Moreover, al-Warraq tells us the story of the birth of a Persian sounding dish, namely, the *Kushtabiya,* which will further illustrate how thorny the subject of influence and borrowing is. One of the Persian kings, the story goes, used to travel a lot, and he used to take with him his cook, who was an Arab. At the end of his riding session, the king would say to the cook, "*gusht biya,*" (bring the meat) and the cook would have ready for him a dish of grilled meat. It so happened one day that the king came back hungry and the grill fire was not ready yet, so his Arab cook had to improvise. He prepared a fast dish by putting the prepared meat pieces, oil, chopped onion, salt and ground spices in a frying pan. He then weighed the meat with a heavy plate, and let it cook fast under high heat, frequently sprinkling the meat with water to keep it from drying out. It came out deliciously moist, a happy medium between frying and grilling. The king liked it and it became his favorite dish. The cook called it *Kushtabiya,* and developed some variations on it. People started making it with meat and fat of sheep tail, and called it *Kusht,* which in its final version, vinegar, juice of sour grapes, or murri (fermented sauce) mixed with lime juice were added to it (216).

Of the twenty-two sweet and sour dishes al-Baghdadi gives in his stew chapter, only seven are given Persian names, the rest are called after the down-to-earth souring agent added to the dish. Yet, it was mostly these foreign dish names that kept on resounding in their poems, stories, and chronicles. The storytellers of the *Arabian Nights,* for instance, enchanted and hooked their readers and listeners by describing profusely the ways and means of the aristocracy, of their lavish feasts, their rich desserts, dripping with honey, and the exotic dishes of the *sikbaj* and *nirbaj* and *zirbaj.* It is my belief that a name of a dish such as, say, *husrumiya* (from *husrum,* sour grapes), would have hardly elicited any dribbling on the part of the audience, although it was basically cooked the same way. In modern terms, these dishes were as hip and faddish perhaps as cream sauce à la king, and pie à la mode were in the fifties and sixties, or the café au lait, and the chai tea were afterwards.

Medieval Affinities with Ancient Mesopotamian Cooking

I probed the origin of the word *tannour* (domed clay oven). Because the word is mentioned in the Qur'an, I assumed it was of Arabic origin. Somebody told me it was derived from the Hindi word "tandoor," and an old Arabic dictionary suggests the word was probably of Persian origin. Finally I checked books on the history of ancient Mesopotamia, and to my surprise the word turned out to be of Sumerian origin. They called it "tannouru."

This kind of knowledge was not available before the middle of the nineteenth century. In fact very little was known about the ancient civilizations of Babylon and Assyria, and of the Sumerians practically nothing was known. After the fall of Nebuchadnezzar, the region was ruled subsequently by the Persians, Greeks, Parthians, and the Sassanides, up until 636 AD, when the Muslim Arabs defeated the Persians and took hold of the region. However, throughout this period the culture itself "remained Mesopotamian, in custom, organization and in the language of the root population, whose Arabic is descended from the Aramaic spoken across the Near East in early Christian times, which in its turn comes from the Semitic Akkadian" (Wood, 34-5). Some of the ancient cities did not go into oblivion until much later, such as the ancient Mesopotamian sacred city of Nippur, which remained active and effective up until the fourteenth century, AD.

As we have seen in the previous sections, the most significant ancient culinary testimonies we have from the entire ancient Near Eastern region, to this day, are the Babylonian recipes written around 1700 BC. The world knew about them only as late as 1982 AD.

Admittedly the gap between that ancient era and the Abbasid one is too wide to expect names of dishes to have survived, and gastronomically speaking almost nothing is known of any developments that might have taken place during the interim. But now with the newly excavated evidence and accumulated information, we can possibly speak of a culinary continuity with regard to cooking techniques and even survival of some dishes.

Continuity is clearly evident in the fact that stew remained a staple dish. It was prepared, broadly speaking, the same old way: cuts of meat (the red and the white were sometimes combined) were browned in dissolved fat from sheep tail. Water was then added to it, with lots of onion and garlic, leeks, lots of spices, aromatics, and herbs, that were added at different stages in the cooking process. To these would be added some thickening agents such as milk, soured yogurt, grains, flour, bread crumbs or nuts The stew was then simmered over a prolonged period of time to let flavors blend and sauce thicken.

The tradition of cooking sour and sweet and sour stews is also evident in both cuisines. In the *Assyrian Herbal*, there is a description of an Assyrian "lubu" stew (Arabic *lubya*, black-eyed beans) which uses "beans, apricots, clean salt, bread [crumbs?], kidneys, etc" (197). Apparently the Babylonians preferred to have their stews rather on the sour side. A number of the Babylonian recipes called for vinegar and "andahsu" the green and sour variety of plums. Besides, the practice of balancing the sweet and the sour in savory dishes was featured, as we have seen, in one of the Babylonian elaborate recipe for the francolin birds. Vinegar, "andahsu" and honey were included in the ingredients for making this pie-like dish. They clearly indicate that the taste for the sour and the sweet and sour in savory dishes was not exclusively Persian. The medieval cooks exploited the possibilities to the full. They used vinegar, sumac, sour citrus fruits, quince, unripe sour fruits such as grapes and apples, and sour vegetables such as *ribas* (rhubarb). They were sometimes balanced by adding date syrup, honey, *julab* (syrup flavored with rose water) or sugar.

In the Babylonian recipes we also find frequent references to "siqu" (fermented fish sauce) and "kisimmu" (*kishk*, yogurt and wheat grains mixed and dried, and stored). The "siqu" was used the same way we use, for instance, Worcestershire sauce or soy sauce today--to add flavor and zest to the dish. The medieval Baghdadi cooking called for "murri" which was also fermented sauce basically made from grains. Moreover, they hankered after pickled locusts the way their predecessors did. In his chapter on relishes and pickles, al-Warraq gives a recipe for making it. The live locusts were let suffocate in brine, and were then layered with salt and spices in a jar. Water in which the locusts suffocated was poured to cover. Then the jar was sealed with mud and kept aside for a while (102). As for the ancient "kisimmu," unlike the "murri," it never went out of use. Now as of old it is crushed and added to soups and stews, to thicken and to flavor. We still call it *kishk*, and the Turkmans in northern Iraq call it *kisham*. The resemblance of the name to the ancient "kisimmu" is uncanny.

It is also interesting to see how the ancient Mesopotamians' love of relishes and condiments has evolved. In the Babylonian recipe "pigeon stew," there were directions that "before the broth cools, serve it accompanied with garlic, greens and vinegar" (Bottϑro, *Mesopotamian Culinary Texts*, 12). We still believe, as people in medieval times did, that having sour condiments with food helps the digestion.Our small bowls of pickled vegetables and *anba* (pickled mango) testify to this. In the medieval times the dieticians recommended having vinegar and pickles with grilled and fried meat. Collectively they called such digestive condiments, *sibagh* and *kawamikh*. They were vinegar based sauces and dips.

The ancient Mesopotamians' love for bread never slackened. The *tannour* has always been as versatile as ever. Besides baking the same old simple flat breads, called *khubuz mei* (water bread) and a myriad of "improved" breads of different shapes and hues, it was also used as an oven for grilling meats, simmering pots, and baking pastries. The medieval dry *khushkananaj* cookies so much resembled the ancient Mesopotamian "gullupu" cookies. Both were basically dough made of wheat flour, sesame oil, and water, filled and baked in the *tannour*. The traditional *Kleicha* cookies made these days in Iraq are not different from these, either. Flour was also used in other ways. There was even an indication that they made pasta of some sort. In the Babylonian recipe of "Spleen Broth" Tablet 4644, there were directions to add to the simmering stew "bits of toasted 'qaiatu-dough'," which I suspect were a kind of fine noodles (see Babylonian recipes above for more details). By the medieval era there were already several types of pasta cooking in their pots, such as the *itriya, rishta*, and *sha'riyya*. The ancient semi solid flour-based "muttaqu" (*halwa* made with toasted flour, sesame oil and honey) metamorphosed into the numerous medieval *khabees halwa*, and the traditional condensed flour puddings of the present day.

With so much bread being made in the region, it is not surprising to learn that a practical dish like *thareed* should have been a staple ever since ancient times. As we have seen in the Babylonian recipes, bread was incorporated into the dishes in several ways. Breadcrumbs were added as a secondary item to thicken sauce. They were also added as a principal ingredient, such as the "crumb stew" (tablet 4644). They were added as a last cooking stage, *a la thareed*, exactly like what we have been doing throughout all these millennia. In al-Warraq's cookbook there is a dish called *al-thareeda al-Iraqiya* (Iraqi *thareed* dish) which has a striking resemblance to the Babylonian "crumb stew." Meat along with, water, milk, onion, vinegar, and spices were simmered in a pot, to which breadcrumbs were added in a final stage (208-9). Another similar dish (name is missing) describes a meat preparation which also calls for adding breadcrumbs in its last stage (al-Warraq, 178).

The ancients also used bread in more ingenious ways. The Babylonian Tablet 8958 contained recipes for bird dishes cooked in white sauce and enclosed in pie crusts. One of them in particular, the francolin pie, called for elaborate layering of a pie bottom crust topped with a layer of prepared porridge, and followed by a layer of batter made of flour and aromatic beer. It was then spread with leek, garlic, honey, butter, and the cooked birds. It was covered with a top pie crust and baked in the oven. There is a recipe in al-Warraq's tenth-century cookbook that bears a telling resemblance to this ancient bird preparation. The medieval dish is called *tannouriya* (baked in clay oven). A pan with high sides was lined with a thin layer of bread dough. Then chickens, which had first been cooked in water and salt, were laid flat on the lined pan. They were sprinkled with cilantro, minced onion, cloves, cinnamon and pepper, and drizzled with wine vinegar and *murri* (fermented sauce). If these were not available, the recipe went, they might be substituted with juice of raisins and pomegranate.

39

A good amount of clarified butter or oil was spread, along with five beaten eggs. The top was covered entirely with a flattened round of bread dough, making sure to seal it with the dough lining the side of the pan. It was lowered into the *tannour*, and cooked until done (253).

In dishes such as the Babylonian francolin pie of Tablet 8958, we can also see the seeds for what might later have developed into the much more elaborate and varied medieval Baghdadi dish, the *judhaba*. The basic idea behind it was to prepare a bread pudding, sweetened with sugar, honey or *julab* (syrup flavored with rose water). Then it was enclosed between two flat thin breads, and baked in the *tannour*, with a skewered chunk of meat or a chicken suspended over it. The instruction in al-Baghdadi's recipe was to suspend the chicken "in the oven, and watch: then, when the fat is about to run, place the *judhab* under it" (209, more on *judhab* in the following section).

The purpose of cooking to people of the Middle East has never been to satisfy the physical needs of the body only. The haute cuisine, and this is what we are largely dealing with in describing the ancient and medieval cooking, has been, more often than not, an occasion for display and showmanship. That might well have been the incentive behind the creation of the Babylonian bird pie dishes in tablet 8958 that were prepared with utmost care, and with an eye on presentation. After painstakingly garnishing the dishes, the cook would clad them with a crust and serve them. One imagines that when the diners uncovered the edible crust, they would behold some lovely birds cooked to perfection in white sauce. That might well have been the incentive behind the medieval *maghmoumat* (the covered), according to which the dish was entirely covered with a disc of bread, and baked. Chapters 74 and 91 in al-Warraq's cookbook deal with such dishes. There was also the *Makhfiya* (the hidden), in which whole boiled egg yolks were hidden inside meatballs (al-Baghdadi, 194). The *Madfouna* (the buried) was eggplant stuffed with a mixture of meat, onion and spices and then "buried" and simmered in broth.

Medieval Culinary Techniques

Cooking to the medieval Arabs was recognized as an art. In the preface to his thirteenth century cookbook, al-Baghdadi says that "a cook should be intelligent, acquainted with the rules of cooking, and that he should have a flair for the art" (33). A prerequisite to these was the personal hygiene of the cook. He particularly elaborated on this saying the cook "must keep his nails constantly trimmed, not neglecting them, not allowing them to grow long" (33). Next comes thorough cleanliness of kitchen utensils and pots. Al-Warraq emphasizes this point by saying that what differentiates between the food of the Caliphs and that of the ordinary people was not ingredients as much as the utmost care taken in cleaning the ingredients as well as the pots. Some even went as far as saying that if it were left to them, they would recommend using a new pot every time they cooked a dish (al-Tujibi, 31).

Al-Warraq gives an extensive list of the kitchen utensils and gadgets that any cook worth his salt should have handy. Stone pots were recommended for prolonged stewing, and metal ones for brief boiling. Iron pans are the best for frying fish for they ensure a crisp skin. There should be separate knives and cut boards for cutting meat and vegetables. Metal mortar and pestle is good for grinding spices, and stone ones should be used for pounding meat. He does not even neglect to mention small items such as geese feathers for glazing pastries, and pieces of clean cloth to wipe the inside of the *tannour*.

The fresher the vegetables and herbs are the better. "Expired" seasonings and spices are out of the question. When buying cinnamon, for instance, the bark should be "thick and luxuriant, strong-scented, burning to the tongue" (Al-Baghdadi, 33). An important rule for good cooking is removing the scum when the pot boils, otherwise the dish will be spoiled.

The key word to the medieval cooking was harmony, and this was no less manifested than in the stew dishes they prepared, where the sour agents, such as vinegar, sumac and sour fruits and vegetables, had to be carefully balanced with the sweet, mainly date syrup, honey and sugar. A rule of thumb, "seasonings are used freely with plain dishes and fried and dry foods, but sparingly in sour dishes that have their own broth" (Al-Baghdadi, 33).

The stew recipes all started with the initial stage of melting chunks of sheep's tail fat. Choice cuts of meat were braised first briefly, then water was added. The stew would then simmer over an extended period of time. All the while the pot was tended to. Vegetables and sometimes a chicken might be added half way through cooking. To thicken the stews all kinds of agents were added such as ground nuts, breadcrumbs, yogurt, *kishk* (yogurt and grains dried, and crushed when needed), milk, and crushed chickpeas. The most common spices used were coriander, cumin, cloves, cinnamon, cardamom, mustard, and ginger. The herbs were mostly parsley, cilantro, dill, mint, leeks, and basil. The aromatics and colorants were rose water, saffron, mastic, ambergris, and camphor. These and much more were added to the pot at different stages of cooking, sometimes with quite a liberal hand.

What attracts the attention in al-Baghdadi's stew recipes is his fondness of the seasoned succulent meatballs, which undoubtedly reflected not only his own private preferences but also a general culinary trend that was initiated much earlier. They were called *kubab* (plural of *kubba*, ball*)*, and were made by pounding meat into paste, and mixing it with herbs, spices and sometimes egg white, as a binder. They were added to the simmering stews, that is, in addition to the meat chunks already cooking in the pot. This was probably one of the ingenious and most practical ways of using the not so tender cuts of meat. They varied in size and shapes, some were a little smaller than oranges, whereas others were small and round like hazelnuts (*bunduqiyat*). The *Rutabiya* (like dates) had small longish *kubabs*, each of which was stuffed with a whole almond to make it look like a date (al-Baghdadi, 195). The meatballs were sometimes called *mudaqaqat*, because meat was always pounded first.

The Medieval Baghdadi cooks used vinegar in many of their dishes, to add zest and flavor to food and to tenderize meat. The preservative and tenderizing qualities of the vinegar were exploited to the full. Besides pickling vegetables, it was also used for preserving meat, called *mamqour.* Meat was also steeped in it and then cooked, such as in *masous* dishes. They used it in their stews along with other souring agents such as sumac, sour pomegranate, unripe grapes, lemon juice (*leimoun*), or lime juice (*leimo*). From this practice stemmed the need sometimes to balance the sourness with sweet agents, such as sugar, honey, and date syrup, and hence the category of the sweet and sour dishes. This also explains the need to add good amounts of fatty substances to their dishes. Fats were mainly melted sheep tail, and clarified butter (*samn*). Fat helped cut the sharpness of the vinegar, but it also helped make their dry (sauceless) dishes nicely moist. However, there is an indication that not all the fat used while cooking the dish was served. In the last stage of cooking, the pots were always kept on low heat for an "hour" to rest, during which period all the extra fat would come up and was skimmed. Instructions in al-Baghdadi'd dish of *Ma' wa Hummus* urged to "pour off the fat" (47). In al-Warraq's *faloudhajat* desserts (similar to Turkish Delight) there were also instructions to throw away the oil that separated from the thickening mixture (242-5).

As a last touch to the sweet and sour stew dishes, al-Baghdadi did not fail to mention spraying the pot with "a little" or "a trifle" of rose water. The fact that just a small amount of this fragrant substance was used indicates that it was just meant to give a light pleasant aroma to the pot, especially if we know that spices in the sweet and sour stews were supposed to be used "sparingly." They have "their own broth," al-Baghdadi explains (33). The practice of spraying the pot with a little rose water, therefore, might well have been al-Baghdadi's personal preference, or a contemporary trend. Al-Warraq's cookbook, written two hundred years earlier did not make mention of this culinary habit. However, because al-Baghdadi's book was our only significant testimony on the medieval Baghdadi's cuisine, that is up until, 1987, people think that adding rose water to the stew pot was a matter of course rather than a trend or an option.

41

In the grilling domain the medieval cooks fully exploited the conventional means. They grilled strips of meat and called the dish, *kebab*. They were also fond of grilling whole stuffed, goat- kids or sheep, which we nowadays call *qouzi*. They did these mostly in the *tannour*. They also grilled their meats the rotisserie way. The dishes were called *kardhabajat*, and there are several recipes for preparing them in al-Warraq's book. Sometimes there were instructions to half cook the meat in water and then bake it, because the cuts were not tender enough. It was the custom to serve grilled meats accompanied with simple condiments and sauces, which served as dips. Collectively they were called *sibagh*. The purpose of these relishes was to "cleanse the palate of greasiness, to appetize, to assist the digestion, and to stimulate the banqueter" (al-Baghdadi, 205). *Sibagh* was vinegar mixed with sumac and ground almond, or crushed raisins and pomegranate seeds, or mustard and garlic. Such grilled dishes and other "hamburger" patties dishes cooked on the stove come within a category that al-Baghdadi called *nawashif* (dry dishes), which is still an important component in our modern daily diet.

No discussion of the medieval Baghdadi cuisine is complete without including the sweet and savory *judhaba*, of which al-Warraq gave nineteen recipes in his cookbook, and al-Baghdadi, eight. It was a popular fast "carry out" food, sold in the food markets of medieval Baghdad. Here is how it was prepared. First of all there was the bread part. The simplest kind was to put breadcrumbs, broken pieces of bread, or even stuffed *qata'if* (crepes) in a wide tray with not so high sides, called *joudhaban*. Then a sweet substance and a liquid were poured to cover the bread. They could be any combination of the following: honey, *julab* (syrup flavored with rose water), sugar, water, milk, and eggs. Ground nuts or toasted poppy seeds might be sprinkled, and the whole dish might be perfumed and colored with rose water and saffron. Alternatively, a thin (*riqaq*) bread could be spread in the bottom of the *joudhaban* (a wide pan with slightly high side), on which sweet apricots, bananas, sweet melon chunks, black mulberries, or pounded raisins were put, then layered with sugar, sometimes with some additional honey, and sometimes with eggs. The whole arrangement was then to be covered with another layer of thin bread. Now we come to the more exciting part. The *joudhaban* would be lowered into the *tannour*, and a plump chicken or a side of lamb would be suspended on top of it. The meat was not supposed to touch the dish, and hence the name *judhab* or *judhaba*, which is derived from *judhba*, the distance between two objects. According to the directions al-Baghdadi gave, the *joudhaban* was to be put under the grilling meat only when its fat started to run (209) so that the bread mixture underneath would receive and sop up all the falling fat.

The most inventive of these *judhaba* dishes by far was *Al-Mansouriya* (after the Caliph al-Mansour). Pancake-like yeast batter was made and poured into the *joudhaban*. The pan was then placed in the *tannour* under the suspended meat, which had just started to drip its fat. A long reed was stuck in the batter, and honey was to be slowly poured through the reed into the cooking batter. As it rose, the batter would develop air pockets that eventually would be filled with honey, while at the same time sucking up all the fat drippings of the meat. Al-Warraq's comment was that it would be as delicious as honey combs (240).

As to how this dish was served, the only directions given were to invert the bread casserole on a platter and serve it with the meat. However, from one of the medieval stories in al-Hamadani's ninth-century *Maqamat*, we get the clue that meat prepared this way was to be sliced very thinly (72), similar to the way grilled meat is cut for the *shawirma* sandwiches of today.

Besides the conventional ways of cooking, the medieval Baghdadi cooks sometimes had to go out of the ordinary when faced with a challenge. Delicate batters with a high percentage of eggs were cooked in hot water baths, to prevent them from burning. The prepared mixture was poured into a pot, which in turn was put in a larger one. Water was poured all around it, and was covered and let simmer (al-Warraq, 268-9). For their sandwiches they usually used the regular flat breads on which they spread the filling, rolled tightly, and then sliced into discs. They also baked round thick discs of bread in the *furn* (brick oven), removed the pith, filled them with sandwich stuffing, pressed them very well, and then cut them into smaller portions. I have also come across a recipe that instructed the baker to put inside a portion of bread dough, and before baking it, a latticed metal disc with slightly raised sides, called *ward mushabbak*. The instructions as to what to do next were very succinct, most probably because the cooks back then knew what to do. It is my assumption that after baking, the device would be removed leaving behind a pocket in the bread big enough for stuffing (*Wasf al-At'ima al-Mu'tada*, 381)

There were directions in one of al-Warraq's recipes to create a steam cooker. In a dish called *dakibriyan*, which he said was a Persian name meaning "grilling in a pot," six holes were made all around the middle of the high wall of a pot. Then three sticks were inserted through these holes. They should be long enough to stick out of the pot, so that a rack was created inside the pot. The holes were completely closed with mud from the outside. Water was poured until it reached the level just below the sticks. A whole side of lamb was rubbed with salt and oil, and put on the sticks. The pot was then covered with a lid, and tightly blocked with mud to prevent any steam from escaping. The pot was put on top of medium high heat, until done (Al-Warraq, 225).

Vegetables were highly esteemed, and were described as the ornament of the table. Some of the new vegetables gave rise to new dishes, such as the eggplant dishes known as *al-Buraniyat*. They were named after Buran, the wife of the ninth-century Abbasid Caliph al-Ma'moun. She is believed to be the originator of these dishes. Obviously most of the vegetable dishes were cooked with meat, and the vegetarian dishes were called *muzawarat*, (counterfeited dishes), and were recommended for sick people, and Christians during Lent. For ordinary consumption, they were used as side dishes.

The medieval Baghdadi cuisine was also characterized by its array of appetizers served in a number of small bowls and plates that are tellingly reminiscent of our modern time *mezza* dishes, usually served with drinks. The word *mezza* itself in Arabic means either to eat or drink in small amounts, or to describe a *mezz* taste, which verges on the sour side.

The medieval *kawamikh* were *mezza* dishes in both senses of the word. First of all they were served in *sakareej* and *jam* (small bowls) brought to the tables, five or six of them, for the diners to nibble on, to whet their appetites before the main dishes were brought in. One *kamikh* type was made from a basic ingredient prepared from molded bread or a mixture of bread and milk left to ferment over a long period of time, to which different spices and herbs were added, such as caraway, cloves, cinnamon and *reihan* (sweet basil) or rose petals. The *kawamikh* might simply be *mukhalalat*, that is pickled vegetables, such as eggplant, turnips, mint leaves, olives, and capers seasoned with spices and herbs. They might be *rabeetha,* which were pickled small fishes, or pickled locusts for the making of which there is a recipe in al-Warraq's book (chapter 40). They might also be a dip of thin paste made of ground almonds, mustard and vinegar, or *simply milh mutayyab* (spiced or seasoned salt). Rock salt was first kept in a hot oven for a whole day, then it was crushed, and added to a variety of spices such as coriander, and toasted seeds of sesame, nigella, hemp, poppy, cumin, and fennel, pomegranate seeds, and juniper berries (*habbat khadhra*). It was sometimes attractively colored yellow with saffron, or red with sumac juice, or green with chard juice. Or it could be made *muza'tar* by adding thyme to it (al-Warraq, 52, al-Baghdadi, 207-8).

Of the side dishes served before the main hot meal, there were the *bawarid* (cold dishes), which could be meat or vegetarian cold dishes. The *bawarid* meat dishes were invariably served with *sibagh*, (also called *sulus*, plural of *salsa*, after the thirteenth century) which were basically sour-based dips, seasoned and sometimes thickened with ground nuts. In the Baghdadi cookbooks many recipes were given for these.

Vegetarian side dishes included the *baqila bi khal* (boiled fava beans, drained and drizzled with oil and vinegar), for instance, and the *badhinjan mahshi* dishes (perhaps wrongly interpreted as *muhassa*, which means mashed). They were mostly made of finely chopped boiled eggplant, mixed with other ingredients such as ground nuts, sesame seeds, sesame oil, vinegar, pomegranate juice, and sometimes fried onion. They also served boiled and drained vegetables such as eggplant, gourd,

43

Swiss chard, and fava beans, seasoned with spices, mixed with yogurt and drizzled with hot sesame oil (Al-Baghdadi, 205-6, al-Warraq, 115). Grilled chicken was sometimes served with a cold side dish of *khubuz maftout* (crumbled bread), soused in vinegar and oil, and served with chopped cucumber pulp, mint, tarragon, thyme, parsley, and sometimes aged cheese (al-Warraq, 125-6), which beyond doubt was one of the ancestors of today's *fatoush* salad. In al-Warraq's chapter on dairy products, I also came across an appetizer made by mixing yogurt with garlic, onion, tarragon, chopped parsley and mint, the chopped crunchy lower stalk of romaine lettuce, and chopped cucumber, to be served with oil. To my great surprise it was called *jajiq* (96), and lo and behold! We found an ancestor for our *jajeek* appetizer, so well known these days in the entire Mediterranean, and Middle Eastern countries.

While all kinds of fancy dishes were cooking in Baghdad, the homely and comforting traditional dishes were still in demand. For instance, the *madhira* dish, meat simmered in flavorful yogurt sauce, deemed the wonder healer of maladies. There were the grain and pulse dishes made into soups and pottages, such as soups, *aruz* (rice cooked in milk and sugar), *mujaddara* (lentil and rice dish), *itriya* and *rishta* (thick noodle soups), *adasiya* (lentil dish). Or the *harisa* (whole wheat grains simmered with lamb, and pounded), which is still esteemed as a comfor dish in the Arab world. Other dishes were the *Kurdiya* (simmered suckling lamb), the *kibbayat* (stuffed pieces of sheep tripe, simmered in broth), and the *akari'* (simmered lamb trotters), which are still around. The simple *thareed* (pieces of bread sopped in rich broth) was deemed the master of all dishes. It was sometimes lavishly garnished for formal presentations. Interestingly we still garnish our *thareeds* with fried eggs sunny-side up, as they used to do in medieval times (*Anonymous Andalusian Cookbook*, 73), except that today we do it only with vegetarian *thareed* varieties.

Culinary artistic complexity was not only sought after in flavor. Contrary to the above mentioned straightforward honest dishes, the medieval Baghdadi cooks sometimes cooked with an aim to surprise, deceive or intrigue, which gave rise to a host of stuffed dishes such as *mahshiyat* (stuffed vegetables), *maghmouma* (the covered), *madfouna* (the buried), *mukaffana* (shrouded), or *makhfiya* (the hidden). An honest sounding dish such as *al-rutabiya* (cooked with dates) was meant to play a trick on the eaters by serving them a stew containing long and small stuffed meatballs that look like dates, along with real stuffed dates (al-Baghdadi, 195). They even made the process of cooking an entertaining show, such as watching chickens cooking in a glass pot with their heads bobbing gently up and down along with colorful spice grains and pulses (Marin, 212).

The rich and scrumptious desserts that were made and consumed during the period were amazing. I get dizzy by just going through the endless list of all kinds of *aruzziyat* and *muhallabiyat* (sweet puddings of rice and cornstarch), *khabees* and *faloudhaj* (condensed halwas), *natif* (nougat), *ha'is* (date halwa), *halwa yabisa* (candies), *lauzeenaj yabis* (marzipan), and *lauzeenaj mugharraq* (baklawa). The list for desserts fried and soaked in honey or the cheaper *julab* (rose water syrup) is endless. There were *zilabiya* (fritters), *asabi' Zeinab* and *halaqeem* or *qanawat* (tubular cookies, prototypes of cannoli), *qata'if* (pancakes), *kunafa* (shredded dough), *luqmat al-qadhi* (fried balls of dough), and *furniyyat* and *shahmiyyat* (cakes drenched in syrup). They made cookies such as *khushkananaj* (cookies stuffed with nuts and dates), *mutabbaq* (sanswich cookies), *aqras mukallala* (crowned rounds, i.e. cookies with toppings), and so on. And for those who could not afford such delicacies there were always dates, either fresh or dried.

In presentation they took great measures to decorate the dishes so that they might elicit the ooh and aahs of the prospective eaters. Special molds were used to make impressions on cookies, colored sugar was drizzled to make the dessert look as vivid as a *bustan* (orchard), as they used to say. There are instructions in one of al-Warraq's recipes to color the *halwa* and shape it like a dome, and drizzle it, while still hot, with a caramel-like *natif*. Then a *sauma'a* (similar to a minaret) is shaped in the middle, colored differently and drizzled with a different kind of caramel. As for savory foods, such garnishes as pomegranate seeds, chopped mint and parsley, boiled eggs neatly sliced with a thread, and cucumber slices, were artistically arranged. A casserole dish such as *narjisiya* (meat omelet), usually taken from stove to table was presented in an attractive way: the middle part of a thin *riqaq* bread was cut out first. It was then fitted into the pan, so that it draped like a skirt to hide the blackened sides of the pan (al-Warraq, 182).

Evidently there were no set rules for the number or times of meals per day. The Abbasid Caliph al-Ma'moun, for instance, used to have three meals in two days, the first one mid-day, the second early morning of the following day, and the third, in the evening. He also preferred having early lunches in the summer for three reasons: cooler breeze, colder water, and less flies. Early lunches in the winter were also recommended because the nights were long. The recommendation was to have two meals a day following the verses in the holy Qur'an, which promise the dwellers of Paradise an early lunch and an evening dinner. Breakfasts were nowhere mentioned. Apparently such early meals seem to be a modern concept in our dietary habits. We also have to assume that each meal proper had, more or less, the same components: *Kawamikh* dishes to whet the appetite, and dry (*nawashif*) and cold (*bawarid*) dishes, invariably accompanied with *sibagh* (sour-based dips), to be followed by the hot dishes. Then followed desserts. Cheese was recommended as a digestive, and to cleanse the palate after dessert. Exercising before the meal was approved, but it was to be avoided on a heavy stomach. Any way the golden rule was to eat when hungry, otherwise food would eat you (Al-Warraq, 19, 29, 31, 64).

Post Medieval Era

After the Mongolian attack, Baghdad lost its glory. From the sixteenth century to the end of First World War the whole region was politically dominated by the Ottoman Turks. It was a period when doing and calling things the Turkish way was a fashion statement, and an indicator of high life. Some of the medieval *mahshi* (stuffed) dishes started to be called dolma, a generic Turkish word for "stuff," which can be used in contexts other than culinary. A pillow may be stuffed with cotton and called "dolma." The medieval meatballs, which adorned so many of their stew dishes for so long, were no longer called *kubab* (rounds of meat) but *kufta*. The *maqaniq* and *qadid* (sausages, and jerked meat) were called *bastirma*, and the ancient dish of simmered heads of sheep and calf started to be called *pacha*. The medieval *louzenaj*, those dainty thin pastries stuffed with almond and sugar, and soaked in syrup, have developed into baklawa dessert (so far it is not certain where the name came from).

During the medieval times, Baghdadis used to make *riqaq* breads (paper-thin breads), and used them in stuffing and draping food. They were fine breads always referred to as *waraq* or *awraq* (leaves or paper, see for instance al-Warraq, 265). In medieval Andalusia, such thin sheets of dough were sometimes called *wouriqat*. They were sometimes stuffed with cheese, meat or fish, and were called *mujabbana*, and *mukhabbaza*. They also layered thin sheets of dough and stuffed them with chicken. The resulting savory sweet pie so much resembled the *pasilla* Moroccan dish of today (for more details see chapter 14, on savory pastries).

During the Turkish era and onwards, similarly stuffed pastries were called *bourag*, and the origin of this nomenclature is still obscure. However, based on what we know today of the medieval Baghdadi and Andalusian cooking terminology, it is my contention that the word might have been derived from the Arabic, "*waraq*" (sheet of paper, or leaves) Thin layers of bread were called *awraq al-riqaq* (paper-thin breads). In Andalusia, they used to bake flaky pies called *muwarraqat*, some of which were made by layering large sheets of thin dough called *riqaq* or *wureeqat* (as thin as paper or leaves). Another possibility for the naming could simply be linked to the ingredient, *bouraq* (borax).

Bouraq (borax or sodium borate) was used in the days of the ancient Greeks for preserving food. In the medieval Arabic cookbooks this substance was mentioned only with relation to bread and the crispy translucent *zilabya* (fritters), as in al-Warraq's tenth-century book (35, 269). In the thirteenth-century *Al-Wusla ila'l-Habeeb* of Allepo, *bouraq* was mentioned in a sandwich recipe which called for leavened bread "worked with borax," purchased from the baker (Rodinson, *Studies*,159). As al-Warraq's recipes show, this ingredient was used sparingly, "as much as salt," possibly for its preservative qualities, but what is more important to keep bread crisp. Naming baked foods after a leavening ingredient is quite a common practice. People of the northern city of Mosul, for instance, make cookies with baking soda, and simply call them *soda*. Similarly the traditional Irish bread leavened with soda is called "soda bread" (for more details see chapter 14, on savory pastries). Evidently, during this period the Baghdadi cuisine lost neither its luster nor popularity. The mere fact that many augmented manuscript copies were made of al-Baghdadi's thirteenth-century cookbook, between the fourteenth and eighteenth centuries, and that one of them was beautifully done "on the order of a Turkish sultan" (*Wasf al-At'ima*, 277) is testimony enough.

Around the sixteenth century, an important New World vegetable came to the region that revolutionized the way our stews started to be cooked. This vegetable was the tomato. It gradually replaced most of the souring agents previously used, and also rendered the use of ground nuts as thickening substances, and a seasoning such as murri, or a colorant such as saffron unnecessary. Stews nowadays are mostly cooked the same old way, albeit with a little less fat. In fact it was only relatively recently that the majority of the people abandoned the melted fat of the sheep tail, and switched to healthier types of oil. The stews are now mostly thickened, colored and soured with tomato juice with the help of a squeeze of lemon juice, a pinch of *leimoun doozi* (citric acid), or *noomi Basrah* (dried lime). Sometimes a pinch of sugar is also added to balance the final taste. Of the few medieval white (tomatoless) stews that survived, *margat mishmish*, or as some people call it *margat turshana* (apricot stew), is the favorite.

Rice now is more widely used than before. It is as important in our diet as bread is. The medieval cookbooks gave rice recipes, such as *aruzziyat*, but these were largely porridge-like dishes, cooked with meat and sugar. We also know that they cooked rice the same way we cook it today. They called it *ruz mufalfal*, plain fluffy rice with separated grains (Al-Baghdadi, 44). It was offered as a side dish with stew, as we still do to this day. Moreover, al-Baghdadi's cookbook gave variations on the plain rice. As we still do today it was mixed with lentils and sometimes with mung beans. However, rice was too expensive to be a daily staple in the medieval diet, it was largely the dish for special occasions such as feasts and weddings. One of the *Arabian Nights* stories tells how for a wedding five kinds of rice were cooked, each colored differently.

A good number of the medieval traditional dishes are still simmering in our pots, such as the *thareeds* of broken pieces of bread sopped in rich broth, and garnished with fried eggs sunny-side up. There are also the stuffed lambs and chickens, *akari'* and *kibbayat* (simmered trotters, and stuffed tripe of lamb and calf, we now collectively call, *pacha*), and *harisa* (mashed shelled wheat with meat). Most of the *nawashif* dishes (dry dishes) the medieval Baghdadis enjoyed, as side dishes, are still very popular, along with some of the condiments they served along with them. Today's *jajeek*, *fatoush* (from *fateet* or *maftout*, crumbled bread), and puréed hummus and eggplant dishes, are testimony to that. The same thing can definitely be said of their innovative *awsat*, *shata'ir*, and *bazmaward* (sandwiches), now more commonly known as *laffa* (wrapped), or the more hip, *sandaweech*. Their innovative eggplant and gourd *mahshi* dishes and *madfouna* (stuffed foods) still adorn our tables. The *kubba* dishes (stuffed foods), for which the Iraqi cuisine is famed, undoubtedly had their seeds, as we have seen, in the medieval stuffed *kubab* (meatballs), and possibly much earlier. Most of the traditional desserts, cookies, and cakes available at confectioners' now, or the ones prepared at home, were handed down to us from the medieval times, and in some cases, even much earlier than that.

In the following chapters the vast array of recipes and accompanying information will give further glimpses on everyday-life culinary practices in Iraq, both past and present. So hold on tight to your flying carpets, for it is time now to set out on our culinary tour, and as the Iraqis say, *B'Alif Afya* (may you enjoy in a thousand healths).

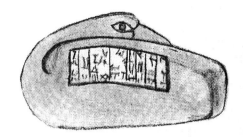

A stone weight of about 5 pounds, made of black stone,
late third millennium BC (Iraqi Museum).

Weights and Measures

In their daily lives and trade transactions, the ancient Mesopotamians needed to measure correct quantities for different purposes including cooking. Balances were used, some of which were small enough to measure a shekel (almost a gram), and others were large enough to measure a man. Incidentally, we know this from a document in which a captive prisoner was to be freed by paying what equaled his weight, silver. Portable metal balance scales were used with weights made of stone or bronze, beautifully carved or cast into forms of animals such as ducks and lions.

By volume, the largest measure was "emer" (literally a donkey load, which, interestingly is still used nowadays to measure vegetables and fruits such as melons purchased in bulk, we call it *himil*, i.e. a donkey's load). Other measures and weights were:

Emer = 10 sutu (=5 bushels)
Sutu = 10 qu
Qu (= 3 pints or 2 litres)
Gun (= 30 kilograms)
Manu or mina (=500 grams)
Sila (= 1 litre)
Gur (= 300 litres)
Gin (= 8 grams)

We know the value of these measures because the excavated storage jars were marked with their capacity.

As for the weight measurements during the Middle Ages, evidently the portable metal balance scales with sets of metal weights were still in use. Venders use them now in weighing bulky produce. The medieval weighing system was adopted by the surrounding regions, and was transmitted even to northern Europe by the Norse traders who had trading relations with Baghdad.

In the trading and shopping transactions and cooking, the following measures were used, some of which are still used in different parts of the Arab world, such as *ratl* and *uqiya*:

Makouk = 3 *keilecha* (= bushel = 36 litres)

Keilacha= 1 7/8 *mann*

Mann=2 ratl

Ratl = 12 *uqiya* (= 16 ounces = 1 pound = 1 pint = approx. 1/2 kilo)

Uqiya = 10 *dirhams* (= approx. 1 ounce = 37 grams)

Dirham (named after the silver coin) (= weight of silver coin) = 6 *danaq* (= 3 grams)

Danaq= 1/6 *dirham* (= 1/2 gram)

Dinar (named after the gold coin)= *mithqal* (= 41/2 grams)

Even though the decimal system with its kilos and grams was later on adopted, some weights and measures of the past still linger in our everyday life usage such as the *chela* (=keila), *mann, himil, uqiya, mithqal*. Moreover, we still use the universal and timeless *hafna* or *kaff* (handful), or *ma hamalat al-raha wal asabi'* (what the palm and the fingers can hold). For a smaller amount, *ma hamalat ru'us al-asabi' madhmouma* (what the fingers can pick up when they are put together, i.e. a pinch, al-Warraq, 75, 150).

The Sumerian King, Shulgi, holding the balance

49

CHAPTER ONE
BREAD

CHAPTER ONE

BREAD

خـبـز

"THE GLORY OF LIFE"

Eat bread, Enkido, the glory of life,
Drink wine, Enkido, the custom of the land.
(The Epic of Gilgamesh)

In a cookbook that seeks to trace the origins of a modern cuisine back to its ancient roots, what's more appropriate than opening it with a chapter on bread, believed to be the world's oldest prepared food?

Baking with the Ancient Mesopotamians

They ate a lot of bread in ancient Mesopotamia. We know this from a Babylonian letter written by a grumpy son, who was surprised that his parents were not sending him new clothes at a time when in their house "wool is used up like bread." (Oppenheim, 84) Indeed, so important was bread in their lives that they thought of it as the epitome of life, as shown in the lines quoted from *The Epic of Gilgamesh*, above.

Archaeological records show that the ancient Mesopotamians made more than 300 kinds of bread, both unleavened and leavened. They baked plain and improved breads, which came in different shapes and colors, and were spiced differently. The ancient records classify these breads as large and tiny, long and short, fresh and dry, black and white, excellent and ordinary. The improved bread was called "ninda" to which fatty ingredients were added, such as sesame oil, butter, lard, mutton fat, and even fish oil. The oils themselves were sometimes seasoned and flavored, most probably, to mask the rancid taste that fat quickly acquired in hot weather. The Sumerians described these improved oils as oils "made good." Date syrup and honey were sometimes added as sweetening agents. The better quality breads, the ones baked with the "noble fat" (clarified butter), were reserved for the gods and the royalty. The Sumerians also made what they called "gug," or "kuku," in the Akkadian, which was a kind of rich pastry (more on this in the cake and cookie chapters). (Limet, 133)

In making these breads they used a variety of grains of which barley and wheat were the most popular. By the first millennium BC, the Akkadian texts mentioned white barley, small grain barley, and pearl barley. It was not the ideal grain for making successful bread because it is very low in gluten content. Therefore it was mostly used in baking unleavened breads on the heated exterior walls of upright clay cylinders (Bottèro, *Cuisine of Ancient Mesopotamia*,39). When, at times, ovens were not available they baked bread on heated stones, or made an arrangement of stones and hot ashes and buried the flattened dough in it to bake what they used to call "akal tumri" (bread using ashes). A scene in an Assyrian relief of Ashurbanipal's campaign shows unleavened bread being prepared: an Elamite prisoner is kneeling by the fire, tossing a flat disc of bread between his hands, the way people still do to this day, and another disc is already placed in the ashes (Levey, 48).

The Ancient Mesopotamians were soon to learn the value of wheat. It had more gluten in it than the rest of the grains they grew. From then on the baking of leavened bread went hand in hand with the unleavened variety. For a start it might have taken one or two neglectful housewives to forget to immediately bake the dough they kneaded, which gave it enough time to pick up yeast from the air. They must have noticed that dough had puffed, and when baked, gave them bread which was more appetizing, lighter in texture, and easier on the digestion.

Cooking on direct heat worked well with unleavened bread, but not so when it came to leavened varieties, which needed less intense heat and more humid cooking environment. By the third millenium BC, domed clay ovens were built to provide better conditions for baking leavened bread. Such ovens were actually found in many excavated sites in the region, such as Tell Asmar, Nippur, Ur, and Namrud.

The technique of baking bread in a clay oven is simple: fire is built in the bottom of the clay oven, and the flattened leavened dough is pressed or slapped onto the oven's inner hot wall, above the smoldering fires. In ancient Mesopotamia these ovens were known as "tanuru," from which the Arabic *tannour* was derived. In one of the verses in the holy *Qur'an*, Noah's Flood is described as having started with eruptions of water metaphorically referred to as an erupting *tannour* (Chapter: Hud, verse 40). The image evoked is that of an erupting volcano, and for those of us who have seen a *tannour* being prepared for baking bread, this image is quite familiar. When brushwood is lighted in it, flames of fire, 6 to 7 feet high, would shoot out of the upper opening of the oven. Then the fire would soon die down, leaving smoldering coals in the bottom, hot enough to heat the oven's inner wall. The flattened discs of bread would then be slapped on the hot interior walls of the *tannour*. When the top opening is closed with a cover, enough humidity, generated by the baking breads, would be trapped to allow them to puff, developing the characteristic lovely bubbles. The humid environment inside the *tannour* also enabled them to bake all kinds of dainty cakes and cookies.

Sumerian Diplomacy

Clay ovens to the Sumerians were indispensable. They had to keep them constantly burning and in tip-top shape. An extinguished *tannour* was a bad omen. As shown in the following piece of wisdom, the older the ovens got, the more care they needed:

Be gentle to your enemy as to an old oven

To make breads they had to grind the grains. They tried toasting them first. His helped make the grains less hard, but it spoiled their gluten. Gradually their milling and grinding techniques so much developed that by the first millennium BC they had two main types of mills, the hand-operated ones, and the animal-turned ones. The hand mills were made of two round flat stones, stacked together. The top one was rotated with the help of a stick placed in a vertical slot near the outer edge of the disc. In the Akkadian it was called "tee'inu," from which the Arabic *tahuuna* (grinder) is derived (the verb was "teenu," cf. Arabic *tahan*). This is still in use in rural areas. We call it *majrasha* (grinder). By using different kinds of stones they were able to produce several degrees of grinding, to meet the different demands of their busy kitchens. The groats were used for making porridges, such as tikku-flour, which according to the directions given in the Babylonian recipes, was not kneaded but mixed with beer and added to the dish. Finer grains were soaked first, then kneaded, such as sasku-flour, and ziqqu-flour (Bottèro, *Mesopotamian Culinary Texts*, 8-15). The finely ground grains, used for more delicate pastries, were more expensive and hence within the reach of the affluent only. The following Sumerian proverbs clearly demonstrate this fact.

"In my budget there is no place for any one to bake cakes."
"Fine flour is appropriate for women and the palace"
(Gordon, 65)

As to how these breads were actually made, there is ample information in the Babylonian recipes of bird pies (Bottèro, *Mesopotamian Culinary Texts*, 11-15). Interestingly, the whole process was summarized in a letter written by Bel-ibni, a general of Assurbanipal's army. "They grind its grains, sift [the flour], knead [the dough], … and bake. They eat [this bread] and live thereby" (Levey, 48). That's it!

As to how this bread was served, it had the same uses for them it still has for us today. They ate it by itself with a drink, they broke it to pieces and used it to scoop their stews. Sometimes the bread itself served as a plate on which other cooked foods were put. The Ethiopians still serve their food, even in the most affluent restaurants, in this way, using their flat sour *anjera* bread simultaneously as a plate and a scoop.

All the aforementioned varieties of breads were baked at home, however, there is also evidence that in the big ancient cities of Mesopotamia, bread making was a flourishing organized industry. Apprentices were to serve their masters, the "nuhatimmu," for 15 months to learn the tricks of the trade (Levey, 48).

The Epic of Gilgamesh

Although this epic is believed to be at least 5000 years old, we knew of it only in the mid-nineteenth century. Cuneiform tablets on which it was written were unearthed in several sites in Iraq. The epic was written as a series of 12 tablets, all of which were found in fragments. But because there were several copies of each tablet, archaeologists were able to use fragments from different sites to put the epic together. Most of the tablets found in ancient Babylon and Assyria were written in Akkadian. The most famous and most complete collection up to date is the one found at Nineveh and is translated by George Smith.

The epic's stories of creating humans from clay, the serpent that steals the secret of eternal youth, and the Great Deluge, they all bear striking resemblance to stories in the Bible and Qur'an. The epic also depicts one of the earliest quests in search of immortality. But at the same time it deals with common human experiences such as friendship, hatred, ambition, fear of death, and the urge for adventure.

Gilgamesh was the king of the ancient Babylonian city of Uruk (the Biblical "Erech"), situated between the Tigris and Euphrates rivers in Southern Mesopotamia. "He who saw everything to the ends of the world," as the title of the poem put it, Gilgamesh was two-thirds god and one-third man. He was strong, brave and handsome, and cared for Uruk, around which he built the famous wall. When he became increasingly arrogant and oppressive, the people of the city prayed to the gods for help. The goddess Aruru created a strong opponent out of clay, and called him Enkido, a noble hairy savage who lived in the steppe among the wild beasts:

[He] was wont to eat only plants with the gazelles,
Only to drink water with the wild,
Only to suck the milk of the wild creatures.

Instigated by Gilgamesh, the prostitute of the temple seduced him and thus introduced him to civilization:

They set bread before him.
He was bewildered, and looked on it, and marveled.
Enkido understood not how to eat bread,
To drink wine he had not learned.
    Then the priestess opens her mouth and says to Enkido:
      "Eat bread, Enkido, the glory of life,
Drink wine, Enkido, the custom of the land."
    Then Enkido ate bread till he was full,
Then he drank wine, seven beakers.
His spirit lost itself, he grew merry,
His heart rejoiced and his face glowed.

The two heroes battled, and Gilgamesh found an equal opponent in Enkido, so they became friends, and set out together in a series of adventures. But Enkido got sick and died. Gilgamesh, overcome by grief and the realization that he too would die, set out on a journey seeking immortality. On his way he stopped at an inn house where he asked for food and drink. Siduri, the cup-bearer or the bartender, offered him food and wine and with it a sound piece of advice, which by all measures was the first literary presentation of the *carpe diem* theme (seize the day):

"Gilgamesh, whither runnest thou?
Life, which thou seekest, thou will not find.
When the gods created mankind,
They allotted to mankind Death,
But Life they withheld in their hands.
So, Gilgamesh, fill thy body,
Make merry by day and night,
Keep each day a feast of rejoicing!
Day and night leap and have thy delight!
Put on clean raiment,
Wash thy head and bathe thee in water,
Look cheerily at the child who holdeth thy hand,
And may thy wife have joy in thy arms!"

But Gilgamesh continued with his quest, and crossed the Waters of Death to find Utnapishtim, the man who had achieved immortality. Utnapishtim was the survivor of the Great Flood. In pity, he told Gilgamesh where to find the plant of eternal youth. So Gilgamesh dove into the bottom of the sea; he found the plant, but exhausted, he fell asleep. A serpent stole the plant while he was asleep. Finally Gilgamesh realized the inevitability of death, and that immortality came from the good a person achieved in his life.

Sumerian Foods Mentioned in the Epic of Gilgamesh:

Caper buds, wild cucumber, ripe figs, grapes, several edible leaves and stems, honey, meat seasoned with herbs, and bread--a kind of pancake made of barley flour mixed with sesame seed flour and onions (Trager, 7). While travelling, Gilgamesh carried chickpeas with him, as the following lines show:

They dug a pit in the sunlight.
Then Gilgamesh went up on the mountain.
He poured out his chickpeas into the pit.
"Oh, Mountain, grant (me) a dream..."
(Levey, 50)

Baking with the Medieval Baghdadis

During the medieval times, the milling industry flourished in the Islamic world to the extent that "water mills were used everywhere (Hassan and Hill, 214). This advanced technique made possible the production of a variety of flour grades, the most important of which were white flour and semolina (*samid* derived from the Akkadian "samidu"). The outcome was a myriad of breads that adorned the tables of the Caliphs and the commoners alike. Hospitality was judged by how much bread was served with the meal. Aesthetically, the beauty of the *sufra* (dining table) was measured by the number and variety of breads displayed on it. Writing from thirteenth-century Andalusia, the anonymous cookbook writer commended the caliphs of al-Mashriq (the Abbasid caluiphate, the center of which was Baghdad) for their love of bread. They would command their bakers to make a variety of breads, beautifully displayed on huge trays, and they would make their pick as their appetites dictate (*Andalusian Cookbook*, 53).

As a general rule they thought of leavened bread (*mukhtamir*) as being easier on the digestion than unleavened variety (*fateer*). Wheat flour was preferred to barley flour in making bread, for the latter, they believed, produced poor quality bread that is dark, heavy, and prone to crumbling. The qualifications of best bread are given in one of the amusing passages of tenth-century satirical Baghdadi writer Abu Hayyan al-Tawheedi. Singing praises of the Baghdadi bread, he explains that, to begin with, it is made of excellent flour, white with a tinge of yellow, and when kneaded, it is as elastic as gum, stretches like *kandar* (Arabic gum), and sticks to the fingers. When eaten, it squeaks between the molars, and is so chewy that it exhausts the jaws. You feel full just by looking at, and a single morsel would gratify your heart's desires (151-2).

Baking bread reached such a specialized stage that they knew more than thirty kinds of bread. Though they were all round and flat, they, nevertheless, were made of different flours, some were leavened, others were not, and were spread to varying thicknesses. Some were baked in the *tannour*, some in the *furn* (brick oven), and others spread on hot surfaces metal, earthenware, or marble. *Khubz al-ma'* (water bread) was basically the *tannour* bread that had been baking for millennia, and continued to bake to this day. It was usually made of soft dough. Sometimes they made it fancier by sprinkling the top with nigella seeds such as *Khubuz jazmazij*. *Khubz al-baneej*, was made of a stiffer dough, and was sprinkled with sesame and aniseed. It was made thicker when baked in the brick oven. *Al-khubz al-ma'rouk* was characterized by excessive kneading and hence the epithet, *ma'rouk* (from *'araka*: knead). Indeed, dough became so elastic, so the poem al-Warraq quoted went, that if you tugged a small piece, it would bounce back faster than the strike of fate (34-5).

They also prided themselves on baking the unleavened *riqaq* breads that were extremely large and thin. In fact they were so thin that they were referred to as *awraq*, or *wureqat* (as thin as leaves or paper). They made different varieties of this bread, and were baked differently. The *labiq* was the thinnest, and was baked in the *tannour*, one at a time. The other way for baking the *riqaq* was using hot surfaces. *Khubz al-milla* was unleavened *riqaq*, rolled out with a long dowel as thin as possible and baked on hot ashes or *milla*, which was a domed earthenware disc, fitted on fire. This variety of bread was mostly prepared by rustics, nomadic, and settled Bedouins. In urban areas finer *riqaqs* were usually baked on *tabaq*, a big round iron plate. For this bread they used batter similar in consistency to pancake. They poured it in small quantities on the hotplate, and allowed it to spread and flatten as thin as possible. With this kind of device they were also able to make rice bread. People in rural Iraq, especially in the southern marshes, still make *khubuz tabaq* the same old way.

They also knew how to make puff pastry. They would roll out dough *riqaq* way, brush it with oil or butter, fold it, roll it out again, and repeat the procedure all over again. When baked, bread would be puffy, and look layered, and they called it *muwarraqa* (leafy). *Awraq al-riqaq* (leaves or sheets of thin bread) were proudly displayed on the medieval *sufras* (dining table), a testimony on the skill of the baker, and the good taste and hospitality of the host. They were spread in piles all around the table, or were rolled or folded on appetizing herbs. These thin breads were also used the same way we use fillo dough, to enclose other dishes, such as in making the *maghmoumat* and *judhabat* (for more details, see Introduction).

For sandwiches they used the regular flat breads, and just rolled them around the filling, or they baked a slighter thicker bread in the brick oven, and emptied the inside of its pith. There is also evidence that they used a simple device, a latticed metal washer-like disc (*ward mushabbak*) when baking bread for sandwiches. It was put inside the bread before baking it, and was removed after baking. The function was to create a pocket inside the bread to put the sandwich filling in (al-Baghdadi, 381-2). They also baked *khubz al-malla* and *tulma*, which were rustic breads baked in the *malla*, (a pit with hot ashes).

Besides baking at home, which is normally a woman's job, people also had the option of buying their breads from commercial bakeries with large ovens (*afran*), usually operated by men. The baker, called *khabbaz* or *farran*, was always subject to inspection by *al-muhtasib* (inspector), for quality control (Hassan and Hill, 219).

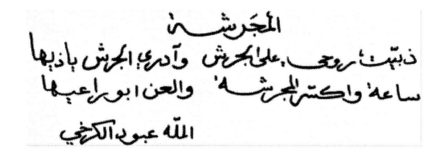

I threw myself into grinding, even though I know it would do me harm.
After a while, I would break the grinder, and curse its owner.
(The Iraqi poet, al-mulla Abbud al-Karkhi)

Curious Bread from al-Waraq's Tenth-Century Baghdadi Cookbook

Besides the regular traditional flat breads, the book contains some unusual bread recipes. The most interesting is *khubz al-quanani* (bottled bread). The recipe goes as follows:

Make soft dough from wheat flour. Pour some oil into wide-mouthed, heatproof bottles, and pour dough into the bottles after you spray the inside with rose water. Let bottles sit upright on a tile put on the smoldering coals in the bottom of the *tannour* (domed clay oven). Let heat be moderate. To test for doneness, insert the tip of a fresh date, if it comes out clean, bread is done. Take bottles out of the oven, and break them. The resulting breads will be shaped like bottles. If wished, moisten the breads with a mixture of milk, mastic and rose water, or milk and honey, or just leave plain (al-Warraq, 34).

The two dancers of Samarra (9th century AD)

The Modern Baking Scene

The bread-making scene has undergone little changes over the centuries, a testimony on the practicality and workability of those ancient and medieval ways of baking. Rolling out unleavened dough thin, and baking it on *saj* (domed metal plate) is still done in northern Iraq, by the Bedouins both nomadic and settled, and dwellers of the southern marshes. As for the leavened flat bread, it is still baked in the same clay ovens as of old days, except that some of the modern *tannours*, especially the commercially operated ones, are fuelled with gas or kerosene. But there is nothing like the genuine traditionally baked bread touched by the smoky aroma of the smoldering coals of brushwood. The baker, normally the woman of the house, wraps the palms of the hands up to the elbows with pieces of cloth to protect her hands from the heat of the fire. The woman takes the fermented balls of dough one by one, and flattens them by wetting her hands and flipping the enlarging disc from hand to hand. The dough, as if by magic, gets bigger and thinner. She then puts it on a slightly domed bread cushion, even up the edges, and slaps the disc against the hot inner walls of the *tannour*. The breads, 8 to 10 breads a batch, will soon develop golden small bubbles all over their faces, and within 5 minutes the baked breads start to peel away from the wall, and are ready to be picked up with long-handled tongs, and spread on a huge wicker basket.

The bread is normally consumed immediately while still warm. The kids of the house get a treat, tiny breads called *hannunat*, a gesture of love and caring. A better treat in the good old ignorant days would have been hot bread spread with *dihin hur* (clarified butter), and sprinkled with sugar. Sometimes those breads are rolled around fresh herbs and greens, and distributed among neighbors in fulfillment of a vow (*nidhir*) that a member of the family has made when a problem is solved or a wish is fulfilled. This is called *khubuz'l-Abbas*, after the name of a Muslim *Imam*.

By the sixties, the number of commercial bakeries in Iraq increased noticeably. Besides the traditional flat bread, specialized bakeries also started baking *sammoun*, which is the domesticated version of French and Italian breads. However, prior to that, almost every household used to have a *tannour* installed, usually with working surfaces built on both sides. The *tannour* should always be kept outside the house, such as at a corner in the porch, the garden, or on the multi-functional roof terrace of the house.

In the western world where most of the roofs are sloped, and are good only for installing TV antennas and satellite dishes, the function of Middle-Eastern flat roofs might not be fully comprehended. A few sentences on their function might not be amiss.

Besides serving as a "bake house," the roof, on warm sunny winter days and cool summer evenings could be used as a playground for kids, especially in houses without gardens. However, rope jumping was not allowed, but who would listen, we even played soccer and basketball over there. For a change of scene, people might picnic up there, such as having an early breakfast on breezy summer mornings, or lunch on warm winter days. It is also a good place for drying up the laundry, and is perfect as a quiet study room. It is also the place where some young men called the *mutyerchiyya* (the pigeon-fliers) practice their hobby of rearing and flying domesticated pigeons by whistling and waving to them with a brightly colored piece of cloth, a hobby often deemed frivolous. While watching television the other day, I was amused to see that some people still practice this hobby on the roofs of skyscrapers in New York.

During the cool summer nights, the roof even serves as an open air "bedroom." It is a pleasant thing to do, except on occasions when a dust storm takes the sleepers by surprise, covering everything, including the sleepers themselves, with a film of fine reddish dust, or when mosquitoes are in the mood for late "dinner." This naturally does not mean that people sleep in public as mistakenly thought by one of the visitors to the area (Fagan, 44). The high walls, usually built all around the roof, help give the sleepers a kind of enclosure and a sense of privacy. As a further protection from the prying eyes of neighbors or the blood thirsty mosquitoes the beds sometimes are enclosed with white muslin called *kulla*. For the thirsty sleepers there is the cool water of *tunga,* the earthenware porous pitcher, with its mouth always covered with a piece of muslin to keep water clean. As for the sleepless, there is always the beautiful crowded night sky to enjoy. However, I most of the time ended up sleeping with my glasses on, for I liked to doze off with the clear sight of the twinkling stars filling my eyes.

Uses of Bread

A meal is not complete without the warm and crispy rounds of bread. Sometimes the bread is a dish by itself, as when it is rolled for a sandwich. It is also an eating utensil used for scooping food off a dish. Indeed, this has always been the case with bread. A recurrent ancient scene depicted on cylinder seals and plaques, is that of seated figures, scooping food from plates with pieces of "tanuru" bread. The flat breads sometimes function as plates on which other cooked foods are put.

Bread is not called the staff of life for nothing. Indeed, it is an emblem of life itself, as one of the names of bread, *eish* (living), connotes. Passing away is sometimes euphemistically expressed by saying that the person "has eaten all his bread." According to the ethical social codes, you are supposed to remain faithful with whom you've shared bread and salt. This connection between bread and salt was established millennia ago. We know this from a Sumerian proverb on poverty:

If you have bread, you have no salt,

If you have salt, you have no bread.

Bread is symbolic of God's bounty, and should be treated with all due respect. As kids we were cautioned against stepping on bread for it is *haraam* (forbidden) to do this. If a God-fearing person comes across a piece of bread on the floor he is supposed to lift it up, make a kissing gesture, lift it up to his forehead, in acknowledgement of God's bounty, and put it away from the feet of careless walkers. Throwing away bread is also *haraam*. Indeed, this might explain the existence of a wide variety of dishes that use stale bread, which is characteristic of the Arabo-Muslim cuisine, in general.

Tannour (domed clay oven)

Tips for Making Good Bread

- In making the following breads, be flexible. If you get rather soft dough, add a little more flour. If dough feels rather stiff, add a little more liquid. But as a general rule, slightly sticky dough, though difficult to handle, will yield more tender and porous bread.

- Bread flour is recommended for making breads since it has higher gluten content than all-purpose flour.

- All-purpose flour can substitute bread flour. However, it absorbs a little less moisture than bread flour or whole wheat flour. In this case leave a little of the liquid aside and see how much you're going to need.

- When using all-purpose flour, you may add more gluten to the dough by using 1 to 2 tablespoons of **gluten flour**, available at specialty stores.

- Whole wheat may be used in making these breads. The best ratio is 1/3 whole wheat to 2/3 white flour.

- Wheat bran is partially ground husk of wheat. In the recipes it is given as an option. However, it is better to give it back to the flour. It is high in fiber content, and adds flavor, and texture to the bread.

- The function of sugar in making these breads is mainly to feed the yeast, tenderize texture, and help brown the crust.

- Salt, on the other hand, helps control the rise of dough. Too much salt will slow down action of yeast, and not enough will weaken gluten structure.

- Semolina is made from durum wheat, which is high in protein and gluten. It is often called for in recipes, for sprinkling on working surfaces and baking pans. I prefer it to regular flour because it does not burn easily.

- Water, in some recipes can be substituted with milk or buttermilk. Use same amounts.

- If dough feels resistant and springs back when flattening or shaping breads, it always helps to let it rest for 10 minutes.

- Toasting nuts and seeds used in making these breads is not necessary but is recommended, for it will give breads a wonderful aroma. Toast in the oven at 350 degrees F. for 10 minutes, or use a skillet over medium heat, stirring frequently, for 5 to 10 minutes.

- If you do not have the time to deal with dough after making it, you have the option of slowing down the process by using only one third of specified yeast, and use liquids at room temperature. Prepared like this, dough will take about 8 hours to ferment if kept at room temperature, and longer if kept in the refrigerator. Actually slow rising will improve the texture of breads. When ready to use, put dough in a warm place to bring it back to life.

I prefer to do the slashing of breads immediately after shaping them. Slashing after they rise is rather risky, since this might cause them to deflate.

To make bread with a good crisp crust, the moment you put it in the oven spray it with a fine mist of water. Spray the inside of the oven, too, but avoid lamp or electric wires. Repeat twice for the first 5 minutes of baking.

Unless otherwise mentioned, glaze breads just before baking in order not to inhibit rising.

There are many ways for glazing the breads, each of which will give a different effect:

1. For a shiny and clear glaze, and to help secure seeds on top of bread, whisk 1 egg white, and 1 tablespoon water. For a shinier look, glaze again 10 minutes before bread is fully baked.

2. For a chewy crust, dissolve 1 teaspoon cornstarch in 3/4 cup cold water. Bring to a boil, stirring until mixture starts to thicken slightly. You can also microwave the mixture for 90 seconds, stir, and let cool.

3. Brush the bread with milk just before baking. This will brown the crust without the gloss.

4. For a soft crust, glaze breads with milk or melted butter as soon as bread is taken out of the oven.

Iraqi Flat Bread

(Khubuz al-Tannour)

(Makes 8 flat breads, 15 inches across)
(Or 15 flat breads, 9 inches across)

This leavened bread is as ancient as the Sumerian civilization itself is, and the way it is prepared and baked now have undergone little changes. Up until recently, the way to leaven the bread was to use a piece of dough, called *shunga,* as a starter, usually reserved from the previous day's baking. It would then be incorporated into the new batch.

The components of the bread are quite basic: wheat flour, salt, starter (yeast) and plain water. That is the reason why it has also been called *khubuz Mei* (water bread). What makes the difference is the kind of flour used. Compared with the commercially made *khubuz*, the homemade bread is denser in texture and a little darker in hue, because it is mostly made of whole wheat. Unfortunately, up until recently, this was not considered a virtue in bread. Dough used in making this bread should be soft and rather wet, so that when it is flattened and slapped into the inner wall of the hot *tannour*, it will generate humidity, which, in turn, will cause the face of the *khubuz* to develop attractive bubbles, characteristic of this bread.

I have never used a *tannuor*, nor have I ever tried making *khubuz al-tannour* myself, that is until I came with my family to the United States. It was nowhere to be found, and we missed it a lot. So driven by necessity, I started experimenting in my small kitchen, with the help of hints from a friend. The major problem was how to prevent it from sticking to the pan, because no oil is used in making or handling the dough, just pure water. Another problem was how to flatten the dough. My first attempts to emulate the way of the masters by flipping the dough from hand to hand to enlarge the disc and then slapping it onto the pan were a disaster. Most of the flattened discs ended up falling on the floor, or acquired pathetically funny shapes. Sprinkling the surface of the pan with flour, before flattening the dough on it, didn't work either, because the flour burnt, and triggered the smoke detector. Semolina flour helped a little but was too messy. At last, and in an epiphanic moment, the idea came to me--use parchment paper! My problems were solved, and ever since baking *khubuz al-tannour* in the convenience of my kitchen has become just a breeze.

A Note on Parchment paper:

I have experimented with paper other than parchment, such as wax paper, aluminum foil, and brown paper, but results were not satisfactory. Besides, parchment paper is reusable until it becomes brittle. The most economical way to get parchment paper is to buy it in bulk from paper warehouses. Look them up in your phone book under "paper," and call them and ask. You can get 1000 sheets, 16 by 24 inches, for about $31,50. This might sound a lot of paper and money, but it is a once in a lifetime purchase. You can share them with friends, too.

3 tablespoons dry yeast
9 cups warm water (it should feel comfortably warm to the dipped finger)

5 pounds (20 cups) flour (for example: 12 cups white bread flour, 7 cups whole wheat flour, and 1 cup wheat bran)
2 tablespoons salt, preferably sea salt

A little semolina or wheat bran for sprinkling on work surface
Preheat oven to 500 degrees F.

1. In a medium bowl, mix dry yeast and warm water. Stir with a spoon, and set aside at a warm place for 5 minutes.

2. Meanwhile put measured flours and wheat germ in a big deep container. I use a plastic container 10 inches in diameter and 5 to 6 inches deep. Mix in salt.

3. Make a well in the middle, and pour in yeast mixture. Stir liquid into the flour in a circular movement, with a wooden spoon, until all flour is incorporated into liquid.

4. Wet both hands with warm water, and start kneading lightly, wetting the hands every time dough gets too sticky to handle, until dough pulls away from sides of bowl, and is less sticky to handle, about 6 minutes. The finished dough should be soft and look rather wet. This soft consistency will make it easier for the bread to develop those characteristic bubbles all over the surface. Smooth surface of dough with wet hands. Cover bowl and let rise in a warm draftless place for about 45 minutes. If you are using the same size of container I suggested, the risen dough should come up to its rim and touch the inside of the lid.

5. Fifteen minutes before baking, preheat oven to 500 degrees F. If you have a baking stone put it on lowest shelf of oven as soon as you preheat the oven, otherwise it might crack if you expose it to sudden change of temperature.
   If you do not have a stone, put big cookie sheet **upside down** on lowest shelf then you preheat oven to let it heat up. Put second shelf on highest level in the oven.

6. While dough is fermenting, prepare parchment paper. Cut out circles a little bigger than size of bread you are going to bake.

7. After dough has risen, punch it lightly with wet hands. Sprinkle generously two big trays or a big working space with semolina or wheat bran. Divide dough into 8 parts or 15, and form each into a ball (it does not have to be perfect), and place them on trays or working space. Always handle this dough with wet hands.

8. To flatten breads, put one cut out parchment paper on an inverted tray, and place it on a warm place. My favorite spot is the stovetop. In stead of tray you may use a big piece of hard cardboard, or any flat and solid transferable board.
   Put one portion of dough on paper. With moistened fingertips flatten with swift jabs to all directions until a thin disc about 15 inches in diameter is formed (or 9 inches). Let the marks of your

fingertips show on the surface. Moisten your fingers as often as you need while doing this. In fact the more moisture the better, for this will create humidity in the oven while baking, which is good for this bread. You might want to keep the disc to rest for 5 minutes, but this is optional.

9. Open the oven door and draw out one third of the lower rack. Transfer flattened dough with the help of tray or hard cardboard, to the level of the lower rack. Swiftly transfer disc with paper by pulling it from the uncovered edges of the paper into the heated stone or inverted pan. If the paper happens to fold or wrinkle while transferring, smooth out folds so that it lays flat.

10. Immediately start working on the second piece, repeating the same procedure. After about 5 minutes of baking, transfer first baking bread to upper shelf, also with the help of the uncovered edges of paper. By now it should have developed bubbles on its face. Put second piece on the stone or inverted pan. Flatten the third piece and get it ready for baking. Repeat the same procedure with the rest of the pieces.

11. Have ready, a big wicker tray or rack. As soon as the first bread on the upper shelf is nicely browned, especially the bubbly parts, in about 4 to 5 minutes, take it out of the oven. Peel paper off the baked bread, and put it in wicker basket or rack. Reuse parchment paper if it is still in good condition. Avoid stacking finished breads while still hot, as this will cause the attractive bubbles to deflate. You can do this when they cool off.

The whole procedure should go fast because each bread would take less than 10 minutes to bake. Keep breads in plastic bags to prevent them from frying out. Freeze for future use any amount you cannot consume in 2 or 3 days. To heat frozen bread, put in the oven at 350 degrees F. for 5 to 7 minutes or until hot. It will taste as fresh as newly baked bread.

بَين الجرف والمـاي حــنطة زرعــوني
لا كـالوا الله ويـاك لا وَدّعـوني

Like wheat planted between the riverbank and water, was I left stranded.
They neither said "God be with you," nor bad me farewell.
(A folkloric Iraqi song)

Variations on Iraqi Flat Bread

From the basic recipe above, you can make the following assortment of breads. Be creative and make your own variations.

Sesame or Nigella Seeds Bread

After you flatten the breads sprinkle the surface lightly with dry toasted sesame seeds, or nigella seeds (see Glossary).

Bread with Herbs and Cheese
(Makes two big breads)

Make delicious aromatic bread by mixing the following ingredients with the dough before flattening it on parchment paper. The amount given is enough for making 2 large breads. After punching the dough as directed in step 7, add the following to what equals two portions of dough:

3/4 cup shredded mozzarella cheese
3/4 cup crumbled feta cheese
3/4 cup grated Romano cheese
1 cup chopped parsley
1/2 cup chopped mint
1/4 cup chopped fresh dill or 1 tablespoon dill weed
2 tablespoons *za'tar* (see Glossary) or fresh thyme
Some optional herbs such as chives and basil

Mix well. Incorporate into dough, then divide into two portions (or more if smaller breads are desired). Prepare and bake bread as directed above.

Spicy Bread with Meat and Vegetables
(Kubuz Uruq, or Khubuz Laham)

(Makes 4 big breads)

By adding ground meat, chopped vegetables, and spices you will get tasty and nourishing bread. You might call it the Iraqi counterpart for pizza, in which meat and vegetables are mixed with the dough itself.

The bread is called *Khubuz Laham* because of the meat added to it. As to why it is called *Khubuz Uruq* there is no one "official" theory. Some think the word *uruq* is derived from the Arabic verb "to branch like veins," which describes the way the bread looks when mixed with the vegetables and meat. Others believe it is from *'iraq*, meat scraped from the bones (al-Tawheedi, 335, n. 1). I think that the nomenclature might be taken further back to the Ancient times when vegetables in the Akkadian were called "arqu." Besides, there is a hint in one of the Babylonian recipes that the practice of mixing meat with dough was already known. There were directions to clean sasku-flour and "add it to the meat, which you have first chopped" (Bottèro, *Mesopotamian Culinary Texts*, 15)

To make this delicious bread, mix the following ingredients with **half** the fermented dough, divide it into 4 portions, and bake, following the same procedure, except that this bread will take a little longer to bake to allow meat to cook well.

Traditionally lots of chopped fat from sheep tail is added. A lighter touch is given here by replacing it with olive oil. (Omit meat if you want to make it vegetarian.)

> 1 1/2 pounds lean ground beef
> 2 cups parsley, chopped
> 2 medium onions, chopped
> 2 teaspoon salt
> 1/2 teaspoon black pepper
> 1 tablespoon *baharat* (see Glossary)
> 2 teaspoons ground cumin; whole seeds may also be used
> 1 teaspoon ground coriander
> 1 teaspoon curry powder
> 1/2 teaspoon chili powder, or to taste
> 3 tablespoons olive oil

Traditional Ways of Using Flat Bread

* Serve bread warm with the traditional dip of *dibs wa rashi* (date syrup drizzled with tahini).

A Kurdish Treat:

Serve it warm with a dip of drained yogurt (see Chapter 2, dairy products), or roll it around warm toasted walnuts. Serve it with sweet hot tea.

Khamee'a:

Boil a cup of milk with 1 teaspoon sugar. Put in a bowl. Cut a piece of hot freshly baked bread into bite size pieces, and add to the milk. Traditionally it is drizzled with sizzling clarified butter.

During the medieval times, such a dish was called *thareed al-laban*. It was made from boiled sheep milk, and done exactly the same way (*Anonymous Thirteenth-Century Andalusian Cookbook*, 112)

Bread Simmered in Tamarind Sauce (Tishribaya or Mahroog Isib'a (his finger is burned):

A very delicious way of consuming stale Iraqi flat bread is to make *Tishribaya*, nicknamed "his finger is burned." Apparently people eating this dish end up getting their fingers burnt. It is so delicious they could hardly wait for it to cool off a little. Incidentally, the Syrians seem to be as impatient as their Iraqi neighbors are. They also have a dish called *hiraaqat isba'u* (burning of his fingers), but it is made of lentils simmered in pomegranate or tamarind juice, with dumplings, fried garlic, and onion (Charles Perry, Correspondence).

2 tablespoons oil
1 to two medium onions, chopped
1 teaspoon curry powder
1/2 teaspoon turmeric
1 clove garlic, grated
1 teaspoon salt
1/4 teaspoon black pepper
1/2 teaspoon chili pepper, or to taste
2 heaping tablespoons tomato paste, or 1/2 cup tomato sauce
1 tablespoon tamarind syrup, may substitute with 1 tablespoon pomegranate syrup, see Glossary
1/2 plain big Iraqi flat bread, broken into pieces

For garnish: dry mint, and yogurt

1. In a medium heavy pot, heat oil and sauté onion until transparent, about 6 minutes. Add curry powder and turmeric a few minutes before onion is done, and stir until aromatic.

2. Add garlic, salt, pepper, chili, tomato paste or sauce, and tamarind syrup. Stir together for a few minutes.

3. Add bread, and cover with hot water by up to 2 inches. Stir briefly to allow bread to mix with spices. Bring to a quick boil, then reduce heat to medium-low, and let simmer, covered, until most of the liquid evaporates, about 20 minutes. Fold twice while simmering.

4. Transfer to a big platter, sprinkle with dry mint, and drizzle with yogurt. And don't forget to let it cool off a little!

جيث أشجر التنور
العذرية طاحت
مدني يا بعد الروح
حسن أمي صاحت

I came to light the *tannour*, and the flower fell.
Let go of me, soul of my soul, I hear my mother calling.
(An Iraqi folk song)

Turkumani Treats

The *Turkumans* are an Iraqi ethnic minority that resides in the northern region, particularly in the city of Kurkuk. Their cooking has a lot in common with the general Iraqi cuisine. Nevertheless, they do have some specialties in which grains and yogurt are used.

The **Mastawa** is a soup-like dish in which shelled wheat is simmered in yogurt, with lots of mint. **Kishkak** is another soup in which *kishk* (also called *kasham*) is used to make a hearty soup, flavored with mint. *Kishk* is dough made of yogurt and bulgar, shaped into patties and dried, and used to flavor sauces. The fact that they also call it *kasham* is testimony enough to its ancient origin. In the Babylonian stew recipes a similar concoction was called "kisimmu," and the similarity is uncanny (see Introduction for more details).

Belamaj is an interesting dish prepared by browning flour in oil, and adding liquid to it to make gravy of medium consistency. It is flavored with a little sugar, cinnamon, and garlic, and poured on broken pieces of fresh flat bread. It is reminiscent of the medieval flour based soups, and resembles the American traditional breakfast treat of biscuits with gravy.

Karawan Asha is a simpler version of the *Tishribaya* (pieces of flat bread cooked in flavorful sauce, see recipe above). As the name suggests, it must have originally been one of those practical dishes in which people used stale or dry bread while travelling in caravans. It is basically onion browned in oil. Water or broth, lemon juice, salt, pepper and broken pieces of stale or dry flat bread are added. It is to be simmered until most of the liquid evaporates and bread is pleasantly moist. (For information on the *Turkumani* dishes I am indebted to my friend Amal al-Toma, who is a *Turkuman* herself, and is an excellent cook in her own right.)

69

They Ate a Lot of Bread in Mesopotamia

Following is a letter from a grumpy Babylonian son to his mother, from which we incidentally learn that the Mesopotamians used to consume a lot of bread:

Tell the Lady Zinu: Iddin-Sin sends the following message:

May the gods Samas, Marduk, and Ilabrat keep you forever in good health for my sake.

From year to year, the clothes of the [young] gentlemen here become better, but you let my clothes get worse from year to year. Indeed, you persisted in making my clothes poorer and more scanty. At a time when in our house wool is used up like bread, you have made me poor clothes. The son of Adad-iddinam, whose father is only an assistant of my father, [has] two new sets of clothes while you fuss even about a single set of clothes for me. In spite of the fact that you bore me and his mother only adopted him, his mother loves him, while you, you do not love me!

(Oppenheim, *Letters from Mesopotamia*, 84-5)

Barley Bread

(Khubuz al-Sha'eer)

(Makes 2 breads)

Barley bread was one of the earliest breads to be baked on the ancient land of Mesopotamia. Though people in rural areas never stopped making it, in the big cities it unfortunately grew out of vogue for the last two or three decades. It was looked down upon as being too rustic for city slickers. It became synonymous with poverty. Utter depravity was when you cannot even afford barley bread.

Barley flour is now believed to make healthy and tasty bread that is rich in cholesterol-lowering soluble fibers. In texture barley bread is denser than wheat bread because it lacks the glutinous proteins that help bread to rise and acquire a light texture. Therefore when baked, barley bread cannot develop those attractive bubbles that appear on the face of baked flat wheat bread. To help it rise, I add a little wheat bread flour, wheat bran and gluten. The following proportions make 2 big (14-inch) flat barley breads:

1 tablespoon dry yeast
3 cups warm water

4 cups barley flour
1 cup white bread flour
1 cup wheat bran
1 tablespoon gluten, optional (but it does help the texture a lot)
1 teaspoon salt

1/4 cup sesame seeds, dry toasted, for sprinkling on bread

1. Dissolve yeast in water, and set aside in a warm place for 5 minutes.

2. In a big bowl, mix the flours, bran, gluten, if used, and salt, and make a well in the middle of flour mixture.

3. Pour yeast mixture, and follow the same instructions in making Iraqi flat bread, above. The finished dough should be rather soft. When kneading you will notice that dough will feel funny, like kneading a piece of clay. This is because barley dough does not have enough gluten in it.

4. Let dough rise for about 1 hour in a warm place, then punch down and divide into 2 portions. Follow the same instructions of Iraqi bread with regard to heating the oven and shaping the breads. However when shaping, make sure to put deeper impressions of your fingertips on the surface, this will help give the bread a more interesting look. Sprinkle with toasted sesame, and allow shaped discs to rise for about 15 minutes.

5. Bake as directed in Iraqi flat bread.

Flat Bread with Dill
(Khubuz bil- Shibint)

(Makes two 10 to 12-inch flat breads)

I developed this bread to incorporate two of my favorite ingredients, dill and potatoes. It is in fact a variation on the traditional flat bread. Though I always like to use wheat bran and whole wheat in my breads, for this recipe I use unbleached bread white flour, mainly for the sake of contrast between the fresh greenness of the dill and the attractive ivory whiteness of the dough.

2 medium potatoes (about 8 ounces), peeled, cut into cubes, boiled until cooked, then drained. Reserve 1 cup of drained liquid, keep warm. Mash drained potatoes and let cool
2 tablespoons dry yeast
1 teaspoon sugar
1 cup warm water

4 1/2 cups unbleached white bread flour
2 teaspoons salt (preferably sea salt)
1 packed cup fresh dill, chopped
1/4 cup olive oil

Toasted sesame seeds, optional
Preheat oven to 450 degrees F.

1. In a small bowl dissolve dry yeast and sugar in 1 cup warm water, and set aside at a warm place until foamy, about 5 minutes.

2. In a big bowl mix flour and salt, and make a well in the middle. Add mashed potatoes, dill, olive oil, yeast mixture, and reserved cup of drained potato liquid. With a wooden spoon, stir mixture in a circular movement to incorporate flour into the other ingredients. Then with oiled hands (for it will be sticky) knead mixture for about 6 minutes. The final dough will be rather on the soft and sticky side. Oil on both sides and let rise, covered, in a warm and draft-free place for about 1 hour.

3. Punch dough down, and divide into 2 equal parts. Prepare 2 circles of parchment paper, about 12 inches in diameter, and place them on a transferable flat surface, such as a big tray turned upside down, or a piece of hard cardboard. With oiled hands, spread each dough portion on the parchment paper, spreading and flattening as you go to make a flat disc 1/2 to 3/4 inch in diameter. Make sure to leave your fingerprints on the entire surface for this will create an interesting surface when baked. **If parchment paper is not available** then generously oil 2 big cookie sheets and shape each portion into an oval 1/2 to 3/4 inch thick. Sprinkle with sesame seeds if wished. Let rise in a warm place for about 30 minutes (my favorite spot is the top of the stove). No need to cover the rising breads because surface will stay moist from the oil used in spreading dough.

4. If you have a baking stone, put it on the lower rack when you turn on the oven. **If you do not have a stone**, then just turn a big cookie sheet upside down, and place it on the lowest oven rack. When ready to bake, transfer risen flattened dough with the support used underneath it, and lower it to the level of the stone or the upside down cookie sheet. With the help of the parchment paper transfer the

disc to the oven. If dough is flattened on a cookie sheet, then put the flattened dough with the cookie sheet on the stone. If no stone is used then place the cookie sheet on the center oven rack. Meanwhile get the other batch ready.

5. Let bread bake for about 10 minutes, or until the surface nicely browns in spots. Take out of the oven and let cool on a rack or a flat wicker tray. Repeat with the other portion.

Variation: Spicy Dilled Flat Bread

This variation will result in excitingly spicy and aromatic bread. To the dough add the following in step 2:

1 medium onion, chopped or thinly sliced, then sautéed in 2 tablespoons olive oil until nicely caramelized, about 10 minutes. (Deduct oil used here from the 1/4 cup oil called for in the above recipe, so that it will not be too greasy). Towards the end of cooking the onion, add 1/2 teaspoon of whole seeds of caraway, cumin, and aniseeds or fennel, each. This will allow the seeds to toast a little before using.

You can also add 1/4 cup chopped dried tomatoes, and 1/4 cup chopped pitted olives.

Bread, European Style

(Sammoun)

Samoun is the Iraqi domesticated version of the French and Italian bread styles. It started to be popular in the early fifties, especially among city dwellers. Unlike the Iraqi flat bread, this variety is only commercially baked for it requires big ovens for baking it. The bread is traditionally shaped into diamonds, a little bit bigger than the palm of the hand, puffy and wide in the middle, and tapered into two rounded crisp ends. But it also comes in other shapes, such as baguettes and buns. When making sandwiches, the inside is usually scraped out. Flat bread, by contrast, is rolled around the filling, nothing is wasted.

The Iraqi *samoun* has the same desirable chewiness in its texture, characteristic of its prototype, but the crust is not as hard. This, in fact, is not a bad thing taking into consideration that *samoun* is mainly used for sandwiches.

The following recipe would enable you to make, within a few hours, bread similar in appearance and texture to the Iraqi *samoun*. If you prefer the slow-rising method, then go to next recipe.

3 tablespoons dry yeast
1 tablespoon sugar
1/2 cup warm water

8 cups white bread flour
1 cup wheat bran, optional
1 tablespoon salt

3 cups water, or 2 cups milk or buttermilk and 1 cup water
1/4 cup oil

For glazing: 1 egg white whisked with 1 tablespoon water; or 1 teaspoon cornstarch dissolved in 3/4 cup cold water and cooked until slightly thickened, stirring frequently, or microwaved for 90 seconds. Use milk if you are not interested in giving the bread a glossy look.

Sesame seeds, dry toasted, optional
Semolina flour, or wheat bran to sprinkle on baking sheets, optional
Preheat oven to 450 degrees F.

1. Dissolve yeast and sugar in 1/2 cup warm water, and set aside, 5 minutes.

2. In a big bowl mix flour, bran, if using any, and salt. Make a well in the middle.

3. Pour yeast mixture, water and oil into the well. With a wooden spoon incorporate liquids into flour in a circular movement. With slightly oiled hands knead dough for 6 to 7 minutes. The finished dough should have a soft to medium consistency. Oil dough on both sides, and set aside, covered, in a warm draftless place. Let dough rise until doubled in size, about an hour.

Shaping and Baking Sammoun Bread

Preheat oven to 450 degrees F. Punch down dough. The number of breads made depends upon shapes and sizes chosen. The following are some suggestions and guidelines, and remember to handle dough with slightly oiled hands:

1. To make traditional **diamond shaped** *sammouns* with two nipple-like ends, divide dough to **10 portions**, and let rest for 10 minutes. Quickly roll one portion between the palms until it becomes 7-to-8-inches long log. Lay it flat on greased baking sheet, sprinkled with semolina or wheat bran, if wished. Using the fingers, flatten to broaden the middle part, and make it look diamond-shaped with two nipple-like ends.

Repeat with rest of pieces, leaving space between pieces to allow for expansion. With a very sharp knife or a razor blade, make 2 diagonal slashes, or one long slash in the middle. Allow to rise, loosely covered with a kitchen towel, at a warm place, for about 30 minutes. My ideal spot is the top of the range and places around it.

When ready to bake, brush pieces of bread with chosen glaze, and sprinkle lightly with dry toasted sesame, if desired. Put pan on middle shelf of the oven. Using a spray bottle filled with warm water, spray the breads, the interior of the oven, and the oven door (avoid the bulb if there is any), and quickly shut the door to entrap the moisture you have created inside the oven. Repeat the spraying twice during the first 5 minutes of baking. The total baking time is 15 to 18 minutes, or until the breads are golden brown. Immediately transfer breads to a big paper bag lined with a kitchen towel, and partially close the opening to allow some of the steam to escape. For a crispier crust, let breads cool on a wicker basket or a rack.

2. To make **buns** after punching dough, divide it into **18 to 20 portions,** depending on how big you want them. Form into smooth balls as follows: hold a portion in one hand, and with the other pull the sides towards the center of the piece. Put the ball, smooth side up, on a baking sheet, greased and sprinkled with some semolina, if wished. Leave a good space between portions. Let rest for a few minutes, then flatten the balls with oiled fingers to 3/4-inch thick discs. If it springs back, let it relax a little further, and try again. Make 2 slashes on the surface with a sharp knife or razor blade. Let rise, covered, for about 20 minutes. Then brush with glaze, spray with water, and bake exactly as described in the diamond-shaped *sammouns*, above.

3. To make **baguette-like** *sammouns*, after punching dough, divide it into **8 pieces**. Let them rest for 10 minutes, then flatten each into a rectangle 1/2-inch thick, and roll from the longer side in a Swiss-roll fashion. Seal edge well and taper the ends by rolling slightly. Arrange pieces, seam side down, on prepared greased baking sheets, sprinkled with semolina flour or wheat bran, if wished. Leave space between pieces to allow for expansion. Make 3 long diagonal slashes with a sharp knife or a razor blade. Let rise, covered, for about 30 minutes. Brush with glaze, spray with water, and bake as described in diamond-shaped *sammouns*, above.

4. You can also make **flat *sammouns*,** impressively huge and attractively dimpled. It is good for dipping and scooping.

After punching dough, divide it into **4 or 6 parts**, depending on how big you want them to be. Form portions into balls and let them rest for 10 minutes.

On a surface generously sprinkled with semolina or wheat bran, roll out a portion with a rolling pin to a disc, 1/2-inch thick. If dough resists and springs back, let it relax for a few minutes, and try again. Transfer flattened disc to a big cookie sheet that has been greased and sprinkled with semolina, or to a round of parchment paper, put on a flat surface. Let it rest while you do other portions. Let discs rise, loosely covered, for about 20 minutes.

Preheat oven to 450 degrees F. When ready to bake do the following, **only** to the one or ones that are ready for the oven: Brush with chosen glaze, sprinkle with dry toasted sesame or nigella seeds, if wished.

You can also turn them into foccacia breads, by sprinkling the breads with your choice of toppings, after brushing surface with olive oil, instead of the suggested glazes. The topping can be a mixture of grated Romano cheese and crumbled feta cheese, with some dried thyme, or *za'ter*, rosemary, chopped herbs such as mint, basil, parsley and dill, pitted and chopped olives, slices of tomatoes or roasted bell pepper, sautéed sliced onion, or whatever.

Now after glazing or spreading the topping on the surface, with wet fingertips, lightly make some impressions like dimples on the surface, avoiding the border of the circle by 1 inch. You need to do this quickly so that bread does not deflate. Immediately put dough disc in the oven. If using parchment paper, transfer disc with the help of a hard transferable surface, such as the back of a big tray, and put it on a baking stone or a cookie sheet turned upside down. Spray bread and oven 2 or 3 times during the first 5 minutes of baking. Bake for 15 to 17 minutes, or until puffy with dimples, and nicely browned in patches.

Spread (do not stack) baked breads on a flat wicker basket or a rack, let cool for a few minutes then serve. When breads are cool, keep them in plastic bags, and freeze the amounts you cannot consume within 2 days.

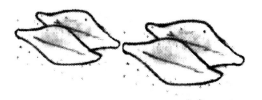

Slow-Rising Sammoun Bread

Since the joy of bread is having it fresh and warm, I find the following recipe quite convenient. Prepare dough at night, allow it to slowly ferment during the night, and have it ready for baking in the morning. Thus on a weekend morning you'll be able to treat your family to piping hot bread right from your oven. Alternatively, you can prepare the dough in the morning and bake it in the evening at your convenience. Besides, using less dry yeast, and allowing bread to ferment along a considerably longer period of time yields better quality bread, more porous, and chewier in texture.

In the big cities bread is usually purchased before a meal is served to ensure its freshness. I remember when we were sent to the neighborhood bakery at noontime, the line seemed to be a mile long. Not that we minded. The wait was whiled away by chattering with friends and neighbors, and as we got nearer to where the action was, the aroma of baking the bread filled the place, and was deliciously intoxicating. Mesmerized, we would be watching the breads, glazed, slashed, and popped into the huge oven. As a batch came out of the oven, we would cringe at the annoyingly gritty sound made when breads rub against each other, as they were thrown from the baking trays to the big bread wicker box. It was not unusual to get home with blistered fingertips from handling the hot bread, and with some *sammouns* with their crispy ends chewed away.

1 tablespoon dry yeast
1 tablespoon sugar
4 cups water, room temperature

9 cups bread flour
1 cup wheat bran, optional
1 1/4 tablespoons salt
1/4 cup oil

For glazing: 1 egg white whisked with 1 tablespoon water; or 1 teaspoon cornstarch dissolved in 3/4 cup cold water and cooked until slightly thickened, stirring frequently, or microwaved for 90 seconds. Use milk if you are not interested in giving the bread a glossy look.

Dry toasted sesame for sprinkling on breads, optional

1. Dissolve yeast and sugar in water, and set aside for 5 minutes.

2. In a big bowl mix flour, bran, if used, and salt. Make a well in the middle, and pour in yeast liquid and oil. Using a wooden spoon, stir mixture in a circular movement, until well incorporated. With oiled hands knead briefly for about 6 minutes, or until you get a smooth and soft dough. Oil dough on both sides and set aside, covered, at room temperature for 8 to 9 hours.

3. When ready to bake, punch dough down, and shape and bake as described in **Bread, European Style (*Sammoun*)**, given above. If dough is too elastic to handle after punching because it is cold, let it rest, for a while, at a warm place. Besides, with this kind of bread you need to let the shaped breads rise at a really warm place to give the cold dough a boost.

Have Your Bowl and Eat It

An interesting way for shaping bread is to make it look like a bowl so that it could hold food. This way you can eat the contents of the bowl as well as the bowl itself. This will save you the trouble of doing some dish washing.

Make dough for the bread bowls by following directions given in **Bread, European Style (Samoun)**. The size of the bread bowls depends on your preference and purpose. I use cereal bowls as molds to make bread bowls to contain soups that are rather thick in consistency (nearly all the recipes given in the soup chapter can be put in these bowls).
Alternatively, you can fill bowls with salad garnished with beans and boiled eggs to make it a complete meal. Following is how to make the bowls:

Grease or spray the back of small ovenproof bowls. After dough has risen and is punched, take a portion the size of a small orange (for cereal bowl size), flatten it on a surface sprinkled with semolina, and drape it on the inverted greased bowl. Pull the sides to cover the entire surface. Set it aside, covered, for about 30 minutes. Then glaze and sprinkle with sesame seeds, if wished. Bake as directed in the recipes.

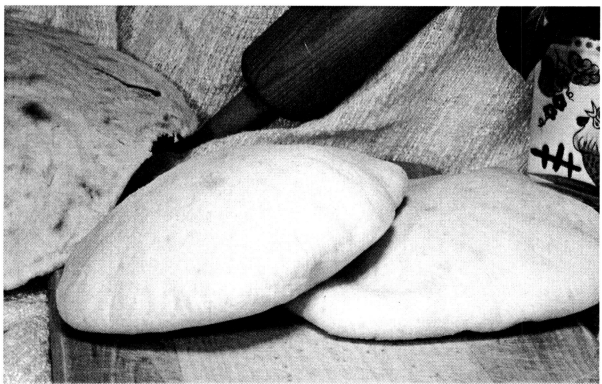

Pocket bread

Arabic Bread
(Al-khubuz al-Arabi)

This variety of flat bread started to make its appearance in Iraq around the late sixties Some people call it *khubuz Lubnani*, others call it *khubus Suri* (from Syria), or simply *khubuz Arabi*, to differentiate it from the indigenous *tannour* flat bread. Like all flat breads, it is very versatile, it can be used as a scoop, or made into sandwiches. The only disadvantage is that it gets dry very quickly, and therefore needs to be stored properly.

In the West this bread is known as pita bread, and it is a little different from the Greek version which, for one thing, does not puff and separate when baked, and is higher in fat content. Although Arabic bread is not hard to come by in the markets nowadays, home baked bread is far more superior in quality, and much cheaper. Following is a recipe for pita bread dough, with some traditional ways of using it:

2 tablespoons dry yeast
1 tablespoon sugar
1/2 cup warm water

9 cups bread flour, either all white, or a blend of 7 cups white and 2 cups whole wheat
1 cup wheat bran, optional
1 tablespoon salt

79

1/2 cup oil
1 1/2 cup warm water
1 1/2 cup warm milk

Semolina or flour for sprinkling the work surface

1. Dissolve yeast and sugar in 1/2 cup of warm water, set aside in a warm place for 5 minutes.

2. Put flour, bran, if used, and salt in a big bowl. Make a well in the middle.

3. Pour yeast mixture, oil, milk and water. Using a wooden spoon, incorporate liquids into flour in a circular movement. With slightly oiled hands knead dough for 7 to 8 minutes. The final dough should be of medium consistency. Oil dough on both sides. Set aside, covered, in a warm draftless place for 45 minutes or until well risen.

4. Punch dough down, and divide it into portions, the size of which depends on what you are going to do with it.

With the prepared dough you can do the following breads:

Pocket Breads
(Makes 12 breads)

1. After punching dough, divide it into 12 portions. Place them on surface sprinkled with semolina or flour, and cover them with a clean piece of cloth.

2. Meanwhile preheat oven to 500 degrees F., and place oven shelf on lowest level. Remove the other shelf. Put a baking stone or a cookie sheet turned upside down on shelf. Have ready 12 rounds or squares of parchment paper, big enough to accommodate an 8 to 9-inches discs of bread.

3. On surface sprinkled with semolina or flour, and with a rolling pin, flatten dough portions one after the other, into circles 8-to-9-inches in diameter, and 1/4-inch thick. While working on a piece keep unflattened portions covered. Place each disc on prepared parchment paper, and put it on a flat surface in a warm place to allow it to rise a little. **Do not stack the flattened discs.** Each piece will need about 10 minutes to rise, and while rising, keep discs from getting dry by covering them with kitchen towels.

4. As soon as you are done flattening, start baking, starting with the ones you worked on first. This will give time to the latter ones to rise. Bake 2 or 3 at a time depending on the size of your oven, by transferring discs with the paper from the working surface to the stone or inverted sheet.

5. These breads cook fast, they might require 5 to 6 minutes, and will puff and develop a pocket. They are done when bottom is slightly browned in patches, and top is almost white. Take breads out of the oven, and immediately put them in a big paper bag lined with a kitchen towel. Partially close bag to allow some of the steam to escape. Repeat with rest of pieces.
When breads are cool, keep them in sealed plastic bags, and freeze any amount you cannot consume within 2 days, and heat as needed.

Note:
If parchment paper is not available, flatten pieces as directed in step 3, and arrange them on greased baking sheets, and let rise and bake as directed above.

Lawash Bread (Thin Flat Breads)
(Makes 12 pieces)

Using the basic Arabic Bread dough given above, you can make thin and pliable *lawash* bread, good for making wrap sandwiches. In Iraq it is called *khubuz rgag*, or *rqaq* or *rgoog*, depending on whether you live in Baghdad, Mosul, or Basrah, respectively. In the Middle Ages such thin pliable breads were simply called *riqaq* (very thin), or *awraq al-riqaq* (as thin as paper). They were arranged on the dining tables or the large serving trays, rolled or in stacks, to be eaten with stews or the dry dishes (*nawashif*). Besides, they were used to cover up other meat preparations, such as in the *maghmoumat* (covered dishes), or *judhabat* (for details, see Introduction), for the same purpose we now use layered fillo dough with savory dishes.

Riqaq, as it is made in northern Iraq, is crisp and brittle. Traditionally a dowel is used to roll out unleavened dough into huge thin sheets, around 24 inches in diameter. A large domed metal plate, called *saj,* placed on direct heat, is used to bake the bread. When first peeled off the *saj,* the bread is soft and pliable, and while still warm, it is folded for easy storage. Once they cool off and harden, they can be stored for months. The bread is used as needed, by reviving it, so to speak, with a sprinkle of water, and covering it with a kitchen towel to soften.

These giant breads are not easy to make, and they require special expertise, a long dowel and a big working space. In Iraq you cannot buy *khubz rqaq* from the regular commercial bakeries, but rather from the small home-run "bakeries." In Baghdad we used to buy ours from women vendors who stacked their featherweight breads in cage-like baskets.

Medium size breads, thin and pliable, can be made quite easily, using simple equipment available in the kitchen. For baking them, I first tried using a pancake pan, but they tended to shrink as they bake, due to the flat surface of the pan. A big all-metal Chinese wok, turned upside down, is the best substitute to the *saj.* I got mine from a garage sale for a dollar, and it has become an indispensable gadget in the kitchen, and even outside it. You may put the wok on the grill and have fresh baked bread cooked outside the house. This is a bonus in summer if you do not want to generate heat inside the house. This bread is great for picnics, too. All you need is a wok put on campfire, and a rolling pin, and there you go, first class bread, fresh, warm and fragrant, right in the middle of the wilderness. Here is how to make it:

1. Prepare **basic dough of Arabic Bread**, and let it rise as directed.

2. Punch dough down and divide it into 12 pieces. Place them on a surface sprinkled with semolina or flour. Keep them covered with kitchen towels, and let rest for about 10 minutes.

3. Meanwhile invert a wok on top of a stove burner on high heat. To check whether it has reached the right temperature, sprinkle a few drops of water on the surface. It is ready when drops sizzle, and form into dancing drops.

4.On a surface sprinkled with semolina or flour, roll out a piece of dough, as thin as possible. Then drape it on the back of the hand and try to stretch it, especially the thick areas, taking care not to make holes. Immediately spread it on the hot wok. After a few minutes, turn the piece over and let it cook for a few more minutes, until it develops blisters on the surface. (Total cooking time for a piece is 5 to 6 minutes.) You might need to lower heat to medium high, if pieces get scorched quickly.

5. Immediately, put baked bread in a paper bag, lined with a kitchen towel, and close the opening. Repeat with rest of pieces. As soon as breads are cold enough, put them in sealed plastic bags, keep them refrigerated, or freeze them for future use.

Arabian Pizza
(Laham bi Ajeen)
(Makes **18 to 20** breads, 7 inches in diameter, or **13 to 14** breads 10 inches in diameter)

This is the Arabic alternative to pizza, and it is what it literally means-- "meat with dough." When I was a kid in Baghdad, not many people knew of it. We used to get it by order from the neighborhood bakery owned by an Armenian, but his version was very basic. The topping consisted of just meat, onions, salt and black pepper. By the seventies, this delicious bread started to gain tremendous popularity. A large number of carryout *Laham bi Ajeen* restaurants mushroomed out in all the major cities in Iraq, to meet the increasing demand. They were baked in brick ovens, and were lusciously moist and tender, but unfortunately too greasy. The following recipe is a much leaner version, in which olive oil replaces fat meat.

1 recipe of Arabic Bread Dough
For the topping:
    1 1/2 pounds ground lean meat, beef, lamb or turkey
    3 medium onions (about 1 1/2 cups) finely chopped and sautéed in 2 tablespoons olive oil
    3/4 cup chopped parsley
    2 medium tomatoes (about 1 1/2 cups) finely chopped
    3 heaping tablespoons tomato paste (one 6-ounce can)
    1 tablespoon pomegranate syrup, optional (see Glossary), or lemon juice
    3 tablespoons yogurt, optional
    1 to 2 cloves garlic, grated
    1 tablespoon *baharat*, (see Glossary)
    2 teaspoons salt, or to taste
    1/2 teaspoon black pepper
    1/2 teaspoon allspice
    1/2 teaspoon cinnamon
    1/4 teaspoon chili pepper, or to taste

Olive oil for brushing the flattened breads
Preheat oven to 450 degrees F.

1. Prepare basic dough as directed in recipe, and while waiting for dough to rise, prepare topping by mixing all topping ingredients in a big bowl.

2. Put one of the shelves on the lowest level, and the other on the highest one. Put a baking stone or an inverted cookie sheet on the lower shelf. Preheat oven to 450 degrees F.

3. As soon as dough rises, punch it down and divide it into 18 to 20 pieces, or 13 to 14 pieces. Place portions on surface dusted with semolina or flour, and cover with kitchen towels.

4. Since dough does not need to rise again, you can start shaping, filling and baking immediately. On surface sprinkled with semolina or flour, roll out a piece to a disc, 7 inches or 10 inches in diameter, about 1/8 inch thick. Place flattened dough on a piece of parchment paper, a little bigger than dough disc. Spread about 1/4 to 1/3 cup of filling (depending upon size of disc) on surface of flattened disc. The filling should cover surface in a thin layer, leaving a 1/4-inch border uncovered. Lightly brush uncovered border with olive oil. **(If parchment paper is not available use greased cookie sheets)**

5. Immediately, and with the help of paper, slide discs into the oven on the hot stone or the inverted baking sheet. Dough is not supposed to puff, and it will take 5 to 8 minutes to bake. You can bake 2 or 3 at a time depending on oven size. While this batch is baking start working on the other batch. You might transfer half-baked ones to the upper shelf, and put some new ones on lower shelf.

6. As soon as you take baked ones out of the oven, stack them **with the parchment paper**, in a big paper bag, lined with a kitchen towel, and partially close the bag. (The parchment paper will prevent the topping from sticking to the bottom of the piece above it.)
   Best when eaten hot from the oven. Any leftovers may be refrigerated or frozen, and warmed up in the oven.

A Vegetarian Option:
Meat can be replaced with two 10-ounce packages of frozen spinach, thawed and excess moisture squeezed out, or 1 1/2 cups of a mixture of crumbled feta cheese and grated Romano cheese, or 2 cups cooked whole lentils, or whatever you fancy.

Filled Pastries
(Fatayer)

Using bread dough for making more elaborate pastries is an old culinary practice. During the medieval times for instance, pieces of dough were spread into discs, filled with cheese, and folded from four sides, leaving the middle open, to let the cheese show. In Andalusia, such pastries were called *mujabbanat* (cooked with cheese, *Anonymous Thirteenth-century Andalusian Cookbook*, 119-20). Today such pastries are traditionally shaped into triangles. But feel free to shape them to your fancy.
   These pastries make an elegant and tasty appetizer. Served warm or at room temperature, they are ideal for buffet parties. They are also quite handy as snacks. Keep them in the refrigerator and heat as needed, or freeze them for future use.
   To make **24 pieces**, you need to make **half the dough recipe**. Here is how to make them:

1. Follow directions for **basic dough of Arabic bread**, and while rising, prepare the filling, using any of the options given below.

2. Preheat oven to 425 degrees F.

3. When dough has risen, punch it down and divide into 24 pieces. Place them on surface sprinkled with semolina or flour. Keep covered the ones you are not working on.

4. On a surface sprinkled with semolina or flour, roll out each portion into a thin disc 3 to 4 inches in diameter, 1/8-inch thick. Put about 1 heaping tablespoon of the chosen filling in the middle of disc. Visually divide disc into 3 sections, and lift and seal 3 edges to form a triangle. Seal ridges of triangle by pinching with fingertips. For the ones filled with meat mixture, I wouldn't close triangle completely, but leave an opening on top to allow more heat to get into the filling. Lift finished ones from the working surface into a greased cookie sheet, with help of a pancake turner, if needed. Bake immediately. They will take around 15 minutes to brown nicely. If wished, lightly brush pastries with melted butter or oil immediately they are taken out of the oven. Serve warm.

To store, when pieces are cold, keep them in sealed plastic bags and refrigerate them, or keep them in the freezer, for future use.

Meat Filling:
Follow recipe for **Laham bi Ajeen Topping**, above.

Spinach Filling:

In a bowl, mix the following:

Two 10-ounce packages frozen spinach, thawed and excess moisture squeezed out
2 medium onions (about 1 1/2 cups) finely chopped, and sautéed in 2 tablespoons olive oil
1/2 cup crumbled feta cheese, or grated Romano cheese
1/4 cup chopped fresh dill, or 1 tablespoon dill weed
1/4 cup chopped dry tomatoes, optional
1 tablespoon lemon juice
1/4 cup chopped toasted walnuts, or whole dry toasted pine nuts
1 teaspoon salt
1/2 teaspoon black pepper
1/2 teaspoon chili pepper, or to taste (optional)
1 teaspoon za'tar, or thyme, optional (see Glossary)

Cheese Filling:

In a bowl mix, the following:

2 cups feta cheese, crumbled (about 8 ounces)
1 cup shredded mozzarella cheese
1 egg, beaten
1 cup parsley, chopped
1/4 cup fresh dill, chopped, or 1 tablespoon dill weed
1/4 cup fresh mint, or 1 tablespoon dried mint, optional
1 teaspoon za'atar (see Glossary), or thyme

Sour Dough Twisted Sesame Rings (Semeat)

Sourdough Twisted Sesame Rings

(Semeat)

(Makes 20 pieces)

This is the Iraqi version of bagels. They are shaped into attractive twisted small rings, encrusted with lots of fragrant toasted sesame, crispy in crust and chewy in texture. They are purchased from wandering vendors who arrange the *semeats* on wicker baskets in tall piles and carry them on their heads.

The traditional method requires a starter, which is easy to make. All it needs is a little stirring, and waiting. Actually, if you plan on baking your own bread regularly, it is a good idea to have a starter lurking in the refrigerator. It will be ready for you whenever you need it, provided you replenish it every time you use some of it. In fact, the starter can be used with all kinds of bread to enhance its taste and texture.

For sourdough starter:
  2 cups bread flour
  2 cups water, room temperature
  3 tablespoons sugar
  1 teaspoon dry yeast

For the *semeat*:
> **2 tablespoons dry yeast**
> **1 tablespoon sugar**
> **1/2 cup warm water**
>
> **6 1/4 cups bread flour**
> **1 tablespoon salt**
> **1/2 cup oil**
> **1 1/2 cups warm water**
>
> **For glaze: 1 egg white whisked with 1 tablespoon water; or 1 teaspoon cornstarch dissolved in 3/4 cup cold water and cooked until slightly thickened, stirring frequently, or microwaved for 90 seconds.**
>
> **About 1 cup sesame seeds, dry toasted**
> **Preheat oven to 450 degrees F.**

1. In a medium glass or plastic container combine all starter ingredients and stir with a wooden spoon until smooth. Cover loosely to allow fresh air to get into the container, and let stand in a warm draftless place for about 2 days. Stir mixture 2 to 3 times a day. Dough should rise; bubble, and separate and smell like sour yogurt. Stir well before using it. If you want dough to develop just a tinge of sourness, then keep starter for 24 hours only.

2. In a small bowl dissolve dry yeast and sugar in 1/2 cup water, and set aside for 5 minutes.

3. In a big bowl mix flour and salt, and make a well in the middle. Pour **1 cup** of sourdough starter (replenish the rest with 1 cup water and 1 cup flour, stir well, then return to refrigerator for future use), yeast mixture, oil, and 1 /12 cups water. With a wooden spoon, stir in a circular movement to incorporate flour into liquids. Then with oiled hands knead for 6 to 7 minutes to make a rather soft dough. Coat dough with oil on both sides and let rise in the bowl, covered, in a warm place for about 1 hour, or until it doubles in size.

4. Punch dough, and divide it into 20 portions, and let rest for about 10 minutes, covered.

5. On a slightly oiled surface form into *semeat* rings as follows: Divide each piece into two parts. Roll each part into a rope about 9 inches long (if dough feels elastic and springs back, let it rest for 5 minutes). Lay 2 ropes next to each other, and wind each rope around the other, curve twist into a circle, matching ends to form a continuous circle. Make sure to seal the ends very well to prevent them from opening while rising and baking. Put shaped pieces aside on a flat surface. After making about 5 ones, brush them with the egg wash or cornstarch mixture, and dip each, face down, in the toasted sesame. Arrange rings in a greased cookie sheet sprinkled with a little semolina, if wished. Leave space between pieces to allow for expansion. Repeat with other batches.

6. Let rise in a warm place for 40 to 45 minutes, covered with a kitchen towel.

7. Bake in middle of preheated oven at 450 degrees F. To create a good crust, using a spray bottle, spray pieces and oven with water. Repeat about 2 or 3 times, for the first 5 minutes of baking. Bake for about 15 minutes or until golden brown. Serve immediately or let pieces cool in a wicker basket

or a rack. Cooled ones can be kept in plastic bags in the refrigerator or freezer. Heat in the oven as needed.

Semeat, Made Easy
(Makes 28 pieces)

This is an easier version when you cannot afford the long wait. Though it does not have that characteristic tinge of sourness in it, it is equally delicious, and makes an excellent light snack.

3 tablespoons dry yeast
4 tablespoons sugar
1 cup warm water

10 cups bread flour
1 tablespoon salt
1/4 teaspoon ginger powder

1/4 cup oil
3 cups warm water

1 egg white whisked in 1 tablespoon water, or 1 teaspoon cornstarch dissolved in 3/4 cup cold water, and cooked until slightly thick, or microwaved for 90 seconds.

Sesame seeds, dry toasted, for sprinkling
Preheat oven to 450 degrees F.

1. Dissolve yeast and sugar in 1 cup warm water, and set aside for 5 minutes.

2. In a big bowl combine flour, salt and ginger. Make a well in the middle.

3. Pour in yeast mixture, oil and the 3 cups warm water. Using a wooden spoon, incorporate liquids into flour in a circular movement. With oiled hands knead for 6 to 7 minutes until you get a smooth dough. Let rise in a warm draftless place for about 1 hour.

4. Punch dough down, and divide into 28 portions.

6. Shape and bake as described in the Sourdough Twisted Sesame Rings given above.

Variation: Semeat with Cheese and Olives:
Prepare dough as directed above. After dough rises, punch it, and add to **half** of it the following ingredients:

3/4 cup pitted and chopped olives
1/2 cup crumbled feta cheese or mozzarella cheese
1/4 cup chopped fresh mint, parsley, and dill, each

Knead the ingredients into the dough. Let it rest for 10 minutes, then divide into 14 portions. Shape and bake them as directed above.

Sweet Breads
(Chureck)

Chureck is the sweet rolls of Iraq. The most traditional ones are shaped like flattish circular or oval window panes, about 12 inches across, with four big holes. Smaller oval-shaped ones with no holes in them are stuffed with dates or cheese and parsley. The name of the bread itself, *chureck*, goes back in origin to the Old Persian *charka* (wheel). In the Iraqi dialect the wheel is still called *charikh*.

2 cups milk (or one 12-ounce can evaporated milk diluted with enough water to make 2 cups)
1/3 cup oil, or 1/2 cup butter (one stick)
1 1/2 cups sugar

2 eggs
1/2 cup milk or orange juice
1 teaspoon rose water or 1 teaspoon ground cardamom, or both
1 teaspoon ground *mahleb* (see Glossary), optional

2 tablespoons dry yeast
1 teaspoon sugar
1 cup warm water or milk

10 cups all purpose white flour
1 teaspoon salt

1 egg, beaten, for brushing the pastries, or use 1 egg white whisked with 1 tablespoon cold water

About 3/4 cup dry toasted sesame seeds for sprinkling on the pastries
Preheat oven to 375 degrees F.

1. In a small saucepan, bring to a boil milk, oil or butter, and sugar, and keep hot.

2. In a medium bowl, beat eggs, and whisk in 1/2 cup milk or orange juice. Add a little of the hot milk mixture, stirring all the time, to prevent it from curdling. Slowly pour in the rest of milk mixture, stirring constantly. Allow to cool, until comfortably warm. Add rose water or cardamom or both and *mahleb,* if used.

3. Dissolve yeast and sugar in 1 cup warm water or warm milk, and set aside in a warm place for 5 minutes.

4. In a big bowl, mix flour and salt. Make a well in the middle. Pour milk and egg mixture prepared in step 2, and yeast mixture. With a wooden spoon, stir mixture in a circular movement to incorporate liquids into flour. With oiled hands knead for about 7 minutes. The final dough should be rather soft and sticky in consistency. Coat with a little oil on both sides, and let rise in a warm draftless place for about an hour.

5. Punch down dough, let rest for about 10 minutes, then divide and shape as suggested below, on slightly floured surface.

6. Arrange shaped pieces on greased baking sheets. Let rise, covered, in a warm place for about 30 minutes. When ready to bake, carefully brush with beaten egg and sprinkle generously with sesame.

7. Bake in a preheated oven at 375 degrees F. for about 20 minutes, or until nicely browned. Allow to cool on a rack or a flat wicker basket. Refrigerate or freeze any leftovers, in sealed plastic bags.

Suggestions for Shaping Chureck

Lovers' Window (Shubbak'l-Habayeb): (makes 4 pieces or more if smaller pieces are desired)

To make these beautiful *churecks*, punch dough and divide it into 4 pieces, and let it rest for about 10 minutes. On a slightly floured surface, roll out each piece into a disc, round or oval, about 12 inches in diameter, and 1/4-inch thick. Transfer the disc to a greased cookie sheet. **Visually** divide it into 4 quarters, and with the index fingertip make a hole in the middle of each quarter, thus creating four holes. Widen and enlarge these holes with the fingers until the piece looks like a window frame, the panels of which are about 1 1/2-inch wide. Set aside, covered, in a warm place, let rise for about 30 minutes. When ready to bake, carefully brush pieces with beaten egg, and sprinkle generously with dry toasted sesame Bake and store as directed above.

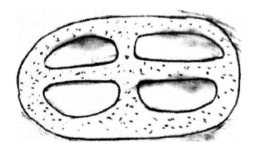 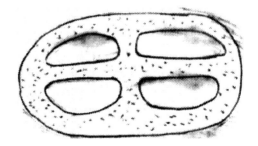

Chureck with a Filling: (makes 12 pieces)

After punching dough in step 5, divide it into 12 balls. Make a hollow in each ball, and fill it with about 1/4 cup of one of the fillings suggested below. Close the ball very well, and with a rolling pin flatten it into an oval, 1/2-inch thick and 8-inches long. Transfer pieces to a greased cookie sheet. Allow to rise for about 30 minutes. Just before baking, brush pieces with beaten egg, and make impressions with the fingers on the surface of each, avoiding the borders. Bake as directed above.

Cheese filling:

1 cup parsley or fresh mint, chopped, or a combination of both

2 cups shredded mozzarella cheese. Get rid of extra salt by soaking cheese in cold water for 30 minutes, changing water at least once in the process. If available substitute with *jibna hilwa* (sweet cheese) available at Middle-Eastern grocery shops

Combine ingredients, and use as directed.

Date Filling:
>   **2 cups dates, pitted and chopped**
>   **1 tablespoon butter**
>   **1/2 teaspoon whole toasted coriander seeds**
>   **1/2 teaspoon cinnamon**
>   **1/2 teaspoon toasted aniseed or fennel**
>   **1/4 cup water**

Mix all ingredients in a skillet or a heavy medium pot, and cook on medium heat, stirring and mashing with a wooden spoon until mixture softens and looks like a thick paste.

Chureck with Currants or raisins: (makes 16 pieces)

Add 1cup currants or raisins to flour mixture in step 4. After punching dough in step 5, divide it into 16 portions, and shape into balls, knots, crescents, pretzels, or whatever. Arrange pieces on a greased baking sheet, and set aside, covered in a warm place to rise for about 30 minutes. When ready to bake carefully brush the pieces with beaten egg, and sprinkle with sesame Bake and store as directed above.

The Sultan's Turban

(Imamat al-Sultan)
(Makes 12 pieces)

Forming pastries and confections into turbans is as old as the Mesopotamian cuisine itself is. Such shapes were called "kubbushu" (rounded) in the Akkadian (Levey, 49). In modern times our model is the sultan's huge turban.

This recipe will guarantee you splendidly shaped buns, delicately flavored with cardamom, with a hint of sweetness. Due to the way it is handled, this pastry is as flaky as croissant but without the excess fat. The handling technique is not new either. In the thirteenth-century *Andalusian Cookbook* there is a pastry recipe called *muwarraqa* (leafy), according to which dough is rolled out thin, and smeared with melted butter. Then it is rolled up into a reed-like shape that is twisted into a coil (119). According to this medieval recipe the coil was then flattened into a thin disc, but we are not going to do this, because we want the pastries to puff up and look like turbans. Nevertheless, it will still be *muwarraqa* (leafy) in texture.

>   **2 tablespoons dry yeast**
>   **2 teaspoons sugar**
>   **Two 12-ounce cans evaporated milk, warmed (may substitute with 3 cups whole milk**

>   **8 cups all-purpose flour**
>   **1 teaspoon salt**
>   **1 teaspoon ground cardamom**

>   **2 beaten eggs, at room temperature**
>   **1/2 cup oil**

90

1/4 cup melted butter

About 1/4 cup milk for glazing, for a glossier glaze use egg-white wash
Preheat oven to 375 degrees F.

1. Dissolve yeast and sugar in warmed evaporated milk, and set aside for 5 minutes.

2. Mix flour, salt and cardamom in a big bowl, and make a well in the middle. Pour in yeast mixture, beaten eggs and oil. With a wooden spoon, and in a circular movement, incorporate liquids into flour. With slightly oiled hands knead dough for about 7 minutes. The final dough should be on the soft side. If it is too sticky to handle sprinkle it with a little flour as you knead. Let dough rise, covered, in a warm draftless place for about an hour.

3. Punch dough down, and divide it into 12 portions. Let rest for 10 minutes.

4. With a rolling pin, roll out each portion into a circle, about 8 inches in diameter, 1/4-inch thick. Lightly brush surface with melted butter. Roll circle in a jellyroll fashion. Then elongate the roll as much as you can without tearing it, by holding it from both ends, and swinging it up and down allowing it to hit the working surface lightly as it swings down, until it is about 15 inches long. Coil the rope, and secure the end by tucking it underneath the coil, so that it will not open up while rising and baking.

5. Arrange pieces on a greased baking sheet, leaving space between pieces to allow for expansion. Let rise for about 45 minutes. The pieces will rise and form a turban-like shape.

6. When ready to bake brush pieces with milk or egg-white wash, and bake in preheated oven at 375 degrees F. in the middle of the oven, for 12 to 15 minutes or until golden brown. If wished brush them lightly with butter as soon as they come out of the oven.

Let pieces cool off a little, on rack or flat wicker basket. Serve warm, and refrigerate or freeze leftovers in sealed plastic bags.

بالعـــافيه

CHAPTER TWO
DAIRY PRODUCTS

CHAPTER TWO

DAIRY PRODUCTS

Up until the sixties, city people did not have to go to the stores to buy milk. A moveable dairy, so to speak, used to deliver fresh unadulterated milk every evening. *Um al-haleeb* (the milkmaid) would come with her cow, her bucket and funnel, and milk the cow right in front of her customers' eyes, and using a funnel, she would pour foamy warm milk into their bottles. But all that ended with the advent of commercially pasteurized milk products.

Whereas milking in the contemporary scene is an exclusively feminine occupation, in ancient Mesopotamia it was allotted to men. In the Sumerian milking scene frieze, which goes back to the period around 2900 BC, a calf is placed at its mother's head to make the cow yield milk more readily. A milkman is sitting at a stool behind the cow near a shed made of reeds. A little way off another man sits at a stool rocking a large narrow-necked jar lying on its side to make butter fat coagulate. To his left, two men are shown as straining the resulting buttermilk. Today's peasants make butter by rhythmically swinging suspended *shichwa*, a bag made of dried sheepskin.

In the ancient texts best quality milk, rich and creamy, was referred to as "yellow milk." Milk in general was mostly consumed as soured milk (yogurt), butter and cheese. Fresh milk has a short shelf life, so to speak, in hot climates. Judging from the Babylonian recipes, It was frequently used in making rich and nourishing white sauces for their meat stews and bird "pies." To prolong the shelf life of butter, and prevent it from getting rancid, it was made into "samnu" (clarified butter), from which the Arabic *samn* was derived.

By the Middle Ages manufacturing dairy products was an already a booming business, and in Baghdad's markets the shoppers had the leisure to choose from a wide selection of cheeses, ranging from fresh white cheeses to aged varieties, such as *halloum*, *jibin roumi*, and *jibin deinouri*. Indeed, so available and so affordable was it that having a meal of "hot bread and a slice of cheese" was an emblem of simple and unpretentious living (Burton, *Arabian Nights*, vol. 6, 235).

Homemade Yogurt

(Liban)

Yogurt is commonly made from cow's milk, but in the southern region a richer variety is made from buffalo's milk. Prior to the days of pasteurization, the sight of *labbanaat* (yougurt female sellers) balancing six or seven piers of yogurt containers on their heads was quite a familiar sight in the market places. This is a thing of the past now, only to be seen in folkloric pictures and dances.

In the northern region an excellent quality yogurt is made from sheep's milk. It is abundant in springtime when the pastures are luscious green. It usually comes with a creamy top, about 1/4 inch thick, with slightly smoky taste that is intoxicatingly delicious. It is known as *liban Arbeel* (yogurt of *Arbee*l, a northern Kurdish city). Indeed, so well-known and loved is *liban Arbeel* throughout Iraq that, according to a standing joke, when an out-of-towner in Baghdad asked for directions to the Ministry of Defense, he was told it was behind *Liban Arbeel* dairy shop.

During the hot summer, a thirst-quenching drink, called *shineena*, is made from diluted yogurt. A dish of rice with a side of yogurt makes a light and cool summer meal, enjoyed by high and low. To some foreigners this might sound a little strange. The Englishman, for instance, who spent some time in the southern marshes of Iraq, in the fifties, protested that a dish of rice and yogurt was the most primitive food he had yet encountered (Maxwell, 135). In fact it is the simplest and healthiest dish ever devised by man. People have faith in its medicinal value as a cure for diarrhea, and, if we are to believe old wives' tales, rice and yogurt taken together negate each other's calories. I haven't seen this scientifically verified anywhere, but I'd like to believe in it.

Though yogurt is readily available in the supermarkets, the homemade variety is tastier and cheaper, as well. The key to good yogurt is temperature. You need to experiment with it until you get the hang of it. Start by making a small batch (2 to 3 servings) following instructions below. Powdered milk, called for in the recipe, will thicken yogurt and give it a creamier texture, especially when low fat milk is used.

> **2 cups milk, whole, low fat or skim**
> **4 tablespoons powdered milk**
> **2 heaping tablespoons yogurt, beaten, and at room temperature**

1. Bring milk and powdered milk slowly to boil, and set aside and let cool to 110 degrees F. If you do not have a thermometer, use one of the following means: put a few drops of the milk on the inner side of your wrist; it should feel comfortably warm. Or immerse two thirds of your pinky in the milk you should be able to count up to 10 before you feel a gentle sting of heat.

2. Gently stir in the prepared yogurt. Transfer milk into a glass bowl or keep it in the same pot. Set aside at a warm draftless place. Cover pot or bowl with several layers of cloth, such as clean kitchen towels, and leave undisturbed for 6 to 8 hours. My favorite place is the oven (**do not turn heat on**). When set, remove covers and refrigerate.

If yogurt fails to curdle and set, it could be that milk was not warm enough to begin with, or the place was not warm enough. The remedy is to expose it to more warmth. Put it on top of a warm stove, or in a barely warmed oven.

If yogurt develops small curds with lots of whey, it could be that milk was too hot, or the place where it was kept was too warm. In this case you'd better use it for making cheese following instructions in White Cheese recipe below.

Note: After you gain more experience in making yogurt, you can make a bigger quantity as in the following:

1 gallon milk
3 cups powdered milk
2 cups yogurt, beaten, and at room temperature

Follow the same method suggested above.

A Medieval Battle of the Bulge

I was surprised to learn that medieval Baghdadi women had their own fights with the bulge. The tenth-century Baghdadi cookbook writer, al-Warraq, gives a regimen for the *niswan* (women, he did not mention men) who want to lose some weight. The key ingredient is yogurt. It works like this:

Have 16 ounces (2 cups) of diluted yogurt early in the morning. Repeat the dose after three hours. At midday eat a dish of *zirbaja* stew (sour meat stew cooked with oil, onion, and chickpeas) using partridge, goat, or young chickens, and 3 glasses of the yogurt drink. For the rest of the day, sniff on aromatic herbs, and snack on aromatic spice seeds. Keep on doing this for ten days eating nothing but bread and stew cooked with partridges and quails, i.e. lean meat, besides the yogurt drinks, spices and herbal sniffs. (44)

A Sumerian Proverb on the Obvious

Can one conceive without intercourse?
Can one get fat without food?
(Kramer, History Begins at Sumer, 118)

Drained Yogurt (Yogurt Cream Cheese)

(Liban Nashif)

Making cheese can be traced back to prehistoric man who kept milk in bags made of skins and stomachs of different animals, thus accidentally bringing milk into contact with rennet, an important substance in making cheese.

To circumvent the highly perishable quality of milk, the ancient Mesopotamians preserved it as cheese. They knew about twenty kinds of cheese, a clear indication of their sophistication in processing dairy products. For the royal table, many varieties were offered such as "white", fresh, rich, flavored, sweetened, and sharp cheese. The basic variety might well have been similar to our fresh cream cheese. It also came in numerous shapes, as one can tell from the several fired, porous clay molds, discovered in the kitchens of the palace of the ancient city, Mari. (Though some believe they were bread molds, (*Ebla to Damascus*, 229-33)

Cheese was even considered a treat that has a healing power. In an elaborate Sumerian composition, believed to be the oldest lullaby known from the ancient Near East, the wife of the Sumerian King Shulgi, is bribing her sick child into sleeping:

U-aa-u-a

Sleep will fill your lap with emmer,

I--I will make sweet for you the little cheeses,

Those little cheeses that are the healer of man. (Kramer, 330)

Drained yogurt (cream cheese) is the most basic, and it keeps fresh much longer. This is especially important in springtime when milk is abundant and villagers have to be versatile in processing their dairy products. Now, they drain the yogurt in cotton sacks. In the Middle Ages, however, yogurt was put in unglazed earthenware jars and sprinkled with salt, then liquid filtered through the pores over a period of time. It was identified as *qanbarees*, and sometimes *shiraz*. (Al-Warraq, 95).

Start with a small batch at first until you get the cheese consistency desired. Your choice of yogurt will determine the richness of the resulting cheese.

> **Cheese cloth or 1 layer of big coffee filter**
> **2 cups yogurt**
> **1/2 teaspoon salt**

1. Line a small sieve with 3 to 4 layers of cheesecloth or a layer of coffee filter. Fit sieve into a bowl.

2. Put yogurt and salt in the lined sieve; and with a spoon make a kind of well in the middle to facilitate the dripping process. Let yogurt drain overnight or until it becomes thick. Let it drain in the refrigerator if you want a mild tasting cheese, or keep it at room temperature for a tart taste.

Suggestions for Serving Drained Yogurt

It is served as a breakfast dish or an appetizer. The following are nice ways for serving it.

* Spread drained cheese on a small plate in about 1-inch layer. Drizzle with olive oil, sprinkle with za'tar (see Glossary). Garnish with olives and wedges of tomatoes. Serve with warm bread. (Makes 2 servings)

* Form it into 6 walnut-size balls (handle with slightly oiled hands). Roll them in toasted and chopped walnuts and za'tar, arrange them on a tray, and let dry for about an hour. Serve arranged on a platter, drizzles with olive oil, and serve with crackers. (Makes 3 servings)

Yogurt balls would stay much longer if you put prepared balls in a clean jar, cover them with olive oil and some nigella seeds (see Glossary), and keep them in the refrigerator until needed.

*You may also shape drained yogurt like a butter stick, coat it with a mixture of toasted chopped nuts and za'tar, and let dry for about an hour. To serve, drizzle with olive oil.

White Cheese

(Jibin)

White cheese sandwiches are traditionally served for breakfasts and light suppers. It is usually served with sliced cucumber, olives, and sprigs of fresh mint. The saltiness of the cheese is nicely balanced with sweet tea in winter and chilled watermelon cubes in summer.

In the local markets, you can find the mild soft white cheese, *jibin Arab* (cheese of the Arabs). *Jibin dhafayir*, is braided white cheese that is studded with aromatic nigella seeds (see Glossary), and in texture is similar to mozzarella cheese. Its homeland is the southern port city of Basra. In the Western supermarkets, it is sold as Armenian cheese. The aged and hard *jibin Akrad* (cheese of the Kurds) is similar in texture to Romano cheese, and is mostly used for cooking purposes. *Jibin w'shari* is an aged variety similar to blue cheese or Roquefort cheese. It is flavored with chopped green stems of fresh garlic, and is kept in sheepskin bags. It is pungent, and has a sharp and mellow taste, which you either love or hate. At any rate you wouldn't catch a child eating it.

In trying to adapt the recipes in the book to what is readily available in the markets, the best substitute for white fresh cheese may be feta cheese. For cooking purposes a combination of crumbled feta, shredded Romano and mozzarella cheese may be used.

You can make a small chunk of white cheese using yogurt as follows: (2 servings)

2 cups yogurt
2 tablespoons lemon juice or white vinegar

1. Put yogurt and lemon or vinegar in a small pot. On medium heat bring to a boil stirring gently until it starts to curdle. Turn off heat and let it stand aside until cool enough to handle.

2. Line a colander with 3 to 4 layers of cheesecloth and let it hang over the sides. Fit colander into a bowl.

3. Pour curdled yogurt into the colander, and let whey drain into the bowl. Gently stir yogurt to help drain more of the liquid. Gather ends of cheesecloth and twist them to help curds form into a disc. Put a heavy weight on the disc. A bowl with some water in it will do the trick. Leave for a few hours. When set, remove cloth, and sprinkle cheese with a little salt, if desired. Keep cheese in a covered container. For softer cheese, weigh down the cheese with a plate only.

Making Cheese Using Rennet

In supermarkets rennet is usually stacked with jam making ingredients. To make one pound of cheese you need:

10 cups milk
2 tablets rennet, dissolved in a little cold water

1. Heat milk until it is warm enough to the touch. Test by putting a few drops on the inner side of the wrist. If it just feels warm without scorching, this is the right temperature. Or dip your pinky in the milk for 10 seconds, you should feel noticeable warmth.

2. Away from heat quietly stir in the dissolved tablets, and set pot aside, covered and draped with a big towel or small blanket, or whatever, to keep it warm, for a few hours. This will allow milk to solidify. Drain as described in steps 2 and 3 above.

If, for some reason, milk fails to solidify, return milk pot to heat, and bring it to a quick boil. You will notice that milk solids separate from whey. Set aside until cool enough to handle, and drain as in steps 2 and 3 above.

Tip:
The best way to keep white cheeses, such as feta, fresh as long as possible after opening the package, is to keep it submerged in brine (1 teaspoon salt for 4 cups water), sprinkle with a few nigella seeds (see Glossary). Keep covered under refrigeration.

To use, take the amount needed, rinse it in water to get rid of salt. For softer texture, keep it submerged in somewhat hot water for a minute or two.

Thick (Clotted) Cream.

(Geymer)

Geymer is the solidified skimmed cream of the heated and then cooled buffalo or cows milk. Buffalo milk yields a thicker and richer cream, more commonly available in the southern region, where buffaloes are more abundant. People in the northern city of Mosul pride themselves on their *geymer abu sha'ra*. It is thick and yet so pleasantly chewy, that when you lift a small amount with a spoon it makes an elastic trail, as fine as a hair.

Geymer is made into sandwiches with date syrup, honey or jam. A winter breakfast treat may be *geymer* and *kahi*, which is a paper thin sheets of dough, folded, fried or baked, drenched in syrup, and decked with a generous slab of cream. *Kahi* is usually purchased from specialized bakeries.

Since *Geymer* is white, creamy, and luscious, comparing the beloved's cheeks to *geymer* is a common metaphor in folkloric songs and poems. I recall a song, in particular, in which the lover vows to make his beloved's *geymer*-like cheeks, his breakfast.

Geymer is a definite no for people watching their cholesterol and weight, but I am including it here because it is a very traditional breakfast item in Iraq. In the pre-cholesterol- conscious days, people used to have it almost every day, especially in winter. It would be purchased early in the morning from the neighborhood grocery shop, or from the door to door female peasant vendors. As they go from one street to another, balancing their big trays of *geymer* on their heads, they periodically announce their merchandise at the top of their shrill voices, *"Geymer Yooo."* They would cut slabs of cream with a knife, sometimes with a safety pin, and as a treat, would pour on it some milk.

Nostalgic Iraqis outside their homeland have been trying to make this breakfast delicacy, and some have been able to duplicate the original with great success. I have tried many of their versions, but the best recipe, so far, is the one developed by my hospitable friend Khaula Dhiyab, who in her turn learnt the basics from an Iraqi cook. The key to good *geymer* is using unpasteurized milk. So if you are one of those lucky ones, who have access to a dairy farm, go ahead and use it. Boiling the milk will definitely kill the germs. But if you have access to supermarket milk only, the pasteurized is preferred to the ultra pasteurized variety.

Geymer is quite easy to make, but it requires patience. Here is how to make it:

1. You need equal amounts of heavy cream and whole milk (pasteurized gives better results than ultra-pasteurized). To make 4 servings, use 1 pint (2 cups) heavy cream and 1 pint (2 cups) whole milk, use the empty heavy cream container to measure milk, to have equal amounts of both.

2. Put milk and cream in a heavy pot. Size of pot will determine the thickness of the *geymer* slab you'll be getting. A wide pot will yield a thin layer, a relatively smaller one will yield a thicker slab.

3. On medium-high, heat mixture until it starts to rise, but do not let it boil over, so you need to watch it.

4. Away from heat and in a draftless warm place, cover the pot with a colander turned upside down to create a dome on top of the pot. Cover the pot very well with a big towel or a small blanket, or whatever, and set it aside for about 6 hours to overnight.

5. Remove coverings and colander, put regular lid on pot, and refrigerate for 24 to 36 hours.

6. Run a knife around the entire edge of the solidified top to dislodge it from the pot. Then use a wet big pancake flipper to fold the *geymer* disc so that the soft bottom is enclosed in the drier surface layer. This will enable you to have a neat slab of *geymer*. Transfer it to a slightly deep dish, and drizzle with some of the remaining milk. Serve immediately along with warm bread and jam, honey or date syrup, or refrigerate it for later use.

7. Repeat the same procedure with the remaining milk. Whatever milk remains from the second time you can make cheese or yogurt with it, following the recipes provided in this chapter.

يَمّ العجون السود ما جوزنخ أنا
ختِّج الكيم انا آتريك منه
من ورة التنور تناوشني الرغيف
يا رغيف الحلوة يكفيني سـنه

Of you, black-eyed beauty, I would not let go,
Of your cream-like cheeks, I would my breakfast make.
From behind the *tannur*, she tosses me a bread,
The bread of the beautiful one would sustain me for a year.
(An Iraqi folk song)

Bribery in Ancient Mesopotamia

Clarified butter must have been a desirable commodity in ancient Mesopotamia. Here is a letter written about 3500 years ago in which the writer is trying to bribe his brother with clarified butter and a ram:

A letter from Nabu-ahhu-iddina: To my brother Nabu-usallim:

May the gods Bel and Nabu, the Lady of Uruk, and the goddess Nana ordain well-being and good health for my brother.

See I am sending you by Ibni-… one container with clarified butter, and at the same time I have sent you a beautiful ram. But you too must do something to help me; go into the office of the scribe of the palace and investigate those complains that are being made there (against me), and report to me. Do not be negligent.

What is this that I keep hearing every day about the gold?

(Oppenheim, 192-3)

Yogurt Maids, iraq.net

101

CHAPTER THREE
VEGETARIAN APPETIZERS AND SALADS

1. Vegetarian Appetizers:

2. Salads

CHAPTER THREE
VEGETARIAN APPETIZERS AND SALADS

الزلاجات والمقبلات

When everything is cooked, remove the meat from the fire, and before
the broth cools, serve it accompanied by garlic, greens and vinegar

(A Babylonian recipe of pigeon stew, ca 1700 BC)
(Bottèro, *Mesopotamian Culinary Texts*, 12)

With all the vegetables and greens the ancient Mesopotamian kitchen garden offered, it should not be surprising to learn that salads and appetizers were an important component of their menus. The vegetables were the mainstay of the poor people's diet who could not afford the more expensive meat. When a person was utterly poor they said, "in his stomach the vegetables are too little" (Levey, 50).

Members of the onion family such as onions, leeks, shallots, and garlic were basic ingredients in their diet. The excavated lexical and economic texts sometimes specified different characteristics for these crops. For instance they had sharp onions, sweet onions, and those "which have a strong odor." It is amazing how many of the "table" or salad vegetables, with their names, survived to this day. Lettuce, for instance, was called "khassu" in the Akkadian, from which the Arabic *khass* was derived. Apparently romaine lettuce with its characteristic tender heart (known as *lib* in the Iraqi dialect, cf. Akkadian "libbu") is the only variety that stood to the test of time. Roots and leaves of radishes and cucumber, as well as greens such as mint (Akk. "ninu", Ar. *ni'na'*), leeks (Akk. "karasu", Ar. *karrath*), thyme (Akk. "zateru", Ar. *za'tar*), and *rishad* (Akk. "erishtu"), an herb that grows exclusively in the region, these and much more, have always been staple items in the Mesopotamian diet, especially for the not well to do families who had to eke out their meals with them.

Though the medieval diners did not think much of vegetarian dishes, they called them *muzawwarat* (counterfeit), they, nevertheless, valued them as accompaniments to the main meat dishes. Vegetables, they said, were the ornament of the table. Sliced cucumber and lemon, olives, mint, parsley, seeds of sour pomegranate, and much more were arranged artistically so that the dish would look like a *bustan* (orchard) as they said.

103

Nawal Nasrallah

They also loved to nibble on all sorts of *bawarid* (cold dishes) side dishes, both vegetarian and with meat. They were served before the main hot meal. The meat cold dishes were always accompanied with *sibagh* and *kawamikh,* which were vinegar based sauces, relishes, pickles, and condiments, thickened with nuts and seasoned with mustard and other spices. They were believed to aid the digestion, and whet the appetite. The vegetable side dishes were both cooked and raw, and were usually seasoned with herbs, spices, vinegar, oil, and sometimes yogurt. All these, in addition to nuts and sour fruits such as pomegranate seeds, were served in the medieval drinking parties, as well. They were collectively called *naql* or *nuql* (move from one thing to another), because the revelers switched repeatedly from drink to these foods, have a bite or two, and back to drink. They were indeed the precursors of the modern *mezza* platters customarily served in drinking parties, such as Hummus, *Baba Ghanouj, Taboula, Lablabi* (boiled chick peas), *Bagilla* (boiled fava beans), *jajeek* (yogurt salad), sliced cucumbers, pickles, hearts of romaine lettuce, olives, and other vegetables.

Salad today is usually served with the main dishes. Dressing for the daily bowl of salad is quite simple-- a squeeze of orange of Seville juice (*raring*) with a little olive oil, salt and pepper. When *raring* is not in season, lemon juice, or date vinegar (similar to balsamic vinegar) might replace it.

The following appetizers are all vegetarian, for more varieties with or without meat see chapter 14, on savory pastries, and some variations on breads in chapter 1.

Tip:
When handling a big amount of eggplant, pomegranate, beet, or hot peppers it is advisable to protect your hands by wearing disposable kitchen gloves, as they cause discoloration or irritation to the skin.

1. VEGETARIAN APPETIZERS

Puréed Chickpeas with Tahini
(Hummus bi Tahina)

(Makes 8 servings)

They dug a pit in the sunlight.
Then Gilgamesh went up on the mountain.
He poured out his chickpeas into the pit.
"Oh, Mountain, grant (me) a dream..."
(Ancient Mesopotamian epic, Levey, 50)

The nutritious potentialities of chickpeas (*hummus*) were acknowledged when in the epic of Gilgamesh it was chosen as one of the victuals he carried with him on his journeys. In the medieval times other potentialities were attributed to it such as aphrodisiac ones. There was the belief that it increased the sexual appetite and number of sperms. They also recommended it for nursing mothers. As for cooking purposes, it was sometimes crushed and used as a thickening agent in stew dishes, and was boiled to tenderness and served with vinegar and oil, as we do today.

The medieval cooks also discovered its compatibility with *tahini*. In the augmented copy of al-Baghdadi's cookbook, entitled *Wasf al-At'ima al-Mu'tada* (fourteenth century), there is a dish called *hummus kisa* (chickpea blanket), in which we see the ancestor of our *hummus bi tahina* in the making. In this medieval version the chickpeas were cooked and mashed, then mixed with *tahini*, oil, vinegar, pepper, aromatic spices, parsley, mint, nuts, coriander, toasted caraway seeds, *za'tar*, salted lemon, and salt. The mixture was spread in thin layer in a container, and set aside overnight, to let it dry out a little, and was used (al-Baghdadi, 383).

Although it is readily available in stores, both fresh and canned, the homemade *hummus* is definitely much tastier and cheaper. Whole chickpeas can be used, but skinned split variety gives a creamier texture, and cooks much faster. Canned cooked chickpeas may be substituted if you want to make *hummus* in just five minutes.

1 1/2 cups yellow split chickpeas, picked over and washed, (will make 3 cups mashed chickpeas); or two 15-ounce cans cooked whole chickpeas, drained, reserve liquid
2 to 3 garlic cloves, grated
1/2 cup fresh lemon juice
1 teaspoon salt, use less salt if using canned chickpeas
1/2 to 3/4 cup *tahini* (see Glossary)

For garnish: olive oil, olives, chopped parsley, chili powder, sliced tomato, some whole cooked chickpeas, (optional)

1. (Note: Although split chickpeas do not need to be soaked, doing so for 30 minutes will cut down cooking time considerably.) In a medium pot cover chickpeas by about 3 1/2 cups of cold water. Bring to a quick boil, skimming if needed. Lower heat to low, and let simmer, partially covered, 40

to 45 minutes, or until chickpeas look mushy, and most of the liquid has evaporated. Do not drain. Let cool **completely**. Mixture will look watery when hot, but it will be firmer when cold.

2. If using **blender** or **food processor**, put cooled chickpeas or canned variety in a blender or food processor, and purée for a minute or two. If canned chickpeas look rather dry, add about 1/4 cup of the reserved liquid. Add garlic, lemon juice, salt and *tahini*. Blend for a few more minutes or until mixture looks smooth, lighter in color, and of spreading consistency. If it looks rather dry, add a little of the reserved liquid or just plain cold water. Check for salt and lemon juice. Chill at least one hour before serving.

3. **If making hummus by hand** (This method is not recommended for whole canned chickpeas, since the masher is not strong enough to mash skins of chickpeas), mash chickpeas with a potato masher until smooth. Add garlic, lemon juice, salt and *tahini*. Mix well with a wooden spoon, wire whisker, or an electric mixer until smooth, lighter in color, and of spreading consistency. Chill at least 1 hour before serving.

4. Remedies for not so perfect *hummus*:
*If it is a little thick and heavy in texture, add some cold water or reserved chickpeas liquid, and adjust seasoning.
*If the consistency is good but it still needs more tartness, use a little of the unsweetened lemonade powder (see Glossary).
   *If the taste of chickpeas still overpowers, add a little more *tahini*, until you get a balanced taste.
   But as a rule, you would get a balanced taste and the right consistency if you use the amounts and methods suggested above.

5. To serve, spread *hummus* on a plate in a layer about 1-inch thick. Smooth surface with back of spoon, making trenches as you do so. Pour a little olive oil in trenches, sprinkle with chili, and decorate with parsley, tomato slices and whole cooked chickpeas, if wished. Serve with warm flat bread. Romaine lettuce leaves can also be used as garnish and as scoops.
   Under refrigeration *Hummus* will keep well for 4 to 5 days. Garnish the amount needed just before serving.

Variations:

Spicy Hummus:
Make it as spicy as the medieval cooks used to make it.
   To the ingredients given above add 1 teaspoon whole cumin seeds, 1/2 teaspoon whole coriander seeds, 1/2 teaspoon caraway seeds. Dry toast these spices in a skillet until fragrant, a few minutes. Then coarsely crush and add in step 2 or 3.
   If you are a lover of hot food add to the ingredients 1/2 teaspoon coarsely crushed chili pepper in step 2 or 3.

* Try the Hummus recipe given above with other kinds of beans of your choice.

Puréed Eggplant with Tahini
(Baba Ghanouj)

(Makes 6 servings)

This is a tasty and healthy way of serving eggplant. Traditionally eggplant is roasted to tenderness in the clay oven, *tannour,* which gives the vegetable a delightful smoky taste. They are also grilled on smoldering charcoal. It is then peeled, mashed and mixed with a little *tahini.* For convenience most people bake it in an oven, which gives a satisfactory result, but unfortunately without the smoky taste. I have also tried a very short cut by cooking it in the microwave, but I do not recommend it. Eggplant does not like to be rushed.

As for the name *baba ghanouj,* meaning "the pampered father," Lebanese folklore has it that it was originated by a dutiful daughter who used to pamper her old toothless father by fixing him a treat of puréed eggplant.

Historically the popularity of grilled eggplant did not pick up until after the thirteenth or fourteenth centuries. We know this because in all the extant Baghdadi medieval eggplant recipes there is not a single one that calls for grilling the vegetable. The general method was to parboil it first to get rid of the bitterness, and then fry it, or boil it until fully cooked, and do other things with it. The nearest recipe we have to our modern *baba ghanouj* was thirteenth-century *Buran* dish, in which fried eggplant was mashed and mixed with garlic, coriander seeds, salt, and yogurt (Arberry, 191).

When first introduced around the ninth century, the eggplant was received with reservation. It was too bitter to be trusted. It gradually gained popularity as cooks devised ways for getting rid of the bitterness. On the whole they believed that boiling and frying it was less harmful than grilling it (al-Warraq, 55). Despite such lukewarm reception, it enjoyed a fair share of interest. There were even those who thought it was sexy. Al-Warraq's tenth-century cookbook gives six recipes of eggplant cold side dishes, in addition to an excerpted poem in praise of this wonderful (*'ajeeb*) vegetable, the taste of which was compared to saliva exchanged by kissing lovers (116). In the thirteenth century books we notice an increase in the number of eggplant dishes. Grilling eggplant must have gained popularity at some point after thirteenth or fourteenth centuries when people got over their fears of the vegetable itself. Perhaps not totally. Even today when people get quick-tempered in the heat of summer they put the blame on eating eggplant. We also believe that a distressed person should not eat it because it will cause hives.

1 large eggplant (about 1 1/2 pounds)
1/4 to 1/2 cup *tahini*, see Glossary
1/4 cup lemon juice
1 to 2 garlic cloves, grated
1/2 teaspoon salt, or to taste
1/2 teaspoon cumin, ground

For garnish: olive oil, olives, chili powder, chopped parsley, sliced tomato, pomegranate seeds, preferably the sour variety, optional

1. Wash eggplant and pierce at 2 or 3 places so that it will not burst in the oven. Bake in preheated oven at 450 degrees F. for about 45 minutes. After it cools off, cut off the stem, and peel. Discard the liquids and as much as you can of the seeds. Mash pulp with a fork.

2. Put mashed eggplant in medium bowl. Add *tahini,* lemon juice, garlic, salt, and cumin. Mix well with a fork or spoon until well blended. Refrigerate at least 1 hour before serving.

3. For a creamier texture use blender or food processor. After peeling the eggplant as directed in step 1, purée it for a few seconds. Add rest of ingredients as in step 2. Blend for 1 or 2 minutes or until smooth. Refrigerate for at least 1 hour before serving.

4. Spread mixture on plate in layer about 1-inch thick, drizzle with olive oil, sprinkle with chili, and garnish to taste. It will keep well 3 to 4 days under refrigeration. Spread and garnish just before serving.

Variations:

* For a lighter touch replace *tahini* with yogurt or sour cream. You may also use half the amount of *tahini*, and replace the other half with yogurt or sour cream. To give depth to taste, add 1 teaspoon balsamic or red wine vinegar.

   * For elegant presentations cut big celery stalks crosswise into 1 1/2-inch pieces, and fill ridges with the mixture.

Spicy Puréed Eggplant
(Misaqua'at Betinjan)

(Makes 4 servings)

Unlike the Mediterranean "mosaka," the Iraqi *misaqua'a* is true to its meaning which is "cooled off." In this respect it is more akin to the medieval eggplant *bawarid* (cold) dishes. The tenth-century writer al-Warraq gave six such recipes, three of which, called *badhinjan mahshi* (literally stuffed eggplant, perhaps meaning mixed with other ingredients) were accredited to the ninth-century Abbasid prince Ibrahim Ibn al-Mahdi. In one of them eggplant was boiled until fully cooked, finely chopped, then mixed with fried onion, a little vinegar, sugar, ground almonds, saffron, caraway, and cinnamon. The whole mixture was then drizzled with a little oil (115).

Today there are two version of "cooled off" eggplant. In the following recipe eggplant is grilled or baked first:

> **1 large eggplant (about 1 1/2 pounds)**
> **2 tablespoons olive oil**
> **1/2 teaspoon salt**
> **1/4 teaspoon pepper**
> **1 garlic clove, grated**
> **1/2 teaspoon ground cumin**
> **1/2 teaspoon coriander**
> **1/2 teaspoon coarsely crushed chili pepper**
>
> **For garnish: chopped parsley, tomato slices, pomegranate seeds, preferably the sour variety, optional.**

1. Grill or bake eggplant as instructed in step 1, in Puréed Eggplant with *Tahini*, above. Put it in a medium bowl.

2. Heat oil until it sizzles, and pour it on eggplant.

3. Add salt, pepper, garlic, cumin, coriander and chili. Mix well.

4. Spread mixture on a plate in a layer about 1-inch thick. Garnish with parsley, tomato and pomegranate seeds. Serve cold with warm bread.

Variation:
Like in the medieval version, coarsely chop 1 medium onion and sauté it in the oil in step 2, and add it to the eggplant with the oil.

Nawal Nasrallah

Browned Eggplant with Yogurt
(Misaqua'at Betinjan bil Laban)

(Makes 4 to 6 servings)

The versatility of the eggplant was fully exploited by the medieval cooks of Baghdad, that is, once they learnt how to get rid of its bitterness, which caused many people to be suspicious of it at first and avoid it. It was used in stews, stuffed, fried, pickled, and made into vegetarian *bawarid* (cold) side dishes. Pairing fried eggplant with yogurt proved to be so successful that it is still one of the favorite ways of serving eggplant. In the tenth century, small eggplants were soaked in salted water first, then drained and fried in oil, and sprinkled with a little pepper, *murri* (fermented sauce), and caraway (al-Warraq, 115-6). In the thirteenth -century cookbook, *Buran* was fried eggplant, mashed and mixed with garlic, coriander, salt and yogurt. There is another recipe in the same book, called *badhinjan bil laban* (eggplant and yogurt) which is basically parboiled eggplant and yogurt (Arberry, 191, 206).

Today, we take the best of each medieval recipe. Fried eggplant slices are kept intact, and are arranged on a plate, and drenched in yogurt flavored with garlic and some spices. It's a simple and beautiful dish, great for hot summer days. Today, an identical dish, called *Buran* is still cooking in countries as far removed from Baghdad as Afghanistan.

1 large eggplant (about 1 1/2 pounds)
Flour for coating eggplant slices, optional
Oil for frying

1 1/2 cups yogurt
1 to 2 garlic cloves, grated
1/2 teaspoon salt
A dash of cumin, and a dash of coriander, optional

For garnish: Chili pepper, chopped parsley, sliced tomato.

1. Wash eggplant, cut off stem and peel it into stripes. Cut crosswise into 2 parts, then cut each part lengthwise into 1/4-inch-thick pieces.

2. Soak eggplant pieces in warm salted water for about 1/2 hour. Put a heavy plate on the pieces to keep them submerged.

3. Drain eggplant pieces and fry them in a skillet or oven fry them by brushing or spraying them with oil, and baking or broiling them in a hot oven, turning once. **To prevent eggplant from sucking up a lot of fat while frying, coating the drained eggplant slices in flour on all sides does help a lot.**

4. Mix together yogurt, garlic, salt, and cumin and coriander, if used. Stir well.

5. On a flat big platter arrange eggplant pieces in a single layer (pieces may overlap a little). Spoon yogurt mixture all over. Sprinkle with chili, and garnish with parsley and tomato. Serve with warm bread.

110

If the amount is more than you can consume in one sitting, refrigerate eggplant pieces and yogurt in two separate containers. Combine and garnish just before serving.

Swiss Chard or Spinach with Yogurt
(Silıq bıl Laban)

(Makes 4 servings)

One of the popular medieval ways of serving the *bawarid* (cold) vegetarian dishes was to boil the vegetables, mix them with yogurt, and drizzle them with oil. The most commonly used vegetables were gourd, eggplant, fava beans, herbs, such as mint, *kurrath* (celery leaves), parsley, spinach, and stalks and leaves of Swiss Chard (al-Warraq, 118, Arberry, 206). They were first boiled, and then mixed with drained yogurt, with spices and a drizzle of oil. These dishes were recommended as relishes "to awaken and stimulate the appetite" (Arberry, 206).

The following recipe is inspired by such medieval yogurt dishes. Spinach or chard can be used. If chard is your choice, use the green part of the leaf only. The ribs and stalks can be used for something else, such as soup.

1 bunch fresh spinach (about 1 pound), coarse stems discarded, and leaves washed and drained. Swiss chard may be substituted.

1 cup plain yogurt
1/2 teaspoon salt
1/4 teaspoon black pepper
2 cloves garlic, grated
1/2 cup green onion, finely chopped with the tender green part (about 1 small bunch)
1/4 cup radish, preferably white variety, such as dykon, shredded
2 teaspoons fresh tarragon or 1/4 teaspoon dried
1 teaspoon vinegar, preferably balsamic
2 tablespoons olive oil

1. In a medium pot, wilt spinach or chard leaves in water clinging to it, 3 to 4 minutes. Stir once or twice. Sprinkle with cold water to refresh leaves, let drain well in a colander. Chop fine.

2. In a big bowl mix spinach or Swiss chard with rest of ingredients. Refrigerate for about an hour, and serve garnished with wedges of tomato, if wished.

Puréed Fava Beans, Medieval Style
(Bagilla Mahrousa)

(Makes 4 servings)

The following is inspired by al-Warraq's *baridat al-baqli* (cold fava beans dish, 117-8).

2 cups fresh or frozen fava beans
3 tablespoons olive oil
1 medium onion, finely chopped

2 to 3 garlic cloves, grated
1/2 teaspoon salt
1/4 teaspoon black pepper
1 teaspoon ground cumin
1/4 cup lemon juice
1/2 cup ground pistachio, optional
For garnish: chili powder, chopped parsley, olives, and slices of tomato.

1. Put fava beans in a medium pot and cover with cold water. Bring to a boil, then lower to medium, and let boil gently for about 15 minutes, or until tender. Drain beans, reserve some of the liquid, in case you need it. When beans are cool enough to handle, peel and purée in blender or food processor.

2. Sauté onion in oil until it starts to change color. Set aside 2 tablespoons for garnish. Add rest of browned onions to the mashed beans along with garlic, salt, pepper, cumin, lemon juice, and ground pistachio, if used. If mixture is dry, add a little of drained liquid in which beans were cooked.

3. Spread mixture on a plate in a layer about 1-inch thick. And garnish with the browned onion, chili, parsley, olives and tomato slices. Drizzle with olive oil, if wished. Serve with warm bread.

Fava Beans with Vinegar
(Bagilla bil-Khal)

One of the simplest medieval methods of serving fava beans as a cold dish was to boil it, drain it, and drizzle it with oil and vinegar. Al-Warraq boils the vinegar first with onion juice, and seasons it with coriander, cumin, cloves, caraway, and other spices. Chopped parsley is used as a garnish (117). Al-Baghdadi's version is even simpler:

Take green beans as soon as firm, and peel off the outer skin [i.e. the jackets]: then boil in salt and water until cooked. Dry, and pour on a little sesame oil: cover with good vinegar, and serve (Arberry, 208).

Tender Chickpeas
(Lablabi)

(Makes 6 servings)

This is a popular snack and appetizer nationwide, especially in wintertime, when it always smells as though there is a pot of *lablabi* cooking somewhere in the neighborhood. It is sold by vendors, given as a healthy snack at schools, cooked at home, and served as *mezza* with drinks at restaurants and bars. People believe in the magical power of its warm broth in curing colds and sore throats. It is an affordable source of protein and carbohydrates, a great energy booster. It is even reputed to have an aphrodisiac power.

2 cups uncooked whole chickpeas, washed, soaked overnight, and drained
1 cube chicken bouillon, or 2 cups unsalted chicken broth, optional
1/2 teaspoon curry powder
1/4 teaspoon turmeric
1 teaspoon salt, use less if bouillon is used
For garnish: lemon juice, olive oil, chopped parsley or mint

1. Put drained chickpeas in a medium pot, along with bouillon or broth, curry powder and turmeric. Add enough cold water to cover by 3 to 4 inches. Bring to a quick boil, skimming if needed. Reduce heat to low and let simmer gently, covered, until chickpeas are tender when squeezed, do not let them get mushy, about 45 minutes. Add salt half way through cooking.

2. Serve hot in small bowls, with some of the liquid. Drizzle with olive oil, lemon juice and garnish with chopped parsley or mint.

Simmered Fresh Black-eyed Peas
(Loubya Maslouga)

(Makes 4 servings)

This is a favorite summertime appetizer or a side dish. While in season, fresh black-eyed peas in the pod (also known as cowpeas) are cooked almost every day to be devoured before the meal or with it. The best *loubya* grows on the small islands (*jazra*) that come into existence as the water level of the river Tigris declines in the summer. It has been growing in the region ever since antiquity. In The Akkadian it was known as "lubu". The best substitute is asparagus beans or string beans sometimes found in farmers markets in the summer or oriental stores year round.

1 pound fresh black-eyed peas in the pod
1 teaspoon salt
Crushed dry mint

1. Wash beans, leave whole, and do not cut off ends. In a medium pot, arrange and stack beans lengthwise like untied bunches to prevent them from getting squished while handling, since they become very tender when cooked. Invert a plate on the beans to keep them submerged. Pour enough

hot water to cover by 2 inches. Bring to a quick boil, then lower heat to medium low, and let simmer gently, covered, for 20 to 30 minutes or until tender but still intact. Add salt about 10 minutes before beans are done.

2. Use a pancake turner to take beans out of the pot and into a flat dish. Sprinkle with mint and serve warm or cold with a drizzle of vinegar or lemon juice, if liked.

3. These beans are usually eaten with the fingers since most of them come with tough threads or strings that have to be discarded. The way to do it is to pick up a bean with the fingers, eat it until most of the bean is in the mouth, press it between the lips or front teeth, and pull the threads with the index finger and thumb. Have fun!

A Medieval Appetizer of Black-eyed Peas
(Barıdat Loubya)

Al-Warraq's tenth-century cookbook includes two simple *bawarid* (cold) dishes that call for dried black-eyed peas. They are very good as they are, but you can improvise by adding chopped vegetables such as onion, tomatoes, grated garlic, and so on. The beans are boiled and drained first. They are then put in a bowl, and some lemon juice, sour grape juice or sumac juice was poured on them. Sumac juice is made by soaking whole seeds of sumac in hot water for 30 minutes, and drained. Juice is used, and seeds are discarded. A last touch would be a drizzle of oil.

In the second recipe, after cooking and draining the beans, they are put in a bowl, and sweet vinegar, mustard, and oil, in equal amounts are poured on the beans. For garnish, a good amount of walnuts, chopped parsley and rue are sprinkled on them (al-Warraq, 120).

2. SALADS
(Zalata)
Tossed Colorful Salad

Though, admittedly, there is no big breaking news in a recipe called "Tossed Salad", it seems that every culinary culture has its own favored combination of vegetables, or ways of presentation. The typical Iraqi salad is composed of a variety of vegetables finely chopped or shredded. Big chunks of vegetables in a salad are a sign of sloppy workmanship. Healthwise, of course, fine chopping of vegetables is only acceptable if the salad is consumed right away, since cut vegetables are to be exposed as little as possible to oxygen. Having a bowl of a variety of finely chopped vegetables, though, makes it easier to meet the 5-a-day- servings requirement, and it makes the task of munching and crunching on the vegetables less tedious and a much faster and enjoyable one.

Choice of vegetables is determined by their availability, though it is customary to use romaine **lettuce** in winter and **cucumber** in summer, in its two types, the regular dark green variety, and the pale green thin-skinned ribbed cucumber called *ta'rouzi* (identified in the West as Armenian or Japanese cucumbers).

Tomatoes or **beets** are finely diced and added for their bright red colors, otherwise the salad would be considered anemic, and will be given two thumbs down. Also added are chopped or thinly sliced **onion**, shredded or thinly sliced green **cabbage**, chopped **parsley**, **lemon pulp**, cubed boiled **potatoes** or boiled **white beans**, shredded **yellow, orange or purple carrots**. Yes, purple carrots.

Purple carrots are crisp, and sweeter than the regular yellow variety. It has been growing in the region ever since antiquity. I first became aware of the fact that purple carrots are not readily available in other parts of the world, when, in the late seventies, I took an American wife of a visiting professor on a tour in the college of Arts where I was teaching English in Baghdad. In one of our stops to take some refreshments she was thrilled to see some of the female staff members were fighting the battle of the bulge by munching on purple carrots. She actually took a piece to show it to her husband. Later on in a letter she told me that was the highlight of her visit.

In fact, as late as 1996 purple carrots were still news making vegetables in the United States. The purple carrots are called "BetaSweet carrot, and "with up to 3 mg of beta carotene per ounce--about twice the level of an average carrot--the BetaSweet represents a new frontier in nutrition" (Stephanie Lyness, *Food and Wine*, June, 1996). They are now sold in some of the American supermarkets as "maroon carrots."

Occasionally the salad would be garnished with pitted **olives** and wedges of **boiled eggs**, or sprinkled with **Za'tar** (see Glossary). With a warm piece of bread, a salad prepared like this can make a healthy satisfying meal by itself.

Tip:

Using lemon pulp in a salad is more exciting than lemon juice. The easiest way to get lemon pulp is to peel the entire lemon using a sharp paring knife. Then slash each section in half lengthwise, and scrape out pulp with the knife, discarding seeds if any.

Salad Dressings

For every day use a simple and light salad dressing is used. Olive oil and vinegar in the ratio of one part olive oil to two parts vinegar are mixed with the salad before serving it. In wintertime fresh lemon juice or the sweet and sour juice of orange of Seville (*rarinj* or *narinj)* would substitute the vinegar. A sprinkle of salt and black pepper are also added.

Olive oil can be flavored with herbs. In a small glass jar put washed and thoroughly dried sprigs of thyme, dill and mint, lemon zest, 2 skinned cloves of garlic, and a few olives.

Following are more elaborate salad dressings for special occasions.

Vinegar and Mustard Dressing
(Khal wa Khardal)

The following is a medieval salad dressing from the thirteenth-century Baghdadi cookbook. Such relishes were called *sibagh*, and were usually served with grilled meats to aid the digestion. Here is the original recipe:

> Take sweet almonds, peel, and chop up fine [or grind]: then moisten with sour vinegar until making a thin paste. Grind mustard fine, and mix in as required, then serve (Arberry, 207).

The consistency of this dressing is like that of the prepared mustard, and it is very nice with hamburger and *kufta* sandwiches, or grilled meats. Here is how to make it. Quantities are my improvisation.

1/4 cup unskinned almonds, toasted and ground
1/2 cup balsamic vinegar
2 tablespoons prepared mustard
A dash of salt and black pepper

Mix all ingredients and set aside to allow flavors to blend for 15 minutes. If a thinner consistency is required, just add a little cold water until desired consistency is attained, and adjust salt and pepper.

Salsa, any one?

The medieval dieticians believed, as we still do, in the power of sour agents to digest heavy foods, "to cleanse the palate of greasiness" and apptize" (Arberry, 205). This belief can be traced back to ancient culinary practices in the region. One of the Babylonian recipes, for instance, suggests that the prepared dish might be accompanied with greens, garlic, and vinegar (Bottèro, *Mesopotamian Culinary Texts*, 12).

In the medieval era this practice developed into a whole category of condiments, called *sibagh,* usually served in *sakarij* or *jam* (small glass bowls). True to the literal meaning of the word, they were dips (the verb *sabagha,* means "dip'. It also means "baptize", John the Baptist, was called *Yohanna al-Sabbagh*). The fact that a variety of these dips were presented in small bowls for communal use necessitated that they stay clean for all eaters. One of the severely criticized types of diners was the *qatta'.* He was what we might describe today as the double dipper, the eater who dipped a morsel into the *sibagh* bowl, had a bite, then dipped again.

Al-Warraq gives a good number of these dips, some served with grilled fish and others with grilled chicken, but the basic ingredients for both were more or less similar. A sour base such as, vinegar, or sour pomegranate juice was mixed with mustard, garlic, spices, herbs, crushed onion, sometimes oil, and raisins. The sauce was thickened with ground nuts, and was balanced with a little salt and sugar.

Al-Warrap also gives a recipe that travelers can use when they are on the road. It was made of one part raisins, and two parts pomegranate seeds to be pounded with a little pepper and cumin, and made into patties. When needed, a patty would be dissolved and thinned with vinegar.

He also gives a recipe for a rich gravy dip. It was made by collecting the dripping fat of a rotisserie chicken, and mixing it with juice of sweet and sour pomegranate, mixed with *murri* (fermented sauce), and thyme. Ground meat of ten walnuts would give body to the gravy. He highly recommends it, it is delicious, he says, good, wonderful (*'ajeeba*), and commonly used (83-6).

Around the thirteenth century these *sibagh* started sometimes to be called *suls* or *sulus* (plural of *salsa*). Some researchers conjecture that the word *salsa,* describing this old condiment, might have filtered to the culinary vocabulary through the Romance, during the Crusaders wars. The word *sulus* was found in the thirteenth-century Syrian cookbook *Al-Wusla ila'l Habeeb* (the way to the lover's heart) believed to be written by Ibn al-Adeem, and the augmented copies of al-Baghdadi's cookbook, *Wasf al-At'ma al-Mu'tada* (description of familiar foods). The *sulus* recipes given in both books were all served in separate bowls with dishes of grilled fish and meat. (Rodinson, "Venice, The Spice Trade," 211, and Perry, "The Salsa of the Infidels," 499-502). They were quite similar to the *sibagh* (dip) recipes given by the earlier Baghdadi writers during the tenth and thirteenth century.

The terms *sulus, salsa, sibagh,* and *kawamikh* gradually disappeared from the Arabic vocabulary, except for *salsa,* which came back to us, once again as a loan word.

Spicy Orange Juice Dressing

Try this spicy, fruity and chunky salad dressing. The sweet and sour orange of Seville (*rarinj* or *narinj*) is perfect for making this dressing, but since it is hard to come by, orange juice can be substituted.

1 cup orange juice

1 teaspoon whole cumin seeds
1 teaspoon whole anise or fennel seeds

1 teaspoon *za'tar*, see Glossary, or dried thyme
2 tablespoons lime or lemon juice
1/2 cup, parsley, finely chopped
1/4 cup pitted olives, chopped (about 8 olives)
1/4 cup olive oil
A dash of salt and black pepper
1/4 teaspoon crushed chili pepper, optional

1. Reduce orange juice on medium-high heat to 1/4 cup, about 15 minutes. Set aside to cool thoroughly.

2. In a small skillet toast cumin and aniseeds until fragrant, about 2 minutes. Grind them.

3. Mix reduced orange juice and ground seeds with rest of ingredients. Let steep for about 15 minutes, and use.

Easy Salad Platter

If you are not in a chopping, dicing and shredding mood, there is always the alternative of making a nice platter of sliced vegetables and whole greens and herbs. Indeed, they are even sometimes rolled in a piece of flat bread and enjoyed as a quick snack by themselves. That was also the way greens and herbs were served during the medieval times. They were folded in *riqaq* (thin) breads and artistically arranged on the dining table, between platters and other breads.
It may include any of the following:

*__Tomato__ wedges
*Sliced **green pepper**, hot or sweet
*__Green onions__, whole, or **white onions**, cut into wedges.
*__Radish__ both red and white. The white variety tastes like dykon radish, and in Iraq it is called American radish, for it is believed that the seeds are imported from the States.
*__Radish leaves__ while still young and tender
*Sprigs of flat-leaved **parsley** (known In the States as Italian parsley)
*Sprigs of tender **mint** and **sweet basil** (*rihaan)*, and the tender young small leaves of **leeks** (*kurrath)* also known as "garlic chives" or "table leeks". ***Rishshad*** is an herb that grows exclusively in Iraq. Its leaves are smaller and lighter in color than parsley, and it has a sharp peppery taste.

Bulgar Salad
(Taboula)

(Makes 4 servings)

This refreshing and nourishing salad is known almost everywhere. However, the vegetables to bulgar proportions might vary from one country to the other, and even from one household to the other. In Iraq it is not consumed on every day basis, but rather reserved for parties and big gatherings. The secret to a good *taboula* is fine chopping.

3/4 cup bulgar #1, see Glossary
1 large bunch parsley, finely chopped (about 2 cups)
1 cup tomatoes, finely diced (about 2 medium ones)
3/4 cup finely chopped cucumber, optional
3/4 cup green onion, finely chopped with the tender green stalks
1/4 cup mint, finely chopped, optional
1/2 cup fresh lemon juice
3 tablespoons olive oil, or to taste
Salt and pepper to taste
A dash of chili pepper, optional

For garnish: olives, leaves of the heart of romaine lettuce

1. Wash bulgar and soak it in warm water until it softens, about 30 minutes. Drain very well, and set aside.

2. Mix bulgar with rest of ingredients except for garnishes. Refrigerate at least an hour before serving. This salad will stay good for about 2 days under refrigeration.

To serve put salad in a bowl and garnish with olives and lettuce leaves.

Salad with Toasted Pita Croutons
(Zalatat Fatoush)

(Makes 4 servings)

This is one of the delicious ways in which not so fresh bread is ingeniously used in the entire Middle-Eastern region. The word *fatoush* is closely linked to the old tradition of crumbling bread and using it in *thareed* dishes. Bread used for such purposes would be called *fateet*, or *khubuz maftout*. From al-Warraq's tenth-century cookbook we learn that they sometimes served *thareeds* as cold side dishes or salads, he calls them "*khal wa zeit*," dishes(vinegar and oil). They were prepared to accompany grilled meats. Of these he gives four recipes, the principal ingredients of which are a sour agent, oil, crumbled bread and chopped vegetables and herbs.

In one of the recipes, for instance, he soaks dry bread (*ka'ak*) in vinegar chilled in ice, and is balanced with a little sugar. Oil is added as needed, and chopped cucumber pulp and fresh thyme are sprinkled all over. It is served with hot *farareej* (young chicken). In other recipes he uses *ragheef sameedh* (high gluten bread) broken to pieces. In another, he used chilled sour grape juice, enriched with ground almond. He also adds chopped mint, parsley, onion juice, pieces of aged cheese, and decorates the top with discs of sliced cucumber, like *dirhams* (coin), and broken pieces of ice (125-6).

The reason why we use stale bread in this salad is because it can soak up the liquids without disintegrating. However, if you do not happen to have stale bread, use fresh, by all means, and toast it in the oven until it is nicely crisp. If you like to use cheese as in the medieval recipes above, stuff the bread with cheese and toast it, before using it in the salad, as directed below.

For the Bread (croutons):
    1 pita (pocket) bread, separated to make pieces
    1/4 cup crumbled feta cheese, and grated Romano cheese, each
    1/4 cup toasted and chopped walnuts
    1 teaspoon *za'tar*, see Glossary, or thyme

    1 large bunch parsley, finely chopped (about 2 cups)
    2 medium tomatoes, diced
    3/4 cup diced cucumber
    3/4 cup diced green onion with tender green stalks
    1/4 cup fresh mint, chopped, optional
    1/4 cup balsamic vinegar
    1/4 cup olive oil
    A dash of salt and black pepper
    8 olives, pitted and chopped
    1 tablespoon sumac, see Glossary

    Preheat oven to 450 degrees F.

1. Prepare croutons: Spread inner side of pita bread with cheese, sprinkle with walnut and *za'tar* or thyme. Cap it with the other half. Cut bread into 1-inch pieces and arrange in one layer on a baking sheet. Bake in the middle of the oven, at 450 degrees F. for about 10 minutes, or until they are well toasted. Allow to cool.

2. In a large bowl mix all ingredients, and refrigerate for about 30 minutes before serving.

Lentil Salad
(Zalatat Adas)

(Makes 4 servings)

This is a refreshing variation on *taboula*, in which whole lentils replace bulgar.

1 cup uncooked whole lentils with shells on, picked over, washed and drained (2 cups cooked)
2 to 3 garlic cloves, whole and unskinned

1/2 cup green onion, chopped with the green stalks, or regular onion sliced thinly and sautéed in 1 tablespoon olive oil until it caramelizes
2 medium tomatoes
1 cup parsley, chopped
1/4 cup fresh mint, chopped, optional
1 medium carrot, grated
2 tablespoons olive oil
3 tablespoons vinegar, (cider or balsamic), or lemon juice
1 teaspoon cumin, ground
1/2 teaspoon chili pepper, or to taste
1/2 teaspoon salt
1/4 teaspoon black pepper

2 eggs, boiled for garnish

1. In a medium pot, cover lentil and garlic with cold water by an inch. Bring to a quick boil, skimming any foam that might form, then reduce heat to low and let simmer, covered, for about 20 minutes, or until lentil is cooked but still firm (al dente) and most of liquid has evaporated. Avoid overcooking it. Add a little hot water if needed while simmering. Allow lentil to cool.

2. Take out cooked garlic cloves, and squeeze out pulp, mash it with back of the spoon and mix it with the lentils.

3. In a big bowl, combine lentils with green onion, tomatoes, parsley, mint,if used, carrot, olive oil, vinegar or lemon, salt, peppers, and cumin.

4. Garnish with wedges of boiled eggs. Refrigerate for about 30 minutes to allow flavors to blend.

Variation: Bean Salad

Replace lentils with white beans, black-eyed peas, or fava beans (small variety known as *fool mudammas*, see Glossary). Soak beans overnight, drain, cover by 3 to 4 inches of cold water, bring to a quick boil, and then lower heat and simmer for about 35 to 40 minutes, or until cooked but intact (al dente). Or use two 15-ounce cans of beans, rinsed and drained.

Yogurt Salad
(Jajeek)

(Makes 4 servings)

Apparently yogurt salad was a popular appetizer during the middle ages. In the tenth-century Baghdadi cookbook there is a recipe for what was named in the medieval book as *jajiq.* It was made by combining yogurt with chopped vegetables such as cucumber, lettuce hearts, mint, tarragon, onion, garlic, and parsley, and drizzled with oil (96). Nowadays this simple salad is made throughout the entire Mediterranean and Middle-Eastern region as a *mezza* or a salad dish. It takes only a few minutes to make, and is especially good in the summer as an appetizer, or a cool sauce to be paired with hot dishes.

> **2 cups plain yogurt**
> **2 cups finely diced cucumbers**
> **2 garlic cloves, grated**
> **1/4 teaspoon salt**
> **2 tablespoons finely chopped fresh mint, or 1 teaspoon crushed dried mint**
> **1 teaspoon fresh dill finely chopped, or 1/2 teaspoon dill weed, optional**

In a medium bowl stir yogurt until creamy. Add cucumbers, garlic, salt, mint, and dill, if used. Stir well and refrigerate for about 30 minutes before serving. It is not a good idea to keep leftovers for more than a few hours since cucumbers will lose their crunchiness.

Variations:

* If you want to make yogurt salad of a thicker consistency, drain 3 cups of yogurt using a sieve lined with cheese cloth or coffee filter. Fit it into a bowl, to receive the drained liquids. Let yogurt drain for a few hours, and use as directed above. For a thicker consistency you can drain cucumbers, too, by sprinkling them with a little salt and letting them drain in a colander for an hour. The cucumbers will lose their crunchiness, but the salad will stay good for a longer period of time.

* To give more color to Yogurt Salad, add 1 tomato, chopped, and drained for 15 minutes, to the basic recipe above.

Beet Salad
(Zalatat Shuwander)

(Makes 4 servings)

Beets in Iraq are wintertime vegetables, and they come in very handy when tomatoes are scarce in that season. The potentialities of beets have been fully exploited. In pre-tomato times it was used to add an interesting hue to the stews. It is now simmered and eaten as a snack, its liquid is made into a delicious drink (see chapter 21, on beverages). It is pickled (see chapter 20, on pickles), and made into jam (see chapter 20, on jams), and last and not least, it is used to make beautiful salads.

Beets can be boiled or baked. I prefer the latter since it helps keep flavor and nutrients locked in. Beets contain a high amount of folate, fiber, and potassium. Some researches even suggest that the substance which gives the beets their crimson color, is a powerful cancer-fighting agent (*Bon Appetit*, December, 1999, 268). So keep the good tradition going!

3 medium beets (about 1 1/2 pounds)
2 tablespoons olive oil
Juice of 1 lemon (about 1/4 cup), or 1/4 cup vinegar, cider or balsamic
1/4 teaspoon salt
1/4 teaspoon black pepper
1 cup parsley, finely chopped

For garnish: 1/4 cup yogurt or sour cream, and 1/4 cup broken walnut pieces, toasted

1. Wash beets well (**neither peel them, nor cut off the ends since this will cause them to "bleed"**), put them in a medium pot, and cover with cold water by 2 inches. Bring to a quick boil, then reduce heat and simmer, covered, on low heat for 40 to 45 minutes or until they are cooked but still firm. Test by inserting a fork. Or you have the option of baking them in the oven. Just wrap them very well in foil, and bake in a preheated oven at 450 degrees F. for 60 minutes or until tender. Let cool.

2. Peel beets by rubbing the peel between the fingers under running water. You might need to use the knife if skin does not peel off easily. Cut off both ends, and chop beets into small pieces.

3. In a big bowl, mix diced beets with oil, lemon juice or vinegar, salt, pepper, and parsley. Refrigerate for about 30 minutes.

4. Serve cold in individual bowls, drizzled with yogurt or sour cream, and sprinkled with toasted walnuts.

This salad keeps well, under refrigeration, for 2 to 3 days. However, drizzling it with yogurt and walnuts should be done just before serving.

Rainbow Salad
(Zalatat Qows wa quzah)

(Makes 4 servings)

This is a beautiful salad in which beets and other vegetables are combined to make a colorful platter.

1/2 head of romaine lettuce, washed and drained
3 medium beets (about 1 1/2 pound) cooked and peeled (see directions above in Beet Salad), slice them, put aside 10 slices of equal size, chop the rest into small cubes
2 tablespoons olive oil
2 tablespoons vinegar, cider or balsamic

1/4 teaspoon salt, sugar, black pepper, mustard powder, each

3 eggs, boiled and cut into quarters
10 thin slices of dykon radish
Chili pepper, to taste

1. Thinly slice lettuce. Add diced beet, olive oil, vinegar, salt, sugar, pepper, and mustard. Gently mix, and spread on a big platter.

2. Decorate edge of platter by alternating slices of beets with slices of dykon radish, overlapping a little. Arrange egg quarters in a decorative way in the middle space. Sprinkle lightly with chili pepper.

This salad should be served immediately, because beets might discolor the radish and the eggs.

Carrot and Cabbage Salad
(Zalatat Lahana wa Jizar)

(Makes 4 servings)

The following is a nice and easy way for consuming these healthy vegetables, that is, other than having them boiled or steamed.

3 cups white cabbage, finely shredded or thinly sliced
2 cups carrots, shredded
1/4 cup vinegar, cider or balsamic
3 tablespoons olive oil
Salt and pepper to taste
1 cup parsley, finely chopped

In a big bowl, mix all ingredients. Refrigerate for about 30 minutes. If wished drizzle with a little yogurt or sour cream.

Simple Potato Salad
(Zalatat Poteita)

(Makes 4 servings)

This is the Iraqi version of the potato salad. It can make a refreshing and nourishing lunch by itself.

4 medium potatoes, boiled with skin on
2 medium tomatoes, chopped
1 cup cucumber, chopped

1/2 cup parsley, chopped
1/2 cup green onions or white onion, finely diced
3 tablespoons olive oil
3 tablespoons vinegar, cider or balsamic
Salt and pepper to taste

For garnish: slices of boiled eggs, dilled yogurt (1/2 cup yogurt combined with 1 tablespoon chopped dill), and chili pepper

1. Skin boiled potatoes and cut into small cubes.

2. Mix potatoes with tomatoes, cucumber, parsley, onion, oil, vinegar, salt and pepper. Refrigerate for about 30 minutes.

3. Serve in a bowl. Garnish with sliced eggs. Drizzle with dilled yogurt, and sprinkle with chili pepper.

Relish of Pickled Mango with Tomatoes ('Anba wa Tamata)

(Makes 4 servings)

If you want to give a bland dish or a sandwich a good kick, make the following relish in a minute, provided you already have bought the *'anba* (Indian pickled mangos) from the store (for a home made substitute for the pickled mango, see chapter 20, on pickles). The Iraqis' love for this spicy hot stuff is apparently not a new trend. Eleventh-century writer al-Tha'alibi, for instance, tells in his *Lata'f al-Ma'arif* (interesting tidbits of knowledge) that the Abbasid Caliphs used to import huge amounts of the preserved mango.

1/2 cup chopped tomato
1/2 cup pickled mango, mild or hot, available at Middle Eastern grocery shops

Combine ingredients, and serve in a small bowl. Eat sparingly.

Hot Pepper Salsa (Salsat al-Filfil al-Har)

The following sauce can replace the relish given above. Because it is hot and thick in consistency, it stays in the refrigerator for a long time. The color of salsa will greatly depend on whether you use green or red hot peppers, or both.

1 pound red chili peppers, cored and seeded
1 pound red bell pepper, cored and seeded
1 teaspoon honey or brown sugar

1 teaspoon salt
1 teaspoon cumin seeds, toasted and crushed
1 teaspoon *za'tar*, see Glossary, or dried thyme
2 cloves garlic, grated

2 tablespoons white or cider vinegar
2 tablespoons olive oil

1. In a medium pot cover peppers in hot water, and bring to a quick boil. Reduce heat to medium and cook gently for 15 minutes. Drain peppers, and set aside to cool.

2. Purée peppers in a blender or food processor. Then transfer them to medium pot. Add honey or brown sugar, salt, cumin, *za'tar* or thyme, and garlic. Let simmer, uncovered, for 25 minutes. Stir the peppers several times while simmering. Cool completely.

3. Pour mixture in a **glass** jar. Stir in vinegar. Pour olive oil on top to cover the whole surface. Refrigerated, it will keep for about three months.

To serve, stir mixture, take out amount needed, and return rest to refrigerator. Use sparingly.

Note: If you want to use this salsa as a dip, add to it a little white vinegar and cold water, until the desired consistency is attained. Adjust seasonings. Do this just before serving.

126

Village panorama.
An illustration by al-Wasiti of Baghdad, from 13th century Maqamat al-Hariri.
Bibliothèque Nationale (MS Arabe 5847)

CHAPTER FOUR
SOUPS

CHAPTER FOUR
SOUPS

الشُّورُبَة

(Shorba)

An Excavated Sumerian-Akkadian list attests to the fact that soups were an important dish on the menu of the ancient Mesopotamian diners. They knew the liquid form, such as broths, as well as the thick and nourishing soups similar to today's *kishk* soup (basically bulgar soup. This Akkadian document included over a hundred kinds of soup, which by definition were dishes prepared by cooking food in water. The thickening ingredients the Sumerians used included chickpeas, lentils, barley flour, and emmer flour, which are still used to this day. The flour soups for instance, were known as *harira* during the medieval times, as they still are today in North African countries. Some soups contained mutton fat or oil, honey, or meat broth. Others were made with a vegetable base (Limet, 136,145). They even made fish soups (Gordon, 99).

There have been conjectures as to where the name of *shorba* came from. In the medieval books, many words were used to designate soup, such as *hasa'*, *sakhina*, *harira*, and *shorba*. Of these, the last one is the only word in use now in the colloquial Iraqi. There is the theory that it is originally a Persian word, from *shor*=salty, and *ba*=cooked with water. In al-Warraq's tenth-century cookbook, there is a recipe for meat broth or soup, cooked with pasta-like triangular pieces of thin dough (*shawabeer*). He gave it the name, *ma' wa malh* (water and salt, 200-1), which in effect is the same as *shorba*.

Going back to the Akkadian texts, meat broth was called "mei sheri" (meat juice or broth, Limet, 146). In Bottèro's "Culinary Tablets at Yale," it was called "shiru" (11). *In The Assyrian Herbal*, we learn that "juice" in the Akkadian was "pa" (Thompson, 181). The similarity between these and *shorba* is revealing. The widespread belief that the word, *shorba*, infiltrated to the Arabic during the Ottoman rule is unfounded because there is no indication, in the first place, that the word *shorba* fell out of use at any time. Al-Baghdadi's thirteenth-century cookbook, for instance, included a rice soup recipe called *shorba* (44), and the fifteenth-century Damascene cookbook, includes a noodle-soup, called *sha'riya wa-shorba* (Perry, 20). I believe that *shorba* has been around ever since ancient Mesopotamian times.

Soups have the reputation of being the poor people's favorite dish because they are filling and cheap. Nevertheless, they can be made wonderfully delicious, nutritious, and healthy, and fit for kings. And in today's mad race for finding the surest and fastest diet to lose weight, soup should top the list. A bowl of lentil soup, for instance, with a piece of bread and a bowl of salad is all that the body needs for a meal. We, like the rest of the world, also consider soup as a kind of comfort food, and believe in the magical healing power of the chicken soup. In fact it has recently been proved that this is not a myth, chicken soup especially when cooked with the skin has some antiviral substances that can neutralize cold viruses.

Because most of the soups we usually make are quite substantial, what with the vegetables, grains, pulses, optional cuts of meat with bones and meat balls put in them, it is not customary to serve the soup before the meal as an appetizer. It is the meal itself, to be had with salad and warm bread. It is sometimes served to complement a scanty main dish. During the summer it is hardly ever made, and there is no such thing as cold soup in our cuisine. Probably the only time that soup may herald a main meal is during *Ramadhan,* the month of fasting. The soup customarily served on such occasions is lentil soup, which warms the body and prepares it for the big meal awaiting it after the long hours of abstaining from food and drink.

Lentil Soup

Lentil Soup
(Shorbat Adas)

(Makes 6 servings)

This is by far the mother of all soups, rich in nutrients and is a good source of iron. In *The Assyrian Herbal*, a study of ancient vegetable drugs, there was frequent mention of lentils and lentil soup (Akk. "mei ushshe" i.e. lentil cooked in liquid). The Assyrians also referred to it as "vegetable of the lungs", from which may be inferred that lentil soup was believed to be a remedy for colds (Thompson, 114). Al- Warraq, in his tenth-century cookbook, says that lentil dishes help with the phlegm, and is beneficial to the ailments of the chest (55). We still swear by it.

From the Baghdadi medieval cookbooks we learn they used yellow lentils, both shelled and unshelled in cooking their *adasiyyat* (from *adas*=lentil), which were soup-like dishes. Al-Warraq gives four of these, with and without meat (167-8). Following is al-Baghdadi's thirteenth-century recipe for *Adasiya*:

> Cut up meat, and dissolve the tail as usual. Put the meat into the oil, and fry lightly until browned: then throw in a little salt, cumin, and brayed dry coriander, and cover with water. When nearly cooked. Add beet [Swiss chard] washed and cut into pieces four fingers long. When thoroughly boiling, add as required lentils, cleaned and washed, and keep a steady fire going until the lentils are cooked. When set smooth and definitely cooked; add as required fine-bruised garlic, stirring with a ladle. Then leave over a slow fire: and remove. When serving, squeeze over it lemon juice. (45)

They also used to give body to the soup by adding noodles. In al-Baghdadi's *Rishta* soup recipe, besides lentil, he added peeled chickpeas, and *rishta*, which is spaghetti-like noodles "made by kneading flour and water well, then rolling out fine and cutting into thin threads four fingers long", 45)

For making lentil soups today, we use shelled yellow (or red) lentil variety, which is very convenient since it does not need soaking.

2 cups shelled yellow or red lentils
2 teaspoons salt
1/2 teaspoon black pepper
1/2 teaspoon curry powder, optional
1/2 teaspoon turmeric, optional
2 tablespoons tomato paste, or 1/2 cup tomato sauce, optional
1/2 cup broken vermicelli noodles (2 balls)

2 tablespoons olive oil
1 medium onion, finely chopped
1 heaping tablespoon whole wheat or all-purpose flour
1/4 cup lemon juice
For garnish: chopped parsley

1. Put lentils in a medium heavy pot, and cover with cold water by 3 to 4 inches (about 10 cups). Bring to a quick boil, skimming froth as needed. Lower heat to low and let simmer, covered, until

lentil is thoroughly cooked, about 30 minutes. For a creamy texture whisk the mixture with a hand whisker until smooth, a few minutes.

2. Add salt, black pepper, curry powder, turmeric, and tomato paste, if used, and broken noodles. Stir well. Keep simmering, and stir occasionally to prevent soup from sticking to the bottom of the pot, until soup is nicely thickened, about 15 minutes.

3. Meanwhile in a small skillet sauté onion until it is golden brown. Add flour and fold until flour changes color and is fragrant. Ladle some of the soup into the skillet, and stir to dislodge any flour and onion that might have stuck to the skillet. Pour the contents of the skillet back to the soup pot about 5 minutes before soup is done. Add lemon juice.

Ladle soup into bowls; garnish with chopped parsley; and serve with warm bread.

Variations:

* Toast bite-size pieces of flat bread, and sprinkle them on top of soup in the bowl, just before serving.

* Add to the soup, chopped spinach, (one 10-ounce package frozen or one pound fresh) along with the rest of the ingredients in step 2.

Meatballs
(Ras al-Asfour or Kuftayat)

The custom of adding small meatballs to soup and stew dishes goes back to the medieval times. They called them *kubab* (plural of *kubba*), and they ranged in size from the very small (as small as hazelnut, and called them *bunduqiyat*), to the big (as large as oranges of Seville, and called them *narinjiyat*). As for today, we make them as small as sparrows' heads, and hence the name *ras al-asfour*, sometimes generically referred to as *kuftayat*.

Add these beautiful spicy meatballs to the soups about 10 minutes before soup is done. Here is how to make them:

1/2 pound ground lean meat
1 small onion, grated
3 tablespoons flour, breadcrumbs, or rice flour
3/4 teaspoon salt
1/2 teaspoon black pepper
1/4 teaspoon allspice
1/4 teaspoon ginger powder and curry powder, each, optional
1/4 teaspoon chili pepper, or to taste
Preheat oven to 450 degrees F.

Combine all the ingredients and knead lightly. With wet fingers, form into small balls (as small as sparrows' heads). Shallow fry them, or arrange them in one layer on a greased baking sheet, and broil or bake in 450 degrees F. oven. Turn pieces once to brown on both sides, about 15 minutes.

Prepare these balls while the soup is simmering. A time saving tip is to make a bigger number of these balls, and freeze them for future use.

Creamy Mung Bean Soup
(Shorbat Mash)

(Makes 6 servings)

Here is another delicious and nutritious soup that comes only second to Lentil Soup in popularity, and is as ancient as lentil itself is (Thompson, 114). It looks attractively green with specks of broken white grains of rice. (See Glossary for more information on mung beans)

1 1/2 cups whole mung beans, picked over, washed, soaked overnight, and drained
1/2 cup rice, soaked for 30 minutes, broken into smaller pieces by rubbing between the fingers, no need to drain
2 teaspoons salt
1/4 teaspoon black pepper
1 teaspoon ground cumin

2 tablespoons olive oil
1 medium onion, chopped
1 rounded tablespoon whole wheat or all-purpose flour
1/4 teaspoon turmeric
Juice of 1 lemon (1/4 cup)

1. In a medium heavy pot, put mung beans and cover with cold water by 2 inches. Bring to a quick boil, skimming froth as needed, then reduce heat to low, and let beans simmer gently, covered, for 20 minutes.

2. Add rice, salt, pepper, and cumin. Stir well. Bring to a quick boil, then reduce heat to low, and continue simmering, covered, for about 30 minutes, or until beans and rice are cooked to tenderness and soup is nicely thickened. Stir occasionally to prevent soup from sticking to the bottom of the pot.

3. While soup is simmering, in a small skillet sauté onion in hot oil until golden brown. Stir in flour and turmeric and fold until flour starts to brown and is fragrant. Ladle some of the soup into the skillet, and stir to dislodge any flour and onion that might have stuck to the skillet. Pour contents of the skillet back to the soup pot about 5 minutes before soup is done. Add lemon juice
Serve with warm bread and salad.

Variation:

Mung Beans with Bread: By replacing one ingredient with another you will turn this basic soup into a heart-and-bone warming meal to be had in the deepest days of winter. Just omit rice from the recipe, and let soup thicken. Break a piece of flat bread into bite-size pieces, and add to simmering pot when you add onion mixture in step 3.

Cream of Turnip and Swiss Chard Soup
(Shorbat Hamudh Shalgham)

(Makes 6 servings)

Evidently turnips have been used in cooking ever since antiquity. In one of the Babylonian stews, turnip was the principal ingredient in the recipe (see Introduction). In the Akkadian it was called "laptu", from which the Arabic *lift* was derived. During the medieval times turnips were made into delicious white stews, sometimes adorned with spicy meatballs. In al-Warraq's tenth-century cookbook, such dishes were collectively called *al-shaljamiyat* (cooked with turnips). Meat was cooked in water, onion, crushed chickpeas, cilantro, salt, oil, and turnips. The sauce was thickened and enriched with ground almonds, mashed turnips, rice and milk. Lean meat was pounded to paste, seasoned, formed into *kubabs* (meatballs) and thrown into the simmering stew.

In Iraq they are winter vegetables, and are believed to have the power to relieve cold symptoms. The sight of vendors selling turnips simmered in water and date syrup is quite common in wintertime. The aroma emitting from those steaming huge pots of turnips is unforgettable. Delicious and creamy soup is also made from turnips and Swiss chard, which is as ancient as turnip itself is, it has even retained the same name (Akk. "silki", Arabic *siliq*). This same soup sometimes makes the basis for another elaborate dish called, *kubbat hamudh shalgham* (see chapter 11, on stuffed foods).

My family nicknamed this soup, *Shorbat Kuluhu*, (eat it soup) after I told them how the prophet Muhammad recommended eating turnips to his followers saying, "Eat it, and do not tell your enemies about it." It is that good! So next time you catch a cold, you know what to do.

1 onion, chopped
2 tablespoons oil
3 to 4 medium turnips, (about 1 1/2 pounds) peeled and cut into 1-inch cubes
1/2 teaspoon turmeric

2 heaping tablespoons tomato paste, or 1 cup tomato sauce
4 to 5 big leaves of Swiss chard, thinly sliced with the stalks (about 3 cups)
1/2 cup rice soaked in cold water for 30 minutes and broken into small pieces by rubbing between the fingers. No need to drain. For a creamier texture substitute with 2 heaping tablespoons rice flour, dissolved in a little cold water
One 15-ounce canned cooked chickpeas, drained, optional
1 1/2 teaspoons salt
1/4 teaspoon black pepper

1/4 cup fresh mint, chopped, or 1 teaspoon dry mint, optional
Juice of 1 lemon (about 1/4 cup)

1. In a medium heavy pot, sauté onion in oil until it starts to brown. Add turnip pieces and turmeric, and fold together for about 5 minutes.

2. Add tomato paste or sauce to turnips, and pour enough hot water or broth to cover by 4 to 5 inches (7 to 8 cups). Mix well, and bring to a quick boil, skimming if needed. Reduce heat to medium low and let simmer, covered, for 10 minutes.

3. Stir in Swiss chard, rice, drained chickpeas, if using any, salt and pepper. Bring to a boil, then reduce heat, and resume simmering, covered, stirring occasionally to prevent soup from sticking to the bottom of the pot, 20 to 30 minutes, or until turnip is tender, and soup is nicely thickened.

4. Add lemon juice and mint 5 minutes before soup is done.

Variation:
Some people prefer to have the soup white. In this case omit tomato paste or sauce and follow same instructions as above.

Tip:
Wash, drain and freeze a few cups of rice, and next time you need crushed or broken rice as required recipes, just take out the amount needed, add some water to it, and crush it between your fingers. The rice grains will fall apart in no time, and quite easily.

The Story of Joha and Turnips

Joha is a popular comic character in Islamic folkloric literature. While at times he is shrewd and funny enough to play practical jokes on people, he is also presented as a naïve person who easily becomes the butt of numerous jokes. The following is my favorite:

Once Joha went to pay homage to the Caliph and as the custom required he took with him a present which comprised of a basketful of *nabug* (jujube fruit about the size of cherries), which by common consent was a very humble fruit. Naturally the Caliph was offended, and gave command that Joha be stoned with each and every jujube fruit he brought with him. Every time he was hit by a jujube, Juha would say, "*Alhamdu lil- lah wal-shukur* (may God be praised and thanked). The Caliph was surprised and asked for an explanation. Joha told him that he was thanking God for listening to his wife who suggested the jujube as opposed to his initial choice, which was turnip.

Spinach Soup
(Shorbat Sbenagh)

(Makes 4 servings)

This soup is light, healthy and easy to make. Milk and flour are used as the thickening agents, and this method of giving body to otherwise watery dishes is a very ancient one (see Introduction).

1 onion, finely chopped
1 tablespoon oil
3 tablespoons flour
3 cups milk
1 pound fresh spinach, finely chopped, or one 10-ounce package frozen chopped spinach
1/4 cup fresh dill, chopped, or 1 tablespoon dried dill weed
1/2 teaspoon coriander
1/2 teaspoon salt, or to taste
1/4 teaspoon black pepper

2 tablespoons whipping or sour cream, for garnish, optional

1. In a medium heavy pot, sauté onion in oil until transparent, about 5 minutes.

2. Add flour and stir for a few minutes until flour is fragrant. Slowly pour in milk, stirring all the time preferably with a wire whisker to prevent lumping.

3. Stir in prepared spinach, dill, coriander, salt and pepper. Bring to a quick boil, then let it simmer gently on low heat, covered, stirring occasionally until it is nicely thickened, about 15 minutes.

Serve in bowls garnished with a swirl of cream or a squeeze of lemon.

Green Soup
(Shorba Khadhra)

(Makes 8 servings)

This soup is inspired by a recipe I found in the thirteenth century Baghdadi cookbook, called *shorba khadhra* (green soup). The main ingredient in the recipe is *kurrath* (leeks), an ancient green that has been growing in the region for a long time, it was called "kurasu" in the Akkadian. But unlike the leeks available in the West, Iraqi variety looks like a bunch of fresh and tender stalks of leeks (no bulbs), and is used as an herb or green. Following is the medieval recipe of al-Baghdadi:

Cut fat meat into middling pieces and fry lightly in dissolved tail. When brown, add salt to taste, fine-brayed dry coriander, pieces of cinnamon, and a handful of peeled chick-peas. Cover with water, and put on the fire: when boiling, throw away the scum. Take two bunches of fresh vegetable leeks, cut small with a knife, pound in the mortar, and throw into the saucepan. Take a portion of red meat, chop up fine with seasonings, adding a handful of

137

peeled chick-peas, washed rice, and a little of the pounded leek: make into cabobs, and throw into the saucepan. When all is cooked, add more water as required. Then take rice, a quarter as much as the water, wash several times, and put into the saucepan: let it continue to boil until thoroughly cooked, a little on the light side. Leave over the fire to settle: then remove (Arberry, 47).

The medieval recipe calls for pounded leeks to give the soup its characteristic color. (I have a friend who grows what's known as "Chinese chives". They are not tubular like regular chives, but look like long spears of grass, and they taste exactly like the Iraqi *Kurrath*) In the following adaptation the bulbous white head that comes with the leeks, will be used to replace the onion which is more commonly used in soups.

1 bunch leeks (about 1 1/2 pounds) choose the smallest leeks available
1 tablespoon oil
3/4 cup split green chickpeas, soaked for 30 minutes and drained, then covered with water and simmered until just cooked (about 20 minutes)
3/4 cup rice, washed, soaked for 30 minutes, then broken between the fingers, no need to drain
1 teaspoon salt
For the meat balls
1/2 pound lean ground meat
3/4 teaspoon salt
1/2 teaspoon coriander
1/4 teaspoon black pepper
1/4 teaspoon cumin

Juice of 1 lemon (1/4 cup)

1. Separate white heads of leeks from green stalks. Wash well. Coarsely chop green stalks, and grind them in a blender or food processor, set aside.

2. Coarsely chop the white part, and in a medium pot sauté them in oil until they soften, about 5 minutes. Add 8 cups hot water, and bring to a boil, then lower heat to medium and continue cooking.

3. Meanwhile combine meatball ingredients, adding 1/4 cup of processed leek, 1/4 cup of the cooked chickpeas, and 1/4 cup of the drained broken rice. Shape into walnut-size balls (about 16 pieces), and drop into the simmering liquid prepared in step 1. Let cook for 5 minutes.

4. To the simmering meatballs in the pot, add remaining ground leeks, chickpeas, broken rice, and 1 teaspoon salt. Stir carefully to mix well. Bring to a quick boil, then reduce heat to low, and let soup simmer, covered, until meat balls are well cooked, and soup is nicely thickened, about 20 minutes. Stir soup several times while simmering to prevent it from sticking to the bottom of the pot.

5. Add lemon juice 5 minutes before soup is done.
Serve in bowls with warm bread.

Cream of Squash Soup
(Shorbat Shjar)

(Makes 4 to 6 servings)

Squash in any of its types makes appetizing and attractive soup. The color is determined by the kind of squash used. It can be light-green, yellow or orange.

1 medium onion, chopped
2 tablespoons olive oil
3 cups chopped squash (zucchini, yellow squash, pumpkin, or butternut squash)
1/4 teaspoon turmeric
2 cups hot water or broth

2 cups milk
3 tablespoons flour, dissolved in 1/3 cup cold water
One cup cooked whole chickpeas
1 1/2 teaspoon salt
1/4 teaspoon black pepper
1/3 teaspoon nutmeg
2 tablespoons fresh dill, chopped, or 2/3 teaspoon dried dill weed
3 tablespoons lemon juice

1. In a medium heavy pot, sauté onion in oil, until transparent. Add squash and turmeric, and fold together for about 5 minutes.

2. Pour in hot water or broth, bring to a quick boil, then reduce heat and let simmer, covered, until squash is cooked but still firm, about 15 minutes.

3. Put pot away from heat. Fit a strainer into a bowl, and pour cooked squash into the strainer. Reserve the liquid. Set aside 1/4 cup of cooked squash. Purée the rest using a blender or a food processor. (Straining squash is necessary to prevent liquid from splashing while blending or processing.)

4. Return puréed squash, reserved chunks of squash, and reserved liquid to the pot. Stir in milk, dissolved flour, chickpeas, salt, pepper, and nutmeg. Bring to a quick boil, then reduce heat to medium low, and let soup simmer, covered, stirring occasionally, until soup is creamy and nicely thickened, about 15 minutes.

5. Add dill and lemon juice 5 minutes before soup is done.
    Serve in small bowls with warm bread.

A Short Cut:
2 cups of canned **pure** puréed pumpkin may replace fresh squash. In this case sauté onion with turmeric as directed in step 1. Then add puréed pumpkin, water, milk, dissolved flour, chickpeas, salt, pepper, and nutmeg. Cook as directed in step 4. Add dill and lemon juice 5 minutes before soup is done.

Vegetable Soup
(Shorbat Khodhar)

(Makes 4 to 6 servings)

Do as directed in Squash Soup, except replace squash with vegetables of your choice, such as carrots, parsley, green peas, potatoes, etc.

Chicken Soup with vegetables
(Shorbat Dijaj bil-Khodhar)

(Makes 4 to 6 servings)

Do as directed in Squash Soup, except replace squash with other vegetables; and instead of water use chicken broth. In step 4 add about 1/2 cup cooked shredded chicken.

Tomato Soup with Rice
(Shorbat Tamata bil-Timman)

(Makes 4 to 6 servings)

Before the arrival of tomato to the region around the beginning of the sixteenth century, this soup was made white, as described in al-Baghdadi's thirteenth-century recipe, *Shorba* (Arberry, 44). Try this modern version. It is smooth and comforting.

> **1 pound lamb (chunks of bone with meat), or chicken**
> **1 onion, chopped**
> **2 tablespoons oil**
> **3/4 cup rice, washed, soaked for 30 minutes and broken by rubbing between the fingers, no need to drain**
> **3 heaping tablespoons tomato paste (one 6-ounce can) or one 15-ounce can tomato sauce**
> **1 teaspoon salt**
> **1/4 teaspoon black pepper**
>
> **For garnish: chopped parsley**

1. Trim meat or chicken, put it in a medium pot, and cover with cold water by 4 to 5 inches. Bring to a quick boil, skimming as needed. Lower heat to medium, and let boil gently until meat is cooked, about 45 minutes, a little less for chicken. Fit a sieve on a bowl and pour meat broth to strain. Reserve broth, and shred meat with fingers, discard bones, or leave them as they are. Set aside. (Tip: if you want to get rid of all fat released in the broth, refrigerate, to solidify the fat.)

2. In a medium heavy pot, sauté onion in oil until golden brown. Stir in rice, tomato paste, salt, pepper, reserved shredded meat, and 5 cups broth. Add plain hot water to make 5 cups if broth is not enough. Mix well, and bring to a quick boil, skimming if needed. Lower heat to low, and let simmer gently, covered, until nicely thickened, about 30 minutes. Stir occasionally to prevent soup from sticking to the bottom of the pot
Serve garnished with chopped parsley.

White Beans Soup
(Shorbat Fasoulya Yabsa)

(Makes 4 to 6 servings)

Beans make healthy and satisfying soups. They are high in fiber, carbohydrates, iron, B vitamins, and folic acid. They also provide a good supply of protein without the fat and cholesterol. Traditionally white beans are used, but other kinds of beans may be substituted.

1 cup white beans, soaked overnight and drained
3 garlic cloves, whole and unskinned

1 medium onion, chopped
2 tablespoons oil
4 tablespoons flour

2 carrots, diced
1 teaspoon salt
1/4 teaspoon black pepper
1/2 teaspoon ground cumin
1/2 teaspoon mustard powder
Juice of 1 lemon (about 1/4 cup)

For garnish: chopped parsley

1. In a medium pot, put beans and garlic, and cover with cold water by 3 to 4 inches. Bring to a quick boil, skimming if needed. Lower heat to low, and let simmer, covered, for about 35 minutes. Set side, until cool enough to handle.

2. Squeeze pulp out of garlic cloves, discard skins. Purée beans and garlic with a potato masher, a food processor or a blender. If too watery, drain, reserve liquid; mash beans then return liquid to it. This will prevent spluttering when puréeing.

3. In a heavy medium pot, sauté onion in oil until golden, about 5 minutes. Stir in flour until fragrant. Add puréed beans slowly, and stir until smooth. If too thick, add hot water as needed.

4. Add carrots, salt, pepper, cumin, mustard and lemon juice. Bring to a boil, then reduce heat to medium-low, and let soup simmer, covered, stirring occasionally until carrots are cooked and soup is smooth and nicely thickened.
Serve in small bowls, garnished with plenty of chopped parsley.

Grains and Beans Soup #1
(Shorbat Burma al- Mosiliyya)

(Makes 6 servings)

Modern Mosul is the cite of the ancient Assyrian capital, Nineva. The reason why the city was called Mosul because it was the "middle-gate." It stood on the way where four great highways met, in particular the junction of Assyria and Babylon (Burton, vol. 1, 82). Mosul was renowned for producing a fabric known in English as "muslin". It is also renowned for some hearty dishes containing barley, wheat, and beans, for this is where they grow in abundance. Here is one of them.

1 cup shelled wheat or barley, washed and soaked overnight, drained
1/2 cup brown or green lentils, unshelled, washed and soaked overnight, drained
1/2 cup dried red beans, or black-eyed peas, washed and soaked overnight, drained
1 pound lamb soup-bones (chunks of bone with meat)

1 teaspoon salt
1/4 teaspoon black pepper
1 teaspoon ground cumin
1 teaspoon prepared *noomi Basrah*, see Glossary, or juice of 1 lemon (about 1/4 cup)

1 medium onion, chopped
2 tablespoons oil

For garnish: chopped parsley

1. Put prepared grains, beans, and soup bones in a medium heavy pot. Cover with cold water by 4 to 5 inches. Bring to a quick boil, skimming as needed. Lower heat to low and let simmer, covered, until meat is cooked and beans are tender, about 45 minutes.

2. Take out meat pieces. Discard bones and shred meat with the fingers. Slightly mash or bruise beans with a potato masher. Return meat to the pot. Add salt, pepper, cumin, and *noomi Basrah* or lemon juice.

3. In a small skillet, sauté onion in oil until golden, about 7 minutes. Add to soup pot.

4. Resume simmering. If soup becomes too thick, add some hot water, and let it simmer, stirring occasionally for 10 to 15 minutes.
Serve in small bowls, garnished with lots of chopped parsley.

Grains and Beans Soup # 2

(Makes 6 servings)

Here is a concoction of beans and grains to make another hearty and delicious soup. It bears a striking resemblance to a tenth-century hearty pottage called *tafsheel*. It is basically a bean and pulse soup that has a porridge-like consistency. The medieval recipe called for a combination of lentil, beans, chickpeas, mung beans, and rice, all to be cooked with meat, Swiss chard, vinegar, mustard, coriander, cumin, pepper, aged cheese and oil (al-Warraq, 170). Although it is largely cooked without meat today, some people like to add small meatballs, known as *ras al-asfour* (sparrow's head), for recipe see p. .

1/2 cup dried red beans or black-eyed peas, washed and soaked overnight, drained
1/2 cup mung beans (see Glossary), washed and soaked overnight, drained

1/2 cup shelled red lentils, washed and drained (see Glossary)
1/2 cup rice, washed and soaked for 30 minutes
2 to 3 garlic cloves, whole and unskinned
1/2 cup peeled and diced tomatoes, fresh or canned

1 medium onion, chopped
2 tablespoons oil
1 teaspoon salt
1/4 teaspoon black pepper
1 teaspoon ground cumin
Juice of 1 lemon (about 1/4 cup)

For garnish: chopped parsley, or fresh or dried dill.

1. Put red beans and mung beans in a medium heavy pot, and cover by 4 to 5 inches with cold water. Bring to a quick boil, skimming as needed. Lower heat to low, and let it simmer, covered, for 15 minutes.

2. Add lentils, rice, garlic, and tomatoes. Continue simmering until beans and grains are soft and tender, and soup in nicely thickened, about 20 minutes. Stir occasionally to prevent soup from sticking to the bottom of the pot. If soup gets too thick, add some more hot water.

3. In a small skillet, sauté onion in oil until golden brown. Add to the simmering soup 10 minutes before it is done, along with salt, pepper, cumin, and lemon juice.

Serve in small bowls garnished with lots of chopped parsley, or a small amount of dill.

CHAPTER FIVE
SNACKS, SANDWICHES, AND SIDE DISHES
(*Nawashif* with Meat)

CHAPTER FIVE
SNACKS, SANDWICHES, AND SIDE DISHES

وجبات خفيفة

(Nawashif)
(With Meat)

In his *Supplement aux Dictionaires Arabes* (ii: 673), the Arabist Dozy states that he does not know the exact meaning of *nashif* (dry) as applied to dishes. For the Iraqis, however, the term has, to this day, been commonly used to designate a wide array of dishes that have no sauce in them, to begin with, or in which sauce is reduced in the course of cooking. They are all invariably served with bread.

In the tenth century cookbook, al-Warraq gives an extensive number of *bawarid* (cold) dishes, meant to be served as a preliminary course before the hot dishes. They cover all sorts of meat, both white and red. The *sibagh* and *kawamikh* were condiments, dips, and sauces usually served with these dishes, to help the digestion.

With all the varieties of breads that have been baking in the region (for details see chapter 1, on breads), it is inevitable that sandwiches have always been an indispensable way of serving food. During the medieval times they were called *bazmaward, ausat* (in the middle), and *wast mashtour* or *shata'ir* (the split), depending on how they were filled.

The tenth-century cookbook writer made a clear distinction between the three kinds of sandwiches. *Shata'ir* were open-faced sandwiches. The *ausat* (sing. *wast*) were made from *furn* (brick oven) bread which was made thicker than *riqaq* breads. The bread was slit open horizontally, and the bottom layer was spread with the filling. The top layer was put back, and was firmly pressed. For presentation, it was sliced into finger-like pieces or other shapes. As for the *bazmaward,* the filling was spread on the entire surface of the *riqaq* bread (flat and thin), which was then rolled tightly, and sliced into discs. (For more details, see Box, A Sandwich for Thought, below)

Today the generic word for sandwich is *laffa* (bread roll), which stemmed from using the traditional flat bread. As for the *samoun,* the European style bread, it is first slashed open along one side, leaving the other side intact. The pith is taken out to make room for the filling.

Sandwiches are an integral part of our menu. We make sandwiches for breakfast with a cup of tea, or have them for brunches, or light suppers. Sandwiches are made at home, or purchased from carry out small restaurants or vendors at the corners of busy streets. The fillings vary, depending upon time, place and occasion. The sandwich of my growing years was *Laffat Anba wa Sammon,* (sandwich of pickled mango). It was the kind of thing to have when you are not really hungry, but would like to snack on something spicy and appetizing. A treat would be to add to it sliced tomatoes and hard-boiled eggs. These sandwiches were sold at movie theatres, at busy areas by street vendors, and even outside school buildings. I remember my friends and I used to buy it after school and munch it on our way home, despite our parents' warning that it was not good to eat it on an empty stomach. We were always betrayed by the distinctive aroma of the pickled mango that had clung to our mouths, hands, and clothes.

The sandwich filling can be as simple as greens and herbs, as common as cheese, *kebab*, and *gus* (shredded meat), as scrumptious as *geymer* (clotted cream) and honey, or as exotic as toasted walnuts.

An Assyrian officer having a hurried meal

Street Food in Medieval Baghdad

Carry out and fast food was a booming business in medieval Baghdad, AD. It was very convenient for travelers and visitors who happened to be passing by the city, as well as residents themselves. It was relatively affordable and even poor people sometimes preferred to eat out rather than put money on fuel in cooking their food at home. From contemporary chronicles we learn that *Souq al-Shawwa'een*, for instance, was specialized in selling all kinds of meat grilled on coals, such as the famous *al- kebab al-Rasheedi* (after Caliph Haroun al-Rasheed), and *kardanaj* (rotisserie) chicken. They were all served with bread and appetizing condiments and relishes, collectively called *sibagh* and *kawamikh*.

The *judhaba* was another delicious choice to make. It was basically meat or chicken grilled in the *tannour*, and served with a sweet bread mixture that was put under the meat, while grilling, to receive all the dripping juices and fat. In the cold days of winter, a wise choice would be a bowl of *hareesa* (mashed shelled wheat with meat) drizzled with sizzling *samn* (clarified butter), and generously sprinkled with cinnamon and sugar. A dish of steaming *thareed* (pieces of bread sopped in rich broth) served with akari' (trotters), *kubbayat* (stuffed tripe), and parts of sheep's head would be a good choice, too.

The diners also had the option of ordering fried foods such as *sanbousaj*, sausages, meat, and fish, collectively called *qalaya*. The *bawarid* (cold dishes) were the dishes to order during the hot days of summer, especially the ones prepared with vegetables and yogurt, such as *jajiq*, and the *awsat* and *bazmaward* (sandwiches).

For dessert there was an overwhelming number of pastries to choose from, but the most popular were the *lauzeenaj* (similar to baklava), *zilabya* (fritters), *kunafa* (shredded dough), and q*ata'if* (thin pancakes). They were all invariably fried and drenched in honey or *julab* (rose water syrup), depending upon how much the buyer could afford to pay. All this food was washed down simply with cold water, or a thirst quenching sweet drink such as *sharab al-zabeeb* (raisin drink), jujube or pomegranate drink.

People who frequented the ready-made food markets were mostly *'awam* (commoners), because it was not fit for the refined upper class people "to patronize the shop of a 'mincer of meats and pies'" (Guthrie, 94). The tenth-century satirical writer Abu Hayyan al-Tawheedi gave us a glimpse of the eating out situation through his protagonist, who vilified supposedly respectable people that go after the *shawaya*, *qalaya* (grilled and fried foods), and *bazmaward* (sandwiches) (56).

Following is a unique episode from the tenth century Arabic picaresque narrative, *Maqamat* by Badi'l-Zaman al-Hamadani. It is an amusing anecdote that incidentally throws vivid light on what eating out was like in medieval Baghdad.

The parasitic protagonist Isa ibn-Hisham, at this point in the narrative, is broke and hungry, and is wandering in the market places of Baghdad, on the lookout for a prey. With his trained eyes he espies a nervous *sawadi* (peasant from rural areas) who obviously has some money on him. He

accosts him, calling him Abu Zeid. The peasant corrects him, saying his name in fact is Abu Ubeid, but Isa reproaches him for having forgetting him, and immediately asks about his father.

The peasant tells him that it has been a while since his father died. At hearing this Isa pretends that he is smitten with the news, and makes as if he is about to tear his garment. The peasant takes hold of his hands, beseeching him not to do this. Having thus broken the ice, so to speak, Isa invites him to have lunch with him at home, but why bother go there since the food market is nearby.

They go to a *judhaba* restaurant, where Isa asks the master to prepare a dish of his juicy grilled meat, sprinkled with sumac water, and decked with *awraq al-riqaq* (very thin breads). They sit and eat to their full as if there is no tomorrow. Isa then orders two pounds of *lauzeenaj*, made the night before, thin crusted, well-stuffed, and drenched in oil, so that Abu Zeid may eat to his heart's desire. They sit down, roll up their sleeves and eat until they wipe out the whole plate. Now Isa suggests that after such a meal what else will they need but a glass of ice water, and he volunteers to fetch some. He goes out and hides where he can see the peasant at a distance. The peasant waits and waits but to no avail, so he decides to leave. The food master prevents him by clutching his sleeves, asking for his money. The peasant tries to explain that he has been invited, but the master does not buy this. So the peasant has no other choice but untie his purse with his teeth, and pay for the hefty meal they had together, saying, "How many times have I told that monkey that I am not Abu Zeid, I am Abu 'Ubeid, but he relentlessly insisted that I am Abu Zeid."

(*Al-Maqama al-Baghdadiya*, 70-3)

Iraqi Sausages
(Bastirma)

(Makes 8 6-inch long sausages)

A brief satiric Sumerian text reveals that the ancient Mesopotamians knew how to fill intestine casings with meat of some kind (Bottèro, "The Cuisine of Ancient Mesopotamia," 37). In the medieval period they were called *maqaniq* or *laqaniq*. Some were made for immediate consumption, such as the ones filled with a mixture of meat and eggs, or chicken. These were usually boiled and then fried. Today we call them, *mumbar* (see chapter 10). Others were filled with a spicy mixture of pounded meat, and were meant to keep for at least a month. Today we call these, *bastirma*.

The *bastirma* makes a hearty delicious breakfast sandwich, usually enjoyed in wintertime. The way we make it today is basically the same. Meat is ground, mixed with lots of spices and garlic, stuffed in intestine casings, and then hung in a ventilated area for a while, away from direct sunlight. The dehydrating process, however, requires dry environment, otherwise meat will go bad. I do not recommend drying the sausages out in the open air, especially in humid areas. It is safer to keep them in the freezer in which case, instead of sausage casings, plastic bags may be used. A dehydrator will do the job just fine, provided you use intestine casings.

In addition to intestine casings, caul, the transparent thin layer that surrounds the stomach, was also used to encase sausage meat. Tenth-century Baghdadi cookbook writer, Al-Warraq, uses it in one of the recipes and calls, *tharb* (57). In the fourteenth-century augmented manuscript of al-Baghdadi's cookbook, lean meat was pounded, with pepper, mastic, cinnamon, caraway, salt and oil, and was made into patties, wrapped in pieces of what by then was called *ghishawa* (thin sheet of caul fat), put in skewers and grilled (375). Nowadays this dish is called *kebab mandeel*.

148

**2 pounds ground meat, 80 % lean, or use 90 % lean meat with
3 tablespoons olive oil added to it**

**4 cloves garlic, or to taste, grated
2 teaspoons salt
1 teaspoon black pepper
1 tablespoon cumin
2 teaspoons ground coriander
1/2 teaspoon allspice
1/2 teaspoon cinnamon
1/4 teaspoon chili pepper, or to taste**

3 to 4 ounces sausage casings (available at meat departments in grocery stores, plastic bags can be substituted, see below

1. In a big bowl combine all ingredients except the casings. Cover the bowl and refrigerate overnight to allow flavors to blend.

2. Fill sausage casings as follows: if you do not have a sausage maker, then use a big funnel or cut-off top of a 1-liter soda bottle. Transfer sausage casing to the spout of the funnel or the neck of the bottle. Tie the end of the casing and start filling it until all the stuffing is used up. Close the other end, and divide the long sausage into 6-inch long pieces either by twisting or using a white kitchen thread. (Do not over-fill pieces) Flatten sausages by pressing with the fingers to make them 1/2 inch thick.

3. Arrange sausages in a single layer on a tray, and freeze. When solid enough, store them in sealed plastic bags, and keep them in freezer until needed.

4. **If you do not choose to use intestine casings**, then do as follows:
    After you mix ingredients and refrigerate them overnight as directed in step 1, with wet hands, take small amounts of meat mixture and form them into small patties. Arrange these pieces on a tray in a single layer, and freeze them. When they are solid enough, freeze them in a sealed plastic bag, and use them as directed below.
    An even easier way of doing it is to put the prepared meat mixture in plastic bags, and flatten them by pressing with the fingers into 1/2-inch thinness. Seal bags and freeze. Whenever you want to cook some, break away the pieces you need, and cook as directed below.

How to Cook Bastirma:
1. Take the amount needed out of the freezer a few hours before actual time of cooking, and let thaw in refrigerator.

2. With a sharp knife, cut pieces crosswise into 1/2-inch wide pieces.

3. Put pieces in a skillet, and cook them, stirring frequently, for about 5 minutes or until they are cooked and nicely browned. Traditionally made *bastirma* will ooze out fat while cooking, but when lean meat is used you might need to help it with a little bit of oil.

How to Serve Bastirma:

*You can have the cooked pieces wrapped in bread as a sandwich, with slices of salad vegetables, and a squeeze of lemon.

*Chop a tomato, and cook it with the sausage pieces. Have it as a sandwich with sliced salad vegetables.

*Prepare it with eggs. Slightly beat a few eggs in a bowl. The number of eggs used depends on the amount of *bastirma* you are cooking. Pour eggs on the cooked pieces of *bastirma*, making sure it covers the meat. Lower heat to low, cover skillet and cook for about 5 minutes or until eggs are set. Divide into wedges and make it into sandwiches along with salad vegetables, and a squeeze of lemon.

An Assyrian officer having a hurried meal

Iraqi Omelet
(Makhlama)

(Makes 4-5 servings)

In the Middle Ages, *al-'ujaj* (omelet dishes) were sometimes called *narjisiyat*, because the set eggs that covered the whole face of the dish looked like narcissus flowers. Sometimes the dish was taken to the table in the same frying pan it was cooked in, after covering the sides with a big and thin *riqaq* bread, in which a hole, as big as the diameter of the pan, was made. Following is a recipe taken from the *nawashif* (dry dishes) chapter in the thirteenth-century Baghdadi cookbook. The medieval recipe *Qualyat al-Shiwa'* (fried roast) uses leftovers of roast meat:

> Take cold roast of yesterday and cut into small pieces. Take fresh sesame-oil, put into frying pan, and boil: then add the roast, stirring. When its fat is melted, throw in fine-brayed coriander, cumin and cinnamon. If desired sour, sprinkle with a little vinegar colored with saffron, and garnish with poached eggs. Leave over a gentle fire an hour to settle: then remove (Arberry, 197).

In some of the medieval omelet recipes, the egg was left undisturbed, sunny side up, such as in the *narjisiya* (like narcissus flowers). Al-Warraq compares them to *'uyoun al-baqar* (cows' eyes). The yolk was sometimes poked with a knife, and lightly mixed with the white to give it a marbled look. On other occasions the meat mixture was scrambled with the eggs, and these were called *muba'tharat*, or *makhlotat* (scrambled, mixed).

Today we still cook it pretty much the same way. It makes a very convenient side dish or a sandwich for brunches, light suppers and picnic lunches. The following basic recipe is with meat, other vegetarian variations are given in the following chapter.

1 pound lean ground meat
2 tablespoons oil
1 onion, chopped
1 teaspoon salt
1/2 teaspoon black pepper
1/2 teaspoon curry powder
1 medium tomato chopped
1/2 cup chopped parsley

6 eggs
Chili pepper, to taste
For garnish: chopped parsley

1. In a big non-stick skillet, cook meat in oil, stirring frequently, breaking down lumps until all moisture evaporates and meat is cooked, about 10 minutes.

2. Stir in onion and fold until it is transparent, about 5 minutes.

3. Add salt, pepper, curry powder, tomatoes and parsley. Mix well and let cook for a few more minutes.

4. With the back of a spoon level surface, make six indentions, and break the eggs into them. Sprinkle surface with chili pepper, if desired. Leave eggs whole, sunny-side-up, or zigzag surface with a knife to break yolks and let them mingle slightly with the whites.

5. Lower heat to low, cover skillet, and let eggs cook slowly until they are set, 5 to 7 minutes. Do not overcook otherwise eggs will develop a leathery texture.

   Alternatively the dish can be cooked in the oven. Simply transfer meat mixture to a greased baking pan, big enough to spread mixture in about 1/2-inch thick layer. Then add eggs as described above, and bake in a preheated oven at 400 degrees F. until set. No need to cover.

6. Cut into wedges, garnish with parsley, and serve as a sandwich, with salad vegetables.

Variation:

*Scrambled *Makhlama*: Another way of presenting the dish, is to beat the eggs, add them to the meat mixture, and fold, scrambling gently over low heat until egg is just set.

Iraqi Burgers
(Kufta)

(Makes 10 Burgers)

Although the name *kufta*, designating balls or patties of ground meat, might suggest a Turkish origin of sort, meat patties, similar to the ones we cook today, were already known to the medieval cooks. They made *kubab* (spicy meatballs) for their stews, fried *muqarrasat* (discs), and *maqloubat* (flipped), in which seasoned pounded meat was shaped into discs, and flipped to brown on both sides. Both were *nawashif* (dry) dishes, served with condiments and bread. To bind the meat particles they added flour, breadcrumbs, and eggs, exactly as we still do to day.

The following is a recipe for simple *kuftas*. I have a friend who adds a little of powdered dried milk for extra calcium, which sounds good.

1 pound lean ground meat
1 medium onion (about 1/2 cup), grated or finely chopped
1/2 cup parsley, chopped
1 clove garlic, grated, optional
1/2 cup bread crumbs
1 egg, slightly beaten
1 teaspoon salt
1/2 teaspoon black pepper
1 teaspoon *baharat*, see Glossary, or 1/2 teaspoon cinnamon
1/2 teaspoon ground ginger
1/2 teaspoon cumin
1/2 teaspoon coriander

Oil for shallow frying

1. Mix all ingredients except for oil. Knead with fingers briefly just to combine ingredients. With wet fingers, divide meat dough into 10 portions and shape into patties, about 1/3-inch thick.

2. Shallow-fry the pieces, pressing them occasionally with a hamburger flipper to help keep them flat, until golden brown. Turn once to brown both sides, about 5 minutes. Drain on white paper towels.

To serve, make into sandwiches with salad vegetables. If wished, serve the sandwich spread with the following refreshing sauce, or any other sauces given after the recipe for Shish Kebab, below.

Yogurt and Garlic Sauce (Salsat Jajeek)

This is a variation on the appetizing *Jajeek* salad (see chapter 3, on salads and appetizers). It is closer to al-Warraq's tenth-century *jajiq* (96). Because yogurt is drained, sauce will be of spreading consistency:

3 cups yogurt drained for 3 hours at room temperature or overnight under refrigeration, use cheese cloth or a coffee filter
1 cup cucumber, grated and drained for 3 hours, or under refrigeration overnight
1/4 cup fresh dill or 1 tablespoon dried dill weed, optional
1 clove garlic, grated
1 medium tomato, seeded and drained, and finely chopped
1/2 teaspoon salt
1/4 teaspoon black or white pepper

Combine all ingredients and use as a spread for sandwiches.

Burgers with Vegetables, Pan Fried
(Uroug or Kebab Tawa, or Shiftayat)

(Makes about 26 small burgers)

In Iraq we make two things that bear the name *uroug*, one is the flat bread with meat and vegetables, and the other is meat and vegetables mixed with dough and fried as patties, and hence the name *kebab tawa* (cooked in a frying pan). The difference is in the proportion of meat and vegetables to dough. (For meaning of *uroug*, and recipe for the bread see chapter 1 on breads).

In the northern city of Mosul these patties are called *sheftayat*. The name in all probability stemmed from a medieval practice of wrapping ground meat mixture in caul fat, the transparent thin layer that surrounds the stomach. The Arabic word for transparent is *shef* (from which, for instance, the name of the fabric chiffon was derived). In Cypress today sausage wrapped in sheets of caul is called "sheftalia" (Wright, 74), which belies its indebtedness to the Arab medieval cuisine.

The medieval cooks knew the technique of lightening up the texture of meat patties by mixing ground meat with eggs and fermented dough. In a thirteenth-century Andalusian recipe of *asfariya* (yellowed with saffron), the patties were made of ground meat, sour dough, eggs, salt, pepper, saffron, cumin, coriander, and enough water to make mixture into soft dough, that was fried by spooning a small amount into hot oil (*Anonymous Andalusian Cookbook*, 25).

Uroug is traditionally made with fermented dough. For convenience sake people switched to flour and baking powder. Both are good, so make your pick. Although parsley is the traditional herb used, feel free to use other herbs like mint, basil, dill or chives.

They are a delicious variation on the regular burgers, and are usually prepared for supper, along with scrumptious slices of fried eggplant, and lots of fresh herbs and vegetables.

1 pound lean ground meat
1 1/2 medium onions (about 1 cup) finely chopped
1 medium tomato (about 3/4 cup) finely chopped
3/4 cup finely chopped parsley
2 eggs, beaten
1 teaspoon salt
1/2 teaspoon black pepper
1 teaspoon curry powder
1/2 teaspoon ground cumin
1/2 teaspoon coriander
1 teaspoon *baharat* (see Glossary)
1/2 teaspoon chili powder, or to taste
1/2 cup water

1 cup flour
1 teaspoon baking powder

Oil for frying
For garnish: sumac (see Glossary), slices of salad vegetables, chopped parsley, and sliced pickles

1. In a big bowl, mix meat, onion, tomato, parsley, eggs, salt, pepper, curry powder, cumin, coriander, *baharat,* chili, and water.

155

2. Add flour and baking powder. Knead lightly with the fingers of one hand for a few minutes. The final dough is to be a little on the soft side in consistency. Add a little more flour if needed. This dough is easier to handle with wet hands.

3. Heat about 1/2-inch deep oil in a medium pan. With wet hands take a piece of the dough, size of golf ball. Put on the palm of one hand, and with the other form it into an oblong patty, about 3 1/2 inches long and 1/3- inch thick (they do not have to be even in shape). Carefully slide the piece to hot oil the moment you finish shaping it. Let them cook until golden brown, turn once to brown on both sides. Remember to wet your hands while handling this meat dough to prevent it from sticking to your fingers. Drain fried pieces on white paper towels put in a colander to prevent them from getting soggy. These burgers cook very fast; the whole process of frying wouldn't take more than 15 minutes.

4. Make into sandwiches with slices of tomatoes, onion, chopped parsley, and pickles. Sprinkle with sumac for a lovely tart touch. Also delicious with slices of browned slices of eggplant and potatoes

Suggestions:

* To prepare *urug* the traditional way, substitute flour and baking powder with 1 cup fermented bread dough. You can use frozen French bread dough or pizza dough available in supermarkets. Thaw according to package directions, and mix it well with the rest of the ingredients.

* To the ingredients given above, you may also add one uncooked medium potato, peeled and shredded.

كل من ماخذ طاوتي .. يبتلي بلوة خالتي

Wiles of Women

I need to explain the meaning of two Arabic words used in the following story.
Tawa: is a loan word meaning frying pan. In standard Arabic it is *miqlat.*
Khala: is "aunt", on the mother's side, *khalti,* is "my aunt".

The story shows that despite the restrictions put on women in the past, they had their way, taking advantage of the same tactics used against them. In this story they are segregation and the veil.

They tell of a beautiful playful wife who had a lover, and wanted to enjoy the forbidden fruits of the affair in her own house. She instigated to the lover to visit her in the house, wearing women's clothes, pretending to be her *khala*. The lover started visiting her fully clad. He would be ushered to the wife's room, and the husband had no right to intrude. When the visit was over, the husband, with all due respect, would usher the *khala* back to her donkey, and escort her home. One day while the husband was on such a mission, he struck the donkey with his stick, a little bit harder than usual, urging it to speed. The poor animal made a sudden lurch that threw the *khala* overboard, on her back, her legs flailing in the air, and wide apart. The husband caught sight of something that made him suspicious, so he immediately turned back home.

When the wife looked at her husband's eyes, she instantly realized what had happened. Before he even had the time to open up his lips, she ran to him crying and wailing at to top of her voice, "My *tawa* is gone, I cannot find my *tawa*, I want my *tawa* back, I wish to God that whatever happened to *khalti* will happen to whoever has stolen my *tawa*." The neighbors heard her and rushed and gathered around her to ask her what had happened. She, between sobs and sniffs, explained that her poor *khala* got ill with a mysterious disease, which caused a hump to develop on her parts. (Zalzala, vol. 3, 82-4)

Whether the husband bought this explanation or not, I will leave it to you to figure out.

MYOB

A Sumerian proverb, cautioning against saying too much, and advising folks to mind their own business, throws light on the fly situation back then. The proverb is, "into an open mouth, a fly enters."

It seems that flies in ancient times were a source of nuisance that had to be swatted or fanned away from the leisurely upper class diners and their food. Such scenes were depicted in the excavated Mesopotamian bas reliefs and seals. Interestingly, the fans we see in these artifacts are identical with the present-day hand woven fans, made from date palm fronds.

A fly-free place was most welcome by all. In an ancient Sumerian poem, a fisherman tried to lure a fish to his bait by telling it he has built a house for it, where "no flies swarm about the liquor bar." (Kramer, *History Begins at Sumer*, 349)

The Baghdadi medieval Caliph, al-Ma'mun preferred to have his lunches early in the day for several reasons, one of which was fewer flies (al-Warraq, 18). Poets, frustrated by the annoying insistence of flies to alight on their food, composed poems in which they beseeched spiders to help them in the hunt (Al-Warraq,10). There was also some talk about a stone, which had the quality to repel flies, no fans and no fly swatters were needed. It was called the flystone, "pretty to look at, and weighing five *dirham*s." We learn this from the tenth-century judge al-Tannukhi in his anecdote of a Persian connoisseur of stones who had been on the lookout for the flystone for years and accidentally found it at a peddler's. To demonstrate its magic power, he went to a "huckster who was selling dates out of a dish, and the flies were buzzing all around." He put it on the plate and all the flies flew away, and "for a time there was not a single fly there" (al- Tannukhi, 205).

An Assyrian king, having a hurried meal.

Hanging Out in Ancient Babylon

Have you ever wondered what life looked like in ancient times, how people used to pass the time, and what the favorite hangouts for ancient Babylonian youths were? Here are some glimpses as conjectured by some of the experts in ancient history:

> Muddy in winter, dusty in summer…the roads [in ancient Babylon] wind without much planning between compact blocks of houses, blank windowless facades pierced by occasional small doors. Here and there, however, little shops grouped in bazaars or set among the houses throw a note of gaiety in the austere scenery. Like the shops of modern oriental *suq*, they consist of a showroom opening widely on to the street, and of one or several back rooms for the storage of goods. Food, clothes, rugs, pots, spices and perfumes are sold in disorderly, colorful and aromatic displays. At intervals, the red glow of a furnace in the smithy's dark workshop, the brick counter of a "restaurant" where one can purchase and eat from clay bowls onions, cucumbers, fried fish or tasty slices of grilled meat, or a small chapel advertised by terra-cotta figurines hung on either side of the doorway. To enter the courtyard, drop a handful of dates or flour on the altar and address a short prayer to the god smiling in his niche takes only a few minutes and confers long-lasting blessings.
>
> Very little traffic in the streets: they are too narrow for carts and even a donkey carrying a bulky load would obstruct most of them. Servants who go shopping, water-carriers, peddlers avoid the sun and hug the shadows of the walls, but in the early morning or late afternoon, a public writer, or a story-teller reciting [epic of] *Gilgamish* would gather small crowds around him at the crossroads, while two or three times a day, flocks of noisy children invade the streets on their way to or from one of the schools. (Roux, 182)

The most popular hangouts for the Mesopotamian juveniles were the public squares, the streets, and the boulevards. We are told that they loitered in such places "perhaps even in gangs." Juvenile rebelliousness, ungratefulness, hatred of education, and dropping out of school, were all problems the Mesopotamian parents had to deal with. We know all this from a Sumerian text, which dates back to around 3,700 BC. (Kramer, *History Begins at Sumer*, 14)

The inns and taverns of ancient times were the places to go to if the ancient youths wanted to hang out with friends or dine out. They were usually run by women, called the ale-wives. The combination of beer, sex and crime earned those ancient inns a bad reputation. Babylonian nuns, for instance, were not allowed to frequent such places. Young men were cautioned against them, such as in the Babylonian wisdom text which warns the youth not to "hasten to a banquet in the tavern lest [he] be tied up with lead-rope," or the father who tells his son, "You must check your appetite and abstain from beer" (Moor, 216-7).

Shish Burger (kebab)

Shish Burger (Kebab)

(Makes 6 kebabs)

Let me start by clearing some of the confusions the name *Kebab* sometimes causes. In Iraq, *kebab* is seasoned ground meat, skewered and grilled. In other Arab countries it is called grilled *kufta*. The Iraqi *Tikka* is cubed chunks of meat skewered and grilled, which is known as kebab all over the world.

The confusion might be traced back to the medieval times when *kebab* was used to designate both types. In the tenth-century cookbook, al-Warraq gives a *kebab* recipe in which meat was thinly sliced, and grilled, unskewered, in a dry frying pan. He called this *kebab khalis* (pure kebab, 106-7). In chapter ten, we understand that *kebab* can be made of fried fat chunks of meat, as well as *mukabbab* (seasoned ground meat formed into *kubab*, i.e. balls), which are either grilled or fried in oil (26).

Kebab (in the Iraqi sense) to the Iraqis is what hamburgers are to the Americans. Specialized restaurants are everywhere in the region. There was a time in downtown Baghdad where two major

160

Kebab restaurants competed with each other, *Tajiraan* and *Al-Shabaab*. They were like the McDonald's and the Burger King of the States. However, the best *kebab* was purchased from the small carryout restaurants at the *suq* (marketplace) next to the holy shrine of *Al-Imam- Al-Kadhum*, a descendant of the prophet Muhammad. As kids our eagerness to pay homage to the place was not motivated by our religious zeal as much as by a much more mundane desire to once again enjoy those delicious *kebab* sandwiches. They came with lots of greens, herbs, onion, pickles, and ice-cold creamy yogurt drink. We would devour those goodies in a picnic-like fashion, sitting on a spread blanket at one of the cool and breezy roofed niches surrounding the huge yard of the shrine. These sandwiches were very greasy, but who cared, they were moist, juicy, and delicious, and that was what mattered at the time. I still recall the feeling of the solidifying fat at the roof of my mouth when sipping the cold yogurt drink after having a bite of the warm *kebab* sandwich. But I guess that's the way it is with fast foods everywhere.

The following recipe is a much lighter version than the traditional *kebab*. Spices are normally kept to the minimum, but if you like them spicy, add the options, too. The way these burgers are shaped, as you'll see, will ensure even cooking inside and out, and will give them a much lighter texture than the solid patties of the regular ground meat burgers. Fat in *kebab* works the same way solid fats work for pie dough. When the solids melt by the effect of the heat, they drip leaving small cavities behind, which gives *kebab* the characteristic light texture. Eighty-per-cent lean meat would give a more genuine texture. Lean meat helped with a little olive oil would give juicier *kebab*. Traditionally skewered *kebab* is suspended on the glowing coals of a brazier, which is a very ancient gadget. The brazier in the ancient Akkadian was called "kinunu" (cf. classical Arabic *kanun*).

1 pound ground meat. The best is a combination of lamb and beef. Add 1 tablespoon olive oil if lean meat is used
1 small onion, grated
1/4 cup flour or bread crumbs
1 teaspoon salt
1/2 teaspoon black pepper

1/2 teaspoon allspice, optional
1/2 teaspoon ginger, optional
1/4 teaspoon chili pepper, optional

For assembling the sandwiches: baguette breads. Flat breads may be wrapped around the *kebab*
Onion relish (see recipe below), slices of tomato, chopped parsley, leaves of sweet basil (*rihaan*) and sliced pickles

1. In a medium bowl, combine meat, onion, flour, salt, pepper, and the optional spices, if using any. With wet fingers knead lightly to combine. Divide dough into 6 portions.

2. For shaping and grilling *kebab*, sword-like 1-inch wide skewers are traditionally used. If they are available, follow this method: Moisten skewer with water and, with wet hands, pierce one meat portion into it. Hold skewer in one hand and hug meat portion with the other, pressing and elongating with the fingers until it is about 5 to 6 inches long. Make dents by pressing between thumb and index finger, so that the shaped *kebab* will not look smooth on surface. Secure the two ends by pressing them well to the skewer. Repeat with the rest of the pieces.

3. To grill, skewers are suspended on a brazier with glowing coals. However, if this is not available, use a regular grill, but to prevent skewers from touching grid of grill, suspend them by crumbling foil paper along the two sides of the grid, about 8 inches apart. Fan *kebabs* as they cook to hasten process of cooking. (Meat might fall off skewers if not enough flour is used in meat dough, or the ends of the shaped meat dough are not well pressed to the skewer as directed above.) These *kebabs* cook fast, about 5 minutes for each side, or until nicely browned, turning once.

You may also broil them hassle-free: Suspend skewers on a baking pan, and broil until golden brown, turning once to brown both sides.

4. When *kebab* is done, hold skewer with a mittened hand, put *kebab* between a folded piece of bread placed on a plate, hold bread down with one hand and pull the skewer with the other, leaving *kebab* behind.

5. **If you do not have the traditional wide skewers, then do as follows:** Preheat broiler and wipe surface of broiling pan with cold water. Use handle of a straight dinner knife to shape kebab as follows: Hold knife blade with one hand and, with the other, moisten handle with water, and pierce a meat portion into it. Shape as described in step 2.

Carefully and swiftly take shaped piece out of the knife, by lightly hugging it between palm and fingers and pulling it out. Arrange shaped pieces on broiling pan leaving a space to allow heat to circulate all around. Broil until surface is browned, turning only once, 16 to 18 minutes.

6. To assemble the sandwich, fill a baguette bread (as long as the *kebab* piece) with one piece of *kebab*. Put some of the onion relish, slices of tomato, parsley, sweet basil, and pickles. Have it with a glass of diluted yogurt (see beverages, chapter 21).

Variation:

Kebab with chickpeas: Instead of flour use 1 cup boiled and drained chickpeas, mashed. Canned variety can be used for this purpose. Add the optional spices for this *kebab*. Follow the same instructions as above.

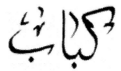

The Ancient Kebab

In the ancient Akkadian language the word "kababu" meant "to burn" or "to char," from which undoubtedly the Aramaic "kabbaba" and the Arabic *kebak* were derived. Evidently during the Middle Ages, the word *kebab* was used to designate both the skewered barbecued pieces of meat and the skewered balls of ground meat .We know this from al-Warraq's tenth-century cookbook. According to him the grilled ground meat variety is easier on the digestion than the grilled chunks of meat (26). They also used to throw into their simmering stews, spicy meatballs called, *kubab*, that were valued as dainty garnishes. It definitely was an ingenious way to use up the not so tender cuts of meat.

Kebab in all its forms was popular during the medieval times. In *Maquamat al-Hariri*, the roguish protagonist, *Abu Zeid*, playfully enumerates *kaffat al-shita'* (the seven *Kaf*s of winter, that is, the seven comforting and soul warming items. In Arabic they all begin with the k-sound, and he contends they have the power to drive away all the discomforts of the cold and soggy wintry days, and they are:

A home, a purse full of money, a brazier, a glass of wine after having *kebab*, a soft "pussy", and warm clothes (*Al-Maqama al-Kurjiya*, 147).

Onion Relish

This simple relish is delicious with all kinds of grilled meat.

Cut a medium onion into halves lengthwise, then thinly slice crosswise. Put in a small bowl, and separate the sliced layers by fluffing between the fingers. Moisten with 1 teaspoon vinegar, and sprinkle generously with sumac (see Glossary). Toss onion to let sumac coat it evenly. Set aside, covered, for 30 minutes, and use as directed.

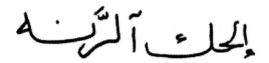

Follow the Ring
(Kebab Allure)

A penniless man was wandering in the streets of Baghdad, and happened to pass by a *kebab* vendor grilling meat. The aroma was so irresistible, that he took a bread out of his pocket, and started eating a piece of that, followed by a sniff of the *kebab* aroma. The *kebabchi* (person who sells kebab) took notice of what the man was doing, and decided to take advantage of him. He asked the poor man to pay for the *kebab* aroma. The man refused, the vendor insisted, they quarreled, and ended up at court. The judge was surprised at the greediness of the vendor and decided to teach him a lesson. He showed him two *dirhams* (metal coins), and struck one with the other, saying, "Do you hear that?" The vendor replied that it was the ring of the *dirhams*. The judge said, "That ring you've just heard is the price of the aroma of your *kebab*. Go and get it."
(Zalzala, vol. 1, 199-200)

Shish Kebab
(Tikkah)

Makes 6 servings)

"Shish kebab," as known in the rest of the Arab and the Western worlds, is called *tikka,* in Iraq. The word is nowhere mentioned in the medieval cookbooks, and there is a possibility it might have been picked up from the Hindi, sometime during the period of the British colonization at the beginning of the twentieth century. It is also possible, however, that, like *kebab,* the word had its origin in the ancient Akkadian. In the Babylonian recipe, the francolin "pie" dish, three degrees of ground grains were called for. The "sasku" and the "ziqqu" where fine enough to knead into dough. The "tiktu," on the other hand, was just blended with buttermilk and poured into the dish (Bottèro, *Mesopotamian Culinry Texts*, 14). The implication is that it was coarsely "cut" and hence cannot be kneaded. Ergo if meat is cut, it is tiktu-meat (cf. Arabic verb qata'a, and its variant, taqta').

During the medieval times the word *kebab* was used when grilled meat was cut into small pieces. For larger chunks of meat, such a whole side of a lamb (*janb*) or a whole animal, they used the generic term *shiwa'*.

Tikka is simply grilled on a brazier like *kebab,* but nothing beats *tikka* baked in the *tanour* to succulent tenderness. However, for more practical purposes, a regular grill or a hot broiler may be used. In Iraq *tikkah* is usually served as a sandwich, unlike the Iranians who prefer to serve it with rice.

3 1/2 pounds boneless leg of lamb, fat and sinews trimmed, and cut into 1 1/2 -inch cubes
For marinade:
   1 small onion, grated
   1 garlic clove, grated
   3/4 cup milk, yogurt, or buttermilk
   1/2 cup olive oil
   Juice of 1 lemon, or 1 tablespoon pomegranate syrup, see Glossary
   1 teaspoon *za'tar*, see Glossary; or thyme
   1/2 teaspoon cumin
   1/4 teaspoon black pepper, cinnamon, cardamom, each
   Crushed chili pepper, to taste
   Coarse salt
   6 small tomatoes, or 3 big ones, quartered
   6 small onions, outer skin removed
   6 hot peppers or 2 bell peppers cut into large pieces

1. Combine marinade ingredients in a glass container. Add meat cubes and let marinate, covered, for 2 hours at room temperature, or refrigerate overnight, but bring to room temperature before grilling.

2. Preheat broiler or light grill (medium-high heat).

3. Drain meat but keep marinade aside, and thread into 12 skewers. Sprinkle lightly with salt.

4. Thread tomatoes, onions, and peppers in separate skewers since they have different cooking times.

165

5. Grill or broil, brushing several times with marinade. **Discard any remaining** quantity. Turn frequently for about 12 minutes or to desired doneness. Grill or broil vegetables until tender and charred at spots.

6.Transfer to a plate, and make into sandwiches with garnishes as instructed in *Kebab* sandwich above. Or serve with vegetarian side dishes (see the following chapter). Any of the delicious sauces and relishes given in this chapter may be served with grilled meat. Condiments are recommended by the thirteenth century Baghdadi cookbook, "to cleanse the palate of greasiness, to appetize, to assist the digestion, and to stimulate the banqueter" (Arberry, 205)

Al-Hisba: the FDA of medieval Times

The *hisba* was a system devised during the Islamic Middle Ages to organize and supervise crafts, standardize and control quality of products, and protect consumer interests against fraud. The *muhtasib*, a government official, was the one who was responsible for carrying out such duties, with the help of his aids and written manuals and guidebooks. Foods sold in markets such as sausages, cured meats, and desserts were no exception. The food manuals would guide the *muhtasib* as to how to detect adulterated food by giving means and ways for doing so. The manual would describe, for instance, how to make artificial honey, *samn* (ghee, or clarified butter), vinegar, olive and sesame oil, and even how to manufacture artificial milk (Hassan and Hill, 230).

Interestingly some of the medieval cookbooks and food manuals contained recipes of "adulterated" dishes the intention of which, in all probability, was not to cheat others as much as to show one's skill in making a certain dish by substituting a key ingredient with a cheaper and commoner one. The tenth -century cookbook writer, Al-Warraq, for instance describes how to make an omelet by substituting eggs with mashed chickpeas. Al-Kindi, in his "Chemistry of Cooked Foods" tells how to make fried liver without liver, sausages without meat, and even dessert without sugar or honey. Adulterated *muh* or *mukh* (bone marrow), for instance, was made of peeled and pounded walnut, and egg white. The mixture was put in a glass, that was fitted in a pot of hot water, and cooked until set (al-Warraq, 91). Vegetarian dishes made for sick people and for Lent were also called *muzayyafa* (counterfeited) because the meat was substituted with vegetables such as truffles.

Grilled Liver, Heart, and Kidneys
(Mi'laag wa Galub wa Chalawi)

Organ meats in Iraq are valued delicacies. Vendors in street stalls and parlors make appetizing sandwiches by grilling cubed livers and hearts of lamb, sprinkled with coarse salt and pepper. They are then stuffed in freshly baked bread with some salad vegetables.

The kidneys require special preparations before grilling them. First remove the membrane surrounding then. Then halve each and remove internal fat and blood vessels. To eliminate odor, soak in salted water (1 tablespoon salt per 1 quart water) 1 to 2 hours under refrigeration. Rinse under running cold water, then dry and grill.

Locusts: Food Fit for Kings

A banquet scene in an Assyrian bas-relief depicts servants carrying choice delicacies to the royal table such as pomegranates and grasshoppers *en brochette*. The latter was very much appreciated by high and low. It was a practical means for using the locusts that invaded Mesopotamia in huge numbers. This and their allegedly pleasant taste and the relative ease with which they were caught made them a convenient source of food. They were made into pickles, and fermented into sauce called in the Akkadian, "siqqu."

The tradition continued up until the medieval times and possibly later. In the tenth-century Baghdadi cookbook there is a recipes for pickling locusts. According to the instructions, after purifying the caught locusts from the dead ones, they are immersed in salted water and kept there until they suffocate. Then they are put in a big earthenware vessel in layers, sprinkling each layer with ground coriander, some other spices, and plenty of salt. Enough water is poured to submerge the locusts. The opening of the vessel is sealed with clay to keep mixture from getting into contact with air, and is set aside for a while (al-Warraq, 102).

Beef Tongue Sandwich
(Sandaweach Lisaan)

Beef tongue makes exquisite sandwiches, juicier and more delicate in taste than beef. Unfortunately not many people know how to cook it or serve it, and quite often than not, it ends up being boiled to toughness, and cut into cubes to be picked up with toothpicks as an appetizer. It deserves a better treatment, and here is how to do it.

1 medium beef tongue
Salt and flour
For Marinade:
1/4 cup olive oil
1/4 cup vinegar
1 teaspoon *za'tar*, **or thyme (see Glossary)**
1/4 teaspoon black pepper, marjoram, caraway seeds, ground ginger, each

1 onion pierced with 6 to 8 whole cloves
2 t o 3 pods cardamom
1 bay leaf

1 teaspoon salt

1. Strike tongue on a hard surface several times until it looks limp and a little longer. This is done to break the muscles. Wash it very well, rub it with salt and flour, and wash it again. Mix marinade ingredients in a glass bowl, and let tongue marinate in it, overnight, turning several times.

2. Put tongue in a big pot with marinade, and rest of ingredients except for salt. Cover tongue by 4 to 5 inches of cold water. Bring to a quick boil, skimming as needed. Lower heat to medium- low and let simmer, covered, until it feels tender when pierced with a fork, about 2 hours. Add salt about 10 minutes before it is done.

5. Take tongue out of the liquid, and let it cool completely. Peel off skin and refrigerate for at least 2 hours. With a thin sharp knife cut it into thin slices and make into sandwiches, with salad vegetables, pickles and olives.

Breaded "Mountain Oysters" (Beidh Ghanam)

Euphemistically known as lamb's eggs in Iraq, these delicacies are usually nibbled on as a snack, not more than 3 to 4 pieces per serving. The way to prepare them is to cut each "egg" into halves, remove the outer skin, and wash the pieces very well. Roll them in seasoned breadcrumbs, and brown them in hot oil. Drain them on a white paper towel, and serve immediately.

This delicacy is known in the States as "Mountain Oyster Fry" and is prepared pretty much the same way, and added into scrambled eggs. According to the food writer M.F.K. Fisher they are believed to be "aphrodisiac and a restorative," adding that she likes to eat them but "never sought them out either on a fixed hour or for a fixed purpose, other than plain pleasurable hunger" (130).

An Assyrian king, having a hurried meal.

169

A Sandwich for Thought

Some claim that John Montague, fourth Earl of Sandwich, invented the sandwich, about two hundred years ago, so that he could eat a meal without having to leave the gambling table. However, judging from frequent references and descriptions of sandwiches in medieval Arabic literature, and recipes given in their cookbooks, the origin of the sandwiches can be pushed back to the eighth or ninth centuries, the beginning of the golden age of the Baghdadi cuisine.

One of the earliest descriptions of a sandwich can be found in al-Mas'udi's tenth-century *Muruj al-Dhahab* (meadows of gold). It is a poem by ninth-century famous poet Ibn al-Rumi (d. 896), which describes the elaborate construction of a *wast* (plural, *awsat*, literally, in the middle). The sandwich calls for two fine quality pithy flat breads, from which the top crusts are removed. The artistically arranged stuffing was put between those two pieces of bread, much like loaf sandwiches of modern times. It is a roast chicken sandwich, garnished with almonds, walnuts, cheese, olives, mint, tarragon, sliced eggs, and salt. The invitation at last was to,

> With watchful eye examine it anon,
> And let thy gaze with pleasure feast thereon;
> But when full satisfied hath grown thy sight,
> Replace the loaf, and eat with appetite;
> With gusto chew, and let thy teeth be filled:
> Destroy in haste the structure thou didst build.
>
> (Arberry, 24-25)

During the medieval times, sandwiches made part of a long list of *bawarid* (cold) or *nawashif* (dry) dishes, served before the main hot meal. They were also consumed as fast food and hurried meals, purchased from the food markets. Around the tenth century at least, specific terms were used describing specific forms of sandwiches. What al-Rumi has just described was called *wast* (plural *awsat*), and was made of bread baked in ovens other than *tannour*. They were rather thick and pithy (*mulabab*) in texture, and when used for sandwiches were slit open horizontally, pith removed, and were filled, and hence the name *wast* (in the middle).

They even made special pocket bread for sandwiches. To make these they used a metal device called *ward mushabbak* (latticed ring) with a domed top and slightly raised sides that was put inside the bread dough, when shaping it. When baked, the washer was removed, leaving behind a cavity in the middle. To serve *awsat*, the filled bread was sliced into fingers or squares or whatever.

Shata'ir or *wast mashtour* (split) were open-faced sandwiches, such as the one made by the prince of epicures, Ibrahim Ibn al-Mahdi. He scraped the top crust and edges of the bread, then spread (*shattara*) the surface with a kind of fermented sauce, that can be replaced sometimes with tahini, analogous to peanut butter of today. It was glazed with walnut oil and toasted on the brazier, then spread with mashed boiled egg yolks, with an optional sprinkle of grated cheese, "this will make it delicious" al-Warraq, adds (58).

As for the *bazmaward,* it was made by spreading filling on a thin flat bread and rolling it tightly. To serve, it was sliced into discs and arranged on a platter. A gorgeous *bazmaward* sandwich roll was made by preparing a mixture of uncooked ground meat, spices, garlic, onion, and eggs. It was put in a thin layer, on a *riqaq* bread that was already spread with a *tharb* (caul fat, the transparent membrane that surrounds stomach). Five whole boiled and shelled eggs were arranged lengthwise in a single file. The *riqaq* was rolled around them. The roll was then secured by winding a piece of clean intestine around it, and was baked in the *tannour.* To serve, it was sliced and presented with condiments (al-Warraq, 57).

Al-Warraq was absolutely consistent in using the word *bazmaward* in relation to sandwiches made from *riqaq* breads, filled, rolled tightly, then sliced into discs. Obviously, the word describes the shape of the sandwich, more than anything else. In his dessert recipe for *khabees* with nuts and sugar, he said the mixture should be spread out flat with a rolling pin, and "rolled the way *bazmaward* is rolled," and is to be "cut the way *bazmaward* is cut" (256). Therefore, I am convinced that the word is not a combination of *bazm* + award (something that brings joy in a party) as Arberry contends (202). It is actually from *buzma* + *ward.* The root verb, *z-m-m* and all its variants convey the action of fastening and tightening. *Al-bazeem* is a strip made of date palm fronds used to tie vegetable bundles. *Ibzeem* is the belt buckle, which keeps the belt tight and in place. In the traditional old-fashioned colloquial Iraqi, *buzma* is the cuff of a garment sleeve, as opposed to loose sleeves. *Al-bazma* also means *al-akla,* food eaten in a small quantity, weighing 30 *dirhams* (3 ounces), to be had in one bite or morsel. That might well explain why the sandwich was also called *muyassar wa muhanna* (easy to eat, see al-Feiruz Abadi, *Al-Qamus al-Muheet*). As for the second part of the word, *ward,* I take it as a description of the sandwich slices which were round like the *ward* (ring or washer).

By the time we come to the thirteenth century as represented by al-Baghdadi's cookbook, the terms *wast* and *bazmaward* seem to have been used interchangeably. The same thing happened to our modern sandwich terminology. The sandwich was to begin with called *laffa,* because traditionally flat *tannour* bread was spread with a filling and rolled (*laffa*) exactly like the *bazmaward.* The term *laffa* persisted even when the sandwich was no longer a roll (*laffa*) but just an ordinary bread slit open and filled like the *awsat.*

171

Shredded Roasted Meat (Gyro Sandwiches)
(Sandaweech Guss)

The medieval Baghdadi cooks knew how to grill meat the rotisserie way, or as they called it *kardhabaj* or *kardanaj*. They skewered chunks of meat or whole chickens, suspended them on open fire, and let them rotate until meat grilled to succulence and almost fell off the bones. It was more like a picnic food where they enjoyed the sight of the revolving meat and the aromas it spreads all around.

The earliest recipes for preparing meat this way occur in al-Warraq's tenth-century cookbook (234). There were not enough directions on how the meat was served, but we do know that the diners normally had it with bread and vinegar-based relishes and condiments, called *kawamikh* and *sibagh*. We are also certain that when serving grilled meat, at least in the food markets, they sliced the meat into fine shreds, served it on *riqaq* (thin and flat) bread, and sprinkled it with sumac water, for zest. (For more details see Box, Street Food in Medieval Baghdad, p.147)

Today, sandwiches of shredded meat of rotisseried lamb, beef and chicken are known in the entire Mediterranean-Middle-Eastern region, albeit served under different names, and there are some differences in preparing them, too. The Greek **Gyro** is a sandwich filled with shaved layers of marinated compressed ground meat, and is drizzled with sour cream sauce. In Turkey it is **Domer Kebab,** whereas it is **Shawirma** in Arab countries surrounding Iraq, and *Guss* (cut) in Iraq.

In the Arab countries it is prepared from thin slices of lamb and/or beef, marinated in oil, vinegar, onion, garlic, bay leaves with some spices and herbs. They are then threaded into a long heavy spit, alternating 3 layers of meat with 1 layer of fat, and arranging them so that they form a conical shape. The bottom layer is kept at place by a special clasp, and the top is garnished with green pepper and tomatoes. The spit is then fixed in a vertical rotisserie, gas or electric. As the meat revolves and roasts, the done parts are thinly shaved or sliced diagonally into a container, using a sharp long knife. The shredded meat is immediately made into sandwiches by wrapping it in flat bread, after drizzling it with tahini sauce. In Iraq, *samoun* (see chapter 1, on breads) is usually used in filling this sandwich.

There is no reason why you cannot enjoy this delicious sandwich in the convenience of your home. The following are down sized, practical recipes that can be prepared without the rotisserie.

Homemade Guss (Gyro) Sandwiches

(Makes 10 sandwiches)

How to Prepare the Meat Method #1:

About 2 pounds lean roast beef, or trimmed lamb, or skinless and boneless chicken, trimmed

For marinade:
>   **1/4 cup vinegar**
>   **4 tablespoons olive oil**
>   **1/2 medium onion, grated**
>   **1 garlic clove, grated**
>   **1 teaspoon salt**
>   **1/4 teaspoon black pepper**
>   **1 teaspoon *baharat* (see Glossary)**
>   **1/2 teaspoon curry powder**
>   **1/2 teaspoon ground cardamom**
>   **1/2 teaspoon whole aniseeds or fennel**
>   **2 bay leaves**
>   **1/2 teaspoon thyme or *za'atar* (see Glossary)**
>   **4 tablespoons Worcestershire sauce**
>
>   **1 tablespoon prepared mustard**
>   **2 tablespoons ketchup**
>   **1/4 teaspoon hot red pepper flakes**

1. Using a sharp knife cut beef crosswise into 1/4-inch thick slices. Then cut each portion into thin strips, as thin as possible. If using chicken cut it into thin strips. It would help a lot if you let pieces of meat solidify a little in the freezer before cutting.

2. In a big bowl, mix ingredients for marinade. Add cut pieces of meat and mix well. Let marinade for about 1 hour at room temperature.

3. Put meat and marinade in a big skillet, or divide between 2 skillets, and cook on high heat, folding and stirring frequently, until all liquid evaporates, and meat starts to nicely brown, about 10 minutes. Discard bay leaves. Alternatively, you can spread meat mixture in a thin layer on a cookie sheet, and bake in a hot oven 450 to 500 degrees F., turning several times while baking, until liquid evaporates, and meat is nicely browned.

How to Prepare the Meat Method #2:

Although the following method is a little more of a hassle than the first method, it nevertheless yields a more authentic texture.

1.Using the same amount and cut of meat given in Method #1, slice meat into thin steaks, and marinate in:

> **3/4 cup buttermilk, or diluted yogurt**
> **2 tablespoons olive oil**
> **1 teaspoon grated lemon rind**

Let meat marinate for 1 hour at room temperature, or refrigerate overnight, but bring to room temperature before using.

2. Stack the slices in threes on a broiling pan to allow liquid to drip down. Discard remaining marinade. Cover loosely with foil paper, and roast in a hot oven until just done, about 20 minutes. Meat does not have to be thoroughly cooked, since it is going to be further cooked.

3. When cool enough to handle, cut stacks of meat diagonally into very thin slices.

4. Mix meat with the marinade ingredients given in Method #1, and immediately sauté in a big skillet, folding frequently until moisture evaporates and meat begins to nicely brown, about 7 minutes.

To Assemble the Sandwich

Get ready:

> **10 pieces of bread, either *sammun*, big sausage rolls, small pita or lawash bread (see chapter 1, on breads)**
> **Thin slices of tomatoes**
> **Chopped parsley**
> **Chopped pickles, optional**
> **Thinly sliced onion mixed with some *sumac***
> **Tahini Sauce, or sour cream sauce, see recipes below**

1. If using *sammun* or the sausage rolls, make a slash along one side and scoop out some of the pith inside, if needed. Fill bread with a suitable amount of prepared meat and cover with slices of tomato. Sprinkle with chopped parsley and pickles, and onion. Drizzle with either of the suggested sauces.

2. To make a neat mess-free bundle of a sandwich using pita bread or lawash, place bread half way up on a triangle of foil paper. Put prepared meat on one half of the bread and cover with slices of tomato. Sprinkle with chopped parsley and pickles, and onion. Drizzle with either of the sauces. Fold the other half of bread on the filling, wrap foil around to prevent it from opening up, and tuck in the bottom of the paper very well, to prevent sauce from dripping down while eating.

Tahini Sauce:

In a medium bowl mix the following ingredients until smooth:

1/2 cup tahini (see Glossary)
Juice of 1 lemon (1/4 cup)
1/4 cup cold water
1 garlic clove, grated
1/4 teaspoon salt

Sour Cream sauce:

In a medium bowl mix the following ingredients until smooth:

1/2 cup sour cream, low fat may be used
1/2 cup cucumber, finely chopped
3 tablespoons tahini
1 garlic clove, grated
1/4 teaspoon salt

Mustard and Vinegar Relish
(Khal wa Khardal)

This relish is an adaptation of a medieval condiment usually served with grilled meat, from al-Baghdadi's thirteenth-century cookbook (Arberry, 207).

1/3 cup whole almonds, toasted and cooled
1 cup chopped parsley
2 cloves garlic, coarsely chopped
1/4 cup olive oil

1/4 cup vinegar
2 tablespoons prepared mustard
1 teaspoon thyme or *za'tar*, see Glossary
1/2 teaspoon salt
1/4 teaspoon black pepper
1/2 teaspoon chili pepper if hot sauce is desired

1. Put almonds, parsley and garlic in a blender or food processor. Blend, adding oil gradually until mixture is well puréed.

2. Add vinegar, mustard, thyme, salt, pepper, and chili, if used. Pulse mixture for a few seconds to blend.
    Use as relish with all kinds of grilled meat.

Eggplant Relish
(Buran)

This relish is named after *Buran*, the wife of the Abbasid Caliph al-Ma'moun (ninth century AD). As given in the medieval recipe it was served with meatballs. Here is the original version:

"Take eggplant, and boil lightly in water and salt, then take out and dry for an hour. Fry this in fresh sesame oil until cooked: peel, put into a dish or a large cup, and beat well with a ladle. Add a little salt and dry coriander. Take some yogurt, mix in garlic, pour over the eggplant, and mix together well." (Arberry, 191)

Following is a modified version to suit the cooking methods of modern times:

1 cup yogurt, drained for 3 hours at room temperature, or overnight under refrigeration, use cheese cloth or a coffee filter
1 big eggplant (about 1 pound) pricked and grilled or baked until cooked and skin charred at some places. Skin and purée

2 tablespoons olive oil
1 clove garlic, grated
1 tablespoon lemon juice
1/2 teaspoon salt
1/4 teaspoon black pepper, cumin, coriander, each
Chili pepper, to taste

Mix all the ingredients and use as a bed for grilled meat.

Cooked Pepper Sauce

1 small onion, finely chopped
2 cloves garlic, grated
2 tablespoons olive oil
1 teaspoon flour
1/3 cup hot water
1/4 teaspoon salt
1/2 teaspoon cumin
6fresh medium hot chilies, grilled or broiled until scorched at some places, then skinned and finely chopped (handle with gloved hands)

1. In a medium skillet sauté onion and garlic in oil until just softened, about 4 minutes.

2. Sprinkle flour on onion and stir briefly.

3. Gradually add 1/3 cup hot water, and stir well. Let mixture simmer on low heat until it is thickened, about 3 minutes.

4. Add salt, cumin, and prepared chilies, and stir until just heated through.

If you do not have the time to grill the pepper, you can just chop it fine, with red bell pepper, and crushed tomatoes. Add mixture in step 3 to allow vegetables to cook a little.

Burger with Vegetables, 155

CHAPTER SIX
SNACKS, SANDWICHES, AND SIDE DISHES
(Vegetarian)

CHAPTER SIX

SNACKS, SANDWICHES, AND SIDE DISHES

وجبات خفيفة (نباتية)

(Vegetarian)

Up until recently, people did not think much of meatless dishes, a legacy we inherited from our ancestors. In the medieval menu there was a whole category of vegetarian dishes known as *muzawwarat*, meaning counterfeited or adulterated dishes. They were usually recommended for sick people, and Christians during Lent, and in this case were sometimes referred to as *ruhbaniyat* (from *rahib*, monk). But to eat a vegetarian dish as an appetizer or a snack was perfectly acceptable. In this case, instead of *muzawarat*, they called them *bawarid* (cold dishes). Vegetables, such as eggplant, gourd, or fava beans, were simply cooked and drizzled with vinegar and olive oil, or mixed with yogurt, or simmered with other ingredients, with lots of onion and oil. Sometimes simple *ausat* or *bazmaward* (sandwiches) were made with cheese and vegetables, or thick yogurt seasoned with herbs and oil.

We still make, more or less, the same side dishes, albeit with less oil, and occasionally enjoy simple snacks. A winter favorite is a dip of *rashi w'dibis* (tahini and date syrup) served with warm fresh bread, or even a small head of romaine lettuce. In the summertime, a snack could be fresh dates, cucumber and yogurt.

Toasted mixed nuts, such as pistachios, almonds, peanuts, chick-peas, hazelnuts, and toasted pumpkin and water melon seeds, collectively called *karazaat*, is the snack for family gatherings, and movie theatres. I particularly remember how we used to anxiously await the exciting chasing scenes in cowboy movies. Not that we were particularly interested in the scenes themselves as much as to hearken to the increasing tempo of the seed cracking caused by the mounting excitement of the audience, whose eyes were glued to the screen. Indeed, those mixed nuts are always associated with fun and happy times. That's why people on mourning are not supposed to be seen eating them in public, except perhaps for the almonds, believed to be beneficial for the digestion. *Lhoom*, which is ground toasted chickpeas or sesame seeds mixed with sugar, makes a satisfactory snack for children, especially those with poor appetites. The medieval counterpart of this was the travelers' victual, *suweiq*, made of toasted grains, ground with almonds and sugar.

Back in the old days when families used to gather around braziers in the cold of winter, walnuts in the shell and chestnuts were roasted amongst the glowing coals. But it was not unusual for some chestnuts to burst all of a sudden, and scatter in smithereens all over the place.

Falafel

(Makes 30 patties)

Falafel is a Middle-Eastern dish well known and loved in most parts of the world. Basically it is ground beans mixed with herbs and spices, shaped into balls or small patties, and deep-fried. Some people use chickpeas only, but using a blend of chickpeas and fava beans would yield falafel that is less dry in texture.

1 cup shelled dry fava beans, washed, soaked overnight and drained,
1 cup whole chick-peas, washed, soaked overnight, and drained
1 cup parsley, finely chopped
1/4 cup green coriander (cilantro), finely chopped
1/4 cup fresh mint, finely chopped, or 1 tablespoon dried mint
1/4 cup fresh dill, finely chopped, or 1 tablespoon, dried dill weed
3 to 4 garlic cloves, grated
1/4 cup grated onion
2 tablespoons za'atar
1 teaspoon ground coriander
1 teaspoon ground cumin
1/2 teaspoon salt
1/4 teaspoon black pepper
1/2 teaspoon chili powder, or to taste
1 teaspoon baking soda
3 tablespoons flour or bread crumbs

Bread crumbs for coating, optional
Oil for deep frying

1. In a food processor or blender, finely grind shelled fava beans and chickpeas.

2. In a big bowl mix ground beans with parsley, mint, dill, garlic, onion, coriander, cumin, salt, pepper, chili, baking soda, and flour. Knead briefly to combine. Let rest for 60 minutes.

3. With wet hands, take walnut-size portions, and form into rounded discs about 2 inches in diameter. Traditional falafil are shaped into balls, but I find rounded discs cook more evenly inside and out. Dip in breadcrumbs if using any. Arrange on a tray in one layer. Allow to rest for 15 minutes.

4. Deep fry in **hot** oil until golden brown, 4 to 5 minutes. (Hot oil will prevent patties from absorbing too much oil)

5. Drain on paper towels put on a rack or a colander to prevent pieces from getting soggy. Serve as appetizers by themselves, or make them into sandwiches as follows:

Fill a warm freshly baked *sammoun* (see chapter 1, on breads) or similar bread with two or three pieces of falafel. Add chopped parsley, and salad vegetables. Drizzle with **tahini sauce** (for recipe see previous chapter, page, 175).

If using pita or *lawash* bread, put bread on a triangle of foil paper, half way up. Put 2 to three pieces of falafel on one half of the bread. Cover with chopped salad vegetables, and chopped parsley. Drizzle with tahini sauce, and fold the other half of bread on the filling. Wrap with the paper, and tuck in the bottom to prevent sauce from dripping.

Baked Falafel

(Makes 18 bars)

To give falafel a lighter touch, you may bake them, and save yourself the trouble of frying. After soaking beans as directed above, do not grind them, but boil them separately by covering them by about 1 1/2 to 2 inches of cold water. Bring them to a quick boil, then reduce heat and simmer until tender. Drain excess liquid, and mash with a potato masher. Mix beans with the rest of the ingredients as directed in Falafel recipe. Grease and coat with breadcrumbs, a 12-by-8-inch baking pan. Spread mixture and brush surface with olive oil, and sprinkle with breadcrumbs.

Bake in a preheated oven at 375 degrees F. for about 20 minutes or until golden brown. Cut into bars, and arrange on a platter with chopped vegetables, accompanied with a bowl of **tahini sauce** as a dip (see p.175 for recipe).

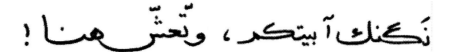

Nibble at Home and Join Me for Supper

A man visited a friend who happened to be having his supper at the time. The friend invited him to join in, but he apologized, saying he is full, he had already had supper at home. The friend insisted that at least he could nibble with him. So the man joined in, and "nibbled" so earnestly that he almost finished the food. The friend could not help but say, "Next time, my friend, nibble at home and join me for supper."
(Zalzala, vol. 3, 321-2)

Lentil Patties
(Kuftat Adas)

(Makes 12 patties)

If you are in the mood for a quick up-lifting sandwich or snack, this is the recipe for you, since it requires no beforehand soaking or preparation. The fried patties will develop a crisp shell, whereas the inside will be melt-in-mouth soft.

1/2 cup shelled lentils, picked over, washed and drained
1 cup water
2 tablespoons rice flour (see Glossary)

1 medium tomato, finely chopped (about 1/2 cup)
1 small onion, finely chopped (about 1/3 cup)
1/4 cup finely chopped parsley
1/4 cup currants or raisins
1/2 teaspoon *baharat* (see Glossary)
1/2 teaspoon ground cumin
1/2 teaspoon salt
1/4 teaspoon black pepper, chili pepper, each

1 egg, beaten
Bread crumbs for coating
Oil for frying

1. In a small pot add water to lentils, and bring to a boil, then reduce heat and simmer on low heat until lentils are cooked and all moisture evaporates, stirring occasionally, about 15 minutes. Add rice flour, and mix and mash with lentils. Set aside until cool enough to handle.

2. Transfer to bowl, and add tomatoes, onion, parsley, currants, *baharat*, cumin, salt, black pepper, and chili. Mix well, and with moist fingers form into well-rounded 12 patties.

3. Dip patties in beaten egg, and then roll in breadcrumbs. Fry in about 1-inch-deep hot oil, until golden brown, turning once to brown the other side. They will cook very fast, so you need to watch them.

4. Drain pieces on white paper towels put on a rack or a colander to prevent them from getting soggy. Serve warm as a sandwich with vegetables and **tahini sauce** (p.175) like in falafel sandwiches, or arrange them on a platter with sliced salad vegetables, and a bowl of tahini sauce as a dip.

Lentil and Rice Patties
(Kuftat Adas wa Timman)

(Makes 24 patties)

Prepared in a jiffy, this vegetarian dish makes a healthy and tasty snack. It can also be served with meat dishes, on the side, instead of mashed potatoes, for instance.

1 cup red shelled lentils, picked over, washed and drained
3/4 cup rice, washed and drained (jasmine rice is good)
2 1/2 cups water

1 medium onion finely chopped.
2 tablespoons olive oil
1 1/2 tablespoon tomato paste
1/4 cup currants or raisins

1/2 cup chopped green onion, with the green stalks
3/4 cup parsley, finely chopped
1/4 cup lemon juice
3/4 teaspoon salt
1/4 teaspoon black pepper
1 teaspoon ground cumin
1/4 teaspoon chili pepper

1/2 cup sesame seeds, dry toasted and coarsely ground

1. Put lentils, rice and water in a medium pot, and bring to a boil, about 5 minutes. Reduce heat, and let grains simmer for 15 to 20 minutes, or until they are cooked, folding several times while simmering. Set aside until cool enough to handle.

2. In a small skillet sauté onion in oil until it starts to brown, about 5 minutes. Add tomato paste and raisins, and stir together for a few minutes.

4. Transfer cooked lentils and rice to a big bowl. Mix in onion mixture. Also add green onion, parsley, lemon juice, salt, pepper, cumin, and chili. Knead briefly.

5. Make into 24 patties or egg-like shapes with two pointed ends (like rugby balls).

6. Roll pieces in prepared sesame, and arrange them on a serving platter.
Serve with sliced vegetables, and Tahini Sauce as a dip (p.175).

Boiled Eggs with Fresh Black-eyed Peas
(A Sandwich for the Nostalgic)
(Abyadh wa Baydh)

This is a simple sandwich that could only have been created by a people to whom everything and anything may be eligible for a filling. It is basically a flat white bread (this is the *abyadh*), rolled around a filling of sliced boiled eggs (the *beidh*) along with simmered fresh black-eyed peas in the pod, salad vegetables and pickles. Here is a description of how it was served by vendors, as seen through the eyes of a foreign visitor, in the late 1950's AD:

> In Baghdad, there is a sort of public smorgasbord called the *abiadh al bedh*, a moving stand piled unbelievably high with hard-cooked eggs, pickles, beetroot, tomatoes, spring onions, and other appetizers. It is gaily decorated and makes a colorful sight on the street corners. A short-order snack from this Oriental hot dog stand is called a *laffa*. The proprietor slices anything you want and rolls it up in a piece of *khubz* or Arabic bread for you to munch as you explore Baghdad. (Rowland, 141-2)

Turnips simmered in Date Syrup

186

Turnips Simmered in Date Syrup
(Maye' al-Shalgham)

(Makes 4 servings)

This is another street-food snack simmered to tenderness, and hence the epithet *maye'* (melting). The small amount of date syrup traditionally used in this snack helps give the turnips a delicately sweet taste. Molasses will give almost the same delicious taste and lovely hue.

2 pounds turnips
1/4 cup date syrup or molasses
1/4 teaspoon salt

Wash turnips, cut off both ends, and cut each horizontally, but not all the way through, leave the halves intact. Put turnips, molasses or date syrup, and salt in a medium pot and cover them by about 2 inches cold water. Bring to a boil, then lower heat and let them simmer until tender, about 30 minutes.
Serve warm sprinkled with a dash of coarse salt, if wished.

Sandwiches of Truffles and Eggs
(Chima wa Beidh)

The early Mesopotamians knew the poisonous and the edible mushrooms as well as the truffles, which are still found in the desert area in the west. In the early Babylonian times they were regarded as a great delicacy, and were dispatched to the king by the basketful.

From the medieval sources we learn they knew the white as well as the black variety, which were usually cooked with meat, aromatics and eggs. They were sometimes used with other ingredients for stuffing kid-goats, or as garnishes. They were particularly useful for Christians during Lent, as they substituted meat in what they called the *muzzawarat* (counterfeit) dishes. They were fried, grilled and made into *kebab*.

The truffle season is very short in the region. They appear only during the short season of spring, the season of showers, thunder and lightning. It was believed that thunder and lightning had a hand in the formation of these delicacies. They actually play an indirect role-- when it thunders, it rains, and when it rains in the desert, the force of the falling water will reveal the truffles buried in the sand. They are then picked up by the Bedouins and sold in the markets of the big cities.

Nowadays they are usually simmered in salted water, cut into slices, and made into sandwiches along with slices of boiled eggs, tomatoes, and pickles. They are also chopped and cooked with rice (see chapter 8, on rice).

187

Iraqi Omelet with Potatoes and Herbs
(Makhlama bil Poteita)

(Makes 6 servings)

This is a delicious vegetarian variation on the traditional Iraqi omelet that is usually cooked with meat (for a recipe, see chapter 5).

2 cups cubed potatoes, fresh or frozen
2 tablespoons oil
1 medium onion, chopped
1/2 teaspoon curry powder
1/4 teaspoon turmeric
1 teaspoon salt
1/4 teaspoon black pepper
1 medium tomato, chopped
1/2 cup chopped parsley
1/4 cup fresh dill, chopped, or 1 tablespoon dried dill weed
1/2 cup fresh mint leaves, chopped
6 eggs
Chili powder to taste
For garnish: slices of lemon, and chopped parsley

1. Spread potato cubes on a baking dish, spray with oil, and broil or bake in a hot oven, turning once to allow both sides to brown, about 15 minutes (or brown in oil in a skillet).

2. In a big non-stick skillet, heat oil and sauté onion with curry powder and turmeric, until onion is transparent, about 7 minutes. Add potatoes, salt, pepper, tomatoes, parsley, dill and mint. Mix well and let cook for a few minutes.

3. Level surface with the back of a spoon, and make six indentations. Break eggs into dents. You may leave eggs whole, sunny-side-up, or zigzag surface with a knife to break yolks and let them mingle slightly with whites.

4. Lower heat to low, and let eggs cook slowly, covered, until they are just set, about 5 minutes. Do not overcook, otherwise eggs will develop a leathery texture.
   Or it can be cooked in the oven. Simply transfer potato mixture to a greased baking pan, big enough to spread in about 1/2-inch layer. Then add eggs as described above, and bake in a preheated oven at 400 degrees F. until set for about 10 minutes. No need to cover.

5. Cut into wedges and serve as a sandwich, with chopped parsley and a squeeze of lemon, along with other sliced salad vegetables of your choice.

Spinach Omelet
(Makhlama bil Sbenagh)

(Makes 6 servings)

This is another beautiful variation on the traditional Iraqi omelet, *makhlama*, normally cooked with meat.

2 tablespoons oil
1 medium onion, chopped
1/2 teaspoon curry powder
1/4 teaspoon turmeric

1 pound chopped fresh spinach or one 10-ounce frozen chopped spinach.
1/4 cup parsley, chopped
1/4 cup fresh dill, chopped, or 1 tablespoon dried dill weed
3/4 teaspoon salt
1/4 teaspoon black pepper
6 eggs
Chili powder to taste

1. In a big non-stick skillet heat oil and sauté onion with curry powder and turmeric, about 5 minutes.

2. Add spinach, parsley, dill, salt and pepper. Stir gently until most of moisture evaporates.

3. Level surface with the back of a spoon, and make six indentations. Break eggs into dents. You may leave eggs whole, sunny-side-up, or zigzag surface with a knife to break yolks and let them mingle slightly with the whites.

4. Lower heat to low, and let eggs cook slowly, covered, until they are just set, about 5 minutes. Do not overcook, otherwise eggs will develop a leathery texture.

Or it can be cooked in the oven. Simply transfer spinach mixture to a greased baking pan, big enough to spread in about 1/2-inch layer. Then add eggs as described above, and bake in a preheated oven at 400 degrees F. until set, about 10 minutes. No need to cover.

Eyes of Eggs

In the medieval Baghdadi cookbooks, poached eggs were added in the last stage of cooking some of the dishes. They resembled what people in the West call "eggs sunny side up." The Baghdadi writers called them "eyes of eggs," and sometimes compared them to cow's eyes (al-Warraq, 179). Today, we still call our fried eggs prepared this way, *bedh ein* (eyes of eggs).

Baked Spinach
(Sbenagh bil Firin)

(Makes 6 servings)

This is for a lazy-day snack, simple and yet so delicious. It is a variation on the traditional Spinach Omelet.

Two 10-ounce packages frozen spinach, thawed, squeeze out extra moisture
1/4 cup fresh dill, chopped or 1 tablespoon dried dill weed
2 medium potatoes, boiled and mashed (about 1 cup)

4 eggs, beaten
1/2 cup crumbled feta cheese
1/4 cup grated Romano cheese
1 teaspoon salt
1/2 teaspoon black pepper
1/4 teaspoon chili pepper, or to taste

1/4 cup bread crumbs
2 tablespoons olive oil
Preheat the oven to 375 degrees F.

1. Mix spinach, dill and mashed potatoes. Spread in a 7-by-9-inch greased glass, baking dish.

2. Mix eggs, cheeses, salt, black pepper and chili pepper. Spread over spinach mixture.

3. Sprinkle breadcrumbs on surface, and drizzle with oil.

4. Bake in a preheated oven at 375 degrees F. 15 to 20 minutes or until set and top is golden. Allow to cool for 10 minutes. Cut into squares and serve warm.

Spinach Simmered in Olive Oil
(Sbenagh bil Zeit)

(Makes 4 servings)

This makes a fast and simple but elegant side dish, to be had warm or cold with meat dishes.

1 medium onion, finely chopped
1/4 cup olive oil
1/2 teaspoon salt
1/2 teaspoon black pepper
1/4 teaspoon chili pepper
1/2 teaspoon ground coriander, optional
2 pounds spinach, washed and coarsely chopped, or two 10-ounce packages frozen spinach
Juice of one lemon (about 1/4 cup)

1. In a medium heavy pot, sauté onion in olive oil until transparent. Add salt, black pepper, chili, and coriander, if used. Stir together for a few seconds.

2. Add spinach. Bring to a quick boil, then lower heat, and allow spinach to simmer until most of the liquid evaporates, stirring occasionally, about 10 minutes.

3. Spread on a platter, and drizzle with lemon juice.

Green Beans in Vinegar
(Fasoulya Khadhra bil Khal)

(Makes 4 servings)

The *bawarid* (cold) vegetarian dishes were an important component in the Baghdadi medieval meal. The vegetables were simply cooked and drizzled with oil and vinegar, and garnished with chopped parsley and mint, as for instance in al-Warraq's tenth-century recipe of *loubyabiya* (bean dish, 169).
Following is how we prepare this dish today:

2 cups green beans, boiled and drained
1 onion, finely chopped
1 clove garlic, grated
1/4 cup parsley, chopped
2 tablespoons olive oil
4 tablespoons vinegar
Salt and pepper to taste

Mix all ingredients together in a bowl, and refrigerate for an hour before serving. Use as a side dish with meat dishes

Baked Green Beans
(Fasoulya Khadhra bil Firin)

(Makes 6 servings)

This is a simple and easy way to prepare beans. It can be served as a side dish or by itself as a snack.

1 pound green beans, both ends cut off. Leave whole or cut into 2-inch long pieces, and then boil and drain. (Two drained 14.5-ounce canned green beans can be substituted)

2 eggs, beaten
3/4 cup milk
1/2 teaspoon salt
1/4 teaspoon black pepper

1/2 cup mozzarella cheese
1/4 cup feta cheese, crumbled, or grated Romano cheese
2 tablespoons bread crumbs

Preheat oven to 375 degrees F.

1. Put beans in an 8-by-6-inch baking pan.

2. Whisk eggs, milk, salt and pepper. Pour on beans.

3. Sprinkle cheeses on bean mixture, and sprinkle breadcrumbs all over the surface.

4. Bake in a preheated oven at 375 degrees F. for 20 to 25 minutes, or until casserole is set, and top is golden brown in patches.

Divide into 6 portions and serve with meat dishes, if wished.

Green Beans Simmered in Olive Oil
(Fasoulya Bil Zeit)

(Makes 4 servings)

Simmering fresh green beans in olive oil will bring out their delicate taste.

1 medium onion, coarsely chopped
1/4 cup olive oil
1 pound fresh green beans, both ends cut off. Leave whole or cut into 2-inch long pieces
2 to 5 cloves garlic, whole and unskinned
1/2 teaspoon salt
1/4 teaspoon black pepper

1/2 teaspoon ground ginger
1 teaspoon sugar
2 medium tomatoes, coarsely chopped; or one 15-ounce can diced tomatoes, do not drain

Juice of 1 lemon (about 1/4 cup)
1/4 cup chopped parsley

For garnish: Lemon slices

1. In a medium heavy pot, sauté onion in olive oil, until it starts to change color, about 7 minutes.

2. Add prepared beans and stir for 5 minutes.

3. Add garlic, salt, pepper, ginger, sugar, and tomatoes. Pour in enough hot water just to cover the mixture, about 2 cups. Bring to a quick boil, then lower heat and let simmer gently for about 30 minutes, or until beans are tender, and sauce is noticeably reduced.

4. Five minutes before beans are done, add lemon juice and parsley,

5. Squeeze pulp out of the cooked garlic cloves, and mash and mix it with the beans.

Serve hot or cold, garnished with lemon slices. Drizzle with yogurt, if wished.

Fresh Fava Beans Simmered in Olive Oil
(Bagilla Khadhra bil Zeit)

(Makes 4 servings)

The season for fresh fava beans is short, so make the most of it while you can, otherwise the frozen variety or even frozen lima beans can be substituted. When fresh fava beans are still tender and young at the beginning of their season, use the whole pod with the beans inside.

1 medium onion, coarsely chopped
1/4 cup olive oil
3 cups fresh fava beans, jacket and skin removed, or 3 cups frozen green lima beans, no need to skin. (Or 1 pound tender and young fresh fava beans, just cut off both ends and pull off the strings from both sides if there are any)

2 cloves garlic, whole and unskinned

1 teaspoon sugar
3/4 teaspoon salt
1/2 teaspoon black pepper, cumin, coriander, each
1/4 teaspoon chili powder, or to taste

1/4 cup lemon juice
1/4 cup fresh dill, chopped, or 1 tablespoon dried dill weed

For yogurt-dill sauce:
1 cup yogurt
2 tablespoons fresh dill, chopped or 1 teaspoon dried dill weed
1 clove garlic, grated
1/4 teaspoon salt

1. In a medium heavy pot, sauté onion in oil until soft, about 5 minutes.

2. Add prepared fava beans and garlic, and stir for a few minutes.

3. Stir in sugar, salt, black pepper, cumin, coriander, and chili. Add hot water just enough to cover the vegetables. Bring to a quick boil, then reduce heat to low, and let simmer, covered, until beans are tender, about 20 minutes.

4. Add lemon juice and dill 5 minutes before beans are done.

5. Stir together sauce ingredients until smooth, and serve beans hot or cold, drizzled with yogurt sauce.

White Beans Simmered in Olive Oil
(Fasoulya Yabsa bil Zeit)

(Makes 6 servings)

Although this is commonly served as a side dish, I find it quite satisfying as a light meal by itself, served with warm bread.

1 cup white beans, washed, soaked overnight, and drained
2 cloves garlic, whole and unskinned

1 medium onion, coarsely chopped
1/4 cup olive oil

2 medium carrots, chopped
2 medium tomatoes, chopped
1 tablespoon tomato paste
1 teaspoon salt
1/2 teaspoon sugar
1/2 teaspoon black pepper
1/2 teaspoon ground ginger
1/4 teaspoon chili pepper, or to taste

1/4 cup parsley, chopped
Juice of 1 lemon (about 1/4 cup)

1. In a medium pot, combine beans and garlic. Cover with cold water by an inch. Bring to a boil then reduce heat to low and simmer, covered, until beans are just done, about 30 minutes.

2. In a small skillet sauté onion in oil until soft, about 5 minutes. Add to the beans pot along with carrots, tomatoes, tomato paste, salt, sugar, pepper, ginger and chili. Continue simmering, until beans are tender, and little liquid is left, about 20 minutes.

3. Add parsley and lemon juice 5 minutes before finished cooking time.

Serve hot or cold

Fried Breaded Cauliflower
(Qirnabeet Maqli)

(Makes 6 servings)

It is not easy to make people get excited about the humble cauliflower, neither in the past when they thought it caused gargles in the stomach (al-Warraq, 56) nor in the present. However, preparing it this way does elevate it a lot. The egg-and-crumb coating makes it deliciously crispy from the outside, leaving the inside soft and succulent. If you want to avoid frying, simply brush or spray them with oil and bake them in a hot oven.

1 small head of cauliflower, broken into florets
2 eggs, beaten
Breadcrumbs seasoned with salt, chili, ground ginger, and black pepper (1/4 teaspoon of each with 1 cup breadcrumbs)

Oil for frying

1. Cook cauliflower in salted water until just done. Drain and let cool slightly.

2. Dip florets in beaten eggs, then coat with breadcrumbs.

3. Fry in 2-inch-deep hot oil until golden brown turning once to allow to brown on all sides, a few minutes. Drain on a white paper towel put on a colander or a rack to prevent pieces from getting soggy.

Serve hot as a snack, or with meat dishes.

Cauliflower Casserole
(Tabsi al-Qirnabeet)

(Makes 6 servings)

Cauliflower here is made succulent by baking it in a light and tasty white sauce. Chopped cabbage may be easily substituted.

2 tablespoons oil
1 medium onion, chopped
1/2 cup flour
4 1/2 cups milk
1/2 cup cheddar cheese, shredded (2 ounces)

1 teaspoon salt
1/2 teaspoon black pepper
1/2 teaspoon ginger powder
1/4 teaspoon chili powder

1 medium head of cauliflower, broken into florets, and partially boiled in salted water, and drained
2 cups elbow macaroni, cooked al dente (1 cup uncooked)

1/3 cup breadcrumbs
2 tablespoons oil

Preheat oven to 400 degrees F.

1. In a medium heavy pot, sauté onion in oil, until it softens, about 5 minutes. Stir in flour and brown lightly.

2. Gradually add milk, stirring with a wire whisk to prevent sauce from getting lumpy. Add cheese, salt, pepper, ginger and chili. Stir over medium-high heat until sauce is smooth and starts to thicken, about 5 minutes.

3. Spread cauliflower florets and macaroni in a 9-by-11-inch casserole.

5. Pour sauce all over cauliflower and macaroni. There should be enough sauce to cover both. Add a little milk if needed. Sprinkle surface with breadcrumbs and drizzle with oil.

6. Bake in a preheated oven at 400 degrees F. for 25 to 30 minutes, or until sauce bubbles, and top is golden brown.
Serve warm, as a side dish, or as a snack by itself.

Macaroni and Cheese Casserole
(Qalab Ma'caroni bil-Jibin)

(Makes 4 servings)

It seems that every country has its own version of this classic dish, but what distinguishes one from the other is the kind of cheese used. The Iraqi variety is made with the local hard white cheese known as *jibin Akrad* (the Kurds' cheese). A mixture of Romano cheese and mozzarella would give almost the same taste and texture. I was first acquainted with the dish as a sixth-grader in a home economics class in one of the elementary schools in Baghdad, and it was love at first bite.

1/2 cup Romano cheese, grated
8 ounces ziti or elbow macaroni, cooked al dente according to package directions, and drained (1 1/2 cups uncooked)
1/2 cup mozzarella cheese, shredded
3/4 cup parsley, chopped

197

1/4 cup fresh dill, chopped, or 1 tablespoon dried dill weed, optional
1/4 cup fresh mint, chopped, or 1 teaspoon dried mint, optional

4 eggs
2 cups milk
1/2 teaspoon salt
1/4 teaspoon black pepper

Preheat oven to 400 degrees F.

1. In a greased 10-by-12-inch casserole layer third of the macaroni, cheese, and herbs in the order mentioned. Repeat the layering two more times.

2. In a medium bowl, whisk eggs, milk, salt and pepper. Pour it all over the layers. There should bee enough liquid to cover macaroni and cheese. If needed add a little more milk.

3. Bake in a preheated oven, at 400 degrees F. for the first 10 minutes. Then reduce heat to 375 degrees F., and bake for 20 more minutes, or until it is set and top is golden brown.
Serve as side dish, or as a light lunch or snack with salad.

Pancakes of Golden Vermicelli Noodles
(Aqras al-Sha'riyya)

(Makes 6 pancakes)

Fine vermicelli noodles made fabulous crisp pancakes, fit for formal occasions.

6 ounces vermicelli noodle balls, keep the balls whole
1/2 teaspoon turmeric

1/2 cup green onion, finely chopped, or regular onion, grated
1 clove garlic, grated
1/4 cup fresh sweet or hot pepper, finely diced, optional
1 medium tomato, finely diced
1/2 cup parsley, finely chopped
1/4 cup fresh dill, chopped, or 1 tablespoon dried dill weed
1/2 teaspoon salt
1/4 teaspoon black pepper
1/2 cup Romano cheese, grated
1/2 cup mozzarella cheese, shredded
4 eggs, beaten

Oil for shallow frying
Thick yogurt for garnish, optional

1.Put noodles and turmeric in a medium pot of boiling salted water. Let cook gently for about 5 minutes or until al dente, stirring frequently but gently to encourage the balls to unravel. Watch noodles carefully lest they should overcook. Drain noodles and allow to cool.

2. In a big bowl mix noodles with the rest of ingredients (except for oil and garnish).

3. Heat about 3 tablespoons oil in a non-stick skillet, and with the help of two spoons put some of the noodle mixture in the skillet, enough to make discs about 3 inches in diameter and 1/3-inch thick. Flatten and shape the pieces with the back of a spoon. Let brown on one side, then carefully flip with a pancake turner to brown the other side. Transfer pieces to a plate, and keep warm until other batches are browned. Drizzle with yogurt, if wished.

These pancakes are very nice with grilled meat dishes. They can also be enjoyed by themselves as a snack.

Eggplant Simmered in Olive Oil
(Betinjan bil-Zeit)

(Makes 4 servings)

This is one of the many scrumptious ways in which eggplant finds itself manifested on a Middle-Eastern table. Traditionally small eggplants are cooked with lots of olive oil. The following recipe is a slimmed down version that calls for the more readily available large eggplants. However, if you are fortunate enough to have access to the small eggplant variety, use them, by all means.

The Baghdadi medieval cooks were still a little suspicious of eggplant. Writing in the tenth century, al-Warraq believes that the worst thing to do is to eat it raw, next comes roasting it, and the lesser of the evils is frying it (55). Their main concern was how to rid them of their unpleasant bitter after taste. The surest method was to parboil, and drain them first. Sometimes it was just soaked in salted water, for a while (al-Warraq, 115) as we do today. Then it was simply fried, and served with vinegar sauce (made of vinegar, oil and garlic) which they believed made it easier to digest. Apparently this method worked well enough to warrant some sexy analogies on the part of the eggplant eaters, such as comparing it to saliva exchanged by kissing lovers (al-Warraq, 116)

Eggplant was also an important item in the medieval *bawarid* (cold) dishes that were prepared with lots of oil and vinegar, reminiscent of today's cold vegetable dishes, such as the following:

> **1 large eggplant (about 1 1/2 pounds), or 8 small eggplants**
> **1 big onion, thinly sliced or coarsely chopped**
> **1/4 cup olive oil**
>
> **2 cloves garlic, thinly sliced lengthwise**
> **2 medium tomatoes, chopped**
> **1/4 cup parsley, chopped**
> **1/4 cup fresh mint, chopped, or 1 teaspoon dried mint, optional**
> **1 teaspoon salt**
> **1/2 teaspoon black pepper**
> **1 teaspoon sugar**

For garnish: One lemon and one tomato thinly sliced
Preheat oven to350 degrees F.

1.Cut off stem of the eggplant, and peel lengthwise so as to give it striped look. Cut it into 1/4-inch slices crosswise and soak in salted warm water for 30 minutes. Drain and fry pieces in a small amount of oil in a skillet. Alternatively, arrange them on a cookie sheet in one layer and spray them with oil, and bake or broil them in a hot oven until golden, turning once, about 20 minutes.

If small eggplants are used just cut off the long stems but keep the heads. Peel eggplants in a striped fashion, and make a slash along each eggplant. Fry or bake or broil them as suggested above, and enlarge the slashes with your fingers, so that each eggplant looks like a boat.

2. In a medium skillet sauté onion in oil until transparent, about 5 minutes. Add garlic, tomatoes, parsley, mint, if using any, salt, pepper and sugar. Cook for about 3 minutes on high heat, folding frequently to mix well.

3. In a 10-by-8 glass baking pan (or any other pan of similar capacity) arrange half the eggplant slices in the bottom, cover with half of the onion mixture. Repeat the layering. If small eggplants are used, arrange them in a single layer in the baking pan, and stuff the enlarged slashes with as much of the onion mixture as they could hold. Scatter the remaining mixture around the eggplants. Decorate with lemon and tomato slices.

4. Add enough hot water to barely reach to three fourths the depth of the vegetables.

5. Bake in a preheated oven at 350 degrees F. for about 90 minutes, or until only 2 to 3 tablespoons of the liquid are left, and the eggplant is tender. Do not rush it let it take its time.

Serve warm or chilled with grilled meat, and cooked bulgar (for recipe see chapter 9, on grains)

Variation:
Substitute zucchini for the eggplant, and follow instructions given above.

Eggplant Sandwich
(Sandaweech al-Betinjan)

(Makes 6 sandwiches)

Eggplant makes easy but bewitchingly delightful sandwiches. The only drawback is that when fried it could get too oily. To prevent it from soaking up oil like a sponge, sprinkle slices with a little flour before frying them. This will help block most of the pores. Our medieval ancestors used to do the same thing.

1 medium eggplant
About 3/4 cup flour for coating, preferably whole wheat

Oil for frying

For assembling sandwiches:
   2 tomatoes, thickly sliced
   1 clove garlic, grated
   1/4 teaspoon chili pepper
   1/4 cup chopped parsley
   2 tablespoons lemon juice, or vinegar
   1/2 cup drained yogurt, (for instructions see chapter 2, on dairy products), optional

1. Cut off stem of eggplant, and peel lengthwise to give it a striped look. Cut into 2 parts crosswise, and then cut each part into 1/4-inch thick slices lengthwise.

2. Soak pieces in salted warm water, and set aside for 30 minutes. Top with a plate to keep them submerged. This is important because it will prevent eggplant from soaking up lots of oil when frying.

3. Drain eggplant pieces, and coat with flour on all sides to prevent eggplant from absorbing excess oil. Fry pieces in 1/2 inch deep oil until golden brown, turning once, about 7 minutes. Drain on a rack or in a colander to prevent fried pieces from getting soggy.

4. Brown tomato slices in a small amount of oil.

5. Arrange eggplant pieces on a big platter in one layer. Arrange fried tomato slices on top. Sprinkle garlic, chili pepper, parsley, and lemon juice or vinegar. Dot with drained yogurt, if wished.

To make into sandwiches, fill a piece of bread with some of the layered vegetables. Or serve the arranged platter as a side dish by itself.

Fried Eggplant Delights
(Betinjan Maqli)

(Makes 5 to 6 servings)

As in the previous recipe, the following way of preparing and frying the eggplant yields crispy pieces that are allowed to absorb as little as possible of the oil. The medieval cooks used to dip prepared eggplant slices in a batter composed of white flour, eggs, and spices, and then fry them (*Anonymous Andalusian Cookbook*, 103)

>**1 medium eggplant**
>**2 eggs, beaten**
>**1 1/4 cups bread crumbs seasoned with 1/2 teaspoon salt, 1/4 teaspoon black pepper, and 1/4 teaspoon garlic powder**
>
>**Oil for frying**

For garnish:
>**1/4 cup parsley chopped**
>**1 medium tomato, thinly sliced**
>**Fresh hot chilies, broiled or grilled, and then skinned**

Yogurt, optional

1. Cut off stem of eggplant, and peel lengthwise to give it a striped look. Cut into 2 parts crosswise, and then cut each part into 1/4-inch thick slices lengthwise.

2. Soak pieces in salted warm water, and set aside for 30 minutes. Top with a plate to keep them submerged. This is important because it will prevent eggplant from soaking up lots of oil when frying.

3. Drain eggplant pieces, and dip each in beaten eggs, then coat with seasoned breadcrumbs. When both sides are well coated, press each piece down against the crumbs in the plate with your palm, and then turn it and press down on the other side.

3. Fry pieces in 1/2-inch oil on high to medium high heat until golden brown, turning only once, about 5 minutes. Drain fried pieces on a rack or a colander to keep them crisp.

4. Arrange pieces on a platter, garnished with parsley, sliced tomato, and skinned chilies. Drizzle with yogurt, if wished

Herbed Zucchini Pancakes
(Aqras al-Shijar)

(Makes 12 pieces)

Zucchini (gourd) is as versatile as eggplant, and in the Baghdadi medieval recipes, it was always given as a substitute for it. The zucchini pancakes are a byproduct, so to speak, of the many stuffed dishes that require the vegetables to be cored out. Instead of throwing the pulp away, it is made into delicious pancakes, to be enjoyed as a snack, or as a side dish. The same thing can be done with eggplant. *The Anonymous Andalusian Cookbook*, for instance, called for a mixture of mashed eggplant, breadcrumbs, eggs and spices to be formed into patties and fried (104).

3 medium zucchinis (about 1 1/2 pounds), grated
1 teaspoon salt

1/2 cup green onion, finely chopped, or white onion, grated
1 clove garlic, grated
1/4 cup fresh dill, chopped, or 1 tablespoon dried dill weed
1/4 cup parsley, chopped
1/2 cup Romano cheese, grated
1/4 cup flour, or bread crumbs
4 eggs, beaten
1 teaspoon cumin
1 teaspoon baking powder
1/4 teaspoon black pepper
1/4 teaspoon nutmeg
1/4 to 1/2 teaspoon chili pepper, optional

Oil for shallow frying

1. In a colander set over a bowl, toss zucchini with salt. Set a plate directly on zucchini, and weigh it down with a heavy pot or a bowl filled with water. Let it drain for 30 minutes. Remove any excess moisture by squeezing out, using hands.

2. Put zucchini in a big bowl, and add the rest of the ingredients, except for the oil and yogurt. Mix well.

3. Heat about 3 tablespoons oil in a medium non-stick skillet. Drop about 2 tablespoons of mixture into skillet. With a pancake turner flatten into 1/4-inch thick pancakes. Cook 2 to 3 minutes on each side, or until golden and cooked through. Fry in batches, adding oil and adjusting heat as needed. Transfer pancakes to a plate, keep warm.

Sprinkle with salt, if wished and serve warm with meat dishes, or as a snack

Baked Zucchini Squares
(Shijar bil-Firin)

(Makes 8 squares)

If you want to avoid the hassle of frying the traditional zucchini pancakes, you can enjoy them baked, but the recipe is to be adjusted as follows:

3 medium zucchinis (about 1 1/2 pounds), grated
1 teaspoon salt

1 medium onion, chopped
2 tablespoons oil
1/4 cup fresh dill or 1 tablespoon dried dill weed
1/4 cup chopped parsley
4 eggs, beaten
1/2 cup Romano cheese, grated
1/4 teaspoon black pepper
1/4 teaspoon nutmeg
1 teaspoon cumin
1 teaspoon baking powder
3/4 cup bread crumbs, divided
Preheat oven to 400 degrees F.

1. Put grated zucchini in a colander fitted into a bowl. Toss it with salt. Set a plate directly on the zucchini, and weigh it down with a heavy pot or a bowl filled with water. Let drain for 30 minutes. Squeeze out excess moisture by squeezing using the hands.

2. Sauté onion in oil until it softens, about 5 minutes.

3. In a big bowl mix zucchini, sautéed onion, with the rest of the ingredients, using only **1/2 cup** of the breadcrumbs.

4. Generously spray or grease a 12-by-8-inch baking pan, and coat with breadcrumbs.

5. Spread zucchini mixture evenly. Sprinkle surface with **1/4 cup** breadcrumbs. Drizzle or spray surface with oil.

6. Bake in a preheated oven at 400 degrees F. for 35 to 40, or until mixture is set and top is golden brown. Let cool in pan for 10 minutes, then cut into 8 squares.

Baked Green Beans, 192

Fresh Fava Beans Simmered in Olive Oil, 195

CHAPTER SEVEN
STEWS

CHAPTER SEVEN

STEWS

مَرَق

(Marga)

A friend of mine never tires of telling us how she once tried to break away from the routine of preparing the familiar dish of *timman wa marag* (rice and stew) for her family of four. She cooked juicy creamed chops with a side of French fries, instead. "They ate these, all right," she says chuckling, but then came the inevitable question, "Okay, now, where is our *timman wa marag*?" This shows how futile it is to attempt to depart from that routine that has been ingrained in our eating habits, and sustained us for more than five thousand years (For history of stew see Introduction). Indeed, why try to do so in the first place? *Timman wa marag* is delicious, healthy, easy, convenient, and economic.

Marga or *marag* is basically vegetables and meat simmered in tomato sauce. The stew is customarily served in a bowl, to be spooned and mixed with rice or sometimes bulgar, with plenty of salad or green onion, fresh herbs, greens, and sometimes spicy condiments such as home made pickles and pickled mango (*'anba*). Such a combination of nutrients makes a reasonably balanced meal. Besides, it can easily be converted into a low-fat meal, or even into a vegetarian dish by passing the meat. Another advantage is that it provides the body with the much-needed liquids. Taken on a regular basis and as a way of dietary life style it is a sure guard against "irregularity."

Marga is an economical dish since it uses a relatively small amount of meat. Big families with a limited budget daily prepare it for lunch, the main meal of the day. Variety is achieved by using different kinds of vegetables, cuts of meat, and rice. No wonder it is a staple and a way of life deeply rooted in our eating habits.

Stew is easy to assemble and does not need much attention on the part of the cook. It can be prepared ahead of time, and some of the stews even improve when refrigerated overnight and then heated, such as okra and white bean stew. With rice and stew nothing is wasted, leftovers are sometimes heated together, with broken pieces of bread to absorb the moisture of the stew. It is not too spicy. In fact spices are either not used at all as in okra stew, or are kept to a minimum, which might explain why we can have this food almost every day. However, for the lovers of spicy food, there is always the complementary bowl of spicy pickles, or pickled mangos.

Tomato the Great

Tomatoes are an essential component in the modern Iraqi cuisine, as they are in the rest of the Mediterranean countries. It is not known exactly when the tomatoes made their appearance in the Middle East, but broadly speaking that must have happened in the sixteenth century. The tomatoes were brought from Peru or Mexico to Europe after 1522, and the earliest record of their consumption in Seville was in 1608. They revolutionized some basic cooking techniques in the Arab cuisine that were prevalent at the time. It replaced most of the thickening, souring, and coloring agents used in making the stews such the nuts, the sour juices of fruits and vegetables, and saffron. According to modern dietary findings, consuming tomatoes in all its forms, especially cooked, is a healthy choice. It is maintained that what makes tomatoes red is a phytochemical called lycopene, which has significant antioxidant qualities. Scientists have found that cooking tomatoes makes them even more beneficial, for heat breaks down the fibrous material within the produce, and makes it release the full potential of the lycopene. Tomatoes also contain folic acid, vitamin C, potassium and beta carotene.It has also been found that the pale yellow jelly-like substance surrounding the tomato seeds might help prevent clots from forming.

So in the light of modern scientific discoveries, serving the traditional dish of rice and stew garnished with meat and served with lots of fresh vegetables almost every day is not a bad idea after all.

Note:

When using tomato paste it is always a good idea (but not a must)to let the tomato paste sauté for about 30 seconds or so in oil. This will give a pleasant depth to its taste, and help get rid of the raw metallic taste of the paste. When you sauté the chopped onion for the stew, add the tomato paste about a minute before onion is done, and stir and mix the two, until tomato paste starts to emit a pleasant caramelized aroma.

Suggested Cuts of Meat for Stews

The traditional cuts of meat usually used for stew are lamb or veal chops or shanks. The advantage of shanks is that they have that flavorful rich marrow, which will give the stew a rich flavor. With lamb shanks you need to have the pieces chopped crosswise into halves before cooking.

The secret in cooking shanks lies in prolonged simmering. First brown them quickly in a small amount of oil for about 10 minutes, turning them to allow juices to seal in on all sides. Pour a small amount of **hot** water, just enough to cover the pieces. Cold water may cause the meat to toughen. Bring to a quick boil, skimming as needed, then lower heat to low, and let it simmer, covered, 1 hour to 1 1/2 hours, or until meat is tender to the touch. The remaining liquid, if any, could be used as part of the liquid added to the stew. Because lamb shanks cannot be completely trimmed of all the fat, it is a good idea to refrigerate them after cooking, to solidify and remove the animal fat.

*Lamb or veal chops are cooked like the shanks, but they need to be trimmed of the fat, and they require a little less cooking time. Indeed, any lamb cuts with bone and meat will do.

*Other cuts or kinds of meat can be substituted such as:
-cubes of trimmed lamb or beef-stew, or lean ground meat.
-Broiled or baked small meatballs, known as *ras al-asfour*, (recipe p.133) can be added to the stew about 15 minutes before it is done.
-Skinned and trimmed chicken pieces such as thighs, drum sticks, tender loins or breasts can be substituted in some of the stews. Sauté them in a small amount of oil, and let them simmer, covered, in the liquid they emit, until they are tender. Add a little more hot water if needed. As a general rule, the breasts cook faster than the thighs.

Mention of the best variety of meat to be used will be made in the relevant stew recipes. **Besides, you can always omit the meat altogether and turn the stews into equally delicious vegetarian dishes.**

Because this kind of food is sometimes spoiled by overcooking, the method given in the following stew recipes is to let meat fully cook before adding vegetables, which normally require less time for cooking.

Okra Stew
(Margat Bamya)

(Makes 4 servings)

In the modern Iraqi cuisine okra the queen of all stews. It is surprising, however, that the Baghdadi medieval cookbooks do not make a single mention of it, even though there is evidence that it grew there and was used in cooking (see Burton, vol. 15, 243). Perhaps it was considered too humble or too slimy a vegetable to be included in the menu of the haute cuisine with which these books mostly dealt.

We know, for sure, that the Ancient Mesopotamians knew this vegetable. They called it "ubanu," (finger, see Campbell, 39. Compare the other English name for okra, "lady's fingers"). Some people today pronounce the vegetable as *banya* instead of *bamya*, which is closer to the original name.

It is a summer vegetable, and before the season is over people usually freeze big quantities to use all winter long. In Iraq, *bamya* stew is cooked at least once a week. In pre-freezer times people used to thread it into strings and dry it.

What puts off many people from dealing with *bamya* is the sticky substance that comes out when it is cut open. It would give the stew a glue-like consistency if not properly treated. The traditional way to get rid of it is to cut off both ends, making sure at least some of the holes show, and wash okras under running water for a long time. I find this tedious and time consuming. **A better way to deal with it is to cut off both ends making sure at least some of the holes show, and wash it briefly. Then partially cook it in boiling water for no more than 5 minutes. Strain it and use it immediately. Alternatively, let it cool and freeze it for future use.**

When buying okras from the market, choose medium-sized ones, about 2 inches long. Choose the ones that do not sound crunchy when gently squeezed between the fingers.

> **4 pieces meat, traditional cuts used are trimmed chops, any cuts with meat and bone may be substituted**
> **1 tablespoon oil**
> **5 to 6 cloves garlic, whole and unskinned**
>
> **3 heaping tablespoons tomato paste (one 6-ounce can) diluted in 4 cups hot water, or one 15-ounce can tomato sauce diluted in 3 1/2 cups hot water, or 4 1/2 cups canned tomato juice.**
> **1 pound okra, prepared as described above (in bold type)**
> **1 1/2 teaspoons salt**
> **1/2 teaspoon sugar**
> **2 tablespoons lemon juice, or to taste**
> **2 to 3 whole fresh small hot peppers, for lovers of hot food**

1. In a medium heavy pot, (4-quart), sauté meat pieces in oil, until browned on all sides, about 10 minutes. Add 1 cup hot water, or just enough to barely cover the meat. Bring pot to a quick boil, skimming as needed, then let meat simmer gently, covered, on low heat, until meat is tender, and moisture evaporates, about 45 minutes. If meat is tender and there is still some liquid in pot, strain it and use it as part of liquid required in the recipe.

2. Add garlic cloves, and stir with the meat on medium heat to allow them to brown slightly.

3. Stir in diluted tomato paste or sauce or juice, and prepared okra. If frozen okra is used, just rinse it under running water and add it. Add salt, sugar, lemon juice, and hot peppers, if using any. Bring pot to a quick boil, skimming as needed, then reduce heat to medium-low, and, covered, simmer gently until okra is done and sauce is delicately rich and thickened. Stir stew gently 2 to 3 times while simmering to prevent ingredients from sticking to the bottom of the pot, 35 to 40 minutes. Adjust salt and lemon juice if needed.

4. Serve stew with white plain rice, or bulgar, and slices of onion and green pepper. The fun part in this dish is eating the cooked whole garlic cloves. There should be at least 1 clove for each serving. To eat it, hold the whole garlic clove between your thumb and index finger and squeeze out the soft pulp into your mouth, discard the skin.

Another popular way of serving okra stew is having it the *tashreeb* way, i.e. putting bite-size pieces of Iraqi flat bread or the Arabic bread (see bread chapter) in a deep dish, and drenching the bread pieces with the stew liquid. Arrange meat pieces and garlic on top.

Stew of White Beans
(Margat Fasoulya Yabsa)

(Makes 4 servings)

Fasoulya yabsa (dried beans) was a staple pulse in ancient Mesopotamia as it still is today. It is one of the winter favorite dishes. It is so popular that it is sometimes just referred to as *yabsa* (dried). Navy beans or great northern beans can be used for this stew, but I personally prefer the navy beans, for they taste as though more flavor is packed into them than the other larger varieties.

2 cups white beans, picked over, washed, and soaked overnight, then drained

> **4 pieces of meat, best choice are trimmed lamb or veal shanks, 2 to 2 1/2 pounds. All other options in Suggested Cuts, above, will do**
> **1 tablespoon oil**
> **1 medium onion, coarsely chopped**

> **3 heaping tablespoons tomato paste (one 6-ounce can) diluted in a little hot water, or one 15-ounce can tomato sauce**
> **2 tablespoons lemon juice, or to taste**
> **1 1/2 teaspoons salt**
> **1/4 teaspoon black pepper**
> **2 to 3 fresh small hot peppers for lovers of hot food**

1. In a medium pot cover beans by 2 inches of cold water. Bring to a quick boil, skimming as needed. Lower heat and let it cook gently, partially covered, just until beans are almost tender, about 45 minutes. Do not overcook, since they will be further cooked in the stew.

2. In another medium heavy 4-quart pot prepare and cook meat as directed in Suggested Cuts above and Okra Stew, step 1.

3. Add onion to meat and stir until onion is transparent, about 5 minutes.

4. Stir in diluted tomato paste or sauce, lemon juice, salt, pepper, and hot peppers if using any.

5. Add beans with liquid in which they were boiled, and stir. There should be enough liquid to cover meat and beans by about an inch. Add more hot water if needed. Bring to a quick boil, skimming as needed. Lower heat to medium-low, and let simmer gently, covered, until meat and beans are tender and sauce is nicely thickened, about 45 minutes. Stir stew carefully 2 to 3 times while simmering. Adjust seasoning and lemon juice if needed. Do not let beans get mushy.

This stew goes well with all kinds of rice, but especially rice and noodles. Serve it with salad and pickles.

Variations:

* When you get to step 5, in addition to beans, add 1 chopped carrot, 1/2 teaspoon coriander, 1/2 teaspoon cumin, and 3 garlic cloves, grated. Garnish with chopped parsley.

* Try the stew with other kinds of dried beans.

Short Cut:

Instead of dried white beans, use two 15-ounce cans great northern beans, rinsed and drained. Add them in step 5.

يَشرب الماى بنص الأكل

Eat All You Can

A peasant came to Baghdad once for some business, and he had only two *rupies* (Ottoman money) on him. He passed by a restaurant where he saw displayed, aromatic dishes of rice, many kinds of stew, and lots of vegetable and meat dishes. It was lunchtime and he was starving, so he desperately tried to strike a deal with the owner, saying, "How much will you charge for feeding me until I am full?"

It was a new business and the owner wanted to attract clientele to his place. He figured out that all the money he had put into that food was not more than four *rupies*, and calculated that the man could not possibly eat more than half his food. So he said, "Two *rupies*!" The peasant gladly accepted, gave him the money, rolled up his sleeves, and fell to the food eating and demanding more and more, until he devoured more than half the food in the whole restaurant. The owner, as a last resort, suggested that perhaps he might be interested in drinking some water. The peasant said, "No thanks, I am not used to drinking water before my stomach is half full." The owner gave him back his money, and asked him to leave.

(Zalzala, vol. 3, 440-1)

Spinach Stew
(Margat Sbenagh)

(Makes 4 servings)

Spinach in Iraq is an exclusively winter vegetable. Spinach stew in winter is like okra stew in summer--it is prepared almost once a week. No need for Popeye the Sailor to promote it. It is one of the few stews that are traditionally cooked without tomatoes, although some people like to cook it red. I personally prefer it green and serve it with yellow saffron rice (see chapter 8). Traditionally, herbs collectively called *ala* are used to give spinach stew a distinctive appetizing aroma. They are chopped parsley, dill, leeks, fresh cilantro, and *halba* which is green fenugreek, using the leaves only, see Glossary.

4 pieces of meat, the best cuts are trimmed veal or lamb shanks, but also see other options given in Suggested Cuts, above
1 tablespoon oil
1 medium onion, coarsely chopped or thinly sliced

2 pounds fresh spinach, finely chopped, or two 10-ounce packages chopped frozen spinach
1 bunch fresh coriander (cilantro), finely chopped
1/4 cup parsley, chopped
1/4 cup fresh dill, chopped, or 1 tablespoon dried dill weed
1/2 cup split chickpeas, soaked for 30 minutes, or 1cup frozen or canned black-eyed peas, or 1/2 cup dried black-eyed peas, soaked overnight
3 heaping tablespoons tomato paste (one 6-ounce can) diluted in a little water, or one 15-ounce tomato sauce (optional)
1 1/2 teaspoons salt
1/4 teaspoon black pepper
1 teaspoon ground coriander
1/2 teaspoon ground cumin
1 tablespoon prepared *noomi Basrah* (see Glossary)
1/4 cup prunes or apricots, halved, optional
2 to 3 fresh whole small hot peppers for lovers of hot food

1. Prepare meat as given in Suggested Cuts and Okra stew, step 1, above.

2. Add onion to meat, and stir until onion is transparent, about 5 minutes.

3. Stir in spinach and rest of ingredients. Fold mixture for a few minutes, or until greens are wilted.
4. Add enough hot water to cover meat and spinach by about one inch, about 3 cups. Stir very well and bring to a quick boil, skimming as needed. Lower heat to medium-low, and allow stew to simmer, until beans or peas are tender, and sauce is nicely thickened, about 40 minutes. Sauce in this stew is normally allowed to reduce more than in the other kinds. Stir 2 to 3 times while simmering, and adjust salt and lemon as needed,

This stew goes very well with all kinds of rice. Have it with turnip pickles (see chapter 20) and spring onions.

Variations:

Spinach -Lentil Stew:
Instead of beans, use 1 cup red, shelled lentils, picked over, washed and drained, no need to soak. Follow same instructions given above.

Spinach-Potato Stew:
Add 1 cup cubed potatoes in step 2.

* Swiss chard Stew:*
Replace spinach with an equal amount of chopped Swiss chard and follow the same directions.

Green Beans Stew
(Marqat Fasoulya khadhra)

(Makes 4 servings)

This is another refreshing winter stew that smells so good. Canned green beans can be used to save time, but I do not recommend the frozen variety, for freezing, somehow, makes beans rather stringy in texture.

4 pieces of meat. Any of the cuts given in Suggested Cuts, above, will do
1 tablespoon oil
1 medium onion, finely sliced
3 cloves garlic, sliced lengthwise

1 pound green beans, washed, both ends cut off, and cut into 2-inch pieces; or one 15-ounce can green beans, drained
3 heaping tablespoons tomato paste (one 6-ounce can) diluted in a little hot water, or one 15-ounce can tomato sauce
2 tablespoons lemon juice
1 1/2 teaspoons salt
1/4 teaspoon black pepper
1/4 teaspoon chili powder, optional
1/4 teaspoon ground ginger

1. Prepare meat as directed in Suggested Cuts, and Okra Stew, step 1, above.

2. While meat is simmering, put prepared beans in another pot and pour enough hot water to just cover them. Bring to a boil, then reduce heat to medium, and let cook gently until they start to change color and are almost cooked, about 15 minutes. If you are using canned beans, skip this step.

3. When meat is done and moisture evaporates, stir in onion and garlic and fold together until onion is transparent, about 5 minutes.

4. Add beans with the liquid in which they were cooked to the meat mixture. There should be enough liquid to cover meat and beans by an inch. Add more hot water, if needed. If drained canned beans are used, add hot water to cover both beans and meat by an inch, 3 to 4 cups.

5. Add diluted tomato paste, or sauce, lemon juice, salt, black pepper, chili, and ginger. Bring to a quick boil, skimming as needed. Lower heat to medium-low, and let stew simmer, covered, until beans are tender and sauce is nicely thickened, about 30 minutes.

This stew goes well with all kinds of rice. Serve it with salad and pickles.

Pea Stew
(Margat Bazalya)

(Makes 4 servings)

Pea stew is cooked like green beans stew except substitute 1 pound green beans with 3 cups peas. Needless to say fresh peas make the best stew, but frozen variety is also good. Since peas cook faster than green beans, there is no need to precook them before using them in the stew. Therefore, skip step 2, and add peas in step 4.

Stew of Green Beans and Potato Cubes

(Makes 6 servings)

This is a variation on the classic way of cooking Bean Stew in which vegetables are cooked the *tabsi* way, i.e. baked in the oven, and the final liquid is more condensed than regular *marga*. The stew may be served from oven to table, and is more suitable for formal presentations.

1 pound lean meat cut into small pieces, or lean ground meat, or 12 pieces chicken tender loins, or 12 drumsticks, skinned
3 tablespoons oil, divided
1 medium onion, chopped
3 cloves garlic, grated
1/4 teaspoon turmeric

1 pound green beans, washed, both ends cut off, and cut into 2-inch pieces, or one 15-ounce can green beans, drained

215

3 to 4 medium potatoes (1 pound), peeled and cut into cubes, and kept in a bowl of cold water until used. Or use 2 cups frozen cubed potatoes
3 heaping tablespoons tomato paste (one 6-ounce can), or one 15- ounce can tomato sauce
1 1/2 teaspoons salt
1/4 teaspoon black pepper
1/2 teaspoon ginger
1/4 teaspoon chili pepper
2 tablespoons lemon juice

Preheat oven to 450 degrees F.

1. In a big skillet, sauté meat in 1 tablespoon oil, and stir until meat is browned and moisture evaporates. Time depends on kind of meat chosen, but drumsticks will definitely take longer than tender loins.

2. Add onion, garlic, and turmeric. Stir until onion is transparent, about 5 minutes.

3. Put prepared beans in a medium pot and pour enough hot water to just cover them. Bring to a boil, then reduce heat to medium, and let cook gently, until they start to change color and are almost cooked, about 15 minutes. If using canned beans, skip this step.

4. Drain potatoes, and sauté them in non-stick skillet in the remaining 2 tablespoons oil, stirring until browned, or spread potato cubes on a well oiled baking sheet, spray them with oil, and bake or broil them in a hot oven, turning once.

5. In an ovenproof 10-by-11-inch glass casserole spread meat mixture in the bottom, then cover it with beans, and top it with browned cubed potatoes.

6. In a medium bowl dilute tomato paste in 3 cups hot water (use liquid in which beans where boiled), or if using sauce, dilute it in 2 cup hot water or beans liquid. Add salt, pepper, ginger, chili, and lemon juice. Mix well. Pour tomato mixture on the layered meat and vegetables. There should be enough liquid to cover them. Add a little bit more hot water if needed.

7. Bake loosely covered in a preheated oven at 450 degrees F. until vegetables and meat are tender, and sauce is thickened, 35 to 40 minutes.

Garnish with chopped parsley, and serve with any kind of rice.

The Emperor's clothes

Here is the story of the sawyer who was daring enough the challenge the whim of the rich.

One day the sawyer was wandering in the streets of Baghdad, hungry and desolate. While passing by a beautiful house, to his surprise, he was accosted by the servants of the house, and was invited to get in and have dinner with their master. He went in, and there he saw the master sitting amongst a number of guests, and servants were coming and going carrying beautiful empty platters. The master would every now and then, and as a true host, entreat the guests to have their full of the delicious "foods" offered, while he himself made as if he was eating. He would describe the excellence and the beauty of the dishes as the empty platters were brought to the table, and encourage them to dig in. Meanwhile the servants "replenished" the guests' glasses repeatedly with their master's illusive wine. All the while the guests were pretending to be enjoying the food and were commenting on its excellence, and our sawyer followed suit. By and by the acting made him feel hungrier than ever, and to the astonishment of everybody, he gave the master a slap on the back of his neck. The master was taken by surprise and harshly rebuked him for doing this. The sawyer apologetically explained that he could not help it, if anything was to blame, it should be the excellent aged "wine" he guzzled, which made him behave irresponsibly.

(*Arabian Nights*, The Story of the Sawyer, the Barber's Brother, 32nd Night. Cited in al-Musawi, 324-5 English translation mine)

Green Fava Beans Stew
(Margat Bagilla Khadhra)

Green fava beans are sometimes hard to come by They start to make their appearance early in the summer, and when they are still young and tender the whole vegetable can be used. But when the pods of the green beans toughen, as they grow larger, fava beans in this case are usually shelled and skinned. Since the two kinds are dealt with differently, two separate recipes are given.

Fresh and Tender Fava Beans Stew
(Makes 4 servings)

4 pieces meat, best cuts are trimmed veal or lamb shanks (2 to 2 1/2 pounds), substitute with any cuts with meat and bone
1 tablespoon oil
1 medium onion, coarsely chopped
3 cloves garlic, sliced lengthwise

1 pound fresh and tender fava beans or one 15-ounce can of chopped green fava beans, drained
1/4 cup fresh dill weed, chopped, or 1 tablespoon dried dill weed
3 heaping tablespoons tomato paste (one 6-ounce can), diluted in a little hot water, or one 15-ounce tomato sauce
2 tablespoons lemon juice
1 1/2 teaspoons salt
1/4 teaspoon black pepper
1/4 teaspoon ground ginger
2 to 3 fresh or dried small hot peppers

1. In a medium 4-quart heavy pot, cook shanks as described in Suggested Cuts, and Okra Stew step 1, above. Cooking time is determined by your choice of meat.

2. While meat is cooking, prepare fava beans as follows: Cut off both ends of pods, and remove strings, if any. Then bunch 4 to 5 pods together, and cut them crosswise into 1/3-inch thick slices. In a medium pot, cover them with hot water, and bring to a boil. Reduce heat to medium-low, and let them simmer for about 30 minutes, or until they change color and are rather tender. If canned green fava beans are used, then skip this stage.

3. When meat is cooked, add onion and garlic, and stir until onion is transparent, about 5 minutes.

4. Add to the meat, fava beans with the liquid in which they were cooked. There should be enough liquid to cover beans and meat. Add more hot water if needed.

5. Stir in dill weed, diluted tomato paste or sauce, lemon juice, salt, pepper, ginger, and hot peppers. Bring to a quick boil, skimming as needed. Then lower heat to medium-low, and let simmer for 40 minutes or until meat and beans are tender and sauce is nicely thickened.

Delicious with white rice and noodles, see chapter8, for recipe.

Stew of Shelled Fresh Fava Beans
(Makes 4 servings)

When the jackets of the green beans toughen, as the pods grow larger, prepare fava beans stew this way:

4 pieces meat, chosen and prepared as in Fresh and Tender Fava Bean Stew
1 tablespoon oil
1 onion, coarsely chopped
3 to 4 cloves of garlic, sliced lengthwise

2 pounds fully grown fava bean pods or 1 pound frozen shelled fava beans
1/4 cup fresh dill weed or 1 tablespoon dried dill weed
3 heaping tablespoons tomato paste (one 6-ounce can), diluted in 3 1/2 cups hot water, or one 15-ounce tomato sauce diluted in 3 cups hot water, or 4 cups tomato juice
2 tablespoons lemon juice
1 1/2 teaspoons salt
1/4 teaspoon black pepper
1/4 teaspoon ground ginger
2 to 3 small hot peppers

1. Prepare meat as in step 1 in Fresh and Tender Fava Bean Stew. Add onion and garlic, and stir until onion is transparent.

2. While meat is cooking, prepare fava beans as follows: Discard jacket of pod, and skin beans by pouring boiling water over them. When beans are cool enough to handle, break the skin from the top with a knife, and press out the beautiful bright green beans. As for frozen beans, let them thaw, and do the same, but no need to pour hot water on them.

3. To the meat and onion mixture, add prepared fava beans, dill, diluted tomato paste, sauce or tomato juice, lemon juice, salt, pepper, ginger, and hot peppers. There should be enough liquid to cover meat and beans. Add more hot water if needed. Bring to a quick boil, skimming if needed. Lower heat to medium-low, and let simmer for about 20 minutes or until meat and beans are tender, and sauce is nicely thickened. The shelled fava beans are very delicate, so watch it, lest they should get mushy.

Note:　If fresh or frozen fava beans are not available, you may substitute with dried, shelled variety. The shelled dried fava beans need to be for several hours, then drained and added in step 3, but they might need more cooking time than the fresh beans.

Fresh Black-eyed Peas in the Pod
With Diced Meat
(Qimat al-Loubya)

(Makes 6 servings)

This stew calls for fresh black-eyed peas in the pod. Longer varieties of these beans are known as string or asparagus beans, available year round in Chinese grocery stores, sometimes in farmers markets in the summer. The asparagus beans plant grows successfully in home vegetable gardens. The nice flowers of this climbing plant would eventually turn into delicate beans. It is a very generous plant.

The way meat and beans are prepared in this recipe is what distinguishes it from other stews. It is diced into small cubes, and hence the name, *qima*. Apparently the word is Akkadian in origin. In *The Assyrian Herbal*, a monograph on the Assyrian vegetable drugs, the word "kima" (make small) often occurs in the Assyrian texts (Thompson, 64). In fact, even the Iraqi name for these beans, *loubya*, is still basically the same. The ancients used to call it "lubbu", and it was a common culinary vegetable. From a cuneiform tablet we learn it was used in a meat dish to which apricot, clean salt, bread, kidneys, and other ingredients were also added. (Thompson, 196-197)

Here is how it is cooked now. Lentils added to the stew will help give the sauce a nice consistency, which is rather on the thick side.

2 tablespoons oil
1 pound trimmed chunk of lamb or beef, cut *qima*-fashion, i.e. small 1/4-to 1/3-inch cubes (One pound lean ground meat may be substituted)
2 medium onions, coarsely chopped
3 cloves garlic, grated
1 teaspoon turmeric

1 pound fresh black-eyed peas in the pod (asparagus beans or string beans can be substituted), cut crosswise into 1/4-inch pieces
1/2 cup red lentils, picked over and washed
3 heaping tablespoons (One 6-ounce can) tomato paste diluted in 4 1/2 cups hot water, or one 15-ounce can tomato sauce diluted in 4 cups hot water, or 5 cups tomato juice.
1 1/2 teaspoons salt
1/4 teaspoon black pepper
1 teaspoon *baharat*, see Glossary
1/2 teaspoon ground ginger
1/4 teaspoon chili, or to taste
1/2 teaspoon ground coriander
2 teaspoons prepared *noomi Basrah*, see Glossary
1/2 cup bite-size prunes, halved or left whole, optional

1. In a medium heavy 4-quart pot sauté meat in oil, stirring occasionally, until all moisture evaporates, and meat starts to brown, about 10 minutes.

2. Add onion, garlic and turmeric. Stir until onion is transparent, about 10 minutes.

3. Fold in rest of ingredients. There should be enough liquid to cover the meat and beans. Bring to a quick boil. Reduce heat to medium-low, and let stew simmer gently, covered, for about 40 minutes, or until beans are tender and sauce is thickened. Stir 2 to 3 times while stew is simmering to prevent it from sticking to the bottom of the pot.

Serve with white rice and noodles (see chapter8, for recipe), salad and pickles.

Stew of Chickpeas and Diced Meat
(Margat Qima)

(Makes 4 servings)

Like the previous stew, this simple and versatile *marga* derives its name from the way meat is prepared, i.e. chopped *qima* way (into small cubes). The chickpeas will give the stew a richly thick consistency, and the prunes, a lovely sweet and sour taste. Traditionally, a variety of small prunes, called *aloucha*, is used. They are tart dried plums that might well have been the same variety used in al-Warraq's tenth-century cookbook, called *khokh al-dub* (the bear's peaches), or the ancient Akkadian "antahsum" (plums) used to sour the Babylonian recipes (see Introduction).

> **2 tablespoons oil**
> **1 pound trimmed chunk of lamb or beef, cut *qima*-fashion, i.e. cut into small 1/3-inch cubes (One pound lean ground meat may be substituted)**
> **2 medium onions, finely sliced**
> **3 cloves garlic, grated**
> **1 teaspoon turmeric**
>
> **1 1/2 cups split chickpeas, picked over, washed, soaked for 30 minutes, and drained**
> **3 heaping tablespoons tomato paste (one 6-ounce can), diluted in 4 1/2 cups hot water, or one 15-ounce can tomato sauce, diluted in 4 cups hot water, or 5 cups tomato juice**
> **1 1/2 teaspoons salt**
> **1/4 teaspoon black pepper**
> **1 teaspoon *baharat* (see Glossary), optional**
> **1 teaspoon cumin**
> **1/2 teaspoon ginger**
> **1/4 teaspoon chili, or to taste**
> **1/4 teaspoon cinnamon**
> **1/2 teaspoon ground coriander**
> **2 teaspoons prepared *noomi Basrah* (see Glossary)**
> **1 teaspoon brown sugar or honey**
> **3/4 cup bite-size prunes, halved**

1. In a medium 4-qurt heavy pot sauté meat in oil, stirring occasionally, until all moisture evaporates, and meat starts to brown, about 10 minutes.

2. Stir in onion, garlic, and turmeric, until onion is transparent, about 10 minutes.

3. Fold in rest of ingredients. Mix well, making sure there is enough liquid to cover meat and beans. Add some more hot water if needed. Bring to a quick boil, then reduce heat to medium-low, and let stew simmer gently, covered, about 45 minutes, or until chickpeas are tender and sauce is thickened. Stir 3 to 4 times while cooking to prevent ingredients from sticking to the bottom of the pot. Sauce in this stew should be thicker in consistency than that of regular stews.

This stew is particularly delicious with white rice, and fresh radish leaves and radishes.

Cabbage Stew
Margat Lahana

(Makes 4 servings)

It is a universally accepted "fact" that there is nothing exciting about cabbage, that homely vegetable, which fills the house with a distinctive odor when cooked. Well, this is so unfortunate, for it is indeed packed with goodness. Besides, it's amazing how many delicious things you can make with one big head of cabbage. The perfect leaves are good for stuffing (see chapter on stuffed foods), the core may be pickled (see chapter on pickles), and the torn leaves can be thinly sliced into an attractive salad (see chapter on salads), or an aromatic stew as in the following:

4 pieces meat, use any of the options given in Suggested Cuts, above
1 tablespoon oil
1 medium onion, chopped
1 teaspoon curry powder

1 small head of green cabbage (1 to 1 1/2 pounds), chopped
3 heaping tablespoons tomato paste (one 6-ounce can) diluted in 3 1/2 cups hot water or one 15-ounce can tomato sauce diluted in 3 cups hot water, or 4 cups canned tomato juice
1 1/2 teaspoons salt
1/4 teaspoon black pepper
1 teaspoon *baharat*, see Glossary
2 to 3 small hot peppers, for lovers of hot food
1 tablespoon prepared *noomi Basrah* (see Glossary), or 2 tablespoons lime or lemon juice
1/2 cup split chickpeas, soaked for 30 minutes and drained, then covered with water and cooked until tender but not mushy, about 20 minutes

1. Prepare and cook meat as instructed in Suggested Cuts and Okra Stew step 1, above

2. Add onion and curry powder to the meat, and stir until onion is transparent, about 5 minutes.

3. Add cabbage, diluted tomato paste or sauce or juice, salt, pepper, *baharat*, hot peppers, if used, *noomi Basrah*, and cooked chickpeas. There should be enough liquid to cover meat and cabbage. Add more hot water if needed. Bring to a quick boil, skimming as needed. Lower heat, and let stew simmer, covered, until cabbage is tender and sauce is thickened, about 20 minutes. Stir 2 to 3 times while stew is simmering to prevent it from sticking to the bottom of the pot.

This stew is delicious served with white rice and noodles (see chapter 8).

Cauliflower Stew
(Margat Quarnabeet)

(Makes 4 servings)

Follow the same instructions given in Cabbage Stew, but substitute 1 small head of cauliflower (about 2 pounds), broken into florets, for the cabbage. Cauliflower will require a little less time for cooking than cabbage.

Stew of Cauliflower and Meatballs
(Tabsi'l Qarnabeet B'ras al-Asfour)

(Makes 6 servings)

The word *tabsi* rather than *marga* is used with stew dishes that are thicker in consistency than the regular *marga*, and are usually simmered in the oven. The following is an elaboration on the regular cauliflower stew. It is more suitable for formal presentation because it can be elegantly served from oven to table, garnished with parsley and lemon slices.

For the meat balls:
> 1 pound lean ground meat
> 1 small onion, grated
> 1 clove garlic, grated
> 1/4 cup parsley, chopped
> 1/3 cup rice flour, all-purpose flour, or bread crumbs
> 1/2 teaspoon salt
> 1/4 teaspoon black pepper, allspice, cumin, ginger powder, each
> 1/4 teaspoon chili pepper, or to taste

For the stew:
> 1 small head of cauliflower (1 1/2 to 2 pounds) broken into florets
> 2 tablespoons oil
> 1 medium onion, chopped
> 1 teaspoon curry powder
> 3 heaping tablespoons tomato paste (one 6-ounce can) diluted in 3 1/2 cups hot water, or one 15-ounce can tomato sauce diluted in 3 cups hot water, or 4 cups tomato juice
> 1 1/2 teaspoons salt
> 1/4 teaspoon black pepper
> 1/4 teaspoon chili, or to taste
> 1 teaspoon *baharat* (see Glossary)
> 2 tablespoons lemon juice

1/2 cup chick-peas, soaked for 30 minutes and covered with water and cooked until tender but not mushy, about 20 minutes

For garnish: 1/4 cup chopped parsley, and lemon slices
Preheat oven to 450 degrees F.

1. Combine meatball ingredients. Knead briefly. With moistened fingers form into meatballs, size of a small walnut each, or as small as *ras 'l asfour* (sparrows' heads). Arrange them in a single layer in a greased baking pan, and broil or bake in a preheated oven (450 degrees F.), turning once to allow both sides to brown, about 15 minutes. (They may be browned in a skillet in a small amount of oil)

2. In a big non-stick skillet, heat oil and add cauliflower and onion. Fold for about 10 minutes or until they start to brown. Add curry powder half way through browning.

3. Spread meatballs and cauliflower mixture in a 10 1/2-by-12-inch glass, baking pan.

4. In the same skillet used for browning cauliflower and onion, mix diluted tomato paste or sauce, or tomato juice, salt, pepper, chili, *baharat*, lemon, and cooked chickpeas. Bring to a quick boil, then reduce heat to medium, and simmer for about 10 minutes. Pour mixture on meatballs and cauliflower. There should be enough liquid to cover them. Add more hot water if needed.

5. Bake casserole, loosely covered, in a preheated oven at 450 degrees F. for about 30 minutes or until sauce is thickened.

Garnish with parsley and lemon slices, and serve with rice and pickles.

Potato Stew (Margat Poteita)

(Makes 4 servings)

This is a delicious way for cooking potatoes. Practically all kinds of meat go well with this versatile vegetable, even fish, or I might say, especially fish (see chapter 13).

4 pieces meat, see options given in Suggested Cuts, above
1 tablespoon oil
1 medium onion, chopped
1 teaspoon curry powder
5 medium potatoes (about 1 1/2 pounds), peeled, cut into 1-inch cubes, soaked in cold water until used

3 heaping tablespoons tomato paste (one 6-ounce can) diluted in 3 1/2 cups hot water, or one 15-ounce can tomato sauce diluted in 3 cups hot water, or 4 cups tomato juice
1 1/2 teaspoons salt
1/4 teaspoon black pepper
1 teaspoon *baharat* (see Glossary)

1 tablespoon prepared *noomi Basrah* (see Glossary), or 2 tablespoons lime or lemon juice
2 to 3 fresh small hot peppers

1. Prepare and cook meat as directed in Suggested Cuts, and Okra Stew step 1, above. Time of cooking will vary according to type of meat chosen.

2. Add onion and curry powder, and stir until onion is transparent, about 5 minutes. Fold in drained potato pieces for a few minutes.

3. Add the rest of ingredients. There should be enough liquid to cover meat and potatoes. Add more hot water if needed. Bring to a quick boil, skimming if needed, then reduce heat, and let simmer, covered, until potatoes are tender, and sauce is nicely thickened, about 40 minutes. Stir 2 to 3 times while simmering to prevent ingredients from sticking to the bottom of the pot.

This stew pairs well with white rice and noodles. Sprinkle with some toasted slivered almonds and currants (see chapter 8, for recipe). Serve with turnip pickles and salad.

Al-Buraniya:
The Mother of all Mosakas

During the medieval Islamic period some of the eggplant dishes were given the name *Buraniya*, after Buran, believed to be the inventor of these luscious eggplant dishes. She was the wife of the Abbasid Caliph al-Ma'moun, who lived in Baghdad during the ninth century AD. Incidentally this was one of the rare dishes attributed to a female gourmet at the time in an otherwise male dominated field.

In the Baghdadi cookbooks, Buran dishes came under different guises. Fried eggplant was called *Buran* (al-Warraq, 115). Fried eggplant, mashed, mixed with yogurt and served as a bed of meatballs, was also *Buran* (al-Baghdadi, 192). What's more to our purpose here is the *Buraniya* stew casserole given in al-Baghdadi's chapter on simple (*sawadhij*) and sweet dishes (191).

It was a casserole of fried eggplant layered with cooked finely chopped meat, onion halves, and meatballs. The dish was spiced with cumin, coriander and cinnamon, and colored and perfumed with saffron. This medieval dish is strikingly similar to the *Musaqa'a* casserole known nowadays throughout the Arab world, and the Greek version, *Mosaka*.

Eggplant Casserole
(Tabsi'l Betinjaan)

(Makes 6 servings)

The eggplant casserole traditionally cooked nowadays is basically similar to the original *Buraniya*, (given in Box above), plus the tomatoes that reached the region around the sixteenth century AD. The dish is called *tabsi* (a Turkish loan word for an oven pan) because it is usually cooked casserole style in a shallow pan, with sauce less in amount and thicker in consistency than regular *marga*.

This stew is as versatile as eggplant itself is. Any meat cut goes very well with it (see Suggested Cuts above). By adding small discs of stuffed bulgar dough known as K*ubbat Burghul* (for recipe see p.329), you can turn it into an exotic dish. Or you can simply pass the meat and serve it as a vegetarian stew.

1 large eggplant, or two medium ones (about 1 1/2 pounds)
2 medium onions, thinly sliced
2 to 3 cloves garlic, thinly sliced lengthwise, or grated
2 tablespoons oil
1/2 teaspoon curry powder
1/2 teaspoon cumin
1 medium bell pepper, sliced, seeds and membranes removed
1 small hot pepper, sliced, for lovers of hot food
1 pound meat of your choice, cooked according to guidelines given in Suggested Cuts above.
3 medium tomatoes, sliced, canned sliced or diced tomatoes can be substituted.
For Sauce:
3 heaping tablespoons tomato paste (one 6-ounce can), diluted in 3 1/2 cups hot water, or one 15-ounce can tomato sauce diluted in 3 cups hot water, or 4 cups tomato juice
1 1/2 teaspoons salt
1/4 teaspoon black pepper
1 tablespoon fresh basil, chopped, or 1/2 teaspoon dried basil
1 teaspoon pomegranate syrup, optional
1/2 teaspoon sugar
1 cup cooked whole chickpeas, optional
For garnish: chopped parsley and lemon slices
Preheat oven to 400 degrees F.

1. Cut off stem of eggplant, and peel lengthwise so as to give it a striped look. Cut it into 1/4-inch slices crosswise. Soak slices in warm salted water, for 30 minutes. Drain well, and fry them in a small amount of oil, or arrange them in one layer in a greased baking sheet, spray or brush them with oil and bake or broil them in a hot oven, turning only once, to allow the two sides to brown, 15 to 20 minutes.

2. In a big non-stick skillet, sauté onion in oil, stirring frequently until it softens. Add garlic, curry powder and cumin. Stir in sliced fresh pepper and hot pepper, if used, for a few minutes.

3. In a large ovenproof 10 1/2-by-12-inch glass casserole, arrange prepared meat and vegetables as follows: Spread cooked meat in the bottom of the casserole. Arrange eggplant pieces on top. Sprinkle onion mixture, prepared in step 2, all over eggplant. Finally arrange tomato slices on top.

4. Prepare sauce as follows: In the same skillet used for sautéing vegetables, put diluted tomato paste or sauce, or tomato juice. Add salt, pepper, basil, pomegranate syrup, if used, sugar, and cooked chickpeas, if using any. Bring to a quick boil, and simmer for about 5 minutes.

5. Pour simmered liquid all over arranged vegetables. There should be enough liquid to cover vegetables. Add some more hot water if needed.

7. Bake in a preheated oven at 400 degrees F., loosely covered, for about 40 minutes, or until vegetables are tender, and sauce is thickened. Garnish with parsley and lemon slices, and serve with rice, bulgar, or warm bread, with fresh greens and pickles.

Zucchini Stew
(Margat Shijar)

(Makes 4 servings)

Zucchini has always been a popular vegetable. In the medieval Baghdadi cookbook it was used in many stew recipes, and it was often given as a substitute for eggplant. We still do the same thing nowadays. Zucchini makes a light and delicious stew, and the fragrance it imparts is wonderful even though spices are kept to the minimum.

4 pieces meat. The best choice is veal or lamb chops or shanks

1 tablespoon oil
1 medium onion, coarsely chopped
1/2 teaspoon curry powder

1/2 cup split chickpeas, picked over, washed, and soaked for 30 minutes, and cooked until just done, about 20 minutes
3 medium zucchinis, (about 1 1/2 pounds) both ends cut off, and cut into 1/2-inch slices crosswise
3 heaping tablespoons tomato paste (one 6-ounce can) diluted in 3 1/2 cups hot water, or one 15-ounce can tomato sauce diluted in 3 cups hot water, or 4 cups tomato juice
1 1/2 teaspoons salt
1/4 teaspoon black pepper
1/2 teaspoon allspice
1 bay leaf
2 tablespoons lemon juice
2 to 3 whole fresh small hot peppers, for lovers of hot food

1. In a medium heavy 4-quart pot cook meat in oil as directed in Suggested Cuts, and Okra Stew. p. 209.

2. Add onion and curry powder to meat and stir until onion is transparent, about 5 minutes.

3. Add cooked chickpeas, sliced zucchini, diluted tomato paste or sauce or tomato juice, salt, pepper, allspice, bay leaf, lemon juice, and whole hot peppers, if used. There should be enough liquid to cover zucchini and meat. Add some more hot water if needed. Bring to a quick boil, skimming if needed. Then reduce heat to low and let simmer gently for about 25 minutes, or until zucchini is tender, and sauce is nicely thickened. Carefully stir stew 2 or 3 times while simmering to prevent ingredients from sticking to the bottom of the pot. Zucchini can easily be overcooked, so watch it.

Serve with white rice and noodles, with lots of fresh greens and spring onions.

Dried Apricot Stew
(Margat Mishmish or Turshana)

(Makes 4 servings)

This stew is a delicious and exotic relic of the way people of the region used to prepare their stews during the pre-tomato days. That's why some people call it *marga bedha* (white stew). It can be traced back to the Babylonian and Assyrian days, as seen in their apricot and bean stew (Campbell, 196-7). It is also reminiscent of the many sweet and sour stews given in al-Warraq's and al-Baghdadi's cookbooks. It was called *Mishmishiya*, from *mishmish* (apricot, al-Baghdadi, 40). Nowadays this stew is mostly popular amongst people living in the middle and southern parts of Iraq, where dried apricot is more commonly known as *turshana* to differentiate it from the fresh *mishmish*.

2 tablespoons oil
1 pound lamb, trimmed and cut into 1-inch cubes, beef can be substituted
1 medium onion, thinly sliced
1/2 teaspoon turmeric
1/4 cup slivered almonds, or walnut coarsely broken into pieces

1 cup dried apricots
1/4 cup raisins, optional
1/4 cup brown sugar
1 teaspoon salt
1/4 teaspoon black pepper
1 teaspoon *baharat* (see Glossary)
1/4 teaspoon ground cardamom
1/2 teaspoon cinnamon
1/4 teaspoon ginger
1/4 teaspoon coriander
2 tablespoons lemon juice
1/4 cup orange juice
1/2 cup split chickpeas, washed, soaked for 30 minutes, and cooked until just done, about 20 minutes

1. In a medium 4-quart heavy pot, sauté meat pieces in oil, stirring frequently until cooked and all liquid evaporates, about 15 minutes.

2. Add onion and turmeric, and stir until onion is transparent, about 5 minutes. Stir in nuts, and allow to brown slightly.

3. Stir in apricots, raisins, if used, brown sugar, salt, pepper, *baharat,* cardamom, cinnamon, ginger, coriander, lemon juice, orange juice, and cooked chickpeas. Add 3 cups hot water to the ingredients. Bring to a quick boil, then reduce heat and let it simmer, covered, until meat and apricots are tender, and sauce has considerably reduced, 45 to 55 minutes.

Serve with white rice, and salad vegetables and greens.

Variations:

*Originally a few threads of saffron are used to give stew an attractive golden hue. If using saffron omit turmeric and add saffron in step 3.

*If you want to do it the medieval style, purée the dried apricots before adding them to the stew. This would give stew a richer and creamier texture. To do this, put apricots in a small pot and cover them with water and bring to a boil. Lower heat, and allow to simmer about 10 minutes. Then purée in blender.

* Instead of the lamb, skinned chicken pieces can be used. Adjust cooking time accordingly.

Pomegranate and Walnut Stew
(Margat Sharab al-Rumman)
(Fasanjoun)

(Makes 4 servings)

As we have seen in the Introduction, the love for the sour, and the sweet and sour goes back to ancient times. To sour stews they added vinegar, and sometimes, sour fruits such as green plums and apricots, and for the sweet they added honey. During the Abbasid era this stew category was fully exploited using all the sour vegetables and fruits available at the time. The *rummaniyat,* for instance used *rumman* (pomegranate), both sweet and sour varieties. Ground nuts were added to give body to the stew. Those medieval pomegranate stews were sometimes given a fashion statement by calling them by Persian names, such as *narbaja* or *narsirk*.

They were all cooked basically the same way. Fat meat both red or/and white was simmered in water, soured with pomegranate juice and wine vinegar, balanced with a little sugar, and seasoned with onion, garlic, cumin, coriander, pepper, cinnamon, ginger, and mastic. Sometimes vegetables were added to it, such as eggplant and gourd, and garnished with the dainty spicy *kubabs* (meatballs). The stew was thickened with ground almonds or walnuts, and was given a final sprinkle of crushed dried mint (al-Warraq, 155,172, al-Baghdadi, 36, 38, 41).

Of all the sweet and sour stews that were simmering in the medieval pots, only a few were handed down to us. In the middle and southern cities of modern Iraq and neighboring cities of Iran, people cook a delicately scrumptious stew known by the Iranian name *Fasanjoun*, or simply *margat sharab al-rumman* (stew of pomegranate juice).

The following is a basic recipe that goes with almost any cut or type of meat you desire to use, and for the version with chicken see, Chicken simmered in Pomegranate Syrup, in chapter 12.

> **4 pieces of meat such as trimmed veal or lamb shanks, or trimmed and skinned chicken breasts, thighs or drumsticks, or meat balls (*ras'l asfour,* for recipe see p.133), or 4 serving-size salmon fillets**
> **2 tablespoons oil**
> **1 medium onion, chopped**
> **1/2 teaspoon turmeric**
>
> **1 tablespoon flour**
> **1 cup toasted walnuts (4 ounces), pulverized in a food processor or blender until oily**
>
> **3 cups water**
> **1/4 cup pomegranate syrup (or substitute with juice of one lime or lemon, 2 tablespoons brown sugar, and 1/2 cup tomato juice)**
> **1 teaspoon salt**
> **1/2 teaspoon cardamom**
> **1/4 teaspoon black pepper, cumin, cinnamon, each**
> **1/4 teaspoon chili powder, optional**
> **2 cups diced vegetables (such as potatoes, or one medium eggplant, peeled, cut into 1/4-inch slices, and soaked in salted warm water for 30 minutes, then drained, and fried or sprayed with oil and broiled on both sides**
>
> **For garnish: 1/4 cup fresh pomegranate seeds, and chopped parsley, or crumbled dried mint**

1. In a medium 4-quart heavy pot, cook cuts of meat following guidelines given in Suggested Cuts and Okra Stew, above. Fish fillets may be sprinkled with salt and pepper and fried or brushed with oil and broiled, and then added to stew in the last few minutes of cooking, in step 3, just enough to let it heat through. If using meatballs, add in step 3.

2. Add onion and turmeric, and fold until onion is transparent, about 5 minutes. Sprinkle flour and ground walnut on the onion, and fold for a few more minutes.

3. (If using meatballs, add them at this stage.) Add the rest of ingredients except for garnish, and stir carefully. Bring to a quick boil, then reduce heat and let simmer gently for about 40 minutes, or until meat and vegetables are tender, and sauce is nicely thickened.

4. Garnish with chopped parsley and pomegranate seeds, and serve with white rice.

Entertainment in the Marshes

The marshes are in southern Iraq where the two rivers, Tigris and Euphrates flow. As recently as Biblical times, the gulf in the south stretched far up the southern part of Iraq, and the two rivers flowed separately into the sea, and did not joint into *shut al-Arab,* as they do today. Life has little changed for the dwellers of these marshes. Their lives basically follow patterns established about six millennia ago, when the first nomadic tribes settled in this watery land. Their reed houses and their few possessions have been excavated at the level just above the virgin silt. Indeed, according to Sumerian myths it was at that place where the world began, when the god Murdokh built a platform of reeds and earth on the face of the universe where all the lands at first were sea. As the centuries went by, the sea receded further south leaving behind areas of seasonal flooding, semi-permanent marshlands, fed by the many tributaries of the two rivers, and a central area of permanent marshes that lie low between the courses of the two rivers (Maxwell, 16).

Like their ancient ancestors, the marsh people of today still build their houses on artificial islands of reeds and mud. Each household is an island by itself, with a barn built for the family's water buffalo, domesticated by the Sumerians around 4000 BC, and are essential to their lives. The modern marsh people, like their predecessors, catch fish, bake unleavened bread in crude ovens, weave mats from the marsh reeds, and build arched huts of reeds. Rice introduced about 1000 BC is still the food staple there. Planted sprout by sprout in shallow paddies, harvested by hand, and carried in *mashhoufs* (canoes) to the neighboring villages and towns (Kramer, *Cradle of Civilization*, 87-93).

The marsh people receive their guests in the *mudhif* (guesthouse in rural areas), and they sometimes entertain them by singing and dancing, usually performed by males, called *sha'ar.* (In other parts of Iraq such entertainment is provided by male and female gypsies, known as *kawliyya*) The following is a unique account of this sort of entertainment, as described by Maxwell:

I realized in the first few seconds that though the marshmen's singing required a co-operative effort from the listener a little akin to that demanded of a hypnotic subject, the impact of the dancing was full and complete and to me irresistible. The rhythm was staccato yet somehow fluid, each movement whether of limb or torso somehow resembling a pause and a pounce. The dance was a narrative, as are many of them, and song and mime was a part of it, all held within the framework of a tight unvarying iambic rhythm. *Ti-tumti-tum, ti-tumti-tum*; the audience took up the rhythm, each stamping out the tune with the heel of an extended right foot, each with his arms outstretched before him and his hands locked with extended fingers to produce a finger-click as loud, literally, as a man may make by clapping his palms together. Even the small children can do this; a shrimp of six years can with his soft baby fingers make a crack like the report of a small pistol.

It seems likely that many hundreds of generations of dancing in the tiny confined space about the hearth of reed huts, with the necessity for the maximum movement in the minimum space, have been responsible for the great development of body-movements opposed to footwork for which there would be inadequate room. ...An important part of every dancer's vocabulary, as it were, is a violent and prolonged shivering of one or both shoulders. Precise and almost acrobatic use of the pelvic muscles lends a sexual flavor to nearly all dancing, the movements ranging from direct crissation to sinuous rolling motions or plain high-speed bottom waggling; this last nearly always draws enthusiastic laughter from the audience. (Maxwell, 47-9).

231

***Sufurtas*, a four-tiered lunch box for rice, stew, salad and dessert**

The Marshes in Southern Iraq
(A painting by Hashim 1989. Permission, Altoma)

233

CHAPTER EIGHT
RICE

CHAPTER EIGHT
RICE

الرُّزّ

(Timman or Ruz)

My grandmother, normally a reluctant socializer, used to go head before feet, as we say in Iraq, whenever we were invited to dinner at our young, newly-married neighbor's house. "I like her rice," she used to say, "she still doesn't know how to cook." And taking into consideration my grandma's remaining three or four teeth, perilously hanging on, it is understandable why our neighbor's sticky and soft rice, which by common standards is a failure, appealed to her. The perfect rice is the criterion of a good cook in Iraq, simply because it is prepared practically every day, and if the cook doesn't know how to prepare this daily staple properly, then what does she know?

Traditionally, the grains of the perfectly cooked rice should be separate and unsoggy, tender and yet have a little of elasticity in them. In the medieval Baghdadi cookbooks, rice prepared this way was called *al-ruz'l mufalfal*. The word *mufalfal* is sometimes wrongly translated as "peppered rice." The word is not derived from *filfil*, meaning pepper, but rather from the verb *falla*, meaning "loosen", and adjective *mafloul*, "loose." Loose tea in the Iraqi Arabic, for instance, is *chai fal*. Therefore, rice cooked this way will result in grains that separate, and are not so sticky.

In her book *Guests of the Sheik*, Elizabeth Fernea tells us how during her first few months of her stay in the remote southern village of al-Nuhra, three local women stood at her door, and after greeting her, one of the women said, "We hear you can't cook rice." "I almost threw a rusty tin can at her," Elizabeth said, "I was so annoyed. But one of them said, 'If you will open your gate, we will come and show you how to cook rice, so your husband will be pleased with your food.'" She did, and they actually taught her how to cook rice:

> We picked over and washed the rice, covered it with cold water, then sat down on the floor to drink tea while it soaked. A large pot of salted water was put on the stove to boil, and the rice was cooked in the boiling water until the grains were separate and tasted right. When the rice was drained, clarified butter was put in the dry pot over fire until it sizzled. Then the rice was poured back into the pot and stirred quickly until each grain was coated with the boiling butter. Then we covered the pot, turned down the heat, and let the buttered rice steam slowly. We drank another cup of tea, and I thanked the ladies profusely.
>
> "We don't want your husband to beat you," said one. "After all, you are here alone without your mother" (78-9).

What Elizabeth Fernea has described is the traditional way of cooking rice, which robs it of almost all nutrients, as the drained liquid is thrown away. I remember my mother used to give us a glass or two of this delicious liquid, and we loved it, but how much can one drink? A more up-dated and healthier method for cooking the rice is to simmer it using a small amount of oil.

The perfectly cooked rice requires the right amount of liquid, which is, more or less, determined by your choice of rice itself. Jasmine variety is aromatic, easy to handle and is good for every day use. With the right amount of water you'll get firm but tender, and barely sticky rice. The Indian basmati rice is characterized by its long and slender grains, which when cooked would separate and expand even more, lengthwise. However, it is less aromatic than jasmine, and unfortunately, if not packaged well, it sometimes smells of the jute sack in which it is kept. When this happens, I get rid of the sack as soon as I buy the rice, let it air for a while, and keep it in a plastic bag. Because basmati rice is aged, you need to soak it longer than you do with jasmine, and you need also to be a little more generous with oil when cooking it. All-purpose long grain American rice can be substituted, its grains nicely separate when cooked, but it lacks the aroma of the jasmine rice.

No rice, however, compares with the native Iraqi *timman anber*, which grows in the marshes of southern Iraq. When lunchtime approaches, all the neighborhoods would be perfumed with the aroma of steaming pots of rice. It is not called *anber* for nothing. In this respect, Jasmine rice is the best alternative.

You must have noticed how easily rice can stick and burn if left unmonitored, producing the most unwelcome smoky stench. Using a generous amount of oil or clarified butter will definitely help prevent such accidents from happening, and what's more, will result in a deliciously crispy crusty bottom layer. In offering rice to guests, there is a protocol that a hospitable hostess needs to heed. The crunchy crust, exciting as it might be, should not make its presence on the rice platter. The hostess should always give the indication that there is more where that came from. However, informally served rice almost always comes topped with pieces of golden brown crunchy crust. The best way to take it out of the pot is to spoon rice out without disturbing the bottom, then remove the crust and put it on the rice either in one piece or broken into chunks.

Unfortunately the rice and its crust come out loaded with fat. To avoid this, it is a good idea to invest in a dependable non-stick pot. You will keep oil to the minimum, and not a single grain of rice will go to waste. What's more, you will get a crust, golden and crunchy, which will come out in one piece by just inverting the pot.

Plain White Rice
(Timman Abyadh)

(Makes 4 servings)

The amount of water used in cooking the rice is crucial, and eye measurement works better with experienced cooks. According to those eye measurements, there should be enough liquid to cover rice in the pot by 1/3-inch. If you prefer to measure by cups then always remember that **every cup of uncooked rice needs 1 3/4 cup liquid, provided you follow the instructions below.**

> **2 cups rice**
> **3 1/2 cups cold water**
> **1 tablespoon oil**
> **1 1/2 teaspoon salt**

1. In a fine-meshed sieve, big enough to hold rice comfortably, wash rice under running cold water. Let it drain then transfer it to a medium bowl. (If the package directions say there is no need to wash it, then skip this stage, and just put the measured rice in the bowl)

2. Add cold water to rice, and **let soak for 30 minutes**. This time is good enough for jasmine and American rice. Aged rice, such as basmati, needs about an hour of soaking.

3. In a medium heavy non-stick pot, pour rice **with the water in which it was soaking**. Add oil and salt, stir lightly with a wooden spoon. Bring to quick boil, covered, on high heat, for 5 minutes or until most of the moisture has evaporated and small holes start appearing.

4. Lower heat to low and gently and lightly fold rice with a fork or a wooden spoon to allow rice grains to expand while cooking. Cover pot tightly, and let simmer for 20 minutes. While simmering, fold rice lightly twice preferably with a fork to allow it to fluff. (Over stirring or folding the rice might cause the grains to break, and make rice glutinous in texture).

How to make the crispy crust:

A non-stick pot is recommended if you want to get the crust in one piece. When rice is almost cooked, say after 15 minutes of simmering and before any of the grains have started to crisp or stick to the bottom of the pot, transfer rice to a bowl. In another smaller bowl, mix 2 tablespoons yogurt, about 2 tablespoons oil and 5 to 6 heaping tablespoons of the cooked rice. Spread bottom of rice pot with this mixture and return rest of the rice, and resume simmering rice for 15 more minutes. This will result in a flavorful crust. Needless to say, the more freely oil is used, the more delicious and crunchy the crust will be. In fact, if a generous amount of oil is used in cooking the rice to begin with, there will no need for doing all this. Just let rice simmer for 10 or 15 minutes more to allow rice in the bottom to crisp and brown in the oil.

Alternatively, if you are cooking a small amount of rice, and do not want to use oil more than is needed, then simply cook rice as directed above. During the last 5 minutes of cooking give heat a boost to high, but you need to watch it lest it should burn, let your nose be the judge. This will result in a thin but crispy crust. To prevent the crust from getting soft or soggy from the steam in the pot, it is essential to invert the rice immediately by putting a plate or tray on top of the pot, and holding both the pot and the plate with both hands. The beautiful delicious crust will be on top in one piece.

Timman versus Ruz

Contrary to the entire Arab world, the majority of people in Iraq call rice, *timman*. The more familiar word, *ruz* is mostly used by the Mosilis (people from Mosul). Evidently the two words were used interchangeably many centuries ago. The ninth-century Abbasid prince of epicures, Ibrahim Ibn al-Mahadi, for instance, uses the word *timman* rather than *ruz* in his poem on a dish called, al-*maghmouma* (the covered, al-Warraq, 186).

Variations:

* Cinnamon Rice:

Give plain rice an appealing color and aroma by adding one rounded teaspoon cinnamon, when you add the salt in step 3. It will do wonders to your rice. It pairs nicely with fish dishes.

* Rice Cooked in Broth:

Instead of plain water, use broth, which will makes rice more flavorful and nutritious. Just substitute plain water with an equal amount of cold broth. You might need to adjust amount of salt, if broth has salt in it.

Rice with Vermicelli Noodles
(Timman bil Sha'riyya)

Add 1/4 cup broken vermicelli noodles (one ball of noodles, lightly crushed between the fingers) to the ingredients given in Plain White Rice. Put oil first in the pot, then add the noodles, and stir in the oil constantly until they are golden brown. Add rice and water as described in Plain White Rice. The rest is the same.

Variation:

*Rice with Almonds and Raisins or Currants:

For a more interesting presentation of rice with noodles, brown 1/4 cup slivered almonds in a little oil, then add 1/4 cup raisins or currants and stir together until currants are heated through. Sprinkle on top of the rice after it is mounded on the serving dish.

Golden Yellow Rice
(Timman Asfar)

Rice can be given an appealing color and fragrance by using saffron or the less costly turmeric. For even distribution of color, steep 1/4 teaspoon saffron in 2 tablespoons hot water for a few minutes, and add it, with the liquid in which it steeped, to the rice is step 3 of cooking Plain White Rice, above.

If turmeric is used instead, put oil first in the pot, then add 1/4 teaspoon turmeric and stir it until it gets fragrant (a few moments). Add rice, salt and water as directed in Plain White Rice, step 3.

For an attractive **speckled white and golden yellow look**, do as follows:

1. Five minutes before rice is done, sprinkle surface of rice with a mixture of 1/4 teaspoon ground saffron, steeped in 2 tablespoons hot water for 5 minutes. Do not disturb the rice.

2. When rice is done, gently fold it to allow color to touch more grains.

3. To achieve the same effect, at a much lesser cost, but without the aroma, use diluted 4-5 drops of yellow food coloring, and use it as directed above in steps 1 and 2.

Variations:
* Aromatic Rice:

A subtle aroma can be given to the yellow rice by adding 1/4 teaspoon cinnamon, and 3 to 4 whole pods of cardamom, when you start cooking the rice. 1 tablespoon rose water may be sprinkled on the rice, after it is cooked.

*Yellow Rice with Almonds and Raisins or Currants:

Brown 1/4 cup slivered almonds in a small amount of oil. Add 1/4 cup raisins or currants, and stir together until currants are just heated through. Scatter this mixture on the rice after it is mounded on a serving plate.

*Molded Rice:

This is a simple and yet elegant idea for formal occasions. Line a mold, such as bundt or tube pan, with browned finely sliced onions, toasted nuts, and raisins or currants. Press cooked rice, White Plain or Yellow Rice, on this layer. Unmold rice onto a serving dish. Fill the center with salad, or some kind of stew with thick sauce. For individual servings use a medium cup or a small bowl as a mold. Simply press rice into the bowl, then unmold it onto the dish. Ladle out some stew all around it, and garnish it with salad.

A Basic Recipe for
White Rice with Meat and Vegetables:
Infinite Variety
(Timman Tachina)

(Makes 4 servings)

Instead of the usual rice and stew, rice is sometimes cooked and simmered with a variety of meats and vegetables. Some people call it *tacheen*, others *tacheena*, but obviously it is ultimately a loan word of sort. It is a convenient one-dish meal usually served with yogurt and salad. It is an ideal meal for hot summer days.

The following is a basic method for making *timman tachina*, to be followed by variations. This dish is usually made with cubed lamb, but other kinds of meat can easily be substituted. (Follow directions given after this recipe for preparing and cooking other kinds of meat). The dish may also be made vegetarian, if you just pass the meat.

2 tablespoons oil
1 pound lamb or beef, trimmed and cut into 1/3- inch cubes (see directions below if other kinds of meat are used)
1/2 teaspoon turmeric

1 medium onion, coarsely chopped
1 teaspoon curry powder
1 teaspoon prepared *noomi Basrah*, see Glossary
1 teaspoon salt
1/4 teaspoon black pepper
1 teaspoon *baharat*, see Glossary
1/2 cup chopped parsley

1 recipe plain White rice, see recipe above

1. In a medium skillet, heat oil, and sauté meat cubes with turmeric, stirring frequently until all moisture evaporates, and meat starts to brown, about 15 minutes.

2. Add onion and curry powder, and stir until onion is transparent and curry is fragrant, about 5 minutes. Add *noomi Basrah*, salt, pepper and *baharat*, half way through cooking. If mixture looks dry, add a little hot water.

3. Put away from heat, and fold in parsley.

4. Cook white plain rice as directed in recipe above

5. When rice is done, empty it into a bowl. Then in the same rice pot, layer rice with the meat mixture, starting and ending with a rice layer. (If you want to make a crunchy crust, mix 2 tablespoons yogurt, 2 tablespoons oil, and 6 to 7 heaping tablespoons of the cooked rice. Spread this

mixture in the bottom of the pot, and then layer the rest of the rice and the meat mixture as described at the beginning of this step.)

Cover the pot and resume simmering on low heat for additional 15 minutes.

Serve with plain yogurt and salad.

Variations:

*If meats other than lamb and beef are used:

1. **Chicken or turkey skinless and boneless breasts or tender loins**: Cut meat (1 pound) into 1-inch cubes, wash and drain. Coat pieces with cornstarch, shaking off excess. Heat 1 tablespoon oil in non-stick skillet, and sauté until meat starts to brown, about 10 minutes. Transfer to a dish, and keep warm. In the same skillet sauté onion in 1 tablespoon oil, with the turmeric and curry powder, as directed in step 2 above. Return chicken pieces when you add parsley in step 3. The rest is the same.

2. **Fish**: Any leftover baked, fried or poached fish may be added. Just break it into chunks, removing any bones and skin. Or you may sprinkle strips of boneless, skinless fish with a mixture of flour, curry powder, salt and paprika, and fry them, or brush them with oil and bake them for 7 to 10 minutes. Avoid overcooking. Add fish to onion mixture when you add parsley in step 3 above. The rest is the same.

3. **Shrimp**: Shrimp needs a special treatment because it tends to release some moisture when cooked especially the frozen variety. Besides it should not be overcooked, otherwise it will suffer a considerable shrinkage, and gets rubbery in texture. Clean and devein 1 pound shrimps. Wash and let them drain very well. Sprinkle with a little flour and curry powder, and cook them in a heated 1 tablespoon oil in a non -stick skillet. Stir frequently until shrimps are opaque in color and are firm to the touch, 4 to 5 minutes. If too much liquid is released, get rid of it to allow shrimps to brown a little without being overcooked. Or take shrimps out, allow liquid to reduce, then return shrimps. Add cooked shrimps when you add parsley in step 3, the rest is the same.

   In addition to the different kinds of meat added to the basic recipe of *Timman Tachina*, given above, delicious and nutritious vegetables and dried fruits may also be added, such as in the following recipes:

Rice with Carrots (Timman bil Jizzar):

To the ingredients specified in the basic recipe, p., add 2 big carrots, diced or cut into thin strips (about 1 1/2 cups). Add them to the meat in step 1, half way through the given time for cooking, to allow the carrots to cook.

Note:

Other vegetables, such as cauliflower cut into florets, chopped cabbage, or peas, may be used instead of carrots. Or make colorful rice using an assortment of vegetables. Add these vegetables in step 1, half way through the cooking time of meat.

Rice with Truffles or Mushrooms (Timman bil-Chima):

Traditionally, the exotic truffles (*chima*) are used in cooking this variety of rice, but mushrooms are substituted because they are more readily available and much cheaper.

Follow same directions given in the basic recipe, p.240, using chopped lamb or beef. Add 1 pound sliced mushrooms, after you sauté onion and add spices in step 2.

Rice with Fresh Black-eyed Peas in the Pod (Timman Bi'l Loubya al-Khadra):

Follow the same directions given in the basic recipe, p.240, but add 1 pound fresh black-eyed peas in the pod or string beans. Here is how to prepare them:

Cut beans into 1/2-inch pieces. Put them in a small pot, and cover them with water. Bring to a quick boil, then lower heat and let them cook, for about 15 minutes, or until they are just done. Drain and add them to the meat mixture in step 2 when you add the *noomi Basrah* and spices. If wished, along with beans, add 3 medium tomatoes, peeled, chopped and well drained.

Suggestion:

If the variety of beans called for in this recipe is hard to come by, simply use tender green beans instead.

Rice with Spinach (Timman bi'l-Sbenagh):

Follow the same directions given in the basic recipe, p.240, but add:

2 pounds fresh spinach, washed and chopped, or two 10-ounce packages frozen chopped spinach, thawed

1/4 cup chopped fresh dill or 1 tablespoon dried dill weed.

Add them in step 2 with the *noomi Basrah* and *baharat*, but let mixture cook, until moisture evaporates.

Rice with Dried Apricots (Timman bil-Mishmish):

Follow the same directions given in the basic recipe, p.240, but add 1/2 cup diced dried apricots, 1/4 cup currants or raisins, and 1/4 teaspoon ground nutmeg. Add them to the meat mixture in step 2 along with the *noomi Basrah* and spices.

Simmered Lamb with Rice
(Quouzi ala Timman)

(Makes 4 servings)

Quouzi, in the proper sense of the Arabian cuisine, is a whole suckling lamb, stuffed with rice, meat, nuts, and dried fruits, with lots of spices and herbs. (For recipe and more information, see Chapter 10)

However in most of the restaurants in Iraq, *quouzi* is a much simpler and modest dish. For practical reasons, instead of a whole lamb, choice cuts of lamb are braised and simmered until the meat almost falls from the bones. It is usually served with rice topped with almonds and raisins. Cooked this way the meat stays lusciously moist in its own sauce. If wished, cook the rice with some of the lamb broth, this will result in flavorful rice.

2 lamb shanks, trimmed and cut into halves, crosswise (ask the butcher to do it for you)
1 tablespoon oil
1 large onion, thinly sliced
2 to 3 cloves garlic, whole
1 teaspoon curry powder
1 teaspoon *baharat* (see Glossary)
2 *noomi Basrah*, whole and pricked at several places, see Glossary
3 to 4 pods cardamom, whole
1/2 teaspoon ground coriander
1/2 teaspoon ground ginger
1/4 teaspoon black pepper
1 1/2 teaspoon salt

One recipe of cooked rice, White Rice with Vermicelli Noodles, or Yellow Rice, topped with browned almonds and currants are good choices.

1. In a medium and heavy 4-quart pot, brown shanks in oil on all sides, about 10 minutes.

2. Add onion, garlic, and curry powder. Stir until onion is translucent, and curry is fragrant, about 5 minutes.

3. Add *baharat*, *noomi Basrah*, cardamom, coriander, ginger, and black pepper. Pour into the pot hot water, enough to cover meat pieces by an inch. Mix well, and bring to a quick boil, skimming if needed. Lower heat to low, and let meat simmer, covered, for about an hour or until meat is very tender. Add salt about 15 minutes before meat is done, because adding it at an early stage will toughen the meat. For a lighter touch, cook meat ahead of time, and refrigerate it to solidify, and remove the fat.

To serve, mound rice on a platter, arrange lamb shanks all around, sprinkle almonds and currants all over, and drizzle with some of the sauce. Put rest of sauce in a separate bowl. Serve with lots of fresh greens, green onion, pickles, and yogurt drink (see chapter 21, on beverages).

243

Red Rice
(Timman Ahmer)

(Makes 4 servings)

Tomato juice gives rice an attractive red or rather orange hue.

2 cups rice, soaked in cold water for 30 minutes, then drained
2 rounded tablespoons tomato paste diluted in 3 1/2 water, or 1 1/2 cups tomato sauce
diluted in 2 cups hot water, or 3 1/2 cups tomato juice
1 1/2 teaspoon salt
1 tablespoon oil

1. About 5 minutes before rice is ready, prepare tomato liquid. Put diluted tomato paste or sauce, or tomato juice in the pot you are going to use for cooking the rice. Let it boil gently for about five minutes.

2. Stir in rice, salt and oil. Allow to boil for about 5 minutes on high heat, or until most of the liquid evaporates. Then reduce heat to low, fold rice gently with a fork to allow for expansion. Let rice simmer, tightly covered, for about 20 minutes, or until grains are cooked. If for some reason the rice looks dry, sprinkle it with a little hot water, and let it simmer for additional 4 or 5 minutes. While rice is simmering, fold it twice, quickly but gently with a fork, to allow rice to fluff and expand while simmering. Because there is tomato in the liquid, the rice might burn easier than plain rice, so watch it.

Yogurt makes an excellent accompaniment.

Variations:

* Red Rice with Browned Onion and Chickpeas: Thinly slice a medium onion, and sauté it in a small skillet in the 1 tablespoon oil given in the recipe above. Add it to the pot when you add the rice. 1 cup cooked and drained whole chickpeas may also be added.

Red Rice with Shanks and Chickpeas
(Timman Ahmer Bi'l-Zinoud wal Hummus)

(Makes 4 servings)

I've always found this dish convenient to cook, for I do not have to worry about the stew. The leftover sauce will do just fine. It is a satisfying and nutritious meal when served with yogurt, and fresh greens and herbs. Moreover, it is the ideal dish for hot summer days. Though traditionally it is cooked with lamb shanks, chicken pieces may be substituted, but you need to adjust cooking time accordingly.

2 tablespoons oil
4 lamb shanks, trimmed, and cut into two parts, crosswise (ask the butcher to do this for you), or 4 veal shanks

2 medium onions, quartered
1/2 teaspoon turmeric

2 rounded tablespoons tomato paste diluted in 3 3/4 cups hot water, or one 15-ounce can tomato sauce, diluted in 3 cups hot water, or 4 cups canned tomato juice

2 to 3 *noomi Basrah*, pricked at several places, see Glossary
1 cup whole chickpeas, picked over, soaked overnight, and drained, or one 15-ounce can cooked and drained whole chickpeas
1 tablespoon salt

2 cups rice, washed, soaked for 30 minutes, then thoroughly drained in a fine-meshed sieve

For garnish: 1/4 cup slivered almonds, or pine nuts; and 1/4 cup raisins or currants

1. Heat oil in a medium pot, and brown shank pieces on all sides, about 5 minutes. Add onion and turmeric, and fold for a few minutes until onion softens.

2. Add diluted tomato paste or sauce or juice to the meat. Add *noomi Basrah*, and drained chickpeas, and stir well. If using canned chickpeas, add it in step 3. Add more hot water to cover meat by 2 inches, about 1 cup. Bring to a quick boil, then lower heat, and, covered, let simmer gently until meat and chickpeas are tender, about 1 hour.

3. Add salt and canned chickpeas, if using any, about 15 minutes before meat is cooked. If you want to get rid of the fat, refrigerate meat and sauce to solidify and remove fat. In this case heat meat and sauce before you start cooking the rice.

4. In a medium heavy 4-quart non-stick pot, put rice, and pour 3 1/2 cups of the sauce. If needed, add hot water to make this amount. Spoon out about half of the chickpeas, and add it to the rice. Stir gently, and let cook on medium high heat, until most of the liquid evaporates, about 5 minutes. Lower heat to low, fold rice gently with a fork, and let simmer, covered tightly, for about 20 minutes.

While rice is simmering, fluff it twice with a fork, to allow grains to expand. This rice burns faster than the plain rice, so you need to watch it.

5. While rice is cooking prepare garnish. In a small skillet brown almonds in a small amount of oil. Add raisins or currants and fold, until currants are heated through.

To serve, mound rice in a serving platter, and surround it with pieces of meat. Sprinkle the surface with the prepared garnish. Put the rest of sauce in a bowl, and serve it with plain yogurt and a bowl of salad. Pickled mango salad (see chapter 3, on salads) is especially good with this dish.

Green Rice with Fresh Fava Beans (Timman Bagilla)

(Makes 4 servings)

Dill and shelled fresh fava beans will give rice a fresh and appealing green color. When out of season use frozen fava beans or lima beans. The dish may be cooked with meat to make a hearty main meal. Lamb, veal shanks, or chicken, are delicious with this kind of rice. Or you may pass the meat, and serve it with yogurt sauce,

2 pounds fresh fully-grown fava beans in the pods, or 1 pound frozen fava beans or giant lima beans, thawed

1 medium onion, thinly sliced
2 tablespoons oil
1/2 cup chopped fresh dill, or 2 tablespoons dried dill weed
1/4 teaspoon turmeric

2 cups rice, washed in a fine-meshed sieve, drained, then soaked for 30 minutes in
3 1/2 cups cold water, do not drain
1 1/2 teaspoons salt
1/4 teaspoon black pepper
1/3 cup raisins, optional

1 recipe Yogurt Sauce, recipe below

Optional: 2 boneless and skinless chicken breasts, cut into 3/4-inch cubes, sprinkled with salt and pepper, rolled in 1/2 cup cornstarch (shake off excess cornstarch), and browned in 1 tablespoon oil in non-stick pan, for about 10 minutes, or until cooked.
**   Or 4 lamb shanks or 4 veal shanks, prepared as in Simmered Lamb with Rice, above, p.243, steps 1, 2, and 3.(You might use the broth to substitute for plain water in cooking the rice.)**

1. Remove pods, and skin fava beans by pouring boiling water over them. When cool enough to handle, break the skin from the top with a knife, and simply slip off the outer skin. If frozen fava beans are used, let them thaw, and do likewise with them. Do not do anything to lima beans.

2 In a medium, heavy, 4-quart non-stick pan, heat oil and stir in onion until it starts to change color, about 7 minutes. Add prepared fava beans or lima beans, dill, and turmeric, and fold for a minute or two.

3. Add rice with the water in which it was soaked. Add salt, pepper, and raisins, if using any. Mix well, and let boil on high heat, for 5 minutes, or until most of the moisture has been absorbed by the rice. Reduce heat to low, and fold rice gently with a fork, to allow it to expand while cooking. Let rice simmer, covered tightly, for 20 minutes. While simmering, gently fold twice with a fork to allow it to fluff.

Serve rice with a bowl of Yogurt Sauce, recipe below, and fresh greens and radishes. If the optional meat is used, arrange it on or around the mounded rice.

Yogurt Sauce:

1 cup yogurt
1 clove garlic, grated
1 tablespoon fresh mint, finely chopped, or 3/4 teaspoon dried mint
1/4 teaspoon salt

Mix all the ingredients in a bowl, and use as directed above.

Green Rice with Dried Split Fava Beans

If fresh fava beans are hard to come by, it may be substituted with dried shelled and split fava beans, available at Middle-Eastern grocery shops.

1 medium onion, thinly sliced
2 tablespoons oil
1 1/2 cups dried split fava beans soaked in cold water for a few hours, then drained.
1/2 cup chopped fresh dill, or 2 tablespoons dried dill weed
1/4 teaspoon turmeric

2 cups rice washed and soaked in cold water for 30 minutes, then drained
1 1/2 teaspoons salt
1/4 teaspoon black pepper
1/3 cup raisins, optional
1 recipe Yogurt Sauce, given in previous recipe

Optional: 2 boneless and skinless chicken breasts, cut into 3/4-inch cubes, sprinkled with salt and black pepper then rolled in some cornstarch, and browned in 1 tablespoon oil in non-stick skillet, for about 10 minutes, or until done
Or 4 lamb shanks or 4 veal shanks, prepared as in Simmered Lamb with Rice, above, p., steps 1, 2, and 3.

1. In a medium heavy pot, sauté onion in oil until it starts to change color, about 7 minutes. Add drained fava beans, dill weed and turmeric. Fold for a few minutes.

2. Add 3 1/2 cups hot water, bring to a quick boil, then reduce heat to medium, and let beans boil gently, covered, until they are almost done, about 5 minutes. Do not let beans overcook. Test by biting into a piece.

3. Add rice, salt pepper, and raisins, if using any, and fold gently. There should be enough liquid to cover rice. Add a little more hot water if needed. Let rice boil for 5 minutes, or until it has absorbed most of the liquid. Lower heat to low, and fold gently with a fork. Let rice simmer for 20 minutes, or until it is done and beans are tender. While simmering, fluff it twice with a fork to allow it to expand while simmering.

Serve dish as directed in the previous recipe.

Rice with Lentils
(Timman wa Adas, or Kichree)

(Makes 4 Servings)

Nutritionists in the West have recently discovered that lentils and rice eaten together is the kind of food good for you-- each helps the other to do its best in the human digestive system. It looks as though this discovery has been made much earlier in the eastern regions of the globe. Wasn't it a pottage of lentil and rice that Esau sold his birthright for? We even have a recipe for cooking it which goes back around eight centuries ago. Equal amounts of rice and lentil were cooked the same way as *ruz mufalfal* (steamed rice with separated grains). The writer called it *mujadara* (al-Baghdadi, 45).

> **1 tablespoon oil**
> **1 medium onion, thinly sliced**
> **1 1/4 cup rice, washed in a fine-meshed sieve, drained, then soaked in 3 1/2 cups cold water, do not drain**
> **3/4 cup red lentils (the shelled variety), washed and drained, no need to soak it**
> **1 1/2 teaspoons salt**

1. In a medium, heavy, 4-quart pot, heat oil and sauté onion until transparent, about 5 minutes.

2. Stir in rice with the water in which it was soaked, drained lentils, and salt. Mix well but briefly, and let boil on high heat for about 5 minutes, or until rice absorbs most of the liquid.

3. Reduce heat to low, and fold rice with a fork to make room for expansion. Let it simmer, covered for 20 minutes or until grains are cooked. While rice is simmering, fold gently twice with a fork, to allow grains to fluff.
Serve hot with a bowl of yogurt, fresh greens, and radishes.

Variation:

*This dish may also be served simmered with lamb or veal shanks. In this case cook meat as directed in Simmered Lamb with Rice, given above, and use the broth instead of plain water to cook the rice.

*Other kinds of lentil may be used, such as brown or green variety. These lentils are unshelled and take longer to cook. Therefore the recipe given above needs to be modified a little, as follows:

1. Soak 3/4 cup unshelled lentils for about 2 hours, and drain.
2. Soak 1 1/4 cups rice in 2 1/4 cups cold water for 30 minutes. Do not drain.

3. In a small pot, cover drained lentils with cold water by 2 inches. Bring to a quick boil, then reduce to low, and let lentils simmer for about 15 minutes, or until they are cooked al dente (i.e. cooked, but still firm). Drain lentils.

4. Cook rice in the water in which it was soaked, as directed in steps 2 and 3 of Rice with Lentils above. Add drained lentils half way through simmering time, in step 3 of Rice with Lentils above.

Rice with Mung Beans
(Timman wa Mash)

(Makes 4 servings)

Mung beans are less known in the West than lentils. The grains are a little bigger, and creamier and nuttier in taste (see Glossary). In the Arabic cuisine it is as popular as lentil is. The recipe in al-Baghdadi's thirteenth-century cookbook calls for using rice and mung beans in the ratio of 3/4 to 1/4, and the instructions were to cook it the same way as *ruz mufalfal* (steamed rice, with separated grains). The dish was simply called *mash* (mung beans, 47).

3/4 cup mung beans, picked over, washed and soaked overnight, then drained
1 1/4 cup rice, soaked in 2 1/4 cups cold water for 30 minutes, do not drain

1 medium onion, coarsely chopped
1 clove garlic, grated, optional
1/4 teaspoon turmeric
1 tablespoon oil
1 1/2 teaspoons salt
1/4 teaspoon black pepper
1/4 cup currants or raisins, optional
1/4 cup chopped pitted dates, optional

1. In a small pot, cover drained mung beans with clod water by 2 inches. Bring to a quick boil, then reduce heat to low, and let simmer for about 15 minutes, or until beans are cooked but still firm. Drain.

2. In a medium heavy, 4-quart pot, sauté onion in oil for about 5 minutes, or until onion is transparent. Add garlic and turmeric a minute before onion is done.

3. Stir in rice with the liquid in which it was soaked, salt and pepper. Let boil for about 5 minutes, or until rice has absorbed most of the moisture. Gently fold rice with a fork to allow it to expand. Reduce heat to low, and let it simmer for 20 minutes. While rice is simmering, fluff it with a fork to make room for expansion.

4. Gently fold in drained mung beans prepared in step 1, raisins and dates, if using any, half way through simmering time of rice.

Serve with a bowl of yogurt and lots of fresh greens and radishes.

Variation:

For meat lovers, this rice may be accompanied with meat cooked as in **Simmered Lamb with Rice**, above. In this case use the broth instead of plain water for soaking and cooking the rice. Alternatively, you may use skinless and boneless chicken breasts, cubed, sprinkled with salt and black pepper, then drenched in cornstarch, and browned in a little oil

Eggplant Upside Down
(Maqloubat Betinjan)

(Makes 6 servings)

This is a dish for elegant occasions. Rice comes out as a mold enclosed in juicy slices of eggplant. Like the rest of the traditional eggplant dishes, it is a relic of the medieval times. In al-Warraq's tenth-century cookbook a *maghmouma* dish (covered) is described in a poem by the ninth-century prince of epicures, the Abbasid Ibn al-Mahdi. He plays on the name of the dish. In category it is *maghmouma* (means both, covered and sad), but it is called *farhana* (happy). The dish is constructed of a layer of meat spread on top of a bottom layer of chopped tallow. On top of this is spread a layer of sliced sweet onion, a layer of rice, a layer of rounds of peeled eggplant, and an optional layer of sliced carrots. The pot is sprinkled with aged *murri* (similar to soy sauce), and chopped fresh cilantro. When it comes to a boil, a whole disc of bread is put on top, and let simmer. The pot would then be inverted on a big tray, thus gladdening the hearts of the hungry when it appears like a full moon in the darkness of night (186).

Today there is no set rule for the order of layering so long as it is inverted in one piece like a mold. The following is the most popular arrangement.

2 medium eggplants (about 2 pounds)

1 tablespoon oil
1 pound lean ground meat, or rump roast cut into thin strips
1/2 teaspoon turmeric
1 onion, thinly sliced
4 cloves garlic, grated

1 teaspoon salt
1/4 teaspoon black pepper
2 teaspoons *baharat*, see Glossary
1 teaspoon ground cumin

    1/4 teaspoon allspice
    1/2 teaspoon cardamom
    2 teaspoons *noomi Basrah*, see Glossary
For the rice:
    2 cups rice, soaked in cold water for 30 minutes, then drained

    2 rounded tablespoons tomato paste diluted in 3 1/2 water, or 1 1/2 cups tomato sauce diluted in 2 cups hot water, or 3 1/2 cups tomato juice
    1 1/2 teaspoon salt
    1 tablespoon oil

    1 cup cooked tubular macaroni such as zitis, optional
    1 green pepper, thinly sliced, and 2 hot chilies, diced, if desired
    2 medium tomatoes, peeled and sliced, optional

1. Remove stems from eggplants, and peel lengthwise in a striped fashion. Slice lengthwise into 1/4-inch thick slices, and immerse in salted warm water for 30 minutes. Drain, and fry in oil, or spray or brush with oil, and broil on both sides for about 20 minutes.

2. Heat oil in a big skillet, and sauté meat with turmeric, stirring occasionally until all moisture evaporates, about 15 minutes. Add onion and garlic, and stir until onion softens, about 5 minutes.

3. Add salt, pepper, *baharat*, cumin, allspice, cardamom, and *noomi Basrah*. Stir for a few seconds to mix, and put away from heat.

4. About 5 minutes before rice is ready, bring tomato juice or alternatives to a boil, in a medium heavy 4-quart non-stick pot, 5 minutes. Add rice and salt and oil. Stir gently to mix, and let boil for 5 minutes or until rice absorbs most of the moisture. Fold gently to prevent it from sticking to the bottom of the pot. Reduce heat to low. Let simmer, covered, for 20 minutes, or until cooked. While rice is simmering, fold it twice with a fork, to allow it to fluff.

5. Grease bottom and sides of a heavy medium pot. The rice pot will do, only you need to empty the cooked rice into a bowl first. Line bottom and about 2 inches of the sides of the pot with eggplant pieces. Spread meat mixture, prepared in steps 2 and 3. Spread cooked macaroni, and arrange pepper and tomato slices, if used, on the meat layer. Spoon red rice on top, and press it with the palm of the hand, or the back of a big spoon.

6. Cover pot and let it simmer on low heat for about 15 minutes to allow bottom to brown.

   7. Let pot cool for 10 minutes then turn it upside down by inverting a big serving plate on the pot. Hold both tightly, and invert rice pot. The rice mold will be transferred to the serving dish, and the eggplant layer will be on top.
    Serve cut into wedges, with a bowl of yogurt, and lots of fresh greens, radishes and pickles.

Variation:

   *Instead of red meat, **chicken** may be used. Prepare it as follows:

Cut 1 pound chicken tender loins or skinless boneless breast into 1-inch cubes. Sprinkle with salt and black pepper and coat lightly with cornstarch, shaking off excess. Brown as directed in step 2 for 10 minutes only. Remove them from skillet, and sauté onion and garlic with the spices as directed in steps 2 and 3. Return chicken to onion mixture. The rest is the same.

*Chicken pieces, such as thighs or drumsticks, simmered to tenderness in salted water can be used instead. In this case arrange them in the bottom of the pot as directed in step 5. Prepare the onion mixture as given in steps2 and 3 without the meat. The rest is the same.

Spicy Rice with Meat (Biryani Iraqi Style)

(Makes 6 to 8 servings)

This is one of the dishes that migrated from the medieval Muslim Arab world to India and later came back to us a much spicier and more aromatic dish under the name, *biryani*. It is well known now in the Arab countries, where each region has developed its own version. Apparently the Iraqi contribution to this dish was using *ras al-'asfour* meat balls (as small as sparrows' heads) along with chicken and eggs. We learn from the extant medieval cookbooks that boiled eggs were neatly sliced with a thread to garnish dishes.

The amount of aromatic and hot spices used is largely left to personal preferences

For the rice:
> **3 cups rice, washed in a fine-meshed sieve, and drained, then soaked in 5 1/4 cups cold water, do not drain**
> **2 tablespoon oil**
> **1 ball vermicelli noodles (see glossary), optional**
> **1 tablespoon salt**

> **2 tablespoons oil**
> **2 medium onions, thinly sliced**
> **4 cloves garlic, grated**

> **1 1/2 pounds meat. Any of the following:**
> ***Lamb or beef cubes, sautéed in a little oil and 1/4 teaspoon turmeric**
> ***Ground meat, made into small meatballs, and fried or broiled, for recipe, see p.133**
> ***Chicken breasts, boneless and skinless, or tender loins, cut into cubes, sprinkled with a little salt and pepper, rolled in cornstarch, and browned in a little oil**
> ***Fish pieces, sprinkled with salt and pepper, and poached or baked in foil until just done (about 10 minutes), boned and skinned, and broken into large chunks**
> ***Shrimp coated with a little flour, and browned in a little oil, do not overcook.**

> **1/2 cup peas, canned or frozen, drained**
> **2 medium carrots, diced or cut into thin strips**
> **4 ounces sliced mushrooms (about 1 cup)**

1 1/2 tablespoons *baharat*, see Glossary
1 teaspoon salt
1/4 teaspoon black pepper
6 to 7 pods cardamom, or 1 teaspoon ground
2 to 4 whole cloves, optional
1 tablespoon *noomi Basrah*, see Glossary
1/2 teaspoon cinnamon
1 teaspoon cumin
4 hard boiled eggs, shelled
3 medium potatoes, cut into small cubes, or 2 cups frozen diced potatoes; browned in a little oil or sprayed with oil, and broiled

For garnish: Brown 1/3 cup slivered almonds in a little oil, and add 1/3 cup currants or raisins and cook just enough to heat raisins through

1. Cook rice as in Plain White Rice, p.237. If vermicelli noodles are used then follow recipe, p.238.

2. Meanwhile, in a big skillet heat 2 tablespoons oil, and sauté onion, stirring frequently, until it starts to brown a little, about 7 minutes. Add garlic about 1 minute before onion is done.

3. Fold in your choice of meat (if poached fish or precooked shrimps are used, fold them in when you add the potato cubes, below). Add peas, carrots and mushrooms, *baharat*, salt, pepper, cardamom, cloves, *noomi Basrah*, cinnamon, cumin, shelled eggs, and about 1/2 cup hot water. Simmer to allow vegetables to cook and flavors to blend, about 10 minutes, or until most of moisture has evaporated. Fold in potato cubes, (and fish or shrimp if using any). The potatoes are kept till the last so that they may not get soggy.

4. When rice is cooked, transfer it to a bowl. If you are interested in making a crunchy crust, mix 2 tablespoons yogurt, 2 tablespoons oil, and 1 cup of the cooked rice. Spread this mixture in the bottom of the rice pot. Layer rice with meat and vegetables mixture, prepared in steps 2 and 3, beginning and ending with a rice layer. Cover pot tightly, and resume simmering for about 15 minutes.

To serve, mound rice on a big platter, garnish with eggs and prepared almonds and raisins. Pickles, pickled mango, or tossed salad are delicious with this rice.

Variations:

Vegetarian Biryani: Omit meat from list of ingredients, and follow instructions given above.

Chicken Biryani: 1 medium chicken, whole or quartered, leave skin on, and prepare as follows:
Put a washed chicken, whole or quartered in a medium pot with 1 whole onion pierced with 4 or 6 whole cloves, 2 bay leaves, 4 pods cardamom, and 1 tablespoon salt. Cover with cold water and bring to a quick boil, skimming as needed. Lower heat to medium and let chicken simmer for about 30 minutes or until chicken is cooked.

Drain chicken, spray or brush it with oil, and broil until it is nicely browned on all sides. Keep warm until the rest of the dish is ready. To serve mound cooked rice and vegetables on a serving platter, and arrange chicken on top with the almond and raisin garnish.

You can use broth in cooking the rice. Replace the amount of water specified for cooking rice with cold chicken broth, after you strain it and remove most of the fat. Since broth is salted, leave out salt in rice ingredients.

Rice Pies
(Parda Palau)

(Makes 6 to 8 servings)

This dish is an elaboration on the *biryani* rice, described above. It is the perfect dish for formal presentations. Today it is the specialty dish of the of the Kurdish people in northern Iraq. As the name suggests, it is rice with vegetables (*pilau),* hidden or enclosed (*parda*) in pastry.

However, covering food with thin bread is not a new technique in the Iraqi cuisine. Its roots go as far deep in history as the ancient Mesopotamian times, as reflected in the Babylonian culinary tablets (see Introduction for details). By the time we come to the medieval times the technique has already reached its zenith in a host of dishes that come under the categories of *al-maghmoumat* and *al-judhabat.*

The idea of the *maghmouma* is to cover with *riqaq* (paper-thin) breads a prepared mixture of meat, vegetables, and sometimes rice. In ninth-century Ibn al-Mahdi's poem that al-Warraq excerpted in his chapter on *al-maghmoumat* (the covered dishes), the poet describes how it is prepared by layering meat with tallow, sweet onion, rice, and peeled eggplant cut into rounds, or carrots, with *murri* (fermented sauce), and cilantro. It was then covered with bread, and cooked until it is done and has released all its fat. To serve, the dish is inverted on a platter. The poet plays on the two meanings of *maghnouma*, covered and sad. He says although it is *maghmouma* (covered with bread), it has never seen a day of sadness, because its name is *farhana* (happy), and it brings joy to the hearts of hungry diners (186).

As for *judhaba* it is meat grilled in the *tannour*, suspended over a sweet versatile bread or rice preparation with nuts, vegetables, fruits, etc, and enclosed in *riqaq* (thin) breads. Apparently the sweet bread part of the dish gradually attained autonomy and was often cooked without suspending meat over it, as in the thirteenth-century Andalusian *judhabat um al-faraj* (for more details see *bourag*, in chapter 14 below). For presentation, the prepared dish enclosed in *riqaq* bread is inverted on a platter, letting the golden brown, crusty bottom layer of bread be on top (al-Warraq, 184-6, 235-41, al-Baghdadi, 208-9).

In the following recipe, you have the option of making your meat pie into one big mold fit for a big gathering, or you can divide it into 6 individual molds. The traditional meat cooked with the rice is usually chicken. Cooking it with shrimps or fish is my improvisation. The Kurds, mountain dwellers of northern Iraq, are not known as devout eaters of shrimp or fish.

1 recipe Biryani Rice, given above, using any of the meat options, or let it be vegetarian
1 recipe Boureg Dough # 1, see chapter 14, on savory pastries, or if not in the mood, use fillo dough, one 1-pound package
About 1/2 cup oil

Preheat oven to 400 degrees F.

1. Cook rice as directed in recipe and cool slightly.

2. Prepare dough as directed in recipe, or follow directions for thawing fillo dough.

3. If you want to make **one big mold**, generously grease 10-inch round pan. Flatten **boureg dough** on a floured surface, and make it as thin as possible. It should be big enough to cover the bottom and sides, and overhang down the edges. If making one large piece is difficult for you, divide it into two parts, and line the bottom and sides with one piece, and use the other one for covering the top after filling the pan with rice.

Fill lined pan with prepared rice, pressing it gently with the fingers or the back or a big spoon. Fold overhanging dough on the rice, to enclose and prevent rice mixture from showing. Generously brush surface with oil.

4. If using **fillo dough**, spread one layer on a working surface, lightly brush it with oil, and spread another layer on it, and brush it with oil. Repeat spreading and brushing using 10 layers. Line half of the bottom and sides of pan with those layers, letting the rest overhang down the edges. Make another stack of 10, (or the remaining sheets), repeating the same process of spreading and oiling. Line the other bottom half and sides of the pan, with this stack, making sure to allow the two stacks to overlap, to prevent filling from showing.

Fill lined pan with prepared rice, pressing it gently with the fingers or the back or a big spoon.

Fold overhanging dough on the rice, to enclose and prevent rice mixture from showing. Generously brush surface with oil.

5. Bake in a preheated oven at 400 degrees F. until dough is crisp and golden brown, about 15 minutes. Cool slightly, then unmold by inverting a big serving dish on the pan, and holding both with both hands, invert mold into plate. If bottom layer, which is now the top, is not crisp enough, return it to the oven and bake or broil it for a few more minutes until it is golden. But you need to watch it, because this dough is thin and it might burn quite easily if left unattended.

Cut into wedges using a long sharp knife, and serve, along with salad, pickles, and yogurt or your choice of stew.

6. If you choose to make **smaller molds**, then do as follows:

The number of molds made depends upon the size of bowls you're going to use. Usually I use 6 ovenproof cereal bowls to make 6 generous individual servings. In fact this is how it is served in restaurants in northern cities, such Arbeel, known in ancient Mesopotamian times as "Arbeela."

7. If using **Boureg dough**, make 1 1/2 recipes of the dough, and divide it into **6 portions**, or according to the number of bowls you've chosen. Flatten each portion as thin as possible, and line the generously greased bowl with this dough. Let it overhang down the bowl edge. Fill each bowl with the rice mixture, and press it with the back of a big spoon. Cover top completely with the overhanging dough. Brush surface generously with oil, and bake as directed above step 5. Baking time depends upon the size of bowls you've chosen, approximately 12 to 15 minutes.

8. If using **fillo dough**, spread stack of sheets on a flat surface, and divide it into two parts crosswise. This will give you about 40 layers of fillo. Divide sheets among bowls used. Layer and oil as described above in step 4. Line bowls with the layered sheets, letting the extra overhang down the bowl edge. Fill with the prepared rice mixture, press and cover completely by folding the overhanging part on the top. Bake as directed above in step 5.

To serve, unmold, and garnish with chopped and sliced vegetables, along with stew of your choice, or yogurt.

CHAPTER NINE
OTHER GRAINS AND BEANS

CHAPTER NINE
OTHER GRAINS AND BEANS

الحُبوبُ والبقُولُ

Bulgar

Bulgar, or *burghul* as it is more commonly known in the Arab countries, makes a nice and nutritious change from rice. It is especially good with eggplant dishes, and stews like okra, potato, spinach and green bean stew. Or enjoy it by itself as a snack. In most of the preceding rice recipes, you can substitute bulgar for rice, thus giving the dishes a whole new look, color, taste, aroma and texture.

Judging from the extant ancient archaeological records, the practice of toasting and then coarsely grinding grains goes back to the Sumerian times, more than 5000 years ago, and possibly earlier. To this day it is common to see people in northern Iraq preparing their winter *moona* (supply) of bulgar on their porches or sidewalks outside their houses, by parboiling, toasting and crushing wheat grains in big containers.

Bulgar comes in different grinds. Coarser grinds such as #2 and #3 are used in cooking bulgar, *mufalfal* way, i.e. with grains separated like rice. It does not need to be soaked, unless specifically required by the recipe because it is parboiled.

A Basic Method for Cooking Bulgar Mufalfal
(Makes 4 servings)

1 tablespoon oil
1/4 cup vermicelli noodles (one ball slightly crushed between the fingers)
2 cups bulgar, #2 or #3, picked over
1/2 cup cooked split or whole chickpeas
1 teaspoon salt
4 cups hot water or broth, in case of the latter, adjust salt

1. In a medium, heavy 4-quart non-stick pot, heat oil, and stir in noodles until golden brown, a minute or two.

2. If wished, wash bulgar in a fine-meshed sieve, under running water, and drain well.

3. Add bulgar, cooked chickpeas, salt and liquid, and mix well. Let boil for about 5 minutes, then reduce heat to low, and let simmer, covered, for 20 minutes, or until grains are cooked. Gently fold twice while simmering to allow grains to fluff.

Serve as a side dish instead of rice. For garnish, if wished, sprinkle it with some browned slices of onion, or browned slivered almonds and raisins.

Most of the rice recipes given in the rice chapter may be adapted for preparing bulgar dishes. Just remember **for each cup of bulgar, 2 cups of liquid are needed.**

Shelled Wheat Berries Simmered with Lamb (Habbiyah)

(Makes 6 servings)

This is another specialty of the northern region. It calls for shelled wheat berries, usually available at Middle-Eastern or international grocery markets. Wheat cooked this way, results in a lusciously creamy texture. It is a meal by itself. Shelled barley may sometimes be substituted, for a change. Traditionally, lamb shanks are used in cooking these grains, but any cuts with bones, veal shanks, or chicken pieces, skinned and trimmed, may be substituted. Alternatively you can pass the meat altogether and have it as a vegetarian dish.

> **1 tablespoon oil**
> **3 medium lamb shanks, halved crosswise. Ask the butcher to do this for you**
> **1/2 teaspoon turmeric**
> **1 onion quartered**
> **1/2 cup whole chickpeas washed and soaked overnight, or 1 cup cooked whole chickpeas**
> **1 tablespoon salt**
> **2 cups shelled wheat berries (one pound), washed and soaked overnight, drained**
> **2 cups tomato sauce, optional**

1. In a medium heavy pot, heat oil and brown shanks on all sides, about 10 minutes. Add turmeric and onion, and stir until turmeric is aromatic, a minute or so. Cover meat pieces with hot water by an inch. Add chickpeas if they are uncooked. Bring to a quick boil, skimming if needed. Lower heat to low, and let simmer, covered, for about an hour, or until meat is cooked. Add salt 15 minutes before meat is done.

2. Remove shanks from broth, and set aside, and measure the remaining broth. You need 8 cups of broth. Add hot water to make 8 cups if needed. Using the same pot, cook the drained wheat and chickpeas if you are using the already cooked ones in the measured broth. (If tomato sauce is used, then use 6 cups of broth only). Bring to a quick boil. Reduce heat to medium, and let pot cook gently, covered, until all moisture evaporates, and wheat is cooked and puffed, about 40 minutes. While wheat is cooking, fold it gently, twice. It should be sticky and creamier in consistency than regularly cooked rice.

3. Return meat pieces to pot, about 5 minutes before wheat is done, to allow it to heat through.

To serve, mound wheat on a serving platter, and arrange meat all around it. Pickles and salad are usually served with this dish.

Al-Hadba', the leaning minaret of Mosul

Shelled Wheat Porridge with Cinnamon and Sugar (Hareesa)

(Makes 6 servings)

This dish is not to be mistaken with the North-African *Hareesa*, a very hot condiment, made principally from mashed chilies, and served with couscous dishes. The word *hareesa* is derived from the Arabic verb *harasa* (to mash, derived from Akkadian "harasu"), and here the similarity ends between the two dishes. Our *Hareesa* is wheat simmered to tenderness and then mashed. This Arabian porridge was and still is a favorite food. Many medieval poems were recited in praise of its merits, and several recipes were given in their cookbooks. It is the kind of dish that, when traditionally cooked, requires slow simmering and almost constant stirring. Here is how people used to cook it in medieval Baghdad:

> Take 6 *ratls* (equivalent of 6 pounds) of fat meat, and cut into long strips: throw into the saucepan, and cover with water. Heat until almost cooked: then take out, strip the meat from the bone, shred, and put back into the saucepan. Take good, clean wheat, shell, clean, grind, and wash: weigh out 4 *ratls*, and put into the pot. Keep a steady fire going until the first quarter of the night is gone, stirring all the time: then leave over a good fire. Put in quartered chicken with cinnamon-bark, and leave until midnight: then beat well until set in a smooth paste- set hard it is spoilt- adding salt to taste. If water is needed put in hot water. Leave until dawn: then stir again, and remove. Melt fresh tail, and pour this over when ladling out. Sprinkle with cumin and cinnamon ground fine separately. It is better when made in an oven [i.e. *tannour*, the domed clay oven) than over an open fire. (Al-Baghdadi, 198-9)

259

In fact this is how it is still cooked during the first ten days of *Muharram* (the first month in the Islamic lunar calendar). The pious Shiite Muslims in middle and southern Iraq commemorate the martyrdom of Imam Husein, the prophet's grandson. Passion plays are enacted, dramatizing the battles that led to his death, and the peak of these ceremonies is the tenth day, known as *'Ashoura* (from *'ashra*, number 10). In memorial of this tragic historical incident, *hareesa* is cooked in big cauldrons, outside the house, and is simmered on wood fire. Men of the neighborhood take turns in stirring and mashing it all night long. By the advent of dawn it will be distributed in big bowls to the neighborhood families.

Hareesa making is not restricted to that period only. People like to enjoy it more often, and make it year round for breakfasts, brunches and light suppers, albeit in smaller amounts, and in the confinement of their own kitchens. Here is how to cook it the "private" way:

> **1 pound lean trimmed pieces of meat. Lamb is the traditional meat to use, but skinned chicken may be substituted**
> **1 pound (2 cups) shelled wheat, washed, soaked overnight, and drained**
> **1/2 teaspoon salt**
> **1 cup whole chickpeas cooked, optional**
>
> **Heated butter, sugar and cinnamon, for garnish**

1. Put meat pieces in a heavy big pot, and cover with 12 cups cold water. Bring to a quick boil, skimming as needed. Reduce heat to medium, and let simmer gently until meat is almost cooked, about 45 minutes.

2. Stir in drained wheat, and salt. Let pot simmer gently, until meat is thoroughly cooked and wheat is very tender. Stir occasionally to prevent ingredients from sticking to the bottom of the pot, about an hour. Add more hot water if needed. It should be of medium consistency.

3. Take meat out, and when cool enough to handle, remove bones, if any, and shred with the fingers into small pieces. Set aside.

4. Mash wheat with a potato masher, or process or blend in batches.

5. Return shredded meat to the pot. Add cooked chickpeas if using any, and resume simmering on low heat. The final porridge should be of medium consistency. Add more hot water if it becomes thick. Stir frequently so that it will not stick to the bottom, and burn.

To serve, pour into bowls. Drizzle with heated butter, and generously sprinkle with cinnamon and sugar.

Note:
This dish can be cooked without meat, and sometimes some milk is added in step 5.

The Qrayas: a Mesopotamian Group Therapy

The *qraya* is a religious reading of the holy Qur'an and the story of martyrdom common in Shiite communities. Such religious ceremonies are performed in memorial of the death of Imam Hussein, grandson of the prophet Mohammed, and religious leader at the time. He went to Kufa to press his claim to the caliphate, and was killed in battle on the plains of Karbala, on the tenth day of *Muharram* (the first month of the Islamic lunar calendar year). His death greatly contributed to the split of Islam into Shiite and Sunni sects in the seventh century AD, which persists in Islam to this day.

Many of the customs of the Shiites are deeply rooted in an Iraqi past much earlier than the seventh century AD. One of these customs is the religious lamentation, especially in its female form, which "offer close parallels with the ancient world." (Wood, 35)

Although such occasions are primarily held for their religious significance, they nevertheless, offer an opportunity for the hardworking women to wear their best clothes, leave the house, socialize, and hence release some of the pressure off their chests. Following is a unique description of the *qraya*, as seen through the keen eyes of Elizabeth Fernea during her stay in one of the southern villages in Iraq, in the late 1950's:

> For the occasion, the women wear their best black. There were some beautiful *abayahs* [black cloaks like garments covering the entire body only allowing hands and face to show] of heavy silk crepe, and a few of the black headscarves were heavily fringed. Many wore a wide-sleeved full net or sheer black dress, the *hashmi*, the ceremonial gown worn for *krayas* and similar religious services. Underneath was a hint of color; as the women seated themselves cross-legged and arranged their *hashmis* over their knees, bright satin petticoats shimmered through the smoky net: green, blue, red. They wore black stockings, and the rows of clogs left at the door were almost all black.
>
> There was a stir: the *mullah* [the professional woman who does the reading] had arrived, a tall woman with a hard, strong face, carrying worn copies of the Koran and her own Book of *Krayas*....The *mulla* sat down and the two young girls [trainees] stood to lead the congregation in a long, involved song with many responses. Gradually the women began to beat their breasts rhythmically, nodding their heads and beating in time to the pulse of the song, and occasionally joining in the choruses, or supplying spontaneous responses such as "A-hoo-ha!" or a long-drawn-out "Ooooooh!" This phase lasted perhaps ten minutes, the girls sank down into their places, and the *mullah* arose to deliver a short sermon.
>
> She began retelling the story of the killing and betrayal of the martyr Hussein, which is told every night during Ramadan and is the beginning of the important part of the *kraya*. At first two or three sobs could be heard, then perhaps twenty women covered their heads with their *abayas* and were weeping; in a few minutes the whole crowd was crying and sobbing loudly. When the *mullah* reached the most tragic parts of the story, she would stop and lead the congregation in a group chant, which started low and increased in volume until it reached the pitch of a full-fledged wail. Then she would stop dead again, and the result would be, by this time, a sincere sobbing and weeping as the women broke down after the tension of the wail.

Abruptly the weeping would stop and everyone would stand, to begin with the third stage. The mullah, flanked by her two novices, stood in the center of the court rocking forward with her whole body at each beat, slowly but regularly, until the

Crowds of women formed concentric circles around her, and they too rocked in unison,
Singing and beating their breasts. Three older women joined the *mullah* in the center, throwing aside their chin veils so they might slap their bared chests.
"A-hoo-ha" sounded the responses.
All her veils flying as she rocked, the *mullah* struck her book with her right hand to indicate a faster tempo, and the novices clapped and watched to make sure that all were following correctly. The circles of women began to move counterclockwise in a near-ceremonial dance. A step to the left, accompanied by head-nodding, breast-beating, the clapping of the novices, the slap of the *mulla*'s hard hand against the book, and the responses of "A-hoo-ah!" "Ya Hussein," they cried. The *mullah* increased the tempo again, the cries mounted in volume and intensity, the old women in the center bobbed in time to the beat, there was a loud slap against the book, a high long-drawn-out chant from the *mullah*, and everyone stopped in her tracks. The three old ladies who had bared their chests readjusted their veils, and many of the women stood silently for a moment, their eyes raised, their open hands held upward in an attitude of prayer and supplication. But the *mullah* was already conferring her novices. The *kraya* was over.

The women began to stream out, smiling and chattering (108-112).
All I can say is, Who needs a shrink after all this!

A Street in the old quarters of Baghdad
(A painting by Wathiq 1989. Permission, Altoma)

263

Beans and Grains Medley (Pottage) (Ashouriyya)

(Makes 10 servings)

Ashouriya is another dish related to the tenth day of *Muharram* (the first month of the Islamic lunar year). It is a variation on the *hareesa,* in which beans and nuts are added. However, according to a folktale deeply rooted in the ancient history of Mesopotamia, the dish might be related to the Deluge, when the dove returned to the ark of Noah and his family. Legend has it that they cooked all the remaining food on board into a sweet pudding, called *Ashurey* (Goodman, 82). In light of this, it might not be farfetched to relate the name of the dish to the ancient city of Ashur, located at the heartland of wheat and barley.

In al-Warraq's tenth-century cookbook, there are three wheat and rice dishes quite similar to the *Ashouriya.* They are categorized as *hintiyat muthallathat* (probably named after the third degree of grinding the wheat, which result in coarse grinds), or the *Makhloutat* (mixed). They are all meat pottages with a number of grains, such as shelled wheat, green wheat (*freek*), rice, lentil, dried beans, both white and red, and chickpeas (145). Sometimes sugar and milk are added (145, 149).

1 cup shelled wheat, washed and soaked overnight, drained
1/2 cup white beans, navy or great northern, washed, and soaked overnight, drained
1/2 cup whole chickpeas, washed and soaked overnight, drained
1/4 cup rice, washed and soaked 30 minutes, drained

1/4 cup slivered almonds, toasted
1/4 teaspoon salt
Sugar, to taste
1 tablespoon rose water, optional

For garnish: walnuts, dried fruits such as raisins, dates, figs and apricots, to taste

1. Put wheat, beans and chickpeas in a big pot and cover by about 12 cups cold water. Bring to a quick boil, then reduce heat, and let cook gently until wheat and beans are almost cooked, about 40 minutes.

2. Add rice, bring to a boil, then reduce heat and continue simmering until rice is tender, about 15 minutes.

3. Add almonds, salt and sugar to taste, and continue simmering until all ingredients are very tender, and mixture is of medium consistency. While simmering, stir occasionally to prevent ingredients from sticking to the bottom of the pot. Stir in rose water if wished

To serve, pour into soup bowls, and garnish with walnut pieces, and dried fruits.

Bulgar Simmered with Lentils
(Kujari 'l-Burghul)

(Makes 4 servings)

A dish of brown lentils simmered with bulgar or rice is well- known throughout the Arab world, although it comes in different guises, and passes under different names. The Egyptians cook it with rice, lentil and macaroni, and call it *Kushari*. People in Lebanon and adjoining countries cook it with lentils and rice or bulgar, and call it *Mujaddara* (literally, having smallpox). The Iraqis call it *Kujari*. In Hindi it is "kedergee", and so on. The earliest recipe for this dish can be traced back to al-Baghdadi's thirteenth-century cookbook. He called it *mujaddara*, and it was a meat dish in which rice and lentils (ratio of one part rice to 1/2 part lentil) are cooked *mufalfal* way, i.e. with the grains separated (45).

Anyway, whatever it is called, this vegetarian dish is wholesome, satisfying and delicious. Lentils, unlike dried beans, do not require soaking. However if you do soak them for two hours, you will cut down cooking time.

> **1 1/2 cups whole unshelled brown lentils, picked over, washed, soaked in cold water for 2 hours, and drained**
> **2 cups bulgar, #2 or #3, washed and drained**
> **1 cup rice, washed and soaked 30 minutes**
> **2 teaspoons salt**
> **1/4 teaspoon black pepper**
> **1/4 teaspoon chili, or to taste**
> **1 teaspoon ground cumin**
> **1 teaspoon ground coriander**
> **1/4 cup olive oil**
> **2 medium onions, thinly sliced**

1. In a medium heavy 4-quart pot, cover lentils by 2 inches cold water and bring to a quick boil, skimming if needed. Reduce heat to low and let lentils simmer gently until almost done, about 20 minutes.

2. Add bulgar, rice, salt, pepper, chili, cumin, and coriander. There should be enough liquid to cover the grains by about 1/3- inch. Add a little more hot water if needed. Bring to a quick boil, then reduce heat to low, and let simmer until grains are cooked, but still intact, about 20 minutes. While simmering fold grains gently two or three times to allow them to fluff.

3. In a medium skillet, heat oil, and stir-fry onion slices until golden brown, about 10 minutes.

4. Five minutes before grains are done, fold in two thirds of the browned onion.

To serve, pile simmered grains on a serving platter. Spread reserved third of browned onion slices on top and drizzle with any remaining oil.

265

Spicy Lentils
(Yakhni'l- Adas)

(Makes 6 servings)

Traditionally this dish is cooked with lamb, but you can pass the meat and still have a nourishing and appetizing meal. Keep spices to the minimum, or use all the varieties suggested below, for a spicier and more aromatic dish. In the neighboring countries, *yakhni* simply means stew. In Iraq it is used to describe stews that are thick and rather mushy in consistency, due to prolonged simmering. The word itself is sometimes used metaphorically. If we describe a piece of news, for instance, as *yakhni*, we mean it is old news. But do not let this discourage you from trying the dish. If prolonged simmering might spoil your news, it does wonders to your lentils.

2 tablespoons oil
1 pound lamb or beef cut into 1-inch cubes

2 medium onions, coarsely chopped
2 cloves garlic, grated
1 teaspoon curry powder
1/2 teaspoon turmeric
1 teaspoon of ground cumin, ground coriander, *baharat* (see Glossary), each
1/2 teaspoon toasted whole anise seeds, ground ginger, each

2 cups red, shelled lentils, picked over and washed
1/2 cup whole, unshelled brown lentils, washed
1 heaping tablespoon tomato paste diluted in 1/4 cup hot water, or 1/4 cup tomato sauce, or 1/4 cup tomato juice
2 medium tomatoes, peeled and chopped
1/4 teaspoon chili powder, or to taste

1 1/2 teaspoons salt
1/4 teaspoon black pepper
Juice of one lemon, or 1 tablespoon *noomi Basrah*, see Glossary

For garnish: 1/4 cup chopped onion browned in 1 tablespoon oil

1. In a medium heavy 4-quart pot, heat oil and sauté meat cubes until all moisture evaporates, and meat starts to brown, about 15 minutes.

2. Add onion, and stir until transparent, about 5 minutes. Stir in garlic, curry powder, turmeric, cumin, coriander, *baharat*, anise seeds, and ginger. Stir until spices are fragrant.

3. Stir in lentils, diluted tomato paste or sauce or juice, chopped tomatoes, and chili. Add enough hot water to cover lentils and meat by about 2 inches. Bring to a quick boil, then reduce heat to low, and let simmer gently, covered, for about 30 minutes, stirring occasionally.

4. Add salt, pepper, and lemon or *noomi Basrah*, and resume simmering for about 15 more minutes, or until red lentil is mushy, whole brown lentil is tender, and sauce is nicely thickened. While simmering, stir frequently to prevent grains from sticking to the bottom of the pot.

266

To serve ladle out into a big bowl, and sprinkle with the prepared browned diced onion. Hot toasted bread or rice is the usual accompaniment to this dish.

Variations:
Spicy Lentils with Spinach:

To the ingredients above, add 1 pound chopped spinach, or one 10-ounce package frozen spinach. Add it to the pot about 10 minutes before dish is done, in step 4.

*Spicy Lentils with Meat Balls:

Instead of meat cubes, prepare meatballs, as directed on page 133. Shape them into small balls, broil or fry them and add them to the pot in step 4.

Flat Bread Sopped in Broth of Fava Beans (Tashreeb or Thareed Bagilla)

(Makes 4 servings)

Bagilla, (fava beans) is the Iraqi counterpart of the Egyptian *fool mudammas.* However, the Iraqi variety is larger and fleshier than the Egyptian beans. It is the dish to serve for brunch on Fridays, the weekend in Islamic countries.

The dish is invariably prepared without meat, and apparently this was how it has always been served centuries ago. In the augmented version of al-Baghdadi's cookbook, *Wasf al-At'ima al-Mu'tada,* (fourteenth century) there is a *thurda* (variant of *thareed*) recipe that calls for boiling fava beans with salt, then sopping broken pieces of bread in its broth, with cumin, sumac, lemon juice, walnut, yogurt, or clarified butter, or oil. (445-6)

During the medieval times, such a vegetarian dish was called *muzayyaf,* or *muzawwar,* i.e, counterfeit. The implication is that only dishes with meat are considered authentic, but they are also given as alternatives for Christians during Lent. In modern traditional standards a vegetarian dish like this was thought of as less prestigious than meat dishes. There was a time, probably up until the mid-fifties, when people used to take their bread to be soaked in a big pot of simmering fava beans fixed by a woman vendor, at the corner of the neighborhood sidewalk. To distinguish which bread belongs to whom, people used to mark their breads with colored threads. When they came to pick up their dishes, *um il-bagilla* (vendor, literally the mother of beans) would ask, "What's your color?"

Though *Tashreeb Bagilla* is definitely no haute cuisine, it can be made quite attractive when garnished with fried eggs sunny-side up, sprinkled with sumac and crushed *butnij* (a kind of wild mint), and drizzled with sizzling hot butter or oil.

Dried fava beans are normally used for making the dish except during the summertime when fully-grown fresh fava beans are available. In this case the pod is discarded, and the beans are simmered until tender. Alternatively, canned fava beans may be substituted The dish is better made with slightly stale bread, so that it will not disintegrate when simmered in the broth.

2 cups dried fava beans (about 1/2 pound), wash very well, then soak in cold water for 24 hours, do not drain.
2 teaspoons salt

1 1/2 Iraqi flat bread or Arabic bread, see bread chapter, preferably rather stale
2 tablespoons olive oil
4 eggs
1 lemon
1 teaspoon sumac, optional, see Glossary
1 tablespoon dried and crushed *butnij* (known in the United States as wild or river mint, see Mint, in Glossary)

1. In a medium pot, put fava beans with water in which it was soaked, add more water if needed to cover beans by 4 to 5 inches (up to 3/4 of the pot). Bring to a quick boil, skimming if needed, 10 minutes. Reduce heat to low, and let beans simmer slowly and gently, covered, for about an hour, or until beans feel soft to the touch. Add salt about 10 minutes before beans are done, since adding it earlier would toughen the beans.

2. To prepare the dish: with a slotted spoon, take out most of the beans and put in a plate, set aside in a warm place. Break bread into smaller pieces, and add them to the bean liquid. Let them simmer for about 10 minutes.

3. With a slotted spoon take out the bread pieces and place them on a big platter. Spread the reserved beans all over the bread.

4. In a medium non-stick skillet, heat oil and fry eggs sunny side up, until just set. It is a good idea to put a lid on the skillet while frying to help eggs set faster without burning. Separate eggs if possible, and arrange them on the beans.

5. Squeeze lemon juice on the entire surface of the dish. Sprinkle crushed *butnij* and sumac all over the surface.
Serve with wedges of tomatoes, green onions, and mixed pickles, preferably pickled chilies.

Short Cut: Use canned fava beans instead of the dried variety. You'll need two 15-ounce cans, do not drain. Add some water and bring to a quick boil, and use as directed above.

Flat Bread Sopped in Broth of Creamy Black-eyed Peas (Tashreeb Loubya)

(Makes 4 servings)

This is a variation on the fava beans dish. Dried black-eyed peas are used in making this humble but delicious dish. Lamb or veal shanks are sometimes cooked with them, but it makes a satisfying meal even without the meat.

2 lamb shanks, cut into halves crosswise, ask the butcher to do it for you, or 4 veal shanks, optional
1 tablespoon oil, if meat is used

1/2 pound (1 1/4 cup) dried black-eyed peas, washed, soaked overnight, and drained. Alternatively use frozen variety (you'll need 1 pound), o r canned variety (you'll need two 15-ounce cans)
1 onion, quartered
2 whole *noomi Basrah* (see Glossary) pricked at several places
4 to 6 whole garlic cloves, unpeeled
1 teaspoon cumin
1 tablespoon salt

1 1/2 Iraqi flat bread 3 Arabic breads, see bread chapter, preferably rather stale
2 tablespoons oil
4 eggs, optional
Dried and crushed *butnij* or mint, see Glossary

1. If optional meat is used, heat oil in a medium heavy pot, and brown meat pieces on both sides, about 10 minutes. Cover with hot water by an inch. Bring to a quick boil, then reduce heat to low and let simmer gently, until meat is tender, about an hour. This can be done ahead of time, since it is going to be added to the beans at a later stage. Besides, this will also enable you to remove fat after it solidifies in refrigerator.

2. In a medium heavy pot put drained beans, onion, *noomi Basrah*, and garlic. Cover with cold water by 3 to 4 inches, and bring to a quick boil, skimming if needed. Lower heat to low, and let beans simmer, covered, until tender to the touch, about 40 minutes. Add salt, cumin, and cooked meat, if using any, with whatever broth is left, about 10 minutes before beans are done, stirring gently. (Frozen beans might need less cooking time, so watch it). If canned variety is used, then let onion, *noomi Basrah*, and garlic simmer in water for about 15 minutes, then add drained canned beans, with cooked meat if used, and let simmer for additional 10 minutes.

3. When ready to serve, take out beans with a slotted spoon, and keep warm.
4. Break bread into smaller pieces and put them in the bean pot. Let them cook gently on medium heat, for about 10 minutes.

5. Spoon out bread pieces into a big platter, with some of the bean liquid. Cover bread with the reserved beans, and arrange meat pieces, if used. Squeeze out *noomi Basrah* all over the surface, making sure to discard peel and seeds.

6. Heat oil in a small pan, and sizzle all over the dish. If eggs are used, which often is the case when meat is not used, in a non-stick pan heat oil and break eggs, and allow them to fry whole, sunny side up. While frying, cover pan with a lid to allow egg to solidify without burning. Arrange eggs on the dish.

7. Sprinkle generously with *butnij* or mint.
Serve with green onions, sliced tomatoes, and pickles, preferably picked hot chilies.

The Problem with Beans

Beans are an excellent nutritional source. They are versatile, tasty, and cheap. They are a good source of fiber and are believed to lower blood pressure and bad-cholesterol levels. They are low in fat and high in folic acid, which helps prevent some birth defects and cancers. But the problem with beans is that our bodies lack the enzyme to break down bean sugars. Bacteria feed on the sugars in the intestines in a natural fermentation process producing, unfortunately, gas. To make the effects of beans on your body less devastating, some think that it helps a lot if you soak beans overnight, rinse and cook them in fresh water. Let them boil for 10 minutes, then lower heat and simmer to tenderness. But then there is always the product "Beano" that comes to the rescue and help digest these troublesome sugars. After all didn't it help the monks keep their vow of silence, as the T.V. commercial goes?

Talking of beans, there is a funny story in the *Arabian Nights,* which deals with the by-product of beans. Richard Burton, the translator, finds the following story very curious, and thinks it is ethnologically valuable. It is the story of "How Abu Hasan brake Wind." The story incidentally gives details on the elaborate wedding customs at the time. The story begins with the wedding of Abu Hasan, a widower who is remarrying following the advice of his friends.

> The whole house was thrown open to feasting: there were rices of five several colors, and sherbets of as many more; and kids stuffed with walnuts and almonds and pistachios and a camel colt roasted whole. So they ate and drank and made mirth and merriment; and the bride was displayed in her seven dresses and one more, to the women, who could not take their eyes off her. At last the bride groom was summoned to the chamber where she sat enthroned; and he rose slowly and with dignity from his divan; but in so doing, for that he was over full of meat and drink, lo and behold! he let fly a fart, great and terrible. Thereupon the guest turned to his neighbor and talked aloud and made as though he had heard nothing, fearing for his life. But a consuming fire was lit in Abu Hasan's heart; so he pretended a call of nature; and, in lieu of seeking the bride-chamber, he went down to the house-court and saddled his mare and rode off, weeping bitterly, through the shadow of the night.

He fled to India, and after many years he longed to go home. Disguised he went, and stayed at the outskirts of the city, listening to people to make sure that his case was forgotten by now. "He listened carefully for seven nights and seven days, till it so chanced that, as he was sitting at the door of a hut, he heard the voice of a young girl saying, "O my mother, tell me the day when I was born; for such an one of my companions is about to take an omen for me." And the mother answered, 'Thou was born, O my daughter, on the very night when Abu Hasan farted.' Now the listener no sooner heard these words than he rose up from the bench, and fled away."

Burton explains that "a *Badawi* who eructates as a civility, has a hatred for this… and were a by-stander to laugh at its accidental occurrence, he would at once be cut down as a 'pundonor.'" To the western world, such an occurrence poses no point of honor, and is ignored. (Vol. 5, 135-7)

Curried Black-eyed Peas
(Kari'l Loubya)

(Makes 4 servings)

Since my mother had a light hand on chilies, my father, a devout lover of hot foods, felt the urge every now and then to prepare us a pot of hot and spicy curry. His dishes were memorably delicious, especially the one made with black-eyed peas. He made it so hot that we felt like smoke was coming out of our ears while eating it.

1/2 pound (1 1/4 cup dried black-eyed peas, washed, soaked overnight, and drained. Alternatively frozen (you'll need one pound) or canned variety (you'll need two 15-ounce cans, drained) can be used
5 to 6 whole cloves of garlic, unskinned

1 medium onion, coarsely chopped
2 tablespoons oil
1 teaspoon turmeric
1/2 teaspoon whole aniseed
2 tablespoons flour

1 1/2 teaspoons salt
1/2 teaspoon black pepper
1 1/2 teaspoons ground cumin
1 teaspoon ground coriander
1 bay leaf
1 teaspoon thyme
1/2 teaspoon chili flakes or powder, or to taste
1 teaspoon prepared *noomi Basrah*, see Glossary

1. In a medium pot, cover beans and garlic with cold water by 2 inches. Bring to a quick boil, then lower heat to low, and let simmer, covered, until tender to the touch, about 40 minutes. If canned variety is used skip this step.

2. While beans are simmering, heat oil in a medium skillet, and sauté onion until it softens, about 5 minutes. Stir in turmeric, aniseeds and flour until fragrant, about 5 minutes. Add 1cup hot water, and mix well, set aside.

3. When beans are cooked (if canned beans are used add them in this step with 1 cup hot water), add onion mixture, salt, pepper, cumin, coriander, bay leaf, thyme, chili, and *noomi Basrah*. Mix well, and bring to a quick boil. Reduce heat to low, and let pot simmer gently for about 15 minutes, or until sauce is nicely thickened and beans are very tender, stirring occasionally to prevent ingredients from sticking to the bottom of the pot.
Serve with warm bread.

271

Succulent Macaroni Simmered in Spicy Tamarind Sauce (Ma'karoni)

(Makes 4 to 6 servings)

In Iraq and most parts of the Arab world pasta is not a staple food the way rice is. It is cooked every now and then for variety's sake. In my growing years, the only types of pasta we had access to were the long tubular macaroni that were broken into smaller pieces before cooking them, besides the vermicelli noodles (*sha'riyya),* and the local toasted small noodles called *rishta.* Spaghetti was the last to reach the region. Both *sha'riyya* and *rushta* are used in soups, and are cooked with rice as garnish. Because *sha'riyya* is much finer and delicate in texture, it is also used in making desserts.

Apparently experimentations with wheat to make pasta of some sort, go back as early as ancient Mesopotamia. In one of the Babylonian recipes written in the second millennium BC, there was already a hint that they knew pasta of some sort (see Box below). As we advance to the medieval times there was mention of *itriya, sha'riyya,* and *rishta* (see Box below). In the tenth-century Baghdadi cookbook, Al-Warraq includes a *ma' wa malh* soup (literally water and salt, basically meat broth) to which were added pieces of *'ajeen* (dough). According to al-Warraq, the dish was the invention of the Persian king, Khasrau. They were made from stiff dough that was rolled out as thin as *riqaq* bread, and were then cut lengthwise into strips, each strip was cut into *shawabeer* (triangles) and thrown into the boiling broth (200-1). These pieces of pasta were called *lakhshat* because they got slippery when cooked (Perry, "Notes on Persian Pasta," 253).

Al-Warraq also included two recipes in which ravioli-like pastas were thrown into a simmering pot of *humadhiya ibrahimiya* (sour stews of Ibrahim Ibn al-Mahdi, the Abbasid prince). *Sanbousaj* pastries were made from stiff and well-kneaded dough. It was stuffed with cooked spicy meat filling, sealed well, and carefully dropped into the simmering pot of stew (156-7). Similar dishes in the medieval Persian were called *joshparag* (boiled pastries?), that later evolved into the *shishbarak* dishes known, to this day, in countries adjacent to Iraq. No further experimentations with pasta were recorded after the medieval period, probably because the availability and popularity of rice rendered further steps not so essential.

The way macaroni is traditionally cooked nowadays is very basic, but the blend of spices added makes it very aromatic.

1 pound lamb cut into small cubes, or lean ground meat
2 to 3 tablespoons olive oil
1 medium onion, coarsely chopped
1 teaspoon turmeric
3 tomatoes, skinned and chopped
3 heaping tablespoons tomato paste (one 6-ounce can), or one 15-ounce tomato sauce
1/4 cup chopped pepper, preferably hot variety
1 cup sliced mushrooms, optional

1 1/2 teaspoons salt
1/4 teaspoon black pepper
1/4 teaspoon dried sage or 1 teaspoon chopped fresh sage
1/2 teaspoon coriander
1/2 teaspoon cumin

1/2 teaspoon ginger powder
1/2 teaspoon ground mustard
2 bay leaves
1 teaspoon brown sugar or honey
1 scant tablespoon tamarind concentrate

10 ounces ziti macaroni cooked al dente according to package directions. Drain, but keep 2 cups of its liquid aside.

1. In a heavy medium pot cook meat in oil, stirring occasionally until meat starts to brown, about 10 minutes.

2. Stir in onion until soft, about 5 minutes. Add turmeric and stir for a few more minutes.

3. Fold in the rest of the ingredients except for macaroni. Stir for a few minutes.

4. Gently fold in the cooked macaroni. Add the reserved macaroni liquid. Let pot simmer gently until ingredients are well blended, and sauce is nicely thickened, about 15 minutes.
   Serve with salad.

Macaroni and Noodles: A Bit of History

We are all familiar with macaroni and traditionally associate it, as a matter of course, with Italian cooking. However, it has been plausibly argued that its homeland might be somewhere else. Clifford Wright's search, the most extensive so far, has led him to the "juncture of medieval Sicilian, Italian, and Arab cultures" as a possible origin for the pasta proper, made from hard durum wheat (622).

Contrary to the belief that macaroni is an Italian loan word, there is the theory that it is of Arabic origin. It describes, the argument proceeds, an old type of pasta made in Tunisia by joining (*qarana*) the two ends of vermicelli-like noodles and, hence the name *maqruna* (two ends attached), which became the generic name for macaroni. Wright withholds his judgment for lack of written evidence (627). It is my hunch though that there should be some credible grounds for this theory, and that calling pasta by this generic name was not exclusively Tunisian. In Iraq up until the fifties, pasta in the southern regions was called *maqarna*, but in more cosmopolitan areas such as Baghdad, that word was already passé. They replaced it with the classier Italicized *ma'karoni*.

As for noodles, the Baghdadi medieval cookbooks mention two kinds. The *rishta* (Persian loan word, literally "thread") was more like fresh noodles. According to the thirteenth-century Baghdadi cookbook "it is made by kneading flour and water well, then rolling out fine and cutting into thin threads four fingers long," (45) and was thrown into the simmering pots of soup or stews.

As for *itriya*, we know that it was "made of dough", "thrown in the pot by handfuls," and was "cooked like *rishta*," as explained in one of the recipes of fifteenth-century al-Mubarrad's cooking-pamphlet (Perry, "Kitab al-Tibakhah," 18). But *itriya* was mentioned in dictionaries and cookbooks much earlier than this one. The word appeared in two ninth-century Arabic dictionaries. In one of them it was described as cloth-like pasta, and the other said it was "a sort of food similar to *hibriya*," (Wright, 623) which was a kind *Yamani* (from

Yemen) silken shawl or wrap worn by ladies. Both seem to be referring to thin sheets of pasta, which seems to be in keeping with the view that it was related to the Greek "itrion", which itself was derived from the pre-Christian Aramaic, with reference to thin sheets of unleavened dough. It seems that at some point after the ninth century those thin sheets started to be cut into thin strips. Al-Idrisi, the twelfth-century Arab geographer, for instance, mentioned the *itriya*, describing it as a kind of vermicelli pasta (Wright, 623). Moreover, the first pictorial representations of pasta occurred in the medieval Latin translations of the Arabic medical eleventh-century treatise of Ibn-Butlan's *Taqweem al-Sihha*. In the manuscript's translations of Venice and Rome it was called "trij" and, in the pictures, it looked like fettuccine. By the fourteenth century the generic name for pasta in Italy was "tria" (Wright, 623).

In his tenth-century cookbook, al-Warraq used *itriya* in a chicken stew called *nibatiyya* (from Nabat, in syria), accredited to Ishaq al-Mausily. According to the recipe, three handfuls of *itrya* made of white dough was added in the last stages of cooking (181). In another sweet *muhallabiya* dish, it was cooked in milk and butter, and sweetened with sugar or honey. Both cases indicate that *itriya* must have had the same uses as those of the delicate *sha'riyya* (fine noodles, as fine as hair). The fact that these noodles were handled in dried form, either made at home and stored or purchased ready made, is evident in al-Warraq's instruction to "take *itriya* and pick it over (*yunaqqa*)" (262). In his chapter on nature of foods made from grains, we also learn for sure that it was made from unleavened dough (*fateer*, 33). The name *itriya* itself might well have been related to the Arabic adjective *tariya* (Arabic root: t-r-a, Aramaic: t-r-y), meaning succulent and tender (in this case, because so thin) which can be taken as a descriptive name of what these delicate noodles looked like after they were cooked. Anyway in modern Arabic the word *itriya* is no longer used, but *rishta* and *sha'riyya* are still with us.

Apparently, in looking for the origin of pasta, research has not gone beyond the Greeks or the Aramean peoples. Earlier attempts, however, may be recognized in the cuisine of ancient Mesopotamia as registered in the Babylonian recipes. In the "spleen stew" there were directions to throw into the cooking pot "bits of roasted qaiatu-dough" (Bottéro, *Mesopotamian Culinary Texts*, 10). To begin with, ancient Mesopotamia is an eligible candidate to be the first creator of pasta, because emmer wheat grew there, even the word semolina was ultimately derived from the Akkadian "samidu." As for the kind of dough mentioned in the recipe, it is my hunch that it refers to some kind of fine noodles. The Akkadian "qatanu," from which "qaiatu" was possibly derived, means, to become thin and fine, usually used in relation to textiles (*Dictionary of American Heritage*). The two ninth-century Arab lexicographers many centuries later used the same textile analogy in describing *itriya*.

The Arabic *qitan*, with its plural, *qaiateen*, is ultimately derived from this Akkadian "qatanu," which means, strings or cords. Ergo, there is the possibility that the qaiatu-dough was flattened thin "qatanu," and was cut into strips like *qaiateen* (strips or cords). The fact that they were toasted before throwing them into the simmering pot confirms the belief that it was not regular bread dough. As we all know from our familiarity with *sha'riyya* (vermicelli) noodles, toasting helps keep them intact and prevents them from getting doughy or disintegrating into the liquid. To this day the local rustic-looking, brown, and small noodles called *rishta* are sold already toasted in the markets of Iraq.

Chicken with Macaroni, 376

Cooked bulgar, 257

CHAPTER TEN
LAMB AND BEEF
AND GROUND MEAT DISHES

1. Lamb and Beef Dishes

2. Dishes with Ground Meat

CHAPTER TEN
LAMB AND BEEF, AND GROUND MEAT DISHES

اللّحُـوم

1. Lamb and Beef Dishes

It is our custom that the main meal dish has got to have some meat in it, whether little or much depends upon how much money you are ready to invest into it. But generally speaking the Arabic cuisine of today is characterized by a moderate consumption of meat, usually taken in combination with lots of vegetables, bread, grains and beans. Indeed, in most of the dishes cooked on daily basis meat is added as a flavoring agent or a condiment rather than the primary ingredient itself. The reason is basically economical. Vegetables are comparatively speaking much cheaper than meat, and they are mostly used to eke the meat out. According to modern studies, this is the healthy thing to do.

With regard to consumption of meat, the medieval diners during the medieval times were much more demanding than their modern counterparts. Vegetarian main dishes, to them, were not real food, they were called *muzayyafat* or *muzawwarat* (false or counterfeit dishes), served as side dishes, cooked for special religious purposes such as Lent, or given to sick people who could not handle meat.

However, when it comes to dinner invitations and other social gatherings, we are as medieval as medieval can be. According to the traditional codes of hospitality, meat is a status symbol. The more meat you offer your guests the more honored and welcomed they feel, and the more appreciated you will be. Vegetarian dishes are not the right stuff for such occasions. A classic Arab peasant feast in general might well be huge trays, heaped with rice and succulent lamb, with lots of flat breads. In more urban areas dishes are more luxuriously prepared. On weddings, for instance, *quouzi* is the traditional dish to prepare. A whole lamb would be stuffed with rice, nuts and raisins, and then rubbed from the outside with a paste of onion crushed with spices like cinnamon, cloves and cardamom. It is browned first in hot clarified butter, and then roasted and served on a mound of fragrant *anber* rice (excellent local variety of rice usually grown in the southern marshes of the region). Around the center tray of *quouzi*, numerous plates of stews, greens, salad vegetables, and pickles would be arranged.

The sheep is also a religious sacrificial symbol. It is usually slaughtered when people perform

the pilgrimage to Mecca, known as *Hajj*, or as a fulfillment of a wish called *nidhir*. Most of the sacrificed meat would be distributed among neighbors and the needy. Whether for religious sacrifice or regular consumption, according to the guidelines of the *halal* method, the Muslim butcher must say *bismillah* (in the name of God) before slaughtering the animals.

Beef is used but mostly in dishes requiring ground meat. Pork is not readily available for it is banned by Islam. There is evidence, however, that on the land of ancient pre-Islamic Mesopotamia, pigs along with sheep, cows, goats and gazelles were consumed.

The domestication of sheep started around the ninth millenium BC in northern Iraq. According to a Sumerian legend, prosperity started in Mesopotamia when the gods "made the ewe give birth to the lamb, and the grain increase in the furrows". Cows and pigs were domesticated a little later. In Sumer, beef and mutton were popular with those who could afford them, but mutton was more commonly used. Of sheep there were many breeds. About 200 Sumerian words designating the various types of sheep have come down to us, although most of them are still unidentified. Of the known types there were, for instance, the "wiry-haired" sheep, fattened sheep, mountain sheep and "fat-tailed" sheep. Of all these kinds only the fat-tailed sheep survived. It is this fat tail that has been providing the cooks for thousands of years with a valuable source of fat, that was looked upon as a great delicacy and high quality fat. In fact, it is not until recently that people in the region started to use less of this fat and more of vegetable oil for health reasons.

An Assyrian seventh-century BC stone relief showing cooks at work in the royal kitchens of Ashurbanipal of Nineveh. Clockwise: a servant opening and airing wine jars, with a swatter in one hand and a fan in the other. Two women preparing food. Two butchers working on a slaughtered animal. A baker tending to his oven. (British Museum)

The rich ancient Assyrians used to keep herds of sheep. As for the poor, one or two were kept mainly for cheese making. In their records they were referred to as "sheep of the roof." The indication is that they were kept on the flat roofs of their houses presumably for lack of pastures or room.

As for cows, they were kept for their meat as well as their milk, dung, and hide, in addition to being used as agricultural laborers. Those destined for food or sacrifice must have been fattened to a huge size, for in one of the letters belonging to the second millennium BC there was mention of an ox intended for a palace offering, which had been made so fat that it could not stand. They were very much like part of the family. It is known, for instance, that in Old-Babylonian households, they were given names just like any other member of the family. Letters sometimes inquire about the health of the cow along with the rest of the household.

Goats were normally herded with sheep, and their meat was acceptable but definitely not a delicacy. It was a regular part of peasant diet. In the modern northern regions of Iraq goat meat is sold along with beef and lamb, but it is reputed to be hard on the digestion. Goats were mostly kept for their delicious milk and their hides, which make excellent liquid containers. The gazelle was considered an important meat especially in the third millenium BC and earlier.

As for pigs, archaeological evidence shows that in the third millennium BC they were a common sight on the streets of Mesopotamia, and they still were up until the 1950's AD. Wild pigs can still be found in the marshes in the south, and there is an island on the river Tigris near Baghdad called *Jazeerat um-al Khanazeer*, (the pigs' island). Evidently it was once inhabited by pigs. However, the pig was rarely presented in art, and was seldom mentioned in ancient texts. It was mostly valued for its fat meat. A Sumerian proverb makes the point that pork was too good for a slave girl. She has to make do with the lean ham. With the advent of Judaism and later Islam, pork was tabooed. This religious prohibition, some argue, has its roots in medical doctrines-- that pork was a dangerous meat in a hot climate, and that this must have been taken into account when the dietary regulations were being formulated.

Archaeological findings also point out to the fact that after the animals were slaughtered they were butchered into these cuts: head, neck, hind legs, breast, ribs, thighs, back tail, heart, stomach, liver, entrails, and kidneys. There is also evidence that it was made into soups, and stews. It was roasted, fried, ground, chopped, pickled, and dried, sometimes after being steeped in a solution of spices (see Introduction for more details).

Simmered Lamb on a Bed of Flat Bread
(Thareed or Tashreeb Laham)

(Makes 4 servings)

The idea of the *thareed* --soaking bread in broth and serving it with meat-- is an ancient one. In one of the Babylonian recipes breadcrumbs were added to the pot as last stage in the preparation of the dish (for more information see Introduction). Islamic tradition has it that the prophet Muhammad singled out the *thareed* as the "master" of all dishes. History has it too, that the prophet's great-grandfather got his nickname al-*Hashim* (the crumbler) when in a year of famine he made bread available for his tribe, *Quraysh*. He brought it by caravan from Syria, and crumbled it and made into *thareed*. The overwhelming number of recipes for making different kinds the dish given in medieval cookbooks is testimony enough on its popularity.

In today's cuisine *thareed* or *tashreeb* is still popular as a traditional dish but it is usually reserved for informal gatherings. The way to eat it is to dig in with the hands, actually three fingers, and enjoy it with lots of condiments.

2 lamb shanks (about 2 1/2 pounds), each halved crosswise (ask the butcher to do this for you), or 4 veal shanks. Any pieces of lamb with bone and substantial amount of meat will do. Trim off excess fat.

> **1 tablespoon oil**
> **1 tablespoon curry powder**
> **5 to 6 cloves garlic, unskinned**
> **2 onions, quartered**

> **1 cup chickpeas, soaked overnight, and drained. Or 2 cups drained canned chickpeas**
> **4 medium potatoes, pealed and cut into big cubes**
> **1/2 teaspoon ground coriander**
> **2 bay leaves**
> **2 to 3 whole *noomi Basrah*, pricked at several places, see Glossary**
> **2 whole chili peppers, optional**

> **1 tablespoon salt**
> **3 boiled eggs, shelled, optional**
> **2 big flat breads, Iraqi style, see Bread chapter, or 4 pita breads**
> **Yogurt Sauce (optional):**
> **1 cup yogurt**
> **1/2 cup chopped parsley**
> **1/2 teaspoon salt**
> **1 clove garlic, grated**
> **1/4 teaspoon crushed chili**

1. In a medium heavy pot, heat oil and brown meat pieces on all sides, about 10 minutes. Add curry powder, garlic, and onion. Stir for a few minutes, or until curry is fragrant.

2. Pour 8 cups hot water. Add chickpeas, potato, coriander, bay leaves, dried limes, and chili peppers, if using any. (Canned chickpeas is to be added about 10 minutes before meat is done) Bring to a quick boil, skimming as needed. Reduce heat to low, and let meat simmer, covered, until very tender and enough liquid is left, about 1 1/2 hours, depending on your choice of meat cuts. Add salt and shelled boiled eggs, if using any, half way through cooking. Discard bay leaves.

3. When ready to serve, break bread into small pieces, and put them in a big dish. Pour enough of the liquid to cover the bread, and arrange meat pieces and the rest of vegetables on top of the bread. Traditionally some hot oil is sizzled on the meat mixture, but this step can be skipped.

4. Prepare the sauce, if used, by stirring parsley, salt, garlic, and chili into the yogurt. Drizzle this sauce on top of the *tashreeb*. Serve with pickles, and sliced vegetables such as onion, tomatoes and cucumber.

A Light Touch:

If you want to get rid of fat completely, cook meat the night before, and refrigerate the pot. The following day, and before heating it, remove the solidified fat on top.

Variations:
* *Tashreeb Ahmer (Lamb Simmered in Tomato Sauce):* Add 3 heaping tablespoons tomato paste (one 6-ounce can) to the liquid in step 2.

Tashreeb of Lamb and Eggplant Simmered In Pomegranate Sauce (Tashreeb Sharab al-Rumman)

(Makes 4 servings)

This is a nice variation on the basic *tashreeb* dish. Instead of *noomi Basra*, pomegranate syrup is used to give the dish a delicious sweet and sour flavor and an attractive hue. Al-Warraq gives a similar recipe in his tenth-century cookbook, in which he adds crushed chickpeas to the broth, to give it some body (155).

> **2 lamb shanks (about 2 1/2 pounds) prepared as instructed in the main *tashreeb* recipe above**
> **3 tablespoons oil, divided**
>
> **1 medium onion, coarsely chopped**
> **1/4 cup pomegranate syrup, see Glossary**
> **1/4 cup yellow split chickpeas**
> **1 teaspoon *baharat*, see Glossary**
> **2 whole chili peppers, optional**
> **1 teaspoon ground coriander**
>
> **4 small eggplants, or 1 big eggplant**
> **1 tablespoon salt**
> **2 big flat breads Iraqi style, or 4 small pita breads, see Bread Chapter**

1. In a medium heavy pot heat 1 tablespoon oil and brown meat pieces on all sides, about 10 minutes.

2. Add onion and stir for a few more minutes.

3. Pour 8 cups hot water, and add pomegranate syrup, chickpeas, *baharat*, chili peppers, if used, and coriander. Let pot simmer, covered, until meat is very tender, about 1 1/2 hours.

4. While pot is simmering prepare eggplant. Just trim the stalks of the eggplants; do not remove them completely. Peel eggplants completely, and quarter them lengthwise but not all the way through, i.e. leave them intact. Soak them in warm salted water for 30 minutes, drain well and then lightly brown in the remaining 2 tablespoons of oil, or brush them with oil and broil them.
If using 1 big eggplant, peel it and cut it into thick slices. Soak eggplant pieces in warm salted water for 30 minutes, then drain and lightly brown in a little oil, or brush with oil and broil.

5. Add salt and prepared eggplant half way through cooking.

6. In a big platter break bread into smaller pieces. Pour enough of the hot liquid to soak bread. Arrange meat pieces and eggplant all over the bread. Serve with sliced salad vegetables.

Head, Tripe, and Trotters

پاچَة

(Pacha)

This dish is for the nostalgic, the curious and the bold, and as for the squeamish, I can only say, you don't know what you're missing! Here is a description of it through the eyes of an American couple, visiting Baghdad in the late sixties:

> Nearby [the hotel] was a restaurant whose stock in trade was *pacha*, the boiled heads, stomachs and trotters of sheep. Outside, a boy cracked bones on a small anvil. Inside, a huge aluminum kettle steamed in anticipation of the midday rush. An early customer ordered a bowl of broth and a second bowl containing broth-soaked bread; he helped himself to side dishes of onion and *turshi*, a mixture of pickled vegetables made attractively pink with beets or beet juice. His meal looked like a balanced, nourishing one, and I reckoned that it cost about 30 cents; for another 15 cents, he could have had pieces of tongue or stomach as well. It suddenly occurred to me that Iraq could be a bargain paradise for retirement (Nickles, 109).

Pacha is definitely not an haute cuisine dish, and you either love it or dread it. As a kid, it was not the dish for me. The parts in it I was able to accept as consumable food were far less than the parts I would put aside untouched, with the result I would end up hungrier than when I started the meal. However, as I grew older and bolder, I discovered some of the joys of eating it. Though even to this day, there are parts I would never dream of eating, such as the eye of the sheep, which to some is considered a delicacy, and is reserved for the honored guests, as is the custom amongst the peasants and the Bedouins.

When introducing a person to this dish for the first time, tripe and trotters pose less of a problem than the head, and if you want to enjoy it really, do not think about it, just eat it. Gavin Maxwell, the British writer who stayed in the marshes in the south of Iraq for a period of time in the mid fifties, describes his first encounter with this dish which obviously was not carefully and meticulously cleaned the way it should be:

> A hospitable sheikh will sometimes kill a sheep, whose boiled and nauseous head is placed among the other dishes to announce the fact. Pieces of flesh from the ears, the hair still attached, are esteemed as a delicacy, and hospitable fingers explore for a guest the gums and palate, producing strips and morsels which would be appetizing if the head were not staring at the eater with those dreadful boiled eyes. (24)

Apparently *pacha* is one of those dishes that have to be introduced with an apology, everywhere. The American food writer M.F.K. Fisher, herself a tripe eater, dedicates in her book *With Bold Knife and Fork*, a chapter to tripe, entitled "The Trouble with Tripe". It is the kind of dish that requires a big pot and plenty of hungry people. She then relates in her familiar amusing manner how once in

Dijon, France, she went to a small restaurant all by herself, for no other members of her family shared with her this interest in tripe. She ordered a dish of tripe for old time's sake. "They were as good as they had ever been some decades or centuries ago... They hissed and sizzles with delicate authority." The place was noisy, and an accordionist that she had last seen in Marseilles added to the wildness. "When he saw me digging into my little pot of tripe," she says, "he nodded, recognizing me as a fellow wanderer" (122, 125).

In the Middle East in general, and Iraq in particular, *pacha* is a very popular traditional dish. Actually some people even have it for breakfast, too. A hefty filling breakfast, no doubt, that will last the whole day. Indeed, it is reputed to be so filling and nourishing that if a person talks too much, his friends will chide him saying, "What's the matter with you? Have you eaten *pacha* or what?"

In the old days, the anklebones (astragali) of trotters used to be "collectible items" for kids. After eating the trotters, these heel bones were washed and given to kids to play a very popular game called *ch'aab*. Indeed, in ancient times, it is believed that they were used as dices for board games. Not only that. Those same bones were also used by spiteful women who wanted misfortune to befall a second favored wife (*dharra*), for instance. The *cha'ab*, in this case, would be put at the doorsteps or thrown over the fence of the target woman. This would do the magic, so they believed.

How to prepare the Pacha:

Thorough and meticulous cleansing of the sheep's head, tripe and trotters is the key to good *pacha*. Luckily in the local markets they can be purchased readily cleaned from the butcher's, which makes the task of preparing this dish much easier. However, people who slaughter a lamb have to start from scratch, the same way our ancient ancestors used to do, as evident in the Babylonian recipe, "goat's kid stew"(Bottéro, *Medopotamian Culinary Texts*, 9). The instructions were to singe the head, legs, and tail first on direct fire to burn the hairs, assumabely after dipping the parts in boiling water several times to facilitate the plucking of the wool first

The tripe should be washed and washed until it becomes white in color, and then cut into squares or rectangles 6 to 8 inches in size (see the following recipe for more details). Some people prefer to cook the trotters only, and a recipe for this dish is included in the thirteenth century Baghdadi cookbook. It was simply called *Akari'* (trotters).

The head requires further treatment. It should be struck on the nose on a hard surface to let all the mucus come out. I used to watch my mother clean the head. She would repeatedly bang it on the nose, saying never stop until you see the worm come out, and actually a white worm would eventually come out. As to why the worm was there in the first place, she could not satisfy my curiosity, it was just an inherited routine. The thirteenth-century Andalusian cookbook, *Fadhalat al-Khiwan* (the best of the dishes) by Ibn Razin al-Tughibi, includes a passage which specifies how to clean the heads of slaughtered sheep. He described exactly the same procedures we follow in cleaning them including instruction to "hit the nose on a stone until the inside worm falls out" (40).

After all this washing, The cleaned parts should be sprinkled with a mixture of salt, curry powder and flour, then washed thoroughly to remove all traces of flour and curry. The cleaned parts are then put in a very big pot, and covered with lots of cold water. Any or all of the following can also be added:

2 to 3 whole onions, skinned
1 whole head of garlic, unskinned, washed
1 tablespoon curry powder
3 to 4 whole *noomi Basrah*, pricked at several places, see Glossary
3 to 4 bay leaves
1 cup chickpeas, washed and soaked overnight, and drained
1 tablespoon salt

1. Put pot on high heat at first to bring it to a quick boil, skimming as needed. Reduce heat to low and let it simmer for 3 to 4 hours, or until tender, especially the tripe pieces. Add more hot water if needed. Do not rush it. When *tannuors* (domed clay oven) were in every household, after the initial stage of boiling and skimming the pot, it was lowered inside the oven and was kept to simmer overnight. If certain parts cook earlier than the others, just take them out of the pot and put them aside.

2. Add salt half way through cooking.

To serve, put broken pieces of bread in a deep dish, and pour enough broth to cover them. Arrange pieces of meat on top, along with chickpeas and *noomi Basrah*. Put the remaining pieces of meat with some broth in a big bowl, as a side. Drizzle with sizzling hot oil, if wished, and/or yogurt sauce (1 cup yogurt, 1/4 cup chopped parsley, and 1 grated clove of garlic, mixed together). Serve with lots of greens, herbs and pickles.

Stuffed Tripe
(Karsha Mahshiya or Kabbayat)

(Makes 4 servings)

Today this dish is the specialty of the northern city of Mosul. It is made of pieces of tripe stuffed with a mixture of spiced ground meat and rice, and simmered until tender, which takes hours. The naming of this delicious treat, *kabbayat*, goes back to the medieval practice of cooking the simple *ma' wa malh* dishes (literally water and salt). These were mostly cooked during the hunting sessions. The resourceful cooks would decorate them with an impressive *qabba* (stuffed tripe, plural *qabbayat*). This Arabic word is derived from *qabqab*, which is the belly or stomach of the slaughtered animal. (This, and all the variants such as *qubba*, *kubba*, etc. can ultimately be traced back to the Akkadian "kubbu," meaning "rounded in shape")

In a *qabba* recipe, al-Warraq gives, meat was pounded with onion, and cilantro. Ground coriander, pepper, cinnamon, chopped leeks, a little rice, and optional liver chopped fine, were mixed with the meat. Tripe was stuffed with the mixture and was sewn closed with thin sticks, and added to the simmering pot of *ma' wa malh.* When served, it was cut open and sprinkled with cinnamon, a little *murri* (fermented sauce), and mustard (129-30).

In al-Baghdadi's thirteenth-century cookbook, the dish has already been incorporated into the fine cuisine of good living. The tripe was cut into smaller pieces and stuffed with basically the same ingredients, that is meat and rice. The result was daintier looking *qibbayat.* A fashion statement was made by calling them by the Persian name, *sukhtur* (sheep's tripe stuffed with meat and rice)

As directed in al-Baghdadi's recipe, much care should be taken in cleaning the tripe, "Take fine sheep's tripe, wash with hot water and soap, then with hot water and citron leaves, then with salt and water, until quite clean. Smear inside and out with saffron and rose water".

Then small *kubabs* were prepared from red meat and rice "twice as much as the meat and about a quarter as much chickpeas," salt, cinnamon, and saffron, coriander, cumin, mastic, pepper, and ginger. Then tripe was "cut into middling pieces" and stuffed, "joining together and sewing up with cotton, or skewering with dry sticks." After initial boiling and skimming, the pot was lowered into the *tannour*, and covered to be left "from nightfall until morning" (199-200).

The way to prepare it nowadays is basically the same:

> **8 pieces of tripe each cut into 6-to-8-inch square (palm-size pieces), cleaned, and ready to be cooked**
> **For the stuffing:**
> **1 cup rice, washed, soaked in cold water 30 minutes, and drained**
> **8 ounces ground meat**
> **1/4 cup slivered almonds, optional**
> **1 teaspoon salt**
> **1 teaspoon *baharat*, see Glossary**
> **1/2 teaspoon allspice**
> **1/4 teaspoon black pepper**

With a white cotton thread, sew tripe pieces into triangles, leaving an opening for stuffing. Mix stuffing ingredients. Fill tripe pieces loosely to allow for expansion, and close the opening. Cook stuffed tripe, following the same instructions given for *Pacha*, above. While simmering, pierce the stuffed tripe with a fork to allow broth to get into the inside of the pieces.

Serve the same way *Pacha* is served.

Simmered Lamb
(Habeet)

(Makes 4 servings)

This is a simple way of preparing lamb, with spices kept to the minimum. It is mostly cooked for gatherings, and special occasions like picnics. The meat would be cut and washed at home, but the simmering part would be done in a big pot set on a campfire for hours until meat almost falls from the bones. In the old days when there was a *tannour* in every household, it was lowered into it and let simmer overnight. That's why perhaps the dish was called *habeet* (the lowered). In all probability this simple dish was initially prepared during the hunting sessions of our ancient and medieval ancestors, using the meat of the wild animals (*wahsh*, plural *wuhoush*) they caught. There is a chapter in al-Warraq's tenth-century cookbook, which gives recipes for such dishes. They were simply called *ma' wa malh* (water and salt), meaning broth (127-31), and were more like survival food.

> **2 pounds lamb, choose cuts with bones and a considerable amount of meat, trimmed**
> **1 tablespoon oil**
> **1 onion, quartered**
> **1 teaspoon *baharat*, see Glossary**
> **2 to 3 whole *noomi Basrah*, pricked at several places, see Glossary**
> **1 tablespoon salt**
> **1/2 teaspoon black pepper**

1. In a medium heavy pot, brown meat pieces in oil, turning frequently to allow to brown on all sides, about 10 minutes. Add onion, and fold frequently, until transparent, about 5 minutes.

2. Fold in *baharat,* and pour hot water enough to cover lamb pieces, about 5 cups, and add *noomi Basrah.* Bring to a quick boil, skimming if needed. Lower heat to low, and let simmer for about one hour and a half, or until meat is so render it almost falls off the bones. Add salt and pepper towards the end of cooking. Serve with bread or rice of your choice (see chapter 8, on rice) with lots of salad.

Aromatic Shanks Simmered in Vegetable Sauce (Znoud bi Salsat al-Khudhar)

(Makes 4 servings)

According to western standards, shanks have the reputation of being humble cuts that make the staple of the peasant kitchen. That's why perhaps they are relatively cheaper than, say, lamb chops. However, recent surveys in food magazines show that shanks are showing up and selling out at the most exclusive restaurants. In Iraq, they have always been looked upon as a delicacy. The succulent bone marrow (*mukh al-'adhum*) will seep into the broth and enrich it, and the rest will be extracted by gently tapping the bone on the plate, or scooped out with a small spoon. This by far is a largely medieval habit that a lot of us are not willing to quit (see Box below).

The shanks, though, need to be cooked the right way. To get succulent and tender meat, prolonged simmering is required. Following is a spicy concoction inspired by the medieval masters.

> **2 lamb shanks, halved crosswise (by butcher), or 4 veal shanks (about 2 1/2 pounds)**
> **1 teaspoon ground aniseed**
> **1/2 cup flour for dredging**
> **3 tablespoons oil**
>
> **1 medium onion, coarsely chopped**
> **2 cloves garlic, grated**
> **1 teaspoon turmeric**
> **1 teaspoon ground coriander**
> **1/2 teaspoon ground cumin**
> **1/2 teaspoon ground cardamom**
> **1/4 teaspoon chili, or to taste**

1 cup chopped carrots
1 cup cubed zucchini
1/4 cup chopped dried apricots
1 cup orange juice
1/4 cup lemon juice

1/2 teaspoon salt
1/4 teaspoon black pepper

For garnish: 1/4 cup chopped parsley, 1/4 cup chopped and toasted walnuts, optional

1. Sprinkle shanks with aniseed, and toss pieces in flour to coat all over.

2. In a medium heavy pot, heat oil, and brown shanks on all sides, about 7 minutes. Transfer shanks to a plate, and set aside.

3. Sauté onion in the same pot, for 5 minutes. If pot looks dry, add 1 tablespoon oil. Add garlic and turmeric and fold for a few minutes. Stir in coriander, cumin, cardamom, and chili if used.

4. Add carrots, zucchini, and dried apricot. Fold for a few minutes.

5. Return shanks. Add lemon and orange juice, and enough hot water just to cover meat and vegetables, about 3 cups. Bring to a quick boil, then reduce heat to low, and let pot simmer, covered, for about 1 1/2 hours, or until meat is very tender, and sauce is thickened. Add salt and pepper about 15 minutes before meat is done.

6. Take out shanks and keep them aside at a warm place. Set aside 1 cup of vegetables, and purée the rest in blender or food processor. Return chunky vegetables to sauce.

To serve, arrange shanks on a plate, and pour sauce all over. Sprinkle chopped parsley and walnuts, if used, on meat and sauce. Serve with a side dish of rice, or bulgar (see chapters 8 and 9 respectively). Freshly baked bread is also good with this dish.

Bone Marrow: A Medieval Delicacy

During the medieval times bone marrow was a prized royal treat comparable to today's *fois gras*, and it was as rich. The anonymous writer of the thirteenth-century *Andalusian Cookbook* says that, "many kings like to eat it and consider it of very good nutrition." Getting the substance out of the bones and collecting a worthwhile amount was time consuming, but it was worth the trouble. The proper protocol for eating them, the Andalusian writer explains, was that "he who comes first and takes them out to the table should not try them until the lord of the table begins to taste them, and should not try any until he gives it to the taste of his friend and him who eats at his side." He also tells the story of a high-ranking officer who went to the king's palace to take his leave of him, and was invited to join for dinner. One of the courses included a portion of bone marrow. The officer got hold of it. Though the king was taken aback, he was certain that the officer's intention was to offer it to him. Instead, "he took it, he put it on a bite of bread, sprinkled it with salt and ate it himself." That was a breach of decorum. The king did not say anything, but when the officer prepared to leave, the king said to him, "There is between us something I need to tell you afterward." (31)

Because the medieval gourmets were never able to have enough of the real thing, many recipes were given for making counterfeit bone marrow using ingredients such as lambs' brains mixed with butter, eggs, milk, and a little sugar, or crushed walnuts mixed with egg white. The mixtures were poured into intestines and boiled like sausages, or were put in special glass marrow containers that were sealed with dough, cooked in a hot water bath, and served with a sprinkle of salt and sugar (al-Warraq, 90-1, *Andalusian Cookbook*, 31-2).

Meat Simmered in Vinegar
(Laham bil Khal)

(Makes 4 servings)

Simmering meat in vinegar is an ancient way of cooking, and our evidence is the extant Babylonian recipes (see Introduction). Vinegar was recognized as having a tenderizing effect upon not so tender cuts of meat. During the medieval times meat dishes cooked in vinegar were called *masous* (soak up). They also made stew in which the souring agent was mainly vinegar, and they called it *sikbaja*. *Mamqour,* on the other hand was meat cooked in vinegar for the purpose of preserving it.

The following is a recipe inspired by this tradition, it is more like a *masous* dish, because little sauce will remain when the meat is cooked.

> **1 1/2 pounds lean lamb, cut into 1-inch cubes, or lean beef stew-cubes**
> **2 tablespoons oil**
> **1 teaspoon turmeric**
>
> **1 medium onion, sliced**
> **1/4 teaspoon chili pepper, or to taste**
> **1 heaping tablespoon flour**
>
> **1 1/2 cup hot water**
> **1/4 cup vinegar, balsamic or cider**
>
> **1 1/2 teaspoons salt**
> **1/4 teaspoon black pepper**
> **1 tablespoon honey**

1. In a medium heavy pot, heat oil and sauté meat with turmeric until browned, about 10 minutes. Take out of pan and set aside.

2. Add onion to pot and sauté until it softens. Stir in flour and chili, if used until flour is fragrant.

3. Mix water and vinegar and slowly add to onion stirring to prevent flour from lumping. Bring to a boil.

4. Return meat and simmer slowly, covered, on low heat until meat is tender, and sauce is thickened and reduced, about 40 minutes. Add a little more hot water if needed. Salt, pepper, and honey are added 10 minutes before meat is done.

Curried Lamb or Beef
(Karı'l Laham)

(Makes 4 servings)

Curried dishes are the specialty of the southern region, especially the port city of Basrah. This is largely due to the Indian influence which is as old as the silk road trade itself. During the medieval times the historian, al-Mas'udi named the city *ardh al-hind* (land of India). Though, as you will notice, curry powder is not used in the recipe, the components of the curry blend are present here, except for the curry leaves.

2 tablespoons oil
1 pound lamb trimmed and cut into 1-inch cubes. Stew beef may be substituted
1/2 teaspoon turmeric
2 medium onions, coarsely chopped
3 cloves garlic, grated
3 medium potatoes, peeled and cut into 1-inch cubes
2 tablespoons flour

1 scant tablespoon tamarind concentrate, see Glossary
2 cups hot water
1 teaspoon ground coriander
1 teaspoon cumin
1/2 teaspoon whole aniseed or fennel
1/2 teaspoon ginger
1/4 teaspoon whole mustard seeds, optional
1/2 to 1 teaspoon chili pepper, or to taste
1 bay leaf
2 to 3 pods cardamom
1 teaspoon salt
1/4 teaspoon black pepper

For garnish: 1/4 cup chopped parsley

1. In a medium heavy pot, heat oil and brown meat cubes, stirring frequently, about 10 minutes.

2. Add turmeric, onion, and garlic, and stir until onion softens, about 5 minutes. Add cubed potatoes, and stir for a few more minutes. Sprinkle flour on the vegetables, and fold until fragrant.

3. Add rest of ingredients, except for garnish. Bring to a quick boil, then reduce heat to low, and let simmer, covered, until meat is tender, potatoes are cooked, and sauce is of medium consistency, about 30 minutes. Stir 2 to 3 times while simmering to prevent sauce from sticking to the bottom of the pot.
    Garnish with chopped parsley, and serve with rice with noodles or yellow rice (see chapter 8).

Chili Fry
(Makes 4 servings)

This foreign sounding dish is probably a relic from the days of British colonization after the First World War. As the name suggests, it is traditionally a hot dish in which lots of hot fresh peppers are used, but you certainly have the option of using sweet peppers instead. It is a delicious comfort food similar to the American hash.

2 tablespoons oil
1 pound lean cubes of meat, preferably lamb
2 medium potatoes cut into small cubes, or 1 cup frozen diced potatoes, optional
1 big onion, coarsely chopped
1 teaspoon curry powder
1 teaspoon turmeric

2 cups chopped tomatoes
3 to 4 fresh chilies, chopped, or 1 medium bell pepper, chopped, or a combination of both
1 heaping tablespoon tomato paste, diluted in 3/4 cup hot water, or 1 cup tomato sauce
1 1/2 teaspoons salt
1/4 teaspoon black pepper

1. In a medium heavy pot, sauté meat cubes in heated oil, stirring occasionally. Reduce heat to medium. Add potato cubes, if used, and continue cooking until all moisture evaporates, and meat is tender, 10 to 15 minutes.

2. Add onions, curry powder, and turmeric. Stir until onion is transparent and curry is fragrant.

3. Add rest of ingredients, and mix well. Bring to a quick boil, then reduce heat to low, and let simmer, covered, until sauce is thickened, and flavors are well-blended, about 15 minutes.

This dish is usually served with bread and salad. If sauce is allowed to evaporate, the chili fry would make a tasty filling for a sandwich, with sliced onion and pickled mango (available at Middle-Eastern grocery shops).

Breaded Lamb Chops
(Cream Chap)

(Makes 4 servings)

It is funny how adopted foreign names sometimes metamorphose in the process. This dish might originally have been "creamed chops", but it finally settled to *Cream Chap*. This happened not only to borrowed dishes but also to proper names of persons. The name *"Kokaz"*, for instance, was popular amongst peasants in the twenties and thirties, the time of British colonization. It is, no doubt, a corruption of the name of Sir Percy Cox who was appointed as high commissioner in Baghdad in 1920. Some peasant girls born during that era were given the name *"Ingireziyye"*, a corruption of "English woman", and some were called *"Amrikiyya."*

About 2 pounds lamb chops (8 rib chops, or 4 lamb or veal loin chops)
Juice of 1 lemon
1/2 teaspoon salt
1/4 teaspoon black pepper, and paprika, each
1 teaspoon thyme

1/2 cup flour for dredging
4 to 5 eggs, beaten
About 2 cups bread crumbs, seasoned with some salt and black pepper
Oil for frying

1. French the chops by scraping clean the bones that protrude beyond the meat, the butcher could do this for you. Trim off excess fat. Pound meat pieces with a mallet, making them as thin as possible without tearing them. Do not let meat separate from the bone.

2. Sprinkle meat pieces with the lemon juice, salt, pepper, and thyme, and set aside for 15 minutes.

3. Dip meat pieces in flour then shake off extra. Dip them in beaten eggs, and then coat them with breadcrumbs, pressing with the fingers, to allow crumbs to stick to the chops until surface is well covered and does not feel wet.

4. Fry in 1-inch deep hot oil, until golden brown on both sides, about 5 minutes for each side. Adjust heat if you notice chops are browning quickly before the inside is done. Drain on white paper napkins put on a rack to prevent pieces from getting soggy.
    Serve hot along with lots of salad, and bread.

Suggestions:
* You may substitute chops with a piece of rump roast, sliced thinly to steaks, and pounded as described above. Or if you want to treat your family to a gourmet dish, prepared in a jiffy, use cubed steaks, instead, but pound them even a little more as described above. These boneless cuts make an excellent filling for sandwiches. After frying, simply slice each piece into 1/2-inch wide strips, and fill sandwich breads with them, along with sliced vegetables.

* Instead of frying, you can bake the chops or steaks by arranging them in one layer on a well-greased baking sheet. Generously spray or brush pieces with oil. Bake in a preheated oven at 450 degrees F., until bottom is browned. Flip pieces to the other side, and continue baking until well browned on both sides.

After removing pieces from pan, spread a layer of sliced boiled potatoes. Sprinkle with some thyme, 2 tablespoons olive oil, and 1/4 cup hot water. Toss potato pieces in the mixture, and bake, turning once, until they are nicely browned

* Instead of red meat use chicken breasts, pound and cook as described above

Grilled Lamb Chops
(Gulbasti)

(Makes 4 servings)

Here is another borrowed name for a very basic and simple meat dish. It is one of the *nawashif* dishes (sauceless dishes) usually ordered at restaurants. If you like to marinate the chops the medieval way, use a little vinegar mixed with crushed raisins and pomegranate seeds, garlic and coriander.

8 rib lamb chops, trimmed (about 2 pounds)

1 teaspoon *baharat*, see Glossary
Juice of one lemon
1 medium onion, grated
2 tablespoons olive oil

1 teaspoon salt
1/4 teaspoon black pepper

1. Pound meat pieces with a mallet. If lean chops are desired, french chops by scraping clean the bones that protrude beyond the meat, all the way down to the eye of the meat.

2. Combine *baharat*, lemon juice, grated onion, and oil in a glass container, and marinade chops in the mixture for 30 minutes.

3. Take chops out of marinade, sprinkle with salt and pepper, and grill on charcoal, medium high, or broil in a preheated hot broiler, turning twice, for about 15 minutes total, or until done but still moist. While chops are broiling, baste them with the marinade. Discard leftover marinade.

Serve immediately with bread, and salad.

Lamb Chops with Lentil
(Dhlou' Ghanam bil Adas)

(Makes 4 servings)

Here is a variation on the basic *gulbasti* if you are not in the mood for grilling, and would like to prepare a dish with some sauce in it. The addition of lentil to the dish is inspired by al-Warraq's tenth-century recipes of *al-adasiyyat* (lentil dishes, 167).

8 rib lamb chops, trimmed
1 tablespoon oil
1 medium onion, coarsely chopped
1/2 teaspoon turmeric
2 cups skinned and diced tomatoes
2 cloves garlic, grated
1/2 teaspoon za'tar or thyme, see Glossary
1/2 teaspoon cumin
1 teaspoon salt
1/4 teaspoon black pepper
2 cups cooked whole lentils (1 cup uncooked), drained, reserve 1 cup of the liquid

For garnish:
1/4 cup chopped parsley and lemon slices
Preheat oven to 400 degrees F.

1. Pound meat pieces with a mallet. If lean chops are desired, french chops by scraping clean the bones that protrude beyond the meat, all the way down to the eye of the meat.

2. In a big skillet, heat oil, and brown chops on both sides, about 2 minutes for each side. Transfer to a dish.

3. In the same skillet sauté onion until it softens. Add turmeric and fold until fragrant.

4. Stir in tomatoes, garlic, thyme, cumin, salt and pepper. Fold for about a minute. Add lentils and the reserved cup of liquid. Mix well.

5. If skillet is not ovenproof, transfer lentil sauce to a medium baking dish, and arrange browned chops on sauce. Cover loosely with foil, and bake in a preheated oven at 400 degrees F. for about 20 minutes or until chops are tender, and sauce is thickened.
   Garnish with parsley and lemon slices, and serve hot with rice, Bulgar or bread.

Suggestion: Any kind of cooked beans may be substituted for lentils.

Stuffed Lamb
(Qouzi Mahshi)

Qouzi is the dish for large gatherings, especially weddings. Depending on how big the occasion is, a suckling lamb or a medium lamb is stuffed and slowly baked to succulence. It is customarily served on a huge mound of cooked rice, and decked with toasted nuts and raisins. The rice may be just white, or it might be multi-colored, partly white, partly yellow with saffron, partly red with tomato sauce, partly brown with cinnamon, and partly green with dill. It was definitely the dish for festivals during the medieval times, and was an emblem of good living, as seen in *The Arabian Nights* in which some lavish weddings are described.

The following recipe will give the interested reader an idea on how such dishes are usually prepared. A more practical and scaled down recipe will follow. However, the idea of stuffing a lamb is not as extravagant as it sounds at first, even by today's standards. A small lamb as required in the recipe below is a little larger than a big turkey stuffed for a Thanksgiving feast, for instance.

> **1 small lamb, about 25 pounds**
> **12 to 16 cups rice, depending on how many are to be served. Wash rice and soak for 30 minutes, cook as directed in White Plain Rice p.237**
> **3 cups slivered almonds**
> **3 cups raisins**
> **3 cups peas, cooked, frozen or canned**
> **3 pounds lean meat, diced and browned in 3 tablespoons oil**
> ***Baharat*, (see Glossary), cardamom, sticks of cinnamon, *noomi Basrah*, allspice, and Salt to taste**

To prepare the lamb: Wash lamb well, and rub with salt and pepper inside and out. Wash in cold water and pat dry. Rub lamb inside and out with a paste of grated onion, salt, pepper, cardamom, cinnamon, and allspice, and set aside.

To prepare stuffing: Brown almonds in a little oil. Fold in raisins, and stir for a few minutes. Add peas, browned cubes of meat and spices. Fold together until well blended. Mix with the cooked rice.

To stuff and bake the lamb: Stuff the cavity of the prepared lamb with some of the rice mixture, and truss it with a thick white thread. Some people prefer to brown the stuffed lamb in clarified butter at first before roasting it; and some just place it on a big baking pan, brush it generously with oil, and bake it in a preheated oven, 450 degrees F. for the first 15 minutes. Then cover with foil paper and reduce heat to 350 degrees F., and continue baking until very tender. Allow 30 minutes per pound. If the oven is too small to contain the lamb, people would stuff the lamb at home, and take it to the neighborhood bakery, to be roasted there. Originally the stuffed lambs used to be baked in the household *tannour*. After stuffing the lamb, 4 date palm leaves would be stripped of their fronds. Two of the resulting sticks would be pierced crosswise through the two sides of the lamb, and the other two are inserted vertically along the body of the lamb, through the neck opening. The hands and legs are tied to the sticks so that the lamb would not slide into the bottom of the *tannour*. The lamb is then put vertically inside the hot *tannour*, the top opening of which was closed with a big lid. Within a few hours, the lamb would be ready. Needless to say, the *tannour* method is the best since heat is locked in, and meat comes out tender and succulent.

To serve, put remainder of rice on a big platter, and put cooked lamb on top. Garnish the dish with slices of salad vegetables, and serve it with stews of your choice.

Recipes Not for the Faint of Heart

The following is a recipe of a royal dish taken from the anonymous Valencian thirteenth-century *Andalusian Cookbook* on the cuisine of Muslim Spain, which was greatly influenced by the haute cuisine of Baghdad during the Abbasid Period. The book contains around 500 recipes. The recipe gives directions on how to prepare a stuffed calf:

> One takes a fat young sheep, skinned and cleaned. It is opened between the two muscles and all that is in its stomach is carefully removed. In its interior one puts a stuffed goose and in the goose's belly a stuffed hen, and in the hen's belly a stuffed young pigeon, and in the pigeon's belly a stuffed thrush and in the thrush's belly another stuffed or fried bird, all of this stuffed and sprinkled with the sauce described for the stuffed dishes [mixture of murri, oil, and thyme]. The opening is sewn together, the sheep is put in the hot clay oven [*tannour*], and it is left until done and crisp on the outside. It is sprinkled with more sauce, and then put in the cavity of a calf, which has already been prepared and cleaned. The calf is then stitched together and put in the hot *tannour*, and left till it is done and crisp on the outside. Then it is taken and presented. (*Aramco*, 40, 5, S-O, 1989: 29)

Nowadays the idea of stuffing an animal with a smaller one has been mostly cut down to a lamb stuffed with a chicken and that with eggs, and the cavities are filled mostly with a spicy aromatic mixture of cooked rice, sometimes ground meat, and toasted nuts and raisins.

If you think that these medieval gourmets went a little bit too far then listen to this: It seems that the trend of stuffing poultry with poultry is the latest gourmet fad in the United States of nowadays. The dish is called "Turducken". It is a Thanksgiving turkey stuffed with a duck, which in turn is stuffed with a stuffed chicken. The trend came from the south where there is a long tradition of stuffing a bird with a bird. What brought this to the attention of people was a *Wall Street Journal* article, 1996 just before Thanksgiving featuring a company that prepares turduckens. Immediately after that the company received 10,000 orders a day, and the company sold 25,000 turduckens for Thanksgiving. Devotees think its taste just blows your mind; skeptics think the idea is disgusting, and paranoids think it is a bacterial contamination nightmare. What do you think?

Scaled down Versions of Qouzi:
Aromatic Leg of Lamb
(Fukhudh Ghanam bil-Firin)

(Makes 10 servings)

For a group of ten diners, a leg of lamb can easily be substituted for the whole lamb, and yet keep its glamour. Incidentally, I discovered that the practice of making small slashes on meat and injecting them with garlic goes back at least to the ninth century (AD, to be precise). Al-Warraq gives a recipe of a *barid* (cold) dish of leg of gazelle, and the instructions were to make slits with a knife, and insert an almond, a pistachio, or a clove of garlic in each slit. The leg was then cooked in wine vinegar, with salt, parsley, rue, citron rind, cinnamon, coriander, and pepper (107).

1 leg of lamb, about 5 pounds, trimmed
4 cloves garlic, sliced lengthwise

For marinade:
3/4 cup yogurt
1 tablespoon grated orange peel
1 tablespoon grated lemon peel
1 tablespoon *baharat*, see Glossary
1/4 teaspoon black pepper
1 teaspoon cumin, coriander, cinnamon, and cardamom, each

3 to 4 sprigs of thyme and mint, each
1 medium onion, sliced
1 tomato, sliced
2 carrots, sliced
2 tablespoons olive oil
1/4 cup orange juice
1 teaspoon salt

5 cups rice, washed, soaked and cooked according to directions in Plain White Rice, p.237
3/4 cup slivered almonds
1 teaspoon oil
1 cup currants or raisins
1/2 teaspoon noomi Basra, see Glossary

Preheat oven to 450 / 350 / 400 degrees F.

1. Trim and wash leg of lamb. Pat it dry. Using a small, sharp knife, make shallow slashes on the leg of lamb about 1 inch long. Fill incisions with garlic slices.

2. Mix yogurt, orange and lemon peel, *baharat*, pepper, cumin, and coriander, cinnamon and cardamom. Rub entire leg with this mixture, and let marinade for an hour at room temperature. Or refrigerate overnight, covered, in a glass dish, but bring to room temperature before baking.

299

3. In a baking pan large enough to hold leg of lamb, spread sprigs of thyme and mint, onion, tomato and carrot slices. Place leg of lamb on this bed of herbs and vegetables, fat side up. Brush with oil. Pour 1/2 cup hot water around the meat.

4. Bake in a preheated oven at 450 degrees F., for the first 15 minutes. Reduce heat to 375 degrees F., and loosely cover with foil. Baste every 20 minutes with the liquid around the meat. Allow 30 minutes per pound. Add a little more hot water if pan gets dry.

5. When lamb is almost done, remove foil, pour 1/4 cup orange juice all over the leg, sprinkle it lightly with 1 teaspoon salt. Raise oven temperature to 400 degrees F., and continue baking until meat is tender and nicely browned. Take out of the oven, and let rest loosely covered for about 10 minutes. Discard the bed of herbs and vegetables.

6. Transfer meat to a big platter, and surround it with the cooked rice. Brown almonds in a medium skillet using 1 teaspoon oil. Fold in raisins and noomi Basra, until heated through. Garnish rice with almond mixture.

Leg of Lamb in Sweet and Sour Sauce (Fukhudh Ghanam b' Salsat Hamudh-Hilu)

(Makes 10 servings)

The following is a sensational variation on the traditional leg of lamb done in the spirit of the medieval cuisine, in which vinegar and dried fruits are combined to give a sweet and sour flavor. It is given a lighter touch though-- most of the fat drippings are removed.

One leg of lamb, about 5 pounds
3 cloves garlic, sliced lengthwise
For marinade:
    3 tablespoons vinegar, preferably balsamic
    1/2 teaspoon caraway seeds
    1/2 teaspoon aniseed
    4 to 5 juniper berries, crushed, optional
    1 tablespoon grated lemon peel
    1 tablespoon grated orange peel
    2 teaspoons *baharat*, see Glossary
    1/4 teaspoon black pepper

    Sliced onion, tomatoes, carrots, with some sprigs of herbs like thyme and rosemary to serve as a roasting bed for the meat, (to be discarded later)
    2 tablespoons olive oil, divided
    1/4 cup orange juice
    1 teaspoon salt
For the sauce:
    1 medium onion, thinly sliced
    1 tablespoon oil

3 tablespoons flour
1 teaspoon brown sugar or honey
8 ounces mushroom, sliced
1 medium pepper, hot or sweet, sliced
2 medium carrots, sliced diagonally
1/2 cup dry apricots, quartered
1/2 cup prunes, quartered

5 medium potatoes, boiled, peeled, cut into 1-inch cubes, and browned in 2 tablespoons olive oil, or sprayed with oil and broiled

Preheat oven to 450 / 350 / 400 degrees F.

1. Trim and wash leg of lamb. Pat it dry, and with a small sharp knife make shallow slits, 1-inch long. Stuff incisions with garlic slices.

2. Mix vinegar, caraway seeds, aniseeds, juniper, lemon and orange peels, *baharat,* and black pepper. Rub leg of lamb with the mixture. Cover it, and let it marinate for 1 hour at room temperature, or refrigerate overnight in a glass container. In this case bring meat to room temperature before baking.

2. Preheat oven to 450 degrees F. Place sliced vegetables and sprigs of herbs in a baking pan big enough to hold leg of lamb. Put meat on top of this bed, fat side up, and rub with 2 tablespoons olive oil. Pour 1/2 cup hot water round the meat. Roast for 15 minutes.

3. Reduce heat to 350 degrees F., and continue roasting, loosely covered with foil, allowing 30 minutes for each pound. Baste meat several times while roasting. Add a little more hot water if pan gets dry.

4. When meat is almost done, pour 1/4 cup orange juice all over the leg, and sprinkle with 1 teaspoon salt. Raise heat to 400 and continue roasting, uncovered, until meat is tender and nicely browned. Take it out of the pan, and keep it loosely covered at a warm place.

5. Strain leftover juices in the pan. Discard solids. Remove as much as you can of fat in the liquid.

6. To make the sauce, in a medium skillet, sauté onion in 1 tablespoon oil until transparent, about 5 minutes. Add flour and stir until fragrant, a few minutes. Gradually add the defatted meat juices, prepared in the previous step, adding more hot water to make 2 cups. Add brown sugar or honey, mushrooms, pepper, carrots, apricots, and prunes. Stir well. Bring to a quick boil, then reduce heat to low, and let simmer until sauce is of medium consistency, about 10 minutes. Stir occasionally.

7. Return meat to baking pan, and surround it with the browned potatoes. Pour sauce on meat and potatoes. Let heat through in the oven for about 10 minutes.

Slice and serve with plain rice, and salad.

Liver Simmered in Tomato Sauce
(Mi'lag bi'l Tamata)

(Makes 4 servings)

Liver tops the list of foods high in iron, but at the same time it is high in cholesterol. However, if one enjoys normal health conditions, I guess it is no sin to enjoy these traditional liver dishes every once in a while.

1 pound liver, cut into 1-inch cubes, washed and drained
1 tablespoon vinegar
1 teaspoon curry powder
1 teaspoon salt
1/2 teaspoon black pepper
1/2 cup flour for dredging
2 tablespoons oil
2 medium onions, coarsely chopped
1 medium green pepper, sweet or hot, chopped
3 medium tomatoes, skinned and chopped
1 tablespoon *noomi Basrah*, see Glossary
2 tablespoons tomato paste diluted in 1 cup hot water, or 1 cup tomato sauce

1. Put liver pieces in a bowl, and sprinkle with vinegar and toss to allow pieces to be covered with vinegar. Mix curry powder, salt, and pepper, and sprinkle on the liver pieces, and toss again. Set aside for 30 minutes.

2. Spread flour on a tray, and dredge the liver pieces in it, allowing pieces to be coated on all sides.

3. In a big skillet, heat oil, and brown liver pieces after shaking off excess flour. (About 5 minutes) Remove from pan, and set aside. Avoid overcooking liver pieces otherwise they will develop a tough texture.

4. In the same skillet, sauté onion until transparent, about 5 minutes. If skillet gets dry, add a little bit more oil. Add tomatoes and pepper, and stir for a few more minutes.

5. Add noomi Basra and diluted tomato paste or sauce. Return liver pieces, and mix well. Bring to a quick boil, then reduce heat to low, and let simmer, covered, until sauce is thickened, about 10 minutes.
    Serve with freshly baked bread, or a side dish of rice or bulgar, with lots of salad.

Liver Simmered in Cumin Sauce
(Mi'lag bi'l Kammoun)

(Makes 4 servings)

Here is another liver dish delightfully aromatic and spicy.

1 pound liver, cut into 1-inch cubes, washed and drained
2 tablespoons lemon juice
1 teaspoon grated lemon zest
1 teaspoon coriander
3 whole pods cardamom, cracked
2 teaspoons cumin, divided
2 tablespoons oil
1 medium onion, coarsely chopped
1 heaping tablespoon flour
1 teaspoon salt
1/2 teaspoon black pepper
1/2 teaspoon crushed chili pepper
2 medium potatoes, peeled, cubed, sprayed with oil, and broiled until golden, optional

1. Put liver cubes in a bowl, and sprinkle with lemon juice, lemon peel, coriander, cardamom, and 1 teaspoon cumin. Toss to allow liver pieces to be coated with the spices. Set aside for 30 minutes.

2. Heat oil in a big skillet. Add liver mixture, and let cook on high heat until all moisture evaporates, and liver pieces start to brown, stirring occasionally, about 5 minutes. Remove from pan, and set aside. Avoid overcooking liver pieces.

3. In the remaining oil, sauté chopped onion until transparent, about 5 minutes.

4. Sprinkle flour and 1 teaspoon cumin, and mix with onion, until fragrant, for a few minutes.

5. Gradually add 1 1/2 cups hot water, stirring to prevent flour from lumping. Add salt, black pepper, and chili pepper. Return liver pieces, and add potatoes, if used. Mix well. Bring to a quick boil, then reduce heat to low, and allow to mixture to simmer until sauce is thickened, 7 to 10 minutes.

Serve with warm bread, or a side dish of rice or bulgar, with lots of salad.

Grumpy Old Men

Here is what a Sumerian husband would say when he felt neglected:

My wife is in the temple,
My mother is down by the river,
And here I am starving of hunger.

(Kramer, History Begins at Sumer, 120)

2. DISHES WITH GROUND MEAT

The Arabian cuisine in general abounds with a variety of dishes that call for ground meat as the main ingredient. Ground meat is very versatile and is more economic than say, steaks. A relatively small amount of meat goes a long way with so delicious and satisfying results, what with all the seasonings, herbs, spices, and vegetables added to it.

During the medieval times pounded meat was a convenient way for using the not so tender cuts of meat, and was creatively incorporated into their cooking. They also believed it was easier on the digestion than having meat in chunks. Al Baghdadi's thirteenth-century cookbook, for instance, offered an interesting collection of such dishes. The *kubabs* (meatballs), made as a supplementary meat ingredient, came in different sizes and shapes. Some were as big as oranges as *al-narinjiya* (from *narinj,* sweet and sour variety of orange). These huge meatballs were dipped in a flavorful sauce, and then thrice taken out of the pot, dipped in egg yolk and returned to the sauce, so that the meatballs would look like oranges (190). On the other extreme, there was *al-bunduquiya* (from *bunduque,* hazelnut). In this case the meatballs were made as tiny as hazelnuts, and were stuffed with a little of boiled and mashed chickpeas. They were then cooked in a flavorful sauce (196-7). Interestingly, to this day, there still is a dish in Spain called "albondigas."

The following recipes, contrary to traditions, call for the leanest meat possible to keep up with the modern tendency to cut down on animal fat. Nevertheless, to retain the traditional juicy texture of the dishes corn or olive oil was added as a substitute. Ground turkey may substitute for ground beef. (For more recipes with ground meat, see also Chapter 5, on snacks and sandwiches with meat, Chapter 11, for stuffed foods)

Scotch Eggs, Medieval Style

(Makes 4 servings)

The idea of boiling eggs and covering them with a thin layer of ground sausage meat, such as in what's called in the Western world as Scotch eggs, goes in fact back to the medieval times. The Baghdadi tenth-century cookbook includes such a recipe. However, taking into consideration that the book was a collection of dishes prepared for the caliphs and high personages, this simple egg preparation was given a lofty twist. It was made in such a way that it came out of the *tannour* as a filled sandwich roll (*bazmaward*) ready to slice and serve. Here is how al-Warrag prepared it:

-Take meat and pound it as you do with sausage meat, let there be with it, a little of kidney fat, onion, herbs, coriander, pepper, caraway, cumin, nutmeg, ginger, and cinnamon.

-Break five eggs, add crushed garlic, and pound together until well mixed.

-Take *tharb* (transparent sheet of caul fat), and spread it on a big *riqaq* (very thin) bread. Let it cover the bread, as much as you can.

-Spread the meat paste all over the surface.

-Arrange five boiled and shelled eggs, lengthwise, in the middle. Roll the *riqaq* bread around it very well. Tie the roll with a length of intestine. Tie the roll to 4 sticks and secure with a thread, so it does not slide down. Lower it into the *tannour* until done, and slice. (57)

305

In the following adaptation I left out the *riqaq* bread part, since I gave boiling the roll as a option.

> **1 pound lean ground meat**
> **1/2 medium onion, grated**
> **1 clove garlic, grated, optional**
> **1/2 teaspoon cinnamon**
> **1/4 teaspoon allspice**
> **1 teaspoon salt**
> **1/4 teaspoon black pepper**
> **1/4 teaspoon nutmeg**
> **1/2 teaspoon ginger**
> **1/2 teaspoon cumin**
> **1/4 cup bread crumbs**
> **1 egg, beaten**
> **6 large eggs, hard-boiled, shelled, and both ends cut off, reserve cut off discs**
> **Preheat oven to 400 degrees F.**

1. Mix all ingredients except for boiled eggs. Knead to form a paste.

2. Divide meat paste into 2 equal parts. Flatten each portion to a 6-by-7-inch rectangle on a piece of kitchen paper. Arrange 3 eggs lengthwise along the longer side of the meat dough. Roll with the help of the paper but do not wrap it with it, seal the seam very well, and tuck in the sides, to hide the eggs inside. Repeat with the other portion of meat paste and eggs.

3. Put on a well-greased baking sheet, decorate tops with the reserved cut discs of eggs, and brush rolls with a little oil or butter. Bake in a preheated oven at 400 degrees F. loosely covered, for 20 minutes, or until cylinders are nicely browned. Let cool for 10 minutes, then cut into slices with a sharp knife.
   Serve with warm bread, pickles and salad. Or as suggested in the tenth century cookbook, serve it with mustard.

4. An optional method for cooking the cylinders is to wrap rolls in cheesecloth, tying both ends with kitchen strings to prevent cloth from opening while simmering. Gently immerse cylinders in boiling salted broth or water. Invert a plate on cylinders to help keep them submerged. Bring to quick boil, then reduce heat to low, and let cylinders cook gently for about 20 minutes, or until meat is cooked. There should always be liquid enough to keep cylinders submerged while cooking.
   Allow to cool, then remove cheesecloth and slice with a sharp knife. Serve with bread, salad and pickles.

Kufta Supreme
(Kebab Mulouki)

(Makes 4 servings)

Mulouki (kingly) is a word usually used to designate excellence. The ingredients in this dish are ordinary but the construction is regal. The way it is traditionally made is to spread pieces of browned bread in the bottom of an oven casserole dish. Fried kebabs and browned onion slices are arranged all over. Chopped tomato and green pepper, preferably hot, will make another layer. The whole thing will be covered with more pieces of fried bread, and tomato juice is poured all over. The casserole is baked until most of the liquid is soaked up, and top is nicely browned.

The idea of lining and covering a pot of a prepared dish with bread before cooking it is quite medieval. Such dishes were called *maghmoumat* (covered), and they were very popular, back then. The tenth-century cookbook writer al-Warraq gives five recipes and a poem in praise of this dish. In *maghmouma tayyiba* (delicious) the instructions were that fat meat was to be cut into very fine slices, "the finest you could get them." Onion was to be thinly sliced like *dirhams* (i.e. rounds) and layered in a pot with the meat and sprinkled with spices and chopped fat. This was to be repeated until all ingredients were used up. The top was to be totally covered with a bread. The pot was then cooked on low heat. To serve, the pot was inverted on a plate. The poem al-Warraq quoted punned on the name of the dish. Although the dish was called *maghmouma* (covered), the poem went, it was far from being *maghmouma* (sad) for it brought joy and happiness to the hungry (184-6).

The following is a simplified and lighter rendition of such dishes.

For the *kufta*:

1 pound lean ground meat
2 tablespoons flour, or bread crumbs
1 small onion, grated
1 clove garlic, grated
1/4 cup parsley, chopped
1/2 teaspoon salt
1/4 teaspoon ginger, cumin, allspice, each

For the tomato sauce:

1 medium onion, coarsely chopped
1 tablespoon oil
1/2 teaspoon turmeric
2 tablespoons tomato paste diluted in 1 1/2 cups hot broth or water, or 1/2 cup tomato sauce diluted in 1 cup hot broth or water
3 medium tomatoes, skinned and diced, or one 15-ounce can diced tomatoes
1/2 teaspoon salt
1/4 teaspoon black pepper

For the yogurt sauce:

1 cup yogurt
1/2 cup chopped parsley
1 clove garlic, grated
1/4 teaspoon salt

2 to 3 flat breads, depending on their size. Lightly brush with oil, and slightly toast in hot oven
For garnish: thinly sliced onion, sprinkled with sumac, see Glossary

1. Preheat broiler. Mix all *kufta* ingredients. Knead briefly, and divide into 8 portions, and shape into *kebab*s by piercing a piece into the handle of a straight dinner knife, elongate by pressing with the fingers. Carefully pull out of the knife handle. Arrange *kuftas* on a broiler pan brushed with water or oil. Broil for about 15 minutes, turning once to brown on both sides.

2. To prepare the tomato sauce: in medium skillet sauté onion in oil, until it softens, about 7 minutes. Fold in turmeric half way through cooking. Add diluted tomato paste or sauce, tomatoes, salt and pepper, and stir. Bring to a quick boil, then reduce heat and let simmer, uncovered, stirring frequently, until it nicely thickens, about 10 minutes.

3. Mix Yogurt Sauce ingredients, and set aside until needed.

5. To assemble the dish: arrange toasted bread in bottom of a rather deep serving platter. Pour tomato sauce all over the bread to moisten it. Add some more hot broth if bread still looks a little dry. Arrange broiled *kuftas* on this bed of bread and drizzle with the prepared yogurt sauce.

Garnish with onion slices. Serve with salad.

Eggplant Rolls
(Laffat al-Betınjan)

(Makes 6 servings)

Succulent slices of eggplant are rolled around spicy *kuftas* and simmered in flavorful tomato sauce. The neat presentation of the dish renders it suitable for formal occasions.

3 medium eggplants, stalks cut off, do not peel. Slice lengthwise into 1/4-inch thick slices, and soak in warm salted water for 30 minutes, drain (you need 18 good full-length slices)

For the Kuftas:
1 1/2 pounds lean meat
3 tablespoons flour or bread crumbs
1 small onion, grated
1 clove garlic, grated
1/4 cup parsley, chopped
1 teaspoon salt
1 teaspoon cumin
1/2 teaspoon chili pepper, or to taste
1/4 teaspoon black pepper, ginger, allspice, each

3 medium tomatoes, skinned and diced, or one 15-ounce can diced tomatoes, do not drain
3 heaping tablespoons tomato paste (one 6-ounce can), diluted in 3 1/2 cups hot water, or 1 cup tomato sauce diluted in 2 1/2 cups hot water, or 3 1/2 cups tomato juice
1/4 cup fresh basil, coarsely chopped, or 1 teaspoon dried basil

1 teaspoon sugar or honey
1 teaspoon salt
1/4 teaspoon black pepper

For garnish: 1/4 cup parsley
Preheat oven to 400 degrees F.

1. Fry drained eggplant slices, let brown on both sides, and drain on white paper napkins. Alternatively, broil after spraying or brushing them with oil, about 20 minutes or until soft and browned in spots.

2. Mix *kufta* ingredients, and knead briefly. Divide into 18 pieces, and form each like a thick finger about 3 1/2 inches long, or the length of your index finger. Broil, turning once to brown on both sides, about 15 minutes.

3. Make 18 rolls by putting a *kufta* finger crosswise at one end of a spread eggplant slice. Roll up the eggplant slice around the *kufta*. This roll is traditionally secured by tying it with a parsley stalk softened in hot water. Arrange finished rolls side by side, seam side down, in a glass baking pan, 11-by-7 inches or approximate size.

4. Spread diced tomatoes on rolls.

5. Add basil, sugar, salt and pepper to diluted tomato paste or sauce or juice. Heat until it starts to bubble, or microwave for 3 minutes on high. Pour liquid all over the rolls. There should be enough liquid to cover them. Add a little hot water if needed.

5. Bake in a preheated oven at 400 degrees F., loosely covered, for about 30 minutes or until sauce is bubbly and nicely thickened.

Garnish with chopped parsley, and serve hot, 3 rolls per serving, with warm bread, bulgar or white rice, and salad or pickles

Eggplant and Kufta Necklace (Maldhouma)

Eggplant and Kufta Necklace
(Maldhouma)

(Makes 6 to 7 servings)

This is a pretty dish in which *kufta* and eggplant rounds are arranged interchangeably so that they look like a threaded necklace and hence the name *maldhouma* (the threaded). For this dish you need small eggplants, about 1 1/2 to 2 inches in diameter. The long Japanese eggplants would be ideal for this purpose.

22 small eggplant discs, 1-inch thick, soaked in salted warm water for 30 minutes, then drained

For the *kufta:*
1 pound lean ground meat
2 tablespoons flour, or bread crumbs
1 small onion, grated
1 clove garlic, grated
1/4 cup parsley, chopped
1/2 teaspoon salt
1/4 teaspoon ginger, cumin, allspice

For the tomato sauce:
3 1/2 cups tomato juice; or 3 heaping tablespoons tomato paste (one 6-ounce can) diluted in 3 1/2 cups hot water; or 1 cup tomato sauce diluted in 2 1/2 cups hot water
1/4 cup fresh basil, coarsely chopped, or 1 teaspoon dried basil

1/2 teaspoon sugar or honey
1 teaspoon salt
1/4 teaspoon black pepper

1. Brown drained eggplant discs in a small amount of oil, or spray or brush with oil and broil.

2. Meanwhile combine *kufta* ingredients in a medium bowl, and knead briefly with wet hands. Form into 20 discs about 1-inch thick and a little bit larger in diameter than the eggplant discs.

3. In an ovenproof glass baking dish about 8-by-12-inches, make rows of "threaded necklaces" by alternating pieces of eggplant with discs of *kufta*, beginning and ending with an eggplant slice, pressing while arranging to keep the "necklace" intact. Curve the rows a little downwards to give it the necklace look.

4. Broil dish for about 7 minutes or until surface is nicely browned.

5. Mix sauce ingredients, and pour all around the rows of "necklace", but do not let the sauce submerge it. Bake in a preheated oven at 400 degrees F. for about 30 minutes or until sauce is nicely thickened.

   Garnish with chopped parsley if wished, and serve hot with rice or warm bread along with some salad.

Kufta Simmered in Dill Sauce
(Raas al-Asfoor bi Salsat al-Shibint)

(Makes 4 to 6 servings)

   This is my family's favorite whenever we want a break from the familiar red stews. It is delicious, light and pretty, and is, believe it or not, so medieval.
   To begin with, the medieval cooks loved to give their dishes some panache by adding those dainty spicy meatballs of different sizes, sometimes using egg white as a binder. Eggs were also used to thicken sauces. For flavor dill was added dried in a bunch and was removed before serving, as in al-Baghdadi's recipe of *mudaqqaqat sadhija* (simple pounded meatballs, 195). In one of al-Warraq's tenth-century recipes called *mudaqqaqa* (the pounded meatballs) the prepared meatballs were thrown into boiling water, to which was added oil, crushed chickpeas, onion, leeks, cilantro, and were simmered until almost done. Then sauce was thickened by adding ground almonds and ten eggs, and was stirred very well and was further simmered until done (195). In another recipe, *al-shaljamiya* (turnip stew) he used turnips for vegetables, and thickened sauce with a combination of crushed chickpeas, ground almonds, rice, and milk (147).

   1 whole onion, skinned and pierced with 6 whole cloves
   2 tablespoons vinegar
   1 bay leaf
For the *kufta*:
   1 pound lean ground meat

        1 small grated onion
        1/2 teaspoon salt
        1/2 teaspoon black pepper, za'tar or thyme, nutmeg, ginger, each
        2 egg whites
        1/2 cup bread crumbs
        1/4 cup fresh dill, finely chopped, or 2 teaspoons dill weed
For the Sauce:
        2 tablespoons cornstarch dissolved in 1/2 cup cold milk
        1/2 cup yellow split chickpeas, cooked and drained
        2 egg yolks
        1 teaspoon salt
        A dash of black pepper

1. In a medium heavy pot pour 6 cups water. Add the whole onion pricked with cloves, vinegar and bay leaf. Bring to a quick boil, and let cook for 10 minutes. Remove bay leaf and onion.

2. Meanwhile mix *kufta* ingredients in a medium bowl. Knead briefly and form into small balls, as small as the sparrow's head, or to taste.

3. Gently drop meatballs into the boiling liquid. Let them cook for 10 minutes on medium high. With slotted spoon take balls from liquid and set aside.

4. To the remaining liquid in the pot, stir in diluted cornstarch. Add the cooked split chickpeas. Continue cooking sauce on medium-high, stirring frequently until sauce starts to thicken slightly, about 5 minutes. Beat egg yolks in a small bowl, and add some of the hot sauce to it and stir, then return it to the pot and stir to prevent curdling. Add salt and pepper. Reduce heat to medium.

5. Return meatballs to the simmering pot, and allow them to cook gently in the sauce, stirring gently, several times, for 10 minutes.
Serve with yellow rice, topped with roasted almonds and raisins (see chapter 8), or bulgar; or serve with warm bread and salad.

Zucchini Simmered in White Sauce
(Shijar bi'l Salsa al-Bedha)

(Makes 5 servings)

This is an elegant dish in which halved zucchinis are stuffed with a meat mixture and simmered in white sauce. It is not as familiar as the traditional tomato stews, but it surely does make a refreshing change. Once again, simmering vegetables in white sauce is a practice so much steeped in our ancient history, as evident in the Babylonian recipes, and the medieval Baghdadi cookbooks, as shown in the previous recipe.

        5 medium to large zucchinis, choose fat ones if possible. Cut off both ends, and split into halves lengthwise. Core out the inside and reserve pulp if it is not seedy

For the filling:
   1 tablespoon oil
   1 pound lean ground meat
   1 medium onion, finely chopped
   2 cloves garlic, grated
   1/4 cup currants or raisins
   1/2 cup chopped parsley
   1/4 cup chopped fresh dill, or 1 tablespoon dried dill weed
   1 teaspoon salt
   1/2 teaspoon black pepper
   1/2 teaspoon allspice
   1/2 teaspoon cinnamon

For the sauce:
   1 tablespoon oil
   2 heaping tablespoons flour
   3 cups liquid, half broth or water, and half milk
   1/2 teaspoon salt
   1/4 teaspoon black pepper

   1/4 cup bread crumbs
   1/4 cup grated Romano cheese, or mozzarella

   Preheat oven to 400 degrees F.

1. Lightly and briefly brown zucchini halves in a small amount of oil. Or Brush or spray with oil, and broil for about 15 minutes, until they start to brown slightly.

2.   In a medium skillet, heat oil and cook ground meat stirring occasionally and breaking any lumps with the back of a spoon until all moisture evaporates and it starts to brown, about 10 minutes. Add onion and garlic and stir until onion is transparent, about 7 minutes. Add currants, parsley, dill, salt, pepper, allspice, and cinnamon. Mix well.

3. Fill zucchini cavities with the meat mixture, and arrange in a rather deep baking pan, big enough to hold the 10 pieces of filled zucchinis in one layer. Scatter the reserved pulp around the zucchini halves, or use it to make another dish like Zucchini Pancakes (see chapter 6, on vegetarian snacks).

4. Prepare sauce: in a medium heavy pot, stir flour and oil until fragrant, about 5 minutes. Add liquids gradually and stir with a wire whisk. Cook on medium heat until it starts to bubble, about 10 minutes. Add salt and pepper.

5. Pour sauce all over filled zucchinis and around them. There should be enough liquid to barely reach the top of the zucchinis. Add a little more liquid if needed. Sprinkle the entire surface with breadcrumbs and grated cheese.

6. Cover loosely with foil paper, and bake in a preheated oven at 400 degrees F. 35 to 40 minutes, or until zucchini is tender, and sauce is nicely thickened. Remove foil 10 minutes before dish is done to allow surface to brown. Serve hot with yellow rice, topped with toasted almonds and raisins.

A Quiz Show from The Arabian Nights

A smart slave-girl called Tawaddud is cross-examined in a battle of wits, in the presence of the eighth-century Abbasid Caliph Haroun Al-Rasheed. She is questioned by the court's most learned philosophers and intellectuals, and needless to say her answers get their unanimous approval. Here are some of her answers concerning food, some of which, even by today's standards, still ring true especially her answers advocating simplicity in preparing food, avoiding overeating, shunning processed meats, and the virtues of wine.

Q. How cometh hurt to the head?
A. By the ingestion of food upon food before the first be digested, and by fullness upon fullness; this is that wasteth peoples. He, who would live long, let him be early with the morning-meal and not late with the evening-meal.

Q. What food is it that giveth not rise to ailment?
A. That which is not eaten but after hunger, and when eaten, the ribs are not filled with it.

Q. What kind of food is the most profitable?
A. That which women make and which hath not cost overmuch trouble and which is readily digested. The most excellent of food is brewis [*thareeda* made of broken pieces of bread, sopped in broth; or bread sopped in milk and meat. Burton in his note comments that the *tharida* of the famous Arab tribe, Ghassan, cooked with eggs and bone marrow, was held a dainty dish].

Q. What kind of meat is the most profitable?
A. Mutton; but jerked meat is to be avoided, for there is no profit in it.

Q. What of fruit?
A. Eat them in their prime and quit them when their season is past.

Q. What sayest thou of drinking water?
A. Drink it not in large quantities nor swallow it by gulps, or it will give thee headache and cause diverse kinds of harm.

Q. What of drinking fermented liquors?
A. Doth not the prohibition suffice thee in the book of Almighty Allah, where He saith, "Verily, wine and lots and images, and the divining arrows are an abomination, of Satan's work; therefore avoid them, that ye may prosper"? And again, "They will ask thee concerning

wine and lots: Answer, "In both there is a great sin and also some things of use unto men: but their sinfulness is greater than their use."... As for the advantages that be therein, it disperseth stone and gravel from the kidneys and strengtheneth the viscera and banisheth care, and moveth the body, expelleth disease from the joints, purifieth the frame of corrupt humors, engendereth cheerfulness, gladdeneth the heart of man and keepeth up natural heat; it contracteth the bladder, enforceth the liver and removeth obstructions, reddeneth the cheeks, cleareth away maggots from the brain and deferreth Grey hairs. In short, had not Allah (to whom be honor and glory!) forbidden it, there were not on the face of the earth aught fit to stand in its stead.

Q. What wine is best?
A. That which is pressed from white grapes and kept eighty days or more after fermentation.

Q. What are the most excellent fruits?
A. Pomegranate and citron.

Q. Which is the most excellent of vegetables?
A. Endives.
(Burton, vol. 5, 221-4)

CHAPTER ELEVEN: STUFFED FOODS

1. THE ART OF MAKING *KUBBA*

2. MORE STUFFED FOODS

CHAPTER ELEVEN
STUFFED FOODS

المُحْشِيّات

(MAHSHIYYAT)

1. The Art of Making Kubba:

K*ubba* is dough made from grains such as bulgar and rice, or potatoes that is usually stuffed with a spicy mixture of ground meat and onion. It is traditionally shaped into balls (hence the name *kubba*) or discs. Though not difficult to make, *kubba* definitely requires a certain amount of skill, acquired by practice. No wonder, of all the dishes it is *kubba* that is the touchstone of a good cook. Skill is measured by how thin the shell of *kubba* is made. "Oh," it would be said *flana* (so and so) "is such a fine cook, she makes her *kubba* as thin as onion skins." As for *kubba* of the novice, alas, it would be gravely reported, if you threw it from the rooftop to the ground it wouldn't break.

The art of stuffing food with food is not new to the Mesopotamian cooks. Indeed, it can be detected back to the Babylonians' bird "pies" prepared by enclosing birds cooked in white sauce between two layers of seasoned dough (for more details see Introduction). The word *kubba* itself, used to designate this kind of stuffed food, may be derived originally from the Akkadian "kubbu," (rounded like a ball or a dome, *qubba*). "Kubbuzu," for instance, was an Akkadian turban-like headdress, a word we still use in relation to headdresses (*kabbuz*).

As we advance in history, the art of making *kubba* becomes more subtle. First of all there were the medieval *kubabs* (singular *kubba*), the spicy and aromatic meatballs that adorned their stews. Al-Warraq's tenth-century cookbook has got a few of them, but there are many in the al-Baghdadi's thirteenth-century book, a testimony to its increasing popularity. More elaborate *kubba*-like dishes were also included. They were meant to be a kind of a pleasant surprise to the eaters. *Al-makhfiya* (the hidden), for instance, is a stew dish containing whole cooked egg yolks that have been enclosed in spicy paste of ground meat, and shaped into a ball. In a dish called *Rutabiya* (with dates) a paste of ground meat is formed into date-like balls, stuffed with peeled almonds, and simmered in broth. When served the dish is garnished with real dates filled with almonds, to further confuse the diners. In another dish called *Bunduqiya* (like hazelnuts) a paste of seasoned ground meat is shaped into small balls, as small as hazelnuts, filled with mashed cooked chickpeas, then simmered in broth. In our modern *kubba*-making practices we have reversed the procedure-- meat is used as the main ingredient in the filling rather than being the main ingredient of the shell itself.

317

وكت دك الكبة، رّعو قربـــدل،
وكت أُكل الكبة: نا بـدقرندل

For the Love of Kubba

When its time for pounding *kubba,* wake up Qarandal! When its time to eat the *kubba,* let poor Qarandal sleep (Zalzala, vol. 3, 383).

Kubba is delicious, no gourmet diner worth his spoon, so to speak, would argue against that. But it is time consuming especially before kitchen gadgets like blenders and food processors were accessible to cooks. What we achieve with a press of a button in a few seconds, used to take hours of pounding using stone mortars and pestles.

The proverb is said when a person feels used. He would be called when his help is needed, but none would think of calling him back when the time comes to share the fruits of his deed with them.

Stuffed rice dough simmered in turnip soup, 323

A General Recipe for the Kubba Filling

Though shells for this type of stuffed food are made from a variety of ingredients, the stuffing for all is the same. Here is how to prepare it:

1 3/4 pounds lean ground meat
1 tablespoon oil
2 medium onions, finely chopped

1 1/2 teaspoon salt
1/2 to 1 teaspoon black pepper
1/2 teaspoon allspice
1/2 teaspoon cinnamon
1/4 to 1/2 teaspoon chili pepper, optional
1/4 teaspoon prepared *noomi Basra*, see Glossary, optional
1/4 cup chopped parsley, optional
1/2 cup blanched, slivered and dry toasted almonds, or dry toasted pine nuts, optional
1/2 cup currants, or raisins, optional

1. Heat oil in a big skillet and cook ground meat, stirring occasionally, and breaking down any lumps with the back of a spoon. When moisture evaporates, add onion and stir until transparent, 10 to 15 minutes, total.

2. Five minutes before meat mixture is done, add the rest of the ingredients, and fold gently.

Note: After making the *Kubba,* you might be left with some filling. You can make delicious sandwiches with it.

Stuffed Potato Dough
(Poteta Chap)

(Makes 18 to 20 pieces)

The meaning of *chap* in this otherwise very Iraqi dish eludes me, though in most probability, it is a corruption of some sort of an English word which might have filtered into the dialect during the time of the British colonization. It is the best guise that potatoes can ever make. The stuffed fried discs are a delight to look at and eat.

2 pounds whole unpeeled potatoes, preferably the starchy variety, such as russet (Idaho) potatoes. Boil, then cool
2/3 cup corn starch (with starchy potatoes use a little less)
1 teaspoon salt
1/2 teaspoon white or black pepper

1 recipe of the filling, p. 319, include optional ingredients
About 1 cup bread crumbs for coating
Oil for frying

1. Peel the cooled boiled potatoes. Cut them into smaller pieces. Put them in big bowl, and add cornstarch, salt, and pepper.

2. First mash the potatoes with a masher. Do not use a blender or a food processor. Then with a moistened hand knead mixture the way you knead pastry dough, until well-blended, about 5 minutes. If mixture is too dry to form into dough (sometimes this happens when potatoes are too starchy), add a little cold water.

3. Divide dough into 18 to 20 pieces, size of a small lemon each. With moistened hands flatten a piece into a wok-like, thin disk.

4. Put about 2 tablespoons of filling in the middle, gather edges, and close the piece into a ball. Then flatten it into a disc, by putting it between the palms of the hands and gently pressing the edges so that it is full in the middle and thinner around the edges. Always remember to handle dough with moistened hands. Put finished discs in one layer on a tray or a big dish.

5. Put breadcrumbs in a flat dish, and coat discs before frying. Shake off excess crumbs.

6. Put about 1/2-inch deep oil in a skillet. When hot, fry discs turning once to brown on both sides, 3 to 4 minutes for each side. If they brown quickly turn heat down a little. Drain pieces in a colander lined with white paper towels or napkins put on a rack to prevent pieces from getting soggy.
Serve warm with lots of salad, and bread. They also make an exciting filling for a sandwich. Fill sandwich bread with a piece or two of *kubba* along with sliced salad vegetables.

Baked Poteta Chap

(Makes 8 servings)

Most of the traditional dishes were fried which is largely due to the fact that ovens were not available in every kitchen that is up until the late 1950's. Nowadays there is no reason why some of the dishes should not be baked. Though frying is fast and easy, baking gives a lighter touch to the food. The following is a lighter version of the traditional stuffed potato dough.

1. Use exactly the same ingredients given in *Poteta Chap* above. Make dough as directed in steps 1 and 2, and prepare filling as directed in the general recipe for the filling.

2. Preheat oven to 375 degrees F. Grease 15-by-10-inch baking pan. Coat generously both bottom and sides with breadcrumbs.

3. Divide dough into 2 parts. Spread one half in the bottom of prepared pan, and cover evenly with the filling. Cover with the second half of dough by taking small portions and flatten and put them on the filling, until the whole surface is covered with dough. With wet fingers lightly press top layer closing any gaps on surface. Smooth and brush it with a beaten egg, and sprinkle lightly with breadcrumbs. Decorate surface with a fork and drizzle with a little oil.

4. Bake in a preheated oven at 375 degrees F. for 40 to 45 minutes, or until surface is golden brown. Let cool for 10 minutes, then divide into 8 pieces, or more if smaller portions are desired.

A Jiffy Treat:

Instead of fresh potatoes, potato flakes may be substituted, which makes the whole process go so fast. To make dough use 6 cups potato flakes, and 4 cups boiling water. Stir with a fork, and then add the rest of the ingredients as directed above.

Stuffed Rice Dough
(Kubbat Halab)

(Makes 22 to 24 pieces)

These beautiful creations are golden and appetizingly crunchy from the outside, but succulently moist from the inside. Although their name links them to the Syrian city of Aleppo, they are, as far as I know, an Iraqi specialty. I once made this dish for friends from Aleppo, and they said they have never seen anything like it before.

Making dough for this *kubba* might prove to be rather tricky at the beginning. I remember when I first started experimenting with it, the finished *kubbas* were soft, and took some odd shapes. To make successful *kubbat Halab* you need to watch for two things:

First choose rice that is rather on the sticky side like jasmine rice, for instance. Basmati rice or American rice are not a good choice because the grains have the tendency to separate when cooked, which is a virtue when rice is cooked to be served as a side dish, but not for making *kubba*. However, adding a little bit of cornstarch to the dough can help greatly in this case. Some people choose to add beaten egg to the dough as a binder, but this will soften the texture, and the *kubba* loses its characteristic crunchiness.

Secondly let rice boil gently in a big amount of salted water, and watch it and test the grains for doneness. Undercook the grains and they will not bind into dough, overcook them and they will be good for nothing.

Although turmeric and cinnamon are given as optional ingredients, their addition to the rice dough will give the *kubba* shell an attractive golden hue and a delicious aroma.

2 cups rice, (jasmine rice is good) washed and soaked in cold water for 30 minutes
2 teaspoons salt
1/4 teaspoon turmeric, optional (1/4 teaspoon saffron might be substituted if you do not mind the extra expense)

321

1/2 teaspoon cinnamon, optional
1/4 cup cornstarch

1 recipe of the filling, **p. 319, use optional ingredients**

Oil for frying

1. Put rice in a medium pot, and cover it by 2 inches hot water, about 9 cups. Add salt, turmeric and cinnamon, if using any. Mix and let boil gently, partially covered, on medium heat, until rice grain is cooked, about 15 minutes. Stir several times while cooking to prevent grains from sticking to the bottom of the pot. Start testing after the first 10 minutes of cooking. Test the grain by eating it. It should be cooked but intact, not chewy, and not mushy. Do not let rice overcook.

2. Strain rice in a metal colander. Put the colander with the rice back into the pot and cover it with a lid, and set it aside until it is cool enough to handle.

3. Transfer rice to a big bowl. Sprinkle cornstarch on rice and knead until mixture is combined into dough.

4. Have a bowl of cold water nearby. Handling with moistened hands, take a small amount of dough, size of a small lemon, and shape into discs as described in the *Potata Chap*, p. steps 3 and 4. Or, **shape it like an egg with two pointed ends (more like an American football)**, which is the more traditional thing to do. To make this shape, hold the ball of dough in one hand and hollow it with the thumb of the other hand until you get an elongated oval shell about 1/4 inch thick and 3 inches long, it does not have to be perfect. Fill and close the opening, and roll it gently between the palms to make it look like an egg but with two pointed ends. Moisten your fingers whenever dough feels sticky. Put the finished ones on a big tray in one layer.

5. Fry them in 1/2 inch of hot oil, turning once, until golden all around, about 7 minutes per batch. Drain on a colander lined with white paper towels or napkins put on a rack to prevent them from getting soggy.

Serve with lots of salad and bread, or make into a sandwich with slices of salad vegetables, and pickles. Pickled Mango Salad is especially good with this dish (see chapter 3).

Kubbat Halab Made, Light and Easy

To avoid frying, simply divide dough into 2 parts, and line a well-greased 10-by-15-inch-baking pan with one half of the dough. Spread filling and cover it with the second half by taking small pieces and flattening them and spreading them on the filling until the entire surface is covered. Spray or brush surface generously with oil. Score all the way down into squares or diamonds. Bake in a preheated oven at 375 degrees F. for 40 to 45 minutes, or until surface is golden brown.

Let stand for 10 minutes, then re-cut and serve with salad and bread.

Rice Patties
Hassle-free Kubbat Halab

(Makes about 24 small patties)

The following is even an easier way for doing *kubbat halab*. It is a lazy day recipe when you have the craving to enjoy something nice with preparation kept to the minimum. Ultimately the taste is the same since the same ingredients are used here, but craftsmanship is absent.

1/2 pound lean ground meat, browned with 1 medium onion, chopped, using 1 tablespoon oil. I sometimes use the leftover *kubba* filling, instead
3 cups cooked rice; leftovers can be used here. Break grains by blending or processing using on/off turns, or simply press by hands
1/2 cup chopped parsley
1 egg, beaten
1 teaspoon salt
1/2 teaspoon black pepper, cinnamon, allspice, each
1/2 teaspoon *baharat*, see Glossary
1/2 teaspoon chili pepper, or to taste
1/4 cup currants or raisins

1. Mix all ingredients and knead into dough.

2. Handling with wet fingers, shape mixture into small patties about 1/2- inch thick, and brown them on both sides in 1/2-inch deep oil. Or simply press dough into a generously greased 12-by-9 inch baking pan. Brush with oil, score into squares or diamonds, and bake in a preheated oven at 375 degrees F. for about 40 minutes, or until surface is golden brown and bottom layer is crispy brown.
    Let set for 10 minutes then re-cut and serve with salad.

Stuffed Rice Dough
Simmered in Turnip Soup
(Kubbat Hamudh Shalgham)

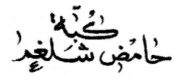

(Makes about 16 pieces)

This is the mother of all *kubbas*. I am using the expression in the medieval sense, which is,"the best of." I imagine had al-Warraq known this dish, he would have called it *"um al-kubab."* Actually he came that close to creating such a dish. In one of his *shaljamiyat* (white stew with turnips) recipes, turnips were cooked in white sauce thickened with crushed chickpeas, ground almonds, milk, and rice. Lean meat was pounded into paste with spices, formed into *kubabs* (meatballs) and thrown into the simmering stew or soup (147-8).

This *kubba* is different from *kubbat halab* in that dough is made from ground uncooked rice pounded with meat. There is only one way to serve it and that is as *kubbat hamudh shalgham*. After shaping the *kubba*, it is simmered in delicious turnip and Swiss chard soup. The soup in this case is served as a main dish (see also *shorbat hamudh shalgham*, chapter 4).

Kubbat hamudh shalgham is everybody's favorite. As kids we used to beg our moms to make it, since it wasn't an easy thing to do-- what with all the pounding and grinding needed to make this dish. It was definitely not the kind of thing to be cooked as often as we would have desired. However, in the age of food processors and blenders, making it is no big deal. Nowadays, rice flour can be purchased ready pounded, and dough can be pulsed in the food processor in a few minutes. This might explain why in the Arab countries, a food processor is called *sit al-bet* (the lady of the house).

In Iraq, this dish is basically a winter treat since turnips and Swiss chard are available in that season only. Still, some people do make it in the summer too, using summer squash and mint instead. Incidentally, al-Warraq, in the same turnip stew recipe I mentioned above, also gave gourd (*qar'*) as a substitute when turnip was not in season (147).

> **1/2 pound (8 ounces) lean beef, ground or cubes, the leanest you can get**
> **2 cups rice flour, white or brown**
> **1 teaspoon salt**
> **1/4 teaspoon white or black pepper**
> **2 to 4 tablespoons cold water, depending on how moist your ground meat is**
>
> **1 recipe** filling, **p. 319**
> **1 recipe** Cream of Turnip and Swiss Chard Soup **(chapter 4)**

1. To prepare dough, put meat in food processor, and pulse it for 10 to 15 seconds, or until it starts to form into a ball.

2. Mix rice flour, salt, and pepper. Add rice mixture to meat in food processor and process on high speed, adding, through the spout, cold water in tablespoons. Stop when you notice a ball of dough starts forming and revolving, 2 to 3 minutes. The final dough would be pinkish in hue, pliable and of medium consistency.

3. Fill 3/4 of a big pot with water, add 1 tablespoon salt, and bring to a boil, getting it ready for boiling the *kubba* pieces.

4. Take a piece of dough, the size of a golf ball, and fill and shape as instructed in Stuffed Potato Dough, steps 3 and 4, p. . Make it as thin as you can, without tearing the shell, otherwise it will be thick when boiled. (Handle dough with moist hands) The traditional shapes are balls, and flattened discs. I personally prefer the balls. They look more appealing in the soup dish. To make the ball, flatten a piece of dough, the size of a golf ball, and put about one tablespoon of filling in the middle. Gather the ends to close it, and roll it between the palms into a ball.

Sometimes while shaping the dough would tear at places, especially when you are trying to make it as thin as possible. The way to fix this is to take a small piece of dough, flatten it between your fingers, slightly wet the torn area, and patch. Put the finished pieces on a tray, in one layer.

5. When water starts boiling carefully and with the help of a slotted spoon put *kubbas* into boiling water, 6 to 8 ones at a time, depending on the size of your pot. Avoid crowding the pot. Carefully stir the pieces to prevent them from sticking to the bottom of the pot. If you notice cracks on the filled piece before you put it in the water, seal them with moistened fingers, otherwise the filling will come out while boiling.

6. Let the pieces boil gently uncovered, on medium high, for 15 minutes. The *kubbas* might start rising after 5 to 6 minutes of cooking, but this does not mean they are done, meat and rice need to take their time to cook. With a slotted spoon take out the cooked pieces, and put them in a big flat dish in one layer. Repeat with the remaining batches.

7. Make soup as directed in the soup recipe, preferably using the liquid you boiled the *kubbas* in. Add the cooked *kubbas* to the soup about 15 minutes before it is done. Stir carefully, and occasionally, until soup is rather thickened.

Serve with bread and salad.

Note:

Instead of turnip and Swiss chard, zucchini may be substituted. Use

2 to 3 medium zucchinis, cubed
1/2 cup chopped fresh mint or 1 1/2 teaspoons dried mint
1 cup cooked chickpeas

Follow method given in preparing Cream of Turnip and Swiss chard Soup.

Stuffed Bulgar Dough
(Kubbat Burghul)

كُبّة بُرغُل

This is the specialty of the northern city of Mosul where wheat grows in abundance. *Kubbat burghul* comes in different sizes and shapes. People of Mosul particularly pride themselves on making the round, flat, thin, and big variety (sometimes they are made as big as 16 inches in diameter). Needless to say, the bigger they are, the more skill and craftsmanship they require. Special big pots and utensils are usually used to facilitate the making and the handling of the big *kubbas* without breaking them. Here we'll make do with whatever is more readily available in our kitchens. However, if you still find this too much of a hassle, you can make the smaller ones which are easier to handle and require no special utensils. The big and the small are given in two separate recipes, for there are some slight differences in preparing them.

1. Flattening and stuffing Big Flat Kubba (Kubbat Mosul)

2. The final shape before cooking Kubba.

Big Flat Kubba
(Kubbat Mosul)

(Makes 3 *kubbas* 9 to 10 inches in diameter)

The following is a practical method for making the flat variety using utensils readily available in every kitchen. If you find that the suggested size of the disc is too big to handle successfully, go ahead, by all means, and make them smaller, 6 inches across, perhaps. You also have the option of making half circles by putting the filling on one half of the disc, folding the other half on top of the filling, and pressing the edge to prevent filling from coming out while cooking. Some cooks use the general cooked kubba filling (given above), but I strongly recommend the uncooked variety of filling, given below, for the big flat discs. The reason is, when the meat filling cooks inside the disc, it forms a binding layer that helps the disc stay intact while cooking and even while cutting into wedges when ready to serve.

For bulgar dough:
>2 cups bulgar #1, picked over but not washed
>1 cup farina, see Glossary
>1 teaspoon salt
>1/2 teaspoon white or black pepper
>12 ounces lean, ground beef, the leanest you can get, 90 % lean is fine

For filling:
>2 medium onions, finely chopped
>1 tablespoon olive oil
>
>1 pound lean ground meat, 90 % lean will do, uncooked
>1 teaspoon salt
>1/2 teaspoon black pepper
>1/2 teaspoon allspice
>1/4 cup slivered toasted almonds, or to taste
>1/4 to 1/2 cup currants or raisins

1. To make the **dough**: Combine bulgar, farina, salt and pepper in a big bowl, and pour over them 2 cups warm water. Mix with a fork, and cover. Let stand for 30 minutes, folding mixture 2 or 3 times while soaking. Test for doneness by taking a small amount of bulgar and pressing it between the fingers. If it forms into dough, it is ready. (If for some reason it still feels dry, sprinkle it with a little bit more warm water, cover, and set aside for 10 more minutes, and test again.)

Put half the meat in a food processor, and pulse for 8 to 10 seconds or until it forms a ball. Add half the bulgar mixture, and turn processor on high speed, until a revolving ball of dough forms, about 2 minutes. Take ball of dough out of the processor, put it in a big bowl, and repeat with the other half of bulgar and meat. Knead the two balls for a few minutes with moistened hands to combine the two batches. The final dough should be of medium consistency, a little more on the stiff side, so that when cooked the *kubba* shell will have a pleasantly chewy texture.

2. To make **filling**: Heat oil in a medium skillet, and sauté onion until transparent, about 5 minutes. Cool and combine with the rest of ingredients.

Here is how to shape the big and flat kubba:

1. Fill with water three quarters of a skillet, 12 inches in diameter or bigger. Add 1/2 teaspoon salt, and bring to a boil. (The skillet should be larger in diameter than the dish you're going to use as a pattern for cutting out the dough)

2. Divide prepared dough into 6 equal parts. Spread a sheet of plastic or parchment or wax paper, big enough to accommodate the 9-inch or 10-inch disc of *kubba*. Wipe the surface of the sheet with moistened fingers. Put a portion of dough on the sheet and press it first with the fingers into a 1/2-inch thick round, then roll it out with a slightly moistened rolling pin. Moisten the rolling pin a little whenever you notice that it is sticking to the dough. Roll the dough into a thin 9 to 10-inch disc, the thinner you get it without tearing it the better. Using an inverted round dinner plate as a guide cut out around it with a sharp knife. Reserve the cut out parts.

3. Spread a little bit less than third of the filling on the disc. Press the filling with your hands, leaving about 1/3 inch around the edge uncovered. Put it aside on a flat surface.

4. Make another circle as described in step 2. Moisten around the edge, lift it with the paper, and flip it on the filled disc. **Do not remove the sheet of paper or plastic, yet**. Press lightly on the disc to get rid of air pockets. Press around the edge very well with the fingers to seal it and prevent the filling from coming out while cooking. Now remove the top plastic or paper sheet, but keep the bottom layer, and set the disc aside on a flat surface to dry out a little while you make the other discs.

5. Repeat the same procedure with the other 4 pieces. With the leftover cut off pieces, make a small disc and fill it with the remaining filling.

6. Due to their size these flattened discs are to be cooked one after the other. So when ready to cook, and water is boiling in the skillet, lift, with wet hands, one disc with the help of the bottom plastic or paper sheet; invert the discs on one palm, and swiftly but carefully slide it into the boiling water in the skillet. Carefully and quickly remove plastic or paper sheet, and gently with a wide spatula press the disc down so that it is totally submerged in boiling water. Let the *kubba* boil gently on medium-high heat, partially covered for 10 minutes. Help the disc stay down at least for the first 5 minutes, by weighing it down with a wide spatula especially at the places where air bubbles seem to be vigorously coming up which might cause the flat disc to break. The disc will float up to the surface when it is done, about 10 minutes.

7. To take the cooked disc out of the skillet in one piece, have a big tray ready near the skillet, and carefully and deftly put a big flat and thin plate under the disc. With the help of the plate and the wide spatula, lift the disc from the water, and place it on the prepared tray. Put it aside, tilting the tray slightly to let the liquid scooped with the disc drain. Let it cool for at least 10 minutes (if you can wait) before serving to allow it to set

8. Repeat with the other 2 discs. However, you need to replenish the boiling water every time you start cooking a new disc, and do not forget to add a little bit more salt.

Serve by dividing the disc into wedges, and have it along with pickles and salad. Olives are especially good with this *kubba*.

Traditionally, after *kubba* is boiled, it is browned in a few tablespoons of oil, which gives it a lovely crispy texture. Alternatively, to cut down on fat put the disc in a generously greased or sprayed baking sheet, brush or spray the surface with oil, and bake in a hot oven until bottom is browned, then broil top until golden brown. This method spares you the trouble of having to flip the disc to brown on both sides.

To refrigerate leftovers, put plastic sheets between the discs to prevent them from sticking to each other, or put them in separate sealed plastic bags. To freeze the discs put each one in a plastic bag, seal and freeze. To serve, let the disc thaw slowly in the refrigerator for a few hours then put it in a greased baking sheet and spray or brush the surface with oil. Sprinkle disc with water and warm it up in a hot oven.

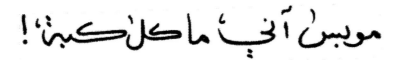

Bonding with Kubba

This is the story of a man who had an amazingly intelligent parrot. Once he invited friends to dinner, and his wife prepared a feast, the crown jewel of which were the flat beautifully huge *kubbas*. In order to cool them off a little, she spread them on a huge tray, and put them in the middle of the house yard. It so happened that *kubba* was the parrot's favorite food. When he saw them spread like this he could not resist the temptation to try some of it. He did not want the wife to take notice that one piece was missing, so he decided to take one bite from each, thus unintentionally spoiling the whole lot.

When his deed (or misdeed) was discovered, his master was so angry with him that he plucked every single feather on his head, to teach him a lesson he would never forget. The parrot was very much hurt and cried bitterly at the loss of his beautiful plumes. After a while he flew to the dining room where the guests were eating, and was consoled to find a bald fellow sufferer. So he alighted on the man's shoulder saying, "Poor soul, have you also eaten *kubba*?"

(Zalzala, vol. 3, 287-8)

Small Discs of Bulgar Dough

(Makes 18 to 20 small discs)

These small discs are much easier to handle. They are versatile and taste as delicious as the big ones.

For bulgar dough:
> 2 cups bulgar #1, picked over but not washed
> 1 cup farina, see Glossary
> 1 teaspoon salt
> 1/2 teaspoon white or black pepper

One recipe general *kubba* filling, **p. 319**

1. To make the **dough** combine bulgar, farina, salt and pepper in a big bowl, and pour over them 2 1/4 cups warm water. Mix with a fork and cover. Let stand for 30 minutes, folding mixture 2 or 3 times while soaking. Test for doneness by taking a small amount of bulgar and pressing it between the fingers. If it forms into dough, it is ready. (If for some reason it still feels dry, sprinkle it with a little bit more warm water, cover and set aside for 10 more minutes, and test again.)

2. Put half the amount of bulgar in a food processor, and pulse until a revolving ball of dough forms, about 2 minutes. Take ball of dough out of the processor, put it in a big bowl, and repeat with the other half of bulgar. Knead the two balls for a few minutes with moistened hands to combine the two batches. The final dough should be of medium consistency, a little bit on the stiff side, so that when cooked, the *kubba* shell will have a pleasantly chewy texture. Now dough is ready for shaping.

3. Take a piece of dough the size of a golf ball, and flatten and fill exactly as in Stuffed Potato Dough, p., steps 3 and 4. Handle dough with moist hands.

3. Fill up 3/4 of a big pot with water, add 1 teaspoon salt and bring to a boil. When discs are ready, put each disc in a slotted spoon, immerse it in the boiling water, and let it slide gently into the water. Cook 6 to 8 ones at a time depending upon the size of the pot and the discs. Carefully stir pieces once to prevent them from sticking to the bottom of the pot. When done discs will float up to the surface and feel tender to the touch, 10 minutes.

4. Take out the cooked ones with a slotted spoon, put them on a tray or a big plate, and allow them to cool slightly before serving. They go very well with warm bread, salad, pickles and olives.

If wished, these small *kubbas* can be browned on both sides in a little amount of oil, either in a nonstick skillet, or in a greased baking pan in a hot oven.

Variation:

You can form dough into small filled balls instead of flattened discs, and use them in soups. Flatten a piece of dough, the size of a golf ball, fill it with about 2 tablespoons meat filling, gather the edges and seal well. Roll it between the palms of the hands to give it a nice regular shape, and boil as directed above.

Eggplant Casserole with Bulgar Dough Discs (Tabsi Betinjan bil-Kubba)

(Makes 6 servings)

This is everybody's favorite. The combination of bulgar dough discs with eggplant gives the dish a festive touch suitable for parties and formal presentations.

1. Prepare eggplant casserole as directed in chapter 7, p.226.

2. Make small filled bulgar dough discs, as directed above. For this casserole you need 12 *kubbas*.

3. Arrange discs and vegetables as follows: First arrange cooked discs in the bottom of the casserole. Top each with a piece of eggplant, and fill in the spaces with the sautéed onion slices and garlic. Top with tomato slices, or chopped tomatoes, and scatter pepper slices on top. Pour the diluted tomato sauce on the vegetables and bake as directed.

Serve with white rice decked with almonds and raisin or bread, along with some salad.

Stuffed Bulgar Dough Simmered in Yogurt Sauce (Kubba Labaniyya)

(Makes 7 servings)

This dish calls for small balls of stuffed bulgar dough. It is delicious and healthy.

> **1/2 recipe** Bulgar dough for small discs, **p.329**
> **1/2 recipe** general *Kubba* filling, **p.319**
> **For the sauce:**
>> **2 cups yogurt, use whole milk yogurt**
>> **2 tablespoons cornstarch**
>> **1/4 cup rice, washed, soaked 30 minutes, and crushed between the fingers, do not drain**
>> **1 cup cooked whole chickpeas**
>> **1 teaspoon salt**
>> **1/4 teaspoon pepper**
>> **2 cloves garlic, grated**
>> **1/4 cup chopped fresh mint or 2 tablespoons dry mint**
>> **1/4 cup fresh dill, chopped, or 1 tablespoon dill weed, optional**

1. Take a piece of dough the size of a walnut, flatten it into a disc, and fill it with 1 teaspoon of the filling. Gather the sides and close it into a ball, then roll it between your palms to make a ball. (Amount of dough is enough to make 28 balls). Cook balls in a pot of salted boiling water. The balls will start floating up after 5 minutes. Take them out with a slotted spoon, and keep aside.

2. In a medium heavy pot, dilute yogurt and cornstarch in 3 cups cold water. Mix well. (Suggestion: the cooled liquid in which the balls were cooked can be used instead of plain water, but then you need to adjust the total amount of salt used in the sauce.)

3. Add rice and chickpeas, and mix well. Bring to a quick boil on high heat, stirring occasionally in one direction, to prevent mixture from curdling. Lower heat to medium, and continue cooking and stirring until sauce bubbles, about 10 minutes.

4. Add cooked stuffed bulgar balls, salt, pepper, and garlic. Simmer on medium-low heat, stirring occasionally, always in the same direction, for about 15 minutes, or until sauce nicely thickens. Add

mint and dill, if used, 5 minutes before sauce is done to prevent herbs from losing their lovely bright green color.

Stuffed Bulgar Dough Baked in the Oven
(Kubbat Burghul bil Firin)

(Makes 18 pieces)

Preparing this *Kubba* is much easier than the traditional individually shaped ones. The filling is enclosed between two layers of dough, spread on a baking pan. Nevertheless, it tastes as good as the individual discs and balls.

For the dough:
> **2 cups #1 or #2 bulgar, picked over but not washed**
> **1 cup farina**
> **1 1/4 teaspoon salt**
> **1/2 teaspoon white or black pepper**
> **1 small onion, grated**
> **1 teaspoon cumin**
> **1/2 teaspoon cinnamon**
> **1/4 teaspoon chili pepper**
>
> **1/4 cup lemon juice**
> **1/2 cup tomato juice**
>
> **12 ounce lean ground meat**
>
> **1 1/2 recipes *Kubba* filling, p.319, using optional ingredients, or use uncooked filling, p.327**

1. In a big bowl mix bulgar, farina, salt, pepper, grated onion, cumin, cinnamon, and chili.

2. In a small bowl mix lemon juice, tomato juice, and 1 1/2 cups warm water. Pour this mixture on bulgar, and follow directions given for making bulgar dough, p.327, step 1.

3. Generously grease 15-by-10-by-2-inch baking sheet, and spread half the dough in the bottom, about 1/4-inch thick. Sprinkle surface with cold water. Spread filling evenly on entire surface. Cover filling with remaining dough, by taking small pieces and flattening them between fingers and placing them on top of filling until entire filling is covered. It is easier to handle dough with moistened hands. An easier way for preparing top layer is to arrange those flattened pieces of dough on a sheet of plastic or paper a little bigger than the baking pan. When an area the size of the baking pan is covered with dough, lift the plastic or paper sheet, and flip it on the filling. Peel off the plastic or paper sheet, and press the entire surface with wet fingers

4. Brush top with 3 tablespoons oil, then sprinkle 3 tablespoons clod water. With a sharp knife score all the way down, into 18 squares or diamonds (or more if it is to be presented as an appetizer). If wished, press an almond sliver in the center of each piece.

5. Bake in a hot oven at 450 degrees F. loosely covered with aluminum foil for the first 10 minutes. Then lower heat to 375 degrees F., and bake for 25 minutes. Remove cover, give surface a light brush of oil and continue baking for 10 more minutes longer, or until top is slightly browned. Let it stand for about 10 minutes before serving. Re-cut, and serve with lots of salad.

Pizza, the Mosuli Way
(Uroug Mosuliyya)

(Makes about 7 servings)

   This is the Mesopotamian counterpart of pizza from the northern region of bulgar, city of Mosul. It is a variation on the filled bulgar dough and is much easier to make. So enjoy the delicious taste and aroma of the traditional *kubba,* hassle free. Traditionally fat meat is used in preparing this dish to give it the desirable moist texture. In this updated version, a little olive oil is substituted.

2 cups bulgar #1 or #2, picked over, but not washed
1 cup farina, see Glossary
2 1/4 cups warm water

1 pound lean ground meat
2 medium onions, finely chopped
1 1/2 teaspoons salt
1/2 teaspoon pepper
1 teaspoon ground cumin
1/2 teaspoon allspice
1/2 teaspoon cinnamon
1/4 teaspoon or to taste, chili pepper
2 tablespoons olive oil

2 rounded tablespoons tomato paste
1 egg, beaten
1 tablespoon olive oil
Blanched almonds for garnish, optional

Preheat oven to 400 degrees F.

1. Put bulgar and farina in a big bowl and pour 2 1/4 cups warm water. Mix with a fork, cover and set aside for half an hour folding 2 to 3 times in the meantime. Test for doneness by pressing a small amount between the fingers. If it is soft and sticky enough to make dough, it is done. If not, then add a little bit more hot water and mix and set aside for 10 more minutes.

2. Add meat, onion, salt, pepper, cumin, allspice, cinnamon, chili pepper, and olive oil. Knead until dough of medium consistency forms.

3. Form into 9-inch discs, 1/2 inch thick (will make 4 discs), and arrange on generously greased cookie sheets, or spread the entire dough on a well-greased large cookie sheet (approx. 18-by-11 inch) in about 1/2-inch-thick layer.

4. Combine tomato paste, beaten egg, and oil, and brush surface of spread dough with the mixture.

5. Score surface into wedges or bars, squares, or whatever, and press a sliver of almond in the center of each portion, if used.

6. Bake in a preheated oven, at 400 degrees F., for 20 minutes, or until surface is golden brown. Re-cut and serve hot with lots of salad and olives.

Cooked Bulgar Dough Stuffed with Meat
(Kubbat Burghul Matboukh)

(Makes 25 to 28 pieces)

This is different from the previous bulgar dough *kubba* in that bulgar used here is cooked first then made into dough. It is delightfully spicy, light in texture, and crunchy to the bite.

> **3 cups bulgar #1 or #2, picked over**
> **6 1/2 cups hot water**
> **1 teaspoon salt**
> **1/2 teaspoon white or black pepper**
> **1/2 teaspoon cumin**
> **1/2 teaspoon coriander**
> **1/4 teaspoon chili pepper, or to taste**
> **1/3 cup cornstarch**
>
> **1 recipe kubba filling, p.319**
> **Oil for frying**

1. Put bulgar in a medium heavy pot and cover it with hot water. Add salt, pepper, cumin, coriander, and chili. Bring it to a quick boil for about 5 minutes. Reduce heat to low and let simmer, covered, until bulgar is well cooked and all moisture has evaporated, about 20 minutes. To test for doneness press a tablespoonful of cooked bulgar between the fingers, if it is soft enough to stick together and form a dough, it is done. Fold 2 to 3 times while simmering to let grains puff out. Set aside, covered, until cool enough to handle.

2. Add cornstarch to cooked bulgar and knead with slightly moistened hands until dough forms.

3. Take a piece of dough size of a small lemon, and fill and shape as described in Stuffed Potato Dough, p., steps 3 and 4.

4. Fry filled pieces in 1-inch deep hot oil, turning once to allow both sides to brown and crisp, about 5 minutes for each side. Drain in a colander lined with white paper towels to prevent pieces from getting soggy. Serve warm with lots of salad.

Note: Instead of frying, bake dough and filling like in *Kubbat Halab* Made Light and Easy, p.323. The final taste is the same but craftsmanship is absent here.

2. MORE STUFFED FOODS

(Al- Mahshıyyat)

Vegetables are stuffed in a variety of ways and in the most alluring and intriguing manner. You see a beautifully simmered piece of vegetable, and you are clueless as to what there is inside. Is it just the pulp, or is it something else? The only way to know is to dig in, and you'll be pleasantly surprised. That was exactly the intention of the medieval cook whose last instruction in a recipe of *badhinjan mahshi* (stuffed eggplant) was to "put them as they are on a platter, whole, as if nothing had been done to them (*Anonymous Andalusian Cookbook*, 103).

Following are the most popular types and methods for stuffing food, particularly vegetables.

Dolma

During the Middle Ages stuffed vegetable dishes were the epitome of good life. The countless *mahshi* recipes in the medieval cookbooks, and the many references to them in *The Arabian Nights*, for instance, bear witness to that. The vegetable that the medieval cooks commonly used was eggplant, to which gourd was always given as a substitute. Those vegetables were usually stuffed with a spicy mixture of ground meat with onion and other ingredients, eked out with peeled and crushed chickpeas. Rice was added to the filling of the stuffed tripe dish, called *kabbayat* (see chapter 10).

At some point during the Ottoman rule, when it was the fashion to call things the *Istanbuli* way, dolma, instead of *mahshi* was used to designate vegetables, including grape leaves, stuffed with a meat mixture that is eked out with rice. *Mahshi* proper, on the other hand, was reserved for stuffed vegetables (leaves excluded) that were simmered lots of sauce.

Dolma in Turkish simply means, "stuffed," and it may be applied to contexts other than culinary. A pillow stuffed with cotton may be called "dolma" An Ottoman palace built right on the seashore that was raised by burying and "stuffing" the land with sand, was called "*Dolma Buqcha*" (literally, stuffed orchard" (Zalzala, vol. 1, 160).

Nowadays dolma is well known in the Arab world and several Mediterranean countries, and each country, more or less, has established its own version. What characterizes the Iraqi dolma is combining an assortment of vegetables in making a single pot of dolma. The variety of flavors, aromas, and colors makes the dish a feast to the senses.

Dolma is the dish for big gatherings. Every household has a special pot for cooking dolma. It is usually heavy, big and wide to make the layering of the vegetables easier. There is no one particular uniform way of cooking it. Some people prefer it white, others like it with lots of tomato sauce. Some pride themselves on how cute and small their dolmas are, whereas others do not mind using bigger vegetables. I remember how a friend used to tease his wife on the size of her dolmas, saying her onion dolmas were good enough to play soccer with.

Sometimes lamb rib chops are put in the bottom of the pot to simmer in the flavorful dolma juices. Fresh green fava beans are sometimes scattered in the bottom of the pot, or between the layers of the stuffed vegetables. Lovers of bread would put pieces of flat bread on top of the pot towards the end of cooking time, and let it soak up some of the liquid, and when the pot is turned upside down, the bread will be in the bottom. I have never realized how steeped in tradition this practice was until I had access to al-Warraq's tenth-century cookbook. Covering pots with bread in this fashion was called *maghmouma* (the covered). A favorite accompaniment with dolma is plain yogurt.

Preparing a big pot of dolma might be somewhat time consuming, but it is time well spent. Leftovers refrigerate very well (dolma with meat would stay as long as 3 days and the vegetarian variety 5 days). Heat leftovers in the microwave for 3 minutes or on the stove after sprinkling them with water. It would smell and taste as though you have just cooked it. The mere idea of going to the vegetable market hunting for the suitable vegetables, small and evenly shaped is exciting enough. To go home and handle this plethora of vegetables is an added pleasure. The entire kitchen will be replete with the vegetable aromas, so enticing and so wholesome.

When households were big, dolma making was always a family affair, especially during the summertime. I remember how in the late hours of the morning we would all go out and gather around a table under the grape arbor-- a splendidly cool and shaded breezeway, an oasis in the midst of summer scorching sun. The children were given the task of picking the tender leaves growing on the grapevines, whereas the grown ups were to do the coring and the stuffing of the vegetables, under the supervision of mother who would be sipping her daily *finjaan* of Arabic coffee and smoking her morning cigarette. However, the most tedious time was the waiting, as lunchtime approaches. It was not easy what with all the alluring aromas escaping from the simmering pot and filling the air with a promise of a feast. When at long last it was decided that the pot was done, the dolma would be inverted on a huge tray, to be followed by more torture, waiting until it gets cool enough to handle and devour. Then the onslaught begins, three grape-leaf dolmas, one zucchini, half an eggplant, one onion, etc, etc, and you wish you have two stomachs to eat to your heart's desire.

The traditional way of cooking dolma calls for not so lean ground meat and requires that some of the vegetables be slightly fried before stuffing them. Keeping up with the modern trends of cooking, in the following recipes lean meat is used and the vegetables may be left raw, or brushed or sprayed with oil and broiled. In order to retain the original texture and flavor, olive oil is added to the filling.

Vegetables Used for Stuffing Dolma, How to Prepare and Stuff them

Cored Vegetables

This category includes **eggplant**, **zucchini**, **yellow squash**, **cucumber**, **bell pepper** (green, red, and yellow), **banana peppers**, or any big size variety of hot peppers, **tomatoes,** and sometimes **potatoes.**

Choose small and rounded vegetables, but if these are hard to come by, medium-sized vegetables may be used. In this case eggplant, zucchini, yellow squash and cucumbers are cut into 2 or 3 parts depending on their size. Use a corer to core the eggplant, zucchini, yellow squash, and cucumber to 1/4-inch thick shells. Whatever you core out do not throw away, use it for making other dishes or simply dump it in the bottom of the dolma pot, and let it simmer with the dolma. When coring, always try to keep a base for each piece. If this is not possible especially with the middle parts, use slices cut off from the vegetables, and press them into the bottom to make bases. As for potatoes, choose medium sized ones, peel them, cut off one top, and core out the inside, leaving a shell about 1/4-inch thick. Keep them in cold water until needed, to prevent them from getting discolored.

After coring, prick these vegetables at 2 or 3 places with a pointed knife to allow some of the dolma-liquid get into the filling while simmering. Then sprinkle pieces with salt and set aside for about 15 minutes. Lightly fry eggplant, zucchini, yellow squash, and cucumber, or brush them with oil and broil them until they soften, or just leave them alone.

As for tomato, cut a 1/4-inch slice off the stem side, but not all the way, leave top attached, to be used later on as a lid. Use a spoon or knife to remove pulp (add pulp to filling after chopping it). Sprinkle tomato shells with salt and invert, to allow them to drain. Do not prick the tomatoes.

Use a sharp pointed knife for the peppers. Cut off the upper stem, set it aside to be used as a lid for stuffed pepper. Discard seeds and membranes, and prick at several places.

To fill all these vegetables, stuff them loosely to allow for expansion of rice while cooking, unless otherwise indicated. Close the openings with cut off tops. If they are divided, the first thing to try is to fit the smaller pieces into the slightly bigger ones. You can mix and match. Those that are of equal opening size, close their openings with discs cut off from the pulp or the bottom of the vegetable piece. This is to ensure that filling will not come out while simmering.

Onions

Choose medium-sized rounded or longish onions. Under running water, with a sharp pointed knife, core out the two ends of the onion especially the root part since this will make separation of layers easier. Slash the onion lengthwise only to the center. This way you will be able to fill an onion layer and overlap its cut edges to make it look like a filled rugby ball. Remove the brown outer skin and blanch the onions in boiling water for about 5 minutes. This will soften the onion and makes the separation of layers possible without tearing them. Drain onions, and when cool enough to handle, separate layers until you reach the heart of the onion. Do not throw it away, chop it and use it in the filling.

Stuff onion layers with the filling rather loosely, or as directed in the recipe. Slightly overlap the edges to keep the stuffing inside while cooking.

Grape Leaves

If you are lucky enough to have fresh grape leaves, wash them, cut off stems and stack them in a big rather deep pan. Pour hot water to submerge them and set aside for 30 minutes. The leaves will change color, and will be tender enough to use. In the old days, it was only possible to make grape-leaves dolma in the spring and summer, but with the advent of freezers, it is possible to enjoy them all year round. To, freeze them, treat them as described above, then drain and freeze them in plastic bags. To thaw, take them out of the freezer and soak them in warm water. Grape leaves kept in brine are available in the grocery stores, but you need to wash them in several changes of water to get rid of salt, then drape them over the edge of a colander to drain. Cut off stem, if wished.

To fill a grape leaf, lay it flat on a plate or a working surface, vein side up. If the leaf is torn or small, overlap it with another one. Put about 1 tablespoon filling near stem side of the leaf, fold the two sides on the filling, they do not have to cover the entire filling. Roll leaf towards the direction of other end. Arrange finished ones snugly side by side in the pot, seam side down. Or you can roll it the *buqcha* way (like a bundle). Simply put stuffing in the middle of the leaf, and fold the 4 corners of the leaf to enclose the stuffing.

Swiss Chard

In Iraq it is only possible to make this kind of dolma in wintertime, because freezing spoils Swiss chard. The huge leaves are divided into smaller pieces in the following manner: Cut off the stems (do not throw them away, arrange them in the bottom of the dolma pot or on top of the stuffed vegetables, and let them cook with dolma). The medium sized leaf can be divided into 3 parts-- Cut across the top third of the leaf, i.e. at the place where the spine is still thin and pliable, then divide the rest into 2 parts, lengthwise, along the spine. If the leaf is not big enough, just divide it into 2 parts crosswise. Any torn portions can be put on top of the layered stuffed vegetables in the dolma pot.

To fill Swiss chard pieces: for the upper third, put stuffing in the middle and fold it like a bundle, or roll it like you do with grape leaves. For the lower parts with the spine, spread filling along the spine, and roll it like a cigarette. Arrange snugly in the pot, seam side down.

Cabbage Leaves

Discard outer layers. With a sharp pointed knife, core out the bottom of the cabbage. Go as deep as you can, to make it easier to separate the leaves. Put whatever leaves you manage to separate without tearing, along with the rest of the head, in a big pot of boiling water, and let boil gently for about 5 minutes, or just enough to soften leaves and make them more pliable, then take them out and drain them. When leaves are cool enough to handle, separate as many as you can, and return the rest to the boiling water, repeating the same process until you get to the core. Do not discard it, but put it in the bottom of the dolma pot, and let it simmer with the rest of the filled vegetables.

To fill small leaves, cut off the hard area attached to the core part, and trim the spine flat. Lay the piece flat on the working space, soft side down. Spread stuffing along the core end, and fold both sides to enclose the filling. Fold the core end towards the other end of the leaf. To fill the big leaves, divide each into two, at the place where the spine is thin and pliable enough to fold. Slice off the thick part of the spine on the upper half to make it flat. Lay it on a flat working space, soft side down, put filling along the wider end, fold the sides on the filling, and roll like a cigarette. As for the lower part with the thicker spine, slice off the spine, and if it is big enough divide it into 2 pieces along the spine. Put filling along the spine side and roll like a cigarette. Arrange snugly in the pot seam side down.

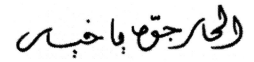

As Cool as a Cucumber?

A countryside bumpkin once visited a relative in Baghdad. They sat together and started talking about the countryside and what grows in it of sweet fruits and appetizing vegetables. "Particularly cucumbers," the relative emphasized. "They are healthy, and have an amazing quality to cool down body heat, and extinguish the heat of summer." The villager was impressed by that, and took a mental note of it.

The following day, the relative offered a huge platter of dolma (stuffed vegetables) for lunch, and they sat together to eat. Amongst the many stuffed vegetables, the villager saw a cucumber, and immediately remembered what his relative told him about it. So he picked it up, and greedily stuffed it into his mouth. To his dismay it was so spicy, that he felt his mouth was on fire. He gulped a whole glass of ice-cold water, and said, looking at his relative with the corner of his eyes, "cucumber is hot in the inside, and yet they say it is cool!" (Zalzala vol. 2, 69-70)

Dolma of stuffed cabbage leaves

Baghdadi Dolma

(Makes 6 to 8 servings)

People in the middle and south of Iraq, particularly in Baghdad, prefer their dolma cooked "white", i.e. without tomato sauce. The souring agent they use can be lemon juice when in season, or citric acid (see Glossary). To add a more exciting flavor to the dish, some cooks replace lemon juice with *noomi Basrah* or tamarind (see Glossary).

For the filling:

> **1 pound lean ground meat**
> **2 1/2 cups rice such as jasmine, washed, soaked in cold water for 30 minutes, and drained**
> **1 medium onion, finely chopped, and sautéed in 2 tablespoons oil**
> **1/2 cup parsley, chopped**
> **1/2 cup chopped fresh dill, or 2 tablespoons dried dill weed**
> **1/4 cup fresh mint, chopped, or 1 tablespoon dried mint, optional**
> **4 to 6 cloves garlic, finely chopped or grated**
> **1/4 cup currants or raisins, optional**
> **2 tablespoons salt**
> **1 teaspoon black pepper**
> **1 tablespoon *baharat*, see Glossary**
> **Juice of 2 lemons, or 1 tablespoon citric acid**

For the bottom layer in the pot:

> **2 to 3 tablespoons oil**
> **2 to 3 lamb chops, trimmed, or 4 to 5 chicken drum sticks, optional**
> **1 cup shelled fava beans, fresh or frozen, optional**

Vegetables to be filled: (prepare and stuff as directed above)

> **2 small eggplants or 1 medium divided into 2 parts**
> **4 small squash and zucchinis, or 2 big ones divided into 3 pieces, each**
> **3 medium onions**
> **2 tomatoes**
> **1 to 2 medium peppers**
> **1 medium cucumber, divided into 3 parts**
> **20 grape leaves, or 1 small bunch Swiss chard, or 1 head of cabbage, or a combination of leaves. (There is no hard and fast rule in the choice of vegetables, it all depends on your personal preference and whatever is readily available.)**

For the simmering liquid:

> **2 1/4 to 2 1/2 cups hot water**
> **1 teaspoon salt**
> **1/4 cup lemon juice**

1. In a big bowl mix all filling ingredients. If mixture looks a little dry, add about 1/4 cup water or as needed (I usually use the drained liquid of the rice, if needed).

2. Prepare the dolma pot: The perfect dolma-pot is big, wide and heavy-bottomed. If you do not have such a pot, use 2 medium-size heavy- bottomed pots, and divide stuffed vegetables between the two,

making sure to include all kinds of vegetables in each pot. Put oil in the bottom of pot or pots, and sprinkle fava beans, lamb chops or chicken drumsticks if used, along with pulp of cored vegetables, and cut off Swiss chard stalks, if wished.

3. Always start by stuffing onion shells, and arrange them side by side in the bottom of the pot, following directions given above. Then fill cored vegetables, making sure to close the openings as directed. The top layer is normally reserved for stuffed leaves. The entire assortment of stuffed vegetables shouldn't come up to more than 3/4 of the depth of the pot. Cover stuffed vegetables with Swiss chard stalks and the remaining leaves. Invert a heat- proof plate, a little smaller than the pot, on top. This helps keep vegetables in place when dolma starts to boil.

4. Put pot on high-heat stove burner. Mix simmering liquid ingredients, and pour on vegetables (there should be enough liquid to cover vegetables when pressed firmly down with the inverted plate). Firmly press inverted dish several times to let air bubbles come up.

5. Bring pot to a quick boil, for 10 minutes. Lower heat to medium-low, and let simmer, covered, for 45 minutes or until liquid is absorbed. Let pot cool down and vegetables set, for about 15 minutes. To hasten the procedure, put pot in a sink half filled with cold water and leave for 5 minutes.

5. To unmold pot, remove inverted plate. Invert a large tray or platter on pot. With both hands holding both pot and tray or platter (if still hot wear oven mittens) turn pot upside down. This is to transfer dolmas onto the plate or tray. If this sounds too risky for you, then just wait for the dolmas to cool down, and with a big spoon, carefully transfer them to a big platter, taking care not to cause them to break or tear. For more formal presentations, arrange dolma pieces in an attractive way on a platter, using the perfect, unopened ones, after removing any grains of rice that might have clung to them,
Serve warm with bread and yogurt.

Suggestions:

*The way to make dolma greatly depends on personal preference. Some like to have all the liquid evaporate, which makes it suitable for an impressive presentation. On the other hand, some prefer to have it with some sauce in it.

The way I like to have it is to add a little bit more than the required amount of liquid. About 15 minutes before it is done I remove the inverted plate and replace it with a piece of flat bread, and press on it with a spoon so that it soaks up liquid from the pot. When the cooked dolma is inverted on the tray or platter the bread will be in the bottom, and it will absorb most of the dolma liquid. Yummy!

*To give the dolma a true Baghdadi flavor, replace lemon juice of the simmering liquid with 1 teaspoon ground noomi Basra or 1 tablespoon concentrated tamarind.

341

Dolma the Mosuli Way
(Al-Dolma al- Mosuliya)

(Makes 6 to 8 servings)

People in northern Iraq, especially in the city of Mosul, prefer to make their dolma red, using tomato sauce or the more exotic sumac liquid extracted from sumac berries. The way to get the sumac liquid is to crack whole sumac berries and soak them in hot water for about 30 minutes (do not boil), then press well to extract all the juice. The berries are to be discarded (see Glossary). When sumac is used no other souring agents, such as lemon juice or citric acid will be needed in making the dish.

The following is the Mosuli version of dolma using the more readily available tomato paste. However, if you want to give it a true Mosuli flavor, sprinkle the stuffed vegetables with about 1 teaspoon ground sumac, before placing the platter on the stuffed vegetables and before pouring the prepared liquid on the vegetables. In this case reduce, a little, the amount of tomato paste called for the simmering liquid, in the recipe below

For the filling:

> 1 pound lean ground meat
> 2 1/2 cups rice such as jasmine, washed, soaked 30 minutes in cold water, and drained
> 1 medium onion, chopped, and sautéed in 2 tablespoons oil
> 1/2 cup parsley, chopped
> 1/2 cup fresh dill, chopped, or 2 tablespoons dill weed
> 1/4 cup fresh mint, chopped, or 1 tablespoon dried mint
> 4 cloves garlic, grated
> 2 tablespoon salt
> 1 teaspoon black pepper
> 1 tablespoon *baharat*, see Glossary
> 3 heaping tablespoons tomato paste (one 6-ounce can). Do not substitute
> Juice of 2 lemons or 1 tablespoon citric acid, see Glossary

For the bottom layer of the pot:
> Use oil and any of the ingredients suggested in the Baghdadi Dolma

The vegetables:
> Use the same amounts suggested in Baghdadi Dolma, and prepare and fill them as suggested above

For the simmering liquid:
> 2 heaping tablespoons tomato paste diluted in 2 1/2 cups hot water, or one 8-ounce can tomato sauce diluted in 1 1/2 cups hot water, or 2 1/2 cups tomato juice
> 1 teaspoon salt

1. In a big bowl, mix filling ingredients. If mixture looks a little dry add about 1/4 cup water or as needed (I usually use the drained liquid of the rice, if needed).

2. Put oil in the bottom of pot with any of the suggested ingredients for bottom layer, if any.

3. Fill vegetables and arrange them in pot as described in Baghdadi Dolma.

4. Combine simmering liquid ingredients, and cook the dish as directed in Baghdadi Dolma. (Remember, when adding the liquid, pour enough just to cover vegetables when pressed firmly down with the inverted plate).

Vegetarian Dolma Simmered in Olive Oil (Dolma bil Zeit)

(Makes 8 servings)

For people who have a long tradition of believing that dishes without meat are counterfeit and not real (*muzawwara, muzayyafa*), it is not surprising to learn that such a healthy and delicious dish as *dolma bil zeit* is not given the due attention it deserves. It is usually presented warm or cold as a side dish, or *mezza* (small platters to be had with drinks). I myself can never have enough of it, it is deliciously succulent, and is packed with goodness. Besides it is very convenient since it keeps good, refrigerated, for about 5 days. For vegetarians, I guarantee this dish is heaven.

For the filling:
  3/4 cup olive oil, divided. (For maximum flavor, use extra virgin olive oil)
  1 medium onion, finely chopped
  4 cloves garlic, grated
  2 cups rice, such as jasmine, washed, soaked for 30 minutes in clod water, and drained
  1/2 cup split chickpeas, cooked but still firm, and drained, optional
  3 heaping tablespoons tomato paste (one 6-ounce can)
  1 1/2 tablespoons salt
  1/2 teaspoon black pepper
  1 tablespoon *baharat*, see Glossary
  3/4 cup parsley, chopped
  3/4 cup fresh dill, chopped, or 2 to 3 tablespoons dried dill weed
  1/2 cup fresh mint, chopped or 2 teaspoons dried mint
  1/2 cup toasted pine nuts, optional
  3/4 cup lemon juice (about 2 big lemons), divided
  1/2 cup currants or raisins, optional

For the vegetables:
  50 fresh grape leaves, or one 16-ounce jar of grape leaves kept in brine, or 2 bunches of Swiss chard. But you can also use other vegetables, especially zucchini, cabbage, onion, and peppers both hot and sweet. Prepare and fill vegetables as directed above

1. To prepare filling, sauté onion in **1/4 cup olive oil** until soft, about 5 minutes. Add garlic and stir for few moments. Fold in rice until well coated with oil.
2. Away from heat fold in the rest of filling ingredients using only **1/2 cup lemon juice**. If mixture looks a little dry add about 1/4 cup water or as needed (I usually use the drained liquid of the rice).
3. Fill vegetables as directed above, and arrange them in a heavy-bottomed medium to large pot (depending on vegetables used. Filled grape leaves and Swiss chard take less space). Fill the vegetables rather looser than you do with other types of dolma, since the filling is mostly rice, and it needs more room to expand while cooking.

4. Invert a heatproof plate a little bit smaller than the pot on the stuffed vegetables.

5. Pour remaining **1/2 cup olive oil**, **1/4 cup lemon juice** and about 1 1/2 cups hot water (there should be enough liquid to completely cover vegetables when pressed firmly down with the inverted plate). Press inverted plate several times to let air bubbles come up.

6. Bring to a boil, 10 minutes. Then reduce heat to low and let simmer gently for 45 minutes, or until liquid is absorbed.

7. Turn off heat and let dolma settle and cool down, for at least 30 minutes. Invert it on a tray or plate as directed in the previous dolma recipes. Arrange on a platter and decorate with slices of lemon and serve warm or cold.

Suggestion:
If planning to present this dish as an appetizer, use grape leaves only, because they are small and uniform in size.

Variation:
Instead of chickpeas use 1 cup cooked brown or green lentil. Add them in step 2. Additions like these help make this dolma a complete meal, what with all the protein they bring along with them. Shredded carrot makes a nice addition, too. Add it in step 2.

أگر حيلة ندارى؟ ... چرا لغلف ميكوني؟

The Benefit of the Doubt

Our elders in Baghdad tell the following anecdote:

An Iranian villager was traveling in Iraq and happened to reach one of the cities at noon. He went to a restaurant and asked the owner to offer him the best he had on the menu. A beautiful dish laden with dolma was proudly put on the table for the villager to enjoy. He looked suspiciously at it and asked for another dish. The owner was surprised and assured him that it was very delicious. The villager looked at it again suspiciously, and said in Iranian, "*Agar hilat nadari, chara laflaf mikuni?*" (If no cheating or deceit was involved in making it, then why is it stuffed and wrapped like this?)

The moral: It is sometimes wise not to give suspicious matters the benefit of the doubt.
(Zalzala, vol. 1, 161-2)

Aromatic Sausages Stuffed with Rice and Meat (Mumbar)

(Makes 6 to 8 servings)

According to ancient texts, the practice of stuffing sausage casings (lamb and beef intestines) goes back to the Sumerian times. Al-Warraq's tenth century cookbook includes six recipes for different kinds of *maqaniq* (sausages), some fried, some baked in the *tannour* (clay oven), and some simmered in aromatic liquid as in the following recipe. The medieval cooks were quite inventive in filling the casings. In one of the recipes, for instance, they used a spicy mixture of mashed eggplant (*Anonymous Andalusian Cookbook*, 103). In another, they used a mixture of pounded chicken breast, cheese, leeks, and walnut. Egg white was added as a binder (al-Warraq, 88).

Lamb casings are normally used for stuffing, for they yield small sausages. If these are not available, beef casings may be substituted.

For the filling:
> **1 medium onion, finely chopped**
> **3 cloves garlic, grated**
> **2 tablespoons oil**
> **1 pound lean ground meat**
> **1 1/2 cups rice (such as jasmine), washed, soaked in cold water for 30 minutes, then drained**
> **1/2 cup chopped parsley**
> **1 1/2 teaspoons salt**
> **1/2 teaspoon black pepper**
> **2 teaspoons *baharat*, see Glossary**
> **Juice of 1 lemon, about 1/4 cup**
> **2 heaping tablespoons tomato paste diluted in 1/4 cup water, or 1/2 cup tomato sauce**
>
> **About 3 ounces sausage casings, available at meat departments, wash before using to get rid of brine**

For the simmering liquid:
> **Water enough to fill three quarters of a big pot**
> **2 whole *noomi Basrah*, pricked at several places, see Glossary**
> **1 whole small onion, outer skin removed and pricked with about 6 whole cloves**
> **2 bay leaves**
> **1 tablespoon salt**
> **Vegetables, such as carrots and zucchini, for flavor**
> **Oil for browning, optional**

1. Sauté onion in oil until soft, add garlic and fold for a few moments. Set aside to cool, then in a big bowl, mix it with the rest of the filling ingredients.

2. If you have a sausage stuffer, use it to fill the casings, if not, fill them with a big funnel. First transfer the casing to the spout of the funnel, tie the end with a kitchen thread, then start pushing the filling through the opening of the funnel spout into the casing, gradually releasing the casings as you

do so. Run your fingers along the sausage to distribute filling evenly. **Fill casings loosely to allow rice to expand while cooking**. Overfilled sausages might burst while cooking. (You can make your own "funnel" by cutting a plastic 1-liter soda bottle using the side with the neck.)

3. When stuffing is done, divide the long loosely filled casings into portions about 4 inches long, using a kitchen thread. Make sure to leave enough room in each portion to allow rice to expand while cooking. Leave the sausages linked.

4. In a big pot let simmering liquid ingredients come to a boil. Coil sausage links in the pot. Bring pot to a quick boil. When sausages puff out, after about 10 minutes, pierce them with a pin or needle at one or two places to allow some of the moisture get into the inside of the sausages. Reduce heat to medium-low. With pot partially covered, let it simmer gently for about 45 minutes, or until casings are tender. While cooking, make sure there is always enough liquid to cover sausages.

5. When done, turn off heat and let stand in pot for 15 minutes before serving.

To serve, divide into individual sausages, cutting at the points were the threads are. Put them in serving dish, and drizzle with a little of the liquid in which they simmered. Have them hot with bread and salad.

Some like to brown the pieces in a small amount of oil before serving to make them look even more appetizing.

The Best of Stuffed Vegetables
(Sheikh Mahshi)

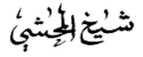

(Makes 4 servings)

Some call this dish *sheikh mahshi*, others call it *sheikh al-mahshi*, and the addition of the "*al*" makes all the difference. The former means "stuffed chieftain", whereas the latter means "the chieftain, i.e. the best of the stuffed food". The first is justified since the principal vegetable used in stuffing is eggplant. The green stems and the bulging black body of the vegetable might have inspired a playful mind into giving it this name. On the other hand, the second nomenclature might well be attributed to the fact that, unlike dolma, the main ingredient in stuffing this dish is meat, which makes it superior to other stuffed dishes.

In medieval Baghdad, the dish was known as *Madfuna*, (the buried). According to the medieval recipe, eggplants were cored and stuffed with finely ground meat, cooked with peeled and coarsely ground chickpeas, and seasonings. The stuffed eggplants were then put in a pot, having first put a little chopped onion in the bottom. The broth was colored with saffron, sprinkled with coriander and cinnamon, and sprayed with a little rose water (al-Baghdadi, 193). *Madfuna,* as cooked today, is eggplant, zucchini or cucumber, stuffed with a spicy mixture of ground meat and rice, and then simmered with lots of tomato juice. It is a midway between dolma and *Sheik Mahshi.*

Sheik Mahshi is cooked as follows:

For the filling:

>   **1 pound lean ground meat**
>   **1 tablespoon oil**
>   **1/2 teaspoon turmeric**
>   **1 medium onion, finely chopped**
>   **2 cloves garlic, grated**
>   **1/4 cup chopped parsley**
>   **1/2 teaspoon salt**
>   **1/4 teaspoon black pepper**
>   **1 1/2 teaspoons *baharat*, see Glossary**
>   **1/4 teaspoon cinnamon**
>   **1/4 teaspoon allspice**
>   **2 tablespoons dry toasted pine nuts, optional**
>   **1/4 cup currants or raisins, optional**
>   **1/2 cup cooked split chickpeas, optional**

For the vegetables:

>   **This dish requires vegetables that are small in size. The most commonly used vegetables are eggplant and zucchini, but you can also use cucumbers, peppers, and even potatoes or tomatoes. If small eggplants and zucchinis are not available use medium ones, and divide each into 2 portions crosswise. You'll need about 3 to 4 pounds of vegetables, allow at least 3 pieces per serving. Core vegetables as directed in the introductory part to dolma, p. 337. Sprinkle them lightly with salt, and set aside for 30 minutes. Lightly fry them, or spray or brush with oil and broil them on both sides. The aim is to soften them.**

For the liquid:

>   **Juice of 1 lemon (about 1/4 cup)**
>   **1/2 teaspoon salt**
>   **1/4 teaspoon black pepper**
>   **1/2 teaspoon honey or sugar**
>   **3 heaping tablespoons tomato paste, (one 6-ounce can) diluted in 4 cups hot water, or one 15-ounce can tomato sauce diluted in 3 cups hot water, or 4 cups tomato juice.**

1. To prepare filling, heat oil in a big skillet and sauté meat stirring frequently and breaking big lumps with a spoon. When all moisture evaporates, about 10 minutes, add turmeric, onion, and garlic, and stir frequently until onion softens, about 10 minutes. Remove from heat and add the rest of filling ingredients.

3. Fill prepared vegetables. No need to stuff loosely here, since filling is cooked and there is no rice to expand. Make sure to close the openings with lids made from slicing off tops of vegetables. This will prevent stuffing from coming out while cooking.

4. Line a heavy wide pot 10- to-11 inches in diameter with some of the cored out pulp, if wished, and arrange stuffed pieces in a single layer. If one pot is not enough, divide between two smaller pots. Secure vegetables with an inverted heatproof plate.

5. Add lemon juice, salt, pepper, and sugar or honey to diluted tomato paste, sauce or juice. Pour this mixture all over stuffed vegetables. There should be enough liquid to cover the vegetables.

6. On direct heat, bring pot to a boil, 10 minutes, then reduce heat to low, and allow to cook gently, until sauce nicely thickens, about 45 minutes. You can also arrange filled vegetables in a glass baking dish and bake, covered, in 400 degrees F. oven, until sauce nicely thickens, about 30 minutes.

Serve hot with white rice and salad.

Variation:

Add 1 cup rice, washed, soaked for 30 minutes and drained, to the filling mixture given above. Fill loosely to allow for expanding rice. This will make the *Mahshi* more like the *madfouna* as it is cooked in modern times.

Eggplant fans, 349

Fancy Ways for Stuffing Eggplant, Using the Sheikh Mahshi filling

*Eggplant Boats:

This is only possible with small eggplants. For the amount of filling given above, you need 6 to 8 small eggplants. Cut off the stem and peel the eggplant so as to give it a striped look. Slash one of the sides in the middle, do not go all the way down, and leave about an inch from the top and an inch from the bottom. Soak pieces in warm salted water for 30 minutes. Drain and fry them or spray or brush with oil, and broil. The aim is to soften them.

Enlarge slashes in eggplant using fingers of both hands to give them the semblance of a boat. Fill them with prepared stuffing and arrange on a baking dish, filled side up. Pour on them the prepared liquid (given above), and bake as instructed in the recipe above. Garnish with parsley.

*Eggplant Fans:

This can be done with small and medium eggplants. Cut off stems and peel in a striped fashion. Cut the eggplant lengthwise at 4 places, going from the bottom all the way up to about 1 short of the stem. Soak, fry or broil as described in the above recipe.

Lay each eggplant on the baking dish, and put the filling between the cut slices, all along the eggplant, and try to open up the layers to make it look like a hand fan. Cover with the prepared liquid given above. Bake as directed above.

To serve, garnish with chopped parsley and serve with rice and salad

*Eggplant Nests:

Small and medium eggplants can be used to make nests. Cut off the stems and peel the eggplants in a striped fashion. Cut each into 2 parts lengthwise. Hollow out the middle of each part. Soak and fry or broil as directed above.

Fill cavities with meat filling given above. Put a slice of tomato on each piece, over with the prepared liquid (given above), and bake as directed above.

To serve put half of a boiled egg, domed side up, on each piece and sprinkle with chopped parsley. Serve with rice or bread, along with some salad.

*Eggplant Rolls:

This way of presenting eggplant is especially ideal for the more readily available big eggplants. The larger, the better.

Cut off the stem of a big eggplant. Peel it in a striped fashion. Slice it lengthwise into 8 pieces 1/4- inch thick, each. Lightly fry or spray or brush with oil and broil until soft. Lay each slice flat on a working surface, and spread with some of the filling. Roll eggplant slice around the filling, jelly-roll fashion. Arrange rolls in an ovenproof glass baking dish. Pour the prepared liquid (given above) all over the rolls. Sprinkle with 2 tablespoons Romano cheese and 2 tablespoons breadcrumbs. Bake as directed above. Garnish with chopped parsley.

Stuffed Zucchinis
Simmered in Yogurt Sauce
(Shijar bi'l Salsa al-Labaniya)

(Makes 8 servings)

Cooking with milk and yogurt is an ancient Mesopotamian way of enhancing flavors in the cooked dishes, as shown in the Babylonian recipes (see Introduction). In the thirteenth century Baghdadi cookbook a whole chapter is given to dishes cooked with yogurt and milk. The *Labaniya*, for instance, is composed of cut meat cooked with chopped onion and leeks to which is added cut eggplant, coriander, cumin, mastic, cinnamon, and some sprigs of mint. Then yogurt and ground garlic are added, with a sprinkle of dry mint (42).

In the following recipe zucchinis are stuffed with meat and a little rice then simmered in a delicate and delicious sauce made from yogurt, seasoned with mint and garlic, like in the old days. It makes a very pleasant dish for elegant presentations.

16 small zucchinis, or 8 big ones, about 4 pounds

For the filling:
1 medium onion, finely chopped, sautéed in 2 tablespoons olive oil
2 to 4 cloves garlic, grated
1 1/2 pounds lean ground meat
1/2 cup rice, washed, soaked in cold water for 30 minutes and drained
1/4 cup parsley, chopped
1/4 cup fresh mint, chopped, or 1 tablespoon dried mint
1/4 cup fresh dill, chopped, or 1 tablespoon dried dill weed
1 tablespoon salt
1/2 teaspoon black pepper
1/2 teaspoon allspice
1/2 teaspoon nutmeg
1/2 cup currants or raisins, optional
1/4 cup dry toasted pine nuts, optional

For the sauce:
2 1/2 cups yogurt
2 1/2 rounded tablespoons corn starch
4 cups cold water
1 teaspoon salt
1/4 teaspoon black pepper
1 clove garlic, grated

For garnish: chopped fresh mint, or crushed dry mint
Preheat oven to 400 degrees F.

1. Cut zucchinis into halves crosswise. Core out pulp using an apple corer, leaving about 1/4-inch thick shells. Keep some of the pulp pieces to be used as lids for the filled zucchinis. Use the rest of pulp in other dishes requiring shredded zucchini (see chapter 6, on vegetarian snacks and side

dishes). Prick shells with a sharp pointed knife at 2 or 3 places to allow sauce to penetrate while simmering. Lightly sprinkle with salt, and set aside for 30 minutes. Then lightly fry or broil zucchini pieces after spraying or brushing them with some oil.

2. In a big bowl mix filling ingredients.

3. Fill zucchini halves and seal using some of the cored out pulp. Arrange pieces in a single layer in a big glass ovenproof baking dish, big enough to accommodate stuffed pieces in one layer. Set aside.

4. Prepare yogurt sauce by diluting yogurt and cornstarch in 4 cups cold water. Add salt, pepper, and garlic, and mix well until smooth. Cook on moderate heat, stirring frequently in one direction (to prevent it from curdling) until it starts to bubble, about 10 minutes.

5. Pour sauce on the arranged stuffed vegetables and bake, loosely covered, in a preheated oven at 400 degrees F., until sauce is nicely thickened, about 45 minutes.

Serve hot sprinkled with mint, fresh or dry, along with yellow rice.

Sumerian Spite

Who would have thought our Sumerian ancestors could have been that spiteful? The following are curses, which in all probability were uttered by women. We incidentally learn that baking was a woman's job, and that a menstruating woman was considered unclean, and hence not fit to make bread:

"May her bread be as bread (made by an) unclean woman, so no man eats it!"

May his food, though it be plain eggs, clog his wind-pipe.
May his food, though it be plain 'bone' (-fish), pierce his wind-pipe.
(Gordon, 457)

CHAPTER TWELVE
POULTRY

CHAPTER TWELVE
POULTRY
(AL-TUYOUR)

الطُّيُورُ

The ancient Mesopotamian ate a lot of birds. Game was plentiful. There were ducks, geese, and many kinds of pigeons, excluding perhaps the doves, which, though domesticated, were tabooed. They were thought of as belonging to the goddess Ishtar, and during religious festivals worshippers fed them crumbled cakes made especially for such occasions. Some of the wild marsh birds were domesticated as pets such as the ibis, crane, and herons of which seven varieties were mentioned in the ancient records. The pelicans were trained for fishing, and the fields were the home of birds like thrushes, blackbirds, sparrows and larks. The partridges and francolins were bred in the countryside. Chicken was the last to reach the scene, it was definitely known by the first millenium. The chicken reached Greece around 600 BC by way of Syria where it was called the "Akkadian" bird.

The Akkadian language abounds with terms and occupations related to birds. There was the "feeder of birds", "bird keeper", "fattener of poultry", "poultry farm" and so on. The wild ducks and geese were netted by fowlers, and the domesticated varieties were kept for food outside the houses. They were fattened on barley, sometimes in the form of dough. An entry made for one day at the palace at Ur included a suckling pig delivered for roasting, two wood pigeons, one duck, and one pigeon, which were definitely destined for the rich royal stew pots and the fabulous pie dishes (see Introduction for details on the Babylonian bird recipes).

By the medieval times chicken was already the queen of all birds par excellence. In *The Arabian Nights*, for instance, a browned stuffed chicken was the epitome of affluence and luxury, a status which the chicken enjoyed up until the present time. Commenting on the injustices of life, a modern rhymed proverb laments the fact that whereas some people eat chicken, others eat dust (*nas takul dijaj, w'nas titlaga'l ajaj*). Other domesticated and game birds were also available to the medieval diners, such as geese, partridges, francolins, and sparrows.

In the tenth and thirteenth century Baghdadi cookbooks, the general method for cooking chicken the *mutajjan* way (fried chicken) was to simmer it in water first, then fry it in different kinds of oil, with lots of spices and herbs, especially coriander. This ensured that the chickens would not toughen when fried. There was also mention in their books that chickens were better chased until fatigued before slaughtering them as a means for tenderizing the meat (*Wasf al-At'ima al-Mu'tada*, 375). Generally speaking, the same recipes used for cooking red meat were also applicable to chicken. For instance they used them in concocting their cherished sweet and sour dishes using vinegar, sumac juice, lemon juice, sour grape juice and pomegranate juice, balanced with a little sugar, date syrup or honey. The sauces were sometimes thickened with ground nuts and bread crumbs. For garnish, poached eggs, sunny-side up, were used. As for grilling, plump chickens or young chicks called *farareej* were preferred, and were usually roasted in the *tannour*. Grilled chickens stuffed with a mixture of rice, meat, nuts, spices, and sometimes truffles were quite popular. Another way for grilling the chicken was by skewering it, and letting it revolve on top of fire, a harbinger to our modern rotisserie chicken.

It was customary to serve grilled chicken with *sibagh*, which were sour sauces and dips made of vinegar, pomegranate juice, mustard, ground walnuts, raisins, mashed onion, garlic, a little sugar, and some spices. Such condiments were believed to help digest the meat.

The present day basic methods for cooking chicken have undergone little changes. Up until the early sixties, only locally grown free-range chicken was available in the markets, and they required prolonged cooking because their meat was tough. The following chicken recipes are adjusted to a more tender variety. However, if you happen to have free-range chicken, then my advice to you is to emulate the ways of the medieval cooks in tenderizing their birds-- chase your chicken until it drops with fatigue before you slaughter it.

Trial by Water

A cuneiform bilingual (Sumerian and Akkadian) dictionary, written around 1900 BC, enumerates, amongst other things, some food and drink items, one of which was a bird called "ezitu." The decipherers of these tablets were unable to identify the bird with a modern counterpart. However, to people who have grown in modern Iraq the name of this bird sounds familiar. To this day, a very common bird called *ziti* can still be seen around the region. It is a small bird distinguished by the rapid wagging of its tail. It must have been around for a long time, for I remember my mother used to tell us a funny fable of a bird called *ziti* and his friend, who happened to be an ass (both physically and metaphorically). This story must have been told by generations of mothers before her. Oh, how we used to bug her to tell it to again and again.

One night, the story goes, it was the turn of an ass and a *ziti* bird to guard a field of clover against the attacks of other animals. During their night shift they felt hungry and ate the whole crop of clover. In the morning they claimed that some animals came and ate it all. They were taken to the riverside, and were made to stand at the edge of a very steep cliff, overlook and swear they didn't eat the clover themselves. The *ziti* came first and said, "*Zitu, zit,* I haven't eaten it. If I had, let God make me blind. *Zitu, zit,* if I had done it, may all my bones break to pieces when I throw myself down the cliff." The bird threw itself down the cliff, and flew away. When the ass saw this, he was encouraged by what he saw, and when his turn came he swore that he hadn't eaten the clover, if he had, let God blind him, and break his bones when he threw himself down the cliff.

And down the cliff the ass plunged.

Interestingly, trial by the water ordeal was an Ancient Mesopotamian practice. It constituted the second item in Hamurabi's codes of law, "If any one bring an accusation against a man, and the accused go to the river and leap into the river, if he sink in the river, his accuser shall take possession of his house. But if the river prove that the accused is not guilty, and he escape unhurt, then he who brought the accusation shall be put to death, while he who leaped into the river shall take possession of the house that had belonged to his accuser."

Flat Bread Sopped in Broth of Simmered Chicken (Thareed or Tashreeb Dijaaj)

(Makes 4 servings)

The following recipe is a traditional dish that requires the chicken to be simmered to tenderness with spices and vegetables, and then served with bread soaked in its broth, with garnishes. The dish is as old as the Mesopotamian civilization itself is. It always has been a kind of comfort dish, so much liked by high and low. In the extant medieval Arabic cookbooks, of both *al-Mashriq* (Abbasid Caliphate in the east) and *al-Maghrib* (Ummayad Caliphate in Andalusia in the west) there is an overwhelming number of recipes for *thareed* dishes. (See Introduction for more details) Al-Warraq's *ma' hummus* (chickpeas in broth), for instance, was prepared for the Caliph al-Ma'mun. It was basically plump young chickens, simmered in broth, with chickpeas, onion, seven cubes of white hard cheese, and pepper. For presentation, broken pieces of bread were sopped in the rich flavorful sauce, pieces of the cooked plump young chickens were arranged around the plate along with the simmered cheese, onion pieces, and seven poached eggs (sunny side up). The whole dish was then drizzled with sizzling hot oil, and taken to the table.

1 whole chicken, cut into serving size pieces or 4 thighs, skinned and trimmed
2 medium onions, quartered
4 to 5 cloves garlic, whole and unskinned
2 to 3 whole *noomi Basrah*, see Glossary, pricked at several places
1 tablespoon salt
4 to 5 whole pods of cardamom
2 bay leaves
1 tablespoon curry powder
1 teaspoon ground coriander
2 medium potatoes cut into big cubes
1 cup chickpeas, soaked overnight, and drained, or 2 cups cooked, or canned chickpeas

2 boiled eggs, shelled
1 to 2 flat breads, Iraqi variety or Arabic bread (see bread chapter)

For garnish: Sumac, see Glossary, and/or Yogurt sauce made by combining 1 cup yogurt, 1/2 cup chopped parsley, 1/4 teaspoon salt, and 1 clove garlic, grated

1. In a medium heavy pot, put chicken, onion, garlic, noomi Basra, salt, cardamom, bay leaves, curry powder, coriander, cubed potatoes, and chickpeas (if using cooked chickpeas add them in stage 2). Cover with cold water by 3 inches. Bring to a quick boil on high, skimming as needed, then reduce heat to medium-low, and let simmer gently, covered, until chicken is done, 40 to 45 minutes.

2. Add eggs (and canned chickpeas if used) about 15 minutes before chicken is done.

3. In a deep big dish, break bread into bite size pieces and drench with chicken broth. Arrange chicken on top along with potatoes, chickpeas and eggs. Sprinkle with sumac, or drizzle with yogurt sauce.

For a traditional touch, drizzle with a little sizzling hot oil, if you do not mind the extra calories, and serve with slices of salad vegetables, and pickles.

An illustration by al-Wasiti of Baghdad, from 13th-century Maqamat al-Hariri.
The host is tending to the needs of his guests. The helper is carrying a dish of, what looks like, chicken.
Bibliothèque Nationale (MS Arabe 5847)

Chicken Supreme
Dijaaj Muluki

(Makes 4 servings)

Muluki (literally "kingly") stands for excellence in quality. This dish is a variation on the traditional *thareed* or *tashreeb*. Chicken is baked, and as a casserole, it can be served from oven to table, and hence rendered suitable for more formal presentations.

4 chicken thighs, skinned and trimmed, or 12 drumsticks, skinned
1 medium onion, quartered
2 bay leaves
5 to 6 whole pods of cardamom
1 teaspoon salt
1/4 teaspoon black pepper

2 tablespoons oil
2 medium onions thinly sliced
1 cup mushrooms, cut into halves
1/2 teaspoon salt
1/4 teaspoon black pepper
1/2 teaspoon coriander
1/4 teaspoon crushed chili pepper, or to taste

1 flat Iraqi bread, or 2 Arabic bread, preferably stale (see Chapter One on breads)
1 tablespoon sumac, optional (see Glossary)

1. In a medium pot, put prepared chicken, quartered onion, bay leaves, cardamom, salt and pepper. Add cold water just enough to cover. Bring to a quick boil on high heat skimming as needed. Reduce heat to low and let gently simmer, covered, until chicken is just cooked, about 35 minutes.

2. Meanwhile, sauté sliced onion in oil, until golden brown, about 7 minutes. Add mushrooms, and stir briefly. Add salt, pepper, coriander and crushed chili. Set aside.

3. In an ovenproof deep dish, big enough to hold chicken pieces in one layer, arrange broken pieces of bread to cover the bottom. Spread half of the onion mixture on bread and arrange cooked chicken pieces on top. Spread rest of the onion mixture on chicken. Sprinkle generously with sumac, if wished.

4. Strain chicken broth and skim fat, if you like, by spreading a folded white paper towel on the surface of the broth and lifting it quickly. Repeat until you get rid of fat. Pour broth on prepared chicken casserole enough to come up to half the depth of the baking dish. Cover with foil.

5. Bake in a preheated oven at 400 degrees F. for about 30 minutes, or until most of liquid has been soaked up by bread. Remove foil the last 10 minutes of baking to allow surface to brown.
   Serve with salad, and pickles. If wished drizzle with yogurt sauce made by combining 1 cup yogurt, 1/4 cup chopped parsley, 1/4 teaspoon salt, and 1 clove garlic, grated.

Madhira: "a Very Miracle of Food"

Madhira was a typical medieval meat dish, simmered in yogurt-based sauce, along with onion, mint, and spices, such as coriander, cumin, mastic and cinnamon. During the Middle Ages this was believed to be a "good for you" kind of food.

Cooking meat with minted yogurt sauce is still a favorite dish in the Middle-Eastern cuisine in general. Following are verse lines composed in the ninth century AD, enumerating the benefits of *madhira*.

Madhira cannot rivaled be
To heal the sick man's malady:
No wonder this our meal we make,
Since, eating it, no law we break.
'Tis as delicious as 'tis good--
    A very miracle of food.
    (Arberry, 28)

Cornish Hens Simmered in Cumin Sauce (Dijaj bi'l-Camoun)

(Makes 4 servings)

This is an aromatic dish perfumed with a blend of spices, the most prominent of which is the ancient spice cumin. It is more usually prepared with regular whole chicken, but Cornish hens are more appealing for festive formal presentations. Chicken drumsticks can also be substituted, which in fact makes it suitable for casual dining and buffet dinners, very popular amongst kids of all ages.

For marinade:
> **3 tablespoons olive oil**
> **3 to 4 cloves garlic, grated**
> **1 medium onion, thinly sliced or coarsely chopped**
> **1 small onion, grated**
> **2 teaspoons cumin**
> **1/2 teaspoon turmeric**
> **1/2 teaspoon ginger**
> **1 teaspoon coriander**
> **3 to 4 pods cardamom**
> **1/2 teaspoon prepared *noomi Basrah*, see Glossary**
> **1 teaspoon thin strips of lemon rind**
> **1 tablespoon pomegranate syrup, or tamarind concentrate, or a substitute, see Glossary**
> **1/2 cup parsley or fresh cilantro, chopped**

1 teaspoon salt
1/2 teaspoon black pepper
1/2 teaspoon chili pepper, or to taste

2 Cornish hens or 12 chicken drumsticks, leave skin on

3 medium potatoes cut into 1/3-inch-thick slices
1/2 cup frozen or canned peas, optional
1 carrot diagonally sliced, optional
1/2 cup pitted olives, whole or halved
2 to 3 whole small chili peppers, optional

1. In a big bowl mix marinade ingredients.

2. Wash hens very well and rub them inside and out with marinade mixture. Tie legs of Cornish hens with a kitchen thread. Set aside for 30 minutes.

3. In a medium pot, put hens or drumsticks, the marinade, and potatoes. Pour 2 1/2 cups water and bring to a boil skimming as needed. Reduce heat to medium and let boil gently, partially covered for 30 minutes or until chicken is almost done. Turn whole hens half way through cooking.

4. Remove hens or drumsticks and potato slices from liquid and put them in a large ovenproof glass baking dish. Brush them lightly with oil, and let them brown in a hot oven, about 450 degrees F. or a hot broiler, turning hens several times to allow all sides to brown (turn drumsticks only once). If oven or broiler is hot enough browning will take about 15 minutes

5. Meanwhile, to the remaining liquid in the pot add peas and carrots if any. Add olives, and chili peppers, if any. Bring to a quick boil then reduce heat to medium-low and let sauce boil gently until vegetables are cooked and sauce is richly thickened, about 20 minutes.

6. As soon as hens or drumsticks and potatoes are browned take them out of the oven, remove threads from hens, and pour sauce with the vegetables all over them

Serve with rice and noodles topped with toasted nuts and currants (see chapter 8), along with salad.

Chicken Simmered in Tomato Sauce
(Dijaaj bil-Salsa al-Hamra)

(Makes 4 servings)

In this dish, chicken is simmered in tomato sauce, and balanced with a little bit of sugar. The skin is left on the chicken pieces to protect meat from hardening while browning. Remove skin after browning, if wished.

4 serving size chicken pieces, 1 1/2 to 2 pounds, trim, leave skin on

2 tablespoons olive oil
1 medium onion, coarsely chopped
2 cloves garlic, grated
2 tablespoons flour
One 15-ounce can tomato sauce
1/2 teaspoon sugar, or honey
1 teaspoon salt
1/2 teaspoon black pepper
1/2 teaspoon *baharat*, see Glossary
1/2 teaspoon coriander
1/4 teaspoon allspice

Preheat oven to 400 degrees F.

1. In a big preferably non-stick frying pan heat oil and sauté chicken pieces until browned on both sides, about 10 minutes. Transfer to a plate, and set aside.

2. Sauté onion and garlic in the same oil until onion is transparent, about 5 minutes. Add flour and stir until fragrant, about 2 minutes.

4. Mix tomato sauce, 1 cup water, sugar, salt, black pepper, *baharat,* coriander and allspice. Gradually add to flour mixture stirring until it starts to bubble, 2 to 3 minutes.

5. Arrange chicken pieces in an oven proof deep dish and pour tomato sauce mixture all over. Bake covered in a preheated oven at 400 degrees F. 35 to 40 minutes, or until sauce nicely thickens, and chicken is tender.

Serve with white rice and salad.

Chicken Drumsticks Baked in Fig Sauce
(Afkhadh al-Dijaj bil-Teen)

(Makes 4 servings)

This is another delicious dish prepared à la Medieval Baghdadi cooking. Prunes can be substituted for figs. Skin is to be left on chicken for maximum flavor, and for protection while cooking. Feel free to remove it before serving the dish.

12 chicken drumsticks, do not remove skin
1 teaspoon salt
1/2 teaspoon black pepper
2 tablespoons oil

1 medium onion, coarsely chopped
1 clove garlic, grated
1 cup tomato sauce (one 8-ounce can)

2 cups broth or water
16 dried figs, prunes may be substituted
1 scant tablespoon coriander
1/2 teaspoon salt
1/4 teaspoon black pepper

For garnish: 1/4 cup chopped parsley
Preheat oven to 400 degrees F.

1. Sprinkle drumsticks with salt and pepper and brown on both sides in heated oil in a big non-stick skillet, about 12 minutes. Remove drumsticks from skillet and arrange in a single layer in an ovenproof glass pan (approx.7 1/2-by-12-inches).

2. Leave 1 tablespoon oil in the skillet and discard the rest. Sauté onion and garlic until transparent, about 5 minutes.

3. Add tomato sauce, broth or water, dried figs, coriander, salt and pepper. Bring to a quick boil, stirring occasionally, about 5 minutes. Pour onion mixture all over the drumsticks. Bake, uncovered, in a preheated oven, at 400 degrees F., for about 35 minutes, or until chicken is tender, and sauce is nicely thickened.

Garnish with chopped parsley and serve with rice or bulgar of your choice (see rice and grains chapters for suggestions).

Chicken Legs Simmered in Balsamic Vinegar (Dijaj bil Khal)

Makes 4 servings)

Simmering meat in vinegar has been a favorite method for cooking ever since ancient times. The Babylonian recipes are our best testimony (see Introduction, for details). The tartness of the vinegar is usually balanced with a little bit of honey or sugar. During the medieval era such dishes were called *mamqour* (marinated in vinegar), or *masous* (soaked up). The chicken skin is kept while cooking for flavor and protection. It can be discarded before serving.

4 chicken legs, trimmed, or 12 chicken drumsticks, leave skin on
Salt and black pepper for seasoning the chicken
2 tablespoons oil

1 medium onion, coarsely chopped
1/2 teaspoon turmeric
1/2 cup diced carrots, peas (frozen or canned), sliced mushrooms, each
2 medium potatoes, cubed
1/3 cup vinegar, preferably wine vinegar, as in the medieval recipes
1 teaspoon honey, or sugar

1 cup broth or water
1 teaspoon salt, coriander, thyme, each
1/2 teaspoon cardamom, allspice, each
1/4 teaspoon black pepper
2 bay leaves
For garnish: 1/4 cup chopped parsley, or coarsely ground pistachio

1. Season chicken pieces with salt and black pepper, and brown in oil using a non-stick skillet, big enough to hold chicken pieces in one layer. Brown on both sides, about 10 minutes. Transfer chicken pieces to a plate.

2. Sauté onion in the remaining oil until transparent, about 5 minutes. Add turmeric, carrots, peas, mushrooms, and potatoes. Fold for about 3 minutes.

3. Pour vinegar into the skillet. Add honey or sugar, and let boil with vegetables quickly for about 2 minutes.

4. Return chicken pieces to the skillet and add broth or water, salt, coriander, thyme, cardamom, allspice, black pepper, and bay leaves. Bring to a quick boil, then reduce heat to low and let chicken simmer, covered, until tender and sauce is nicely thickened, about 30 minutes. Half way through simmering, turn chicken pieces once.

Garnish with chopped parsley, or give it a medieval touch by sprinkling ground pistachio on the top. Serve with rice or bulgar (see chapters on rice and grains for suggestions).

Chicken Curry
(Kari'l-Dijaj)

(Makes 4 servings)

Besides the usual staples of rice and tomato-based stews, sometimes dishes are given a kick, whether gentle or vigorous depends upon the region and personal taste. Generally speaking people from the south, especially Basrah, like their food on the spicy side. The best spices are found in the traditional *souks* of this southern port-city, which has been the pass-road for spice traders ever since ancient times. The following is a light version of the chicken curry using cubed chicken breasts.

1 pound skinless and boneless chicken breasts, or tender loins, cut into 1-inch cubes, sprinkled lightly with salt and pepper
2 tablespoons cornstarch
2 tablespoons oil, divided

1 medium onion, coarsely chopped
2 cloves garlic, grated
1 teaspoon curry powder
1/2 teaspoon turmeric

3 medium potatoes, peeled and cut into 1-inch cubes
2 tablespoons flour

1 scant tablespoon tamarind concentrate, see Glossary
2 cups hot water
1/2 teaspoon ginger
1 teaspoon salt
1/4 teaspoon black pepper, whole mustard seeds, whole fennel or aniseeds, each
1/2 teaspoon ground coriander, ground cumin, each
1/2 to 1 teaspoon chili pepper, or to taste

1 bay leaf
2 to 3 pods cardamom
1/2 cup canned or frozen peas, or vegetables of your choice

1. Sprinkle chicken cubes with cornstarch. In a medium non-stick skillet brown chicken in 1 tablespoon oil stirring frequently for about 10 minutes or until chicken is cooked. Set aside in a plate.

2. In a medium heavy pot sauté onion in 1 tablespoon oil, and stir until onion is transparent, about 5 minutes. Add garlic, curry powder and turmeric about a minute before onion is done. Add cubed potatoes and stir for a few minutes. Sprinkle vegetables with the flour and stir until fragrant, a few minutes.

3. Add the rest of ingredients, mix well, bring to a quick boil, then reduce heat to medium low and let simmer until sauce is of medium consistency and vegetables are cooked. Stir 2 to 3 times while cooking to prevent sauce from sticking to the bottom of the pot, about 30 minutes.

4. Add the chicken, and cook for 5 more minutes, or just to heat it through.
Serve with rice and salad.

Chicken Simmered in Pomegranate Syrup
Dijaj bi Sharab al-Rumman (Fasanjoun)

(Makes 4 servings)

This is a tomato-free dish popular in the southern region of Iraq, especially in Najaf and Karbala. Cooking with sour pomegranate juice, and thickening the sauces with walnuts was not new to the region. The medieval Arabic cookbooks abounded with stew and sauce recipes in which countless sour agents were balanced with sweet substances. Dishes soured by adding *rumman* (pomegranate), similar to this dish, were simply called *Rummaniyat*. The Persian name *fasanjoun*, must have filtered to the region at a later date.

In the late 1950's, Elizabeth Fernea spent around two years in al-Nuhra, one of the southern Iraqi villages. In her admirable *Guests of the Skeik*, she describes the way *fasanjoun* was cooked by the wife of the Sheik.

Fasanjan was a worthy delicacy to celebrate our release from the rain. The preparation took hours. First the walnuts were pounded and pounded in a mortar until nothing was left but the oil. The chicken was jointed and browned in the oil and then a little salt was added and water in which dried pomegranate seeds had been soaking. In this fragrant broth the chicken cooked slowly until the broth thickened to nut-brown sauce and the chicken fell from its bones. Walnuts and dried pomegranate seeds and salt proved to be an unexpectedly delicious combination of flavors. I told Selma that it was excellent and she smiled. (271)

This was how it was traditionally prepared. Nowadays it does not have to take that long. Here is how to prepare it the light and easy way:

4 serving size pieces of chicken, skinned and trimmed, about 2 1/2 pounds
3 to 4 pods cardamom

1 medium onion, coarsely chopped
1 tablespoon oil
1 cup walnut halves (about 4 ounces), toasted, then pulverized in a blender or food processor until oily
1/4 cup pomegranate syrup, see Glossary for substitution
1 1/2 teaspoons salt
1/4 teaspoon black pepper
1/4 teaspoon chili flakes, or to taste
1/2 teaspoon coriander
3 cups chicken broth

For garnish: 1/4 cup chopped parsley, 1/4 cup fresh pomegranate seeds, if available, and lemon rind cut into thin long strips

1. In a medium pot put chicken pieces and cardamom, and cover with cold water. Bring to a quick boil on high heat, skimming as needed. Reduce heat to low and let simmer gently until chicken is just cooked, about 30 minutes. Transfer chicken pieces to a plate, and reserve the broth.

2. In a medium heavy pot, sauté onion in oil until it starts to change color, about 7 minutes. Add pulverized walnuts, pomegranate syrup, salt, pepper, chili flakes, chicken broth, and chicken pieces. Bring to a quick boil on high heat, then reduce heat to medium low and let the pot boil gently, covered, stirring 2 to 3 times until sauce is nicely thickened, about 20 minutes. If chicken is done and sauce still needs to be cooked, take it out and let sauce boil gently until
it is of medium consistency.
Garnish chicken and sauce with chopped parsley, pomegranate seeds, if available, and lemon rind strips, and serve with white or yellow rice along with some salad.

Al-Fustuqiya

This is an interesting medieval sweet chicken dish, named after *fustuq* (pistachio), the thickening and coloring agent in the recipe.

Take breasts of chickens, and half-boil in water with a little salt. Drain off water, and take flesh off the bones, pulling it into threads. Then put it back into pot, and cover it with water. Take peeled pistachios as required, and pound it in the mortar. Add it pot and stir. Let it simmer. When almost cooked, throw in as much sugar as the pistachios. Keep stirring until set, then remove (al-Baghdadi, 197).

Chicken with Walnut and Bread Sauce
(Dijaj bil Sharkasiya)

(Makes 6 servings)

Although the name *Sharkasi* (*Circassian*) suggests a foreign origin, we now know that the technique of thickening sauces with breadcrumbs is as ancient as Babylon itself, if not earlier (see Introduction, for details). As for using nuts as thickening agents, the medieval Arabic cookbooks, whether of Islamic East (*al-Mashriq*) or the Islamic West (*al- Maghrib*) testify to the fact that it was already a common cooking practice.

> **1 medium chicken, about 2 1/2 pounds, cut into pieces, skinned and trimmed**
> **1 teaspoon salt**
> **1/4 teaspoon black pepper**
> **1 medium onion, quartered**
> **1 carrot cut into big pieces**
> **1 bay leaf**
> **3 to 4 pods of cardamom**

For walnut and bread sauce:
> **6 to 8 slices of fresh loaf bread, crust removed**
> **2 cups chicken broth**
> **1 cup toasted walnut halves (about 4 ounces), pulverized in a blender or food processor**
> **1/2 teaspoon salt**
> **1/4 teaspoon chili pepper, or to taste**
> **1 clove garlic, grated**
> **1 teaspoon coriander**
> **1/4 cup lemon juice**

For garnish: 1/4 cup chopped parsley, diced vegetables, some broken pieces of toasted walnuts,

1. Put chicken pieces, salt and pepper, carrot, onion, bay leaf, and cardamom in a medium pot and well cover with cold water. Bring to a quick boil on high heat skimming as needed. Reduce heat to low and let simmer gently until chicken in done, 30 to 40 minutes.

2. When cool enough to handle, take chicken out of broth, discard bones, and with fingers shred meat into small chunks. Set aside.

3. Strain broth, and if wished, get rid of fat, as suggested in Chicken Supreme, above, step 4. Set aside.

4. To prepare sauce, soak bread in 2 cups of broth, then process or blend it, along with ground walnut, salt, chili pepper, garlic, coriander, and lemon juice, for a minute or two or until a smooth medium sauce forms.

5. Mix 1/3 of the sauce with the prepared chicken as a binder and mound it on a plate, or for an elegant presentation mold it into a shape of your choice. Drizzle rest of sauce on top and all around chicken. Garnish with chopped parsley, sliced vegetables, and broken toasted pieces of walnut. Serve warm or cold, with bread, and salad.

Rotisserie Chicken, Medieval Style

In addition to the commonly known ways of grilling meat either in the *tannour* or on open fire, *kebab* way, evidently the medieval Baghdadi cooks grilled big chunks of meat or whole chickens in revolving skewers, suspended on open fire. Food cooked this way was called *kardhabaj* or *kardanaj*. The tenth-century cookbook writer, Al-Warraq, gives several such dishes. One of them was made for the Caliph al-Mahdi. A plump hen was salted very well, and rubbed with oil and *rakhbeen* (?). Then it was skewered and let revolve, frequently basting it with the mixture of oil and *rakhbeen,* using a feather. The chicken was then divided into pieces, and arranged on a platter.

To aid the digestion grilled meats were always served with condiments or sauces, called *sibagh*. The *sibagh* prepared for this dish was composed of ground pistachio, mixed with sugar, vinegar, liquid from cucumber pulp, salt, oil, and chopped mint. The sauce was then poured on the chicken, and set aside to let chicken absorb the sauce. Before serving, chopped cucumber pulp, chopped mint, and oil were spread all over.

In another recipe the sauce offered with the rotisserie chicken was sour juice of unripe grapes mixed with thyme, parsley, and other herbs. Al-Warraq recommended it as a summer dish.

One of the ways to protect the chicken skin from scorching, was to wait until the rotisserie chicken drips its initial liquids, then while it revolved, the cook would baste it with pancake-like batter, using a feather, until it is completely covered. The batter would eventually dry out, crack, and was discarded. After that the revolving chicken was basted with murri (fermented sauce), pepper and oil, until fully cooked (Al-Warraq, 71, 218).

Grilled Cornish Hens
(Farrouj Mashwi)

(Makes 4 servings)

It has always been the custom to choose the *farouj or farareej* (young hens) for grilling, because they are more tender than the native fully-grown hens. In the medieval cookbooks there is a considerable number of recipes for grilling *farareej* and plump chickens, with *sibaghs*-- the sour-based sauces thickened with nuts and perfumed with spices and herbs.

Even by today's standards the *sibagh* idea still sounds really good, and is worth trying. Make your own by combining any of the following ingredients:

Choose either wine vinegar or pomegranate syrup and combine it with toasted nut, mustard, grated cucumber, onion and garlic, chopped parsley, mint or cilantro. Spice it with pepper, coriander, ginger, mustard, and salt

2 Cornish hens
For marinade:
2 tablespoons oil
Juice of 1 lemon
1 small onion, grated
1 to 2 cloves garlic, grated
1/2 teaspoon *baharat*, see Glossary
1/4 teaspoon chili pepper, or to taste
1/2 teaspoon thyme, or *za'tar*, see Glossary
For garnish: 1 tablespoon sumac, see Glossary, onion slices, 1/4 cup chopped parsley

1. Wash hens and with a sharp knife cut open flat from the back. Remove backbone and rib bones. Pound a little with a mallet to flatten pieces.

2. Mix marinade ingredients and rub hens with it on both sides. Set aside for about 2 hours at room temperature or refrigerate overnight, but bring to room temperature before using.

3. Put hens flat in a hinged fish grill and sprinkle with salt and black pepper. Grill on medium high heat, turning several times while cooking until browned on both sides, about 30 minutes
The flattened hens can also be broiled. Put hens flat on a broiling pan, and broil, turning twice to allow to brown on both sides. Brush with oil if you notice they are getting dry.

Variation:
You can also cook flattened hens in a skillet on the stove, the medieval way. They called chicken cooked this way, *al-dajaj al-mutajan*, and was cooked in an earthenware skillet (al-Warraq, 74).
Cook them one after the other if you do not have a skillet big enough to hold both of them flat. Heat about 1 tablespoon oil in a big skillet and put in hens flat. To help keep them flat while cooking, put a heavy weight on them, such as a heavy flat plate. Cook on medium heat, basting with the oozing juices occasionally, and turning at least twice until they are tender and nicely browned. Put hens in a serving platter. Mix sumac and onion and arrange around hens. Sprinkle with chopped parsley. Serve with warm bread and salad such as *taboula* or *misaqa'a* (see chapter 3, on salads).

Chicken Shish Kebab
(Dijaj Mashwi)

(Makes 4 servings)

Since fully-grown chicken nowadays is tender enough, there is no reason why we should restrict grilling to young hens. The following marinade will yield succulent and fully flavored grilled chicken.

4 pieces (about 1 3/4 pounds) chicken boneless and skinless breasts, trimmed and cut into 1 1/2-inch cubes, or 12 drum sticks (about 3 1/2 pounds), leave skin on

For marinade:
1 cup buttermilk, or milk mixed with 1 tablespoon lemon juice
1 small onion, grated
1 clove garlic, grated
2 tablespoons to 1/4 cup olive oil (depending on how lean chicken is)
1/2 teaspoon *za'tar* (see Glossary), or thyme
1/2 teaspoon coriander
1/4 teaspoon chili pepper, or to taste
1 tablespoon honey, optional
1 teaspoon grated lemon rind
Salt and pepper
For garnish: 1 tablespoon sumac (see Glossary) mixed with thinly sliced onion, and 1/4 cup chopped parsley

1. Combine marinade ingredients in a bowl and add prepared chicken pieces. Let marinade coat pieces on all sides. Set aside for 2 hours at room temperature, or refrigerate overnight, but bring to room temperature before grilling.

2. Thread chicken pieces into skewers (make 8 skewers if chicken breast is used, and 4 skewers if drumsticks are used). Reserve marinade for basting.

3. When grill is ready, sprinkle chicken with salt and black pepper, and grill on medium high heat. Turn skewers frequently to allow to brown on both sides, and baste several times with the reserved marinade to keep chicken moist, about 15 minutes for breasts, and 25 minutes for drum sticks, or until tender. When done, brush with a little oil if they look dry.
  You can also broil them in the oven about 2 inches from source of heat. Arrange skewers on a broiling pan. Turn skewers once to allow chicken to brown on both sides. Broil until well browned and tender, about 10 to 15 minutes on each side, and a little bit longer for the drum sticks. Baste several times while broiling and brush with a little oil if chicken looks dry.
  Serve kebab on a bed of the onion-sumac mixture. Sprinkle with chopped parsley. Delicious with warm bread and salads like *taboula* or *hummus* (see chapter 3, on salads), and grilled tomatoes and onion slices.

Chicken or Turkey Stuffed with Rice
(Dijaj Mahshi)

(Makes 6 to 10 servings)

The tenderizing effects of brine were recognized by cooks in the past. In the tenth-century Baghdadi cookbook, there is a meat recipe that requires the cut meat to be kept in brine from the time of morning prayer to around brunch time, that is around five hours. The meat was then washed very well and cooked (al-Warraq, 218). That was what our Christian neighbor used to do to her Christmas turkey before roasting it in the oven. However, this might not be necessary for the roasting birds available in today's markets. The suggested proportions for the brine:

For each quart (4 cups) of cold, add 2 tablespoons coarse salt and 1 tablespoon sugar. The brined bird has to be refrigerated for about 6 hours. When ready to cook, do not forget to rinse the bird inside and out with cold water, otherwise it will taste too salty. Discard the brine.

1 big chicken, or a medium turkey
Mixture for rubbing the bird:
    1/2 cup vinegar
    1 tablespoon salt
    2 tablespoons lemon juice
    1 teaspoon pepper
    1/2 teaspoon cinnamon
    1/2 teaspoon nutmeg
    1/2 teaspoon *za'tar*, see Glossary, or thyme
    1 teaspoon coriander
For stuffing:
    1 tablespoon oil
    1 onion, coarsely chopped
    2 cloves garlic, grated
    1/2 teaspoon turmeric
    1/2 cup frozen or canned peas, diced carrots, chopped mushrooms, each
    1 cup diced potatoes browned in 1 tablespoon oil
    1/2 cup currants or raisins
    1/2 cup slivered almonds, toasted
    1 tablespoon *baharat*, see Glossary
    1/2 teaspoon cardamom
    1/2 teaspoon cinnamon
    1 teaspoon prepared *noomi Basrah*, see Glossary
    1/2 teaspoon ginger
    1 teaspoon salt
    1/2 teaspoon black pepper
    1/2 teaspoon chili pepper, or to taste
    2 cups rice preferably basmati or American rice, washed, soaked in cold water for 30 minutes, drained, and cooked as directed Plain White Rice, p. 237

1/2 cup yogurt, for coating the bird
Preheat oven at 425 degrees F.

370

1. To prepare the bird: Rub washed bird with vinegar and salt inside and out and let stand for 30 minutes. Drain and dry. Then rub it with lemon juice. Mix the spices and rub them into the bird inside and out. Set aside bird in a colander fitted on a bowl, at room temperature, until ready for stuffing.

2. In a large skillet sauté onion, garlic and turmeric in the oil until onion is transparent, about 5 minutes. Add peas, carrots and mushrooms. Pour in about 3/4 cup hot water and let simmer on medium heat about 10 minutes, or until vegetables are cooked, and liquid evaporates. Mix in browned potatoes, currants, almonds, *baharat*, cardamom, cinnamon, *noomi Basrah*, ginger, salt, pepper, and chili pepper. Gently fold this mixture into cooked rice.

3. To stuff the bird: Pat cavities dry with white paper towels and fill very well with the rice mixture, for rice is already cooked. Close openings by sewing them with a white thread. If stuffing a turkey, fill the neck cavity also. Tie legs together. Put stuffed bird on the roasting rack, breast side up. Tuck wings under bird and tuck neck skin under the back. Discard any filling that came into contact with the uncooked bird while filling it.

4. Coat bird with yogurt. Bake in a preheated oven at 425 degrees F. for the first 15 minutes. Reduce heat to 350 degrees F. and bake allowing 30 minutes for each pound. While bird is roasting, baste occasionally with the dripping juices until it is nicely browned.

Allow to set for about 15 minutes before carving. Remove threads and serve on a platter surrounded with the remaining rice stuffing.

Note:

Some people prefer to bake the bird first until it is almost done, and then stuff it. According to this method, wash and rub the bird as directed in step 1. Roast it as directed in step 4. Prepare the filling as directed in step 2. When bird is almost done, take it out of the oven and allow it to cool slightly. Lift the bird up, to drain the cavity, then fill it very well with the stuffing, no need to close it, just cover it with a sheet of foil paper. Return to oven and resume baking until bird is thoroughly cooked and nicely browned, basting as needed.

The Pregnant Chicken

The Pregnant Chicken

(Makes 6 servings)

This is an amusing method for stuffing chicken, which I learnt from my friends in Mosul, in northern Iraq. We were once invited to dinner, and there it was in the middle of the table a huge stuffed bird. At first glance I thought it was a huge duck, but I was corrected, it was an ordinary chicken, stuffed in the cavity, as well as between the skin and the meat. The chicken looked hilariously puffy, and we nicknamed it the "pregnant chicken. The advantage of putting the filling between the skin and the meat is that the skin on the roasted chicken would crisp to perfection.

Later on I discovered, so much to my surprise, that stuffing chicken between the skin and the meat is not new. In the thirteenth-century *Anonymous Andalusian Cookbook*, there is a chicken recipe called *al-dajaj al-Abbasi* (Abbasid chicken), which as the name indicates, is a loan dish from the Baghdadi cuisine. There are instructions to stuff the chicken between the skin and the meat, and the interior (36). They separated the skin from the meat after they cleaned the chicken from the feathers, before opening it up, by blowing very hard through the neck, until the skin was separated. If there were still any undetached areas, a meat skewer was pushed through the neck, and very carefully the skin was detached (Rodinson, 161)

To prepare this dish, you need a medium to large chicken, about 5 pounds. Get it ready for stuffing as directed in the recipe for stuffed chicken above step 1. Prepare stuffing as in step 2. When you come to fill the chicken, follow these instructions:

372

Hold the chicken with one hand and with the fingers of the other hand, starting with the neck part, separate skin from meat going down slowly all the way to the thighs, and taking care not to pierce the skin with the nails. This will create a pocket to hold stuffing between meat and skin.

Fill the regular cavity with the stuffing, and fill it well since the rice is cooked. Sew closed the cavity. Then fill the pocket you created with as much filling as it could hold, pushing the filling down to the thighs, the breast area, the wings, and the back. Sew closed the neck opening to prevent filling from coming out.

Remove any of the filling that might have stuck to the outer part of the chicken. Place the prepared chicken on a greased broiler pan, and spray it lightly with oil or rub it with yogurt. Discard any filling that might have come into contact with the uncooked chicken.

Bake the chicken as directed in Stuffed Chicken, step 4.

Stuffed Chicken Simmered in Tomato Juice,
and Buried in Rice
(Tibeat)

(Makes 4 to 6 serving)

This is a traditional dish prepared for the Sabbath by the Jewish families in Baghdad. The slow simmering was traditionally done in the *tannour* (domed oven). Due to the prolonged time of cooking the rice develops a very delicious crunchy crust. The following recipe is given a lighter touch.

> **1 medium chicken, about 4 pounds, washed**
> **1/4 cup lemon juice (juice of one lemon)**
> **Salt and pepper, for rubbing the chicken**
>
> **2 medium onions chopped, divided**
> **3 tablespoons oil, divided**
> **1 medium tomato, skinned and chopped**
> **1 1/2 teaspoons salt, divided**
> **1/4 teaspoon black pepper**
> **1 teaspoon *baharat*, see Glossary**
> **1 teaspoon coriander**
> **2 cups rice, washed and soaked in water for 30 minute, then drained, divided**
>
> **1 cup tomato juice, or 1/2 cup tomato sauce diluted in 1/2 cup water, or 1 heaping tomato paste diluted in water to make 1 cup**
> **4 eggs, boiled and shelled**

1. Rub chicken inside and out with lemon juice, salt and pepper. Set aside.

2. Chop gizzards, and in a medium skillet, sauté them with **one chopped onion** in **1 tablespoon oil**, until browned, about 10 minutes. Add chopped tomato, **1 teaspoon salt**, black pepper, *baharat*,

coriander, and **1 cup rice**. Mix well stirring for a few minutes, and put away from heat. Set aside until cool enough to handle.

3. Pat dry chicken inside and out very well with white paper towels. Stuff cavity with prepared rice mixture. Do not pack, allow some room for expanding rice. Sew closed cavity, and tie legs with a kitchen thread.

4. In a medium non-stick pot sauté the other chopped onion, and stuffed chicken in **2 tablespoons oil**, turning chicken to allow it to brown on both sides, taking care not to pierce the skin, about 15 minutes.

5. Add tomato juice, or diluted tomato sauce or paste. Bring to a quick boil, then allow chicken to boil gently on medium heat until liquid evaporates and chicken browns, about 15 minutes. Do not cover pot at this stage.

6. Pour about 4 cups hot water. Add eggs and bring to a quick boil. Then reduce heat to medium-low and let simmer, partially covered, until chicken is cooked and 2 cups of liquid is left, about 45 minutes. Turn chicken half way through simmering to allow it to cook on all sides.

7. Remove chicken and eggs from sauce. Get rid of fat in sauce, if wished.

8. Add the remaining 1 cup rice and 1/2 teaspoon salt to the sauce. Bring to a quick boil, for 5 minutes, then reduce heat to low, and let simmer until the rice is almost cooked, about 15 minutes. Push some of the rice to the sides of the pot and place the chicken in the middle of the pot and surround it with rice and eggs. Traditionally, at this stage, the pot would be placed in the *tannour* to simmer for a few hours. But for more practical reasons continue simmering the pot on very slow heat for about 60 minutes, or until crust forms in the bottom of the pot. (You may simmer pot, covered in, in the oven, if pot is oven proof-- no plastic or wooden handles or knobs to burn)

To serve, put the chicken in the middle of a platter and surround it with rice and halved eggs. Break crust into chunks and arrange it around the platter. Serve with salad and pickles.

Chicken with Red Rice
(Dijaj bil Timman al-Ahmer)

(Makes 6 servings)

This is an easier version of the *Tibeat*, in which chicken pieces are used, instead of the whole stuffed bird.

> **6 chicken pieces of your choice, about 3 pounds skinned and trimmed**
> **2 tablespoons oil**
> **1 medium onion, coarsely chopped**
>
> **One 6-ounce can tomato paste diluted in 6 cups hot water, or 6 cups tomato juice (one 46- fl. ounce can)**
> **1 teaspoon prepared *noomi Basrah*, see Glossary**

1 teaspoon coriander
1 tablespoon salt
1/2 teaspoon black pepper
4 to 5 cardamom pods
1 bay leaf

2 cups rice, washed, soaked in cold water for 30 minutes, drained
For garnish: sliced boiled eggs, toasted slivered almonds, and currants or raisins

1. In a non-stick skillet brown chicken pieces in oil, turning once to allow to brown on both sides, about 6 minutes. Arrange browned pieces in bottom of a heavy medium pot.

2. In the remaining oil in skillet, sauté onion until transparent, about 5 minutes. Scatter onion on chicken pieces in pot.

3. Add tomato juice or diluted tomato paste, *noomi Basrah* coriander, salt, pepper, cardamom and bay leaf. Bring to a quick boil, then reduce heat to medium low, and let simmer until chicken is tender, about 40 minutes.

4. Take out chicken pieces, and set aside at a warm place until serving time. Measure remaining liquid; you need 4 cups for cooking the rice, the rest can be served in a bowl as extra sauce. Put drained rice in a heavy medium pot. Pour measured 4 cups of liquid, and bring to a quick boil, about 5 minutes. Reduce heat to low, fold rice gently, then let it simmer, covered, for about 20 minutes, folding rice gently twice or three times while simmering to allow it to fluff.

To serve, put rice in a platter and surround it with chicken pieces. Garnish with egg halves, almonds and currants or raisins. Put any leftover sauce in a bowl and serve it with rice accompanied with a bowl of yogurt or pickled mango salad (see chapter 3).

Variation: Some vegetables can be added to the sauce while chicken is simmering in step 3. My choice is cubed potatoes, sliced mushrooms, sliced pepper, either sweet or hot, and peas, frozen or canned.

Easy Fruity Baked Chicken
(Al-Bustaniya)

(Makes 4 to 6 servings)

This is a dish inspired by *al- bustaniyat* (from *bustan*, fruit orchard) dishes, al-Warraq gives in his tenth-century cookbook. In his version, he cuts chicken breasts into finger-like strips, and adds to them juice of sour green plums, and chopped peaches. When brought to a boil, he adds spices, oil, a little sugar, wine vinegar, and ground meat of 5 walnuts. In its last stage, he breaks eggs into it (163-4). Following is my easy fruity version of *bustaniya*:

2 pounds skinless, boneless chicken breasts cut into 1 1/2-inch cubes, or strips
1/2 cup green onion, chopped with the green part

6 chopped dried apricots, dried prunes, dried figs, each
10 green or black olives, stones removed
1/2 teaspoon grated orange peel
1/2 cup toasted walnut, broken into pieces, or ground
1 cup orange juice
1 tablespoon pomegranate syrup
2 tablespoons olive oil
1 teaspoon coriander
1/2 teaspoon ginger
1/4 teaspoon cardamom
1/2 teaspoon whole aniseeds
1 teaspoon salt
1/4 teaspoon black pepper

Preheat oven to 400 degrees F.

1. Mix all the ingredients in a bowl, and let marinade at room temperature for 1 hour.

2. Spread mixture in a baking pan big enough to hold mixture in a thin layer.

3. Bake in a preheated oven at 400 degrees F., loosely covered, until chicken is cooked, about 20 minutes. Fold mixture 2 to 3 times while baking.

3. If remaining sauce is rather thin, remove chicken pieces and fruits from sauce, put them in a platter, and keep warm. Then put sauce in a skillet and reduce it on medium-high heat, until it nicely thickens. Then pour it on the chicken pieces.
Serve hot, with bread and salad, or rice of your choice (see chapter 8).

Chicken with Macaroni
(Dijaj bil-Ma'karoni)

(Makes 4 to 6 servings)

We learn from the Babylonian recipes that the ancient Mesopotamians were the first people to make white sauce. They enriched and thickened their meat and bird broths by adding milk, and breadcrumbs (see Introduction for more details). During the medieval times dishes cooked in white sauces, made of milk, yogurt and flour, such as *al-ragheeda* and *al-madheera*, were already part of an inherited long tradition.

Following is a basic chicken and macaroni dish simmered in milk, and enriched with cheese. The list of pasta dishes is rather limited in the Iraqi cuisine of today, and when used, it would most likely be the zittis, those tubular luscious pastas. The following recipe calls for cooked chicken, which makes it very useful for using up chicken or turkey leftovers. The white sauce in which chicken simmers is a basic form of béchamel sauce. To cut down on calories, you may use skim milk, and defatted broth, but please use regular cheese. To give the dish a lovely smoky taste, I sometimes replace cheddar with 3 ounces smoked Gouda cheese, cut into cubes.

1 medium onion, coarsely chopped
2 tablespoons oil
1/2 cup flour
2 cups chicken broth
2 cups milk
3/4 to 1 cup shredded cheddar cheese, about 4 ounces
3/4 teaspoon salt
1/2 teaspoon black pepper
1/4 teaspoon nutmeg

2 cups cooked chicken shredded into chunks with the fingers (remove skin and bones
8 ounces (about 2 cups) uncooked macaroni (such as zitis or elbow), cooked al dente
according to package directions and drained.

Preheat oven to 400 degrees F.

1. In a heavy medium pot (do not use non-stick because you do not want it to scratch) sauté onion in oil until transparent, about 3 minutes.

2. Add flour and stir until fragrant and slightly browned, about 5 minutes.

3. Carefully add broth (it will splatter) and stir with a wire whisk to prevent lumps from forming. Add milk and cheese and stir mixing well. Let sauce cook gently over medium heat until of medium consistency, stirring occasionally, about 10 minutes. Put away from heat.

4. Add salt, black pepper, nutmeg, shredded cooked chicken and cooked macaroni. Mix well.

5. Grease 11 1/2 -by-7 1/2-inch baking dish (or approximate size) and spread chicken mixture.

6. Bake in a preheated oven at 400 degrees F., uncovered, for about 30 minutes, or until sauce is thickened and top is crispy and golden brown. Serve as a main dish with lots of salad.

Note: To make this dish from scratch could leave you with a mountain of pots to wash. To avoid this, what I usually do is simmer chicken pieces in a medium heavy pot, then take out cooked chicken pieces, and cook pasta in the broth. When pasta is cooked, I strain it and reserve the remaining broth for cooking the sauce. The same pot, no need to wash it, can be used to prepare the sauce.

Chicken and Spinach Delights
(Dijaj bil-Sbenagh)

(Makes 6 servings)

This is a light and tasty way for preparing chicken breasts. The combination of spinach, olives and cheese is a delight to the palate as well as the eyes.

3 boneless and skinless chicken breasts, about 2 1/2 pounds. Divide each piece into 2 portions,
For marinade:
> **2 tablespoons honey**
> **1/4 cup orange juice**
> **1/2 teaspoon nutmeg**
> **1/2 teaspoon cumin**
> **1 teaspoon coriander**
> **1/4 teaspoon ginger**
>
> **2 tablespoons olive oil**
> **2 medium onions, thinly sliced**
> **2 packages 10-ounce frozen spinach, thaw according to package directions, squeeze out extra moisture**
> **1/2 cup grated Romano cheese**
> **1/2 cup sliced olives, stones removed**
> **2 tomatoes, sliced**
> **1/2 cup shredded mozzarella cheese**

Preheat oven to 400 degrees F.

1. Pound each piece of chicken with a mallet, flattening as much as possible. If pieces are too thick to begin with, first butterfly them, then pound them.

2. Combine marinade ingredients in a big bowl. Add flattened chicken pieces and let them be coated with the marinade. Set aside for 2 hours at room temperature, or refrigerate overnight, but bring to room temperature before using.

3. Take chicken pieces out of marinade and let drain a little. Discard marinade.

4. Heat oil in a big non-stick skillet. Brown chicken pieces on both sides keeping pieces flat by pressing with a spatula (this will help them lay flat while baking in the oven). The chicken will brown quickly because of the sweet marinade. Turn over as soon as bottom side is browned, they do not need to be fully cooked.

5. In the remaining oil and liquid, sauté onion slices until they brown and start to caramelize, about 10 minutes.

6. Arrange browned chicken pieces flat and in one layer in a baking pan, leaving a little space between pieces. Divide spinach among the 6 chicken pieces, covering the entire surface of each piece with it. Then sprinkle onion slices on the spinach.

7. Sprinkle each portion with Romano cheese and sliced olives. Arrange about 2 to 3 slices of tomato on each piece.

8. Loosely cover with aluminum foil, and bake in a preheated oven at 400 degrees F. for about 35 minutes, or until chicken is tender and some liquid is released. Remove foil and sprinkle mozzarella cheese on each portion. Broil for about 5 minutes, or until cheese is bubbly and browned in patches.

Delicious with rice or warm bread and salad.

CHAPTER THIRTEEN
FISH

A detail from the Standard of Ur, ca 2000 BC

CHAPTER THIRTEEN

FISH

(SAMAK)

سمَكٌ

Around a hundred different types of fish were mentioned in Sumerian texts, thirty of which were tentatively identified. In a Sumerian amusing poem a devout lover of fish addresses his beloved fish in the following manner:

My fish I have built a house for you, I have built a granary for you,
In the house there is food, food of top quality,
In the house there is drink, drink of well being,
In your house, no flies swarm about the liquor bar,
The house smells sweet like a forest of sweet-smelling cedar,
By the house I have placed beer, I have placed fine-quality beer,
    I have placed there honey-beer and sweet cookies.
    (Kramer, *History Begins at Sumer*, 348-9)
Some interpret the poem as an attempt of a fisherman to lure the fish to his bait or net.

In the third millenium BC, full use was made of this natural resource. It was salted and dried, a method that is still in use nowadays in the marshes of the south. The marsh dwellers call it *gbab*, and they normally desalt it and cook it with rice, in a dish they call *masmouta*. Fish also was smoked, as well as consumed fresh. The roes were preserved separately and eaten as a delicacy. They were the caviars of the Sumerians. Out of fish they made fermented sauce for both kitchen and table use similar to the oriental fish sauce. Some archaeologists even suggest that fish was a popular "carry out" food in the narrow winding streets of cities like Ur, where vendors with stalls offered fried fish with onions and cucumbers to hungry diners (Roux, 182).

During the Sumerian times fish was an important source of food and fishing was considered a respectable profession, for fishermen were well attested as temple servants. In their records there were freshwater fishermen and saltwater fishermen. Different methods for catching fish were mentioned, such as using harpoons, nets, and wires. The way big fishes were carried by those fishermen, as evident from existing bas-reliefs, seals and other artifacts, was to let them hang from a cord threaded through their gills. In one of these bas-reliefs a temple attendant is portrayed as carrying a big vessel in one hand, and two fishes threaded through their gills, in the other. Amulets in the shape of two fishes strung together were found at Uruk (Buren, 106). To the modern Mesopotamians, carrying large fishes in this manner is a very common sight along the banks of the rivers Tigris and Euphrates.

Allusions to fish were made, as well, in the Sumerian hymns and incantations. A hymn in praise of the goddess Ishtar of Uruk associates the goddess with fish. It joyfully proclaims that as a result of

381

Ishtar's favor prosperity and plenitude gladdened the land, and the channels were filled with fish. They swarm with fish as if with dates. Another hymn describes a festival in honor of Ishtar: the table was laden with butter, milk, dates, cheese, and seven fishes. The number seven was not probably a specification of quantity as much as a magical number to suit the religious rite (Buren, 112).

However, during the second half of the reign of Hammurabi, mention of fish, more or less, disappeared from texts, and the word "fishermen" in the Neo-Babylonian era was synonymous with "lawless people". One of the reasons could be that people escaping justice at the time used to find refuge in the southern marshes, the homeland of fishermen. This was by no means an indication that people stopped consuming fish. Herodotus, for instance in his relation of his visit to Babylon (Book I, lines 200 ff.) mentions that there were tribes in Babylonia who ate nothing but fish.

Fish from the river Tigris was highly valued by the medieval Baghdadis because they believed that the best fish came from running cold water sources, with stony riverbeds. Euphrates followed in excellence. Top quality fishes were *shabout* (carp)*, bunni,* and *zajar* (now called *dhakar*), fishes with which we are still familiar.

The preferred medieval method for cooking the fish was frying, because they believed it was easier on the digestion, and alleviated its harmful effects. Fried fish was prepared by sprinkling it with flour and salt and frying it in sesame oil. Sour based sauces and dips (*sibagh*) were always offered with the fish to further aid the digestion. Vinegar was the basic ingredient used in most of these sauces to which might be added garlic, onion, mint, parsley, mustard, caraway, thyme, raisins, walnuts, almonds coriander, pomegranate seeds, or sumac.

Fish was preserved for a few days the *mamqur* way, by poaching it in wine and then keeping it in wine vinegar. A specialty of the ninth century AD Aabbasid caliph Al-Mahdi was to put a live fish in a big container full of juice of red grapes, and let the fish swim and drink of this juice until the liquid noticeably decreases. Then the fish is taken out of the juice, cleaned and baked, and served with sauce (*sibagh*) made from wine vinegar, parsley, mint and caraway (al-Warraq, 80) Fish tongues were a treat. Hundreds of them would be cooked to make a dish fit for a caliph.

The main source for shrimp has always been the gulf in southern Iraq. The port city of Basrah is its sole distributor. Interestingly, the tenth-century Baghdadi cookbook includes around six interesting shrimp recipes. It was chopped with onion and used along with spices as a filling for *sanboosa.* It was cooked, then drizzled with oil and sprinkled with sumac, and was browned with onion and spices, with vegetables. In the recipes it was called *roubyan,* as it is still called to this day (al-Warraq, 122-3)

Of the commercially important fishes that are still swimming in the two rivers the medieval favorites still hold their ground, especially the *shabout* (carp). The British called it "the salmon of the Tigris" for, apparently, besides their delicious flavor, both swim against the current. There are the *bunni* and *gittan.* There is also the huge "the monster of Tigris," *biz,* found in the river Tigris only. In English it is sometimes called "the fish of Tobias." There is the *mangout* (the spotted), the counterpart of the trout, the *mizlaaj* (sole), and the less popular scavenger fish *Jurri* (catfish).

The southern marshes are famous for their *subour* (shad). It is a medium-sized fish, very flavorful, but unfortunately infested with sharp tiny bones. That's probably why in the first place it was called *subour* (patience). As an attempt to understand why such delicious fish has that many bones, folklore has it that when God created the *subour,* they wanted to be distinguished from other kinds of fish so they mediated to the Prophet's cousin Ali. God granted them their request; He gave them a necklace of bones. The gulf itself provides the region with shrimps, and round flat fishes with cute little faces and significantly fewer bones, known as *Zubeidi* (pomfret).

Is it Done?

Cooking time given in the following recipes is approximate, depending on the size and thickness of the cuts. As a general rule fish cooks faster than other kinds of meat, so there is always the danger it might overcook, which results in dry, and sometimes stringy or rubbery texture. To test for doneness, there is the rule that fish is cooked if it flakes when you probe it with a fork. However, this might prove to be a little late sometimes. So to be on the safe side the best way is to gently insert a pointed knife in the thickest area of the fish piece. If the knife slides all the way down without resistance, the fish is done, which might be a little less than 10 minutes, depending on the thickness of the cut. If you feel some resistance, let it cook for a little bit longer, and test again.

A detail from the Standard of Ur, ca 2000BC

383

Fishing by Hafidh al-Doroubi, iraqiart.com

Barbecued Fish
(Samak Masgouf)

One of the most popular ways for preparing fish, especially in Baghdad, is by grilling it the *masgouf* way, a method that in all probability goes back to the times of ancient Mesopotamia. In some ancient Sumerian texts, fish was described as being "touched by fire", and "placed upon the fire", which possibly means placed on the glowing coals. The *masgouf*, as we shall see is cooked in two stages, first it is touched or licked by fire, and then it is placed on the fire. In the Mesopotamia of modern times, *masgouf* is basically a picnic treat that requires a certain skill. In the summertime, particularly on moonlit nights, picnickers make a huge campfire along the banks of the Tigris, or on the many small islands, known as *jazra*. Those small islands spring out into existence when the Tigris' level drops down. The *masgouf* may also be ordered at the open-air restaurants along the river Tigris. In the summertime, the sight and the taste of the *masgouf* has never failed to fascinate foreign visitors to the area. In the amusing memoirs of two American twin sisters, who visited Iraq in the late thirties, the *masgouf* is given exceptional significance. "No wonder," they said, "this part of the world had become the cradle of civilization when its inhabitants could think up a dish like this." The twins then go on to describe how they ate it:

> We rolled up our sleeves, and with our fingers we slid the tender meat off the backbone of the fish and scooped it up. It was a dish worthy of an Escoffier. Everyone had a lot of fun except the [British] ambassador. He, too, sat on the ground, but he was wearing a hat and balancing a plate of fish on his knees drawn up in front of him. He ate with a fish knife and fork. Suddenly we looked around and saw that we were the only ones who were eating the *masgouf* in the proper fashion, or the improper fashion, depending on which way you looked at it. We wondered if a hot dog would also be honored with knife and fork under these circumstances. We were afraid we would never achieve that admirable ability of the British to translate into their own terms everything that came their way.

(Heffman, 57-62)

Another American guest, visiting the region in the late sixties, describes the *masgouf* as prepared at one of the *casinos* (outdoor cafes) at *Abu-Nuwas* Street, a promenade along the river Tigris:

> The best food in Baghdad is *masgouf*, fish barbecued beside the Tigris and eaten outdoors along the riverside… With our host and hostess we looked into several fish stalls and chose a live *shabout* (a popular kind of fish)… It was split and cleaned, seasoned with rock salt and paprika, and placed beside the fire with nine or ten others, all impaled on sticks arranged in a circle around the crackling twigs. The cook used a long stick to push the burning wood toward one fish or another as the breeze shifted the flames.
> It takes an hour for the fish to cook… At last the *shabout* was brought on a large, oval plate, garnished with tomato slices and wedges of raw onion and accompanied by several loaves of Arab bread. "You must eat the fish with your hands," said our hostess, "so you can feel the bones." But I remembered a better explanation of the custom: "Eating with knife and fork is like making love through an interpreter." We all tore off pieces of bread, searched out succulent morsels of *shabout* and ate, alternating mouthfuls of fish with bites of tomato or onion. (Nickles, 110)

Well, they left very little for me to say, except that I should admit that they are justified in all the fuss they made about eating the fish with the fingers. The region's fresh fish has a lot of tiny bones, as

385

sharp as pins, and can only be felt with the fingers. It is to be regretted, however, that nowadays, fish is not readily available or even affordable as it used to be in the good old days. Unfortunately, too, much use and abuse have drained the two rivers of such a nutritious natural resource, and a dish like *masgouf* might well be beyond the means of many pockets.

How to Prepare the Masgouf

The keyword to *masgouf* is freshness. Traditionally, the fish is slaughtered only when fire is ready for barbecuing. In the outdoor cafes they are either kept alive in large basins, or tied with a cord through their gills and kept in the river water until ready to cook. People choose their fish the way lobsters are chosen in restaurants and supermarkets.
Here is how to prepare it:

1. Fresh fish is cut lengthwise **from the back** all the way down without removing or breaking the backbone. The fish is then butterflied, cleaned, washed and sprinkled with coarse salt and black pepper. Two 1-inch-wide slashes are made on the outer skin of the side that has the backbone, for it is heavier than the other side. The fish is going to be hanged on two stakes; therefore, those two slashes should be so spaced that the fish stays open and balanced while cooking without falling.

2. Big fire is made from brush wood and date palm leaves that will give fish that distinguished delicious smoky taste. Around the fire, sticks are then stuck in the sand about one foot away from the flames, two sticks for each fish, or one forked stick, and the distance between them should be the same distance between the two slashes made on each fish.

3. The fish is then hung on these two sticks by inserting their pointed tips into the prepared slashes on the back of the fish between the skin and the flesh. The inside of the fish is to face the flames with the whole fish a little curved so as to receive as much heat as possible. Because the fish needs to be "licked" by the fire, so to speak, the inside of the fish is to face the blowing wind.

4. It takes about an hour for the fish to cook. During the last 10 minutes of cooking, the fish is laid down on its back right on top of the ashes and embers that are raked together.

5. The fish is then put on a big tray, garnished with slices of tomatoes and onion. Sometimes it is topped with a prepared sauce consisting mostly of chopped parsley, tomatoes, onions and garlic, with tamarind sauce and curry powder. *Masgouf* is usually eaten with bread, especially the Iraqi flat breads, and accompanied with pickled mango, as a relish.

Fish Bones

"My husband heaps up (grain) for me, my son metes it out for me--Would that my darling husband would pick the bones from the fish (for me)"
(A Sumerian proverb)

The speaker is a Sumerian woman who had it all, but still pines for the times when her husband used to do those personal, caring, little things for her, perhaps during their honeymoon. Nowadays, such a woman might win our sympathy, but the Sumerians meant this to be a sarcastic comment on unreasonable selfishness (Gordon, 465-6).

Grilled Fish

(Samak Mashwi)

When cooked at home, the *tannour* (clay domed oven) was traditionally used for barbecuing the whole butterflied, fish with skin on to prevent fish from getting dry while cooking. The fish would be put flat in a long-handled hinged fish grill, and put vertically in the *tannour* to cook slowly in the smoldering coals. However, for the less romantic, here is a more practical method for enjoying grilled fish:

1 whole medium-sized fish, butterflied or a fillet, in either case leave skin on to keep fish from drying out
For marinade:
1 onion, grated
2 cloves garlic, grated
1 teaspoon cumin
1 teaspoon coriander
1/4 cup lemon juice

Salt and black pepper for sprinkling

1. Mix marinade ingredients and rub with it the prepared fish on both sides. Set aside for 30 minutes at room temperature.

2. Put the fish flat open in an oiled hinged fish grill. Sprinkle salt and pepper on both sides Grill on medium-high heat, skin down. When skin starts to brown, baste surface with any leftover marinade, or oil, and turn the fish to allow it to brown on the other side. Time greatly depends upon the size and thickness of fish, but avoid overcooking it. If meat flakes easily when probed with a fork, it is done.
Remove fish from hinges, sprinkle it with sumac (see Glossary) if liked, or squeeze lemon juice all over the surface. Serve with bread, salad, and pickled mango.

Baked Fish Stuffed with Sumac Mix
(Samak Mashwi bil-Summaq)

(Makes 4 servings)

This recipe is adapted from the thirteenth-century Baghdadi cookbook. Originally fish is to be baked in the *tannour,* but the regular oven will do the job just fine. Although the recipe calls for a whole fish, which would be a nice thing to have, I sometimes use the whole tail part of a medium to big salmon, slash the skin and fill it and tie it the way I normally do with a whole fish.

> **2 1/2 to 3 pounds whole fish such as a small salmon or 2 big trouts, butterflied. Keep skin and make 2 to 3 diagonal slashes on the outer skin on both sides**
> **2 tablespoons oil**
> **1/2 teaspoon turmeric**

For the stuffing:
> **1/2 cup sumac, see Glossary**
> **1/4 cup za'atar or thyme, see Glossary**
> **1/2 teaspoon coriander, cumin, cinnamon, each, optional**
> **4 cloves garlic, grated**
> **1/2 cup toasted walnut, chopped**
> **2 tablespoons oil**
> **1/2 teaspoon salt**
> **About 3 tablespoons water**
> **Preheat oven to 450 degrees F.**

1. Rub fish with oil and turmeric inside and out.

2. Mix stuffing ingredients, it should have a paste-like consistency. Add a little water if needed. Fill the inside of the fish with it. Secure the fish closed with a kitchen thread, or wooden picks.

3. Put in a greased baking sheet and bake in a preheated oven at 450 degrees F. for about 20 minutes, or until flesh is flaky when poked with a fork, and skin is nicely browned. (Cooking time depends on how thick and big the fish is)

Fish Fillet on Sea of Amber Rice
(Samak bil Timman al-Asfar)

(Makes 4 servings)

This is a beautiful dish-- the fish with its crispy topping is surrounded with golden yellow rice decked with browned noodles, raisins, and toasted slivered almonds. The whole combination is extremely aromatic, and on top of all this, it can be done in only **30 minutes**. Traditionally fish is always served with yellow rice partly for aesthetic reasons and partly for a very practical purpose. Because the domestic fish comes with lots of bones, some of which are as tiny and prickly as thorns, it will be easier to see the bones if the rice is yellow rather than white. Some people like to serve fish with rice cooked with lentils, which also serves the same purpose. In the recipe below the less expensive turmeric is used to color the rice, but if saffron is available, by all means use it. In this case use 1/4 teaspoon saffron, steep it in 3 tablespoons hot water for about 5 minutes, then add it in step 1, when you add water to the rice. In this case omit turmeric.

For the rice:

>**1 tablespoon oil**
>**1/2 cup broken vermicelli noodles (2 balls)**
>**1/2 teaspoon turmeric**
>**2 cups rice, washed and soaked in cold water for 30 minutes, drained**
>**3 1/2 cups hot water**
>**1 1/2 teaspoon salt**
>**3/4 teaspoon ground cardamom**
>**3/4 teaspoon cinnamon**
>
>**2 pounds salmon fillet, skinned**
>**A dash, each, of salt and pepper, flour, and a little lemon juice or sumac for rubbing the fish**

For the fish topping:

>**1 tablespoon oil**
>**1 medium onion, coarsely chopped**
>**1/2 teaspoon turmeric**
>**1 teaspoon curry powder**
>**2 cloves garlic, grated**
>**1 to 2 medium tomato, chopped**
>**1/2 cup tomato sauce, optional**
>**1/2 to 1 teaspoon tamarind concentrate or *noomi Basra*, see Glossary. If not available substitute with 1 tablespoon Worcestershire sauce**
>**1/2 teaspoon cumin**
>**1/2 teaspoon coriander**
>**1 teaspoon salt**
>**1/4 teaspoon black pepper**

For garnish:

>**1 teaspoon oil**
>**1/4 cup slivered almonds**
>**1/4 cup raisins**
>**1/4 cup parsley, chopped**
>**Preheat oven to 450 degrees F.**

389

1. To cook rice, put oil and noodles in a medium heavy pot and stir on high heat until noodles are browned. Stir in turmeric when noodles start to brown. (Total time for browning noodles, a few minutes) Add drained rice, hot water, salt, cardamom, and cinnamon. Let boil on high heat for 5 minutes. Lower heat to low and let rice simmer, covered, for 20 minutes. Fold rice gently 2 to 3 times while simmering to allow it to fluff.

2. Rub the fish fillet with salt, pepper, flour and lemon juice or sumac, and set aside for about 10 minutes. Then lay it flat on a greased baking dish, skin side down. Spray or brush lightly with some oil. Bake in a preheated oven at 450 degrees F. (Total cooking time around 10 minutes, or until it is flaky when poked with a fork. Do not overcook fish.)

3. While rice is simmering, and fish is baking in the oven, prepare the topping. In a medium skillet heat oil and sauté onion with turmeric and curry powder, until onion is transparent, about 5 minutes (add turmeric and curry powder the last minute of cooking the onion to avoid burning the spices). Add the rest of topping ingredients and let cook for about five minutes or until sauce is thickened. Spread topping on the baking fish fillet about 5 minutes before fish is done. To crisp the topping, broil it for a few minutes.

4. In a small heavy pot brown slivered almonds in oil, stirring constantly, a few minutes. Stir in raisins about a minute before almonds are done.

To serve, carefully transfer the fish fillet, in one piece, to a big oval platter, surround it with the cooked yellow rice, sprinkle almond-raisin mixture over the rice, and sprinkle chopped parsley over the dish.

Fried Fish á la Haroun al-Rasheed

(Makes 4 servings)

In an *Arabian Nights* story the Abbasid Caliph of Baghdad, Haroun al-Rasheed, disguises as a fisherman for his amusement. He catches fish, and volunteers to fry it himself for two young lovers in an orchard. For seasoning he used salt, saffron, wild marjoram and cumin. When fish was fried, he put it on a banana leaf, and gathered from the garden wind-fallen fruits, limes and lemons. (From the story of "Nur al-Din Ali and the Damsel Anees al-Jalees", vol. 2, 33). This was how the medieval eaters preferred to have their fish, for they thought frying was lighter on the digestion. In books of professional cooks, such as al-Warraq's, fish was first lightly coated with flour and salt before frying, which was probably done to prevent the oil from spattering while fish is frying. We still fry our fish almost the same old way. He is how we do it:

1. Coat 4 serving-size skinned fish pieces with a mixture of:
    1 teaspoon salt
    1 teaspoon curry powder
    1 teaspoon cumin
    1/4 cup flour
    1/4 teaspoon paprika, for color and flavor, optional

(This mixture will help give fish pieces a protective and aromatic coating)

2. Fry coated fish pieces in hot 1/2-inch deep oil, turning once until golden on both sides. While frying help keep pieces flat by putting a wieght or using a hamburger flipper. Total cooking time 5 to 10 minutes, depending on how thick fish is.

To avoid frying, coat fish pieces with the suggested mixture above, brush or spray the pieces with oil, and bake in a hot oven, about 450 degrees F. until meat is flaky, and coating is golden brown, around 10 minutes, depending on how thick fish pieces are (avoid overcooking fish).

To serve sprinkle with some sumac, see Glossary, or squeeze some lemon juice.

Suggestion:

When oven frying, I sometimes add about 2 tablespoons of sesame seeds to the flour mixture, Coat the fish with this mixture, and press it with the hand to help the seeds adhere to the fish. The seeds will toast while baking, and give the fish a very appetizing aroma.

Browned Fish with Tahini Sauce
(Samak bil Rashi)

(Makes 4 servings)

I found this delicious recipe in the thirteenth-century Baghdadi cookbook, it was called *Samak Maqli bi-Khal wa-Rashi (*fish fried with vinegar and tahini), and here is the original recipe:

> Take salted fish, wash thoroughly in water, then dry, and fry in sesame oil. Put into the frying pan a good handful of whole dry coriander. Now take good vinegar as required, pour on top of the sesame meal, and knead by hand, adding the vinegar little by little until the required consistency is obtained, not too light and not too heavy. If desired, some fine-ground mustard may be added, but this is not necessary. Take the salt-fish out of the frying pan hot, put on top of the meal, and then pour over it the sesame oil remaining in the frying pan, together with the coriander. Sprinkle with fine-ground cumin, coriander and cinnamon, and also walnuts. It may be eaten either hot or cold (Arberry, 203-4)

The quantities suggested below are my improvisation.

4 serving-size fish fillets, skin removed, salmon or any white fish will do, coated and pan-fried or oven-fried as suggested above in Fried Fish à la Haroun al-Rasheed

1 tablespoon whole coriander seeds, or to taste
1/3 cup tahini
2 tablespoons vinegar
1 tablespoon prepared mustard
A dash of salt
About 1/4 cup cold water
1 clove of garlic, grated, optional
1/4 cup toasted walnuts, broken into small pieces

A dash of cinnamon and cumin, optional

1. Fry coriander seeds in a little oil, and drain.

2. Mix tahini, vinegar, mustard, salt, water, and garlic if used, and to make a sauce of spreading consistency. Add a little more water if needed.

3. Spread tahini sauce on the serving plate. Arrange fish pieces on the sauce. Sprinkle coriander seeds on the fish and garnish with toasted chopped walnut and a sprinkle of cumin and cinnamon, if wished.

Baked Fish with Yellow Rice and Raisin Sauce (Samak bil Timman wal Kishmish)

(Makes 4 servings)

This is another delicious and aromatic fish dish that can be prepared in about **30 minutes**. Traditionally saffron is used to add this attractive golden hue to the rice, but in the following recipe the less expensive and more readily available turmeric is used. If you want to use saffron steep 1/4 teaspoon in 3 tablespoons of hot water for 5 minutes, then add it to the rice when you add water in step 2, in this case omit the turmeric.

> **2 pounds salmon fillet, with or without skin, or 2 medium trouts, butterflied, keep skin on**
> **1 teaspoon curry powder**
> **1 teaspoon cumin**
> **1 tablespoon flour**
> **1/2 tablespoon salt**
> **1/4 tablespoon black pepper**

For the rice:
> **1 tablespoon oil**
> **1/2 teaspoon turmeric**
> **2 cups rice, washed, soaked in cold water for 30 minutes, drained**
> **3 1/2 cups hot water**
> **1/2 teaspoon cinnamon**
> **3 to 4 pods cardamom**
> **1 teaspoon salt**

For the raisin sauce:
> **1 teaspoon oil**
> **1 medium onion, coarsely chopped**
> **1/2 teaspoon turmeric**
> **1 teaspoon curry powder**
> **1 tablespoon tomato paste, or 1 tablespoon flour**
> **1 medium tomato, diced, optional**
> **3/4 cup water**
> **3/4 cup currants or raisins**

1 teaspoons prepared *noomi Basra*, see Glossary
1 teaspoon *baharat*, optional, see Glossary
1/2 teaspoon salt

Preheat oven to 450 degrees F.

1. Rub fish with a mixture of curry powder, cumin, flour, salt and pepper. On a greased baking sheet place fish flat, skin side down, and if a whole fish is used open it up, skin side down. Spray or brush surface with oil and bake in a preheated oven at 450 degrees F., until fish is flaky when probed with a fork, and surface is crispy, about 10 minutes. Avoid overcooking the fish.

2. While fish is baking, prepare the rice. In a medium heavy pot put oil and turmeric and stir for a few seconds until turmeric is aromatic. Add the rest of ingredients, and let boil for 5 minutes, on high heat. Reduce heat to low, and let rice simmer, covered, for 20 minutes. Fold rice 2 to 3 times while simmering to allow it to fluff.

3. Meanwhile prepare raisin sauce. In a small heavy pot sauté onion until transparent, about 5 minutes. Stir in turmeric, curry powder and tomato paste or flour, and stir for a few moments, until fragrant. Add the rest of ingredients, and let simmer on low heat about 10 minutes or until sauce thickens.

To serve, put baked fish in a big oval platter, and surround it with yellow rice. Drizzle fish and rice with raisin sauce.

Layered Fish
(Mutabbag Samak)

(Makes 4 servings)

This is a traditional dish that calls for fried pieces of fish attractively layered with rice and raisins. To give it a light touch you can oven fry the fish.

1 1/2 pounds white fish fillet or salmon, skin removed, and cut crosswise into 8 pieces
1 teaspoon curry powder
1 teaspoon cumin
1 tablespoon flour
1/2 teaspoon salt
1/4 teaspoon black pepper
For the rice:
2 cups rice, washed, soaked in cold water for 30 minutes, drained
1 tablespoon oil
3 1/2 cups hot water
1 teaspoon salt
1/2 teaspoon cinnamon, optional
For the raisin mixture:
1 medium onion, coarsely chopped
1/2 teaspoon turmeric

1/2 teaspoon curry powder
1 tablespoon oil
3/4 cup golden raisins, or any other kind of raisins or dried fruits
1/4 cup slivered and toasted almonds
1 teaspoon prepared *noomi Basrah*, see Glossary
1/2 cup parsley, chopped

1. Coat **fish** pieces with a mixture of curry powder, cumin, flour, salt, and pepper. Fry fish pieces until crisp, or brush or spray them with oil, and bake them in a hot oven, 450 degrees F, until crisp and flaky, about 10 minutes. Avoid overcooking the fish.

2. Prepare **rice**: In a medium heavy pot, put all the rice ingredients, and let them boil for 5 minutes on high heat. Lower heat to low and let it simmer for 20 minutes. Fold rice gently 2 to 3 times while simmering to allow it to fluff.

3. Prepare **raisin mixture**: In a medium skillet, heat oil and sauté onion with turmeric and curry powder, until onion is transparent, about 5 minutes. Add raisins, almonds, and *noomi Basrah* and about 1/4 cup water. Stir for a few minutes until most of moisture evaporates. Do not let mixture get dry. Put away from heat and fold in parsley.

4. To assemble the dish: empty cooked rice into a bowl. Using the same rice pot, put about a third of cooked rice as a bottom layer. Arrange half the fish pieces on rice, and spread half raisin mixture on fish. Repeat layering of rice, fish and raisins. Top with the remaining third of rice. Return pot to stove and let it simmer on low heat for about 15 minutes to allow a crunchy crust to form in the bottom of the pot. A non-stick pot will make the task of unmolding the rice much easier.

To serve, unmold the layered rice by putting a big platter on the pot, and holding both with both hands, turn pot upside down. For more casual occasions just carefully spoon out the layered rice with fish and raisins into the serving dish.
Serve with lots of salad.

Note:

Instead of boneless and skinless fish fillets, fish with bones and skin can be substituted. Just sprinkle it with salt and pepper and then poach it or enclose it in a pocket of aluminum foil and bake it in a hot oven, about 10 minutes or until flaky when probed with a fork. When cool enough to handle discard skin and bones, and break fish into big chunks and layer with the rice and raisin mixture as directed in step 4.

Besides, drained liquids from preparing fish this way can be used as flavorful broth in either cooking the rice or raisin mixture or both.

Fish Baked in Tamarind Sauce
(Samak Mashwi bi'l Tamur-Hindi)

(Makes 4 servings)

This is an easy and fast dish, but you'll be amazed at how tasty the tamarind will make the fish. Obviously we do not believe that fish and tamarind do not get along well in the stomach, unlike the Egyptians who believe that combining *samak, laban, tamrihindi* (fish, milk, tamarind) is the epitome of incongruity.

1 1/2 pounds fish fillet, skinned and sliced crosswise into 4 serving size pieces.
Salt and pepper for sprinkling on the fish

2 tablespoons olive oil, divided
1 medium onion, coarsely chopped
2 cloves garlic, grated
1/2 teaspoon curry powder
2 medium tomatoes, diced
1/4 cup parsley, chopped
1 scant tablespoon tamarind concentrate
1/2 teaspoon salt
1/2 teaspoon chili pepper, or to taste
1/4 teaspoon black pepper
2 tomatoes, thinly sliced, or 1/2 red bell pepper thinly sliced

Preheat oven to 450 degrees F.

1. Sprinkle fish pieces with salt and pepper and set aside.

2. In a medium skillet heat 1 tablespoon oil and sauté onion, until onion is transparent, about 5 minutes. Stir in garlic and curry powder a minute before onion is done. Add diced tomatoes, parsley, tamarind concentrate, and salt. Mix well.

3. Spread half of the mixture in the bottom of an ovenproof glass-baking dish. Arrange fish pieces in one layer on top of it. Spread the remaining mixture on the fish. Arrange tomato or pepper slices on top.

4. Drizzle with 1 tablespoon oil, and bake uncovered in a preheated oven at 450 degrees F., for about 10 minutes, or until fish is flaky when probed with a fork. Broil the top for a few minutes to let tomatoes brown a little. Avoid overcooking the fish.
    Serve with rice or warm bread, with lots of salad.

Fish Baked in Pomegranate Sauce
(Samak bi Sharab al-Rumman)

(Makes 4 servings)

Pomegranate and walnuts combine in this recipe to give sauce a rich, medieval texture.

1 1/2 pounds fish fillet, skinned and divided into 4 serving size pieces
1/2 teaspoon cumin
1/4 teaspoon black pepper
1/2 teaspoon salt
2 tablespoons olive oil, divided

1 medium onion, coarsely chopped
1/2 teaspoon crushed chili pepper, or to taste
1/2 teaspoon coriander

1 scant tablespoon pomegranate syrup, diluted in 2/3 cup water
1/2 cup walnut halves, toasted and ground
1/2 teaspoon salt

For garnish: 1/4 cup parsley, chopped
Preheat oven to 450 degrees F.

1. Rub fish pieces with cumin, black pepper, and salt. Quickly brown pieces on both sides, in 1 tablespoon oil, about 5 minutes (they don't have to be fully cooked). Take out of skillet, and keep warm

2. Add 1 tablespoon oil to the skillet, and sauté onion until transparent, about 5 minutes. Fold in chili pepper and coriander.

3. Spread half the onion mixture in the bottom of an ovenproof glass baking dish. Arrange fish pieces on top. Spread the remaining onion mixture on the fish.

4. In a small pot, put diluted pomegranate syrup, walnuts and salt. Bring to a quick boil, a few minutes. Pour it all over the fish and bake in a preheated oven at 450 degrees F. for about 10 minutes, or until fish is flaky when probed with a fork, and sauce is nicely thickened. Avoid over cooking the fish.
   Garnish fish with chopped parsley, and serve with rice and salad.

Fish Stew
(Margat Samak)

(Makes 4 servings)

Cooked in simple tomato sauce, the fish stays deliciously moist and succulent, and potatoes pair very nicely with it. Unfortunately, in its original region, Iraq, it is not a very popular type of stew. The river fish is full of bones, which makes it a rather hazardous dish to cook this way. That's why I have never really had enough of it. But with the availability of boneless fish fillets in the markets here, there is no reason why we should not enjoy it as often as we wish. Here is how to prepare it:

1 1/2 pounds boneless and skinless fish fillet, cut into 4 serving-size pieces
1/2 teaspoon salt
1/4 teaspoon black pepper
2 tablespoons lemon juice

1 medium onion, coarsely chopped
2 tablespoons oil
1/2 teaspoon turmeric
3 medium potatoes, peeled and cut into 1-inch cubes

3 heaping tablespoons tomato paste (6-ounce can), diluted in 4 cups hot water; or 15-ounce can tomato sauce diluted in 3 cups water, or 4 cups tomato juice
1 teaspoon prepared *noomi Basrah*, see Glossary; or 2 tablespoons lime or lemon juice
1 1/2 teaspoon salt
1/4 teaspoon black pepper
1/4 cup coarsely chopped parsley

1.Sprinkle fish pieces with salt, pepper, and lemon juice. Set aside.

2. In a medium heavy pot sauté onion in oil until translucent, for 5 minutes. Add turmeric and potatoes and fold for a few minutes.

3. Add diluted tomato paste or sauce or juice, *noomi Basrah*, salt and pepper. Bring to a quick boil, then reduce heat to medium low, and let simmer for about 20 minutes, or until potatoes are just done.

4. Arrange fish pieces in the bottom of the pot. Bring to a boil, then resume simmering for about 10 minutes, or until fish is done, depending upon the thickness of the fish pieces, but as a rule, cooked fish flakes when probed with a fork. Overcooking the fish will toughen it. Stir in parsley a few minutes before fish is done
Serve with rice and salad.

Fish Curry
(Karı'l-Samak)

(Makes 4 servings)

Curries are cooked whenever we crave something spicier than the regular stew. Being on the crossroads of the spice trade ever since ancient times, the Mesopotamian cuisine has always abounded in aromatic dishes that sometimes tend to be on the hot side, and this is one of them.

1 1/2 pounds boneless and skinless fish, cut into 4 serving-size pieces
1/2 teaspoon salt
1/4 teaspoon black pepper
2 tablespoons oil, divided

1 medium onion, coarsely chopped
2 cloves garlic, grated
1 teaspoon curry powder
1/2 teaspoon turmeric
3 medium potatoes, peeled and cut into 1-inch cubes
2 tablespoons flour

2 cups hot water
1/2 teaspoon ginger
1/4 teaspoon whole mustard seeds, optional
1/4 teaspoon whole aniseed or fennel
1/2 teaspoon cumin
1/2 teaspoon coriander
1 teaspoon tamarind concentrate, see Glossary
1/2 to 1 teaspoon chili powder, or to taste
1 1/2 teaspoon salt
1/4 teaspoon black pepper
1 bay leaf

1. Sprinkle fish pieces with salt and pepper. Heat 1 table spoon oil in a medium non-stick pot and brown fish pieces briefly on both sides to seal them, about 3 to 4 minutes. Transfer to a plate, and set aside.

2. In the same pot, heat 1 tablespoon oil and sauté onion until transparent, about 5 minutes. Add garlic, curry powder, turmeric and cubed potatoes. Stir for additional 3 to 4 minutes. Sprinkle flour and stir to coat the vegetables until fragrant, about 3 minutes.

3. Add the rest of ingredients and bring to a quick boil. Reduce heat to low, and let simmer, covered, for about 20 minutes, or until potatoes are just done.

4. Return fish pieces to the simmering curry, and let them be submerged in the sauce. Simmer for additional 10 minutes, or until fish is flaky when probed with a fork.
Serve with white rice with noodles, or rice of your choice with salad.

Sweet and Sour Salmon Simmered in Almond-Prune Sauce
(Samak bi Salsat al-louz wal-Injas)

(Makes 4 servings)

The following dish is inspired by the medieval Baghdadi cuisine, which had a penchant for combining the sweet and the sour. They also believed, as we still do, that vinegar and other sour agents aid the digestion especially when conjoined with fish. The medieval *sibaghs* were sour sauces to be had with fish, and were made by combining a number of ingredients such as sour pomegranate juice, vinegar, raisins, ground almond or walnut, a little sugar or honey, garlic, mustard, and spices (Al-Warraq, 83-4).

This fish dish is intoxicatingly delicious, and yet unbelievably simple and fast. The fish is briefly broiled first. Then cooking is finished on top of the stove. The sauce is thickened and flavored with an appetizing combination, of prunes, almonds, honey, mustard, pomegranate syrup, and vinegar.

Have a feast in just **30 minutes**-- prepare white rice with noodles while fish is cooking.

1 1/2 pounds salmon fillet, skinned, and boned, and cut into 4 serving-size pieces
1/2 teaspoon salt
1/2 teaspoon black pepper
1 tablespoon prepared mustard, such as Dijon
1/4 cup honey

1/4 cup cider or balsamic vinegar
1 cup water
2 to 3 sprigs fresh thyme, or 1/2 teaspoon dried thyme or *za'tar*, see Glossary
1/2 teaspoon ginger
1/2 teaspoon salt
1/4 cup unskinned almonds (about 28 ones), toasted, and ground
1/2 cup coarsely cut green onion, with the green stalks
12 prunes, whole or halved
1/4 teaspoon crushed chili pepper, or to taste
1 tablespoon pomegranate syrup, see Glossary

Preheat broiler

1. Sprinkle salt and black pepper on fish pieces, and arrange them in one layer in a heavy skillet with ovenproof handles.

2. In a small pot mix honey and mustard, and brush surface of fish pieces with almost half of it.

3. Broil fish in the skillet for about 7 minutes or until surface is golden brown and bubbly. Remove from broiler. Do not turn over fish pieces.

399

4. While fish is broiling prepare sauce: To remaining honey and mustard in the small pot, add vinegar, water, thyme, ginger, salt, ground almonds, onion, prunes, chili pepper, and pomegranate syrup. Mix well, and bring to a quick boil, about 3 minutes.

5. As soon as fish comes out of the broiler, spread sauce on and around the fish, and continue cooking on top of the stove this time, on medium heat. Let fish simmer in the sauce, covered, 7 to 10 minutes, or until sauce is nicely thickened and fish is flaky when probed with a fork.

Serve with white rice with noodles, and salad.

Fish with Eggs
(Samak bil Beidh)

(Makes 4 servings)

As suggested in al-Baghdadi's thirteenth-century cookbook, one of the many ways to prepare *tirrikh* fish (dried and salted) was to fry it, debone it, cut it into bite-size pieces, then cook it with eggs and lots of spices (Arberry, 204-5). The following dish is inspired by such recipes. In our modern kitchens, we can certainly substitute with canned salmon or tuna.

2 cups cooked fish, cut into bite-size pieces; or three 6-ounce cans chunk tuna, drained
1/2 cup breadcrumbs
1 medium onion, diced and sautéed in 1 tablespoon oil
4 eggs, slightly beaten
1 tablespoon vinegar or lemon juice
2 tablespoons tahini
1/2 cup chopped parsley
1/4 cup olives, stoned and sliced
1/2 teaspoon salt
1/4 teaspoon black pepper
1/2 teaspoon coriander
1/2 teaspoon cumin
2 fresh chili peppers, diced, or 1/2 teaspoon ground chili

Preheat oven to 375 degrees F.

1. In a big bowl mix all ingredients, taking care not to crush fish. Put a little of the breadcrumbs aside for lining the pan.

2. Grease 8-by-8-inch baking dish. Sprinkle lightly with some breadcrumbs. Spread fish mixture, and bake in a preheated oven at 375 degrees F. for about 35 minutes, or until dish is set and surface is golden brown. Let set in pan for 10 minutes before cutting into squares.

Serve with warm bread and salad.

Shrimp with Rice
(Timman Roubyan)

(Makes 4 servings)

The southern port of Basrah has been the main source for shrimps. When the season is plenty, it is usually transported to other inland cities such as Baghdad where these moustached creatures, quite often than not, end up being cooked with rice, or made into a delicious curry. However, the problem with shrimps, especially the frozen variety, is that they tend to release some moisture that will sometimes spoil the texture of the dish, or if left to cook until all moisture evaporates, the shrimps themselves will overcook, get stringy in texture and shrink considerably. In the following rice recipe I have managed to avoid this by cooking shrimps separately until just done.

2 cups rice, washed, soaked in cold water for 30 minutes, drained
3 1/2 cups cold water
1 tablespoon oil
1 1/2 teaspoon salt

For the shrimp mixture:
2 tablespoons oil, divided
1 pound medium-sized shrimps, cleaned and deveined

1 medium onion, coarsely chopped
1/2 teaspoon turmeric
1 teaspoon curry powder
1 teaspoon prepared *noomi Basrah*, see Glossary
1 teaspoon salt
1/4 teaspoon black pepper
1 teaspoon *baharat*, see Glossary
One 10-ounce package frozen chopped spinach, thawed according to package directions, optional

1/2 cup parsley, coarsely chopped

1. In a medium heavy pot, preferably non-stick, put drained rice, water, oil, and salt. Bring to a quick boil, and on high heat let cook for 5 minutes, uncovered. Reduce heat to low and let rice simmer, covered, for 20 minutes. While simmering gently fold rice 2 or 3 times to allow it to expand and fluff.

2. While rice is simmering cook shrimp mixture. In a big skillet heat 1 tablespoon oil and sauté shrimps until just cooked, 4 to 5 minutes (avoid overcooking them). Take out with slotted spoon and set aside.

3. Add the second tablespoon of oil to skillet and sauté onion until transparent, about 5 minutes. Add turmeric, and curry powder a minute before onion is done. Add *noomi Basrah*, salt, pepper, *baharat*, and spinach if used. Stir for about 5 minutes or until moisture almost evaporates. Away from heat, fold in shrimps and chopped parsley.

4. When rice is done, transfer it to a bowl. Then layer it in the rice pot with the shrimp mixture as follows: Put about fourth of the rice in the bottom of the pot, then cover it with about third of the shrimp mixture, and continue layering. The last layer would be that of rice. Return pot to stove, and allow it to simmer on low heat, tightly covered, for about 5 minutes.

To serve, carefully spoon out the rice using a big spoon, your scoops should include both rice and shrimp mixture. Serve with yogurt and lots of salad.

Shrimp Curry
(Karry al- Roubyan)

(Makes 4 servings)

The following is the Basrawi (from Basrah) version of cooking shrimps the curried way. Basrah, being the only port city in the entire Mesopotamian region, has always been famous for its spicy hot delicious dishes, especially when it comes to fish and shrimps. The shrimp curry is supposed to be smoky-hot and highly aromatic, but feel free to adjust the quantities of spices to suit your palate.

> **2 tablespoons oil**
> **1 medium onion, coarsely chopped**
> **2 cloves garlic, grated**
> **1 teaspoon curry powder**
> **1/2 teaspoon turmeric**
> **3 medium potatoes peeled and cut into 1-inch cubes**
> **2 tablespoons flour**
>
> **1 teaspoon tamarind concentrate, or 1 teaspoon prepared *noomi Basrah*, see Glossary**
> **2 cups hot water**
> **1/2 teaspoon ginger**
> **1/4 teaspoon whole mustard seeds, optional**
> **1/4 teaspoon whole aniseed, or fennel**
> **1/2 teaspoon coriander**
> **1/2 teaspoon cumin**
> **1/2 to 1 teaspoon chili powder, or to taste**
> **1 teaspoon salt**
> **1/4 teaspoon black pepper**
> **1 bay leaf**
> **1/4 cup coarsely chopped fresh pepper, any variety**
>
> **1 pound shrimp, cleaned and deveined**

1. In a medium heavy pot, heat oil and sauté onion until transparent, about 5 minutes. Add garlic, curry powder and turmeric about a minute before onion is done.

2. Add potato cubes and stir for a few more minutes. Sprinkle flour on vegetables and stir until fragrant, about 3 minutes.

3. Add rest of ingredients except for shrimps and bring to a quick boil. Then reduce heat to medium-low and let cook gently, covered, until sauce is of medium consistency, and potatoes are done, about 15 minutes. Stir 2 to 3 times while cooking to prevent sauce from sticking to the bottom of pot. Add a little more hot water if needed.

4. Add shrimps and cook just until they are done, about 5 minutes (if precooked, just until heated through. Avoid overcooking, otherwise shrimps will be rubbery in texture, and will shrink a lot.
Serve with rice of your choice, and salad.

Sweet and sour salmon simmered in almond-prune sauce, 399

CHAPTER FOURTEEN
SAVORY PASTRIES

CHAPTER FOURTEEN
SAVORY PASTRIES
(al-MAWALIH)

المَوَالِح

There has always been plenty of room on our tables for desserts as well as savory pastries. The fourteenth-century augmented manuscript of al-Baghdadi's cookbook, *Wasf al-At'ima al-Mu'tada* (the description of familiar foods), for instance, includes a recipe of *aqras mumallaha* (salty cookies). The writer comments that, "this is made so that the appetite may incline to the salty taste, rather than the sweet, so it is served among the sweet dishes" (431). Without dispute, the most popular savory snack during the medieval times was *sanbousaj*, those small stuffed pastries made of thin wrappers. The medieval Andalusian cuisine, which was largely influenced by the Eastern style (Abbasid region, the center of which was Baghdad), offered a wider variety of such savory snacks. The meat pies were called *mukhabbaza*, their cheese pies were *mujabbana*. The puff pastry they made was called *muwarraqa* (leafy), or *musammana* (with clarified butter). Today, the *sanbousa*, and *bourag* (filled pastries made of thin layered dough) are the first items that come to mind when we think of serving savory pastries, but there are a lot of other options, as you will see. Usually they are served as side dishes, or as afternoon snacks with hot sweet tea. (There are more savory pastries in chapter 1, on breads)

405

Sanbousa

سُنبُوسَه

(Makes about 40 pieces)

Sanbousa was the queen of snacks during the medieval times. The earliest description of this pastry can be found in a ninth-century poem composed by Ishaq ibn Ibrahim al-Mousili. It is a *sanbousa* recipe in verse as recorded in tenth-century *Murouj al-Dhahab* (meadows of gold) of al-Mas'udi the famous Arab historian. Al-Mousili praises it as the most delicious of *al-ma'kal al-mu'ajjal* (fast food). Following is an excerpt from Arberry's translation of the poem (parenthetical comments are mine):

If thou would know what food gives most delight,
Best let me tell, for none [other than *sanbousa*] hath subtler sight.
Take first the finest meat, red, soft to touch,
And mince it with fat, not overmuch;
Then add an onion, cut in circles clean,
A cabbage [the word in the poem is *kisfara,* cilantro], very fresh, exceeding green,
And season well with cinnamon and rue;
Of coriander add a handful, too,
And after that of cloves the very least,
Of finest ginger, and of pepper best,
A hand of cumin, muri just to taste,
Two handfuls of Palmyra [Tadmur, city in Syria] salt; but haste,
Good master, haste to grind them small and strong.
Then lay and light a blazing fire along;
Put all into the pot, and water pour
Upon it from above, and cover o'er.
But when the water vanished is from sight
And when the burning flames have dried it quite,
Then, as thou wilt, in pastry [*riqaq* = thin sheets of bread dough] wrap it round
And fasten well the edges, firm and sound;
Or, if it please thee better, take some dough,
Conveniently soft, and rubbed just so,
Then with a rolling-pin let it be spread
And with the nails its edges docketed.

The poem goes on describing how the filled pieces are fried, and then arranged in a crystal platter, around a small bowl of sharp mustard (Arberry, 25-6). From another poem we also learn that meat in the filling might be young chicken. In al-Warraq's recipe, an option is given to add dried fruits and nuts. He further suggests eggs can be used for garnish as in parties and feasts (89). There was also the option of using a sweet nut filling, and dipping the pastries in syrup after frying them.

In al-Warraq's chapter on *himadhiyat* and *rummaniyat* (stews soured with citrus and pomegranate), two recipes of *himadhiyya Ibrahimiyya*, called for boiling the meat filled *sanbousaj* pastries that were made from rather stiff, well kneaded dough. When the prepared sour stews were cooked, the *sanbousaj* pastries were carefully dropped into the broth, and were simmered just enough to cook them (156, 7). The fact that al-Warraq gives two recipes for cooking the pastries in broth indicates that it was a common practice rather than a whim of a cook. This is significant because in these simmered ravioli-like pastries might lie the beginnings of the *shishbarak* (and any of its variants), so popular to this day in countries surrounding Iraq. It is not far fetched to suggest that even the name itself might have evolved from *sanbousaj* usually associated with the word *shawabeer*, singular *shabour* (triangle). Indeed, in the augmented manuscript of al-Baghdadi's cookbook, *Wasf al-At'ima*, the merging of the two terms seems to already have started. *Sanbousaj*, in the book, was sometimes called *shanbousaj* (386, n.10).

The name *sanbousaj*, itself, was a loan Middle Persian word meaning "triangular." Apparently when the pastry was first made it was shaped into triangles. Dough was rolled out very thin (*riqaq*), cut into squares (*shabouran*, 2 triangles), and filling was put in the middle. The square was then folded into a *shanbour* (triangle, *Wasf al-At'ima*, 379). The words, *shabour* and plural *shawabeer* were originally used of "a style of hair-dressing favored by women and fops of Baghdad, in which the hair was brought down to a point between the eyebrows, in the form of a triangle" (Arberry, n. 5, 210).

Besides the triangles, *sanbousaj* was rolled into other shapes, as well, such as squares and rectangles, probably similar to the *bourag* rolls. When made into what al-Warraq calls *Ali al-Babaki*, yeast dough was rolled out thin, and was cut out into rounds with a cutter. Filling was put in the middle, and the pieces were folded, forming half moons. The seams were sealed by twisting the edges with the fingertips (al-Warraq, 89) exactly as we do today. They also used the thin *qata'if* breads as wrappers for the pastry (*Wasf al-At'ima*, 386).

The following *sanbousa* recipe is a thoroughly modern one, for mashed potato is used in making the dough. If you feel too lazy to make the dough yourself, use spring-roll wrappers available in oriental stores and some general grocery stores. The homemade dough will yield pastries that are soft in texture. The spring-roll wrappers will result in crispier pastries, although a little oilier (you will need 20 sheets).

For the dough:
>2 medium potatoes, boiled and mashed
>2 cups all purpose flour
>1/2 teaspoon salt
>1/4 teaspoon ginger
>1/2 cup yogurt

For the filling:
>1 pound lean ground meat
>1 tablespoon oil
>1/2 teaspoon turmeric
>1 medium onion, finely chopped
>1 heaping tablespoon tomato paste, or 1/4 cup tomato sauce
>1/2 cup parsley chopped
>2 tablespoons lemon juice, or 1 teaspoon sumac, see Glossary
>Some diced cooked vegetables, optional
>1 teaspoon salt
>1/4 teaspoon black pepper
>1 teaspoon cumin
>1 teaspoon coriander
>1 teaspoon *baharat*, see Glossary
>1/2 teaspoon whole mustard seeds
>1/2 teaspoon ginger
>1/2 teaspoon allspice

1/4 teaspoon chili pepper or fresh hot peppers chopped fine, or to taste

Oil for frying

1. To make **dough**, combine mashed potatoes, flour, salt and ginger. Rub between the fingers until mixture resembles breadcrumbs. Add yogurt and knead for a few minutes until you get dough of medium consistency. Set aside, covered.

2. To prepare the **filling**, heat oil in a medium skillet and cook meat, stirring occasionally, and breaking any lumps with the back of a spoon until all moisture evaporates, about 10 minutes. Add onion and turmeric and continue cooking, stirring most of the time, until onion is transparent, about 5 minutes. Fold in the rest of the filling ingredients, and cook for further 5 minutes, stirring most of the time. Set aside to cool slightly.

3. The most traditional shapes of *sanbousa* are triangles and half moons. My suggestion is if you have made the dough yourself shape pastries into half moons. If you have chosen to use spring-roll wraps it is easier to make them into triangles. Here is how to shape both kinds:
To make half moons, break away a walnut-size piece of dough and on a well-floured surface roll it out into a circle, as thin as possible (sprinkle with as much as needed of flour to prevent dough from sticking to working surface). Cut out into a 3-inch circle using a cutter. Put about 1 1/2 tablespoons of the filling on one half keeping clear of the edges. Then fold it to make half a circle, and press and twist all along the seamed edge to keep filling from coming out while frying. Set aside in a well-floured tray, and repeat with the other portions arranging them in one layer.
To shape into triangles, cut stack of 20 square spring-roll wrappers into 2 sets of rectangles. Put about 2 tablespoons of filling on one of the corners of each rectangle, then fold the sheet three times (like rolling a flag) to form a triangle. Secure the seam side following package directions. Arrange pieces in a single layer on a slightly floured tray.

4. Heat about 1/2 inch of oil in a medium skillet, gently shake off excess flour, and fry pieces turning only once to allow both sides to brown, about 5 minutes. Put browned pieces in a colander or a rack put on a tray to allow excess fat to drip down.
Following the medieval custom, serve these pastries piping hot with **Mustard Dip**, prepared as follows:
Mix together 1/4 cup balsamic vinegar, 1 tablespoon prepared mustard, 1 tablespoon ground walnuts, and a dash of sugar.

Variations:
* Vegetarian Sanbousa:
Replace meat with diced cooked vegetables such as potatoes, peas, cabbage, and cauliflower. Start by cooking the onion as described in step 2, then fold prepared vegetables with rest of ingredients.

* Chicken Sanbousa:
This is very useful when you've already got leftover cooked chicken. Just replace meat with 2 cups shredded cooked chicken. Start by cooking onion as described in step 2. Add chicken with rest of filling ingredients.

* Fish Sanbousa:

Substitute meat with 2 cups shredded cooked fish. Canned salmon or tuna can be used but make sure to drain fish well, and remove skin and bones in the case of salmon. Start by cooking onion as described in step 2. Then fold in fish with rest of filling ingredients.

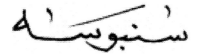

Sanbousa

Filled Rolls (Bourag)

Bourag is basically baked or fried rolls, filled with meat, cheese or vegetables. It is usually served as a snack, a side dish, or an appetizer. It is a variation on the *sanbousa*, the favorite "carry-out" and "fast food" of medieval times. However, it usually thinner than the *sanbousa* and crispier, which indeed might well have been the reason why this pastry was called *bourag*, in the first place.

It is my contention that these pastries owe their name to an old additive and dough enhancer called *bouraq al-'ajeen*. In English this substance is borax, or sodium borate. Nowadays it is banned as a food item, but in the past it was used as a preservative, and was even mixed with honey and given to teething infants on their soothers. What is more to our purpose, it was added to batters in small quantities (the same way we use salt) to keep cooked pastries nice and crispy. We know this from some of al-Warraq's tenth-century pastry recipes. In his chapter on breads and cookies, he makes mention of adding a small amount of *bouraq al-'ajeen* to *al-barazij* breads, which were supposed to be huge, round, white, thin and crisp (35-36). In his chapter on syrupy desserts *zalabiya* (fried fritters), *bouraq* was added to batters made of white flour and cornstarch, and were meant to be as thin as *qata'if* batter. Al-Warraq makes it quite clear that *bouraq* helps keep the fried fritters from getting leathery in texture. Indeed, he recommends adding more of the substance as a remedy to bad *zalabiya*, due to using "expired" yeast (268-9, see also Box, Medieval Leavens in chapter 17). In the thirteenth-century cookbook *Al-Wusla* of Aleppo, *bouraq* was also mentioned with relation to breads. The sandwich recipe called for bread that has been "worked with borax." (Rodinson, "Studies", 159). Calling a pastry product after the name of a leaven is quite a common practice in the baking world, an example on this is the Irish soda bread.

Making pastry sheets as thin *as nassem al-saba* (eastern breeze) or grass hoppers' wings, as the Arab ninth-century poet Ibn al-Rumi put it, was an art that the medieval cooks mastered to make their dainty *lauzeenaj* (baklawa), *qatai'f* (thin crepes), *sanbousaj* (filled pastries), and *riqaq* (thin breads). Filling sheets of thin pastry and shaping them into rolls, just like the basic variety of *bourag* was a common culinary technique of which we have records dating back to the ninth century. For instance, the *lauzeenaj* was filled and rolled, and the *sanbousaj* in one of its familiar shapes was filled and presumably folded to shape into rectangles.

Indeed, *bourag* might even have etymologically evolved from the medieval Baghdadi thin breads proudly referred to as *waraq* or *awraq al-riqaq* (paper-thin sheets of breads). They were eaten by themselves with stew dishes, made into rolled sandwiches. They were spread with butter and layered with a filling to create the most sensuous dishes. In al-Baghdadi's thirteenth-century recipe of *judhab khubz al-qata'if*, the thin *qata'if* crepes were sprayed with a little rose water and layered with ground almonds or pistachio and sugar. When the pot is full, a little sesame oil is sprinkled on top, and syrup is poured. Being prepared for a *judhaba*, the pot was then put in the *tannour* under a suspended grilling plump chicken, to let it receive all the fats and juices of the chicken (208). Moreover, the *Anonymous Thirteenth-Century Andalusian Cookbook* includes a pastry dish called *um al-faraj* (named after the female cook, the mother of al-Faraj, literally, joy), which the anonymous author accredits as an Eastern dish (from the eastern Abbasid region, the center of which was Baghdad). Fine layers of *riqaq* pastry are made by pouring thin batter (similar to *qata'if* batter) on a hot iron plate. The accumulated paper-thin sheets were made into what now is called *pastilla* in Morocco (see Box, Mother of Joy).

The Mother of Joy
Um al-Faraj, an Eastern Dish

This medieval dish is named after the female cook um al-Faraj (the mother of al-Faraj, literally, joy) who apparently was famous for making it. The significance of the dish lies in the fact that it describes the making of a savory and sweet pastry that is now considered the signature dish of the Moroccan cuisine, namely the *pastilla*. It also testifies to the fact that fine paper-thin pastries (*wureiqat*, or *awraq al-riqaq*) were successfully made and used in pastries both sweet and savory as early as the ninth century, and that these were the precursors of the *bourag* pastries known today all over the Middle East.

The dish is included in the thirteenth-century *Anonymous Andalusian Cookbook*, and is categorized as a *judhaba sharqiyya* (i.e. from the eastern Abbasid caliphate of Baghdad). *Judhaba*, to begin with, was a popular medieval Baghdadi dish prepared by suspending a chunk of lamb, a plump chicken, or even a piece of cheese in the clay oven, *tannour*, and letting it drip on a sweet bread-pudding-like preparation, so that it soaks up all the juices. In this Andalusian version, the chicken is enclosed in the pastry itself as follows.

1. Paper-thin *riqaq* sheets are made by pouring thin batter (like that made for *kunafa* or *qata'f*) on a hot iron plate, until the "necessary amount" is accumulated. This was an old well-established practice, the earliest records for which go back to the ninth century AD.

2. Filling is made by cooking plump chicken breasts with salt, oil, pepper, cinnamon, and spikenard.

3. An earthen pot is greased with fat and lined, both bottom and sides, with two sheets of dough big enough to overhang the sides. The surface is dusted with sugar, ground almonds, spikenard, cloves, and cinnamon ("a handful in all"). The surface is then dribbled generously with oil, and sprinkled with rose water in which musk and camphor are dissolved. The layering is repeated in the same order until half the pot is full (they line the bottom only).

4. The cooked chicken breasts are rubbed with saffron that has been dissolved in rose water, and are spread on the lined layers. The chicken is topped with the thin sheets of dough, as done before, in step 3. "Don't stop doing this until the pot is full and the chicken remains buried in the middle" the instructions go.

5. The surface is dusted with plenty of sugar, and sprinkled with oil and rose water. The overhanging first two layers are folded over the whole surface, to cover top completely. Pot is then covered with a fitted lid, and is sealed with dough.

1. The pot is baked in the *tannour* until done. When the seal is broken, it will give off a perfumed aroma. The dish is then inverted on a big platter and is served. The author praises it for its "nutrition and beautiful composition" (117-8).

411

Bourag

To make these delicious *bourag* pastries, you can prepare the dough yourself, or use fillo dough or spring roll wrappers, available at oriental stores and some general grocery supermarkets. As a general rule, homemade dough and spring roll wrappers are shaped into rolls and **fried**. Store bought fillo dough may be shaped into cylinders, triangles, or layered, and **baked**.

Bourag Dough ('Ajeen al-Bouraq)

(Makes 22 pieces)

This dough may be substituted with spring roll wrappers, and in this case, follow package directions for rolling and sealing.

> **2 cups all-purpose flour**
> **1 teaspoon baking powder**
> **1/4 teaspoon salt**
> **2 eggs, beaten**
> **2/3 cup water**
> **2 tablespoons hot oil**
>
> **Flour or cornstarch for spreading on work surface**
> **Oil for frying**

412

1. In a medium bowl combine flour and salt. Stir in eggs and water to make a medium to soft dough. Knead lightly.

2. Drizzle hot oil all over the dough and knead lightly. Leave aside for 10 minutes.

3. Divide dough into 22 walnut-size pieces, or depending on how big you want your rolls to be.

4. On a surface generously sprinkled with flour or cornstarch, roll out pieces into very thin rounds using a rolling pin.

5. Put about 2 tablespoons of filling of your choice (filling recipes will follow) along one corner of the disc. Fold about 1 inch of the sides on the filling to contain the filling, then roll all the way down. Arrange filled pieces, seam side down, in one layer on a flat surface sprinkled with flour or cornstarch.

6. Shake clinging flour or cornstarch off pieces and fry them, seam side down, in 1-inch deep hot oil. Turn once to allow both sides to brown, about 5 minutes total. Let drain in a colander lined with white paper napkins to prevent them from getting soggy, or put on a rack placed on a tray to allow excess oil to drip.
   Serve hot with salad.

Light Touch: Before frying, brush pieces with a mixture of 1/4 cup milk and 1 beaten egg. This will help reduce the amount of oil absorbed by the pieces while frying.

Easy to Make Bourag Dough

(Makes about 30 rolls)

The following is an easy method for making the dough. It needs neither kneading nor rolling out, all you need is a non-stick skillet about 6 inches in diameter. This method is in fact a relic of one of the medieval techniques used to produce thin sheets of bread. Simple batter, made of flour or flour and cornstarch, was poured in small amounts on a hot iron plate called *tabaq*. They used this method to make *riqaq* (thin) breads, *qata'if* (crepe) breads, and the super thin breads for the *louzeenaj* (similar to baklawa).

    1 1/2 cups corn starch
    1 1/2 cups all-purpose flour
    1/2 teaspoon salt

    1 1/3 cups milk
    2 2/3 cups water
    2 eggs, beaten

1. Sift cornstarch, flour and salt into a big bowl.

2. Mix milk, water and eggs, and stir into dry ingredients using a mixer at medium speed. The final mixture will be a little thinner than pancake mix.

3. Put a small non-stick skillet, about 6 inches in diameter, on medium heat.

4. Pour a small amount of batter, 3 to 4 tablespoons, into the pan and tilt to all directions so that batter covers the whole surface. If you notice some holes, try to patch them with a little of the batter. When the piece starts to come away from the sides of the pan, which will be only in a matter of seconds (about 30 seconds), remove it and spread it on a tray. Repeat procedure until batter is used up.

5. Put some filling of your choice (filling recipes will follow) on one side of the circle. Turn once to cover the filling, then fold both sides, and roll all the way down, and press seam to seal it. Put finished ones on a tray in a single layer.

6. Fry in 1-inch deep hot oil until golden brown, 3 to 4 minutes, and drain in a colander lined with a white paper towel, to prevent pieces from getting soggy, or on a rack put on a tray to allow excess oil to drip down.
Serve hot with salad.

Light Touch: Before frying the pieces brush them with a mixture of 1/4 cup milk and 1 beaten egg. This will help reduce the amount of oil absorbed by pieces while frying.

Suggested Fillings for Bourag

Meat Filling
1 pound lean ground meat
1 tablespoon oil
2 medium onions, finely chopped
1 tablespoon tomato paste, optional
1 teaspoon salt
1/2 teaspoon black pepper
1/2 teaspoon allspice
1/2 teaspoon cinnamon
1/4 teaspoon chili pepper, or to taste, optional

1 cup chopped parsley

1. In a big skillet heat oil, and cook meat, stirring occasionally and breaking meat lumps with the back of a spoon until all moisture evaporates and meat starts to brown, about 10 minutes.

2. Add onion and stir together until onion is soft, about 5 minutes.

3. Mix in tomato paste, if used, salt, pepper, allspice, cinnamon, and chili, if used, and stir for a few minutes. Put away from heat and let cool slightly. Fold in parsley, and use as directed.

Cheese Filling

Traditionally grated white hard cheese called *jibin Akrad* (Kurdish cheese) is used to fill the *bourag*. When cooked, it is deliciously stretchy and slightly salty. A combination of mozzarella, feta, and Romano cheese will give almost the same desirable texture as well as taste.

2 cups shredded cheese, a combination of mozzarella, feta, and Romano cheese
1 egg white, beaten
1/4 teaspoon black pepper
1 cup chopped parsley
2 tablespoons fresh dill, chopped or 1 teaspoon dried dill weed, optional

Mix all ingredients and use as directed.

Spinach filling

1 medium onion, finely chopped
1 tablespoon oil
1 10-ounce package frozen chopped spinach, thawed, squeeze out excess moisture

1/2 cup crumbled feta cheese, or Romano cheese
1 egg, beaten
1/2 cup chopped parsley
2 tablespoons fresh dill, chopped or 1 teaspoon dried dill weed
1/4 teaspoon salt
1/4 teaspoon black pepper
1/4 cup chopped toasted nuts, optional

1. In a medium skillet heat oil, and sauté onion until transparent, about 5 minutes.

2. Add spinach and stir together until all moisture evaporates, a few minutes. Set aside to cool.

3. Mix with rest of ingredients and use as directed.

Note: If you like your *bourag* to be spicier, then any of the *sanbousa* filling recipes given above may be substituted.

Making Bourag with Fillo Dough

The homemade *bourag* dough and spring roll wrappers are at their best when fried. If you prefer to bake *bourag*, the option is to use fillo dough, available at most grocery supermarkets. The following two shapes are the most popular:

Bourag Rolls:

You need one 1-pound package fillo dough. This amount is enough to make around 20 pieces depending upon how many layers there are in a package. If everything you need for making *booreg* is ready and you are working at a relatively cool and draftless place (avoid fans), you can fill a sheet without having to cover the rest with a damp cloth, as directed on the package. However, if you find that dough is getting dry then, by all means, go ahead and cover it with a clean kitchen towel, no need to wet it.

Work on one sheet at a time. Spread it on a dry flat surface and lightly brush half of it with oil, fold it, and brush half of it and fold it again. Now you have a piece with 4 layers. Put about 2 tablespoons of filling along the narrower side keeping about one inch of the three other sides clear of the filling. Brush with oil the rest of the piece. Turn the top onto the filling, roll once, then fold in one inch of both sides onto the rolled part, and continue rolling all the way down. This way of rolling the dough prevents filling from seeping out of the sides while baking as it gives more thickness to the sides.

Arrange rolled pieces on a greased baking sheet, seam side down. Brush them lightly with oil, and bake in a preheated oven at 375 degrees F. for 20 minutes or until golden brown.

Best when served piping hot from the oven.

Bourag Triangles:

Use one sheet for each triangle. Brush lightly with oil two thirds of one sheet, lengthwise, and fold the unbrushed third on the center third, then fold the other third. Put about 2 tablespoons of filling on one of the corners, and brush lightly with oil the rest of the piece. Fold the corner on the filling, to form a triangle. Then fold again and again maintaining the same triangular shape, until you get to the other end (like folding a flag).

Arrange triangles on a greased baking sheet, and brush pieces with a little oil. Bake as directed above in *Bourag* Rolls.

Puffed Bourag
(Bourag Muwarraq)

(Makes 20 pieces)

Creating puff pastry was a technique already known to the medieval Arab cooks, and the Andalusian cookbooks, in particular, were the most explicit in explaining this art. Al-Tugibi, author of the thirteenth-century Andalusian cookbook, *Fidalat al-Khiwan* (the best of the dishes) makes big *khubz muwarraq* by rolling out dough thinly using a long dowel. The thin sheets are spread with clarified butter, then folded, and the operation is repeated several times. He also gives the option of stacking three small discs of dough, spreading each with clarified butter while layering. The stack is then rolled out as thin as possible (45). This is still our option today when we want to make *bourag* that is light and puffy in texture.

3 cups all-purpose flour
1/2 teaspoon salt
1 egg, beaten
3/4 cup water
2 tablespoons oil

One recipe filling of your choice, p.414-5
Oil for frying

1. Mix flour and salt in a medium bowl. Make a well in the middle.

2. Combine liquid ingredients and pour mixture into the well. Stir with a fork at first, then knead into a dough that is rather on the soft side and slightly sticky, about 5 minutes.

3. Divide dough into 10 pieces and let them rest for 10 minutes.

4. On a surface well dusted with flour or cornstarch roll out one piece into a 1/4-inch-thick circle 5 inches in diameter, and brush its top with some oil. Repeat with 4 more pieces, stacking them, but do not oil the top of the fifth piece. Make a second stack with the remaining 5 pieces.

6. On a surface sprinkled with cornstarch or flour, roll out the two stacks separately to get 2 thin sheets, as thin as you can get them.

7. With a sharp knife divide each sheet of dough into 10 squares. Put about 2 tablespoons of filling in the center of the square. Fold 3 corners of the square on the filling, then roll down firmly into a roll. Fry rolls in about 1-inch-deep hot oil until golden brown, about 5 minutes. Rolls will nicely puff while cooking. Let pieces drain in a colander lined with a white paper towel or on a rack. This will prevent pieces from getting soggy. Serve hot with lots of salad.

Cheese and Parsley Squares
(Murabba'at al-Jibin wal-Krafus)

(Makes 18 servings)

This is a kind of savory baklawa in which fillo dough is layered and filled with a cheese mixture. The blend of cheeses used gives the filling a delightful taste, and a good texture. The medieval cooks have long recommended mixing cheeses for the perfect texture. They said if you use only sheep cheese, which is flaky in consistency like fetta, it would disintegrate and become runny in texture. And if you use cow's cheese only (similar to mozzarella) it would melt and bind in one mass letting all its moisture run out (thirteenth-century *Anonymous Andalusian Cookbook*, 119).
For the filling:
    1 1/2 cups shredded mozzarella cheese, about 6 ounces
    1 1/2 cups crumbled feta cheese, about 6 ounces
    1 cup parsley, chopped
    1/4 cup fresh dill, chopped, or1 tablespoon dill weed
    3 eggs, beaten

1/2 teaspoon nutmeg
1/4 teaspoon black pepper

One 1-pound package fillo dough
About 1/2 cup oil for brushing

Preheat oven to 350 degrees F.

1. In a medium bowl, mix filling ingredients.

2. Grease 10-by-15 inch baking pan. The pan should be slightly smaller than fillo dough sheets. Spread a fillo sheet on the pan allowing the extra to line up the sides. Brush it lightly with oil, top it with another layer and brush it with oil. Repeat until you stack about 10 sheets or half the package.

3. Spread filling on layered sheets.

4. Layer remaining sheets following same procedure. This time try to tuck in the sides very well to contain filling.

5. Score top sheets into squares with a sharp knife, and spray with water to prevent pastry from curling up.

6. Bake in a preheated moderate oven, at 350 degrees F. for 45 to 55 minutes, or until pastry is crisp and golden. Let it set in pan for 10 minutes, then re-cut all the way down along the scores.

Zucchini Squares
(Murabba'at al-Shijar)

(Makes 18 pieces)

The following is a delicious way for preparing zucchini. A slightly modified version of this recipe has won me the second prize of the *Gourmet* cooking contest, "Milk on the Menu" in February 1997.

1 1/2 pounds zucchini, shredded (about 3 medium ones)
1 teaspoon salt
2 medium carrots, shredded
1/2 cup dried tomatoes, soaked in hot water, then drained and chopped, optional
1/4 cup plain yogurt
5 eggs, divided
1/2 teaspoon salt
1/2 teaspoon black pepper
1/2 teaspoon nutmeg
1 tablespoon fresh dill, chopped, or 1 teaspoon dill weed
1 cup bread crumbs, divided

One 1-pound package fillo dough
About 1/2 cup oil, for brushing

1 cup milk
A dash of pepper
1/4 cup grated Romano cheese
Preheat oven to 375 degrees F.

1. Put zucchini in a colander and sprinkle with 1 teaspoon salt and let drain for 30 minutes. Press out excess moisture.

2. Put zucchini in a big bowl and mix with carrots, dried tomatoes, if used, yogurt, 3 eggs, salt, pepper, nutmeg, dill, and 1/4 cup breadcrumbs. Set aside.

3. Grease 15-by-10 inch baking pan (the pan should be a little smaller than fillo sheets).

4. Spread one sheet, allowing it to line up the sides a little to contain the filling. Brush very lightly with oil, and sprinkle very lightly with breadcrumbs. Repeat brushing and sprinkling with 9 more sheets, or half the package.

5. Spread filling prepared in steps 1 and 2. Cover with remaining sheets repeating the same procedure of spreading, oiling and sprinkling with breadcrumbs. Tuck in sides to contain filling.

6. Mix remaining 2 eggs, milk, a dash of pepper, and grated cheese. Pour mixture over top fillo sheet. Sprinkle with remaining breadcrumbs.

7. Bake in a preheated oven at 375 degrees F. for 45 to 55 minutes or until golden brown.

8. Let set for 10 minutes, then with a thin sharp knife, cut into 18 squares.
Serve warm as a snack by itself, or as a side dish.

Cheese Crescents
(Ahıllat al-Jıbın)

(Makes 36 pieces)

From simple yeast dough you can make wonderful savory cookies that are a pleasure to look at and to eat, as well. And like most yeast pastries they are much lighter than the regular cookie dough.
For the dough:
   1 teaspoon dry yeast
   A pinch of sugar
   2/3 cup warm milk

   2 1/2 cups all-purpose flour
   3/4 teaspoon salt

1 egg, at room temperature, beaten
1/2 cup oil
For the filling:
    About 2 cups shredded cheese of your choice
    3/4 cup finely chopped parsley

    1 egg, beaten, for glazing
    Sesame seeds
    Preheat oven to 375 degrees F.

1. Dissolve yeast and sugar in milk and set aside at a warm place for 5 minutes.

2. Mix flour and salt in a medium bowl. Make a well in the middle and pour yeast mixture, beaten egg and oil. Stir in a circular movement with a fork to incorporate flour into liquids. Knead for about 5 minutes to make dough of medium consistency. Set aside, covered, at a warm draftless place, for 45 minutes.

3. Punch down dough and divide it into 9 pieces, the size of a big egg each. On a slightly floured surface roll out each portion into a circle 6 inches in diameter and 1/8-inch thick. Divide each into 4 parts.

3. Mix cheese and parsley and put a small amount of the mixture on the wider end of each triangle and roll down firmly to the tip. Curve the two pointed sides inwards to shape like a crescent.

4. Arrange on a greased baking sheet, leaving a space between pieces. Brush with beaten egg and sprinkle with sesame seeds. Let rest for 10 minutes.

5. Bake in a preheated oven at 375 degrees F. for 12 to 15 minutes or until golden brown.

Cheese Bundles
(Buqach al-Jibin)

(Makes 36 pieces)

These tiny delicately spiced bundles are delicious with soft drinks or hot sweet tea.

For the dough:

    1 tablespoon dry yeast
    2 teaspoons sugar
    1/4 cup warm water

    3 1/4 cups bread flour
    1 teaspoon salt

    2 eggs, at room temperature, reserve a little of the white for glazing
    1/4 cup oil
    1/2 cup warm milk

For the filling:

    8 ounces crumbled feta cheese, or one 8-ounce package cream cheese
    1 tablespoon milk
    1/4 teaspoon salt, nutmeg, black pepper, chili pepper, each
    1/4 cup finely chopped parsley
    1/4 cup green onion, finely chopped
    5 pitted olives, chopped
    Preheat oven to 375 degrees F.

1. Dissolve yeast and sugar in water and set aside at a warm place for 5 minutes.

2. Put flour and salt in a medium bowl, mix, and make a well in the middle. Pour yeast mixture, eggs, oil and milk, and stir in a circular movement with a fork to incorporate flour into liquids. Knead for about 5 minutes then let dough rise, covered, at a warm draftless place for 45 minutes.

3. Meanwhile prepare filling, cream cheese and milk together. Stir in rest of filling ingredients.

4. Punch down dough and on a slightly floured surface roll it out to a 15-by-15-inch square, about 1/4 inch thick. If dough resists, let it rest for 10 minutes and try again.

5. Divide into 36 squares (2 1/2-by-2 1/2-inch squares). Trim edges if needed. Put about 1 tablespoon of filling in the middle of each square. Join the four corners of square and pinch them firmly together to form a bundle.

6. Arrange bundles on a greased baking sheet leaving a space between pieces. Brush with whisked reserved egg white. Sprinkle with a little chili powder, if wished. Let pieces rest for about 10 minutes. Bake in a preheated oven at 375 degrees F. for 12 to 15 minutes or until golden brown.

Spinach Roll
(Laffat al-Sbenagh)

(Makes 2 rolls, 10 slices each)

This flavorful and beautiful pastry comes out of the oven an already filled sandwich that just needs to be sliced and served. The Baghdadi medieval cooks used to make sandwich rolls quite similar to this. It was called *bazmaward* (for more information, see box "A Sandwich for Thought" in chapter 5). The amount the recipe yields is enough to satisfy a crowd. You can freeze one piece for future use, or just cut the amounts of ingredients given by half.

For the dough:
> 2 tablespoons dry yeast
> 1 teaspoon sugar
> 1 2/3 cups warm milk
>
> 6 cups flour
> 1 teaspoon salt
> 1/2 teaspoon nigella seeds, optional
> 2 eggs, at room temperature, beaten
> 1/3 cup olive oil

For the filling:
> 2 medium onions, finely chopped
> 2 tablespoons oil
> Two 10-ounce packages frozen chopped spinach, squeeze out excess moisture
> 1/2 teaspoon salt
> 1/4 teaspoon pepper
> 1/4 cup fresh dill, chopped, or 1 tablespoon dill weed
> 3 eggs, boiled and coarsely chopped
> 3/4 cup shredded cheese, mozzarella, feta, or Romano, or a mixture
> 1/4 cup toasted and chopped walnuts
> 1/4 cup stoned olives, chopped or sliced
>
> **Milk and sesame seeds for glazing and sprinkling the rolls**
> **Preheat oven to 400 degrees F.**

1. To make dough, dissolve sugar and yeast in warm milk, and set aside in a warm place for 5 minutes.

2. In a big bowl put flour, salt and nigella seeds, if using any. Make a well in the middle and pour yeast mixture, eggs and oil. Stir in a circular movement with a wooden spoon to incorporate flour into the liquid. Knead for about 5 minutes then oil both sides and let rise, covered, at a warm draftless place for 45 minutes.

3. Meanwhile prepare filling: sauté onion in oil until soft, about 5 minutes. Add spinach, and fold frequently until all moisture evaporates, a few minutes. Put away from heat and add rest of the filling ingredients. Set aside.

4. Punch down dough and divide it into 2 parts. Roll out each into a 12-by-9-inch rectangle, 1/3-inch thick (if dough feels resistant and elastic let it rest for 10 minutes). Spread half of the filling on the surface leaving about 3/4 inch of the edges clear of filling. Roll the rectangle starting with the long side, jelly- roll fashion. Seal seam and tuck in sides. Transfer, seam side down, to a greased cookie sheet. Repeat with the other batch and put on the baking sheet leaving a space between the two pieces to allow for expansion. With a sharp knife make 3 or 4 shallow diagonal slits. Let rise, covered with a clean kitchen towel, at a warm place for 30 minutes.

5. Brush rolls with milk and sprinkle with sesame seeds. Bake in a preheated oven, at 375 degrees F. for about 35 minutes or until golden brown. It should bake well otherwise center will remain doughy.

Let cool slightly then divide into 1-inch slices.

بيض مصبّغ .. وكلّه فد طعـــمُ

Eggs Might be Varicolored but they all Taste the Same

There once was a clerk who was married to a beautiful and intelligent woman. The judge for whom the clerk worked had his eye on the wife, so he sent her husband on an errand, and went to the woman's house pretending that he had some business with her husband. The wife immediately understood his intention, but she welcomed him, guided him to the guests' room and offered to serve him dinner until her husband came back. After a while the maids entered with an array of dishes, thirty in all, not a single one has a resemblance to the other. He started tasting the dishes one after the other, but to his amazement they all tasted alike. He got up, apologized to the woman, and ashamedly left the house.
(Zalzala, vol. 1, 381)

Chili Meat Flat Pie (Khubzat al-Lahm al-Mufalfal)

(Makes 16 wedges)

Flat pies are usually filled with jam and served as dessert (see chapter 18, cookies), but sometimes my family prefers to have it filled with some more serious stuff, such as meat and vegetables. Since it is mess-free, it has always been a winner for picnics. Use less chili for mild hot. The resulting crust is flavorful and flaky despite the fact that its fat content is lower than traditionally made pies.

Historically speaking, pie making was an ancient culinary technique that goes back to the ancient Mesopotamian era (see Introduction). During the medieval times, pies filled with a mixture of red meat, chicken or even fish were called *mukhbbazat* (from *khubz*, bread) and the ones filled with cheese were *mujabbanat* (from *jubn*, cheese). Puff pastry was sometimes used, and was called *muwarraqa* (leafy) or *musammana* (with clarified butter) as in the thirteenth-century *Anonymous Andalusian Cookbook* (44, 119-20).

For the pie dough:
>3 cups all-purpose flour
>1 teaspoon baking powder
>1/3 teaspoon salt
>1/4 teaspoon ginger
>2/3 cup oil (or 1/2 cup butter and 1/4 cup oil)
>3/4 cup milk

For the filling:
>1 tablespoon oil
>1 medium onion, finely chopped
>1/2 teaspoon turmeric
>2 tablespoons tomato paste
>2 to 3 small fresh chilies, chopped (or 1 medium chopped bell pepper, and 1/2 teaspoon chili powder)
>1/2 teaspoon salt
>1/4 teaspoon black pepper
>1/2 teaspoon cumin
>1/2 teaspoon allspice
>1/4 cup raisins or currants, optional
>1/4 slivered almonds, or pine nuts, optional
>1/4 cup parsley, chopped
>8 ounces ground lean meat

>1 tablespoon milk for glazing, and 1 tablespoon sesame for sprinkling on the pie

>Preheat oven to 375 degrees F.

1. Make **dough**: in a big bowl mix flour, baking powder, salt and ginger. Add oil (or butter and oil) and rub lightly between the fingers until mixture resembles breadcrumbs. Pour in milk and stir first to incorporate flour into milk then knead very briefly to make dough of medium consistency. Set aside, covered.

2. Make **filling**: in a medium skillet heat oil and stir in onion and turmeric until onion is transparent, about 5 minutes. Add the rest of filling ingredients except for parsley and meat, and cook for further few minutes stirring to mix well. Away from heat, mix in parsley and meat.

4. Divide dough into 2 parts. With a rolling pin flatten a portion until it is as big as a big dinner plate, and about 1/8-inch thick. Grease a flat ovenproof big dinner plate and line it with the dough disc. Trim the edge with a sharp knife. Spread filling on the disc leaving about 1/2 inch of the edge free of filling. Flatten second portion of dough like you did with the first one and cover filling with it. Trim

off edges with a sharp knife and press with the handle of a knife at 1/3-inch intervals to give it a decorative look and to keep the two layers sealed while baking.

5. Prick top disk with a fork at several places. Brush with milk, and sprinkle with sesame seeds.

6. Bake in a preheated oven at 375 degrees F. for about 50 minutes, or until it is nicely browned. Let cool for 10 minutes, then cut into 16 wedges, and serve with salad.

Olive Bars
(Asabi' al-Zeitoun)

(Makes 22 bars)

This quick bread makes a delicious and healthy snack that looks so colorful and appetizing. I like to have it for breakfast with sweet and hot tea.

> **1/2 cup olive oil**
> **2 eggs**
> **1 cup yogurt**
>
> **3 1/2 cups flour**
> **1/2 teaspoon baking soda**
> **2 teaspoons baking powder**
> **1/2 teaspoon salt**
> **1/2 cup milk**
>
> **3/4 cup olives black and green, pitted and chopped**
> **1/4 cup chopped roasted red pepper, or dried tomatoes, soaked in hot water then drained and chopped**
> **1/2 cup chopped fresh mint, may be substituted with fresh parsley**
> **1/4 cup grated Romano cheese, or shredded mozarella cheese**
>
> **About 1/4 cup quick oats or wheat bran for lining the baking pan**
> **Preheat oven to 375 degrees F.**

1. In a medium bowl beat together oil, eggs and yogurt, about 2 minutes.

2. Sift together flour, baking soda, baking powder and salt. Add to oil mixture alternately with milk and stir briefly until mixture is well blended, about 2 minutes. (Mixture will be a little on the thick side)

3. Fold in olives, roasted pepper or dried tomatoes, mint or parsley, and cheese.

3. Grease a 10-by-15-inch baking pan and sprinkle bottom and sides with quick oats or bran.

4. Spread mixture evenly in pan. Even up surface with slightly oiled fingers. Decorate surface with sliced olives, strips of roasted pepper and mint leaves, or to your fancy.

5. Bake in a preheated oven at 375 degrees F., for 20 minutes, or until golden brown. Let cool for 10 minutes then cut into 22 bars.

Poppy Seed Pinwheels
(Furrarat al-Khishkhash)

(Makes 40 pieces)

The bright red corn poppies have been growing in Mesopotamia ever since time immemorial. In *The Assyrian Herbal*, a pharmaceutical monograph on the Assyrian vegetable drugs, the narcotic quality of the plant was recognized. Poppy was recommended, for instance, as a soothing drug for toothache (57). A distinction; however, has to be made between the **opium poppy** plant and the bright red **corn poppy**. Opium extracted from the seed capsule latex of opium poppies contains the powerful morphine, still used for pain relief but is considered unsafe for internal use because of its highly addictive nature. The bright red corn poppies also have some sleep inducing qualities but they are not addictive (McIntire, 177). The corn poppy still grows in abundance on the hillsides of the northern region. The seeds were used in cooking, and the red petals and the seeds were used to aid relaxation and sleep. In Arabic it is called *khashkhash* after the rattling sounds that the seeds make when they dry in the pod. The thirteenth-century Baghdadi *Khashkhashiya* sweet and spicy stew called for poppy flour, and ground fresh or dried poppy seeds. It was also used toasted in small amounts the same way nuts were used, as in the sweet *judhab* dishes (al-Baghdadi, 195-6, 208).

In the following recipe I am trying to revive this medieval practice in making these delicious cookies. Poppy seeds give them a delightfully nutty texture. Toasting the seeds will bring out their flavor.

> **1/2 cup toasted poppy seeds**
> **1/3 cup milk**
>
> **4 cups flour**
> **1/2 teaspoon salt**
> **1/2 teaspoon baking soda**
> **1 teaspoon baking powder**
> **1/2 teaspoon ginger**
> **3/4 cup oil**
>
> **1 egg, separated**
> **1 cup shredded mozzarella cheese**
> **1/2 cup milk**
>
> **Preheat oven to 375 degrees F.**

1. In a small pot mix poppy seeds and milk, bring to a boil, then lower heat and let simmer until milk evaporates, about 10 minutes. Set aside to cool.

2. In a medium bowl, combine flour, salt, baking soda, baking powder and ginger. Add oil, and mix by rubbing between the fingers until it resembles breadcrumbs.

3. Add whisked **egg white,** cheese and milk to flour mixture and knead briefly to make dough of medium consistency.

4. Divide dough into two parts. Roll out one part into a rectangle about 1/4-inch thick. Spread surface with half of the prepared poppy seeds in step 1. Roll firmly from longer side, jelly roll fashion. With a sharp knife, slice log into about 20 1/3-inch wide pieces. Press each piece flat on cut side and transfer with the help of spatula to a greased cookie sheet. Repeat with the other piece of dough. Add 1 tablespoon cold water to the remaining egg yolk, beat a little, and brush cookies with it.

5. Bake in a preheated oven at 375 degrees F. for 15 minutes, or until golden brown.

Cheesy Cookies

Cheesy Cookies
(Biskit al-Jibin)

(Makes 48 pieces)

The beauty of these cookies is that they can be conveniently cut out into any shape you like. The cookies are not rich and they make a nice change from the familiar sweet cookies.

5 cups flour
1/2 teaspoon salt
1/2 teaspoon baking soda
1 teaspoon baking powder
1 cup oil

1 cup shredded mozzarella cheese
1/3 cup milk
3 eggs

Sesame seeds and/or chili powder for sprinkling on cookies
Preheat oven to 375 degrees F.

428

1. In a medium, bowl combine flour, salt, baking soda and baking powder. Add oil and mix by rubbing with fingers until mixture resembled breadcrumbs.

2. Make a well in the middle and add cheese, milk, and beaten **2 eggs and white of the third one**. Reserve yolk for glazing. Knead mixture for a few minutes to make dough of medium consistency. Let it rest for about 10 minutes.

4. On a slightly floured surface flatten dough with a rolling pin to 1/3-inch thickness. Cut into shapes with cookie cutters or molds, and arrange them on a greased baking sheet. To the reserved egg yolk add 1 tablespoon cold water, beat a little then glaze cookies with it. Sprinkle with sesame seeds and/ or chili pepper, to taste.

5. Bake in a preheated oven at 375 degrees F. 12 to 15 minutes, or until golden brown.

Dill Weed Balls
(Kurat al-Shibint)

(Makes 60 balls)

Dill gives these flaky cookies an extraordinary aroma. I usually shape them into balls, but for impressive presentations I use a small wooden mold.

> **1/2 cup oil**
> **1/2 cup melted butter**
> **1 cup yogurt**
> **3/4 cup fresh dill, chopped or 3 tablespoons dried dill weed**
> **3 eggs, divided**
>
> **4 1/2 cups flour**
> **1/2 teaspoon salt**
> **1 1/2 teaspoons baking powder**
>
> **Preheat oven to 375 degrees F.**

1. In a medium bowl beat together oil, butter, yogurt, dill weed and **2 eggs and yolk of the third one**, reserve egg white for glazing.

2. Mix flour, salt, and baking powder, and add to oil mixture. Stir with a fork first to moisten flour, then knead briefly to form medium dough. Let rest for 10 minutes.

3. Break away pieces, size of walnuts, and roll them between fingers to shape into balls.

4. Arrange balls on a greased baking sheet. Brush them with reserved beaten egg white.

5. Bake in a preheated oven at 375 degrees F, for 15 to 20 minutes, or until golden brown.

Spicy Sesame Sticks
(Asabi' al-Simsim)

(Makes 16 sticks)

These sticks are very nice with dips or hot sweet tea.

2 1/2 cups all purpose flour
1/2 teaspoon salt
1/2 teaspoon baking powder
1/2 teaspoon whole toasted caraway seeds or aniseeds
1/4 teaspoon ginger
1/4 teaspoon cumin

1/2 cup oil
2 tablespoons yogurt
2 eggs, divided

3/4 cup toasted sesame seeds
Preheat oven to 375 degrees F.

1. In a medium bowl mix flour, salt, baking powder, caraway or aniseeds, ginger and cumin.

2. Make a well in the middle and add oil, yogurt, and beaten **1 whole egg and one egg white**, reserving yolk for glazing. Stir mixture with a fork first to moisten flour then knead briefly for a few minutes to make dough of medium consistency.

4. Divide into 16 balls the size of a walnut each. Let rest, covered, for 15 minutes.

5. Roll each piece into pencil-like sticks.

6. Add 1 tablespoon cold water to reserved egg yolk and beat together. Put sesame in a flat dish.

7. Brush each stick with egg wash and roll in sesame allowing pieces to catch as much as possible of the sesame.

8. Arrange sticks in a greased baking sheet and bake in a preheated oven at 375 degrees F. for about 15 minutes, or until golden brown.

Cheese crescents, 419

431

CHAPTER FIFTEEN
DESSERTS

CHAPTER FIFTEEN
DESSERTS
(al-Halawıyyat)

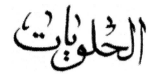

LIGHT PUDDINGS, HALWAS, AND CANDIES

(Only) when he has eaten the food let him give (his) verdict (on it)!
(A Sumerian proverb, ca 3500 BC, Gordon, 456)

Introduction

Arabian desserts in general might strike the Western palate as being too rich and sweet. This might be true, but they are usually reserved for special religious and social occasions and gatherings. For every-day dessert, fresh fruits are almost always the choice after a main meal or between the meals. Most probably the sweet tea normally served after every meal satisfies the sweet tooth in many of us.

Fruits in the region are seasonal. Watermelon and cantaloupes are consumed in huge amounts in the summer, for they help replenish the liquids our bodies lose in the hot dry season. At best, the watermelon is sweet and red, but when buying it, *caveat emptor*. It is safer to buy it *'ala shart al-sikeen* (on the condition of the knife)-- the vendor would choose the melon himself and prove its excellence by cutting out a wedge to show how red and good it is. Watermelons are usually cut open an hour or so before the meal to allow them to cool naturally. In the old-fashioned houses the cut melons used to be kept next to the *badgeer* (a chimney-like cooling passage). Towards the end of summer melons similar to honeydew, greenish and rather crunchy, but as sweet as honey, start to appear in the market. They are called *bateekh Samarra* (melons of Samarra), after the place where they grow abundantly. They are the harbingers of the fall.

Grapes come in different shapes and colors, such as the long and slender variety called *des al-anza* (goat's dugs). Unfortunately our grapes have lots of seeds in them, which gave rise to a word of wisdom you'd better heed: "do not rush things, but deal with them the way you eat grapes, *habba, habba* (one grape at a time)." That's why our *zabeeb* (sultanas) and golden raisins come with lots of seeds. Only *kishmish* (raisins) is seedless.

Nectarines and apricots have a very short season. Different kinds of plums and cherries, such as *goaja*, and locally grown white small apples (more like crab apples) are more commonly eaten while green and tart, with a sprinkle of salt, as appetizing snacks. They are mostly consumed on the household level, and no hostess worth her name would think of presenting her honored guests with

433

such humble, but nevertheless scrumptious stuff. Cucumbers, small, smooth and crunchy, are also snacked on, they are even classified by some as fruit.

Dates start appearing in mid-summer, some golden yellow, some radiant red, and some half golden and crunchy, and half brown, soft and honey-sweet. It is estimated that about 450 kinds of dates are grown in the region but only several kinds are commercially significant, such as *khistawi, zehdi, barhi,* the ruby-colored *barban,* and the giant *majdool* dates, known in California as "madjool." Dates need a lot of heat and humidity to ripen that's why the best dates are grown in middle and southern Iraq, especially in Basrah. Indeed date palm groves growing in Basrah inspired the most beautiful poetic imagery ever composed by a contemporary Arab poet. Badir Shakir al-Sayyab, a native of the city of the date palms himself, compares, in his poem *Inshudat'l-Matar* (an ode to rain), the gracefully long black eyelashes of his beloved's beautiful eyes to two date palm "forests" growing along the banks of the river, at the time of dusk.

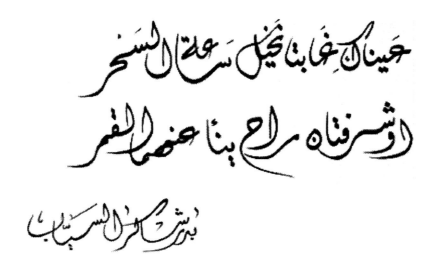

During the month of August dates fully ripen. All it takes is a few bouts of humidity to do the job. A joke is told of the legendary despot, Quaraquosh, the *wali* (governor) of Iraq during the Ottoman occupation, that he once complained of the hot humid weather in Iraq in August. When he was told it was so in order to ripen the dates. He decreed that all date palms be cut off.

Traditional accompaniments with ripe dates are yogurt drink and cucumbers, a prefect balance of colors, tastes, and nutrients. A considerable amount of the ripened dates is dried and kept, so that it may be enjoyed all year round. Basrah is especially famous for its *tamur mu'assal,* (chewy dried dates preserved in their "honey" and mixed with some toasted sesame). My father, a Basrawi himself, used to entertain us with the anecdote of the British soldier who commended the *Basrawi* "chocolate," but complained it always came filled with stones.

434

Singing Praises of Dates

"Our dates are smooth and snub-nosed; your teeth sink into them; their stones are like birds' tongues; you put a date into your mouth and you find the sweetness in your ankles".

That was how a date-lover Bedouin once described dates.
(Ibn al-Jawzi, *Tales of Dupes and Gullibles*, cited in Gelder, 41)

Towards the end of summer figs, both black and white, and pomegranates as well, make their appearance. Fig trees grow successfully in household orchards but mostly in the north where the surplus is preserved by threading them into strings and drying them, or making them into jam for winter. Pomegranates come in different varieties. Sour ones are mostly used for cooking purposes, semi-sweet and sweet pomegranates are consumed as fruit, and the best and sweetest variety grows in Shahrabaan, in the eastern region of Iraq.

Like figs, apricots are highly perishable. They are enjoyed fresh for a limited period of time, but are mostly preserved by drying the whole fruit (*turshana*), to be consumed as a snack, or added to some traditional dishes. It is also mashed, then spread in thin layers in huge trays and dried under the scorching sun of summer. The sheets would then be wiped lightly with oil and folded to be sold as *qamar'l deen* (literally, the moon of religion), a chewy fruit leather. It is consumed as a sweet snack or made into *sherbet* (a cold drink), popular during *Ramadhan*, the religious month of fasting.

If you have a passion for vegetables and fruits, shopping in the local market places may prove to be the most fun time you can ever think of spending. There you lose yourself in the hustle and bustle of the shoppers, the fresh earthy smells of the products that have just arrived directly from the farms and orchards. The venders chant the excellence of their produce at the top of their voices, using some catchy phrases. I particularly remember a smart vendor advertising his sweet pomegranates by saying at the top of his voice, " *'eba hilu!*" (that is, the only "flaw" in his pomegranates was they were too sweet!)

الرُّمّانُ؛ فِرْ عَلِيَّ   يُلمجِكَ عَلَيَّ الرُّمّانِ
وَ آدُونِي لِلأَهْلِيَّ؛   طَلَبها الحُلُو مَارِيدَه

Pomegranates hovered around me. The lemon tree came to my aid,
That sweet one, I do not want him. I want to go home!
(An Iraqi folk song)

435

Citrus fruits are for winter, although some farmers prolong the period of their availability by keeping them in holes under the ground to sell them at a higher price when they become impossible to get in the summer. This method of preserving fresh fruit is called *"jafur"* (keeping in pits), and it must have been quite an old one. Citrus trees thrive in the entire region, but the oranges of Diyala, a city west of Baghdad, are especially sweet and have very thin peels. Household gardens are usually bordered with citrus trees in addition to date palms and other fruit trees. The aroma of the citrus trees blossoms wafting through the fences, while walking in the streets in springtime, is an unforgettable memory.

Two kinds of citrus trees are unique to the region. The first is orange of Seville (*rarinj*) which is a thick-skinned, sweet and sour variety, mostly used for cooking purposes instead of lemon juice. It also yields excellent jam and sherbet. The other variety is as big as an orange but as yellow as a lemon. It is just sweet, that's why it is called *noomi hilo* (sweet lemon). People believe in its soothing effect on skin rashes.

The Ancient Scene:

To go back in history, it is plausible to argue that the ancient scene regarding fruits and desserts in general does not differ substantially from the modern one. Excavators at Ur, a site in the southern part of modern Iraq, inhabited from the Ubaid period (ca. 4500 BC) until about 400 BC, found small crab apples sliced crosswise and threaded in strings. Date stones were also found, evidence that date palms were quite common in the area as far back as 50,000 BC, and that they played a predominant role in Sumerian economic life. The network of irrigation canals in southern Mesopotamia provided ideal conditions for palm cultivation. The palms clung to the canal banks, leaving the open land free for other crops. Literally every single part of the palm was used in one way or another. From early second millennium BC Sumerian lexicographical lists, we learn of about one hundred and fifty words for the various types of palms and their different parts. The date palms were shown in a Neo-Assyrian relief of Ashurbanipal and his queen feasting in a garden at Nineveh. Interestingly, the early archaeologists in the nineteenth century mistook the germinating date palm, a symbol of fertility in Assyrian sculptures, they mistook it for pineapple. In the words of Herodotus, date to the Assyrians was their "food, wine and honey." Although nowadays date palms cannot be successfully grown in the modern northern region, date palms grew in Nineveh as late as the Middle Ages.

In ancient times date palms were so productive that they were cheaper than grain, which made dates a staple food for the poor. The fruits were eaten fresh, but they were also pressed to let juice ooze. This juice was allowed to evaporate into thick syrup called "daspu" (honey-sweet) in the ancient Akkadian (cf. Arabic *dibs*). This syrup was sometimes referred to as "lal" (honey). The real honey was known and used by those who could afford it. The cheaper and more readily available thick date syrup was used for puddings and sweetmeats as an alternative for honey. Cane sugar was not yet known in the region. The dates were dried and compressed for winter use, and sometimes were chopped up and mixed with flour for pastries. In the early fourth century BC, Xenophon, who had been to the region, commented on the size and succulence of the dates- their color was like amber, he noted, and the Babylonian villagers dried them and kept them as sweets.

The new foliage sprouting from the crown of an old date palm was eaten as vegetable. The ancient Sumerians thought it had a "peculiar pleasant taste" though it had the tendency to cause headaches. Nowadays this part of the date palm is known as *jummar,* and it is deemed a delicacy. Since the tree dies after this part is taken, this was normally done with trees past their prime.

Artificial fertilization of the female date palms was known and practiced in Sumerian times. To do this the farmers had to climb up those tall trees, but this was no big deal since the surface of the trunk is rough. The normal method of climbing to the top was for the climber to tie a rope around both the trunk and his body. Then he would lean back and literally walk to the top, the rope being raised at each step so as to hitch itself on the projections immediately above. This can be seen on a fresco from the palace of Mari dating from the beginning of the second millennium BC. And this method has not changed a bit. Nowadays you can still see the date palm climbers "walking" up the date palms for fertilizing as well as gathering the crops. Listen to what an American twin said when they saw the date palm climber for the first time in Baghdad, in their 1940 memoirs, *Our Arabian Nights*. They saw an Arab walk right up their tallest date tree.

> At least it looked as if he did…. [And] when he started climbing, he passed a short length of wire round the trunk of the tree and attached it to a red scarf, in which he sat hammock fashion. Then with every step he took, he hooked the wire one notch higher on the tree. There was a fraction of a second between jabs of the wire, when the man's contact with the tree was the soles of his feet. It was fascinating to watch (140).

The Tree of Life

The concept of the Tree of Life started in ancient Mesopotamia and the date palm was one of the most ancient symbolic forms of it. To the Assyrians it was a symbol of fertility. The ancient *Epic of Gilgamesh* refers to it with veneration, "And did you not love Ishullanu, the gardener of your father's palm grove? He brought you baskets filled with dates without end; every day he loaded your table."

To this day it is still the custom among Muslim villagers in Iraq and other Muslim countries to adorn the gates of their houses with palm leaves on religious festivals. Whereas references to the tree in the Old Testament are scarce (the only reference to it was in the description of Jerico as the "city of palm trees," the Qur'an abounds with references to it. In S*urat Mariam* (chapter on Mary), for instance, when labor came to Mary:

"She withdrew herself to a remote place. And the throes [of childbirth] compelled her to betake herself to the trunk of a palm tree. She said, Oh, would that I had died before this, and had been a thing quite forgotten! Then [the child] called out of her from beneath her; Grieve not, surely your Lord has made a stream to flow beneath you; and shake towards you the trunk of the palm tree, it will drop on you fresh ripe dates."

Date-palm climber. Lands and Peoples vol. III.

Excavated cuneiform texts indicate that the Sumerian orchards included other fruit trees such as pomegranate, apple, peach, fig, apricot, plum, grapevines, and citrus trees. All these were inter-planted with the higher date palms, and together they formed a canopy for vegetables and herbs that required more attention and care. This way of organizing trees for maximum shade and protection is described in a Sumerian poem which tells the story of a gardener called Shukallituda, whose diligent efforts at gardening at first had met with nothing but failure. After doing a lot of scrutinizing, and being guided by divine omens, he came up with the technique of planting shade trees in a garden or grove to protect the smaller plants from wind and sun (Kramer, *History Begins at Sumer*, 70-2). This method is still followed by modern farmers, and it explains why dates are almost always mentioned in conjunction with other fruits. References to fruit trees in the Qur'an, for instance, always include dates with other fruits such as grapes, and pomegranate. Even the names of some of these ancient fruits underwent very little changes throughout all these millennia. Compare, for instance, the Akkadian "Kamissaru" (pears) with the Arabic *kummathra*, "supulgar" (quince) with the Arabic *safarjal*, or "andahsu" (plum) with the Arabic *'injas*.

The ripe and half-open pomegranate displaying its many seeds was the symbol of fecundity and eternal life in ancient times. In ancient Babylon and Assyria they were served at marriage banquets. The Assyrians, in particular, thought highly of them. They figured on many of their monuments and jewelry. They were also used for medicinal purposes. In *The Assyrian Herbal*, pomegranate rind was prescribed as a "stomach binder". Three kinds were mentioned: the sour, the sweet, and the very sweet (called "daspu" i.e. sweet as honey, 177). The pomegranates also yielded a highly prized drink.

The Assyrians knew many varieties of figs, which were a staple dietary item. Fig-syrup was used as a sweetener. The fruit itself was preserved by drying. For medicinal purposes fig juice was used as a stomach wash, and a cake or lump of figs was applied to boils. The fig tree was revered by all religions. To the Hebrews it was a symbol of peace and abundance, to the Christians it was a sacred tree because Jesus desired to eat figs on the way to Bethany. To the Muslims it was called the Tree of Heaven. Figs were deemed sacred for God swore by them and the olives in the opening verse of *Surat al-Teen* (the chapter of "Figs") in the Qur'an.

Since the ancient Mesopotamians were concerned with the laying-out of fine parks and orchards, a tremendous variety of other fruits were also grown. Several Assyrian kings showed keen interest in botany and introduced exotic trees and plants into their parks. The earliest evidence for cultivating quince for instance is in Mesopotamia. Other fruits like plums and especially cherries were mentioned by the Assyrian king Sargon II (722-705 BC). The Akkadian word for cherries was "karshu" (cf. Arabic *karaz*), and Sargon associated it with the word "sumlalu", i.e. sweet smelling. He mentioned they grew in the Kurdish mountains in the north of the region. Scholars believe that the Akkadian name has survived into European languages such as the Greek "kerasos", and the German "kirsche". Apricots were first cultivated in the region, and in the Akkadian it was known as "armanu". It is now believed that the Latin word "armeniaca" and its derivatives do not indicate that the fruit originally came from Armenia but that it is a loan word from the Akkadian. (Thompson, 179).

Peaches originated in the orient and reached the Fertile Crescent as early as the third millennium BC. It must have been from this region that the Greeks and Romans came to know of them. Citron and lemon trees also grew on the land of Mesopotamia ever since antiquity. Lemon pips were found in excavations at ancient Nippur (4000 BC). Apparently they were brought to the land from the Far East. The Sanskrit word for orange "naranj" is still used even nowadays to describe a special variety of orange, sweet and sour with a more than usual bitter rind. These are known as the oranges of Seville, for the Arabs brought them to Spain during the eighth century AD.

Mulberry (*tukki*) and jujube (*nabug*) trees were also found on the land of Mesopotamia ever since ancient times, delicious to nibble on, but they were and still are of no significant commercial value. They are usually grown in orchards as shade trees. Children, in particular, enjoy climbing and picking up those small and exotic fruits. If fruits are too high to reach, they throw stones at them, an utterly irksome way for gathering crops, particularly when done to other people's trees. Mulberry in its white and red varieties is eaten fresh, and made into attractive jam and drink. As for the jujube or lote tree (*shajarat al-sidr* or *nabug*), archaeology has proven that it was as common in ancient Msopotamian household gardens as it is nowadays. We are told that syrup was made out of the fruit, and when dried it yielded a tasty sweetmeat. The tree itself was mentioned in the Qur'an as one of the paradisal trees, and it has always been shrouded with superstitions. It is believed to be the dwelling house of all kinds of demons such as the *ginni* and *si'lua* (male and female demons), and superstitious people believe that cutting off a jujube tree brings bad luck. Some people even claim they heard loud shrieks when they cut down their jujube trees. Its leaves were believed to have a peculiarly pure quality. There are many varieties of the fruit, and Herodotus commented on the similarity in flavor of jujube to dates, and right he was. To this day there is a particular variety called *nabug Khistawi* after the name of an excellent kind of dates. The fruit, unlike the more commonly rounded varieties, is longish in shape like a date, but a little smaller, and when ripe it is as brown and as sweet as a ripe date. Apparently jujube had more uses in earlier days. In the Middle Ages it was used to make a delicious cold drink, and was used in stews.

Nuts such as almonds, walnuts and pistachios were also available in ancient Mesopotamia, and were widely used in cooking and snacks. The poisonous quality of bitter almonds was recognized, although small quantities of its oil were prescribed for their medicinal value as emollient, demulcent and laxative, as well as in enema. Confections, on the other hand, were flavored with "almond flavor", or what was called "spirit of almond" (in Arabic it is still similarly called *rouh al-lowz*). Almond in the Akkadian was called "luzu", from which the Arabic *lowz* was derived (Thompson, 132, 182). Pistachio was cultivated in the gardens of King Merodach-baladan of Babylon. It was used for its oil, or eaten fresh and used in confections as it is used nowadays. Shelled pistachios, nuts and salted seeds were some of the items mentioned in the menu of the huge banquet the Assyrian king Ashurnasirpal II prepared for his 69,574 guests in ninth century BC (for more details see Box, p.617).

Manufactured Desserts:

Making pastries and confections was a flourishing business in ancient Mesopotamia. They were made at the palace and temple kitchens, as well as in bazaars, by professional confectioners, called "episanu". Confectioners attached to temples were specialized in making the sacred cakes consumed in large numbers at times of religious festivals. Menus prepared for the gods invariably included a course of dessert at the end of the meal. They also made the cakes that the worshippers of the goddess Ishtar crumbled and left for her doves. The principal ingredients used for making these cakes were mostly different kinds of flour, date syrup, honey, butter, sesame seeds, sesame oil, and the so much valued rose water, called "hilu" in the Akkadian. Evidently roses were abundant in the region, and evidently rose water was made in the ancient temples (see Glossary). They also valued cardamom for its flavor and medicinal properties.

Confectioneries in Ancient Mesopotamia were mostly sweetened with honey and syrups derived from dates and figs. In making desserts, a product such as sesame proved very handy, indeed. Sesame seeds grew abundantly in the entire region, in the Akkadian it was "samasamu"(cf. Arabic *simsim)*. Though some desserts were made using the seeds themselves, the principal consumptive value of the plant was in its fine oil, which was a staple in the people's diet until recently.

Their pastries and desserts included the "qullupu" which was dough made of sesame oil and wheat, filled with raisins or dates and baked. People in the region have always been baking cookies pretty much similar to these, such as the medieval Baghdadi *khushkananaj*, and the traditional *kleicha* cookies of modern times. They also made a kind of semi solid pudding from flour, sesame oil and honey, called "muttaqu," and it was often mentioned in their literature mainly as offerings to the temples. It sounds so much like many of the medieval and modern Iraqi *halawa*. As for the "mirsu" (cf. Arabic verb *maras*, to mash), a mixture of dates mashed with clarified butter and honey, its counterparts would be the medieval date dessert *ha'is*, and *halawat tamur* of nowadays. They shaped their pastries in many interesting ways, such as pillars as in the "makatu", or turbans as in the "kubbusu", (from which probably the Iraqi *kabbuz,* head cap, was derived).

Although sugarcane was early introduced into the subcontinent (India) and was of considerable importance there by the fifth century BC, it spread very slowly westwards. It was introduced to Mesopotamia around the fourth century AD, and it was not until the eighth century AD, when the Islamic rule spread it along the Mediterranean, that cultivation of sugarcane began on the shores of North Africa, Sicily and Spain. The rest of Europe had to wait eight more centuries before sugar became common.

The word "candy" is borrowed from the Arabic *quand,* which is a hard crystalline mass formed by evaporating or boiling sugarcane. The cane juice was clarified by boiling it with egg white, which coagulated, trapping impurities, and was then skimmed off. The remaining liquid was boiled down until most of the water had evaporated. The resulting thick, sticky mass was poured into cone-shaped clay molds, where it crystallized into raw sugar. The cones were inverted for a few days so that the molasses could run off through a hole in the tip. Finally, wet clay was packed over the wide end of the cone and its moisture was allowed to seep through the crystals for eight to ten days. This washing action removed most of the remaining impurities. The final product was a cone-shaped sugar mass usually wrapped in blue paper to make it appear whiter. It was sold whole to be grated as needed by the cook.

The availability of sugarcane, date syrup and honey by the middle ages brought about an array of confections and cookies as evident from the extant cookbooks and literature of the time. There was the *zilabiya* (fritters immersed in syrup), for instance, for which many recipes were given in the contemporary cookbooks. There were the almond pastries, the *qata'if,* sweetmeats, nougat, candies, oven-baked cookies, cakes drenched in syrup and much more. Rice puddings and custards flavored with saffron and rose water, or fine noodles cooked in honey and nuts were more likely to be made at home.

Nowadays basically similar types of desserts and *halwa* are still cooking in the region, but as a general rule they are not consumed on daily basis. Some of them are more customarily enjoyed with guests, to be had with tea or coffee during the evening visitations and dinner parties. Some pastries are associated with the religious month of *Ramadhan*, such as *baklawa* and *zilabya. Kleicha* cookies are made for the two religious feasts, the small one at the end of *Ramadhan,* and the big one after the pilgrimage to Mecca is performed. Besides, a box of *baklawa* and *zilabya*, or *mann al-sama* (manna), or *halqoum* (Turkish delight), purchased from one of the specialized confectioneries, would make an acceptable gift between friends on such social occasions as graduations, circumcisions, and birthdays.

Medieval Cannoli

In al-Warraq's tenth-century cookbook there is a recipe for small stuffed tubular pastries, called *halaqeem* (like gullets, i.e. tubes). Unleavened dough is made of flour and oil, and is wound around a cleaned long reed, which is then sliced into about one-inch pieces. Red, yellow, green, and blue food colors are used to color the pieces that are to be then baked in the *tannour*. When done, the reeds are removed and the resulting tubes are stuffed with a mixture of walnut and sugar. The tips are sealed by dipping then in melted sugar, and then are sprinkled with colored sugar. Al-Warraq says they will look like a *bustan* (colorful orchard, 276). The reason why they are made small is because they are used for decorations.

In the thirteenth-century *Anonymous Andalusian Cookbook*, there is a similar recipe, called *qanawat* or *qananeet* (tubes). Dough yellowed with saffron is made into thin flat breads that are wound around reeds and are cut small or big, as desired. They are then fried. After removing the reeds the tubes are stuffed with a mixture of nuts and sugar bound with honey (132).

In both recipes we clearly see the origin of what later was called cannoli, the famous Italian pastry.

Other kinds of pastries such as *churek* (sweet dough pastry), *ka'ak* and *bakhsam* (dry cookies like biscottie) are very popular but are too humble to be presented on formal occasions. They are exclusively bought from special bakeries that carefully guard their recipes. The most famous is *Ka'ak al-Sayyid*. My recipes of these traditional pastries are my improvisation, but they are close enough.

You'll notice that the traditional types of dessert are usually fried and soaked in syrup, or simmered on stovetops. Cookies up until the late fifties were baked in the t*annour* (clay domed oven) or at the neighborhood bakery. That's why they were baked in big quantities. Europeanized types of cakes were mostly purchased at bakeries. However, as gas stoves with ovens increasingly became more common in the average kitchens, cakes of all types started to be made at home, and cake making became the favorite pastime of the leisurely modern Mesopotamian young ladies.

One last note. In the following recipes I tried to develop some reasonably low fat desserts, without sacrificing the taste. Most recipes replace the traditional ghee, butter, margarine, or shortening with liquid oil such as corn oil or **extra light** olive oil, which has less saturated and trans fats, infamous for being artery-cloggers. Though some of them still have to be fried. These can be made less frequently and just for the fun of it when there is a big crowd to entertain, or they might be served in smaller portions after a light meal. It is comforting to learn that recent studies have proved that a little fat is good for you. It helps prevent strokes, for instance. But it is safer to go by the golden rule: moderation, and not deprivation, something of everything is good. Besides, keep in mind that it is what you take in a given period of time, such as a whole week, that really matters. In other words enjoy some today and make up tomorrow. (Did I hear somebody say, "yea right!")

SIMPLE AND LIGHT PUDDINGS

Light and tasty desserts are made from basic ingredients such as cornstarch, rice and milk, and the "perfumes of Arabia" will give them a tremendous lift. All it takes is a pinch of saffron, some cardamom or cinnamon and a tablespoon of rose water or orange blossom water.

Milk Pudding
(Mahallabi)

(Makes 6 generous servings)

A warm bowl of *mahallabi* in winter or a chilled one in summer is always welcome for dessert. The way we make it today is much lighter than the traditional medieval *muhallabiyya*. One of al-Warraq's tenth century recipes, for instance, is a custard-like pudding that calls for 30 eggs.

7 cups milk
1 1/3 cup sugar
1 to 2 cardamom pods

3/4 cup cornstarch, or rice flour, or a combination of both
1 cup cold water
2 tablespoons rose water, or to taste
For garnish: 2 tablespoons shelled and ground pistachio

1. In a heavy medium pot, bring milk, sugar, and cardamom pods to a boil, about 10 minutes.

2. Dissolve cornstarch or rice flour in cold water and pour it slowly into the boiling milk, stirring all the time lest it should get lumpy. Lower heat to medium and stir until mixture bubbles and starts to thicken, about 5 minutes. The pudding should be thick enough to cover the back of a metal spoon. Put away from heat and stir in rose water. Discard cardamom pods if wished

3. Pour into individual bowls, and immediately garnish with pistachio before a skin develops on the surface. Serve warm or chilled with fruit compote.

Variations:
Cocoa Pudding: Add 3 1/2 tablespoons cocoa powder and dissolve it with cornstarch in step 2.

• *Marbled Pudding:* Create a marbled look by adding 2 tablespoons of cocoa or chocolate powder diluted in a little water to a third of the *mahallabi*. Pour the white mixture first then add the brown mixture in a swirl. With a wet knife, zigzag the brown mixture.

Rice Pudding
(Mahallabi al-Timman)

(Makes 2 servings)

Unlike the regular rice puddings cooked in other parts of the world, our version is very simple and basic. It is a comfort food, nourishing, delightfully scented, and not so sweet. Slow cooking is best for this pudding.

The medieval version was called *aruzza*, and it was sometimes enriched with meat and colored with saffron. A poem was once recited to the Abbasid Caliph al-Mustakfi (tenth century AD) singing its praises:

O Glorious *aruzza!* What a boon,
Thou cook as lovely as high heaven's moon!
Purer than snow that hath been furrowed twice
By handiwork of wind and frosted ice;
Set out in ordered strips upon the dish,
White as the whitest milk that heart could wish,
Its brilliance dazzles the beholding eye
As if the moon ere even shone in sky;
While sugar sprinkled upon every side
Flashes and gleams, like light personified.
(Arberry, 27)

Here is how to prepare it:
1/2 cup rice, such as jasmine, washed, soaked in water for 30 minutes, break rice grains by rubbing them between your fingers, do not drain
3 cups water
1/4 teaspoon salt

2 cups milk
1/4 cup sugar, or to taste
1 tablespoon rose water, or 1 teaspoon cardamom, or both
For garnish: ground cinnamon

1. Put rice, water and salt in a medium heavy pot and bring to a boil. Reduce heat to medium and let simmer 15 to 20 minutes, or until liquid is absorbed. Stir 2 to 3 times while simmering.

2. Add milk and sugar and let simmer gently, stirring occasionally until pudding is of medium consistency, 15 to 20 minutes.

3. Add rose water and/or cardamom. Pour into individual bowls, and decorate surface with cinnamon. Serve by itself or with fruit compote

Saffron-gold and Milky-white Pudding
(Zarda wa Haleeb)

(Makes 4 servings)

This is a spectacular pudding fit for formal presentations. A shallow platter is filled half with fragrant saffron-yellow rice pudding and half with white rice pudding, and the surface is decorated with ground cinnamon. The yellow part of the dessert, *zarda* (meaning yellow), is well known in the neighboring countries. Besides, judging from the many references to the *zarda* in *The Arabian Nights* it seemed to have been a favorite dish amongst people in the middle ages. However, it is the combination of the white and yellow puddings that gives this dessert a touch of originality indigent to the region. Since only the yellow part is sweetened, the traditional way to enjoy this dish is to combine the two portions in each mouthful.

1 recipe Rice Pudding above, omit sugar

1/2 cup rice, washed, soaked in water for 30 minutes, then break rice grains by rubbing between fingers, do not drain
6 cups water
1/4 teaspoon salt

1 teaspoon saffron, steeped in 1/4 cup hot water
1/4 cup corn starch dissolved in 1/2 cup cold water
1 cup sugar
1 to 2 tablespoons rose water
For garnish: ground cinnamon

1. Prepare rice pudding as given in the previous recipe.

2. Prepare saffron pudding, put rice, water and salt in a medium heavy pot. Bring to a boil, then reduce heat to medium and let cook gently until rice is thoroughly cooked, 20 to 25 minutes.

3. Mash saffron in hot water with a spoon to get as much color from it as possible, and add it to the cooked rice with the liquid.

4. Add dissolved cornstarch and sugar, stir well and resume cooking gently on medium heat. Stir occasionally until pudding nicely thickens, about 15 minutes. Add rosewater.

5. To assemble a dish: Fill a rather flat plate half with the white rice pudding and half with the yellow saffron pudding. Decorate surface with ground cinnamon.

FRUITY DESSERTS

Besides eating fruits fresh there are some nice ways of serving them as desserts, as well. This works especially well with dried fruits, and versatile vegetables such as pumpkin and carrots.

445

Golden Pumpkin Strips
(Shara'h al-Shijar al-Ahmer)

(Makes 4 servings)

Serve this attractive dessert in a transparent bowl with a dollop of cool whip or vanilla ice cream.

2 pounds pumpkin pulp, cut into 1/2 -inch thin strips
1 cup sugar
3/4 cup water
1/4 teaspoon salt
3 whole cardamom pods
1/4 cup toasted broken walnut

1. In a heavy medium pan layer pumpkin strips with sugar.

2. Add water, salt and cardamom and bring to a boil. Then reduce heat to medium and cook until pumpkin is tender and liquid is considerably reduced, about 15 minutes. Fold frequently and gently while cooking.

3. Allow to cool, then chill. To serve, empty into a serving bowl, and sprinkle with walnuts.

Stuffed Dates
(Tamur Mahshi)

(Makes 20 pieces)

Dates by themselves make an excellent dessert, natural and wholesome. However, for special occasions, they can also be made into attractive and elegant dessert.

20 pitted dates
20 toasted almonds, or toasted walnut halves, or more depending on size of dates

1/2 cup water
1/2 cup sugar
3 tablespoons cocoa powder
1 teaspoon rose water

1cup all-purpose flour or wheat
1/4 cup butter
1/4 teaspoon ground cardamom
For garnish: ground pistachio or shredded unsweetened coconut

1. Stuff pitted dates with toasted nuts.

2. Make medium syrup by boiling water, sugar, and cocoa powder until syrup starts to cover back of a metal spoon, about 10 minutes. Add rose water and let cool.

3. Meanwhile, in a small skillet melt butter, and add flour. Stir all the time until flour is fragrant and evenly browned, about 5 minutes. Add cardamom.

4.Dip each filled date in syrup and roll it in toasted flour. Let dates pick as much as possible of the flour. Spread remaining flour on a dish and arrange dates on this bed. Sprinkle with ground pistachio or shredded coconut, and serve with coffee.

Variation:
Dip stuffed dates in melted chocolate, white or dark, or both.

Apricot Delight
(Halawat al-Mishmish)

(Makes 4 servings)

Sweet and sour dried apricots make an appealing dessert garnished with cream and sprinkled with bright green broken pistachio.

> **20 dried apricots (about 1 cup)**
> **1 1/2 cup water**
> **1/3 cup sugar**
> **1 teaspoon grated lemon peel**
>
> **1 tablespoon rose water**
> **1 cup cool whip**
> **Shelled pistachio, some broken into small pieces and some left whole**

1. Put apricots, water, sugar and peel in a small heavy pot. Bring to a boil, then lower heat to low, and let simmer gently until mixture becomes syrupy, about 35 minutes.

2. In a blender or food processor purée apricot mixture. Chill for a few hours.

3. Mix in rose water and cool whip. Spread on a serving dish and decorate with some cream and pistachio, to your fancy.

Nawal Nasrallah

Apricot Balls
(Kurat al-Mishmish)

(Makes 15 balls)

Dried apricots are packed with goodness. You can make some nice and simple desserts with them. These apricot balls make an almost guilt-free snack that you and your guests can nibble on.

20 dried apricots (about 1 cup)
3/4 cup shredded sweetened coconut, divided
1 teaspoon rose water

In a blender or food processor puree apricots, 1/2 cup coconut, and rose water for about 3 minutes or until the mixture starts to gather into a ball. If apricots are not soft enough, adding a little orange juice will help. Form into 15 balls about 1 inch in diameter each. Roll them in the remaining 1/4 cup coconut, and set them aside overnight at room temperature to allow them to dry out.

Apricot "Truffles"
(Kurat al-Mishmish)

(Makes 20 balls)

This is another apricot snack packed with goodness what with all the dried apricots and the powdered milk called for in this recipe. They are tasty, not so sweet, and delightfully chewy. If you want them a little bit sweeter, add the optional sugar. I first made this delightful dessert by accident. I was planning to make the apricot balls, but the dried apricots I had were not soft enough, so I soaked them in orange juice for a few hours. When I puréed them with the coconut, I got a wet mushy mixture. So I kept on adding dried milk until mixture formed into a ball. It tasted so good that ever since it became a favorite.

20 dried apricots (about 1 cup). Soak in orange juice for a few hours, then drain
1/2 cup sweetened shredded coconut
1 tablespoon grated orange peel
3 cups dried milk (such as Nido). If milk is grainy, press it through a sieve
1/4 cup powdered sugar, optional
1 tablespoon rose water

For coating: ground nuts, or shredded coconut
For garnish: 20 shelled whole pistachios, and about 2 ounces melted chocolate

1. In a blender or a food processor blend drained apricots, coconut, grated orange peel, powdered milk, powdered sugar, if used, and rose water. Process or blend on high speed for about 2 minutes, or

448

until mixture starts to form a ball and looks like thick paste. If mixture looks is a little dry add some of the drained orange juice, or rose water.

2. Form into 20 small balls, about 1 inch across. Roll balls in nuts or coconut. Press a shelled pistachio in the center of each, and drizzle with melted chocolate. Set aside to set.

Stuffed Prunes
(Injas Mahshi)

(Makes 5 servings)

Prunes prepared this way are transformed into a refreshing dessert served chilled and garnished with a dollop of whipped cream. Brewed tea adds enticing depth to the stuffed prunes.

20 prunes, soaked overnight in hot brewed tea
20 walnut pieces, toasted

1/2 cup packed brown sugar
1 tablespoon lemon juice
1 tablespoon rose water, or brandy if wished

For garnish: whipped cream

1. Drain prunes, and reserve the liquid.

2. Stuff prunes with walnut pieces.

3. In a small pot combine sugar, lemon juice, and 1 cup of the reserved liquid, if not enough is left add water to make one cup. Bring to a quick boil, then reduce heat to medium and let cook gently for about 10 minutes.

4. Add stuffed prunes carefully to the syrup, and let simmer gently for about 20 minutes. Dessert is done when syrup is of medium consistency. To test put a drop of syrup in a cold plate. It should keep its domed shape even if you shake the dish a little.

5. Allow to cool to room temperature. Add rose water or brandy, then chill for a few hours. Serve in small bowls garnished with cool whip.

CANDIES AND CONFECTIONS
Halawa

The following traditional rich desserts are steeped in sugar and oil, and lots of history. They have been cooking in the region for centuries by professional confectioners and house makers alike. The

449

ancient Mesopotamian date desserts, for instance, still have their counterparts in our kitchens, and most of the halwa made during the medieval era can still be found at the traditional confectioners'. Their basic ingredients are flour, cornstarch, oil, nuts, and sweeteners such as dates, date syrup, honey, and sugar. Aromatics are mostly rose water, cardamom and mastic. The great number of the halwa recipes in the Baghdadi medieval cookbooks is testimony enough on the popularity of this kind of food. Unfortunately, delicious as they are, they come loaded with fat and sugar. The following recipes have been adapted to suit a more updated diet.

Date Sweetmeat
(Halawat al-Tamur)
(Makes 8 servings)

This is the most ancient halwa ever prepared in Mesopotamian kitchens for dates were plenty and cheap. To begin with, they were stored in vats in dry places to be used all year round. In the ancient cuneiform texts they were sometimes referred to as "fresh" or "pitted", they were crushed and made into jam, but also into "daspu," (date syrup, cf. Arabic, *dibs*) which was quite useful in making desserts. In Sumerian cuneiform tablets, a certain type of pastry called "girilam" was mentioned frequently. It was a preparation of mashed dates and sesame oil, sweetened with honey and bound together with a small amount of flour (Limet, 134). Another sweet preparation was referred to as "mirsu of honey, ghee, and dates" (Levey, 49). The Arabic language retained the Akkadian word "marsu," meaning, "mash". In the medieval cookbooks, we find similar date *halwas* called *marees*.

In the Baghdadi medieval cookbooks this type of halwa was called *ha'is* (al-Baghdadi, 214) or *hays* (al-Warraq, 259). It was prepared by mixing fine bread or cookie crumbs with pitted dates, ground almonds and pistachios. The mixture was to be kneaded with some sesame oil or butter, then formed into *kubabs* (balls) or discs, to be dusted with sugar. It was highly recommended as travel food for pilgrims on their way to Mekka.

In modern times no sweeteners are added to this sweetmeat. Flour used here is toasted to enhance the aroma of the dessert and to give the dessert a more interesting texture. Besides, the toasted flour helps balance the sweetness of the dates. Traditionally the flour is browned in lots of clarified butter.

> **1/2 cup flour**
> **1/4 cup butter**
> **2 cups pitted dates (1 pound)**
>
> **1/2 teaspoon ground cardamom**
> **1/2 teaspoon coarsely ground toasted aniseeds or fennel**
> **1/2 teaspoon whole coriander seeds**
>
> **1/4 cup toasted nuts of your choice**

1. In a heavy skillet dry toast flour until it starts to change color and emit an aroma, about 7 minutes on medium high. Transfer toasted flour to a container.

2. On medium heat, and in the same skillet, put dates and butter and mash them with the back of a wooden spoon. While stirring, folding and mashing, gradually sprinkle in the toasted flour,

450

cardamom, aniseeds and coriander, about 10 minutes. If dates look dry and hard to mash, add a little hot water until dates soften.

4. Spread the date mixture on a flat platter, and level the surface with the back of the spoon. Press nuts in a decorative way on the surface and crimp all around the edge like a pie. To serve, cut into thin wedges. Or spread in a pan, and cut into squares or triangles.

Easy Spicy Date Sweetmeat
(Madgouga)

(Makes 8 servings)

This dessert is originally pounded in a mortar and pestle, and hence the name *madgouga* (the pounded). A dry variety of dates called *ashrasi,* is usually used. You may substitute with any kind of dates that are on the dry side.

1/2 cup flour
2 cups pitted dates (1 pound)
1/4 cup tahini

1/2 to 1 teaspoon cardamom
1/2 teaspoon coarsely ground toasted aniseeds
1/2 teaspoon crushed coriander seeds

1/2 cup toasted nuts
1 tablespoon toasted sesame seeds

1. To dry toast flour, put it in a heavy skillet and on medium high heat, fold it until it changes color into tannish brown and is fragrant, about 7 minutes.

2. Put dates, tahini, and toasted flour in a food processor or blender. Blend or process until mixture forms a ball, about 2 minutes. If it looks rather dry add a little bit more tahini.

3. Take out of the blender or processor, and fold in cardamom, aniseeds, and coriander.

4. Press half the date mixture onto a flat plate forming a 7-inch disc. Arrange toasted nuts all over the surface. Cover with the remaining date mixture. Press sesame seeds into the surface, crimp all around the edge, and cut into thin wedges. Alternatively you can form date mixture into small balls. Stuff each with a piece of nuts, and roll it the toasted sesame.

Vermicelli noodles

Sweet 'n Golden Vermicelli Noodles
(Halawat Sha'riyya)

(Makes 4 servings)

Vermicelli noodles can make an elegant dessert easy to prepare and rewardingly delicious. In the stories of *The Arabian Nights* it is always included whenever refined desserts are mentioned and good living is invoked. Do not be tempted to try it with noodles other than vermicelli, though. I once experimented with the local rustic noodles called *rishta*, which are darker in color and coarser in texture. My family ate it all right, but when I asked how it was, they politely said it was good, but don't make it any more. The moral is: never underestimate the power of a fine noodle.

2 tablespoons butter
6 ounces vermicelli noodles, slightly broken between the fingers (about 7 balls)
2 cups hot water

1 1/4 cups sugar, or brown sugar, make sure to pack the cup when measuring
A pinch of salt

452

1 teaspoon ground cardamom, and/or 1 tablespoon rose water
For garnish: coarsely chopped toasted nuts

1. Melt butter in a heavy pot. Fold in broken noodles and stir constantly until golden brown, about 5 minutes.

2. Carefully pour in hot water for it will sputter.

3. Let noodles simmer on low heat, covered, until they start to soften, 4 to 5 minutes.

4. Add sugar and salt and stir well to allow sugar to dissolve. Let simmer on medium-low until all moisture is absorbed, stirring frequently lest it should stick to the bottom of the pot, about 15 minutes.

5. Put away from heat, add cardamom or rose water. Spread on a flat plate evening up top with back of a spoon. Sprinkle with chopped nuts.

Halwa of Toasted Flour
(Halawat Taheen)

(Makes 6 servings)

This is another dessert that has been cooking in the region ever since ancient times. The Akkadian texts tell of a sweet dish called "muttaqu," made of flour, sesame oil, honey and water (Levey, 49). In the medieval times it came to be called *khabees* (the mixed) using basically the same ingredients as we still do to this day. There were many variations on the medieval *khabees*, some were white and others were yellow with saffron, some were solid and others *ratib* (moist). Elaborate decorations were also suggested for impressive presentations.

The toasting of flour called for in this recipe prevents it from getting glutinous and doughy while simmering, and it gives the dish an alluring aroma. However it requires constant attention since it is so easy to get the flour burnt. Toast it less than required and the dessert will be weak in aroma and pale in color. Toast it longer than required and you end up having a good-for-nothing blackened mixture. In all probability it was this kind of tricky dessert that the contemporary Iraqi folkloric poet Mudhaffar al-Nawwab had in mind when he composed his poem "*Lil-Rel wa Hamad*" (For the train and Hamad). In this poem the "burnt up" soul of a frustrated lover is compared to *halawa* cooked at night, assumably in a dimly lit cottage.

1 1/2 cups sugar
3 cups water

1/4 cup butter
1 1/2 cups all- purpose flour or whole wheat
1 teaspoon ground cardamom, or 1 tablespoon rose water, or to taste
For garnish: toasted slivered almonds, or toasted walnuts

453

1.In a medium pot dissolve sugar in water and let boil for 5 minutes.

2. In a heavy medium pot, melt butter and add flour. Stir well on medium heat until flour changes color into medium brown and becomes fragrant, 10 to 12 minutes.

3. Put pot away from heat, (as it will splutter) and gradually pour syrup, stirring constantly with a wire whisk to prevent lumping.

4. Return pot to stove and, on medium heat, continue cooking and stirring until it thickens, about 5 minutes. If it thickens too fast, add a little hot water and continue cooking.

5. Stir in cardamom or rose water, and immediately spread on a flat plate, evening up the surface with the back of a spoon. Garnish surface with toasted nuts.

Halwa of Mastic
(Halawa Mastakıyya)

(Makes 8 servings)

In al-Waerraq's tenth-century dessert section this halwa was called *khabbees abyadh* (white halwa). It called for cornstarch dissolved in some water, and was flavored with mastic. When spread on a platter it was beautifully decorated with a dome made of honey *natif* (nougat, something like caramalized honey), that was drizzled while still hot. Triangles of colored sugar, and almonds colored red, yellow and green along with pistachios were arranged on the dome (246).

1 1/2 cups sugar
2 cups water
1/4 teaspoon cream of tartar or citric acid, or 1 teaspoon lemon juice
1/2 cup cornstarch
2 pieces mastic, or 1 tablespoon mastic cream, see Glossary
1/4 cup toasted almonds or walnuts

1. In a heavy pot dissolve sugar in water and let boil for about 5 minutes. Add citric acid or lemon juice. Put away from heat.

2. Dissolve cornstarch in a little cold water and, away from heat; add to the syrup stirring with a wire whisk.

3. Return pot to heat and continue cooking, stirring all the time, until it thickens, about 10 minutes. Add mastic and nuts, and stir for a few more minutes.

5. Spread mixture on a lightly greased platter, or individual plates. Sprinkle top with icing sugar or ground nuts.

Dental Care in Ancient Mesopotamia

The ancient Mesopotamians were well aware of the association between excessive sweetness in food and tooth decay. The ancient "Incantation against Toothache" tells how after heaven and earth and the rivers were created, the worm goes weeping before the sun god Shamash, and its tears flowing before Ea, god of water, saying,
"What wilt thou give me for my food?
What wilt thou give me for my sucking?"
Shamash promises to give it the ripe fig and the apricot. But the worm does not like this and answers back,
"Of what use they to me, the ripe fig
[And] the apricot?
Lift me up and among the teeth
And the gums cause me dwell!
The blood of tooth I will suck,
And of the gums cause to dwell!
The blood of tooth I will suck,
And of the gum I will gnaw
Its roots!"
Obviously, the ancients saw that the sweet dried fruits were excellent pastures for the small white worms, which the simple imagination associated with the tooth nerve. And the legend continues to this day. One of the expressions used describing a decayed tooth is *sin mdawwid* (i.e. a tooth having worms in it).

Needless to say, the worm was punished for its rebelliousness, for there are instructions for the dentist to extract the decayed tooth where the worm dwells (Pritchard, vol.1, 75-6).

As for less drastic cases of tooth decay, evidently they used gum to fill cavities, and applied poppy seeds to soothe toothache. Cardamom seeds were also used for the same purpose, and as breath freshener, as we still do to this day (Thompson, 118, 178-80). Recent research confirms that cardamom can help prevent cavities.

Halwa of Toasted Rice Flour
(Halawat Timman)

(Makes 8 servings)

During the medieval times rice in desserts was mostly prepared *aruzziya* way (rice pudding), and none of the condensed *khabees* halwas given in the extant medieval cookbooks called for rice. Using rice in such halwas must have developed later on when rice became more commonly used.

It is important to toast the rice to perfection, as this will give the dessert a delicate golden hue and a wonderful aroma.

1 cup sugar
5 cups water

3 tablespoons butter, or oil
1 cup rice flour

1 teaspoon cardamom, or /and 1 tablespoon rose water
For garnish: almonds, slivered and toasted

1. In a medium pot, dissolve sugar in water and boil for 5 minutes.

2. In a heavy medium pot melt butter and fold in rice flour. Stir constantly until rice starts to change color and emit a pleasant aroma, about 10 minutes.

3. Put pot away from heat, for it will splutter, and gradually pour in syrup, stirring all the time with a wire whisk or a wooden spoon to prevent lumping.

4. Return pot to heat and continue cooking, stirring frequently, until mixture thickens, about 15 minutes. Add cardamom or rose water, 5 minutes before it is done.

6. Spread onto 4 cereal bowls, and garnish top with toasted nuts.

Halwa of Golden Shredded Carrot
(Halawat Jizar)

(Makes 8 servings)

This is one of the scrumptious ways in which the humble but versatile vegetable has been used in the region. It is a very popular dessert sold at confectioner's as well as made in households. The tenth-century Baghdadi cookbook gives a recipe for this dessert, called *khabees al-jazar* (halwa of carrots). Honey was used as a sweetening agent (253).

It is usually made red or yellow depending upon the color of carrots used. During the medieval times other fruits and vegetables such as qar' (gourd), apples, dates, and white poppy seeds, were also used the same way.

456

2 pounds carrots, shredded (9 to 10 medium ones)

2 cups sugar
2 tablespoons lemon juice

1/4 cup butter
1/2 cup cornstarch
1 to 2 teaspoons cardamom, or 1 tablespoon rose water, or both
For garnish: toasted walnuts or pistachio, and shredded coconut

1. Put carrots in a medium pot and add water just enough to cover carrots, about 3 1/2 cups. Bring to a boil then reduce to medium and let simmer until carrots soften, about 30 minutes. Drain in a colander fitted on a bowl, and press down extra moisture. Reserve liquid.

2. Make syrup by dissolving sugar in 2 cups of the reserved liquid, if not enough, add more water. Let it boil until medium syrup forms, about 10 minutes. To test put a drop on a dry cold plate. If it forms a ball that keeps its shape in spite of tilting the plate to different directions, it is done. Add lemon juice.

3. Meanwhile, in a heavy medium pot, melt butter and stir in cornstarch until it starts to change color, about 10 minutes. Fold in drained carrots and mix well.

4. Pour syrup into carrot mixture and continue cooking on medium heat, stirring occasionally until mixture is thickened and carrots are transparent, about 30 minutes. Add rose water or cardamom, or both.

5. Spread mixture on a big flat plate, or 8-by-8-inch pan. Decorate with toasted nuts and coconut, and cut into wedges or squares.

Turkish Delight
(Halqoum)

(Makes around 30 pieces)

This delicious chewy candy caught the fancy of the Western world and as anything coming to them from the east during the Ottoman rule it was called Turkish. Actually the Turks themselves called it *rahat lokum*, derived from Arabic, meaning something swallowed with ease.

Chewy candy made from sugar, corn starch, and oil, and flavored with mastic was already a common dessert during the time of the Abbasid Caliphate, from the ninth century AD and upwards. In the tenth-century Baghdadi cookbook a whole chapter was dedicated to similar desserts called *faloudhajat mu'allakat*. It was chewy halwa to be differentiated from *falouthaj gharf*, which was softer in consistency and was meant to be scooped. The name *faloudhaj* was an Arabized form of the Persian *paluda*, meaning the strained, most probably due to the fact that in the final stage of cooking the halwa mixture was strained of its separating oil. Basically it was made by boiling honey and sesame oil, thickened with cornstarch until chewy in texture. Toasted almonds were added, and mixture was stirred until it threw off its oil, which was to be discarded. It was then spread on a big plate oiled with pistachio or almond oil, and sprinkled with sugar mixed with ground mastic (al-Warraq, 242).

In the modern scene such delights are usually purchased from specialized candy stores. But it is fun to prepare at home. It may be made quite attractive by using different colors and flavors besides the traditional mastic flavor.

The following is an easy and fast recipe that yields delicious *halqoum,* studded with toasted nuts.

> **1 1/2 cups sugar**
> **2 cups water**
> **1/4 teaspoon cream of tartar or citric acid, or 1 tablespoon lemon juice**
>
> **1/2 cup cornstarch dissolved in a little cold water**
> **2 small pieces mastic, or 1 tablespoon mastic cream, see Glossary**
> **1/4 cup toasted almonds or walnuts**

1. Put sugar and water in a medium heavy pot, and on high heat bring to a boil, stirring until sugar completely dissolves, about 5 minutes. Add cream of tartar or lemon juice.

2. Put pot away from heat, and add dissolved cornstarch, stirring vigorously to prevent cornstarch from lumping.

3. Return pot to heat and continue cooking on medium high stirring all the time until mixture becomes very thick, about 10 minutes. Stir in mastic and toasted nuts. To test for doneness, take a small amount and rub it between your fingers. If it does not stick, it is done.

4. Spread mixture into a greased 6-by-4- inch pan. Set aside at room temperature for about 12 hours. Turn it onto a flat surface sprinkled with cornstarch. Cut into squares using edge of a thin metal pancake turner. Roll pieces in some cornstarch to coat on all sides, and let dry in one layer for 12 more hours.

Variation: Sujuq (sausage-shaped *halqoum*): In the city of Mosul, in northern Iraq, an interesting variation on *halqoum* is available in the markets. It is shaped like sausage links and filled with walnuts. The liquid used in making these *halqoums* is grape juice, which gives it a very attractive hue and a delicious flavor. The way to make it is to thread walnut halves through strong threads about 4-foot long each, and the first and last pieces of walnuts are tied securely at each end to hold them firmly. The walnut strings are dipped into the *halqoum* mixture, then removed and set aside to cool and set. The process is repeated at least three times until walnuts are well covered. They are then hung to dry for a few days, and are finally rolled in cornstarch.

An easy way for preparing this variation on *halqoum* at home is to use grape jelly. Any other kind of fruit jelly may be substituted to give it a different flavor. You can also skip the threading of walnuts part. Just add nuts to the mixture, they'll still taste the same. Here is how to make it:

> **1 cup grape jelly**
> **1/4 cup sugar**
> **1/4 cup cornstarch, diluted in a little cold water.**
> **1/4 cup toasted nuts**

1. In a medium heavy pot bring jelly and sugar to a boil, about 5 minutes.

2. Add diluted cornstarch and stir vigorously to prevent lumping. Continue cooking until mixture is very thick, about 5 minutes. Stir in nuts.

3. Spread mixture in a greased 8-by-8-inch pan. Set aside at room temperature for 12 hours. Cut into bars or squares, and roll in cornstarch to prevent them from sticking to each other. Arrange in one layer on a tray dusted with cornstarch, and set aside for 12 hours.

Sesame Fingers
(Simsimiyya)

(Makes 32 bars)

In all probability our present day *simsimiyya* was the most ancient candy ever to be concocted on the land of Mesopotamia, where sesame grew in abundance We know at least that in the tenth century Baghdadi cookbook, something similar was made. The recipe was called *al-luluwi* (like pearls). It called for two pounds of honey to be boiled until it thickened. Then hulled sesame, as much as honey could take, was to be stirred into it. It was poured on a greased piece of marble, and when cold, it was broken into pieces (al-Warraq, 279).

Toasting the seeds is the key to fragrant and delicious *simsimiyya*. Following the way of the ancients, the sweetening agent used here is honey.

1 cup honey
2 cups well-toasted sesame seeds
1 teaspoon rose water

1. In a small heavy pot bring honey to a boil, then let cook gently on medium high heat until it starts to thicken, about 5 minutes.

2. Fold in toasted sesame and rose water. Immediately pour into a greased 8-by-8-inch pan and spread evenly with the back of a spoon.

4. When cool and hardened, cut into bars using a sharp and thin knife.

Variations: Instead of sesame seeds, other nuts like shelled pistachio, toasted hazelnuts, shredded coconut, may be substituted.

Almond Brittle
(Sahoun)

Al-Warraq's tenth-century cookbook includes a candy recipe similar to what we nowadays call *sahoun*. He names it *al-Wathiqi*, after the name of the Abbasid caliph who invented it or who used to like it a lot. It is a variation on the *natif* (nougat). One pound honey, one pound red sugar, and a little rose water are boiled until mixture thickens. Then 6 grams of saffron, and 1 pound skinned nuts are added. The mixture is then poured on a greased piece of marble, and when cold, is broken into pieces (279).

Nowadays, this translucent candy studded with toasted almonds is the specialty of the southern city of Basrah. It is usually purchased from confectioner's, and is alluringly spread in huge trays. Although traditionally toasted skinned almonds are the nuts to be used, other nuts of your choice may be substituted.

1 1/4 cup sugar
1/4 cup water
1 cup toasted skinned whole almonds

1. Put sugar and water in a small heavy pot, and bring to a boil stirring to allow sugar to dissolve.

2. Lower hear to medium, and wipe the inside walls of the pot with a wet brush or napkin to get rid of crystallized grains of sugar. Allow to cook undisturbed until sugar turns into golden brown, but be careful not to let sugar burn.

3. Add almonds and immediately pour onto a greased flat pan and spread it into a thin layer. When cool break into smaller pieces.

Almond Pastry (Marzipan)
(Lauzina)

(Makes 15 pieces)

Baghdad is reputed to be the homeland of the marzipan. Almonds that originated in central Asia were transported to the Mesopotamian region thousands of years ago, and with the arrival of cane sugar around the fourth century AD, marzipan became one of the favorite desserts at the time.

During the medieval period two kinds of almond dessert were known: *lauzinaj mughrraq* (drowned in almond oil), and *lauzinaj yabis* (dry). The former was similar to baklawa, and it will be described in the following chapter. As for the latter, there is a recipe in al-Warraq's tenth-century book for *lauzinaj yabis* in which ground almond is cooked in syrup until thick. It is scented with rose water, and kneaded with the hand and rolled like a cucumber, and is divided to sections. A simpler version is called *halwa* and is done by mixing ground toasted almonds, and ground sugar with rose water until stiff dough forms. Using carved wooden molds the dough was shaped onto small *qareesh* and *qarees* (kinds of fish, 257, 265- 6). In the thirteenth-century book it was called *samak wa aqras* (fishes and discs). Other shapes such as cocks and lambs were also made (al-Baghdadi, 212). In another recipe called *shawabeer* (triangles), a mixture of toasted almonds, pistachio, and hazelnuts was added to toasted flour-based halwa, spread, and cut into triangles (214). In another almond recipe, though called *faloudhaj* (the strained, the refined), it is actually more like *lauzeenaj yabis*, made of ground almonds and sugar. The finished halwa was shaped as "melons, triangles, etc." (211). The "etc." would also include squares, and it is quite likely that at some point the rhomboidal shape became characteristic of the candy, and eventually gave its name to the geometric shape itself. Maxime Rodinson, a supporter of this view, argues that the recipe for this dessert was translated into Latin and Italian late thirteenth and fourteenth centuries, and that "lozenge" and its variants "displaced the word rhombus" ("Venice and the Spice Trade", 210). And today this is all that remained of the old *lauzeenaj* glory.

In modern Iraq you can still see vendors in the old bazaars selling diamond-shaped white or colored candy called *lauzena*, that has no *lauz* (almonds) in it. As growing kids we used to find the name so enticing but the taste so disappointing, and wondered why on earth it was called *lauzena*. Little did we know then that it was the shape, stupid! How could we know that, when another dessert, namely the diamond shaped baklawa, some time in the past, replaced the *lauzenaj*, and itself became the promoter of the rhombus?

Following the footsteps of the medieval cooks, my recipe calls for both ground almonds and ground pistachios. This will make an appealing roll of *lauzena* paste. One more thing-- to save yourself time and trouble, use canned almond paste, available in the baking isles in most of the supermarkets. Another reason why I prefer the canned variety is that neither my grinder nor food processor was able to give me the desirable paste-like texture needed for making these dainty cookies. There is also a recipe below for making this candy from scratch, in case you have a grinder with blades sharp enough for this kind of task. The pistachio filling is inspired by al-Warraq's recipe for *khabees yabis maftout* (dry and brittle halwa) that was originally shaped while still moist into discs, cucumbers, or melons (258).

3/4 cup finely ground pistachio (about 4 ounces)
3/4 cup powdered sugar
2 tablespoons rose water

One 8-ounce can pure almond paste (or follow instructions in note, below)
2 tablespoons corn syrup or honey for glazing
Preheat oven to 350 degrees F.

1. Mix pistachio with sugar, and moisten with rose water to form into dough-like mass.
2. On a flat surface sprinkled with powdered sugar roll out almond paste into a 4-by-15-inch rectangle. Shape pistachio dough into a thick pencil-like roll 15 inches long (handle with hands sprinkled with powdered sugar). Place pistachio roll in the middle of the almond rectangle. Wrap almond dough firmly around pistachio dough overlapping edges a little. Press all along the seam to prevent it from opening up. Put this roll on a greased baking sheet seam side down. Press sides and the top so that the roll would look like a long cube. Decorate top with the blunt edge of a knife.

3. Bake in a preheated oven at 350 degrees F. about 20 minutes or until nicely browned. It will be soft at this point but it will firm up when cool. While still warm, brush the log with corn syrup or honey. Set log aside for 24 hours. Cut crosswise into 15 fingers 1-inch long each. Store in an airtight container for 3 days before using.

Note: If you want to make almond paste yourself, then follow this recipe:
1 1/2 cups whole almonds (about 8 ounces)
1 3/4 cups powdered sugar (about 8 ounces)
2 to 4 tablespoons rose water

1. Skin almonds by blanching them in hot water. Rub off skins and let almonds dry completely. Then grind them using a blender or food processor. It is better to put a little granulated sugar when grinding as this will prevent almonds from getting oily.

2. Mix almonds and icing sugar. Start by adding 2 tablespoons rose water, then add just enough to make a comfortably pliable dough. Do not be tempted to add more than is needed.

Use as directed above in step 2.

461

Mann al-Sama

(Makes about 25 pieces)

Today m*ann al-sama* (heavenly-sent manna) is an exclusively Iraqi candy the main ingredient of which is the *manna*, mentioned in the Bible and the Qur'an, as God-sent food to the people of Israel during their wanderings in Sinai Desert. We know from *The Assyrian Herbal*, a monograph on the Assyrian vegetable drugs, that oak-like trees growing in northern Mesopotamia, near Mosul and Suleimaniya of modern day, provided manna, which they made into a paste, ate for food and used for medicinal purposes. The allusions to manna in the Assyrian cuneiform medicinal texts match the Biblical references in Exodus, chapter 16. In the Akkadian it was called "supalu," and the Assyrians called the medicine made from it, "a drug of flour," "a drug of the ground," "a drug of dough paste," "gum of dough," and described it as something round, something which exudes, and also "Earth of the Moon-Crescent" (Thompson, 268-9). Our present day knowledge of the way it formulates, how it is gathered and used, corresponds perfectly with both versions.

We know that tamarisk and oak-like trees in northern Iraq exude manna through their barks in the form of sap as the result of punctures made by tiny insects during June and July. The sap falls on the leaves and down the ground into the bushes beneath the tree or on the ground. According to the Bible it is like white frost, the size of coriander seeds. The manna is then gathered early in the morning before the ants get it, and the sun melts it, and hence the Assyrian expression "Earth of the Moon-Crescent," and Biblical "bread of heaven." Manna, when gathered and is still in its rough form, is a sticky hard darkish mass with impurities such as leaves, twigs, and pebbles. After boiling and purifying it, it is then kept in pots, or shaped into small cakes, or milled. In this form it will keep indefinitely. It tastes delicately sweet, like "wafer made with honey."

Getting rid of all the impurities in the gathered manna, is a time-consuming task, and that's why most people now prefer to buy it ready-made. In the good old days, housewives used to hire experts to come to the house and prepare it for them. After purifying it, it is usually flavored with cardamom, kneaded with pistachios, almonds, or walnuts and shaped into balls the size of a golf ball each. Flour is used to keep the pieces from sticking to each other. For the special religious occasion of *Khidhr Elias* (Ilyas) the Iraqi Christians make a delicious variety on the regular *mann al sama*, shaped into balls in which the walnuts are not mixed with it but rather filled inside it like *kubba*. It is a little harder and chewier than the regular type.

To give you an idea how this confection is prepared by the experts, here is a curiosity recipe I found in Rowland's chapter on Iraq, in *Good Food from the Near East,* 1950. The technique of using eggs to purify syrup is quite a medieval one. It was used in making candy called *natif* (nougat, the Arabic word *natif* is derived from root *n-t-f*, to purify).

12 pounds manna
100 eggs
3 pounds almonds
Flour

1. Soak manna in hot water overnight to help it dissolve. Strain through fine cheesecloth.
2. Put on low heat, in a very big pot.
3. Add 25 eggs, and stir. The mixture will be clear in about 30 to 45 minutes. Strain it again. Soil and dirt will be removed with the coagulated eggs.
4. Return to heat, bring to a boil. Add whites of remaining 75 eggs. Stir constantly over low heat for five to six hours, until manna becomes a light-colored paste. It is ready when the spoon is lifted from the pan and the manna adhering to it breaks off.

5. Meanwhile toast almonds, and add them to the manna.

6. Form into flat cakes or balls about 2 inches in diameter. Roll each piece in flour, and when cold, place in layers in tins or boxes with plenty of flour between the pieces.

Genuine *mann al-sama* is hard to come by, it is chewy in texture and looks rather tan in hue. Most of the stuff sold at confectioners' is adulterated, much like what you will be getting in the following recipe, which I have adapted from a nougat preparation. The taste is quite similar to the cardamom-flavored original *mann al-sama,* it only lacks its characteristic chewiness.

Nougat was a favored candy during the middle ages. The tenth-century Baghdadi cookbook dedicates a chapter to the making of *natif* (nougat) made from honey and egg whites, and mixed with nuts and dried fruits (al-Warraq. 278-280).

2 cups sugar
1 1/2 cups corn syrup
1/4 teaspoon salt
1/4 cup water

2 egg whites
1 teaspoon ground cardamom
1/4 cup butter, softened
1 1/2 cups toasted whole unskinned almonds or broken walnuts, or whole shelled pistachio
Flour

1. Put sugar, corn syrup, salt and water in a medium heavy pot and bring to a boil stirring to allow sugar to dissolve. Keep cooking undisturbed until medium syrup forms. You can tell by placing a drop on a cold dry plate. It should keep its shape when the plate is tilted, 4 to 6 minutes.

2. While syrup is cooking, start whipping egg white on high speed until stiff and glossy peaks form.

3. While whipping pour a quarter of the syrup in a thin continuous thread over the egg white.

4. Return syrup to heat and continue cooking until heavy syrup forms, about 4 minutes. Resume pouring syrup in a thin thread on the egg white while still whipping until mixture is thick. If mixture is too thick for the beaters, continue beating with a wooden spoon.

5. Fold in cardamom, butter and nuts, and mix well until butter is well incorporated into the mixture.

6. Spread mixture into a greased 8-by-8 inch pan sprinkled with flour. Leave in pan for about 12 hours. Form mixture into about 25 balls, the size of a golf ball each. Sprinkle pieces liberally with flour to prevent them from sticking to each other, and set aside for a day or two to allow to harden.

CHAPTER SIXTEEN
DESSERTS WITH SYRUP

CHAPTER SIXTEEN
DESSERTS WITH SYRUP

حلويات بالشيرة

Sugarcane was introduced to the Mesopotamian region around the fourth century AD, before that the most important sources for sweetening agents were the date syrup and the more expensive honey. By the eighth century pastry making reached a high level of sophistication and refinement. A large number of fried pastries dipped in syrup were developed by the medieval cooks due to the fact that they were easily prepared in the convenience of the medieval ordinary kitchens that did have ready access to ovens the way we do now. A few of the pastry dishes were lowered into the *tannour* instead of frying them, and others were sent to the neighborhood commercial *furn* (brick oven). Al-Warraq, in one of the recipes recommends sending the prepared dough to *tannour khabbaz al-Rusafi* (a baker on the eastside of Baghdad), which must have been a famous bakery back then (260). Most of the recipes in al-Warraq's cookbook call for warmed honey to drench the fried pastries, and that is because his book deals with the haute cuisine of the caliphs and princes. The majority used simple syrup or *julab*, syrup made of rose water and cane sugar.

Most of these medieval pasties are still popular in the entire Middle East such as baklawa, *zilabya*, *kunafa*, and *qata'f*, and can be purchased from specialized confectioneries. However, with the availability of ingredients like fillo dough, *kunafa* and light corn syrup, making such sweet delights becomes an easy and enjoyable pastime.

Baklawa

Of the entire array of the Middle-Eastern desserts, baklawa is, by far, the most widely known confection outside its region of origin. And what is its region of origin? Nobody knows for sure. Neither do we know where the word baklawa came from. In the Turkish texts the word first occurred in the sixteenth century in its archaic form, *baqlagu.* However, around the ninth century in medieval Baghdad a delicate pastry called *lauzeenaj* was made, which might well have been one of the earliest ancestors of baklawa.

As described by the eloquent protagonist of tenth-century *Al-Risala al-Baghdadiya* (Baghdadi Tract), the best *lauzeenaj* was made from *raqeeq al-riqaq* (the thinnest of the thin bread, *riqaq*). It was perfumed with mastic and rose water, well stuffed with almonds and sugar, and fried in almond oil. When you eat it, it should melt in your mouth even before chewing it (al-Tawheedi, 162-3). The Baghdadis were so much fond of it that they called it *ahjar al-janna* (the stones of paradise). The pastry wrappers were so delicate that the medieval poet Ibn al-Rumi compared them to *naseem al-saba*, the gentle eastern breeze.

The tenth-century Baghdadi cookbook gives a recipe for making these thin wrappers, usually called, *waraq* (paper). Thin batter was made of cornstarch, water and egg white, and was poured in small quantities onto a hot metal plate called *tabaq* (37). The same hot plate was used for baking the thin *riqaq* breads, *kunafa* (shredded dough), and *qata'if* crepes.

When speaking of the medieval *lauzeenaj*, however, we must differentiate between the dry kind, *lauzeenaj yabis*, which was more like marzipan of ground almonds and sugar bound with rose water, and the baklawa-like variety called *lauzeenaj mugharraq* (immersed in oil and syrup). As given in the two Baghdadi medieval cookbooks, the filling was made by binding ground sugar and nuts such as almonds, walnuts and pistachio, with rose water, just like marzipan. The thin sheets of dough were wrapped around the stuffing like a roll, and were cut into smaller pieces, as desired, and immersed in fresh almond or walnut oil, and syrup. For garnish they were sometimes sprinkled with ground pistachio (al-Warraq, 265-6, al-Baghdadi, 211).

As to how that pastry might have been the ancestor of our baklawa, I need to point out first that although the layered baklawa, cut into diamonds is the most familiar type, baklawa similar in shape to the medieval *lauzeenaj* is still equally common along with other shapes, as you will see in the following recipes. A thin sheet of dough is rolled around a nut filling, and is cut to smaller pieces is nowadays called *asabi' al-'arous* (the bride's fingers). Besides, in the story of "The Porter and the Three Dames" in the earliest Arabic manuscript of *The Arabian Nights,* one of the desserts the dame buys is *kul wa'shkur* (eat and be thankful, Mahdi, vol.1, 127). A recipe in the same name was given in the thirteenth-century *Al-Wusla ila'l-Habbeb* of Aleppo (Rodinson, "Studies in Arabic Manuscripts", 142). Rodinson is right in identifying it as baklawa still known in the Arab countries.

Layering thin sheets of dough and using nuts for a filling was also commonly practiced during the medieval period. For this type of thing they used flour-based *awraq al-riqaq* (paper-thin breads) and not the air-thin cornstarch mixture. To make them so thin, they either prepared thin batter and poured small amounts of it on a heated metal plate, called *tabaq*, or they rolled out pieces of dough into very thin sheets (*raffee'an jiddan*, al Warraq, 35) using a long dowel, the same way we do nowadays (al-Warraq, 12). As for layering and stuffing dough with nuts, there is a recipe in al-Warraq's book, which he describes as beautiful pastry (*judhaba maleeha*) called *julabiyya* (drenched in rose water syrup). It is prepared as follows:

Fat is melted first in a pot, then a thin bread is put in the bottom. Pieces of bread sprinkled with rose water are layered with a mixture of ground almonds and sugar. The layering is repeated until the pot is almost full. Julab (syrup) is poured all over, and beaten egg is spread on top as a protective crust while baking in the *tannour*, to be discarded when baking is done. Being a *judhaba* dish, a piece of cheese, or a plump chicken is suspended on the pot while baking, so that it takes all the dripping fats and juices (240).

There is another pastry preparation in the thirteenth-century *Andalusian Anonymous Cookbook*. It is called *judhabat um al-faraj* (named after the female cook, the mother of al-Faraj), and the writer states that it is an Eastern dish (referring to the Abbasid rule in the east, the capital city of which was Baghdad). It was not a *judhaba* proper because the chicken was not suspended on the sweet pastry preparation, it was rather cooked aside and put inside it as a stuffing. What is more relevant here is the layering of the thin sheets of pastry. Extremely thin sheets of *riqaq* are made by pouring small quantities of batter onto a hot metal plate. The dish is constructed by lining a greased pot with two layers of the thin bread. Ground almonds, sugar, and cinnamon are dusted on the thin breads, and are dribbled with oil and rose water, enough to dampen the sugar. The layering is repeated until half the pot is full. The prepared chicken is spread all over, and the layering of thin breads with sugar and almonds is repeated exactly the same way until the pot is full. Then the top would be sprinkled with a lot of sugar and oil. The pot is covered with a lid, sealed with dough, baked and then inverted on a platter, and served (117-8).

Obviously what we see in this dish is the characteristic layering of baklawa, without the chicken of course. Also for those who are familiar with the present day Moroccan sweet dish, *pastilla*, this pastry-chicken preparation is definitely how it all started. Incidentally, many Moroccan cooks nowadays substitute the homemade labor-intensive *wureiqat* (thin leaves of dough) with fillo dough, as we do when making baklawa.

The technique of scoring pastry before baking it, characteristic of the layered baklawa, was also practiced in the medieval period. In the tenth-century cookbook, there is a *shahmiya* (from *shahm*, tallow) pastry recipe in which the dough was spread in the pan and scored with a knife lengthwise and crosswise. When the pastry comes out of the oven, it is re-scored, and honey is poured all over to allow the pastry soak up the syrup (al-Warraq, 260-1).

Julab: Sweet Migration

Julep is widely known as a sweet alcoholic beverage in the southern states of USA. It is traditionally flavored with mint, and served with crushed ice, and is closely associated with the Kentucky Derby. Although there are many recipes for making the drink, they all boil down to Bourbon, mint, crushed ice and syrup. And it was this syrup that gave its name to this thirst-quenching southern drink. During the Abbasid rule in the Middle Ages it was called *julab*, and was made from boiling rose water with cane sugar. In this concentrated form it was used the same way we use simple syrups to drench pastries. It was also added to medicines to make their taste more acceptable. Diluted in water or fresh fruit juices, with ice, it made refreshing drinks, exactly as we still do to this day.

No recipe was given for making it in the Baghdadi cookbooks, probably because it was too well-known to need a recipe. Luckily, the anonymous Andalusian cookbook writer provided us with one. 5 pounds of aromatic rose water were mixed with 2/12 pounds sugar, and boiled down to syrup consistency (136).

The Arabic name for this rosewater syrup was based on the Middle Persian *gulab*, rose water. As syrup it was known all over Europe. In Portuguese it was "julepe," in Latin, "julapium," and "julep" is the French adaptation. The syrup could have migrated to America with all the fluxes of the European immigrants, or it could have been brought over by the African slaves.

Traditional commercial baklawa is usually made sweet and rich, and if you want to have your baklawa and eat it, you'd better make it at home where you are more in control of your ingredients. No, I am not going to go ahead and give you a recipe on how to make your own dough yourself. Life is just too short to learn how to flatten a dough until it is as thin as onion skins, as our grandmothers used to boast, or as thin as *naseem al- saba* (eastern breeze). Fillo dough works just fine.

Since baklawa is shaped and filled in many different ways, it is more practical to divide the process of making it into three stages:1. preparing the syrup. 2. preparing the filling. 3. filling, shaping, and baking the baklawa.

Medium Syrup for Baklawa:

Medium syrup is required for making baklawa. It should be thin enough to be absorbed by the baked pastry but thick enough to prevent baklawa from getting soggy. If you are not in the mood for messing up with syrups, **2 cups light corn syrup may be substituted. However, do not forget to warm it up with some rose water, orange blossom water or cardamom to give it an original flavor.** (Warming up corn syrup before using it, will help make it a little thinner in consistency, and hence easier to be absorbed by the pastry)

As for home made syrup, cook it before or while baklawa is baking in the oven to allow it to cool down before using it.

2 cups sugar
1 3/4 cup cups water
1/4 cup honey
1 tablespoon lemon juice, or 1/4 teaspoon cream of tartar or citric acid, see Glossary
2 whole cardamom pods, or 1 teaspoon rose water, or orange blossom water

1. In a medium pot combine all ingredients except for rose or orange blossom water if using any. Bring to a boil on high heat stirring frequently with a wooden spoon to allow sugar to dissolve. Skim as needed.

2. Reduce heat to medium and let syrup cook gently, uncovered and undisturbed, otherwise it will cloud or crystallize, about 20 minutes. To test, simply put a drop of the syrup on a flat dry saucer and tilt the dish to different directions. If drop keeps its domed shape, it is done. If it goes flat, then you need to cook it more, and test again. Another way for testing syrup is to drop some syrup off the end of the spoon. If syrup is thick enough, the last drop will cling to the tip of the spoon

3. When syrup is done put it away from heat. Add rose or orange blossom water if using any. Allow it to cool before using or use as directed in the recipes.

Fillings for Baklawa

Nut filling: The most commonly used nuts for baklawa are walnuts, pistachios, and almonds. The best way to grind nuts is to use the shredding attachment in the salad shooter or the food processor. In other words use any grinder that allows the nuts to come out after they are ground. The regular coffee grinder, blender or food processor will either pulverize the nuts or leave you with uneven-sized ground nuts.

> **1 pound ground nuts (about 4 cups)**
> **1/4 cup sugar**
> **2 teaspoons ground cardamom**
> **1/2 teaspoon cinnamon**

Mix ingredients in a bowl and use as directed.

Note: Baklawa filled with nuts does not need refrigeration if consumed within 3 to 4 days. Nut-filled baklawa freezes very well. To serve frozen baklawa, take it out of the freezer and allow it to thaw for about 1 hour. If you like to have it warm, heat it in a moderate oven for about 10 minutes. Do not use the microwave oven for heating it.

Cream Filling (Geymer): Traditionally, layered triangles of dough are filled with slabs of *geymer,* which is a kind of thick cream (see Chapter Two on dairy products). Alternatively the following filling gives baklawa a much lighter touch:

> **4 heaping tablespoons cornstarch or rice flour or 2 tablespoons of each**
> **3 tablespoons sugar**
> **2 cup cups whole milk**
> **1 tablespoon rose water**

1. In a small heavy pot mix cornstarch or rice flour or both with sugar. Slowly stir in milk until all solids are dissolved.

2. On medium heat bring to a boil stirring most of the time to prevent mixture from sticking to the bottom of the pot, until mixture thickens (7 to 10 minutes total time of cooking). In consistency the mixture should be thicker than the regular pudding. To test, when dropped from the spoon it should keep its shape.

3. Put away from heat and add rose water. Set aside covered to cool completely. Use as directed in the recipe.
Note: Cream-filled baklawa can be enjoyed warm or chilled. Any leftovers should be kept in the refrigerator. Freezing is not recommended for this baklawa.

Egg White-Nut Filling: This filling is used in open-faced baklawa to prevent the filling from scattering while handling and baking. The toasting of the almonds and walnuts is recommended to bring out their flavor.

> **2 egg whites, stiffly beaten**
> **1/2 cup sugar**

> **1 pound toasted, ground nuts**
> **1 tablespoon rose water, or to taste**
> **1 teaspoon cardamom, or to taste**

Fold ingredients together, and use as directed.

Note: No need to refrigerate baklawa with this filling if it is consumed within 3 to 4 days. Freeze and defrost as directed in Nut Filling given above.

Tips on Brushing Fillo dough

Fillo dough used in making desserts is always brushed with melted butter for maximum flavor. For a pound of fillo dough try to use between 1/2 cup to 3/4 cup melted butter. To reduce the amount of fat used, you can substitute some of the butter with whipped 2 egg whites. Some light varieties of butter may be substituted for regular butter.

Another suggestion. To give the layers a lighter texture and more height and thickness, after brushing each sheet with butter, sprinkle it lightly with breadcrumbs or crumbs of stale cake.

Shaping the Baklawa
Layered Diamonds
(Makes about 25 pieces)

This is the most commonly known shape of baklawa. Indeed some people think that this is the only form that baklawa comes in. In Iraq the rhombus is called baklawa after the way this baklawa is cut.

One 1-pound package fillo dough, thawed according to package directions
1/2 to 3/4 cup melted butter
> **Half recipe of** Nut Filling
> **Half recipe of** Medium Syrup, **given above, cooled**
> **For garnish: ground pistachio, optional**
> **Preheat oven to 350 degrees F.**

1. Brush with melted butter a pan half the size of the filo dough sheets or the nearest in size

2. Lay the stack of fillo sheets flat. With a sharp knife divide into half, crosswise, and stack them together. Because this baklawa goes really fast, you might not need to cover it, but keep it away from draft.

3. Brush one layer and put it flat in the bottom of the pan. Fold any extra dough if you are not using a pan exactly as big as the sheet (but in this case remember to alternate the places of folds, as you stack up, to get an even height of the layers). Repeat the layering and brushing until you get 12 layers stacked. Spread 1/3 of the filling. Layer and brush 8 more sheets and spread the second 1/3 of the filling. Layer and brush another stack of 8 sheets and spread with the last third of the filling. Then cover it with 12 brushed layers or with whatever is left of the sheets.

This might sound like too many layers but in fact the height of the pieces you will end up having will not be more than 1 3/4 inch. To summarize the layering and filling, this is the way it goes:
12 sheets _1/3 filling _ 8 sheets _ 1/3 filling _ 8 sheets _ 1/3 filling _ 12 sheets.

4. Press down the layers very well. Then brush the entire surface with the remaining butter. With a sharp knife score the surface all the way down, into small diamonds. To get diamond-shaped pieces, cut at first lengthwise into strips, then cut diagonal intersecting lines. **Spray the surface with some water to prevent dough sheets from curling up while baking.**

5. Bake in a preheated oven at 350 degrees F. for the first 30 minutes then reduce heat to 300 degrees F., and bake for another 30 minutes or until golden brown. Slow baking is essential in this kind of baklawa because of the too many layers, so don't try to rush it.

6. Take out of the oven and while still hot pour cooled syrup all over the surface. Let it rest for at least 2 hours to give it time to absorb syrup.

7. Re-cut pieces, and arrange them on a serving platter. If you like, sprinkle pieces with ground pistachio.

A tray of baklawa, 474, and kunafa rolls, 479

Small Rolls (The Bride's Fingers)
(Asabi' al-Arous)

(Makes about 80 small pieces)

This way of rolling the dough yields gracefully thin rolls reminiscent of the original medieval *lauzeenaj* pastries, made of almond filling wrapped in paper-thin breads and drenched in almond oil and honey.

One 1-pound package fillo dough, thawed according to package directions
1/2 to 3/4 cup melted butter
One recipe Nut Filling
One recipe Medium Syrup, **given above, cooled**
For garnish: ground pistachio, optional
Preheat oven to 350 degrees F.

1. On working surface lay a fillo sheet flat, brushing half of it crosswise with melted butter. Fold in half, crosswise, and brush the top. Keep the rest of dough covered with a dry kitchen cloth, away from draft.

2. Spread about 2 tablespoons of nut filling on the surface, leaving uncovered about 1/2 inch all around the edges.

3. Slightly fold the top longer edge on the filling. Roll tightly jellyroll fashion, starting from the longer folded topside down to the bottom edge.

4. With the help of a spatula carefully transfer the roll to a greased cookie sheet wide enough to accommodate the roll without bending. Put seam side down.

5. Repeat the same procedure with the rest of the sheets, arranging rolls side by side on baking sheet. You'll end up having around 20 slender rolls. Brush rolls with remaining butter.

6. Bake in a preheated oven at 350 degrees F. for 35 to 40 minutes, or until golden brown. The slower the oven is, the crispier and more evenly baked the baklawa will be. However, comparatively speaking, these should bake a little faster than the layered kind, so watch it.

7. Take out of the oven, and while still hot pour syrup on rolls. Let them rest for at least 2 hours to allow syrup to be absorbed.

9. To serve, trim off ends of rolls, and cut each roll crosswise (diagonally if you wish) into 4 to 5 pieces. Sprinkle with ground pistachio, as desired.

Swirls or Coils
(Suwwerat)

(Makes 20 pieces)

This way of rolling fillo dough yields comparatively bigger pieces.

One 1-pound package fillo dough, thawed according to package directions
1/2 to 3/4 cup melted butter
1 recipe Medium Syrup**, given above, cooled**
1 recipe Nut Filling
For garnish: coarsely chopped pistachio
Preheat oven to 350 degrees F.

1. Divide fillo sheets into halves, crosswise, and stack them.

2. On a flat surface layer 2 fillo sheets, brushing each lightly with some butter. Keep the rest of sheets covered with a kitchen cloth away from drafts while working on one piece.

3. Spread about 2 tablespoons of filling on the layered sheets, leaving about 1/2 inch from all the edges clear of the filling. Slightly fold the uncovered longer edge on the filling. Put a thin long stick or a skewer along the folded edge, and roll, with the skewer still inside, jelly- roll fashion all the way to the bottom. To create a wrinkled look, with the roll lying on the working surface and with the help of the skewer, press the roll from both ends towards the center. The roll will shorten a little. Wrinkling the roll in this way prevents the roll from breaking while twisting it. Carefully take the skewer out, and coil the roll.

4. Arrange coils on a greased cookie sheet, leaving a space between pieces to allow them to brown on all sides. Brush pieces with remaining melted butter.

5. Bake in a preheated oven at 350 degrees F. for 40 to 45 minutes or until golden brown.

6. Take out of the oven, and while still hot, pour syrup on pieces. Set aside for at least 2 hours to allow pieces to absorb syrup.

To serve, press coarsely chopped pistachio into the center of each coil.

Corrugated Rolls
(Burma)

(Makes about 20 pieces)

This way of rolling baklawa yields somewhat large pieces. For smaller portions, divide each into three pieces.

One 1-pound package fillo dough, thawed according to package directions
1/2 to 3/4 cup melted butter
1 recipe Nut Filling
1 recipe Medium Syrup, **given above, cooled**
For garnish: ground pistachio, optional
Preheat oven to 350 degrees F.

1. On a flat surface spread a whole fillo sheet, lightly brush half of it with butter and fold it. Then brush half of the folded sheet and fold it again.

2. Spread about 2 tablespoons of nut filling leaving 1/2 inch of edges uncovered. Put a stick about 1/4 inches across (a broken off handle of a wooden spoon will do, this is what I actually always use.) along one of the short sides. Roll firmly around the stick down to the bottom. Wrinkle the roll by holding roll in both hands, and gently but firmly pushing the roll towards the center to create the wrinkled look. While holding the roll firmly in one hand, take out the stick. Put roll on a greased baking sheet, seam side down. Repeat with the rest of the sheets, arranging them next to each other.

3. Bake in a preheated oven at 350 degrees F. for about 45 minutes or until golden brown.

4. Take out of the oven and while still hot pour syrup and set aside for at least 2 hours to allow it to absorb the syrup.
Serve warm or cold, with the optional sprinkle of ground pistachio.

Winged Squares
(Makes about 36 pieces)

This way of shaping the dough results in very fluffy and crispy baklawas. Traditionally whole shelled and skinned pistachios are used for the filling, but Egg White-Nut filling may be substituted.

One 1-pound package fillo dough
1/2 to 3/4 cup melted butter
1 recipe Egg White-Nut Filling, **or 2 cups whole shelled and skinned** pistachio
1 recipe Medium Syrup, given above, cooled
For garnish: ground pistachio, optional
Preheat oven to 350 degrees F.

1. Stack 10 sheets of fillo brushing each lightly with melted butter. Do not brush the top layer to help pieces stay in shape after forming them.
2. Divide stack into squares. The size depends on how small or big you want your pieces to be, but generally speaking you can divide layered sheets into 18 squares. Put about 1 teaspoon of filling in center of each square. If using pistachio put about 5 to 7 pieces. Firmly lift up four tips of each square and press them together. While baking folded tips will open up a little, showing some of the filling.

3. Arrange pieces on a greased cookie sheet leaving a space between pieces to allow all sides to brown. Repeat same procedure with rest of sheets.

4. Bake in a preheated oven at 350, for about 40 minutes, or until golden brown.

5. Take out of the oven and while still hot pour syrup all over pieces. Set aside for at least 2 hours to allow pieces to absorb syrup. Sprinkle with some ground pistachio, if wished.

Note:
To skin pistachios, after shelling them, soak them in hot water, leave them for about 5 minutes, then rub off the skin. Dry them before using.

Bird's Nest
('Ish al-Asfour)

(Makes about 20 large nests)

These make a very appealing presentation of the dessert. Traditionally the "nests" are filled with whole, shelled and skinned pistachios. The egg white-nut filling is good, too.

One 1-pound package fillo dough
1/2 to 3/4 cup melted butter
1/2 cup ground nuts mixed with 1/2 teaspoon ground cardamom
To fill the nests: 1 recipe Egg White-Nut Filling **or 2 cups whole, shelled and skinned** pistachios
1 recipe Medium Syrup, **given above, cooled**
Preheat oven to 350 degrees F.

1. Lay flat one whole sheet of fillo. Lightly brush with butter half of it. Fold sheet in half crosswise, and lightly brush entire surface. Keep rest of sheets covered with a dry kitchen towel, away from draft.

2. Fold one of the long edges by 1 inch. Brush top of fold with butter, and spread about 1 teaspoon of ground nuts along the fold. Put a long thin stick or skewer along the fold and roll with skewer jellyroll fashion leaving 2 inches of the other edge unrolled. With the roll still on the working surface, gently but firmly push it from both ends towards the center to create a wrinkled look. Slip out the skewer. Overlap both ends to make a ring about 3 inches in diameter. Tuck in the unfolded edge to create a base for the nest. Put on a greased cookie sheet. Repeat with the rest of sheets leaving a space between pieces to allow to brown on all sides. Brush pieces with remaining butter.

3. To fill the nests: If you are using egg white-nut filling put about one tablespoon or enough to fill the cavity in the nest and bake in a preheated oven at 350 degrees F., for about 40 minutes or until golden brown.

4. Take out of the oven, and while still hot pour syrup all over nests and set aside for at least 2 hours to allow pastry to absorb syrup.

5. If using whole pistachios for filling the nests' cavities, bake the nests unfilled. Take them out of the oven, and fill them with the prepared pistachios. Pour cooled syrup all over the pieces and set aside for at least 2 hours to allow them to absorb syrup.

Note:
To skin pistachios, after shelling them, soak them in hot water, leave them for about 5 minutes, then drain them and rub off the skin. Dry them before using.

Cream-filled Baklawa Triangles
(Baklawa bil Geymer)

(Makes about 20 pieces)

The traditional filling used for these triangles is Cream Filling, which is scented with rose water or orange blossom water rather than cardamom, since filling is supposed to look immaculately white.

One 1-pound package fillo dough
1/2 to 3/4 cup melted butter
1 recipe Cream Filling
1 recipe Medium Syrup, **given above, cooled**
For garnish: ground pistachio
Preheat oven to 350 degrees F.

1. Lay a single fillo sheet flat. Lightly brush with butter 2 thirds of the sheet, lengthwise. Fold the ungreased third on the middle third, and then fold the other third on these two layers. Lightly brush surface. Keep rest of sheets covered with a dry kitchen cloth away from draft.

2. Put a heaping tablespoon of cream filling on one end of the strip. Fold tip of strip across the filling to form a triangle, then fold again and again until you get to the other end of the strip. Put triangle on a greased cookie sheet. Repeat same procedure with the rest of pieces, and arrange them on a cookie sheet. Leave a little space between pieces to allow them to brown on all sides. Brush pieces with remaining butter.

3. Bake in a preheated oven at 350 degrees F. for about 45 minutes or until golden brown. While still hot pour syrup on them. Set aside for about 1 hour to allow pieces to absorb the syrup. Sprinkle with ground pistachio, if wished, and serve at room temperature. Or serve chilled. Keep any leftovers refrigerated.

Shredded Dough (Kataifi)
(Kunafa)

Kunafa in Iraq is a somewhat confusing name. If *kunafa* is made baklawa style, that is filled with nuts and drenched in heavy syrup, it is called *baqlawat sha'riyya* or *qatayif*. If the fine noodles are not allowed to brown, it is called *baklawa balluriyya* (like crystal). When it is prepared, as in the rest of the neighboring countries, spread in huge trays, filled with cheese, and kept warm for the day's consumption, it is called *knafa* (as pronounced in the Iraqi dialect).

The main ingredient, *kunafa* looks like very fine noodles, and is usually translated as "shredded dough" because it resembles cereal known by this name. It is available at Middle-Eastern grocery shops, and the package usually identifies it as "kataifi." This is a little confusing because there is another traditional syrupy dessert made of small crepe-like pastries, also called *qata'if* (a recipe for these is given below).

The reason behind this confusion in the nomenclature may be traced back to the Middle Ages when both the *kunafa* and *qata'if* crepes were made from the same batter, and both were cooked on the *tabaq* (heated metal plate). Whereas the *qata'if* crepe batter was poured in a very thin layer on the hot metal plate, *kunafa* batter was dribbled in a swirling fashion from a perforator and onto the hot metal plate. The batter, in the process, would turn into fine "noodles," which were gathered up in bundles, moistened with butter and spread out in layers to be filled and drenched with syrup, like baklawa (see Perry, "What to Order," 232). This cooking technique is still in use today.

First mention of *kunafa* in medieval books was made as early as the ninth century (Wright, 658), and was described in some medieval cookbooks such as *Al-Wusla ila'l-Habeeb* of Aleppo (Rodinson, 142), the appendix (*Ziyadat*) to this book, and the fourteenth-century augmented version of al-Baghdadi's cookbook, *Wasf al-At'ima al-Mu'tada* (453, 436-7). From the recipes given in this book we understand that fresh *kunafa* noodles were usually purchased ready made and not made at home. This undoubtedly was due to the "high tech" equipment or skill needed to make these fine threads of dough. Besides, in all these recipes, *kunafa* noodles were prepared in pretty much the same way. They were cooked in oil, honey, sugar and pistachio, and flavored with rose water and mastic (436-7, 453), similar to the way we still prepare our *halawat sha'riyya* (see, sweet 'n golden vermicelli noodles, chapter 15, above). In other recipes in this book, sometimes the *kunafa* was mentioned where it was obvious that the recipe called for *qata'if* thin breads as in the recipe of *sanbousak hamudh* (sour *sanbousa*, 386).

In the medieval book of *The Arabian Nights*, frequent mention was made to this delicious pastry, such as in the story of "Ma'ruf the Cobbler and his Wife Fatimah," where the kind of syrup used becomes a social status symbol. One day the shrewish wife Fatima demanded of her husband to bring her *kunafa*, and demanded it should be dressed with no less than bees' honey. So much to Ma'ruf's misfortune, the *kunafa*-seller had the cheaper drip-honey only, which was syrup made of water and cane sugar (*'asal kasab*). Ma'ruf was ashamed to reject the dessert because the "pastry-cook was to have patience with him for the price." So he said, "Give it me with drip-honey." The cook, therefore, went ahead and "fried a vermicelli-cake for him with butter and drenched it with drip-honey, till it was fit to present to kings." Ma'ruf took it home, but needless to say, the wife was furious with him and threw the *kunafa* in his face (vol.10, 2-3). Nowadays *kunafa* is more commonly drenched in simple syrup and the chances of having it thrown in our faces because of this are absolutely nil.

Knafa Rolls

(Makes about 35 to 40 pieces)

Knafa rolls are commonly called *baqlawat sha'riyya* (baklawa of vermicelli noodles), and some bakers prefer to fill the rolls with whole pistachios, rather than the ground nut mixture.

For filling:
2 cups walnuts, skinned almonds or pistachio, coarsely ground (about 10 ounces)
1 teaspoon ground cardamom
1/4 teaspoon ground cinnamon
1 tablespoon rose water
1 egg white, whisked

One 1-pound package *kunafa* (shredded dough), thawed according to package directions
3/4 to 1 cup melted butter
1 recipe Medium Syrup, **given above, cooled**
Preheat oven to 325 degrees F.

1. Make filling by mixing all filling ingredients in a medium bowl. The egg white and rose water will help bind filling.

2. Put shredded dough in a big bowl and pour melted butter all over. Working with fingers, coat strands well with melted butter.

3. Take a strand of dough, about 1/8 of the amount. Fluff it with the fingers to loosen it and spread it out on a flat working surface to make a 6-by-8- inch rectangle. Press down surface with fingers. Put about 3 tablespoons of filling along the narrow edge of strand. Put a long skewer along the filling, and firmly roll the strand around it. Press the roll then slide out the skewer. Neaten up the roll by pressing and tucking it. It will look like a 5-inch long cocoon.

4. Put roll on a greased cookie sheet. Repeat with remaining strands. You'll end up having 8 rolls. Leave space between rolls to allow them to brown on all sides.

5. Bake rolls in a preheated oven at 325 degrees F. for about 70 minutes or until they are golden brown (slow baking will ensure that rolls will be cooked inside and out).

6. Take out of the oven and immediately pour half of cooled syrup on rolls. After 10 minutes pour the rest of syrup. Set aside for two hours to allow pastries to absorb syrup.

7. When completely cool, carefully cut each rolls (diagonally if wished) into slices about 1-inch wide or a little wider. Sprinkle with ground pistachio, if desired.

Note:

In the Arab countries it is customary to buy freshly made soft and moist *kunafa*, (shredded dough). The frozen variety tends to dry out. To compensate for lost moisture, sprinkle the shredded dough with a little warm water before adding butter to it.

Layered Knafa with Nuts
(Makes about 24 pieces)

This is an easy and delicious way of using the *kunafa* dough. Different fillings may be used, and each will yield a delightfully distinguished taste and texture.
The following recipe calls for nut filling.

For filling:
2 1/2 cups walnuts, skinned almonds, or pistachio, coarsely ground (about 10 ounces)
1 teaspoon ground cardamom
1/4 teaspoon ground cinnamon
1 to 2 tablespoons rose water

One 1-pound package *kunafa* (shredded dough), thawed according to package directions
3/4 cup melted butter
1/2 cup whipping cream, optional

1 recipe Medium Syrup**, given above, cooled**
Preheat oven to 350 degrees F.

1. Mix all filling ingredients in a medium bowl.

2. Separate and fluff shredded dough by pulling it with the fingers in two opposite directions. It's okay to break some in the process. Put loosened dough in a big bowl and pour on it melted butter. Work with the fingers to moisten dough strands with butter.

3. Spread one third of dough on a greased 13-by-9-inch baking pan. Spread one half of filling on dough and sprinkle with half of the whipping cream, if used. Repeat the layering two more times to make 3 layers of shredded dough and 2 layers of nut filling. With oiled fingers press entire surface very well.

4. Bake in a preheated oven at 350 degrees F. for about 45 minutes or until golden brown.

5. Take out of the oven and immediately pour half of cooled syrup over entire surface. Let stand for 10 minutes then pour remaining syrup. Cover loosely with a clean kitchen towel and set aside for at least 1 hour to allow pastry to absorb syrup.

6. To serve, cut into squares while still in pan, and garnish with some ground or chopped nuts, if liked.
Refrigerate leftovers.

Cream-filled Knafa Squares
(Knafa bil-Geymar)

(Makes 24 pieces)

The combination of golden *knafa* and cream filling in this recipe make a sensational dessert fit for special occasions.

One 1-pound package *kunafa* (shredded dough), thawed according to package directions
3/4 cup butter, melted

1 recipe Cream Filling, **given above**
1 recipe Medium Syrup, **given above, cooled**
Preheat oven to 350 degrees F.

1. Separate and fluff shredded dough by pulling it with fingers in two opposite directions. It's okay to break some in the process. Put loosened dough in a big bowl and pour on it melted butter. Work with fingers to moisten dough with butter.

2. Layer half of shredded dough in a greased 13-by-9-inch baking pan and press it with fingers.

3. Spread filling on entire surface, and cover filling with remaining dough. Press well with oiled fingers.
4. Bake in a preheated oven at 350 degrees F. for 45 minutes or until golden brown.

5. Take out of the oven and immediately prick surface down to the bottom with a fork or skewer to allow syrup to penetrate to the bottom layer. Pour half of cooled syrup over entire surface. Let stand for 10 minutes, then pour remaining syrup. Cover loosely with a clean kitchen towel, and set aside for at least 1 hour to allow pastry to absorb syrup.
To serve, cut into squares while still in pan and garnish with some ground or chopped nuts, if liked. Refrigerate leftovers.

Cheese-filled Knafa
(Knafa bil-jibin)

(Makes 24 pieces)

Cream cheese or mozzarella cheese can be used for filling *knafa*. Try cream cheese for a smooth texture and mozzarella cheese for a more authentic, chewy and rather elastic texture. If you have access to sweet cheese (*jibna hilwa*), usually used in the Arab countries for making this type of *knafa*, then use it by all means.

For cream cheese filling use:
    Two 8-ounce packages cream cheese (reduced fat variety may be used)
    1/3 cup milk
    1 to 2 tablespoons rose water

With an electric mixer, mix filling ingredients until light and fluffy. Follow directions in Cream-Filled *Knafa* Squares, replacing cream filling with cream cheese filling, and do not forget to prick *knafa* as directed in step 5 to allow syrup to penetrate to the bottom layer.

For Mozzarella or sweet cheese filling use:
    2 1/2 cups shredded mozzarella cheese, or sweet cheese crumbled into small pieces
    1/4 cup milk
    2 1/2 tablespoons semolina, see Glossary
    1 to 2 tablespoons rose water, or orange blossom water, see Glossary

To get rid of salt in Mozzarella cheese, soak it in cold water for about 45 minutes, changing water twice, then drain it very well (no need to do this when using sweet cheese). Mix together all filling ingredients.

Use filling following directions in Cream-Filled *Knafa* Squares, replacing cream filling with mozzarella cheese filling, and do not forget to prick *knafa* as directed in step 5 to allow syrup to penetrate to the bottom layer. Refrigerate leftovers.

Golden Translucent Fritters
(Zlabia)

(Makes about 28 pieces)

Zlabia is always mentioned in conjunction with of baklawa. It is shaped like a tubular rosette, translucent and crispy from the outside and yet succulent from the inside. Baghdad is believed to be the originator of this popular dessert. Indeed, even the name itself is said to have been derived from the name of the famous musician and singer, Ziryab (ca. 800 AD) who was an Iraqi in origin (see Box below). This dessert was called *ziryabiyya* after his name. Apparently the name later on settled at *zlabia*.

The tenth century Baghdadi cookbook dedicates a chapter on this famous pastry. The kind that looks like today's *zlabia* was called *mushabbaka* (latticed). The method of making it today has undergone insignificant changes. In medieval times half a coconut shell with a hole pierced in the bottom was used to drip batter and swirls it into the frying pan. Nowadays most people use a funnel. For syrup, the recipes used the more expensive warmed honey. The cheaper *julab* (syrup of sugar cane and rose water) was also used, for those who could not afford honey, as we have seen in the story of Ma'ruf the Cobbler and his Shrewish wife. We also learn from contemporary poems on *zlabia*, and from the thirteenth-century *Andalusian Anonymous Cookbook* that batter was colored into yellow, green or red before frying it.

Following are tips for making the perfect *zlabia*, as suggested by the medieval experts.
*A test to see whether dough has risen: tap on the side of the pot with your finger, you should hear a "thick dense sound" (*Andalusian Cookbook*, 128).
*Oil for frying should be neither too little nor too cold, otherwise it will stick to the pan. Put just enough to cover them when frying (*Andalusian Cookbook*, 128).
*You know you got the right batter consistency, when fried pieces immediately turn into translucent hollow shapes (al-Warraq, 268).
*After dipping fried pieces in warmed honey, put them on crossed woods until they are drained of all honey except what they hold inside (*Andalusian Cookbook*, 128).
* Good *zlabia* should be brittle to the bite. Bad *zlabia* is soft and leathery in texture. This is because batter was not given enough time to ferment, or yeast was not good, or honey was moist (rather on runny side), or humid and cold weather. The remedy is to let batter ferment well, and put honey back to the fire until it looses its moisture. In humid weather do the cooking indoors, and in a warm room. To compensate for the bad yeast, put some more *buraq al-ajeen* (borax used with dough, no longer used in cooking, al-Warraq, 268).

Although the amount of syrup called for in the following recipe might sound outrageous, a good deal of it will be drained.

1 1/2 teaspoon dry yeast
1 teaspoon sugar
3 cups warm water
A few threads of saffron, optional

2 1/2 cups all purpose flour
1/2 cup cornstarch
A pinch of salt
1 teaspoon rose water
Oil for frying
4 cups light corn syrup warmed, and flavored with 1 tablespoon rose water or orange blossom water (or make your own syrup as suggested below)

1. Make batter as follows: In a big bowl dissolve dry yeast and sugar in warm water. Add saffron, if used. Set aside at a warm place for 5 minutes.

2. Using a mixer beat in flour, cornstarch, salt and rose water into the yeast mixture, for about 5 minutes. The final batter should have the consistency of pancake mixture. Let batter ferment in a warm place, covered, for 1 hour. Stir batter several times while fermenting.

3. When ready to fry, have the warmed syrup ready in a pot or big bowl, put it near the stove.

4. In a 10-inch skillet, heat about 1-inch deep oil until it is shimmering hot, and fry the pieces as follows: Have ready a small funnel or a pastry bag fitted with a 1/4-inch nozzle. Blocking the opening of the funnel or pastry bag with a finger while holding it, ladle a small amount of the batter into it. Transfer the funnel or bag to the place where the skillet is. Quickly remove the blocking finger to allow batter to flow down. While pouring move your hand to form a **closed** circle about 3 inches in diameter, then form a kind of cross in the middle making sure it touches the outer circle at several points to prevent it from opening up while frying. The frying fritter will puff and rise almost immediately. Turn piece only once to allow it to cook on both sides, 2 to 3 minutes or until it turns golden. There should not be much of a change in color.

5. Using tongs, take fried fritter out of oil, shake off excess oil, and immediately dip it in **warm** syrup, turning once to coat both sides. Allow the pieces to absorb syrup, about 4 minutes. Lift them out of syrup and place them on a cooling rack (I use my oven's rack), placed on a big tray to allow excess syrup to drain down, and help keep fritters crispy. Let pieces drain on rack until they are no longer sticky when touched with the finger.
Note: It is better to use separate utensils for frying and dipping in syrup. I use tongs for turning the pieces in skillet and two forks for turning them in syrup. Always keep a napkin ready for wiping your fingers because if you are doing it by yourself you can only handle one piece at a time, but time-wise this is not a problem because the whole process goes very fast. Reuse the drained syrup.

6. Arrange drained pieces on a platter in a pile. Sprinkle *zlabia* with ground nuts, preferably pistachio. If syrup is thick enough pieces will stay crispy.

How to Prepare Heavy Syrup for Zlabia:

In a medium heavy pot, combine 4 cups sugar, 2 cups water, 1 tablespoon honey, 2 tablespoons lemon juice, and 1/4 cup rose water. Bring to a boil, stirring with a wooden spoon to dissolve sugar, then leave to boil gently undisturbed until heavy syrup forms, about 15 minutes. To test, put a drop on a cold dish, it should keep its shape.

Ziryab

Born around 789 AD, Ziryab was an Iraqi Kurdish musician, who was given this nickname because he was compared to the blackbird, ziryab. His teacher was the celebrated Ishaq al-Mosuli who was the court musician of the caliph Haroun al-Rashid of Baghdad. So much impressed was the Caliph by Ziryab's talent and originality in singing and playing a lute (*ud*) of his own design that al-Mousili's jealousy was aroused and Ziryab had to quit Baghdad and try his luck somewhere else. In 822 AD Abd al-Rahman II, Caliph of al-Andalus (Spain) in Cordoba welcomed him and bestowed upon him an abundance of gifts. Ziryab, therefore, decided to spend the rest of his life there.

Coming from the highly cultured and accomplished Baghdadi court, he was in a position to have a remarkable influence upon the court and city of Cordoba such as teaching them the art of grand and refined living. He set trends for their social patterns and domestic habits. He showed the courtiers how to dress in silk, and wear white clothes in summer, how to set their hair, and dye their beards. Besides introducing some sophisticated dishes, he taught them the etiquette of eating, how to set the table, how to behave at the table, and how to serve dishes in a succession of courses, rather than presenting them all at once.

(*Encyclopaedia of Islam*)

Zlabiya

Arabian Pancakes
(Qata'if)

(Makes about 20 pieces)

In the Middle Ages, *qata'if* was a delicacy worthy of the caliph's table. Numerous recipes were given in their cookbooks, and poems were composed in their praises. The fillings ranged from the regular walnuts and almonds to the more exotic skinned green walnuts, and chopped date-palm hearts (*jummar*). In many Arab countries, including Iraq, it is still prepared and cooked in the same manner. However, to give these traditional desserts a lighter touch, the following recipe will call for baking the filled *qata'if.*

1 teaspoon dry yeast
1 teaspoon sugar
1 1/4 cups warm water

1 1/2 cups all-purpose flour
1/4 teaspoon salt

About 1/2 cup honey or syrup of your choice
Ground pistachio and whipped cream, for garnish

1. Dissolve yeast and sugar in warm water, and set aside at a warm place foe 5 minutes.

2. Using a mixer, add flour and salt and beat until smooth, 3 to 4 minutes. Batter should be smooth and have the consistency of pancake batter. Set aside, covered, for about an hour.

3. Heat a pancake grill, or a non-stick pan, until very hot, then reduce heat to medium. Stir fermented batter and pour about 2 tablespoons on the pan. Tilt pan to different directions to spread batter into a 4-inch disc. Wait until surface rises, develops bubbles, and looks dry, a few minutes (when done it should come away easily from the pan). If you intend to serve it unfilled, then you need to flip it to the other side. If you want to have it filled, do not flip, but transfer to a plate, and stack.

Unstuffed *qata'if* may be dipped quickly and while still warm in honey or cold syrup, then sprinkled with chopped nuts, and served by themselves or with whipped cream. Or they may be sprinkled with powdered sugar and ground nuts and rolled like cigars, then drizzled with honey or pancake syrup, and sprinkled with more chopped nuts.

Stuffed Qata'if
(Qata'if Mahshiya)

(Makes 20 pieces)

Qata'if discs as prepared in the previous recipe can also be stuffed for more formal presentations. Traditionally these filled pastries are fried, but in the following recipe a lighter option is given.

One recipe of *qata'if* **dough, cooked on one side only**
For filling:
2 cups chopped toasted nuts
3 tablespoons sugar
1 teaspoon cinnamon, or cardamom
2 tablespoons rose water

1/4 cup butter, melted for brushing the pieces
Light syrup, such as pancake syrup
Preheat oven to 350 degrees

1. Cook *qata'if* discs as directed in the previous recipe. Do not flip the pieces, for this will help edges to stick together when filled.

2. Combine filling ingredients. As soon as you finish cooking *qata'if* discs, fill them by putting about 2 tablespoons of filling in the middle of **uncooked** side. Then fold to form half circles. Press edges very well to prevent filling from coming out while baking.

3. Place filled pieces on a greased baking sheet. Brush them with melted butter and bake in a preheated oven at 350 degrees F. for about 10 minutes or until golden brown. (Alternatively, after filling pieces, fry them in 1/2-inch deep hot oil, for 2 to 3 minutes, or until golden brown. Drain pieces on white paper towels.)

5. Dip pieces whether baked or fried and while still hot, in syrup and serve immediately with cream, if wished.

"Soft Folios" of Qata'if

The following poem describes the Arabian dessert *qata'if.* It was recited to the Abbasid Caliph of Baghdad al-Mustakfi in the tenth century AD:

When in my friends the pang of hunger grows,
I have *qata'if*, like soft folios;
As flow of lambent honey brimming white
So amid other dainties it is bright,
And, having drunk of almond-essence deep,
With oil it glitters, wherein it doth seep.
Rose water floats thereon, like flooding sea,
Bubble on bubble swimming fragrantly;
As foliated book, laid fold on fold--
Afflicted hearts rejoice when they behold:
But when divided, like the spoils of war,
    All have their hearts' desire, and sated are.
    (Arberry, 29)

Cream Filled Rolls
Znoud al-Sit (Lady's Upper arm)

(Makes about 24 rolls)

This is a popular delicious dessert that is lavished an equally scrumptious name. In a way, it is a variation on the cream-filled baklawa, except that these rolls are fried, since a slightly thicker dough is used here. A timesaving tip is to use the ready-made spring rolls (not egg rolls) wrappers available in oriental grocery stores instead of making the dough, yourself.

One recipe boureg dough, **p.412, or one package spring roll wrappers**
Two recipes baklawa cream filling, **p.469, cooled**
One recipe Medium Syrup, **p.468, cooled**
Oil for frying
1/4 cup coarsely ground pistachio or shredded coconut, for garnish, optional

1. Prepare dough as directed in recipe, then divide it into 24 pieces. Roll out pieces as thin as possible, and trim off edges to make into approximate 4-by-5 inch rectangles.

2. Put about 2 tablespoons of filling on the shorter side of rectangle, leaving about 1 inch on both sides uncovered. Roll filled side twice (this will help prevent filling from oozing out while frying), then fold both sides about 1/2-inch inwards, and continue rolling all the way down. In their final shape rolls should look plump and rather short. If using spring roll wrappers, follow package directions.

3. Fry rolls in 1-inch deep hot oil, seam side down. Turn once to brown on both sides, about 5 minutes. To drain put them in a colander set on a plate or tray. When done frying arrange pieces in a big platter in a single layer, and while still warm, spoon cooled syrup all over them. Serve hot or cold with some ground pistachio or shredded coconut sprinkled on them, if desired. Refrigerate leftovers.

Golden Balls in Syrup
Or: The Judge's Morsel
(Luqmat al-Quadhi)

(Makes about 50 pieces)

This dessert is so good, it is worthy of a judge, so seems to be the idea behind the naming of this popular medieval dessert. Even today it is still known by this name in the entire Arab world. The thirteenth-century Baghdadi cookbook includes a recipe for this dessert, which goes, "Make a firm dough. When fermented, take in the size of hazelnuts, and fry in sesame-oil. Dip in syrup, and sprinkle with fine-ground sugar" (al-Baghdadi, 213). The *quadhi* (judge) was an important man in the Islamic State. After the Caliph, Wazir (minister) and the *wali* (governor), he was the fourth man in the medieval political hierarchy. He was a man to be feared and revered and anything related to him or coming from him should be good, or so those dessert-promoters seemed to claim. They didn't even spare his body parts, neither the public, such as his *adhan* (ears), nor the private.

2 teaspoons dry yeast
1/4 cup warm water

1 1/4 cups all-purpose flour
1/4 cup cornstarch
1/4 teaspoon salt
2 cups warm water

Oil for frying
One recipe Medium Syrup, **p. 468**

1. Dissolve yeast in 1/4 cup water and set aside for 5 minutes.

2. Mix flour, cornstarch and salt in a big bowl, and make a well in the middle. Pour in yeast mixture, and 2 cups warm water. Stir using a mixer to incorporate liquids into flour. Beat vigorously until batter is smooth, and soft dough is formed. It should be just thick enough to hold its shape when lifted by a spoon. Let rise at a warm draftless place for 45 minutes. Beat dough about 3 times or more while fermenting. This should result in an elastic texture.

3. Deep fry in batches. Heat about 3 inches of oil in a small heavy pot, until medium hot. Fry 5 or 6 at a time by dipping two teaspoons in cold water or oil (this will help dough slide from the spoon easily). Scoop up a level teaspoon of batter and with the other spoon push batter into hot oil. The pieces will rise to the surface immediately and will brown in about 8 minutes. If they brown faster than that this means oil is too hot. Slow browning ensures that fritters will stay crisp. Turn pieces several times to allow to brown on all sides. Take them out of oil with a slotted spoon and let them drain in a colander lined with a paper towel. Fry another batch, and while this is cooking, dip drained pieces for a few minutes and, while still hot, in prepared warm syrup. Lift them out of syrup and arrange them on a serving dish in a pile. Repeat with other batches. Sprinkle them with a little ground nuts and cinnamon, if wished.

The Lady's Navel (or Dimpled Fritters)
(Surrat a-Khatoun)

(Makes about 28 pieces)

This delicious dessert is called "the lady's navel" due to the dimple in the center of the pastry. A deep navel was an emblem of beauty and good living in the old days. In one of *The Arabian Nights* stories a woman was described as being so beautiful that her navel would hold an ounce of benzoin ointment (benzoin is the resin from certain trees in Sumatra and Java used in medicine and perfumery). The *khatoun*, that is the lady of the old affluent household, was always thought of as leading a life of luxury and plenty and hence was always pictured as being plump and "cushiony". To the depraved commoners who might never have had the chance to see a woman's body except in the privacy of their own homes if at all, what else to compare the diverse delicious desserts but to the luscious body parts of the *khatoun*?

2 1/2 cups water
3 tablespoons butter or oil
1/4 teaspoon salt
2 cups flour
3 eggs
1/2 teaspoon ground cardamom

Oil for frying
1 recipe Medium Syrup, **p.468**
For garnish: Cool whip, and ground pistachio (optional)

1. In a heavy pan, bring water to a boil. Stir in butter and salt. Add flour all at once and with a wooden spoon mix until well blended and dough comes away from sides of pan.

2. Cool slightly and beat in eggs one at a time. Dough should be thick, smooth and shiny.

3. With oiled hands take a piece of dough, size of a walnut and roll it into a ball and flatten it slightly. With the index finger make a dimple in the middle, almost like a hole, but not quite.

4. Fry fritters in batches. Start by dipping 4 to 5 pieces into 3-to 4- inch deep oil, 250 degrees F. As the pieces puff out and rise to the surface increase heat to 300 degrees F., and continue frying until pieces are golden brown, about 15 minutes. After each batch lower heat to 250 F. and start all over again. This method is to ensure that pieces will puff and cook evenly inside and out. If oil is too hot to begin with pieces will not puff out and the outside will brown leaving the inside not fully cooked.

5.Drain pieces briefly and roll them in cold syrup. Transfer to a platter and allow to cool completely.

6. To serve, put a small amount of cream in the dimple and sprinkle with a little ground pistachio, if desired.

Um-Hayder's Colander Datlı

(Makes about 3o pieces)

I called this dessert after the name of a friend who suggested this recipe to me. Actually it is not her name *per se*, but as the rules of decorum in our culture dictate, as soon as a married couple have a child, friends start calling them after the name of their first born. *Um* plus the name of the child for the mother, and *abu* plus the name of the child for the father.

Datli is a loan Turkish word used to describe the traditional syrupy pastries, both leavened and unleavened. Many recipes for such desserts were included in the medieval cookbooks, but they were known by different names. In the tenth-century Baghdadi cookbook they were called *zalabia gheir mushabbak* (not latticed), or *zalabia furniyya* (baked). In the unlatticed type flour was toasted in oil and then made into dough by adding water or milk, shaped into rings, fingers and discs, deep fried, and then dipped in syrup (267-70).

In shaping this pastry a colander is used to give it an attractive form, as you'll see.

1/4 teaspoon dry yeast
1 tablespoon sugar
1/2 cup warm water

1 cup all purpose flour
1 cup semolina, see Glossary
1/4 teaspoon salt
1/2 teaspoon ground aniseed
1/2 teaspoon cardamom
1/2 cup oil

Oil for frying, or preheat oven to 375 degrees F.
One recipe Medium Syrup, **p. 468**

1. Dissolve yeast and sugar in warm water, and set aside for 5 minutes.

2. Put flour, semolina, salt aniseed, and cardamom in a big bowl. Add oil and rub together with the fingers until well mixed. Make a well in the middle and pour in yeast mixture. Stir with a fork or a wooden spoon in a circular movement, and then knead lightly to make slightly soft dough.

3. Divide dough into 30 balls (size of a small walnut). Have a **plastic or metal colander with round holes** ready. With your index finger flatten each ball on the inner curve of the colander elongating the piece while pressing. Peel off gently and join together the two sides of the circle. The piece will develop an interesting design from the outside. Fry as you shape

4. To fry the pieces, put about 3-inch deep oil in a small heavy pot. When oil is hot enough start frying (test by dipping a small piece of dough, if it immediately sizzles, oil is ready). Deep fry in batches 5 to 6 at a time for about 7 minutes or until golden brown. If pieces brown fast, this means oil is too hot. Adjust heat accordingly. Drain pieces in a colander lined with paper towel. Fry another batch, and while it is cooking, dip drained pieces, while still warm, in prepared syrup. Keep them for a few moments, then take them out and arrange them in a pile on a platter. Sprinkle with some ground pistachio, if liked.

5. Alternatively, you have the option of baking the pastries. Shape as in step 3. Because they are going to be baked, you can sprinkle the pressed pieces with chopped nuts and cinnamon before pinching the sides. Arrange pieces on an ungreased cookie sheet, seam side down. Bake in a preheated oven at 375 degrees F. for about 20 minutes or until golden brown. Take out of the oven and immediately dip pieces in prepared syrup. Arrange on a platter and sprinkle with some ground pistachio, if liked.

Ali Baba
(Baked Datli with Cream and Pistachio)

(Makes 24 cupcakes or 12 mini bundts)

To the modern Westerners the Babas are those small and light yeast cakes moistened with rum-flavored syrup. Western culinary records attribute the invention of this dessert to a seventeenth-century Polish king. One day he was eating a dry, day-old kugelhopf (a raisin-studded yeast cake) when he had the idea of moistening it with rum, and garnishing it with sweetened whipped cream. He was so much impressed by the result that he called it "Ali Baba", after one of *The Arabian Nights* heroes, thus, probably unknowingly, paying tribute to the first innovators of such moist pastries. Later on simple syrup was added to the cake to balance the strong rum flavor, and the name was shortened to "baba" (Maida Heatter's *New Book of Great Desserts*, 1982, 230-1).

As early as the ninth century such sumptuous pastries were already cooking in the kitchens of the medieval Baghdadis. They were known as *zalabia furniyya* (oven-baked pastry) and *shahmiyya* (cooked with tallow), and were moistened with nothing stronger than honey, sweetened milk, and melted butter. According to one of the recipes in al-Warraq's tenth-century cookbook, fermented batter was put in an earthenware pot and baked in the *tannour* (clay oven). When done it was inverted on a platter, cut into four parts, and moistened with sweetened fresh pure milk. During the Ottoman period this dessert acquired the more exotic Turkish name, *datli*. Nowadays the moistening liquid mostly used is flavored light syrup. In the following recipe perfumed syrup is suggested, but feel free to make your own concoction of spices and flavors.

1 tablespoon dry yeast
1 cup warm milk

4 cups all-purpose flour
1 /2 teaspoon salt
1/3 cup sugar
1/2 cup melted butter
3 eggs, at room temperature, beaten
For Perfumed Syrup:
3 cups water
1 3/4 cups sugar
4 strips lemon zest
3 coriander seeds
1 sprig mint
1 tablespoon lemon juice
1 tablespoon rose water, or orange blossom water

For garnish: whipped cream (any kind will do), preserved fruits and ground pistachio
Preheat oven to 400 degrees F.

1. Dissolve yeast in warm milk and set aside for 5 minutes.

2. In a big bowl combine flour, salt and sugar. Make a well in the middle and add yeast mixture, melted butter and eggs. With a wooden spoon incorporate liquids into flour in a circular movement.

494

Then knead lightly with the tips of fingers to soft and rather sticky dough. Let rise covered at a warm and draftless place for about 45 minutes.

3. Punch dough down and with oiled hands take pieces, size of a walnut each, and shape them into balls and put them in well-greased 24 cupcake molds, or 12 mini bundts. Set aside uncovered at a warm draftless place for about 45 minutes or until well risen.

4. Meanwhile prepare syrup by combining all ingredients in a medium pot. Bring to a boil, stirring to dissolve sugar. Cook for 10 minutes on medium heat. Keep warm and strain before using.

5. Bake cakes in a preheated oven at 400 degrees F. for about 15 minutes or until puffy and golden brown. Allow to cool for 10 minutes. Prick pieces with a fork or toothpick then spoon half of the warm syrup all over the pieces. After 10 minutes, warm remaining syrup and pour it all over the cakes. Allow to cool.

6. When completely cold decorate top with a dollop of cream and preserved fruit. Garnish with ground pistachio.

CHAPTER SEVENTEEN
CAKES

CHAPTER SEVENTEEN

CAKES

(Keık)

الـكـيْـك

In my budget there is no (place for any) one to bake cakes.
(A Sumerian Proverb, Gordon, 66)

The Sumerians were conscious of the superiority of their cuisine. Criticizing the way the Bedouins of the western desert had their food, they said if you gave them flour, eggs and honey for a cake they would not know what to do with them. In addition to such references to cakes, ancient cuneiform tablets going back to the third millenium BC have preserved interesting records with regard to pastry making. We learn that besides the regular breads, they made a better variety by "beating in" various fatty substances, such as vegetable oils and animal fats. Honey was sometimes added. The cakes were made with even higher quality flour and with "noble fat," which might well have been clarified butter. Those cakes took the shape of lumps, rings, crescents, pillars and even turbans. In the first millenium BC date breads were made by dicing dates and mixing them with oil and flour. They were called "takkasu" or "makkasu" (Limet, 137, Levey, 52). There are cuneiform texts that even give the proportions in which the ingredients were to be mixed for cakes made to go to the temple and the palace. Evidently, ordinary people did not enjoy such refined cakes. It was beyond their means. Cakes have always been emblematic of luxury, refinement, grace and beauty. In Iraq today a pretty woman is called *keka*.

A Sumerian text gives the following ingredients for a cake: (From Limet, 134)
1 sila (= 1 liter) butter
1/3 sila white cheese
3 sila first quality dates
1/3 sila Smyrna raisins
    (It is to be assumed that excellent flour would have been added.)
    Here is another Babylonian cake recipe that dates back to the time of Hammurabi:
X sila flour
X sila dates
1/2 sila and 5 gin (1 gin is equivalent to 8 grams) butter
9 gin white cheese
9 gin grape juice
5 gin apples
    5 gins figs

497

Both recipes seem to be reasonably proportioned, and they might well be the prototypes of the fruitcakes as we know them today. In the Sumerian these pastries were called "gug," and the Akkadian "kuku", and the similarity between these words and "cake" and its derivatives worldwide is striking.

The medieval bakers were no less inventive than their predecessors. They made a variety of pastries, which resemble what we call today cakes and puff pastries. Their names ranged from the literal *furniyya* (oven-baked), *shahmiyya* (made with tallow), and *liyiyya* (made with sheep's fat tail, a delicacy by their standards) to the fancy *abu-Lash*. The *furniyyat* were like sponge cakes in texture, and were basically made of thin leavened batter, that is baked in the *tannour*, and drenched in syrup, warm milk, or just sprinkled with sugar. In *shahmiyyat al-khawas* (cake for the elite), batter is made leavened dough thinned with 20 egg whites, and is poured into a pot lined with pounded *shaham* (tallow). While cake is baking in the *tannour*, a stick is inserted at several places to create holes in it. When cake is done, some of these holes are stuffed with ground nuts and dates, and through others honey is poured into the cake, until it is saturated (261, 269). The *liyiyya* is sweet puff pastry that is either sprinkled with sugar or drenched in honey, quite similar to what we call today the Napoleons, except that, instead of butter, pounded fat from the sheep's tail was used. *Abu-Lash* is a layer cake made by arranging thin cakes on a plate, sprinkling them with sugar and pistachio, and drizzling them with sesame oil, syrup and rose water. The layering is repeated until the plate is full (*Wasf al-At'ima al-Mu'tada*, 428-9).

Sindibad's Seven-Layered Cake (Kekat al-Sindibad al-Bahri)

(Makes 16 servings)

This is a unique and sensational cake, a relic of the past. I am sure it will be your favorite, and you will thank me for making it available to you as I am thankful to my neighbor, Um-Zeinab in Mosul, who imparted it to me, and who in turn got it from a friend baker, who in turn learnt it from…, etc, etc, perhaps down to the Middle ages. The mere fact that it calls for bakers' ammonia for its leaven belies its history (see Box below, for more details). My neighbor used to get her ammonia supply from Turkey and split it with me, and the cake was simply called *keik al-amoniac*, after the name of the leaven.

I adapted this cake in honor of the hero of my childhood Baghdad's renowned sailor, Sindibad and his seven fascinating voyages as narrated in *One Thousand and One Nights*, more commonly known in the Western world as *The Arabian Nights*. I knew of Sindibad even before I learnt to read. In the cold winter nights we used to gather around the brazier, eat toasted chestnuts and walnuts and listen to my father narrating the endless wonderful adventures of Sindibad, or Sandabad, as he pronounced it. When bedtime came, the whispers of my eldest sisters planning their own voyages around the world would lull me to sleep. There was also my schoolmate, Nazhat, a born storyteller, who used to tell us the stories of Sindibad during recess, in installments like Shehrazad. While narrating, she would be drawing on the dirt ground maps of continents and seas with a stick. Sometimes she would get all heated up when Sindibad did something irrational that caused him trouble and loss of fortune, and she would let fly some gentle expletives that would make us all roar with laughter. But soon enough the bell would ring us back to the mundane decisions and revisions of the practical problems of life. Brandishing her ruler, our teacher would demand, 8x7= what? -- O gosh, think, quick, is it 65? or 56? Did Sindibab go to school?

My neighbor usually makes the cake with six large layers, and flavors it with vanilla. Like the old recipes, it did not come with the exact measurement of flour, you go by the feel. Such as, you know you have added enough flour when the dough feels as soft as your ear lobe, which always works, by the way. In my version, the cake is constructed of seven layers, and is flavored with cardamom and rose water, the "perfumes of Arabia." Interestingly, ever since ancient times the number seven has always been bestowed some mysterious magical powers. A Sumerian hymn, for instance, in praise of Ishtar, the goddess of Uruk, "joyfully proclaims that in consequence of her favor, prosperity and plenitude gladdened the land." And to celebrate this "her table was laden with butter, milk, dates, cheese, and seven fishes," which is not to be taken as a specification of the precise quantity of fish as much as suggesting the mystic character of the rite (Buren, 112). Besides, seven dots were a recurrent mystical symbol represented in many excavated cylinder seals.

One last remark. Do not let the lengthy instructions discourage you from making this beautiful and unusual cake. It is one of those dishes that are easier to make than to describe.

For the filling:
>   **3 heaping tablespoons flour**
>   **3 heaping tablespoons cornstarch**
>   **A pinch of salt**
>   **2 1/4 cups sugar**
>   **8 1/4 cups milk**
>   **2 eggs, beaten**
>   **1 tablespoon rose water, and 1 teaspoon ground cardamom, or 1 tablespoon vanilla, or to taste**
>   **4 tablespoons butter**

For the dough:
>   **2 eggs**
>   **1/3 cup sugar**
>   **1/3 cup milk**
>   **1/3 cup oil**
>   **1 teaspoon vanilla, and/or 1/2 teaspoon cardamom, or to taste**
>   **1 level tablespoon baker's ammonia, or 1 level tablespoon baking powder (see Box below)**
>   **1/4 teaspoon salt**
>   **2 3/4 cups all-purpose flour**
>   **For garnish: 1/4 cup ground pistachio**
>   **Preheat oven to 400 degrees F.**

1. Since the filling and layering are done immediately after a layer is baked, you need to cook the filling first, keep it warm and then make the dough. To make the filling: Put flour, cornstarch and sugar in a medium heavy pot. Add milk gradually, stirring all the time with a wire whisker to prevent lumping. Add the egg and whisk very well, (you can use a hand-held mixer for this). Bring mixture to a quick boil, stirring most of the time. Then on medium high continue stirring until mixture bubbles and thickens, a little thicker than pudding, 10 to 15 minutes. Put away from heat, add butter and flavorings, mix well and set aside covered, at a warm place. (Note: if, while stirring the pudding, you notice that some has stuck in the bottom, do not attempt to dislodge it as burnt particles will mix with the pudding and discolor it. That's why non-stick pots are not recommended)

499

2. To prepare dough: in a big bowl, combine all dough ingredients, except flour and beat well using a mixer, about 3 minutes. Beat in 1 cup flour using a mixer. Stir in the rest of flour in a circular movement using the fingers of one hand. Scrape off any dough that might have clung to your fingers, and knead **lightly and briefly** with one hand. If it is a little bit too sticky, sprinkle a little more flour, but no more than 2 to 3 tablespoons. The finished dough should be soft and not so sticky. A never-failing simple clue: the perfect dough should feel as soft as your ear lobe.

3. Divide dough to 7 equal parts and sprinkle them with a little flour to prevent them from sticking to each other.

4. Preheat oven to 400 degrees F. Grease at least 2 round baking pans 9 to 10 inches in diameter. I have 5 of these pans, which makes the process of baking and filling faster, or use aluminum pans. However, even with just 2 pans it does not take long since the layers cook real fast. The pans are to be greased only once even though they are going to be used more than once. Have a serving dish a little bigger than the pans and the filling pot ready nearby. I put both of them on top of the stove, and work on the counter top next to it.

5. Lightly dust working surface with flour and roll out a dough portion into a very thin disc as big as the pan, it does not have to be perfect. Transfer disc to pan and press dough lightly to let it cover entire bottom.

6. Bake for 6 to 8 minutes or until golden and browned at spots. While this one is cooking prepare the other piece, and spread some of the filling on the surface of the **empty** serving dish. If you have many pans, you may bake as many as your oven could take at a time. Place them on two shelves, middle and upper third, and arrange them so that they will not be on top of each other. They might not cook all at the same time, so take out the ones that are cooked, and rotate and replace as needed.

7. Take the cooked layer out of the oven and immediately and with the help of a metal pancake flipper, loosen sides and take it out of the pan and lay it on the serving dish, up side up, no need to invert it. **Immediately** cover the entire surface with some of the filling. Repeat with the rest of the layers, so that you end up having a stack of filled 7 layers, and the last layer is to be covered with a generous amount of the filling. Always keep an eye on how much filling and layers are left.

8. Immediately sprinkle with ground pistachio, before pudding develops a skin.
Serve chilled, and refrigerate any leftovers.

Suggestions:
* This cake makes a delicious **birthday cake**, only do not put filling on the top layer, otherwise your added icing will slide down the sides. Let the cake cool completely, and then decorate it with your favorite icing.

* Flavor dough and filling with cocoa powder or instant coffee, and drizzle top with melted chocolate.

* For a pretty presentation decorate the cake with strawberries or any other berries of your choice.

Medieval Leavens

Using a fermented batch of dough as a leavening agent in bread and pastry making was a common practice during the medieval times. In fact it was one of the earliest fermenting and leavening techniques ever used by man. However, the Arabic medieval cookbooks make mention of other natural chemical substances used to enhance the dough. First of all there was the *boureq*, which is borax or sodium borate. Nowadays it is known as a cleaning chemical but in the past it was considered a safe food product. In the days of ancient Greek it was used for cleaning as well as preserving food amongst other things. Borax was also mixed with a honey preparation and given to teething infants on their soothers. In the medieval bread pastry recipes it was given principally as a preservative, and, what is more important, to keep the cooked pastries nice and crispy. For example it was added in small quantities, like salt, to the thin *baraziq* breads that were supposed to be brittle and crisp. It was also added to the *zalabia* (fried fritters dipped in syrup) batter to keep the finished pieces from softening afterwards. In fact the recipe recommends that some more *bouraq al-'ajeen* (used with dough) is to be added if *zalabia* pieces have a leathery texture. That is why I tend to believe that the name of the crisp small pastries of today, known as *bourag*, goes back to this medieval common practice (al-Warraq, 35, 268. See Chapter 14 on savory pastries for more details).

They also used another substance called *natroun*, which is niter, soda niter or sodium nitrate, used in ancient times for alkaline salts, and extracted from vegetable ashes. Niter today is not used as food, but in one of the medieval recipes of pastries similar to doughnut, namely al-Qahiriyya (after tenth-century Caliph al-Qahir bil-Lah), a small amount of this substance was called for (*Wasf al-At'ima al-Mu'tada*, description of familiar foods, 432).

There is also *nashadir*, which is ammoniam bicarbonate, or baking ammonia, also known as hartshorn, which unlike the previous two, is still used in baking but in a very limited manner. In the medieval cookbooks I have come across the substance with relation to vinegar making. It was mixed with crumbled hot bread and thrown into vinegar in order to bleach it without distillation. It was also suggested that *buraq al-jeen* (boric acid, borax) might be added for the same purpose (al-Warraq, 51-2).

501

Bakers' ammonia is an old-fashioned leaven, and is replaced by baking powder and baking soda. In Europe it was used in the sixteenth century to solidify jellies, and no recipe using it as a leaven has been found prior to the eighteenth century. It is still used in the Scandinavian countries, Turkey and a few Arab countries, to keep pastries, such as cookies and crackers, light and crisp. It is safe and completely breaks down into gases when heated without leaving any solid residue. The only drawback is that it gives off an unpleasant (ammoniac) but harmless odor while baking (for the first five minutes or so), which then completely dissipates leaving behind extra crisp pastries and cookies. That is why it is used only with small flat pastries such as cookies, and the layered cake I gave above.

Baking ammonia is sometimes hard to come by, but an equal amount of baking powder may by substituted. The resulting cake will be good, but not as crisp and light as the one with the baking ammonia. I was able to find it at the international isles of major supermarkets such as Stop and Shop and Star Market, but you can easily get it via mail through King Arthur's baking goods. Write to them at:

The Baker's Catalog,

P.O. Box 876,

Norwich, Vt. 05055-0876

Or call toll-free at 1-800 827-6836, or online at KingArthurFlour.com.

One last remark, after using bakers' ammonia, make sure to close the container tightly and keep it in a cool place (refrigerator), otherwise next time you need it you will find nothing more substantial than air in your container, as I discovered so much to my dismay.

A Basic Cake Recipe: Infinite Variety
(Al-Keka al-Asasiyya)

(Makes 24 servings)

This is a recipe that I have developed throughout my baking years and it serves as an all-purpose cake mix. Its versatility easily lends itself to a wonderful variety of cakes fit for all occasions from birthday cakes to simple snacks. In making the cakes, I experimented with corn oil and extra light olive oil instead of shortening or butter and got quite satisfactory results. Though this might not reduce the number of calories, it will definitely make your cake healthier.

The Basic Cake Recipe:
4 1/4 cups all-purpose flour
1/2 teaspoon salt
3 teaspoons baking powder

3/4 cup corn oil or exrta light olive oil
1/4 cup applesauce
2 cups sugar
6 eggs
2 teaspoons vanilla, or 1 1/2 teaspoons cardamom, or both
1 1/3 cups milk
Preheat oven to 375 degrees F.

1. Sift flour, salt, and baking powder into a bowl, and set aside.

2. In a big bowl beat oil, applesauce, and sugar, about 3 minutes. Add eggs one at a time, beating well after each addition, about 3 minutes. Mix in vanilla or cardamom or both.

3. Add flour mixture in 4 batches alternately with milk. Do not over mix or beat, otherwise cake will develop a tough texture. The aim is to let ingredients blend.

4. Pour batter into a greased and floured 10-inch tube pan, or 2 round 9-inch pans or depending upon what you're going to do with the cake.

5. Bake in a preheated oven at 375 degrees F. for about 45 minutes for the fluted pan, and about 20 minutes for the layered cake pans, or until a cake tester comes out clean.

6. Leave to cool in the pan on a cake rack for 10 minutes then invert on rack. Serve plain or decorate, or use and serve as directed in the following recipes.

Note: Any of the toppings and icings suggested in the following recipes may be used to frost the plain basic cake

Energizing Fruit Cake
(Kekat al-Fawakih al-Mujaffafa)

This cake works as an energizer for me. It is high in carbohydrates and fiber, and a slice of this cake in the morning, taken along with a glass of milk, usually would keep me ticking until dinnertime.

> **4 cups dried fruits like currants, raisins, sweetened cranberries, chopped apricots, figs, dates, etc.**
> **1 teaspoon grated orange peel**
> **1/2 cup finely shredded coconut**
> **1 cup hot tea or coffee**
> **1/4 cup brandy, optional**
>
> **1 recipe basic cake mix, reduce sugar to 1 1/2 cups**
>
> **1/2 cup broken, toasted walnuts or hazel nuts**
> **1/2 cup ground, toasted almonds, or 1/4 cup almond butter or peanut butter**
> **1/2 teaspoon cinnamon, optional**
> **1/4 teaspoon nutmeg, optional**
> **Preheat oven to 375 degrees F.**

1. In a big bowl, Soak dried fruits, orange peel, and coconut in hot tea or coffee and brandy, if used. Keep soaked, covered, for a few hours turning mixture several times. Drain, reserving liquid (it may replace part of the milk called for in the cake).

2. In a big bowl prepare cake mix as directed in basic recipe

3. With a wooden spoon stir in drained dried fruits, nuts, and optional cinnamon, and nutmeg.

4. Grease and flour baking pan. For this cake I usually use one long loaf pan 16-by-4-by-4 1/2-inch, but two regular loaf pans can also be used, or a big tube pan. (Suggestion: after greasing pan, line it with rolled oats instead of regular flour) Sprinkle bottom of pan with halves of walnut or whole almonds or hazelnuts. Pour batter and level with a spatula.

5. Bake in a preheated oven at 375 degrees F. for about 70 minutes or until golden brown, and cake tester comes out clean. If surface starts to brown before cake is done cover it loosely with foil paper.

Let cool completely in pan on a rack, then invert and set aside for a few hours before slicing. If wrapped well, this cake can stay good in the refrigerator for more than a week. It freezes very well, too. I cut the cake into serving size pieces, wrap them individually in plastic wrap and keep them in the freezer for future use.

Marble Cake
(Al-KeKa al-Marmariyya)

I have always been a fan of marble cakes ever since my eldest sister first started making them when I was still a child. She always liked to flavor them with cardamom and vanilla, and that is how I still like my cakes to be flavored.

1 recipe of the basic cake mix
2 tablespoons sugar
1/4 cup cocoa powder
Preheat oven to 375 degrees F.

1.Make batter as directed in basic recipe. In a medium bowl set aside one third of the batter.

2. In a small bowl, mix cocoa powder and sugar. Stir in a little milk or water just enough to make mixture into a thin paste, about 3 tablespoons. Stir this paste into the set aside third of dough and mix well until well blended.

3. Grease and flour 10-inch tube pan. Fill pan by adding white batter in tablespoons alternately with teaspoons of brown batter. Shake pan to level surface of batter.

4. Bake and cool as directed in basic recipe.

Suggestion: You may add another shade to the brown by dividing batter into 3 thirds: leave one third white, the second flavor with the cocoa mixture, and the third flavor and color with 1 tablespoon **instant** coffee dissolved in a little of water. Fill pan with tablespoons of white batter alternating with tablespoons of cocoa and coffee mixtures.

A Slice of Rainbow Cake
(Kekat Qous wa Quzah)

This multi-colored cake is a pleasure to look at and to eat. It is especially popular with kids of all ages. It will also make a handsome birthday cake if you decorate it with icing.

1/4 cup currants or raisins
1/4 cup coarsely chopped nuts

1/2 cup graham crackers crumbs
1/4 cup chocolate drink powder such as Nesquick

1 recipe of basic cake mix

Food colorings: red, green and blue, a few drops of each
1/4 cup shredded unsweetened coconut, optional

Preheat oven to 375 degrees F.

1. Grease and flour a 10-inch tube pan or any other pan with similar capacity. Spread raisins and nuts in bottom of pan and set aside.

2. Mix crackers crumbs and chocolate powder. Set aside.

3. Prepare batter as directed in basic cake mix.

4. Divide and color batter as follows: Besides the mixing bowl, have 3 small bowls ready. Put a quarter of batter into each small bowl leaving one quarter in mixing bowl uncolored, but mix with it coconut, if used. Color batter in the 3 bowls by adding a few drops of food coloring into each, so that you end up having 3 different colors of batter.

5. Start by spreading **green** batter in the bottom of pan, even up the surface with a spatula. Sprinkle surface with one third of crumb mixture letting it cover the entire surface.

6. Spread **uncolored** batter on top of the green and spread it evenly with the second third of crumb mixture.

7. Repeat with the **red** batter, and top it with the rest of crumbs.

8. Spread **blue** portion on top evenly.

9. Bake and cool as directed in the basic recipe. Ice and decorate the cake to your fancy.

Note:
You can also flavor each color differently, such raspberry for the red, mint for the green, and aniseed or liquorice for the blue. However, **do this with extreme moderation** so that the final effect would give a subtle blend of all these flavors. Feel free to make your own choice of colors and flavors.

Black 'n White Cake
(Kekat Abyadh wa Aswad)

Make a handsome cake by neatly alternating white layers with chocolate flavored layers.

1 recipe basic cake mix
1/3 cup cocoa powder
1/4 cup sugar

1/2 cup shredded unsweetened coconut to be added to the white mixture, if wished
1/4 cup toasted and chopped nuts to be added to the black portion, if wished

Icing of your choice to assemble the cake (see, for instance, fat free icing below)
Preheat oven to 375 degrees F.

1. Prepare batter as directed in the basic recipe. Divide it into 2 equal portions. Leave one white and the other color with the cocoa mixture as follows: Put cocoa powder and sugar in a small bowl then add a little milk or water (about 1/4 cup), and stir to a thin paste. Stir this mixture into one half of the batter.

2. Grease and flour 2 round 9-inch pans and spread the brown and white batters, separately. Bake and thoroughly cool a directed in the basic recipe.

3. Using a serrated knife halve each round horizontally. Then stack and fill as follows: on a serving platter put top half of black portion, cut side up, and spread with filling. Then put bottom half of white portion cut side down, and cover with filling. Top it with bottom half of black portion, cut side up, and spread it with filling. Finally, put top part of white portion, cut side down. Cover top and sides with the remaining icing.

Chess Board Cake

Another attractive way of doing it is to bake the black and white batters separately in 2 loaf pans. When cool, divide each into 4 parts, horizontally and vertically. Alternate colors for a chess board effect, sticking pieces together with the icing. Cover entire surface with the rest of icing.

Fat-free Icing (Egg-White Icing)
(Talbeesat Bayadh al-Beidh)

This is my favorite icing. It has a meringue-like consistency that requires no fat, and its sweet taste can always be balanced by sprinkling it with chopped toasted nuts. In the commercial bakeries of Baghdad and other large cities in Iraq it is this icing rather than the shortening-based ones that is used for decorating birthday and wedding cakes. In a way, it is a variation on the royal icing, but unlike the latter it does not dry out and get chalky after a while. If you want to keep the icing white it is better to use clear vanilla, or powdered vanilla rather than the regular brown variety. A stand mixer would be helpful in making this icing. The following amount is enough for filling and icing the basic cake. It is a good idea to mix the filling with thoroughly drained and chopped canned fruits.

> **1 1/2 cups granulated sugar**
> **1/4 teaspoon cream of tartar or citric acid**
> **1/2 cup water**
> **2 egg whites**
> **1 teaspoon vanilla, preferably clear liquid or powdered vanilla**
> **1/2 teaspoon cardamom, optional**
> **For garnish: Finely chopped, toasted nuts, optional**

1. Combine sugar, citric acid and water in a medium heavy saucepan. Bring to a boil, stirring until sugar dissolves. Then let mixture boil gently, undisturbed, skimming any froth that might arise, until syrup of medium consistency is reached. You can tell by placing a drop on a cold dry plate. It should keep its shape when the plate is tilted, 4 to 6 minutes.

2. While syrup is cooking, put egg whites in a clean and dry medium bowl. Start whisking until rather stiff. Slowly and in a thin thread pour 1/3 of the syrup, whisking all the time. Return remaining syrup to heat and resume cooking until it thickens but before it starts to change color, 5 to 6 more minutes. Add thickened syrup in a thin thread, whisking all the time.

3. Add vanilla and cardamom, if used, and continue whisking until icing is stiff enough to hold its shape. Use immediately.

4. To color icing it is better to use **paste food coloring** rather than the regular liquid variety to prevent icing from having runny texture.

5. Since this icing is sensitive to humidity, after icing the cake put it in a warm oven until the outside of the icing forms a kind of protective skin. You can tell by touching the surface of the icing. If it does not stick to your finger, it is ready. A hair drier blown on hot but gentle cycle will also do the trick. However, if you are planning to sprinkle nuts on the icing, do this immediately after you ice the cake and before the icing forms a skin.

7-Up Cake
(Al-Keka al-Isfanjiyya)

(Makes 16 servings)

The medieval bakers made *safanj* (sponge) cakes using fermented *zalabia* batter which, when baked, developed a spongy texture ideal for soaking up with syrups, and melted butter. In a simple version the batter was baked in the *tannour*, then turned over a plate, cut into four parts, and while still hot was moistened with fresh milk, and sprinkled with sugar. In some more elaborate preparations they stuck a fat reed (to be removed after baking) in the middle of the batter. The hole was used to pour syrup and melted butter for the cake to soak up (al-Warraq, 269, *Anonymous Andalusian Cookbook*, 132). In another tenth-century preparation simply called, *unlatticed zalabya*, batter is made of flour or cornstarch, milk, and eggs, and is whipped until frothy and reaches the top of *al-qas'a* (bowl). The batter, referred to as *furniyya* (baked in the oven), is put in a pot, which in turn is put inside a larger one. Water is poured so that the delicate egg mixture is baked in a kind of water bath. When done, the cake is overturned onto a *qas'a*, until it cools off. It is then cut to pieces and drenched in milk, clarified butter, and oil. For garnish it is sprinkled with sugar and ground black pepper (al-Warraq, 268-9).

The following is an easy and light sponge cake in which soda drink is used to give it a desirable moist texture. Besides the original lemon flavored 7-Up, you can use other varieties. My favorite is 7-Up flavored with cherry. I decorate the cake with low-fat cool whip and deck it with maraschino cherries to match the flavored 7-Up.

> **3 eggs**
> **1 1/2 cups sugar**
> **1 teaspoon vanilla**
> **1 cup 7-Up (regular only), open can only when ready to use**
> **2 cups all-purpose flour**

1/4 teaspoon salt
1 teaspoon baking powder
Preheat oven to 375 degrees F.

1. In a medium bowl, and using an electric mixer beat eggs until thick and lemon colored, about 5 minutes.

2. Add sugar in three batches beating well after each addition. Add vanilla. Stir in soda drink.

3. Sift together flour, salt and baking powder. Add to egg mixture all at once and stir just until well blended.

4. Grease and flour a 10-cup capacity tube or bundt pan, and shake off excess flour. Pour batter into pan, and bake in a preheated oven at 375 degrees F. for 40 minutes or until cake is springy to the touch and surface is golden brown.

5. Immediately invert pan on a tray or plate sprinkled with icing sugar, do not remove pan. Let cake cool completely in this position, undisturbed. The cake will fall off the pan into the plate or tray after a while. When completely cool, remove pan, and decorate the cake to your fancy.

Domed Steam Cake
(Kek al- Bukhar)

(Makes 12 servings)

   This cake is unique in that it does not need an oven for baking it, but is rather cooked on top of the stove. It is a reminder of how our medieval ancestors used to bake their cakes, that is, besides the *tannour*. In al-Warraq's tenth-century cookbook there is a cake recipe for which a steam pot was created. First, batter was prepared by mixing flour and cornstarch, and whipping them vigorously with milk and eggs. Then the bottom of a big pot was lined with reeds. The batter was poured into a smaller pot, covered with a lid, and placed on the reeds. The big pot was put on fire, water was poured into it, and was simmered, covered, until cake was done. After turning it on a platter, the cake was cut and moistened with milk and melted butter, and sprinkled with sugar, and a little black pepper (269).
   The function of the steam pot in the following cake is to allow steam to gather on top of the cake, thus keeping it moist, which is critical in the dome formation, as you'll see in the following instructions.

   1 2/3 cups flour
   1/4 cup cocoa powder
   1/4 teaspoon salt
   1/2 teaspoon baking soda
   1/2 teaspoon baking powder
   5 eggs, separated
   1 1/2 cups sugar, divided
   2 teaspoons vanilla

509

        1 tablespoon lemon juice, add enough cold water to make 1/3 cup liquid
For the filling:
        Whipped cream of your choice
        Slices of fresh fruit or drained canned fruit
For the topping:
        3 rounded tablespoons cornstarch
        1 cup sugar
        2 cups milk
        1/4 cup cocoa powder
        1/4 cup butter
        1 teaspoon vanilla
For garnish: 2 tablespoons ground pistachio or nuts of your choice, or colorful sprinkles

1. Mix flour, cocoa powder, salt, baking soda, and baking powder. Set aside.

2. Beat eggs yolks in a bowl until lemon colored, about 2 minutes. Gradually add 3/4 cup sugar, 2 minutes. Beat in vanilla, and diluted lemon juice, 1 minute.

3. Add flour mixture all at once and fold lightly and quickly with a wooden spoon just until mixed. Set aside.

4. With clean and dry beaters whisk egg whites until soft peaks form. Gradually add 3/4 cup sugar and continue whisking until peaks stand firm but not dry, about 5 minutes.

5. Using a wooden spoon fold 1/3 of white mixture into yolk mixture. Then gently and quickly fold in remaining egg white mixture in two batches. Fold just until evenly incorporated, try to keep as much air as possible.

5. Pour batter into a medium-sized greased pressure pot. Put lid on but remove pressure valve, and close hole with a piece of paper towel.

6. Cook on very low heat for 40 to 45 minutes or until steam starts to come out of the hole, and a smell of baking cake starts to emit. To test for doneness, insert a thin skewer through the steam hole. If it comes out clean, cake is done. Start testing after 35 minutes of cooking. Do not overcook otherwise surface will set and you will not be able to have it domed.

7. Immediately after it is done, invert pot onto a heatproof bowl, the upper rim of which matches that of pot. Remove the pot and seal the bowl with plastic wrap. The purpose of this is to prevent any steam from escaping while cake is cooling. This will help the cake develop its characteristic domed top. When completely cool put cake on a serving plate domed side up. Cut it into two parts horizontally, and fill it with cream and fruits.

8. The cake is then covered with the hot topping, and here is how to prepare it: Combine dry ingredients of topping in a small heavy pot. Add milk gradually, stirring all the time with a wire whisker to prevent lumping. Cook on medium heat, stirring frequently until it bubbles and thickens, about 10 minutes. Remove from heat, add butter and vanilla and mix well. **Immediately** cover the entire surface of the filled domed cake with the topping. Give the surface an interesting peaky or swirly look. Sprinkle surface with your choice of garnish. Refrigerate for about 2 hours before serving.

Banana and Pistachio Layer Cake
(Kekat al-Mouz wal Fistiq)

(Makes 16 slices)

It is possible that the ancient Mesopotamians knew of bananas. Some of the Assyrian bas-reliefs show, among other food items on the tables, an object which appears to consist of a number of finger-like sections joined at their base somewhat resembling a bunch of bananas. It is certain; however, that it was known and consumed during the Middle Ages. It is once mentioned in the Qur'an as one of the delicious fruits that grow in the Paradisaical Garden of Eden (it was called *talh*, in *Surat al-Waqi'a*, verse, 29). The tenth-century Baghdadi cookbook includes a recipe called *judhabat al-mouz*, made by layering bananas with thin *riqaq* breads, sprinkled with sugar, until the pot was filled, and perfumed with rose water. The pot was then baked in the *tannour*, under a roasting chicken to get all the drippings while it was roasting (al-Warraq, 236). In another thirteenth-century *judhabat al-mouz*, banana pieces were dipped in batter, fried, then immersed in syrup, thrown into pounded sugar, and arranged between two flat breads, and put under a roasting chicken to receive the drippings (Appendix to *Kitab al-Wusla*, in *Wasf al-Ati'ma*, 451-2). They sound so much like the fried bananas sold by vendors in the streets of Thailand and other South-Asian countries. Furthermore, we also learn from the stories in *The Arabian Nights* that banana leaves were used for wrapping groceries. In the modern scene the trees still grow in some gardens, but the bananas they yield are very small and are definitely of no commercial significance.

In the following recipe the cake is perfumed with rose water which, combined with bananas and pistachio, gives it an unusually delicious medieval flavor.

For the cake:
> 1/2 cup oil
> 1 1/2 cups granulated sugar
> 3 eggs
> 1 cup mashed banana (about 3 medium ones)
> 2 teaspoons rose water
> 1 teaspoon vanilla
>
> 2 1/2 cups all-purpose flour
> 2 teaspoons baking powder
> 1/2 teaspoon baking soda
> 1/2 teaspoon salt
> 2/3 cup buttermilk
> 1/2 cup chopped toasted nuts, optional

For the filling:
> 1 cup chilled whipping cream
> 2 tablespoons powdered sugar
> 1 teaspoon rose water
> (Or substitute with 1 cup cool whip; no need to add sugar in this case)
> Thin slices of banana, optional

For the icing:
> 1/2 cup packed brown sugar
> 1/4 cup whipping cream
> 3 tablespoons butter

511

> 1/2 cup powdered sugar
> 1 teaspoon rose water
> For garnish, 2 tablespoons ground pistachio
> Preheat oven to 375 degrees F.

1. **To make the cake**, in a big bowl put oil, sugar, and eggs. Beat well for 2 minutes. Add mashed bananas, rose water, and vanilla, and beat well. Mix flour, baking powder, baking soda and salt. Beat into oil mixture alternately with buttermilk in two batches. Do not over beat, but just until batter is combined. Fold in nuts, if used.

2. Grease and flour two 9-inch round baking pans. Divide batter between the two pans and bake in a preheated oven at 375 degrees F. for about 30 minutes or until cake tester comes out clean and surface is golden. Let stand for 10 minutes then invert and cool completely on cake rack.

3. **To make the filling**, in a small chilled bowl whip cream until it holds soft peaks. Add sugar and rose water and whip until stiff peaks form. Or if using cool whip just add rose water. Cut cakes into halves horizontally. Put one layer, topside down on a serving platter, and cover surface with a third of the filling. Cover it with the bottom half, cut side down and cover surface with third of filling. Cover it with the bottom half of the other cake, cut side up, and spread last third of filling on surface. Cover it with the top layer, cut side down. If using the optional banana slices, arrange them in one layer after you spread the whipped cream on the cake layers.

4. **To make the icing**, in a small saucepan combine sugar, cream and butter and bring mixture to a boil, stirring to allow sugar to dissolve. Boil mixture for about 2 minutes. Let it cool off to room temperature. Add powdered sugar and rose water, and stir until smooth. Immediately spread icing on the top surface of the cake, allowing it to come nicely down the sides like icicles. Sprinkle ground pistachio all over the surface, and chill cake for at least an hour before serving.

Gold 'n Spicy Pumpkin Cake
(Kekat al-Shijar al-Ahmer)

(Makes 16 slices)

This cake is a variation on the Banana and pistachio Layer Cake. Pumpkin gives the cake an appealing golden hue, and the toasted pumpkinseeds give a pleasant crunch to the bite.

For the cake:
> 1/2 cup oil
> 1 3/4 cups sugar
> 3 eggs
> 1 cup canned puréed pumpkin (not pie filling)
> 2 teaspoons rose water
> 1 teaspoon vanilla
>
> 2 1/2 cups all purpose flour
> 2 teaspoons baking powder

       1/2 teaspoon baking soda
       1/2 teaspoon salt
       1/2 teaspoon cinnamon
       1/2 teaspoon ground cardamom
       2/3 cup buttermilk
For the filling:
       1 cup chilled whipping cream
       2 tablespoons powdered sugar
       1 teaspoon rose water
       (Or substitute with 1 cup cool whip; no need to add sugar in this case)
For the icing:
       1/2 cup packed brown sugar
       1/4 cup whipping cream
       3 tablespoons butter
       1/2 cup powdered sugar
       1 teaspoon rose water
For garnish: 1/4 cup shelled and toasted unsalted pumpkin seeds
       Preheat oven to 375 degrees F.

1. **To make the cake,** in a big bowl put oil, sugar and eggs. Beat well for 2 minutes. Mix in pumpkin, rose water and vanilla, and beat well. In a medium bowl sift flour, baking powder, baking soda, salt, cinnamon and cardamom. Beat into oil mixture alternately with buttermilk in two batches. Do not over beat, but just until batter is combined.

2. Grease and flour two 9-inch round baking pans. Divide batter between the two pans, and bake in a preheated oven at 375 degrees F. for about 30 minutes, or until cake tester comes out clean and surface is golden. Let stand for 10 minutes, then invert and cool completely on cake rack.

3. **To make the filling,** in a small chilled bowl whip cream until it holds soft peaks. Add sugar and rose water, and whip until stiff peaks form. Or if using cool whip just add rose water. Cut cakes into halves horizontally. Put one layer, topside down on a serving platter, and cover surface with a third of the filling. Cover it with the bottom half, cut side down, and cover surface with third of filling. Cover it with the bottom half of the other cake, cut side up, and spread last third of filling on surface. Cover it with the top layer, cut side down.

4. **To make the icing,** in a small saucepan combine sugar, cream and butter and bring mixture to a boil, stirring to allow sugar to dissolve. Boil mixture for about 2 minutes. Let it cool to room temperature. Add powdered sugar and rose water, and stir until smooth. Immediately spread icing on the top surface of the cake allowing it to come nicely down the sides like icicles. Sprinkle toasted pumpkinseeds all over surface and chill cake for at least an hour before serving.

Golden Apple Squares
(Kekat al-Tuffah)

(Makes 18 pieces)

This cake is light, delicious and easy to make. Any kind of sweet eating apples will do. Cooking apples are not recommended for this cake because they will not have enough time to soften while baking.

For the cake:

> **3/4 cup oil**
> **1/4 cup apple sauce**
> **1 cup sugar**
> **4 eggs**
> **Grated rind of 1 lemon**
> **1 tablespoon lemon juice**
> **2 teaspoons vanilla**
>
> **2 1/2 cups flour**
> **1/2 teaspoon salt**
> **2 teaspoons baking powder**
> **1/2 cup currants or raisins, optional**

For the topping:

> **5 to 6 medium apples, peeled, cored and sliced into 1/3-inch thick pieces (about 3 pounds)**
> **1/2 cup slivered almonds, or 1/2 cup chopped walnut**
> **2 teaspoons cinnamon**
> **1/4 cup sugar**
> **Powdered sugar for garnish, optional**
> **Preheat oven to 375 degrees F.**

1. In a big bowl beat oil and applesauce with sugar, eggs, lemon rind, lemon juice, and vanilla, about 3 minutes.

2. Sift together flour, salt and baking powder and add them to egg mixture all at once. With a wooden spoon or mixer, stir until well-blended, about 2 minutes. Fold in raisins if using any.

3. Spread batter in 15-by-10-inch greased and floured baking pan. (Instead of flour I like to use quick oats for lining the pan)

4. Arrange apple slices in rows on surface of batter, slightly overlapping pieces. Scatter nuts on surface, and sprinkle cinnamon, then sugar all over surface.

5. Bake in a preheated oven at 375 degrees F. for 35 to 40 minutes or until golden brown.

6. Allow cake to cool in pan on a rack. Do not invert. Cut into squares while still in pan. Sprinkle pieces with powdered sugar if liked.

Spicy Prune Cake
(Kekat al-'Injas)

(Makes 16 slices)

Prune was a valued fruit in ancient Mesopotamia. In *The Assyrian Herbal*, a monograph on Assyrian vegetable drugs, it was mentioned as a kind of conserve always to be eaten with butter and honey (Thompson, 129-30). In the Akkadian it was called "antahsum" (cf. Arabis '*injas*), and in its unripe state, it was used in cooking as a souring agent (see Introduction). The ancients' belief in the "antahsum" medicinal power has been scientifically confirmed in a recent study. The phytochemicals in prunes have the power to kill bacteria. One tablespoon of puréed prunes mixed with one pound ground meat can kill more than 90% of the E.coli bacteria present in the meat within three days (Daniel Fung of Kansas State University, *Parade Magazine*, Nov. 11, 2001, 6). Any way, prunes are delicious and we can eat them for sheer delight, as in this sumptuous cake. Simply sprinkle it with powdered sugar or cover it with chocolate icing for more dressy occasions.

1 1/2 cups prunes (about 10 ounces)

1/2 cup oil
1 1/2 cups sugar
3 eggs
1 1/2 teaspoons vanilla

21/4 cups all- purpose flour
1 1/2 teaspoons baking powder
1/2 teaspoon baking soda
1/2 teaspoon salt
1 teaspoon cinnamon
1/4 teaspoon ground nutmeg
1/4 teaspoon ground cloves

1/2 cup toasted walnut, broken into small pieces
For topping:
1/3 cup sugar
2 heaping tablespoons flour or wheat germ
2 tablespoons chilled butter cut into small pieces
Preheat oven to 375 degrees F.

1. Put prunes in a small pot and cover with water, about 1 1/4 cups. Bring to a boil, then let simmer for about 10 minutes, or until prunes soften. Drain, but reserve drained liquid. Let cool to room temperature.

2. In a big bowl put oil, sugar, eggs and vanilla, mix for 2 minutes. Set aside

3. Sift flour, baking powder, baking soda, salt, cinnamon, nutmeg and cloves, set aside.

4. Cut drained prunes into smaller pieces, set aside. Add enough cold water to reserved liquid to make it measure 2/3 cup.

5. Stir in flour mixture into egg mixture, in two batches, alternately with the measured prune liquid. Stir in walnuts and cut prunes.

6. Pour batter into a greased and floured bundt pan, or a 9-by-13-inch pan for a sheet cake.

7. Mix topping ingredients until crumbly in texture and sprinkle on the entire surface of spread batter.

8. Bake in a preheated oven at 375 degrees F. for 45 minutes for the bundt pan, and about 30 minutes for the sheet cake, or until cake tester comes out clean. Let cool in pan on a rack for 10 minutes, then invert. Either serve plain or decorate as follows:

Variations:
*Sprinkle cooled cake with a little powdered sugar.

* Do not use topping. After cake is baked and cooled drizzle it with simple icing: mix 1 cup sifted powdered sugar and 1 to 2 tablespoons of liquid, such as rose water or milk until of spreading consistency.

*Do not use topping. After cake is baked and cooled cover it with the following simple and delicious
chocolate icing:
- 1/4 cup butter (1/2 stick)
- 1/3 cup cocoa powder
- 1 cup powdered sugar, sifted
- About 4 tablespoons warm water
- 1 teaspoon vanilla or rose water, see Glossary

In a small pot melt butter and stir in cocoa powder. Then using a mixer on medium speed add powdered sugar in batches alternately with water until smooth and of spreading consistency. If mixture looks oily and separated, beat in a little more warm water as needed until icing looks smooth and of spreading consistency. Stir in vanilla or rose water.

Raisin Cake
(Kekat al-Kishmish)

(Makes 16 servings)

If you are a *kishmish* (raisin) fan as I am, you'll love this cake. It is relatively lighter than the traditional cakes, and liquid called for in the recipe may be as sober as milk or tea, or as tipsy as brandy.

- 3/4 cup oil
- 1 cup sugar
- 4 eggs, separated

1 teaspoon vanilla
1 cup raisins
2/3 cup milk, tea, or brandy
1 teaspoon finely grated lemon rind

2 1/2 cups all-purpose flour
1/4 teaspoon salt
2 teaspoons baking powder
Preheat oven to 375 degrees F.

1. In a big bowl mix oil and sugar. Add egg yolk gradually, beating after each addition, about 3 minutes. Add vanilla. Stir in raisins, milk, and lemon rind.

2. Sift together flour, salt and baking powder, and stir into the mixture.

3. In a small bowl and with clean and dry beaters whisk egg white until stiff peaks form but not dry, about 3 minutes.

4. With a wooden spoon fold third of the beaten egg white into the yolk mixture. Then add the rest of egg white in two batches, folding gently and quickly, until well blended.

5. Pour batter into a greased and floured 10-inch tube pan and bake in a preheated oven at 375 degrees F. for about 40 minutes or until a cake tester comes out clean.

6. Let cool in pan on a rack for 10 minutes then invert on a serving plate. When cool sprinkle with powdered sugar, if wished.

Golden Coconut Cake
(Kekat Joz al-Hind)

(Makes 14 to 16 slices)

My passion for coconut goes back to the times when my father used to gather us around him and tell us of the adventures of *Sindibad al-Bahri* (or *Sandabad*, as he used to pronounce it). In one of his voyages, *Sindibad* happened to land on a desert island where a herd of monkeys, stationed on top of palm trees, attacked him by throwing down coconuts at him. We thought that was very funny, and the story would unfailingly stir in us the desire to eat fresh coconut. We loved the ritual of puncturing it first to take out the milk (whey-like liquid), and then hammering the shell to get out the crunchy pulp. We used to eat a lot, only to regret it after a while, when all the fat we gulped down would take its toll on us, and make us feel nauseated.

Coconut in Iraq is also called *joz nargeela*, because the emptied coconut shell was used to contain water for the *nargeela* (hooka). The shell had other uses for the medieval cooks. In al-Warraq's tenth-century cookbook, a small hole was pierced in the bottom of half an emptied shell, and was used as an instrument in making *zalabya*. Nowadays we use funnels.

Here is an easy and delicious cake for you, which comes out of the oven ready with the topping. You also have the option of not using the topping, and filling and icing it any way you like. (You can use any of the fillings or icings scattered in this chapter)

For the cake:
      1/2 cup oil or butter
      3/4 cup sugar
      2 eggs
      1 teaspoon vanilla
      1/2 teaspoon ground cardamom

      1 3/4 cups flour
      1 1/2 teaspoons baking powder
      1/4 teaspoon salt

      1/2 cup milk
      1/2 cup shredded coconut, unsweetened
For the topping:
      1/4 cup melted butter, do no substitute
      1/3 cup sugar
      1/2 cup flour
      1/2 cup shredded coconut, unsweetened
      1/4 cup broken walnut
      1 teaspoon vanilla, or 1/2 teaspoon ground cardamom, or both
      Preheat oven to375

1. In a medium bowl, cream butter or oil with sugar and beat until creamy, a minute or two. Add eggs one at a time beating after each addition. Add vanilla and cardamom, and mix well.

2. Sift flour, baking powder, and salt, and beat into egg mixture in two batches, alternately with milk. Fold in coconut.

3. Grease and flour 8-by-8- inch baking pan. Spread batter evenly.

4. Mix topping ingredients, and spread evenly on batter. Press topping lightly.

5. Bake in a preheated oven at 375 degrees F. for 30 minutes, or until cake tester comes out clean and topping is golden. If topping starts to brown before cake is done, drape it with aluminum foil. Let cake cool in pan on rack, then turn it carefully into the serving dish. If wished, drizzle topping with melted chocolate or powdered sugar mixed with a little rose water or milk, until of spreading consistency.

Iraqi Éclairs

(Makes 22 to 24 pieces)

Éclairs are quite popular in Baghdad and are usually called *keik*. The Baghdadi bakers make the shells crispier and lighter than the European éclairs, and the filling a little thicker and lighter. The following rendition is the nearest I could get to the Baghdadi version. I like to flavor these cakes with the perfumes of Arabia, namely cardamom and rose water. A sturdy mixer like Kitchen aid would really come to your aid in this recipe, since the mixture would be a little stiffer than he regular cake batter (use the flat beaters). Another tip, baking shells in a hot humid oven for the first 30 minutes is the clue to successfully puffed éclairs. Make sure that the filling and the shells are absolutely cool before you fill the cakes, otherwise the steam will soften the shells.

For the shells:
> **2 cups boiling water**
> **2/3 cup oil or butter (or a mixture of both)**
> **1/4 teaspoon salt**
> **1 teaspoon sugar**
> **2 cups all-purpose flour**
> **6 eggs, beaten**
> **1/2 teaspoon ground cardamom, or 1 teaspoon vanilla, or both**

For the filling:
> **1 cup flour**
> **A dash of salt**
> **1 1/4 cups sugar, adjust to taste**
> **5 1/2 cups milk, preferably whole milk, low fat will give good results, too**
> **1 tablespoon rose water (or 1/2 teaspoon cardamom, or 1 teaspoon vanilla, or a combination of flavors, to taste)**
> **1/4 cup butter**

For the glaze:
> **Two recipes of Chocolate Icing in Spicy Prune Cake, p. 516; or two recipes of icing in Banana and Pistachio Layer Cake, p. 511; or make Chocolate Glaze with Powdered Milk using the following ingredients:**
> **1/2 cup water**
> **1/2 cup sugar**
> **1/4 cup butter**
> **1/2 cup cocoa powder**
> **1 teaspoon vanilla or rose water**
> **1 1/3 cups instant dried milk (such as Nido), if lumpy press through sieve to turn into powder**
> **About 1/4 cup powdered sugar, or additional cocoa powder or dried milk if semi sweet glaze is preferred**

> **Preheat oven to 400 degrees F., and put a small pot filled with hot water in the lowest rack to create moisture in the oven**

1. To make shells, in a medium heavy pot combine water, oil, salt, and sugar. Bring to a boil.

2. Add flour all at once and with a wooden spoon stir vigorously until thick dough forms and starts to pull away from the sides of the pot, about 2 minutes. Put away from heat, allow to cool slightly (cool enough not to cook eggs when added).

3. Using a mixer add eggs to flour mixture one at a time, beating well after each addition. Beat in cardamom or vanilla. The finished dough will be soft and sticky, about 5 minutes. If dough climbs up on the beaters of hand-held mixer while beating, push it down with a spoon.

4. With oiled hands, take a small mount (size of a small lemon) and roll it lightly between the fingers to shape it into thick pencils about 3 inches long. Arrange pieces on an ungreased cookie sheet, leaving a space between pieces.

5. Bake in a preheated oven, at 400 degrees F., and don't forget to put a small pot of hot water on the lowest rack to help create moisture. This will help cakes to puff more easily. After 30 minutes lower heat to 325 degrees F., remove the pot and continue baking for about 20 minutes or until pieces are golden brown. Take out of the oven and let cool completely.

6. With a small sharp pointed knife, make a slit along one of the sides. Open it up a little, and put enough filling (method below) to fill the cavity. Cover top with the chosen glaze (see method below), by taking a small amount with a spoon or knife and spreading it on the piece.

To make the filling, in a small pot, combine flour, salt, and sugar. Add milk gradually stirring all the time with a wire whisk. Bring to a boil on medium high heat stirring constantly, then reduce heat to medium and continue cooking and stirring until mixture is thickened, about 10 minutes. Put away from heat and stir in the chosen flavoring and butter. Let cool completely, covered.

To make Chocolate Glaze with Powdered Milk, in a small pot bring water and sugar to a boil and let cook gently for about 5 minutes (do not let liquid thicken into syrup). Add butter and stir to melt it, put away from heat. Using a hand held mixer or spoon stir in sifted cocoa powder until well blended. Add flavoring. Then gradually beat in dried powdered milk. Beat in the powdered sugar or the additional cocoa powder or dried milk just enough to make glaze thick enough to hold its shape.

Suggestions:

*Instead of chocolate icing, caramelized sugar with broken toasted nuts may be used, see p.459 for recipe of Almond Brittle.

*Feel free to flavor the filling with your favorite flavor. I suggest adding 1/2 cup cocoa powder to the filling ingredients. Or you might add 1 tablespoon instant coffee, regular or decaffeinated. Or you might replace some of the milk with already brewed coffee. You can also flavor the filling with 1 tablespoon of your favorite liqueur.

Cream-filled Spirals
(Malawi bil Kream)

(Makes 12 pieces)

This is another favorite cake in Iraq known by the generic name, *kek*. I have called it *malawi* (singular *malwiyya*, spiral) after its spiral shape, reminiscent of the famous *Malwiyyat Samarra*, the spiral minaret of Samarra built by the Abbasid Caliph al-Mu'tasim in the ninth century AD. The *Malwiyya* was ultimately drawn upon the ancient Sumerian and Babylonian Ziggurats.

The cake is easy to prepare at home, if ready-made puff pastry is used. To make the characteristic spiral shapes, bakeries usually use special cone-shaped molds. I make my molds by cutting a pie aluminum pan into halves, folding each to form a cone. Overlap the sides and secure them so that they will not open up while baking.

Apparently medieval bakers were familiar with the techniques of puff pastry. It was called *muwarraqa* (leafy), and *musammana* (done with clarified butter). The first method was to roll out dough very thin, spread it with melted *samn* (clarified butter), fold, and repeat several times. The second method was to roll out dough thin, spread it with *samn*, roll it like a reed, coil it, and then roll it out thin. Both methods create pastry with a lot of layers (thirteenth-century *Anonymous Andalusian Cookbook*, 113, 119). In the fourteenth-century augmented version of al-Baghdadi's cookbook there is a puff pastry recipe called *liyiyya* from *liyya* (tallow), a valued source of fat taken from the fat sheep's tail. Dough is made of special white flour, rolled out very thin, spread with tail fat (which I assume was pounded into paste), and folded. This apparently is repeated several times, for the final dough should be leafy (*yatawarraq*). It is sprinkled with sugar, baked, drenched in melted *liyya* (tallow), and sprinkled with sugar or drenched in honey (435-6).

Here is how to make the spiral cakes:

> **One 16-ounce package puff pastry sheets**
> **1 egg white for glazing, whisked until foamy**
> **1 recipe** éclairs filling, **in recipe above**
> **About 1/2 cup ground toasted peanuts or pistachio**
>
> **Preheat oven to 400 degrees F.**

1. Thaw pastry according to package directions. Divide sheets lengthwise into a total of 12 strips.

521

2. Wind strips around greased aluminum cones, starting from the tip. Secure tip of strip by pressing it to create a pointed top and overlap layers as you go all the way down.

3. Arrange cones, seam side down, on a baking sheet, brush with whisked egg white and bake in a preheated oven at 400 degrees F. for bout 20 minutes or until golden brown and crisp.

4. Allow pieces to cool slightly, then carefully take out of the moulds. (You can reuse the moulds.)

5. Fill the **completely** cool cones, with the **chilled** filling. If cones are filled with a warm filling, the steam from the filling will soften the cones.

6. Immediately dip bottom of cone in chopped nuts to cover filling completely. Serve chilled

No-bake Cake Truffles
(Kurat al-Keik)

(Makes 24 pieces)

Do you have any leftover cake lurking in the refrigerator that no one is interested in? Here is a lovely way of transforming it. As growing kids in Baghdad we used to look forward to Fridays when the little balls of moist dark cake, rolled in white shredded coconut, made their appearance at the neighborhood bakery. They were delicious and the mystique behind their weekly appearance made them all the more desirable. It was many years later that I knew the secret--they were made once a week because the bakers waited until a good amount of stale cake accumulated to make those cake balls.

They are easy to make, and the ultimate flavor is determined by the stale cake used, and flavors and liquids chosen to bind the mixture.

1 1/2 pounds stale cake (10 to 12 slices)
1/2 cup toasted walnut
1/2 cup chocolate or cocoa powder
1/2 cup apricot jam
3 to 4 tablespoons liquid, it could be orange juice, coffee, or even, on special occasions, brandy or rum

3/4 cup shredded, unsweetened coconut

1. Put cake slices in a blender or food processor, and process until cake turns into fine crumbs, a minute or two. Transfer crumbs to a big bowl. Blend or process nuts until coarsely chopped. Add to cake crumbs.

2. Add cocoa or chocolate powder and jam. Mix well.

4. Add liquid and work lightly with the fingers until mixture is moist, but still firm in consistency. To test, take a small amount and press it between the fingers, it should hold together.

5. Moisten hands with orange juice or coffee, and form into 24 balls the size of a walnut each. Put coconut in a dish. Roll each ball as you do it in the coconut. Arrange finished balls in a big dish, in one layer. Set aside at room temperature for about an hour before using.

They are nice to nibble on with coffee.

Gold'n Spicy Pumpkin Cake, 512

CHAPTER EIGHTEEN
COOKIES

CHAPTER EIGHTEEN

COOKIES

(Biskit)

البِسُكت

"Fine flour is appropriate for women and the palace"
(A Sumerian proverb, Gordon, 65)

The ancient Mesopotamians knew about 300 kinds of bread and pastries, some of which were basic types of breads similar to the flat breads still cooking in the region, and others were "improved" by adding different kinds of flours, spices, dried fruits, oil, milk, beer, and sweeteners. Their pastries ranged from the "very large" to the "tiny," and were shaped differently such as rings, pillars, turbans, crescents, hearts, heads, hands, ears, and even women breasts. Around 1780 BC more than 50 different molds were discovered in the palace at Mari, believed to have been used for forming breads into unusual and decorative shapes (though some believe they were cheese molds).

The improved breads, that is pastries to which fatty substances and sometimes honey and dried fruits were added, were called "ninda" in the Sumerian. Pastries made with "excellent flour" and "noble oil" were called "gug" in the Sumerian, and "kuku" in the Akkadian from which, undoubtedly, all our ka'aks and cakes were derived. All these breads and pastries were baked in the clay oven *tannour*, known in the Akkadian as "tinuru." (Bottèro, "The Cuisine of Ancient Mesopotamia," 38, Limet, 133-5, Levey, 49, see chapter 17, for more details on cakes).

Making and consuming pastries at times of religious festivals have always been the custom ever since ancient times. So much in demand were those pastries that confectioneries were attached to Babylonian and Assyrian temples. They made the sacred cookies, consumed in large numbers during religious occasions, and pastries which worshippers of the goddess Ishtar crumbled and left for her doves.

It is interesting to learn that they also made the "qullupu" cookies. Wheat flour and sesame oil dough was filled with raisins or dates and baked in the *tannour* (Levey, 49). Ever since, this type of cookies became the trademark, so to speak, of the bakers in the Mesopotamian region. During the medieval period similar cookies were baked in the ovens of Baghdad. The *raghuneen* cookies were filled with dates or nuts and shaped in wooden molds, and the *khushkananaj* (from Middle Persian, dry bread) were filled with nuts and were shaped like crescents (*mu'arraj*). Today similar cookies are known as *kleicha*, and are still done, more or less, after the medieval, or I should say ancient style. They are closely associated with the religious holidays.

The medieval people were as fond of cookies as their predecessors were, and indeed as we still are. Besides the *khushkananaj* and its variants, they made the sweet *mutabbaqa* (sandwich cookies),

525

the *mukallalah* ((crowned cookies), which were bar cookies with a topping of pistachio and sugar. Some of the cookies were even sensational names, such as *nuhoud al-'adhara* (breasts of virgins) describing simple almond cookies. There were the dry and sweet cookies *ka'ak*, usually shaped like rings, and the thin and crisp *barazij*. Crackers such as *aqras fateet* (crumbly discs), were made of fermented dough, kneaded with oil of skinned almonds, shaped into even discs using cutters, sprinkled with hulled sesame seeds, glazed using a feather, and baked in the *tannour* until browned. They were to be left in the open air for an hour to dry. "When you eat them," al-Warraq says, "they will crumble in your mouth" (37). They also made *aqras jaffa* (dry discs) sprinkled with sesame seeds, and *khubz al-abazeer* (spiced bread). Besides, they also made sure that a platter of *aqras mumallaha* (salted cookies) was available for those who craved something salty in the midst of the sweet cookies orgies.

A wooden Cookie mold

Iraqi Traditional Cookies (Kleicha)

Kleicha are the most traditional cookies in Iraq. Historically they can be traced back to the ancient Mesopotamian "qullupu" pastries, and the medieval *raghouneen*(?) and *khushkananaj* (loan Middle Persian, dry bread) cookies. In texture they tend to lean to the dry side, and are made into different shapes, such as flat rounds (*khfefiyyat*), half moons filled with nuts and sugar, and molded.

Al-Warraq's tenth-century cookbook gives detailed recipes of various kinds of *khushkananaj* cookies. The *ghareeb* (exotic) variety is made by mixing fine sugar, half the amount flour, and sesame oil. The dough is shaped into domed small cookies, using small bowls as molds. The *khushkananaj mu'arraj* (bent), are made from leavened stiff dough, and a filling of ground almonds, sugar, breadcrumbs, camphor and mastic. To shape, a small piece of dough is flattened and shaped like a tongue, as he says (i.e. like an elongated circle). Some filling is spread on the surface, leaving edges clear. The piece is then folded lengthwise and curved (*tuqawwas*) inwards, sealing edges very well. The cookie is bent (*tu'awwaj*) like a crescent. After taking them out of the *tannour*, the pieces are glazed with Arabic glue dissolved in water (*samugh Arabi*, similar to *sahleb*, or arrowroot).

Another way of forming it is to make small portions into circles, put filling in the middle, and fold them into half circles. The edges are twisted with the fingers, exactly as we do today (271-3). The *basandud*, are a variant on the basic *khushkananaj*. The dough is formed into small rounds that are pricked, and baked, then each two are sandwiched with *halwa sadhija* (plain candy, Appendix to *Al-Wusla ila 'l-Habeeb*, in *Wasf al-At'ima*, 465). The *raghuneen* cookies are shaped using a wooden mold, the likes of which we still use to this day. A small piece of leavened dough is rolled out into a round, pressed into a wooden concaved mold, decorated with some geometric designs. A filling of nuts, sugar, and rose water, or dry dates cooked with rose water and sesame seeds or toasted poppy seeds, is put in the cavity of the lined mold. Another circle closes the filled one, and the two are sealed together (277). Today we just gather the ends of the filled circle in the wooden mold, and tap it out of the mold. All these cookies were baked in the *tannour*.

Nowadays *kleicha* cookies are closely associated with the two Islamic feasts, *Id al-fitr* (after *Ramadhan*, the month of fasting), and *Id al-adha* (when the pilgrimage to Mecca is accomplished). Because these cookies have a long keeping quality, people used to make them in big quantities and store them covered in huge wicker baskets.

Kleicha making was a kind of family affair in which both sexes participate. As far as I remember that's about the only food that my brothers were interested in preparing with us girls. The entire day preceding the *Id* would be engaged in making *kleicha*. The kneading would require the muscles of the stronger sex. The whole house would be filled with the aroma of *hawayej al-kleicha* (spices put in the dough). The ones to be stuffed were given to grown ups to make, since they require a certain level of skill. The children were encouraged to make the rolled out unfilled varieties, by cutting them into rounds using the *istikan* (small tea glass), or into other shapes, using molds or their imagination. The surface of these cookies would be indented in an artistic geometric manner using a blunt knife or even the tip of a big key. When baked, they would resemble our ancestors' cuneiform tablets, especially when whole wheat was used in making the dough. When baking time came, huge trays were carried to the neighborhood bakery, where the cookies were baked to perfection. As soon as they cool down, they were put in huge whicker baskets, covered with beautifully embroidered muslin cloth, and stashed at a high place, inaccessible to children. The following day, and for the following weeks we would be gorging ourselves with these delicious cookies.

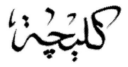

Kleicha: In Quest of a Meaning

Kleicha are the national cookies of Iraq. In texture they are rather on the dry side, and they come in several traditional shapes and fillings, such as the sweet discs *khfefiyyat*), the half moons filled with nuts and sugar (*kleichat joz*), the molded ones filled with dates (*kleichat tamur*). They are all scented with cardamom and sometimes rose water, and glazed with egg wash, that is sometimes scented and colored with a little saffron. We have all wondered, at one point or another, where the name *kleicha* came from, but have not got a satisfactory explanation. However, I think I have put my finger on a clue.

We know now that the ancient Mesopotamians used to make similar cookies called, "qullupu," which in all probability were round in shape ("qullu"), judging from the common Semitic "kull" (whole), and the Greek "kolo" (circle), and "kuklus" (wheel).

During the medieval times, similar cookies were called *raghuneen* (?) and a trendy Middle Persian name, *khushkananaj* (dry bread). The Persian name gradually gave way to *kleicha*, a name which is intriguingly similar to the East European pastries, *kolech*, the filled yeast buns, also characterized by their round shapes.

In the tenth-century Baghdadi cookbook, in measuring flour for making cookies al-Warraq used a dry measure called *keilacha*, a variant on *keil*, which was approximately 4 pounds (36). The *keil* or *keilacha* were also the names of the articles themselves used to measure. As to how this is connected to the naming of the cookies, here is my argument: The *kleicha* cookies were not made year round as we do today in our well-equipped modern kitchens. Up until the sixties or so, they were made twice a year to celebrate the two religious holidays, at the end of *Ramadhan* and the performance of the *hajj*. People used to make them in great quantities and bake them at the neighborhood bakeries, and in measuring ingredients naturally they did not use cups and spoons, but the more practical kilo. In the medieval times the *keilacha* or the larger *makkouk* (=3 *keilachat*) were the measures used. It is my contention that the naming of the cookies stems from such old practices. In other words, the means of measurement itself gradually gave its name to the cookies. Apparently the name lingered, even though the *keilacha* itself is history now, and is replaced by the *kilo*.

This is a common practice in the field of baking. By analogy, the famous European pound cake got its name from the fact that the first bakers in the previous centuries used sugar, butter, and flour, a pound each, for making the cake.

528

Kleicha Dough

(Makes about 25 pieces)

The traditional *kleicha* is usually made with *dihin hur* (clarified butter). The following is a much lighter version, but yields equally delicious cookies. The amount given below is usually doubled or tripled to make an assortment of shapes and fillings.

> **1/2 teaspoon dry yeast**
> **2 teaspoon sugar**
> **2/3 cup warm water**
>
> **3 cups all-purpose flour**
> **1/4 teaspoon salt**
> **1/2 teaspoon cardamom**
> **1/2 teaspoon ground aniseed**
> **1/4 teaspoon cinnamon**
> **1/4 teaspoon whole nigella seeds, optional (see Glossary)**
>
> **3/4 cup oil**

1. Dissolve yeast and sugar in warm water, and set aside for 5 minutes.

2. In a big bowl mix dry ingredients. Add oil and rub mixture between the fingers until it resembles breadcrumbs.

3. Make a well in the middle and pour in yeast mixture. First stir mixture in a circular movement to incorporate liquid into flour. Then knead for about 5 minutes to form pliable dough of medium consistency.

4. Let rise covered at a warm place for about 45 minutes.

5.Punch down, and use as directed below.

Shaping and Baking Kleicha

It is customary to make these cookies in several shapes and with different fillings to satisfy the diverse demands of the family. The shapes are so traditional that they make the *kleicha* instantly recognizable.

1. Walnut-filled Kleicha: For these cookies use walnut filling given below or any of the suggested alternatives. Needless to say the smaller the cookies are made, the prouder the maker would be of her skill and dexterity. But since the tiny ones are time-consuming, the following instructions will yield medium-sized ones. Here is how to shape them: Take a walnut-size piece of dough and with your fingers flatten it to a thin disc. Put about 1 heaping teaspoon of walnut filling (or alternative fillings) in the middle. Fold the disc into half; seal by pressing along the edge. Pinch and twist upwards along the edge to seal it.

2. Date-filled Kleicha: Following are the two traditional ways for shaping the date-filled *kleich*:

1. Take a piece of dough size of a walnut and flatten it with the fingers into a disc. Put a heaping teaspoon of date filling in the middle of the disc. Gather edges and seal them well to prevent date from showing. Form into a slightly flattened ball, make a dent in the middle with the index finger, and shape a kind of border around the upper ridge of the flattened ball, by pinching with an upwards twist. Or if you have the wooden mold put the stuffed piece into the concave, press, and tap out.

2. Alternatively roll out half the dough into a rectangle, one fourth of an inch thick. Fill two thirds of the rectangle, lengthwise, with half of date filling by taking pieces of the filling and flattening them between fingers and spreading them on two thirds of rolled out dough. Fold unfilled third on the middle third, and then turn the other third on the already folded third. Press firmly. With a sharp knife cut into slices about 1-inch wide. Prick them lightly at 2 to 3 places with a fork, and arrange them in baking sheet, bottom side down, i.e. avoid letting the cut-side touch the surface of baking sheet, as this might cause date filling to burn.

3. Filled Flat and Thin Discs: Attractive flat thin discs, about 4 inches in diameter, can also be shaped using date and cheese fillings only. Take a piece of dough, size of a golf ball. Flatten it and put about 1 heaping tablespoon of date or cheese filling in the middle. Gather the edges, and seal them together to prevent filling from coming out. On a flat surface, roll out the piece with a rolling pin to form a flat circle, as thin as it gets without tearing. Prick surface with a fork at several places. You have the choice of sprinkling some sesame on surface of cookies after brushing them with eggs. Bake as directed below.

4. Kleicha Thins (Khfefiyyat): Dough can also be left unfilled (some people choose to add some sugar to the dough, in this case melt 1/4 cup sugar in the amount of water specified). Roll dough to 1/4-inch thinness, and shape into the traditional rounds using the brim of the thin small tea glass known as *istikan* or anything similar. Decorate by pricking with a fork or by denting the surface at several places with the tip of a big key to make cuneiform-like markings. Cookie cutters can also be used. Free-form shapes are sometimes made such as daggers, coiled serpents, dolls, and date palms.

Baking kleicha:

After filling and shaping the pieces arrange them on a greased cookie sheet, leaving a half-inch space between pieces. Let them rest for about 5 minutes at a warm place, then brush them with beaten egg. If wished add a few strands of saffron to the egg, for color and aroma. Bake them in a preheated oven at 400 degrees F. for 15 minutes or until golden brown.

Fillings for Kleicha

The most commonly used fillings are nut and date fillings. The rest are used as variations.

Nut filling: Traditionally walnuts are used for filling these cookies, but other nuts may be substituted. Toasting nuts before grinding will help bring out their aroma.

> **2 cups shelled walnut, or slivered almond, with or without skin (about 1/2 pound)**
> **1 cup sugar**
> **1 teaspoon ground cardamom**
> **2 to 3 tablespoons rose water**

Put all ingredients, except rose water, in a blender or food processor and grind for a few seconds or until coarsely ground. Sugar will prevent nuts from getting pasty. Turn into a bowl and sprinkle mixture with rose water, and stir to allow particles to somewhat stick together. Shape as in #1, above.

Date filling: Traditionally dates are softened by cooking and mashing them with clarified butter (ghee). In the following method dates are softened with liquid. The cocoa powder enhances the taste and color of the dates.

> **1 pound pitted dates, about 2 cups**
> **About 1/4 cup water, or orange juice, depending on how moist or dry your dates are**
> **1 teaspoon cocoa powder**
> **1/2 teaspoon cinnamon**
> **1/2 teaspoon ground cardamom**
> **1/2 teaspoon whole toasted coriander seeds or anise seeds, optional**
> **1/4 cup toasted sesame seeds, optional**
> **1 teaspoon rose water or orange blossom water, optional**

Put dates and water in a heavy skillet or a medium heavy pot. Cook over low heat mashing dates with back of a wooden spoon until they soften. Mix with other ingredients. Shape as in #2 and #3, above.

Coconut filling:

> **2 cups finely shredded unsweetened coconut, slightly toasted**
> **1 cup sugar**
> **1/2 teaspoon ground cardamom**
> **1 to 2 tablespoons rose water or orange blossom water**

Mix ingredients, and shape as in # 1.

Toasted Sesame Filling:

> **2 cups toasted sesame**
> **1 cup sugar**
> **1 teaspoon ground cardamom**

1 to 2 tablespoons rose water

Pulverize toasted sesame and sugar in a blender or a food processor. Mix with cardamom and rose water, and shape as in # 1.

Cheese filling: Cookies filled with cheese are to be kept in refrigerator.

2 cups shredded mozzarella cheese
3/4 cup finely chopped parsley

Mix ingredients together, and shape as in # 1 and #3.

Jam Pie
Khubzat al-Murabba

(Makes 16 pieces)

We always tend to associate pies with Western style pastries, but as we have seen in the Introduction, the pie making technique has its roots in the ancient Mesopotamian cooking. The medieval Baghdadi cooks had their own experimentations. *Al-baseesa*, for instance, is made by mixing flour, eggs, oil, and yeast to make a stiff dough that is left for an hour to ferment. Half of the dough is rolled out into a disc as big as the pan, with an extra for the edges, just like the way we shape the bottom pie crust today. Then a filling of honey and clarified butter is spread on the bottom crust, and is covered with the top layer, and sealed very well. The pan is lowered into the *tannour* to bake. When it comes to serving, the pie is cooled off a little, and is broken to pieces with the fingers and sprinkled with sugar (Al-Warraq, 260). In another pie recipe four centuries later, called *al-shahda* (honeycomb), leavened dough was made of semolina flour, sesame oil, and water, and is rolled out, filled with a mixture of ground almonds and sugar, covered with another sheet of dough, sealing the edge very well. The disc is baked in the *tannour*, and when taken out is put in a bowl, and immersed in thickened honey, sprinkled with sugar and pistachio, and flavored with mastic and rose water (appendix to A*l-Wusla*, in *Wasf al-At'ima*, 462).

The following is an easier version of *kleicha*, which I have devised for a quick treat. My kids call it Frizbee *Kleicha*. If you are in a hurry, or have no patience with yeast dough, you can substitute the traditional *kleicha* dough with this one. It is also a delicious way of using jam that has been lying in your refrigerator for ages. Sugar added to the dough will help it brown when baked.

3 cups all-purpose flour
1 teaspoon baking powder
1 teaspoon sugar
1/3 teaspoon salt
1/2 teaspoon cardamom
2/3 cup oil (or 1/2 cup butter and 1/4 cup oil)
3/4 cup milk

About 1/2 cup jam
A little milk and sugar for glazing

Preheat oven to 375 degrees F.

1. In big bowl mix flour, baking powder, sugar, salt, and cardamom. Add oil (or butter and oil) and rub with the fingers, until mixture resembles breadcrumbs.

2. Add milk and knead briefly with fingers until it gathers into a ball. Let it rest for 10 minutes

3. Divide dough into 2 parts (one a little bit smaller than the other). Roll out into 2 circles the size of a large dinner plate, about 1/4-inch thick. Put the slightly bigger disc on a greased ovenproof flat dinner plate and trim edges with a knife. Cover surface with jam leaving about half an inch of the edge unfilled. Cover with the other disc pressing the two layers gently to get rid of air pockets. Seal the edge in a decorative way, and prick surface with a fork at several places.

4. Brush surface with milk and sprinkle lightly with sugar.

5. Bake in a preheated oven, at 375 degrees F. for 45 minutes, or until golden brown. Let cool, then cut into 16 wedges.

Sugar Cookies
(Skakarlama)

(Makes about 20 cookies)

Shakarlama is traditionally shaped into 4-inch discs studded with the characteristic toasted almond in the middle. The well-made ones are pleasantly brittle, and almost melt in the mouth before you even start chewing them. This is one of those recipes in which you cannot compromise when it comes to fat. Do it when you have a crowd to entertain.

1 cup shortening
1 cup powdered sugar
1 egg white
1 teaspoon rose water or orange blossom water, optional
1 teaspoon cardamom

2 cups all-purpose flour
1 teaspoon baking powder
1/4 teaspoon salt

20 skinned whole almonds, toasted
About 1/4 cup powdered sugar for sprinkling
Preheat oven to 350 degrees

1. Beat shortening in a big bowl. Add sugar, egg white, rose water if used and cardamom. Mix well, using the mixer.

2. Combine flour, baking powder and salt and with a wooden spoon stir them into the shortening mixture. Then lightly knead with the fingers to make dough of medium consistency.

3. Pinch off a piece, size of a walnut. Form it into a ball, flatten a little and put on a lightly greased baking sheet. Repeat with the rest of pieces leaving about one inch between them to allow for expansion.

4. Press an almond on in the center of each piece, and bake in a preheated oven at 350 degrees F. for 20 to 25 minutes, or until they just start to change color at the edges. Take out of the oven and let slightly cool in the baking sheet. Sift icing sugar on the cookies while still warm.

Short Cut:
Instead of shaping cookies into rounds, press dough into a greased 13-by-9-inch baking pan. Score surface into diamonds or squares, and press an almond in the center of each. Bake in a preheated oven at 350 degrees F. for 20 minutes or until surface is golden. Let settle for 10 minutes, then cut into pieces, following scores.

Tahini Cookies
Biskit al-Rashi

(Makes 46 bars)

I have devised this easy version of sugar cookies using my favorite ingredient tahini (*rashi*). You can make them in 5 minutes and bake them in 30 minutes. They are delicately sweet, flaky in texture, and their taste is reminiscent of the traditional *halwa tahiniyya,* known as "halvah". For a more elegant presentation, bars can simply be drizzled with melted chocolate or butterscotch. They can even be made into domino bars as suggested below.

1/2 cup oil
1/2 cup tahini
1 cup sugar
1 egg
2 teaspoons baking powder
1/4 teaspoon salt
1 teaspoon cardamom

2 cups all-purpose flour
1/2 cup chopped toasted walnuts
For decoration: 1 pound melted dark chocolate, 3 ounces melted white chocolate, and
colored mini chocolate chips, optional
Preheat oven to 350 degrees F.

1. In a medium bowl mix oil, tahini, sugar, egg, baking powder, salt, and cardamom. Beat well with a mixer for about 2 minutes.

2. With a wooden spoon, stir in flour and fold in nuts. Knead lightly and briefly just to combine ingredients together into a ball.

3. Lightly grease 13-by-9 inch baking pan and spread and press mixture in pan very well.

4. Bake in a preheated oven at 350 degrees F. for 30 minutes, or until golden brown.

5. Let cool on rack for 15 minutes, then using a sharp thin knife carefully cut into 7/8-by-1 1/4-inch bars (i.e. size of a domino piece). Cool cookies completely in pan.

6. Serve plain, or drizzle with melted butterscotch or chocolate. Or decorate into domino bars as follows: Dip each piece in melted brown chocolate, then decorate like domino pieces using white chocolate and colored mini chips.

Sweet Sesame Ovals
(Ka'ak bil Simsim)

(Makes 42 pieces)

Ka'ak and *bakhsam* are dry cookies usually dunked in sweet hot tea. The traditional Iraqi *ka'ak* are oval in shape, and are profusely coated with toasted sesame. They are not the kind of cookies people would usually make at home. The best place to buy these dunking cookies in Baghdad is a small bakery called *Ka'ak al-Seyyid* (*al-seyyid* is an epithet used to indicate that the family has descended from the prophet Muhammed). It is a family owned business whose well-guarded recipes for making these cookies have passed from one generation to the other.

Several *ka'ak* recipes were given in the medieval cookbooks. They might differ in some details, but they were all sweet, round in shape with the exception of al-Warraq's recipe in which sweet yeast dough was rolled out and cut into squares. They were definitely all dry in texture. Any food item that was supposed to be dry was compared to *ka'ak*. Which explains why they were recommended for travelling. The name of the cookies might ultimately be derived from the ancient Sumerian "gug" or the Akkadian "kuku," which designate refined and dainty pastries that the affluent ancient Mesopotamians used to bake. (*Ka'ak*, in standard Arabic, is the generic name for cake).

It is a good idea to toast sesame seeds before using them in the recipe to allow them to brown nicely while baking. To toast the seeds put them in a skillet, and let them toast on medium heat, shaking and stirring frequently. Or you can toast them in the oven at 350 degrees F., stirring several times, about 5 minutes.

> **1 cup oil**
> **1 1/2 cups sugar**
> **2 egg (reserve one egg white for glazing)**
> **3/4 cup milk**
> **3 tablespoons honey**
> **1 tablespoon vanilla**
> **1 teaspoon ground cardamom**
> **1 teaspoon whole aniseed**
>
> **6 1/2 cups all-purpose flour**
> **3/4 teaspoon salt**
> **4 teaspoons baking powder**
>
> **1 1/2 cups toasted sesame seeds,**
> **Preheat oven to 400 degrees F.**

1. In a big bowl mix oil, sugar and eggs, using a mixer. Stir in milk, honey, vanilla, cardamom, and aniseed.

2. Add 2 cups of the flour, salt, and baking powder, and mix well. With a wooden spoon stir in the rest of flour, then knead briefly to form soft dough.

3. Add 1 tablespoon cold water to the reserved egg white and whisk until frothy. Put sesame seeds in a plate.

4. Divide dough in 42 walnut-size pieces and form each into a flattish oval, 1/3-inch thick and 2 1/2 inch long. Brush each with beaten egg white and dip in sesame seeds to coat on both sides. Let them catch as much as possible of the sesame.

5. Arrange pieces on cookie sheets (no need to grease since sesame will prevent cookies from sticking to pan). Leave a little space between pieces. Bake in a preheated oven at 400 degrees F. for 12 to 15 minutes, then lower hear to 250 degrees F. and let cookies bake and dry out slowly for about 1 1/2 hours.

Iraqi Biscotti #1
(Bakhsam)

(Makes about 40 pieces)

Ka'ak, in Iraq, is always mentioned in conjunction with *bakhsam*(or *baqsam*, standard Arabic *baqsamat*), which is another type of dry cookies, a little less sweet and without sesame. They are double-baked, much like what we call today, biscotties or rusks.

The following recipe calls for dry yeast, but if you are pressed by time follow the alternative recipe given below. Both would yield deliciously crunchy cookies.

> **1 tablespoon dry yeast**
> **1 tablespoon sugar**
> **1 cup warm milk**
>
> **1 cup oil**
> **1 1/2 cups sugar**
> **4 eggs**
> **1 teaspoon vanilla or cardamom, or both**
> **2 teaspoons whole aniseed**
>
> **6 1/2 cups flour**
> **1/2 teaspoon salt**
> **Preheat oven to 425 degrees F.**

1.In a small bowl dissolve yeast and sugar in warm milk. Set aside for 5 minutes.

2. In another bowl, using mixer, beat oil, sugar, vanilla or/and cardamom, aniseeds and 3 eggs and 1 egg yolk. **Reserve 1 egg white for brushing the pieces**. Stir in yeast mixture.

3. In a big bowl, mix flour and salt. Make a well in the middle and pour in liquid mixture. With a wooden spoon stir in a circular movement to help liquids incorporate into flour. Knead for about 5 minutes to form rather sticky dough of soft to medium consistency. Oil dough on both sides, and let rise, covered, at a draftless warm place for about 45 minutes.

4. Punch down dough and form into two regular cylinders, about 15 inches long. Transfer them to a cookie sheet covered with parchment paper. Allow a good space between cylinders for expansion, or

537

put them in 2 separate baking sheets. Flatten cylinders slightly and let them rise, covered loosely, at a warm place for 45 minutes, or until they are double in bulk.

5. Beat reserved egg white until foamy and brush cylinders with it. Bake in a preheated oven at 425 degrees F. for 15 minutes or until cylinders are golden brown. Let them cool on a rack. Then slice into 1/2-inch slices crosswise, using a serrated knife.

6. Arrange pieces on cookie sheets, cut side down, and re-bake at 325 degrees F. for 45 minutes or until golden brown, dry and crisp. Turn pieces once to allow both sides to brown, and rotate position of baking sheets half way through baking.

Iraqi Biscotti #2

(Makes about 48 pieces)

This is an adaptation of the basic cake recipe given in the cake chapter. It is easy to make, and yields crisp and fragrant bicotties.

3/4 cup oil
1 1/2 cups sugar
5 eggs, beaten
1 teaspoon vanilla
1 teaspoon cardamom
2 teaspoons whole aniseeds
1 teaspoon grated orange or lemon rind,
1 cup milk, (or 1/2 cup orange juice, and 1/2 cup buttermilk)

4 1/2 cups all-purpose flour
1/2 teaspoon salt
3 teaspoons baking powder

1/2 cup currants or raisins
1/2 cup toasted broken walnut pieces
Quick oats, wheat germ or semolina for lining baking pan, optional
Preheat oven to 375 degrees F.

1. In a big bowl and using a mixer, beat oil, sugar, eggs, vanilla, cardamom, aniseeds, orange or lemon rind, and milk, about 2 minutes.

2. Sift together flour, salt and baking powder. Add flour mixture to egg mixture all at once, and with a wooden spoon gently stir just until flour is completely incorporated into the egg mixture, do not over-stir. Fold in currants and nuts. Mixture will be slightly thicker than cake batter.

3. Have a 10-by-15-inch baking pan ready by greasing it very well and coating bottom and sides with quick oats or alternatives, if wished. Spread batter into pan.

4. Bake in a preheated oven at 375 degrees F. for 40 minutes or until it is golden brown and cake tester comes out clean. Invert on a rack and let cool thoroughly.

5. With a serrated knife cut it into two halves lengthwise and then cut crosswise into 1/2-inch strips.

6. Arrange pieces, cut side down, in two cookie sheets, and in one layer. Re-bake in a slow oven at 325 degrees F. for about an hour or until pieces are golden brown, dry and crispy. Rotate position of sheets half way through baking and turn pieces once to brown on both sides.

Giant Sesame Cookies
(Baraziq)

(Makes 20 large cookies)

I have been developing this recipe for many years in an attempt to emulate the *Baraziq,* those traditional ready-made crispy and huge cookies encrusted with green pistachio and golden sesame seeds. Apparently my efforts paid off. The recipe won the first place prize of the 1998 annual Holiday Cookie Bake-off, held by the Rhino's Youth Center in Bloomington, Indiana.

In al-Warraq's tenth-century cookbook I found an eligible ancestor for these cookies. It is a recipe for *barazij*, sometimes called *barazeedhaj*. It calls for leavened dough to which is added a small amount of *buraq* (borax). The dough is rolled out into thin big discs (but definitely smaller than the *riqaq* thin breads), that are lightly brushed with the glazing feather (*reesha*), and baked in the *tannour*.

From another recipe and from poems that al-Warraq excerpted we also learn that the *barazij* are made from white flour, they may be sweetened, and they definitely should be round in shape. When baked they are as beautiful as crystal trays (*sawani min al-ballour*). That they should be crisp in texture is attested by the fact that *buraq* was added to the dough. Nobody of course uses this substance any more, but during the medieval times it was added to pastries that were required to stay crisp (35-60).

The cookies can be enjoyed plain, which is the way they are traditionally made. Glazing them with icing perfumed with rose water is my addition. You bite into this crisp cookie, and the rose water scent comes as a delightful surprise. Besides, you can drizzle the immaculately white spacious surface of the glazed cookie with melted butterscotch or chocolate, or you can draw pictures or even write brief messages with chocolate icing.

1/2 cup butter, and 1/2 cup oil (traditionally 1 1/2 cups shortening is used)
1 1/2 cups sugar
2 eggs
1 teaspoon vanilla
1 teaspoon ground cardamom
1 teaspoon ground aniseed

2 1/2 cups all-purpose flour
2 cups semolina
2 teaspoons baking powder
1/2 teaspoon salt

1/2 cup coarsely ground pistachio or walnuts
1/2 cup honey
3/4 cup toasted sesame
For glaze: 1 cup sifted icing sugar, 1 tablespoon rose water, and about 3 tablespoons whipping cream or milk
Preheat oven to 400 degrees F.

1. With a mixer cream butter and oil. Add sugar and beat for 2 minutes. Add eggs and beat 2 more minutes. Mix in vanilla, cardamom, and aniseed.

2. In a separate bowl mix flour, semolina, baking powder and salt. Add to creamed mixture all at once, and with a wooden spoon stir mixture in a circular movement until well incorporated. Knead lightly and briefly until mixture forms into a ball.

3. Divide dough into 20 golf-ball size pieces.

4. Put pistachio, honey and sesame in three small separate bowls.

5. Dip each ball in pistachio first allowing it to pick up as much nuts as possible. Then put it on a greased baking sheet, and flatten it with the fingers to 1/4-inch thickness, shaping it into an oval or round disc. If wished, crimp edges by pinching with thumb and index finger. Brush disc with honey, and sprinkle it generously with sesame seeds. Repeat with the rest of pieces. Leave a space between pieces to allow for expansion.

6. Bake in the middle of a preheated oven at 400 degrees F. for 12 to 15 minutes or until golden brown. Leave in pan for a few minutes and then transfer to a rack using a thin metal pancake turner. Let cool completely and glaze and decorate to your fancy, or serve plain.

7. To glaze the pieces, mix icing sugar, rose water, and enough milk or whipping cream to form a glaze of spreading consistency. Pour on cooled cookies, and set aside until set. Decorate to your fancy.

Aniseed Rings
(Halaqat al-Habbat Hulwa)

(Makes about 20 rings)

These are my favorite cookies, delicately flavored with aniseed, and relatively low in fat, and lightly sweetened.

1/3 cup water
2 heaping tablespoons whole aniseeds

2 1/4 cups flour
1 teaspoon baking powder
3 tablespoons powdered sugar

1/4 teaspoon salt

1/2 cup oil
1 egg, divided
Preheat oven to 375 degrees F.

1. Boil aniseeds and water in a small pot for about 3 minutes. Let steep for about 10 minutes, then strain. Keep liquid and reserve seeds.

2. In a big bowl mix flour, baking powder, powdered sugar and salt. Add oil and rub between the fingers until mixture resembles breadcrumbs.

3. Make a well in the middle and pour strained liquid and beaten **egg white.** Stir with a wooden spoon to incorporate ingredients. Then lightly knead to form dough of medium consistency.

4. Divide dough into 20 pieces, size of a walnut each. Roll each piece like a pencil, half an inch in diameter, overlap ends to form a ring, then seal well to prevent from opening up while baking.

5. Arrange rings in a greased cookie sheet, leaving a little space between pieces. Brush rings with beaten **egg yolk** and sprinkle generously with reserved aniseeds.

6. Bake in a preheated oven at 375 degrees F. for 15 to 18 minutes, or until golden brown.

Nut and Jam Bars
(Biskit al-Joz wal Murabba)

(Makes 60 bars)

These are easy to make cookies in which you can use your favorite jam or use up the small quantities of jam that no one is interested in any more. By doing this you'll end up having a variety of delicious cookies spread with different kinds of jams and nuts. The shredded dough on top of the spread jam will give the cookies an attractive texture.

For the dough:
    3/4 cup oil
    3/4 cup sugar
    5 eggs
    1 teaspoon vanilla or cardamom, or both
    1/2 teaspoon almond extract
    1 teaspoon grated lemon rind
    2 teaspoons baking powder
    1/4 teaspoon salt
    4 1/4 cups all-purpose flour
For the topping:
    2 cups jam of your choice, or use different kinds of jam
    1/2 cup chopped nuts, or shredded coconut, or both
    Preheat oven to 375 degrees F.

1. In a big bowl put oil, sugar, eggs, vanilla or cardamom, almond extract, lemon rind, baking powder and salt. Beat for 2 minutes.

2. Add flour stirring with a wooden spoon to incorporate ingredients. Knead briefly to a rather soft dough and let it rest for 10 minutes.

3. **Put aside about 1/2 cup of the dough** (size of a medium orange) and let it **chill** until needed. Press rest of dough in a greased 17-by-11-inches cookie pan (if dough is sticky handle with floured hands). Prick entire surface with a fork, and bake in a preheated oven at 375 degrees F. for about 10 minutes.

4. Take baking pan out of oven, and **immediately** spread dough with prepared jam. In case many kinds of jam are used, divide into sections and spread each section with a different jam. Using a hand-grater, shred chilled set-aside dough all over the spread jam. Spread nuts all over surface. If using different jams, use different nuts for each section, for more variety.

5. Resume baking for 25 more minutes or until surface is golden and jam is bubbly.

6. Let set for about 10 minutes, then cut into bars.

Nut-filled Crescents
(Ahıllat al-Joz)

(Makes 48 crescents)

This recipe yields a great number of neat, delicately flavored cookies that are filled with nuts of your choice.

For the dough:
> **2 eggs, reserve white of one egg for glazing**
> **1 cup milk**
> **1 cup sugar**
> **2/3 cup oil**
> **1 teaspoon ground cardamom**
> **1 tablespoon grated orange or lemon rind**
> **1 teaspoon orange blossom water, optional**

> **4 1/2 cups flour**
> **2 teaspoons baking powder**
> **1/2 teaspoon salt**

For the filling:
> **1 cup toasted nuts of your choice (about 6 ounces), finely chopped**
> **1/2 cup sugar**
> **1 teaspoon orange blossom water, or any flavor of your choice**
> **1 teaspoon cinnamon**

Preheat oven to 375 degrees F.

1. In a medium bowl put eggs, milk, sugar, oil, cardamom, grated orange rind, and orange blossom water, if used. Beat well with a mixer for a few minutes.

2. In a big bowl mix flour, baking powder and salt. Make a well in the middle. Pour in egg mixture and stir with a wooden spoon to incorporate ingredients. Knead briefly to make dough of soft to medium consistency. If too sticky sprinkle with a little flour. Let it rest for 10 minutes.

3. Meanwhile make the filling: Mix nuts with sugar, orange blossom water and cinnamon.

4. Divide dough into 6 portions. On lightly floured surface roll out each portion into a circle about 8 inches in diameter and 1/4-inch thick. Divide circle into 8 triangles and top the wide edge of each portion with 1 teaspoon filling. Start rolling from the wide edge down to the tip. Curve in tips to form into crescents.

5. Arrange crescents on a greased baking sheet leaving a little space between pieces. Brush with reserved whisked egg white.

6. Bake in a preheated oven at 375 degrees F. for 15 to 20 minutes, or until golden brown.

The Story of Croissant

The crescent and the star are commonly known as traditional Islamic emblems. However, this tradition originated much earlier than Islam. The symbols of the crescent and the eight-rayed stars of the ancient Mesopotamian goddess Ishtar were drawn on so many excavated cuneiform tablets and cylinder seals, and they were believed to have a certain mystical power. Evidently the ancients used to shape some of their pastries like crescents, and in the tenth-century cookbook, dainty crescent-like cookies were made by flattening pieces of dough into rounded oblongs, like tongues, as the writer says. Filling of nuts and sugar scented with rose water was put in the middle of each. Then they were folded, sealed very well, and curved like crescents (al-Warraq, 271-2). As to how this Islamic symbol, the crescent, became the shape of the famous European pastry, the *croissant*, here is the story:

"In 1863 the Ottoman Turks launched an assault on Vienna and were close to succeeding. Inside the city one night during the tense hours before the final assault, a baker, putting his dough in a warm spot to rise, noticed that the puffed-up batter quivered and shook in his bowl. Then, listening tensely he heard a muffled boom. Guessing the Turks had already started their march towards the city, he sent his son running to the military headquarters to tell them the news. Immediately all forces throughout the city were put on the alert. The Turkish attack was met with cannon balls and mortar fire. When finally the Turkish forces were driven out, the baker was given a job in the royal kitchen. To celebrate the victory he created crescent-shaped rolls like the crescent moon on the Turkish banner. The Austrians called them *kipfel*, literally "crescent." Later, when Mary Antoinette became the queen of Louis XIV, she brought the recipe for the crescents with her to Paris, and the French chefs started making the rolls with rich pastry, today known all over the world as *croissant*" (Watson, 154-5).

Almond and Sugar Squares
(Murabba'at al-Louz wal Shakar)

Makes 28 squares)

These cookies were my mother's answer to our nagging request for a jiffy treat, and they are reminiscent of the Baghdadi medieval *aqras mukallala* (cookies with toppings, al-Baghdadi, 213). When she used to make them she basically followed her eye measurements, which unfortunately were not always the same.

> 3/4 cup oil
> 3/4 cup sugar
> 2 eggs
> 1 teaspoon vanilla
> 1 teaspoon ground cardamom
> 1 cup milk
>
> 4 1/2 cups all-purpose flour
> 1/2 teaspoon salt
> 2 1/2 teaspoons baking powder

For the topping:
> 1/2 cup butter, melted
> 1 teaspoon vanilla
> 1/4 teaspoon almond extract
> 3/4 cup sliced almonds
> 1/3 cup sugar
> **Preheat oven to 375 degrees F.**

1. In a medium bowl mix oil, sugar, eggs, vanilla, cardamom, and milk. Beat well.

2. In a big bowl mix flour, salt and baking powder. Make a well in the middle and add oil mixture. Stir in a circular movement with a wooden spoon until thick batter forms.

3. Spread batter in a well-greased 11-by-17 inch cookie sheet. Even up surface with oiled fingers.

4. Mix melted butter, vanilla and almond extract, and spread on entire surface of batter. Sprinkle with almonds and then sugar.

5. Bake in a preheated oven at 375 degrees F. for 15 to 20 minutes or until golden brown, and almonds look toasted. Let cool for about 10 minutes, then cut into squares.

Nutty Factoids

Nuts of all kinds have always been an important component in the cooking of the Middle East, past and present. According to recent scientific studies and findings, this is not a bad thing to do after all. Though packed with fat, nuts are rich in nutrients such as protein and fiber, important vitamins and minerals, and phytochemicals, which are cancer fighting agents, the same agents found in tea, and some vegetables. One ounce of almonds, for example, provides as much protein as one ounce of red meat, but without the bad cholesterol. Besides, almonds are believed to be rich in calcium. In fact most of the fat nuts contain is polyunsaturated fat which helps lower cholesterol and protect arteries from clogging. All it takes is to incorporating two or three ounces of nuts each day into low-fat diet to reduce the risk of heart diseases. Walnut in particular is a good source of heart-healthful Omega-3 fatty acids. Some studies have shown that five small servings of nuts each week can help control high blood pressure.

However, it is so easy sometimes to over eat nuts. The golden rule is to eat them in moderation. When they are called for in a recipe, a useful tip is to dry toast them in order to release their flavor and aroma to make a small amount of nuts go a long way.

A Recipe for the Curious: Medieval Crispy Treats

The following recipe is given in al-Baghdadi's thirteenth-century cookbook. It is called *barad* (hailstone). The puffed, small pieces of crisp pastry are bound together with honey and then cut into pieces. They are reminiscent of the rice-crispy cookies of the modern Western world:

Take best white flour, make into a dough, and leave to rise. Put a basin on the fire, with some sesame-oil. When boiling, take in a reticulated ladle some of the dough, and shake it into the oil, so that as each drop of the dough falls in, it sets. As each piece is cooked, remove with another ladle to drain off the oil. Take honey as required, mix with rose water, and put over the fire to boil to a consistency: then take off, and while still in the basin, whip until white. Throw in the *barad* (hailstones), and place out on a soft-oiled surface, pressing in the shape of a mould. Then cut into pieces, and serve (Arberry, 211).

Rose water and Almond Cookies
(Nuhoud al-'Adhra')

(Makes 25 pieces)

I found this recipe in the fourteenth-century, augmented version of al-Baghdadi's cookbook. They are basically almond cookies, shaped into breasts, so the instructions in the recipe go, and hence the name *nuhoud al-'adhra'* (the virgin's breasts). The recipe calls for equal parts (by weight) of flour, sugar, and almond (*Wasf al-At'ima al-Mu'tada*, 422). The rest of the ingredients are my addition. Here is a small batch using equal parts by weight, converted into volume measurements.

The cookies are delicious and wonderfully aromatic.

1 cup skinless sliced almonds, about 4 ounces, slightly toasted
1 cup flour
1/2 cup sugar
3/4 teaspoon baking powder
1/4 teaspoon salt
1/2 teaspoon ground cardamom

4 tablespoons butter, melted
1/4 cup oil
3 tablespoons rose water
25 raisins
Preheat oven to 375 degrees F.

1. In a food processor, put almonds, flour, sugar, baking powder, salt, and cardamom. Pulse mixture until almonds are finely ground, about a minute.

2. Slowly pour melted butter and oil through spout while machine is on. Add rose water the same way. Mixture will gather into a ball, about a minute.

3. Form into 25 balls the size of a walnut each. Arrange on a greased cookie sheet, and press a raisin in the middle of each.

4. Bake in a preheated oven at 375 degrees F. for 13 to 15 minutes. Do not let them over-bake. They might be a little soft while hot, but they will crisp when cold.

CHAPTER NINETEEN
ICE CREAM

CHAPTER NINETEEN

ICE CREAM

(Dondırma)

الدّوندرمة

Evidently the ancient Mesopotamians used ice in their drinks, although it is unlikely that they manufactured it. Judging from the frequent references to it in literature and cookbooks, the medieval Baghdadis used it in their drinks and in some of their dishes. Al-Warraq, for instance, recommends that the best way to eat fresh and dried dates is to put them in a glass bowl and break some ice on them. He further adds that you might also put ice pieces around a bowl of *shahd* (honey in the comb). Caliph al-Ma'moun, he says, used to do this with dates and desserts. As for al-Wathiq, qata'if pastry was always presented to him chilled with ice (255). However, there is no evidence that they knew ice cream.

In the modern scene there are many specialized places that make top quality ice cream. The most popular are pistachio and *qamar'l deen* (sheets of dried apricot) varieties. It is delightfully chewy in texture and not so rich. Arrowroot or *sahleb* (see Glossary) is usually used as a primary thickening agent besides milk, or/and heavy cream. No eggs are used.

Although supermarkets nowadays abound with ice creams and sherbets of various flavors and kinds, nothing beats homemade ice cream. You can control your ingredients, making it perhaps less sweet. Or you might incorporate your favorite flavors and fruits. Where else would you find ice cream flavored with mastic, cardamom, cinnamon, rose water, or decaffeinated coffee or tea? At home you can use your favorite fruits like cantaloupe, watermelon, apricot (both fresh and dried), or prunes or whatever strikes your fancy. So get your ice cream maker churning, and every now and then surprise your family and guests with an exotic or unusually flavored ice cream.

An ice cream maker comes in handy here (especially the new models that work on dry ice principle), because automatic churning would yield ice cream creamier in texture than the freezing-in-a-pan method.

549

General Methods for Making Ice Cream:

If using an ice cream maker: follow manufacturer's instructions. It is important to **completely chill prepared mixture before churning it.** After ice cream is frozen, transfer mixture to a chilled container and keep it frozen. For easier scooping, take it out of the freezer about 10 minutes before serving.

If using regular freezer:

1. Put prepared mixture in a rather shallow pan, covered, in the freezer until partially frozen. It will be solid to one inch from edges with a soft and mushy center.
2. Blend or process mixture, in batches, until soft but still frozen.
3. Return to pan, cover and freeze until firm, stirring occasionally.
4. To serve: take it out of the freezer, one hour before serving time. Then beat it at medium speed in a bowl until smooth, return it to pan and back to the freezer. 10 minutes before actual serving time take it out of the freezer for easier scooping.

Note: Amounts given below are enough to make approximately 1 quart of ice cream.

Ice Cold Drinks in Ancient Mesopotamia

Although it is not known whether the ancient Mesopotamians manufactured ice, there is evidence that they used it to chill their drinks. An icehouse, dating from about 2000 BC, was found at the palace of Zimri-Lim, ruler of Mari (Hunter, 25). One can safely assume the ice used was the natural snow that fell on the mountains in the northern region, as the following letter indicates. It is from a hospitable king who, around 2500 BC, offered ice and wine to a king who happened to be visiting nearby.

Tell Yasmah-Addu: King Aplahanda [of Carchemish] sends the following message:
There is now ice available in Ziranum, much of it. Place your servants there to watch over it so they can keep it safe for you. They can bring it to you regularly as long as you stay there. And if no good wine is available there for you to drink, send me word and I will have good wine sent to you to drink. Since your hometown is far away, do write me whenever you need anything, and I will always give you what you need.
(Oppenheim, 108-9; and Hunter, 25)

1. Ice Creams

The following recipes are creamier in texture than **Sherbets** and **Ices**. Although low fat dairy products can be substituted, whole milk will definitely yield more delicious ice cream.

Note: When using heavy cream (whipping cream), I recommend whisking the cream before folding it into rest of ingredients. This results in a fluffier and lighter texture.

Basic Recipe for Ice Cream, Chewy and Fragrant

3/4 cup sugar
2 rounded tablespoons arrowroot
1 1/2 cups milk
1 teaspoon vanilla or flavor of your choice such as 1 teaspoon ground cardamom, 1 tablespoon rose water, or 1/4 teaspoon ground mastic, or 1 teaspoon mastic cream, see Glossary

1 cup (one 1/2 pint carton) whipping cream

1. Put sugar and arrowroot in a medium heavy pot. Gradually add milk to sugar mixture, whisking all the time to allow solids to dissolve.

2. Cook on medium heat stirring all the time until mixture thickens, about 10 minutes. It should be thicker than pudding in consistency. Add vanilla or your choice of flavoring. Chill very well (overnight)
3. When ready to make ice cream, whip heavy cream until soft peaks form. Mix with the milk mixture, and churn in an ice cream maker or freezer compartment, as instructed in the general methods above

Variations:

* Before chilling milk mixture, divide it into parts and add a different food coloring to each (you may use cocoa powder, coffee or tea). For a more interesting effect, flavor each color differently. Then chill as directed.

*Add 1/2 cup chopped toasted nuts, half way through freezing, so that they will not sink to the bottom.
It is better to chill nuts before adding to the ice cream.

*Add 1/2 cup finely chopped dried fruits and shredded coconut half way through freezing, lest they should sink to the bottom. It is better to chill them before you add them to the ice cream.

*Add about 1 cup mashed or pureed and chilled fresh fruits when you churn or freeze mixture in step 3.

Dried Apricot Ice Cream with Pistachio
(Dondirmat Qamar'ldeen bil Fistiq)

This is a traditional ice cream that calls for the golden sheets of dried apricots (*qamar'ldeen,* see Glossary). It is attractively speckled with coarsely ground pistachio.

3/4 cup sugar
2 rounded tablespoons arrowroot
1 1/2 cups milk
1 teaspoon ground cardamom, and/or 1 tablespoon rose water, and/or mastic, (see Glossary)

A large piece of dried apricot sheet, the size of a big hand palm, tear into small pieces and soak in 3/4 cup boiling water. Let steep for about one hour, then mash between fingers or with a fork

1 cup (one 1/2 pint carton) whipping cream
1/2 cup coarsely chopped pistachio, chilled

1. Put sugar and arrowroot in a medium heavy pot. Gradually add milk to sugar mixture, whisking all the time to allow solids to dissolve.

2. Cook on medium heat, stirring all the time until mixture thickens, about 10 minutes. It should be thicker than pudding in consistency. Add cardamom and/or rosewater, and the steeped and mashed apricot. Chill very well (overnight)

3. When ready to make ice cream, whip heavy cream, until soft peaks form. Mix with the milk mixture, and churn in an ice cream maker or freezer compartment, as instructed in the general methods above.
Add chilled pistachio half way through making the ice cream.

Variations:
* If dried apricot sheets are not available, substitute with 3/4 cup dried apricots. Put them in a small heavy pot and cover them with 1 cup water. Bring to a boil, then reduce heat and let simmer for about 10 minutes or until apricots are mushy. Puree in blender or food processor, then chill and use as directed above.

*Ice cream with Prunes and pistachio:
Instead of apricot, use 3/4 cup prunes, cover with 1 cup water, and boil, mash and chill as directed above

Green Pistachio Ice Cream with Mastic
(Dondirma bil fistiq wal Mastaki)

Mastic (see Glossary) gives this ice cream a unique flavor, but if it is hard to come by, you can substitute it with cardamom or rose water or other flavors of your choice.

3/4 cup sugar
2 rounded tablespoons arrowroot
1 1/2 cups milk
1 teaspoon mastic cream, or a few pulverized lumps of mastic gum (see Glossary). Or 1 tablespoon rose water, or 1 teaspoon ground cardamom, or 1/4 teaspoon almond essence
A few drops of green food coloring

1 cup (one 1/2 pint carton) whipping cream
3/4 cup coarsely ground pistachio, chilled

1. Put sugar and arrowroot in a medium heavy pot. Gradually add milk to sugar mixture, whisking all the time to allow solids to dissolve.

2. Cook on medium heat stirring all the time until mixture thickens, about 10 minutes. It should be thicker than pudding in consistency. Add mastic or alternative flavors. Chill very well (overnight)

3. When ready to make ice cream, whip heavy cream until soft peaks form. Mix with the milk mixture, and churn in an ice cream maker or freezer compartment, as instructed in the general methods above.
Add chilled pistachio half way through freezing so that it will not sink into the bottom.

Easy Fruity Ice Cream with Condensed Milk
(Dondirmat al-Fawakih bil-Haleeb al-Murakkaz)

1 1/2 cups mashed fresh fruit
One 14-ounce can condensed, sweetened milk, not evaporated
2 cups half and half cream
Flavoring of your choice to suit the kind of fruit used
Food coloring, optional

Mix all ingredients, and chill and freeze either in an ice cream maker or freezer, following instructions given in the general methods above.

Cinnamon Ice cream with Dried Fruits
(Dondirmat al Darseen bil fawakih aL-Mujaffafa)

Tea and cinnamon combine to give this ice cream a uniquely attractive color. The frozen dried fruits will be delightfully chewy.

2 heaping tablespoons arrowroot
3/4 cup sugar
1/2 cup brewed cold tea
1 cup milk

3/4 teaspoon cinnamon
1/2 teaspoon cardamom
1 teaspoon vanilla

1 cup (One 1/2 pint carton) heavy cream, chilled and whipped
1 1/2 cups finely diced dried fruits, shredded coconut, and toasted nuts, moistened with a little brewed tea or brandy, keep chilled
For garnish 1/4 cup raisins coated with chocolate, optional

1. Put arrowroot and sugar in a medium heavy pot. Gradually add cold tea and milk to sugar mixture, whisking all the time to allow solids to dissolve.

2. Cook on medium heat, stirring constantly until mixture thickens, about 10 minutes. It should be rather thick in consistency. Stir in cinnamon, cardamom, and vanilla. Chill, overnight, covered.

3 When ready to make ice cream, fold whipped cream into the chilled milk mixture. Churn in ice cream maker or in freezer compartment, following instructions given in the general methods, given above. Add dried fruits half way through freezing so that they will not sink to the bottom.
   Garnish with chocolate-coated raisins, if wished.

Suggestions:
* Substitute tea with coffee.
* Add about 1/2 cup roasted and mashed chestnuts to the dried fruits and nuts.

Basic Recipe for Ice Cream Sauce

Any kind of juicy fruits can be made into sauce. Your choice of fruit is determined by your special preference, and the kind of ice cream used. It is a good idea to set aside some of the fruit in chunks, to garnish ice cream with them.

1/2 cup sugar
1/3 cup water
2 cups chunks of fruit of your choice
1 tablespoon lemon juice

Boil sugar and water for 5 minutes. Then put syrup along with fruit and lemon juice in a blender or processor. Pulse until smooth.

If soft berries, like black berries or raspberries are used, set aside some of them whole. Add some sugar to the rest of the berries and mash with a fork. Then return reserved whole berries to mashed portion.

2. Milk- Based Ices (Sherbets)

S*herbe* in the Iraqi dialect is a thirst-quenching chilled beverage made from diluted fruit syrups (see Chapter twenty-one on beverages). In the following milk-based ice cream recipes, I'm using the word "sherbet" in the American sense.

Cantaloupe Sherbet

3 cups milk
1 envelope gelatin
1 small ripe cantaloupe, peeled, seeded, and cut into chunks
1/2 cup corn syrup
1/2 cup sugar, or to taste
1 tablespoon rose water

1. In a small pot, away from heat, sprinkle gelatin on **1 cup** milk. Leave for 5 minutes then cook on low heat until dissolved, do not let boil.

2. In a blender or processor, blend cantaloupe with **1 cup** milk in batches, until smooth.

3. Combine gelatin mixture, blended cantaloupe, **1 cup** milk, corn syrup, sugar and rose water. Stir until sugar is dissolved.

4. Churn chilled mixture in ice cream maker according to manufacturer's instructions, or follow freezer method described in the general method, given above. Garnish with sprigs of mint

Sherbet of Arabic Coffee

3 3/4 cups milk
1/2 teaspoon cardamom
3 tablespoons finely ground coffee
1/2 cup sugar, adjust to taste
2 heaping tablespoons arrowroot, dissolved in a little cold milk

1. Bring milk and cardamom to a boil, stir in coffee, and let simmer on low heat for about 5 minutes. Strain milk to get rid of coffee dregs.

2. Return to heat, add sugar and dissolved arrowroot stirring all the time until mixture thickens, about 10 minutes.

3. Chill mixture then freeze in an ice cream maker or freezer, following directions given in the general methods, given above. Garnish with whole coffee beans dipped in chocolate.

Suggestions:

*Any kind of coffee, regular or decaffeinated, can be substituted to suit your personal preference. If instant coffee is used, no need to strain.
* Instead of sugar use one 14-ounce can sweetened condensed milk diluted with milk to make 3 3/4 cups of liquid.

Sherbet of Black Tea

3 3/4 cup milk
1/2 teaspoon cardamom
3 tea bags of your choice, regular or decaffeinated
1/2 cup sugar, adjust to taste
2 heaping tablespoons arrow root, dissolved in a little cold milk

1. Bring milk and cardamom to a boil, dip in tea bags and let simmer on low heat for about 5 minutes.

2. Remove tea bags, and return milk to heat. Add sugar and dissolved arrowroot stirring all the time, until mixture thickens, about 10 minutes.

4. Chill mixture and freeze in an ice cream maker or freezer following directions given in the general methods, given above.

Suggestions:

* Instead of sugar use one 14-ounce can sweetened condensed milk diluted with milk to make 3 3/4 cups of liquid.
* Instead of cardamom flavor tea with a handful of fresh mint sprigs. Let them boil with milk but do not forget to remove them before freezing.

3. Water Based Ices (Slush or Granita) (Azbery)

Azbery is the generic name we use in Iraq to describe all kinds of grainy-textured frozen fruit juices. They are all so refreshing in the heat of summer, and fat free. Both methods, the ice cream maker and the freezer, yield a satisfactory result.

Lemon Ice

1 cup sugar
2 1/4 cups water
1 envelope unflavored gelatin

3/4 cup lemon juice
1 teaspoon grated lemon peel
1 teaspoon rose water

1. Away from heat put sugar and water in a small heavy pot. Sprinkle with gelatin and set aside for 5 minutes.

2. Put pot on low heat and cook stirring all the time until gelatin dissolves, about 5 minutes.

3. Add juice, lemon peel and rose water. Pour mixture into a 9-by-9-inch pan. Cover and freeze as suggested in general method, given above. Or if using an ice cream maker, chill mixture and churn following manufacturer's instructions.

Orange Ice

1/2 cup sugar
1 cup water
1 envelope unflavored gelatin

2 cups orange juice
1 teaspoon grated lemon peel
1 tablespoon lemon juice
1 teaspoon orange blossom water

1. Away from heat put sugar and water in a small heavy pot. Sprinkle with gelatin and set aside for 5 minutes.

2. Put pot on low heat and cook stirring all the time until gelatin dissolves, about 5 minutes.

3. Add orange juice, lemon peel, lemon juice and orange blossom water. Pour mixture into a 9-by-9-inch pan. Cover and freeze as suggested in general method, given above. Or if using an ice cream maker, chill mixture, then churn following manufacturer's instructions.

557

Cantaloupe Ice

1 cup sugar,
1 cup water
1 teaspoon grated lemon peel
2 1/2 cups mashed cantaloupe
2 tablespoons lemon juice
1 teaspoon rose water

1. Put sugar, water and peel in a small pot, and boil for about 5 minutes.

2. Remove from heat and add prepared cantaloupe, lemon juice and rose water. Set aside to cool.

3. Cover and freeze as suggested in the general method, given above. Or if using ice cream maker, chill mixture then churn following manufacturer's instructions.
    Garnish with mint leaves.

Fresh Fruit Ice

Any kind of fresh, ripe and sweet or sweet and sour fruits can be made into ice, such as apricots, peaches, mangos, all kinds of berries, prunes, etc. Mash chosen fruit to make 2 1/2 cups, and follow directions given in Cantaloupe Ice above. Do not forget to adjust amount of sugar used to suit the sweetness or acidity of chosen fruit.

Water Melon Ice

6 cups chunks of peeled, seeded water melon
3 tablespoons icing sugar
1 tablespoon lemon juice

1. In a blender or processor blend all ingredients until smooth. Pour into 9-by-9-inch pan, cover and freeze as instructed in general method, given above. Alternatively chill mixture then churn in ice cream maker following manufacturer's instructions.
    Garnish with thin slices of lemon, and small wedges of watermelon.

Cinnamon ice cream with dried fruits, 554

CHAPTER TWENTY
FOOD PRESERVATION

JAMS

PICKLES

CHAPTER TWENTY
FOOD PRESERVATION

JAMS
(Murabbayat)

المُرَبَّيَاتُ

Man has never been short of devising ways and means for dealing with the surplus of his produce. In *The Assyrian Herbal*, a book which deals with the ancient Mesopotamians' use of plants for medicinal purposes, we learn that some fruits like quince, figs, prunes and cherries were made into a kind of conserve by keeping them in honey. There was a suggestion, too, for how to serve them. They were to be eaten with butter.

In the tenth-century Baghdadi cookbook there were chapters on preserving fruits, and the methods followed did not differ much from how we make jams these days. The jamming season is usually summertime when fruits are plenty and cheap. The way we make them in our hot Mesopotamian summers, is that after we cook a huge amount of jam on the stove, we spread it in somewhat shallow huge containers, covered with muslin cloth, to keep away dust and flies. There they would stay on the flat roof of the house for a week or so, exposed to the dry summer sun, so that jam syrup might thicken, and preserved fruits mellow and mature. This is possible, of course, only at places where the weather is totally dry, otherwise jam gets moldy. However, with the availability of refrigerators this last step can be skipped.

Following is a number of general rules and observations for making jam:
*Use heavy pots for cooking jam.
* Handle cooking jams with a wooden spoon.
*Do not rush jams. Allow them to cook gently and fold gently and frequently to prevent fruits from sticking to the bottom of the pot.
*Skimming is important otherwise jam will develop a cloudy syrup.
*To test for doneness, put a drop of syrup on a dry cold dish. Tilt the dish. If the drop does not go flat, and keeps its domed shape, it is done.

561

*For sour fruits use 2 cups sugar for each pound of fruits and 1/2 cup liquid.

**For less citric fruits, use 1 1/2 cups sugar for each pound of fruits and 1/2 cup liquid.

*For fruits high in moisture, like strawberries and pumpkin, follow same ratio of sugar per pound of fruit, but do not use any liquids. Just arrange fruits in layers with sugar.

*Add lemon juice 5 minutes before jam is done.

* Always let sugar dissolve completely on slow heat at first before letting it boil. If sugar somehow crystallizes after jam is cold, add 1/4 to 1/2 cup water, put back to heat and let cook gently, and retest for doneness.

*A trace of butter or oil added when jam is done will disperse any scum that still remains.

Apple jam, 568

The First "Honeyed" Man

Did you know that the Sumerian wife used to call her husband "honey man"?

Date Syrup
(Dibis)

This is perhaps the oldest form of preserved fruit. To the Ancient Mesopotamians it was known as "dispu" (date-honey) from which the Arabic *dibs* was derived. Date syrup is traditionally served with *geymer* (slabs of thick cream). *Dibis* also makes a delicious winter dip when mixed with a little tahini.

The traditional, and by far the best method for extracting *dibis* is to put a huge amount of fully ripe dates in flat baskets made from date palm fronds. A heavy weight is set on top of the baskets to let date syrup, as clear as honey, ooze down slowly into containers put underneath. A cheaper kind of *dibis* is made by boiling the dates over an extended period of time. They are then strained, and the resulting liquid is put in big containers, and was evaporated and condensed under the scorching summer sun. You can make a small amount of *Dibis,* by boiling a small amount of dates. Strain, and simmer down the resulting liquid. But nothing compares with the traditional cold press method.

Fresh dates are also made into jam. I found the following recipe in the thirteenth century Bahgdadi cookbook, it is called *Rutab Mu'assal* (honeyed dates), and it sounds delicious:

Take fresh-gathered dates, and lay them in the shade and air for a day: then remove the stones, and stuff with peeled almonds. For every ten *ratls* of dates, take two *ratls* of honey: boil over the fire with two *uqiya* of rose water and half a *dirham* of saffron, then throw in the dates, stirring for an hour. Remove, and allow to cool. When cold, sprinkle with fine-ground sugar scented with musk, camphor and hyacinth. Put into glass preserving-jars, Sprinkling on top some of the scented ground-sugar. Cover, until the weather is cold. (1 *ratl* = 1 pound, Arberry, 213-4)

Water Melon Rind Jam
(Murabbat Raggi)

With all the jams cooking in the region, there was a time when the only imported variety was the Australian water melon rind jam. It was good but it lacked the enticing aromas of the cardamom, rose water, mastic, and lots of other spices of the home made varieties. Here is how you can make it at home:

1 pound water melon rind (measure after removing the green outer skin and all traces of pink)
1 1/2 cups sugar
1 strip lemon peel
3 tablespoons honey
A few melon seeds
1 tablespoon lemon juice
1/4 teaspoon mastic, or 1/2 teaspoon mastic cream (see glossary), or 3 whole pods cardamom

1. Cut rind into 1/3-inch strips. Cover in cold water and bring to a quick boil. Reduce heat, and let simmer slowly until transparent, about 30 minutes. Drain, and reserve 1 1/2 cups of liquid.

2. In a heavy pot, completely dissolve sugar in reserved liquid. Add honey and lemon peel, and bring to a boil, skimming as needed. Add drained rind and seeds and boil gently over medium heat, for 15 minutes. Remove from heat, cover, and set aside overnight.

3. Boil again over medium heat, until syrup thickens, about 15 minutes. Test for doneness.

4. Add lemon juice and mastic or cardamom 5 minutes before jam is done. Let jam cool completely then store in a sterilized jar.

Pumpkin Jam
(Murabbat Shijar Ahmer)

Pumpkin is popular for its salted and toasted seeds and the delicious jam it yields.

1 pound pumpkin pulp
1 1/2 cups sugar
1/4 cup walnut halves
1 tablespoon lemon juice
1/4 teaspoon powdered mastic, or 1/2 teaspoon mastic cream (see glossary), or 3 cardamom pods

1. Cut pumpkin into small cubes or strips, layer with sugar and walnut in a heavy medium pot, and set aside overnight.

2. Cook on low heat, stirring gently to let sugar dissolve completely. Skim as needed. Let jam boil gently until syrup is thick and pumpkin is tender and transparent, about 30 minutes. Test for doneness.

3. Add lemon juice and mastic or cardamom 5 minutes before jam is done. Let cool completely and store in a sterilized jar.

Variation:

Grated fresh pumpkin flesh makes a smoother type of jam:

> **1 cup sugar**
> **1/2 cup water**
> **1 cup grated fresh pumpkin flesh**
> **2 teaspoons lemon juice**
> **1/4 teaspoon powdered mastic (see Glossary), or 2 cardamom pod**

In a small pot boil sugar and water until syrup is thick enough to cover the back of the spoon, about 10 minutes. Add grated pumpkin and simmer on low heat until pumpkin is soft and transparent, about 15 minutes. Add lemon juice and flavorings 5 minutes before jam is done. Let jam cool, and store in a sterilized container.

Cantaloupe Jam
(Murabbat Batteekh)

Follow same instructions given in Pumpkin jam above, except substitute 1 pound cantaloupe pulp for pumpkin. The firmer pulp is the better.

Carrot Jam
(Murabbat Jizar)

In the tenth century Baghdadi cookbook there is an array of jam recipes, ranging from delicate rose petals to radishes. Although I haven't ventured to do the latter, other jams, such as carrot jam flavored with ginger and saffron have evidently stood to the test of time.

> **1 pound carrots, shredded, or cut into strips or cubes**
> **2 cups sugar**
> **1/2 cup water**
> **3 pods cardamom**
> **1 tablespoon lemon juice**
> **1/4 teaspoon ground ginger**

1. In a heavy pot, layer carrots with sugar and set aside overnight.

2. Add water, cardamom and cook gently on medium heat, folding and skimming as needed. Make sure that sugar is completely dissolved. Let cook gently until syrup is thick and carrot is tender and transparent, about 30 minutes. Test for doneness.

3. Add lemon juice and ginger five minutes before jam is done. Let cool completely, and store in a sterilized jar.

Beets Jam
(Murabbat Shuwander)

Beets make beautiful jam. I always use it in cookie recipes that call for a top layer of jam.

> **1 pound peeled and shredded beets**
> **2 cups sugar**
> **3 pods cardamom**
> **1 tablespoon lemon juice**
> **1/2 teaspoon ground ginger**

1. Put beets in a medium heavy pot and cover with water. Bring to a boil then let simmer until tender, about 20 minutes.

2. Add sugar and cardamom, stirring well to make sure all sugar grains are dissolved. Let boil gently for about 20 minutes, test for doneness.

3. Add lemon juice and ginger 5 minutes before jam is done. Let jam cool completely, and store in a sterilized jar.

Quince Jam
(Murabbat Safarjal or Hewa)

The Akkadians called quince, "supurgil" (cf. Arabic *safargal*). In the Iraqi dialect it is also known as *hewa*. The ancient Assyrians preferred eating quince simmered in honey, and they had it with butter. Quince needs to simmer slowly, so that pulp may soften and release a wonderful aroma. Its pale flesh will turn to an attractive brownish orange color.

> **3 medium quinces, peeled, cored and quartered**
> **1 3/4 cups sugar**
> **3 pods cardamom**
> **1 tablespoon lemon juice**
> **1/4 cup slivered and toasted almonds**

1. If you like jam to be chunky cut each quarter of quince into thick slices crosswise. Shred quince for a smoother texture. Cover pieces in cold water, about 3 cups. Bring to a boil, then reduce heat and let simmer very slowly, covered, until quince is tender, about 2 hours.

2.Drain, reserving 1 cup of liquid.

3. Dissolve sugar in liquid. Add cardamom, and cook gently over medium heat, skimming as needed, until syrup starts to thicken.

4. Add drained quince and continue cooking gently until quince is tender and syrup is thick, about 20 minutes. Test for doneness.

5. Add lemon juice and ginger 5 minutes before jam is done. Let jam cool completely, and store in a sterilized jar.

Fig Jam
(Murabbat Teen)

Figs grow successfully in the middle and northern regions of Iraq. Top quality varietirs were called *teen wazeeri* (from *wazeer*, minister). Vendors carrying wide wicker baskets full of luscious figs, customarily advertise their merchandise by crying out loud, "*wazeeri ya teen, lawi ya teen*," as they roam the streets of Baghdad, a catchy phrase they must have inherited from their medieval fellow vendors. We know for sure that *teen wazeeri* was a highly valued brand of figs in tenth century Baghdad (al-Tawheedi, 170).

Since figs are highly perishable, it is the custom of the Kurds in the north, where it is most abundant, to preserve the surplus in two ways. Fresh figs are threaded into long "necklaces" and dried. They were also made into jam. Long strings of flattened dried figs and attractive huge jars of golden fig jam are common attractions at the shops in the northern cities.

Fig jam makes delicious dessert. Put 2 to 3 figs in the bottom of a small bowl with some of the golden syrup and pour hot custard (not so sweet) to cover it. Or you can also reverse the order--put the custard first then decorate it with fig jam. Garnish with cream and ground pistachios.

If you happen to live at an area where fresh figs are readily available make jam as follows, if not, then use dried figs as directed in the next recipe.

> **1 pound fresh figs**
> **2 cups sugar**
> **3 pods cardamom**
> **1 tablespoon lemon juice**
> **1/4 cup toasted sesame**

1. In a medium heavy pot, put figs and sugar in layers, and set aside overnight.

2. Put pot on medium heat, add cardamom and let cook gently until sugar dissolves, stirring carefully, and skimming as needed. Make sure all sugar granules are dissolved. Let mixture simmer until figs are transparent and syrup is thickened, about 30 minutes. Test for doneness.

4. Add lemon juice and sesame seeds 5 minutes before jam is done. Let jam cool completely, and keep in a sterilized jar.

Dried Fig Jam
(Murabbat Teen Mujaffaf)

1 pound dried figs
3/4 cup sugar
1/4 cup honey
3 pods cardamom
4 whole cloves
1/2 teaspoon toasted whole aniseed
1 tablespoon lemon juice
1 tablespoon toasted sesame seeds, or 1/4 cup toasted slivered almonds

1. Cover figs in 3 cups water and let soak overnight.

2. Put figs with the water in a medium pot and bring to a boil. Reduce heat and let simmer, covered, for about an hour.
3. Stir in sugar, honey, cardamom, cloves, and aniseeds. Set aside overnight.

4. Bring figs to a boil, then lower heat and let simmer gently for about an hour or until figs are transparent and syrup is thickened. Test for doneness.

5. Add lemon juice and sesame seeds 5 minutes before jam is done. Let jam cool completely, and store in a sterilized jar.

Apple Jam
(Murabbat Tuffah)

For this jam only the locally grown, small and white, sweet and sour apples are customarily used. Excavations have revealed they used to grow thousands of years ago in the region. The ancient inhabitants used to preserve apples by slicing them crosswise and threading them into strings and dry them. Since these summertime apples are small in size, they are usually left whole when used for jam. The best substitute is crab apples or small cooking apples.

1 pound small cooking apples, peel and core out seeds, but leave apples whole and if possible leave stems intact
2 cups sugar
1/2 teaspoon mastic, or 1 teaspoon mastic cream (see Glossary), or 3 pods cardamom
1 tablespoon lemon juice

1. Cover apples with cold water, and cook until half-done and still firm, about 10 minutes.

2. Drain apples and reserve 1/2 cup liquid.

3. Put sugar and reserved liquid in a heavy pot and bring to a boil stirring frequently until sugar dissolves, skimming as needed.

4. Add apples and mastic or cardamom. Continue cooking gently on medium-low until syrup thickens and apples are transparent, about 40 minutes. Test for doneness.

5. Add lemon juice 5 minutes before jam is done. Let cool completely, and store in a sterilized jar.

Plum Jam
(Murabbat Injas)

Plums make tasty and attractive jam. The final color of the jam depends on what kind of plums you're using.

> 1 pound plums, any variety will do
> 2 cups sugar
> 1/2 teaspoon mastic, or 1 teaspoon mastic cream (see Glossary), or 3 pods cardamom
> 1 tablespoon lemon juice

1. Put plums in boiling water for 2 to 3 minutes or until peel come off easily. Remove skin, cut into halves to remove the stone or leave whole with the stone.

2. Cover plums with 1cup water and let boil gently until half done and still firm. Turn pieces over halfway through cooking. Drain plums and reserve 1/2 cup of liquid.

3. Put sugar, mastic or cardamom and reserved liquid in a heavy pot. Bring to a boil stirring frequently and skimming as needed. Make sure all sugar granules are dissolved.

5. Add plums and let cook gently until syrup is thickened, about 30 minutes. Test for doneness.

6. Add lemon juice 5 minutes before jam is done. Let cool completely, and store in a sterilized jar.

Apricot Jam
(Murabbat Mishmish)

Although commercially made apricot jam is available in grocery stores, the special touches given to the homemade jam will definitely make it worth while the trouble.

> 1 pound apricot, cut into halves and remove stones
> 2 cups sugar

3 pods cardamom, or 1/2 teaspoon mastic, or 1 teaspoon mastic cream, see Glossary
4 to 5 toasted whole almonds
1 tablespoon lemon juice

1. Cover apricots with 1cup water and bring to a boil. Half cook, about 3 minutes.

2. Drain apricots reserving 3/4 cup of liquid.

3. Put sugar, cardamom pods or mastic, almonds and reserved liquid in a heavy pot. Bring to a boil stirring frequently and skimming as needed. Make sure all sugar granules are dissolved, about 5 minutes.
4. Add apricots and cook gently until apricots are translucent and syrup is thickened, about 30 minutes. Test for doneness.

5. Add lemon juice 5 minutes before jam is done. Let cool completely, and store in a sterilized jar.

Peach Jam
(Murabbat Khokh)

Follow the same instructions given in **Apricot Jam**, except instead of apricots use 5 medium peaches (about 1 pound), either nectarines or the furry ones. You do not need to peel nectarines but you might want to peel the furry ones (just immerse them in boiling water for a few minutes then peel them).

Mulberry Jam
(Murabbat Tukki)

Mulberry trees have been growing on the land of Mesopotamia ever since ancient times, but the interest was largely in their wood rather that the fruits themselves. We know for instance that the Assyrian king Tiglath-Pileser cut them down "with the double purpose of destroying fruit trees, and supplying himself with wood" (Thompson, 181). The luscious mulberry fruits have never had a significant market value.

The white mulberries are small and sweet, whereas the black ones, called *tukki 'l-Sham*, are much larger, and are sweet and sour. The black variety is preserved in sugar, and as such is sold all year round. I remember as growing kids we used to buy this delicacy from wandering vendors who carried them in huge wicker baskets, balanced on their heads as they walked. As soon as we heard the familiar call coming from afar, "*tuki 'l-Sham, tuki al-Sham*," the nimblest of us would rush out to stop him, and the most eloquent would be begging for money from our parents, and in seconds we would be all out ready for a treat. The man would put down his basket, and put away the muslin that was protecting those rubies from the nosy flies. Each of us would get a handful of the sweetened mulberries heaped on a mulberry leaf or a piece of paper. This treat normally came accompanied with a thorn (from date palm fronds), called *sillaya*, about 3 inches long, which we used as a fork, since the berries were too messy to be handled with the fingers.

The jam is originally made from white or red mulberries. However, any other kind of berries may be used following the same method:

2 pounds berries
3 cups sugar, (or a little more if berries chosen are rather on the sour side)
2 tablespoons lemon juice
2 tablespoons rose water or orange blossom water

1. In a heavy pot, put sugar and berries in layers and set aside, overnight.

2. Cook on medium heat until sugar dissolves completely stirring occasionally and skimming as needed, about 15 minutes.

3. Remove berries with a slotted spoon and set aside. Continue cooking syrup until it starts to thicken, about 10 minutes.

4. Return berries and continue cooking gently until berries are plump and translucent and syrup is like honey, about 10 minutes. Test for doneness.

5. Add lemon juice and rose water or orange blossom water 5 minutes before jam is done. Let cool completely, and store in a sterilized jar.

The First Romeo and Juliet
A Babylonian Legend

If you want to know how red mulberry came into existence, then read the following:

A play within Shakespeare's play *A Midsummer Night's Dream* tells the tragic love affair of Pyramus and Thisbe, which bears noticeable similarities to the playwright's Romeo and Juliet. Shakespeare's source was Ovid's *Metamorphoses* (ca 8 AD). One of the stories in this Roman book tells how in the city of great Babylon the lovely Pyramus and Thisbe lived in adjoining houses from early childhood. They always played together and after they grew older they fell in love. Their parents in the meantime quarrelled, which resulted in a bitter feud, and they forbade any contact between the lovers. They, nevertheless, discovered a chink in the wall dividing the two houses, and every night, when everybody else was asleep, they whispered sweet words to each other through the crack in the wall until dawn. When they said good night, each kissed his side of the wall. One night they agreed to meet on the coming night of the full moon outside the city.

> The tomb of Ninus was the mark they chose
> There they might rest secure beneath the shade,
> Which boughs, with snowy fruit encumber'd, made:
> A wide-spread mulberry its rise had took
> Just on the margin of a gurgling brook.

Thisbe, who arrived first, encountered a lion that had just killed an ox. She fled in terror dropping her veil, which the lion bloodied while tearing it to pieces. When Pyramus arrived later he found the torn, bloody veil, and believing Thisbe dead, killed himself with his own dagger. The returning Thisbe found her dying lover under the mulberry tree, and in her grief plunged his dagger in her own heart. The mingling blood of the two unhappy lovers spurted over the mulberry tree, coloring its fruit red. Ovid concludes:

The whiteness of the mulberry soon fled,
And rip'ning, sadden'd in a dusky red:
While both their parents their lost children mourn,
And mix their ashes in one golden urn.

Orange Jam
(Murabbat al-Burtuqual)

In Iraq citrus jam is sometimes made from fruits that are not easily available in the Western world. *Trinj*, for instance, is a huge citrus fruit mainly purchased for its thick peel that is usually made into jam. *Rarinj* (orange of Seville) is a cheap variety of orange which has a thick peel and bitter rind. Its pleasantly sour juice is made into sherbet (syrup for making a refreshing drink), and its thick peel is thoroughly scraped and made into jam. Orange with a thick peel can be easily substituted as in the following recipe.

7 thick-skinned oranges
3 cups sugar
3 pods cardamom
1/4 cup honey
2 tablespoons lemon juice
1 tablespoon orange blossom water or rose water, see Glossary

1. Wash oranges thoroughly and cut off both ends; divide into halves lengthwise; then cut into thick slices crosswise. Discard seeds.

2. In a big bowl immerse orange sections in cold water. Put a heavy plate on top to keep orange submerged. Set aside, overnight. Drain and discard the liquid.

3. Put drained orange in a heavy pot and cover with water. Let boil gently for 40 minutes. Drain pieces. Reserve 3 cups of liquid.

4. In the same heavy pot mix sugar, cardamom, honey and reserved liquid. Bring to a boil stirring to make sure all sugar granules are dissolved. Skim as needed.

5. Add orange pieces, bring to a boil, then let mixture cook gently for 10 minutes. Cover pot and set aside for 24 hours.

6. Resume cooking the mixture on medium-low heat, stirring occasionally until peels look transparent and syrup thickens, about an hour. Test for doneness.

7. Add lemon juice and orange blossom water 5 minutes before jam is done. Let jam cool completely, and store in a sterilized jar.

For the Love of Oranges or Cucumbers?

I once got a present of a nice jar of marmalade expressly made for the Metropolitan Opera of New York city. Needless to say the marmalade was delicious, but what intrigued me more was the label itself. The marmalade was called "The Love for Three Oranges" after an opera by the Russian composer Sergei Prokofiev, written in the nineteen twenties. It was essentially an adaptation of Carlo Gozzi's eighteenth-century satirical parody of the melodrama, *Fiaba l'amore della tree melarance.*

It is the story of a prince who is cursed by the witch, Fata Morgana to fall in love with the three oranges. This triggered some memories in me. My mother used to tell us the story of "The Love for Seven Cucumbers", which bears an uncanny resemblance to Prokofiev's piece. In her version a prince makes fun of an ugly wicked witch, she gets offended and curses him saying, "May you fall in love with the seven cucumbers." The prince's curiosity is aroused, and he sets out looking for them everywhere. Finally he finds them, and opens one immediately. A beautiful dame comes out of it. She urgently demands some water, but there is none around, so she perishes. This happens to six of them, so he decides to open the last one at the riverbank. The moment he opens up the cucumber a beautiful young woman comes out and urgently asks for water. He scoops some from the river and lets her drink. He falls in love with her and decides to marry her, but asks her to climb up a tree and hide while he goes home, tells his parents, and comes back with an entourage that befits her state. While the prince is away, the witch comes to the place where the princess is hiding. She looks at the surface of the still water, and catches sight of the reflection of the princess's face. Mistaking it for hers, she says, "I never thought I am that beautiful." The princess above hears her and laughs at her. The witch transforms her into a dove and takes her place in the tree. The prince comes back with his parents and followers, he lifts the veil and so much to his dismay he finds an ugly woman instead. Embarrassed, he puts back the veil, resigns to his fate, and takes her with him to the palace to marry her. Eventually the prince discovers the truth, the witch is punished and the prince marries the beautiful princess.

It is quite likely that fables and stories like these were transmitted from Mesopotamia to Spain where, during the middle ages, the Arabs founded a prosperous Islamic rule. The troubadours who flourished in southern France and Spain from the eleventh to the thirteenth century must have played a considerable role in dispersing such stories, amongst other things, to the rest of Europe.

FOOD PRESERVATION:

PICKLES
(Turshi)

Pickling is one of the most ancient methods of preserving food. In the excavated Assyrian cuneiform tablets there were some occasional references to pickled meat. They also made the fermented "siqqu" sauce for kitchen and table use. They made it out of fish, shellfish or grasshoppers, so much similar to the oriental fish sauce. The ancients used to nibble on pickled grasshoppers, and apparently the taste for such "delicacies" continued up until the Middle Ages. In al-Warraq's tenth-century cookbook there is a recipe for making it (102). That was a smart way of using the swarms of grasshoppers that used to attack the region periodically.

The medieval cooks were no less diligent than their ancient counterparts in preserving their surplus of meats and vegetables by keeping them in vinegar. The medieval Baghdadi cookbooks abound with recipes for making vinegar, both simple and herbal, in addition to recipes for pickling fish, beef, poultry, and vegetables. The healing quality of vinegar did not escape them either. Here is a word of wisdom from the writer of the thirteenth century Baghdadi cookbook. He recommends the consumption of pickled substances and vinegar based sauces "to cleanse the palate of greasiness, to appetize, to assist the digestion, and to stimulate the banqueter" (102). Included in his chapter were recipes on pickling vegetables and herbs such as mint, eggplant, and turnips. It is now believed that a small amount of vinegar taken daily helps burn calories, and it is a natural way to counter act the storing up of excess fat within the body.

Nowadays no meal is considered complete without the familiar bowl of *turshi* (pickles) along with salad or a dish of fresh herbs. With the pickled vegetables, some people also like to take a sip or two of the pickling juice. The commercially made pickled mango would sometimes replace the home made pickles with a dish like the *Masgouf* (barbecued fish). We even sometimes have pickles for snacks.

Pickling vinegar in Iraq is made from dates and grapes. Apple cider would make a satisfactory substitute. Because vegetables are kept in undiluted vinegar, they keep for a long time even without refrigeration. The vegetables usually made into pickles are peppers, both sweet and hot, cucumbers, cabbage, cauliflower, green beans, green tomatoes, green grapes, sunckokes (also known as Jerusalem artichokes), lemons, small onions, olives, turnips, beets, carrots, and eggplant.

A General Method for Pickling

Stage One: Wash vegetables and soak them in a briny solution for 2 to 4 days depending on the kind of vegetables to be pickled. Follow instructions below. To make brine: for each 5 cups cold water, mix in 1/4 cup **uniodized** salt.

Here is how to prepare the vegetables, and how long to keep them in the brine

575

Peppers, different kinds: slash them, keep them in brine for 2 days
Cucumbers: slash them, keep them in brine for 2 days.
Cabbage: cut the head into fourths, keep in brine for 3 to 4 days.
Cauliflower: Divide into florets, keep in brine for 3 to 4 days.
Green beans: Keep in brine for 2 days.
Green tomatoes: cut into fourths, keep in brine for 2 to 3 days.
Green grapes: keep in brine for 4 days
Sunchokes (Jerusalem artichoke): wash them very well to get rid of sand, keep them in brine for 3 to 4 days.

Stage Two: Drain vegetables from brine and immerse in prepared vinegar, and here is how to prepare it:

Bring vinegar to a boil and add as many as you like of the following spices and herbs (quantities are left to your special preference):

Pieces of fresh ginger
Crushed chili pepper
Curry powder and turmeric
Bay leaves
Whole seeds of fennel, mustard, cumin, caraway, and coriander
Baharat **(see Glossary)**
Skinned whole garlic cloves
Sprigs of fresh or dry herbs like parsley, basil, mint, and dill
Sliced lemon

Allow vinegar to cool before using it. Keep vegetables in vinegar for about a week before using.

General remarks for making pickles:

*Use non-metal utensils when handling pickles.
*Use glass or earthenware jars to keep pickles, and store jars in a dark place.
*Try to keep pickles always submerged in vinegar solution. I do this by stuffing the empty space between vegetables and the lid with a handful of dried sprigs of mint or any other dried sprigs of herbs. Put as much as it takes.
*Use dry utensils when handling pickles, otherwise white moldy film will form on the surface, which will make pickles look unappetizing. If mold does appear, however, you can still use the pickles, just skim off the white stuff, and rinse pickles before using them.

Stuffed Bell Peppers
(Filfil Mahshi)

Follow rules given above for pickling peppers, but instead of slashing peppers cut them into halves lengthwise, but keep intact by leaving the upper part uncut. Keep them in brine as given in the first stage. Drain, then fill them with the following mixture, which is enough for filling 6 to 7 large peppers:

1 cup chopped parsley, shredded cabbage, shredded carrots, each
1/2 cup chopped onion
1/2 cup dried tomatoes, chopped
1 tablespoon grated garlic
1 tablespoon curry powder
1 teaspoon turmeric
1 teaspoon crushed chili pepper, or 1/2 teaspoon ground chili
1 teaspoon ground ginger
1/2 teaspoon uniodized salt

Fill peppers with the above mixture and tie each pepper with a sprig of fresh parsley, if wished. Arrange peppers in a pickling jar and drench them in the prepared vinegar following directions given above. Keep for about a week before using.

Pickled Turnips and Beets
(Turshi'l Shalgham)

It is amazing how humble vegetables like turnips and beets can be metamorphosed to such a beautiful creation as *turshi'l shalgham*. Turnips and beets have been growing on the soil of Mesopotamia ever since the times of the Sumerians, and possibly earlier. In the ancient Akkadian, turnip was called "liptu" (cf. Arabic *lifti*), and evidently both turnips and beets were used in cooking stews (see Introduction). Beets and turnips are wintertime vegetables, and as long as they are in the market we try to make the most of them: we simmer them with date syrup as a snack; use them in soups; and pickle them in huge quantities.

Traditionally, turnips and beets are preserved in brine and kept in large earthenware jars called *bastouga*. They are left for forty days on the sunny side of the flat roof of the house, to let it mellow under the gentle warmth of the winter sun. However, this method does not seem to work well in other climates, and it has to be adjusted. Besides, who has the patience to wait for forty full days?

The following is a fast method that works anytime, anywhere. Turnips and beets are essential for making this kind of pickles. Beets will give the vegetables a beautiful pinkish hue. The addition of carrots, cauliflower, and sunchokes is optional, but they do add a desirable variety, especially sunchokes. In Iraq they are called *almaaz* (diamonds) which shows how much valued and liked they are (the word is a possible corruption of the Turkish "yerelmasi").

3 pounds medium or small turnips
2 to 3 carrots, or 1 pound baby carrots
1 small head of cauliflower

2 pounds sunchokes (Jerusalem artichokes)
2 pounds beets

Uniodized salt for sprinkling

For the briny liquid:
2 tablespoons uniodized salt
12 cups liquid made from combining liquid in which beet will be cooked and white vinegar (half beet juice and half white vinegar is a good proportion)

4 to 5 juniper berries or corns of black pepper

1. Wash vegetables very well. Cut off both ends of **turnips** and scrape away any brown areas. Do not peel. If turnips are small just cut across, stopping about 1/4 inch short of the other side, leaving the two halves intact. With medium turnips, cut crosswise into halves, then lengthwise into thick slices. Scrape **carrots** and cut them into thick slices, or if baby carrots are used just leave them as they are. Divide **cauliflower** into florets. If **sunckokes** are small just slash them, if they are big cut them into halves.

2.Put turnips, carrots, cauliflower, and sunchokes in a big colander fitted into a bowl. Sprinkle generously with salt, fold vegetables and let them drain overnight. Fold vegetables several times while draining.

3. Meanwhile prepare **beets**: Wash very well, then cut off both ends. Put in a medium pot, and add cold water to fill pot up to three-quarters. Bring to a boil on high heat, then reduce heat and let beets simmer until cooked but still very firm, about 35 minutes. Cool.

4.When vegetables are ready, put them in two large pickling jars.

5.Peel skins of cooked beets by rubbing them between the fingers under running water. Cut beets into thick slices and put them on top of vegetables in jars.

6. Combine beet juice and enough white vinegar to make 12 cups of liquid. Stir salt and juniper berries or peppercorns into the liquid. Pour liquid into jars but do not fill to the brim, leave about 1/2 inch unfilled to allow for fermentation. If liquid is not enough, complement it with a solution made of half white vinegar and half cold water. Close jars and turn them upside down 2 to 3 times to allow color to distribute evenly.

7. Keep closed jars in a cool dark place for about 5 days. Turn jars upside down several times during that period to allow color to distribute evenly.

8. These pickles keep very well for 2 weeks unrefrigerated, and will last much longer if kept in the refrigerator.

Pickled Onions

Pickled Onions
(Turshi 'l Basal)

Small onions make appetizing crunchy pickles. You can pickle them like in the general method given above, or follow this recipe:

> **2 pounds small pickling onions (like pearl onions) washed, both ends cut off, and outer skins removed**
> **Brine made of 1/4 cup uniodized salt dissolved in 5 cups water**
> **6 cups white vinegar**
> **1/3 cup sugar**
> **3 to 4 chili peppers for garnish**
> **A few sprigs rosemary or thyme**
> **A few pepper corns or juniper berries**

1. Keep prepared onions soaked in brine for 2 days.

2. Boil white vinegar and sugar together for 15 minutes. Let cool.

3. Drain onions and add them to vinegar.

4. Put onions with vinegar solution in pickling jars along with chili peppers, herb sprigs and corn peppers. Leave for about 10 days and use.

Pickled Lemon
(Turshi 'l Laymoun)

Lemons make a refreshing kind of pickles. Following is an attractive way for preparing them:

1. Slash **lemons** on 4 sides. Press uniodized **salt** into the slashes, and put them in a colander. Set aside for 24 hours so that lemons may lose their bitterness.

2. Arrange lemons in a jar and cover them with **white vinegar**. Put a few **chili peppers**, **herb sprigs**, and **peeled garlic**. Close jars tightly, and leave them for 2 to 3 weeks.

Relish of Pickled Eggplant
(Anbat Betinjaan)

(Makes about 2 cups)

Anba is a popular condiment in the Iraqi cuisine (for more on its uses and popularity see Chapter Three on appetizers and salads). It is usually made from pickled green mangos, kept in wide-mouthed bottles, imported exclusively from India. In recent years; however, and because of the imposed economic embargo, people were forced to make do with so many substitutes. Here is one of them. Eggplant is used instead of green mangos to make this delicious and appetizing relish. An inventive friend of mine passed on this recipe to me.

1 medium to large eggplant (about 1 pound)
3 cloves garlic, peeled and cut into chunks
1 red bell pepper, cut into strips 2 inches long and 1/4 inch wide
1/2 teaspoon crushed hot chili, or to taste
1/2 cup olive oil
1 1/2 teaspoon uniodized salt

1/2 cup cider vinegar
1/2 cup water
1 heaping tablespoon curry powder
1 teaspoon ground cumin
1 teaspoon whole yellow mustard seeds
2 teaspoons grated fresh ginger, or 1 teaspoon ground dried ginger
1/2 tablespoon arrowroot, diluted in a little cold water

1. Peel eggplant, and cut into strips about 2 inches long and 1/2 inch thick. Discard seeds if any.

2. In a medium pot, put prepared eggplant, garlic, bell pepper, crushed chili, oil, and salt. Bring to a quick boil, then reduce heat to low and let mixture simmer gently until eggplant is cooked, about 20 minutes.

3. Add vinegar, water, curry powder, cumin, mustard seeds, and ginger. Resume simmering, covered, for about 20 minutes. Fold 2 to 3 times while simmering.

4.A minute before you decide to turn off heat, add diluted arrowroot. Mix well and let simmer for one minute then turn off heat.

5. Let mixture cool completely, then store in a sterilized pickling jar, and keep in the refrigerator for about 2 days before consuming, to allow flavors to blend. It will keep for about one month if refrigerated.

Suggestions:
* If green mangos are available substitute eggplant with 3 medium mangos. Peel and cut them into medium chunks. However, since mangos cook faster than eggplant you need to watch it to prevent it from getting mushy. Follow instructions given above.

* Another interesting way of making easy relish is to prepare the sauce without eggplant. When it gets cold, add to it your choice of already pickled vegetables. For a quick treat I sometimes buy jars of pickled baby cucumbers or peppers, drain them completely in a colander, then add them to the sauce after it cools down.

Medieval Food Preservation and Transportation, Using Ice

Preservation using ice was known during the medieval times. In the colder northern parts of the region, icehouses were built. They were shaped like conical domes, and situated against high walls to help keep them cool during the day. Ice formed in shallow ponds around the area was gathered and stored in pits inside these icehouses. Apparently they also had the means to preserve it in the cities to which it would be transported even during the summer, when it would be most needed. From a tenth-century book of anecdotes we learn there were specialized merchants who used to deal with storing and distributing it (al-Tanukhi, 68).

Ice was used to preserve food, and make cold drinks in the summer. Kept this way, fruits such as apples, pomegranates and grapes would stay fresh for months. Cold storage also proved so convenient for transporting foods to Baghdad from distant lands. It was kept fresh by packing it in lead iceboxes (Hassan and Hill, 231).

583

CHAPTER TWENTY-ONE
BEVERAGES

HOT DRINKS

COLD DRINKS

CHAPTER TWENTY-ONE

BEVERAGES

(Al-Mashroubat)

المَشْرُوبَات

Hot Drinks

In Iraq tea is served several times a day no matter what season it is. Loose Ceylon tea is the blend preferred. As for tea bags they are a convenience unheard of in the region, and which at any rate might have received a lukewarm welcome due to the way people are accustomed to brewing their tea. A medium-sized teapot and a large kettle are all it takes to brew the perfect tea, even for a big family. However, in some households, a *samawar* is used to keep the tea-drinking ritual going all day. It is basically a water boiler or a "tea-maker" (in Russian, *sam* means "itself," and *var* "boils"). It is composed of a boiler, which in the old days was fuelled by coal. Most of them nowadays come with electric heaters. The teapot is put on this boiler and tea is allowed to brew slowly by the heat of steam. It is very convenient for large gatherings. In the old days it was the centerpiece around which family members would sit cozily, chatting and sipping hot tea from the small glasses. However, people nowadays use them as a piece of décor and follow the less ritualistic method of the kettle and teapot.

Traditionally, a thick and heavy brew is made by adjusting the teapot on the opening of a boiling kettle, and letting tea gently simmer by the heat of steam. When tea leaves come up to the surface, tea is ready to use. It is then served diluted with boiling water, often with plenty of sugar, in small delicate glasses called *isticans*, which are either fitted in metal holders, or put on small saucers. In northern Iraq the Kurds have the custom of putting a small lump of solid sugar in the mouth and letting it dissolve slowly as the unsweetened tea is sipped, they call it *chai dishlama*. Two or three *isticans* of tea are the average amount served per person.

In the morning tea is normally served in regular cups with some milk. After lunch, the main meal of the day, it is served in *isticans*. The afternoon is another occasion for drinking tea, more or less, like the British high tea. The whole family gets together and enjoys snacks such as *ka'ak* and *bakhsam* (dunking cookies). The kids of course would insist on having their own share of tea, and because tea is believed to be the notorious culprit behind the bed-wetting, they would cunningly be lured into having an extremely light tea, called *fudha wa dhahab* (silver and gold). It is made by filling the *istican* almost to the top with boiling water and some sugar--that will be silver. Then a small amount of tea will gently be poured with the help of the back of a teaspoon so that tea will stay afloat and not mingle with the water--that will be gold. Tea is also served after supper, a light meal, normally between seven and eight o'clock. This obviously sounds like a lot of tea, but in the light of new scientific discoveries this might not be a bad habit after all, except for the sugar, of course.

Tea is sometimes flavored with cardamom or sprigs of fresh mint, but not for breakfast. Sometimes for a change or for medicinal purposes, other teas are served, such as dried lime tea, believed to be good for relieving dizziness, nausea and headaches, and cinnamon tea, usually a winter drink, believed to protect against the cold. During the days when people used to go to public baths, cinnamon tea was the drink to sip after having a bath. Herbal teas are also quite common. Chamomile tea (*chai beboun*) is believed to be good for colds and sore throats. Blue tea (*chai warid mawi)*, made from dried flowers of anchusa (violets?), and flowers shaped like an ox's tongue (*ward lisan al-thor*), are reputed to be good for fevers. *Chai koajarat* is a sour, clear, and ruby-red tea. It is made from hibiscus flowers, and is named after Gujarat, a western India state,

As for coffee, a strong and thick brew is made of it, called *gahwa Arabiya* (Arabic coffee), also known in some parts of the world as Turkish coffee, or after whichever country it is served in. While visiting Cyprus in the early eighties we asked for Turkish coffee at a restaurant in Larnaka, and we were politely but coldly corrected--it is called Cyprian coffee. Arabic coffee is normally made in a *dalla*, a long-handled container with a wide base that tapers at the top. The conical shape helps the coffee to foam while it boils up.

Coffee is made in small quantities, and is usually served in a tiny cup called *finjaan*. It cannot be made in advance since heating it would spoil the foamy creamy top, the mark of good Arabic coffee. It sometimes comes flavored with ground cardamom. Unlike tea, the occasion determines how much sugar to use. In rural areas and at funerals coffee is usually served sugarless (*murra*), on happy occasions it is sweet (*hulwa*), and for daily consumption it is left to personal preference.

Coffee is normally served around brunch time. As for guests it is made whenever they come. A typical way for women to pass the time while socializing is to invert the small cup on its saucer, let the dregs flow down, and wait until they settle forming different shapes and patterns. The connoisseur in the art of reading fortunes amongst them would be asked to interpret those formations. They can be a bundle of money, a prospective journey (*sikkat safar*), a groom (*'arees*), or whatever the imagination dictates.

Up until recently men used to spend the evenings in coffeehouses called *gahwa* or c*haikhana* (teahouse), where they socialize while sipping coffee, different kinds of tea, smoke the *nargeela* (hooka), and play backgammon, domino, or chess. The fun doubles during the month of fasting, *Ramadhan* when a storyteller, *qussakhoun*, entertains customers with exciting stories of romance and heroism. In addition, a very popular ring game, *mheibis,* is often played by teams from different neighborhoods. Men would divide into two parties, covering their hands with a blanket. The ring is put in the hand of one of the participants and the other party has to guess in whose hand the ring is. One of them would stand up and rule out the empty hands by asking them to open them up, thus until guessing is narrowed down to the hand that has the ring. Not an easy task as it sounds. The guessing party has to do a lot of face reading--an excited face, a suppressed chuckle, or an exaggeratedly serious and indifferent face could betray the holder of the ring. The penalty is a tray of *baklawa* and *zlabya* purchased by the losing party to be shared by all. Meanwhile the kids would be doing some trick 'n treating by going from door to door asking for money, singing

Majeena ya majeena, open up your purse and give us some money.

You dwellers of the roofs, will you give us any, or shall we leave?

All they get sometimes is a bucket of water poured on them by the "roof dwellers," and all they could do in return is to scurry away saying,

Oh, we've been drenched in water.

Oh, the stingy ones, they drenched us in water.

قَهْوَة

On Drinking Coffee in the Mudhif
(rural guesthouse)

Coffee prepared in rural areas is thin in consistency and is normally served unsweetened and flavored with lots of cardamom; the more cardamom the more honored the guests are. At the *mudhifs* (rural guesthouses), preparing coffee is usually a man's job. The coffee maker would roast the coffee beans, then, in a brass mortar and pestle, he would rhythmically pound the coffee, most probably, to a tune in his head. The coffee would be served in small cups with no handles, with some more rituals as the following excerpt reveals:

> The mores require that both preparations [grinding and making coffee] should be done in the presence of the guest, and no host would dream of offering previously prepared coffee. ...A servant approaches the seated guests carrying in one hand the coffeepot and in the other doll sized cups. Into the cup he pours about a dessertspoonful, and this the guest drinks- if he can, for it is almost boiling- at a gulp. If he wants no more he shakes the cup quickly as he returns it; it is, in any case, bad manners to drink more than 3 cups before giving this sign (Maxwell, 26).

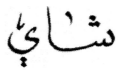

The Perfect Istican Chai

Put 3 to 4 tablespoons of loose tea in a medium teapot and a few whole cardamom pods, cracked a little. Pour a little of the freshly boiled water to rinse the leaves and warm the pot. Quickly pour off water leaving tea in the pot. Then pour hot water into the teapot until it is almost full. Let it brew very slowly on low heat, or remove the lid of the boiling kettle and put the teapot on the opening of the kettle, or brew it on the traditional tea-maker *samawer* if you happen to have one. However, brewed either way, never let it boil over. Tea is ready to use as soon as the leaves come up to the surface. To serve, put sugar to taste first in the *istican* as this will prevent the delicate glasses from cracking when hot tea is poured into them. Pour to about one third of it with the brewed tea, and add

587

hot water enough to come up to the rim. (The proportions of tea and water would vary according to personal preference.) This method is very handy when you want to serve a big number of people, which often is the case in most of the families.

However, to make a ritual-free tea for 2 or 3 people, just put 1 level tablespoon of loose tea leaves in the teapot with 2 whole pods of cardamom cracked a little, and pour freshly boiled water to fill teapot up to three quarters of it. Brew on very low heat or on steam by fitting the teapot on the opening of a kettle of boiling water as described above. However you do it, avoid letting tea boil, as this will cause it to develop a bitter taste.

Old News is Good News: On the Benefits of Tea

Recent research has linked this ancient drink to good health. Like green tea, black tea has been discovered to be rich in antioxidants, those cancer fighting agents, richer, in fact, than most fruits and vegetables. It is also believed that drinking tea could also lower the chances of getting coronary diseases and strokes. Tea is also found to be one of the few natural sources of fluoride. Its antioxidants help prevent gum disease, too. So it does not sound like a bad idea at all to enjoy a cup of tea every now and then (*Food and Wine*, March, 1999).

خـدري الجـاي خـدري

خدري الجاي خدري؛ عيوني ألمن أخدره؟
مالچ يا بعد الروح دوچ مكدرة؟
بعد هواي يا ناس ألمن أنا أصبه؟
محد بعد عيناه يستاهل يشرب به

-Brew the tea, brew it.
-For whom shall I brew it?
-What's wrong with you, dear, you are always sad?
- After my love is gone, folks, for whom shall I pour it?
-After my precious was gone, none is worthy of it.

Tea drinking, painting by Nazar Saleem, 1925-82. iraqiart.com

589

Dried Lime Tea
(Chai Noomi Basrah or Chai Hamudh)

Naturally dried limes, *noomi Basra,* are imported from east Asia to Iraq via the only port city in the country, Basrah (see Glossary). They make a refreshing sweet and sour hot drink tremendously popular throughout the entire region. It is usually served in the traditional Iraqi small transparent glass, *istican.* Here is a recipe for making tea enough for 4 to 6 people:

1. Crack **3 dried limes**. Take all seeds out, as they tend to make tea develop a bitter taste. Put prepared lime in a medium teapot and fill it up to three-quarters with boiling water. Let it brew gently on low heat until it starts to boil, about 5 minutes. Serve the tea sweetened with sugar. If you find it too sour for your taste, dilute it with boiling water. This tea can also be served cold with some ice-cubes, just like the American iced tea.

Cinnamon Tea
(Chai bil Darseen)

Make regular tea as directed above and add to it a small stick of cinnamon or 1 teaspoon ground cinnamon. Let it simmer gently with the tea.

Licorice Tea
(Chai Irg al-Soos)

Though licorice is more commonly consumed as a cool refreshing drink, it also makes a healthy and soothing warm drink. The medicinal qualities of this root have been recognized ever since ancient times in the region. In *The Assyrian Herbal*, a monograph on Ancient vegetable drugs, licorice was mentioned as a healer for asthma, dry cough, and pectoral diseases, among other things. Even the name itself has undergone little changes. What was known as "susu" in the Akkadian is now *sous* (for more details see Glossary).

To prepare this ancient delicious tea, simply mix 1 teaspoon dried orange peel with 1 teaspoon of broken licorice root, and brew like regular tea. Combining equal amounts of licorice root, cinnamon, aniseeds, orange peel, chamomile, and cloves will make even a more aromatic tea. Brew as for regular tea.

Hibiscus Flower Tea
(Chai Koujarat)

Dried Hibiscus flowers make a delicious and beautiful ruby-colored translucent tea. In other parts of the Arab world it is known as *karkady*. At teahouses (*chaikhana*) it is served along with the regular tea and coffee, but at a little higher price. Besides its delicious taste, it has other medicinal benefits. It is believed that it helps women feel comfortable with their sexuality, particularly those who have suffered trauma in the past and are unable to express warmth and love (McIntyre, 42).

To make this exotic herbal tea, put about 1 tablespoon hibiscus flower and a little hot water in a teapot to rinse the flowers and heat the pot. Pour off water quickly but leave the hibiscus in the teapot. Add about 2 cups boiling water and let brew very slowly for about 15 minutes. Serve with sugar to taste. This tea can also be served cold with ice-cubes.

Tea brewing on steam

591

Reading fortune in coffee dregs

Arabic Coffee
(Gahwa Arabiya)

The following is a basic amount enough to make one *finjaan* of coffee. It is traditionally made in a *dalla*, a small long-handled container with a wide base that tapers at the top. A small saucepan with a pouring tip may be substituted.

1 heaping teaspoon finely ground coffee (not instant)
1 level teaspoon sugar, or to taste
1 *finjaan*, (small coffee cup) or 1/3 cup water
    A pinch of ground cardamom, optional

Put coffee, sugar and water in the *dalla*. Stir with a teaspoon to allow sugar and coffee to dissolve a little. Bring to a boil on medium heat, stirring occasionally until coffee starts to rise, and the surface develops a creamy frothy "face." To extract maximum flavor from coffee, as soon as it starts to rise, take *dalla* off heat and allow it to recede, then put it back on heat and let it rise again. Repeat this procedure three times, but avoid letting coffee over boil. Making this coffee takes only a few minutes, so watch it. If it is allowed to boil, coffee will lose its "face" and that's a shame, for Arabic coffee without a face is nothing to be proud of.

If making more than one serving, distribute creamy froth evenly among small cups first, then pour rest of coffee to fill cups almost to the rim.

Note: The thick dregs that will eventually settle down in the bottom of the cup after serving it are not to be sipped. But, by all means, as soon as you are done drinking your coffee, twirl the remaining coffee in your *finjaan*, turn it upside down on the saucer, making a wish while doing so. Wait for about 10 minutes to allow dregs to settle, then ask the *finjaan*-reader in the gathering to read your fortune in it.

Coffee and Tea for the Record

Tea and coffee are so essential in our lives today that one might think that they have been around more than they really are. The beginnings of the cultivation of coffee shrubs, to begin with, are obscure but now we know that the world is indebted to Africa for the coffee bean, such as the Abyssinian (Ethiopian) province of **Caffa**, from which the name of coffee was derived. The Arabs got their coffee beans from Abyssinia across the Red Sea to Arabia through its port of **Mocha** (which gave coffee its second name), and cultivated it in Arabia. Coffee beans cultivated in Yemen were and still are valued for their high quality.

The coffee berries were at first eaten as paste, but the Arabs soon learnt how to brew them as a beverage, which happened around the ninth century. The coffee drink was valued as a stimulant and was called the wine of the faithful, because it had the power to keep worshippers awake and alert. The physicians who believed in the theory of the four humors, wet (water), dry (air), hot (fire) and cold (earth) recommended coffee to dry out humors. They also believed it eliminated constipation and provoked urination, besides other benefits. With such a reputation, I find it rather odd that little mention was made of it in the medieval literature. In the *Arabian Nights*, for instance, while a lot of wine drinking takes place despite the fact that it was a prohibited activity in Islam, not a single mention to drinking coffee was made, or at least as far as I could detect. In al-Warraq's tenth-century huge volume of recipes, only a single mention was made of it, and in passing. It occurs in a poem composed around the ninth century by Abu al-Faraj who describes a day out in the famous picnic spot outside Baghdad, called Huraqa. As a finale to a fresh and satisfying meal in the outdoors, a slave boy, as graceful as a gazelle, serves them piping hot coffee that is reddish-brown in hue, just like the cheeks of the boy who brought it (al-Warraq, 118).

For several centuries coffee drinking was known in the Arab Moslem world only. But it was soon to spread out, and with it spread the coffeehouses, first in Mecca and Medina, then to Cairo, Damascus in Syria. It reached Constantinople in 1554, and from there it spread to other parts of the world (Wason, 149, 152-3, Brothwell, 172-3).

As for tea, in its region of origin, China, it was not until the fourteenth-century AD that the Chinese started using leaf tea and brewed it as we do today. Prior to that, it was compressed into bricks, and crushed to powder that was put in boiling water in cauldrons. By 1500 the first teapots as we know them were made. The white porcelain teacups were favored for they flattered the red-brown color of brewed tea. By the beginning of the seventeenth century, tea reached Europe via the Dutch traders. As for the Middle East, there is no definite date for its arrival, but we do know that the Arabs and Turks were acquainted with it from their trade dealings with the Chinese, and brought it home with them along the Silk Road (Brothwell, 172).

Cold Drinks

Back in the ancient Mesopotamian times the sweet water of the Tigris and Euphrates was part of the meal, and there is evidence that special vessels for chilling water were known. A very simple device was used to filter and keep water cool. Water was poured into a porous unglazed clay vessel, which in turn was placed within a second glazed vessel to retain the filtered water that slowly seeped through the walls of the inner container. Some of this filtered water would inevitably evaporate in the process and keep the water cool. Many earthenware vessels with pointed bottoms were excavated, and it was noted that they must have been placed upon stands of wood or plaited straw. Such simple cooling techniques never fell out of use in rural areas up until now and in the cities up until the early 19-sixsties. The vessel is called *hub* in the modern Iraqi vernacular, a name that evidently goes back to medieval times and possibly earlier. It is a huge porous clay receptacle usually seated on a wooden stand. The water seeping through the pores of the container would evaporate and keep water inside it cool. A small clay pot, called *al-nagout* (the dripper), is put underneath the *hib* to receive the filtered drops of water falling from the bottom of the *hib*. Water accumulated in this pot is exemplary in its purity.

During the summer nights when people sleep on the flat roofs, smaller porous clay jars, called *tunga,* were put on the low walls of the roof, and the mouths of these containers would be covered with a piece of muslin to keep water clean. In the tenth-century Baghdadi cookbook, water cooled this way was called "air-cooled water."

Ice-cold water was also known ever since ancient times, and during the Middle Ages it was a very popular drink. People used to serve it sometimes perfumed, as we indeed still do, with a little of rose water and cardamom. However, the medieval Baghdadi cookbooks caution against drinking too much ice-water with a meal, since it might cause indigestion. Besides ice-cold water Al-Warraq gives many recipes of drinks made from milk and yogurt, or fruit juices from grapes, carrots and lemons, and some alcoholic drinks. Most of these thirst-quenching drinks were flavored with a variety of aromatics such as rose water, saffron and mastic.

Ice itself was brought down to Baghdad from the mountains in the north of the region, it was transported packed in lead ice-boxes and was stored in special basements to be used year round, but especially during the summer.

Nowadays the most popular cold beverage, besides water, is a yogurt drink called *shineena*. It is usually served with the meals, especially in the summer. The *sherbets* (cordials), diluted fruit syrups served with cubes of ice, are definitely the drinks for happy occasions, such as weddings, circumcisions, birthdays and graduations. In the ancient scene juices of fruits like apple, fig, pomegranate and grape, were evidently popular but it is not known whether they were consumed fresh or as cordials. Although nowadays no one would think of making fig juice, for instance, pomegranate juice on the other hand, is still very popular. Up until the near past it was common to see licorice-drink peddlers in the *sougs* (market places) carrying a beautifully decorated container on his back, and tinkling with his small brass bowls to attract attention to his merchandise. Another welcome sight in summer is the tamarind-drink stalls where sweetened tamarind drink is served with lots of crushed ice, much like slush.

As for alcoholic drinks, on the land of barley and dates it should not be surprising that beer and *arak* are the sort of alcoholic drinks consumed in the region. The *arak* is distilled from fermented dates. It looks like clear water when bought, and it comes flavored with mastic. It is not for nothing that it is nicknamed "the lion's milk." Firstly, it looks like milk when diluted, and secondly, it is very strong and crude, and is definitely a man's drink, and a lion-man at that. No self-respecting woman would be caught drinking it. Since abundance of grapes also grow in the region, especially in the north, wine is made for local consumption, especially at monasteries. However the whole region is mostly populated by Moslems, and with the restrictions on the consumption of alcohol, alcoholism is not one of the major social problems, although such problems do exist.

A Sumerian Party
A modern impression of a Sumerian cylinder seal (3rd millennium BC)
Celebrants are imbibing beer through tubes. The lower register depicts people playing music and dancing, and quite possibly singing. University of Pennsylvania Museum of Archaeology and Anthropology.

A Tipsy story

Beer was the drink of choice at the ancient Mesopotamian homes, consumed on daily basis by men and women alike. They believed that it brought joy to the heart and happiness to the liver, and when a new building was built the first brick to be used was made from clay mixed with honey, wine and beer. Another reason for its popularity could simply be attributed to the fact that though water was abundant in the area there was always the fear that it might be contaminated, what with all the laundering and leather tanning that was going on in the rivers (Mieroop, 159).

The earliest beer was Sumerian. Around 40 % of their barley yield was used for beer production, and by the third millennium they knew how to make different kinds of the drink by using a variety of techniques in soaking, crushing, fermenting or sweetening the product. The added spices such as cassia, oils, and aromatic plants helped in its preservation and improving its flavor. They made ordinary and first quality beer, clear and dark, freshly brewed and well-aged, sweet and pleasant with honey and grape juice, and bitter beer. Interestingly the oldest sign for brewer in the Sumerian language had the ideogram for "shim", which stands for "aromatic plant" (cf. Arabic *shim* which is 'to smell'). (Limet, 145, Levey, 55-6)

Brewing beer and drinking, or I might say guzzling it, was an important activity in their lives for it was occasionally depicted in their art. Due to the way beer was made, it came with sediments that had to be filtered while drinking it. For this they used special long tubes made of reeds, with perforated ends. The wealthy coated theirs with gold. As depicted in their seals it was the custom to drink beer from a communal vat.

The oldest beer recipe comes in a Sumerian hymn written around 2800 BC. It is dedicated to the goddess of brewing, appropriately named Nincasa, "the lady that fills the mouth." Brewing was the only craft that was patronized by a female goddess, simply because it was practiced by women only. We know for sure that around 1800 BC, during the rule of King Hamourabi, women were responsible for selling and running alehouses. In his legal code, Hamourabi condemned alewives who over-charge, by throwing them into water. They were also responsible for reporting any illegal activities in their taverns, otherwise they would be burned to death. "Sisters of gods" (priestesses) were prohibited from opening a tavern or frequenting any. The penalty for this was burning to death.

Wine from dates, raisins, and dried figs were also made and were sold in the ancient streets of Mesopotamia by wandering vendors. Wine from grapes was made annually, and was stored in sealed jars. However, it was not as affordable as beer, and there was not enough for the masses. Cultivating grapes was known in Mesopotamia as early as the third millennium BC, especially in the northern regions, that's why it was sometimes called the "mountain beer" (Nemet-Nejat, 158). Many of the early kings and governors recorded that they built irrigated vine terraces, and Sargon II had extensive wine cellars. Mesopotamian wine was reputed to be so good that the king of Ceylon used to import it from Iraq.

But beer remained the drink of the common people until cereals came to be of more value as food, when irrigation spoiled the soil and grain became more difficult to grow. At that stage, the Meopotamians changed their drinking habits and started to drink more of date wine, also called beer, which finally became the most common alcoholic drink.

A Babylonian Cure for the Tipsy

The ancient Mesopotamians used to consume beer, and sometimes wine, on daily basis. In their recorded literature one often comes across descriptions of stages, symptoms, and even warning signs of intoxication. In the poem of the Creation, during a banquet, the gods become talkative and excited under the influence of alcohol. In the *Epic of Gilgamesh*, the temple prostitute introduces Enkido, who is destined to be Gilgamish's companion, to civilization by saying:

"Eat bread, Enkido, the glory of life,
Drink wine, Enkido, the custom of the land."
Then Enkido ate bread till he was full,
Then drank wine, seven beakers.
His spirit loosed itself, he grew merry,
His heart rejoiced and his face glowed
(10-1)
Generally speaking heavy drinking was not frowned at, provided it did not impair their judgment. The intoxicating effects of alcohol were well known and were taken quite seriously.
Drunkenness was treated as a case of poisoning. Here is the diagnosis and the cure:

If a man has drunk too much strong wine, if his head is confused, if he forgets his words, and his speech becomes blurred, if his thoughts wander, and his eyes are glassy, the cure is to take [here follows a prescription containing 11 drugs] and to mix them with oil and wine at the approach of the goddess Gulal [i.e. in the evening]: in the morning before sunrise, and before anyone has kissed the patient [here we learn it was the custom to exchange good-morning kisses] let him take the draught. He will recover (Contenau, 64).

A Wine Recipe from Tenth-century Baghdadi Cookbook

Many recipes for making wine were given in al-Warraq's medieval cookbook despite the fact that the Qur'an strongly stands against consumption of alcoholic drinks. The following recipe calls for raisins and honey as fermenting agents:

Put 50 *ratls* (50 pounds) of raisins, and 30 *ratls* honey in a big pot. Add half the amount of these, water (i.e. 40 *ratls*), and bring to a boil and let cook well. Then strain the mixture, and add 5 *dirhams* (about 15 grams) saffron, and 3 *dirhams* (about 9 grams) mastic, and 1 *daniq* (1/2 gram) *misk*. Put in bottles, and let stay in a shaded place for 40 days, then use (309).

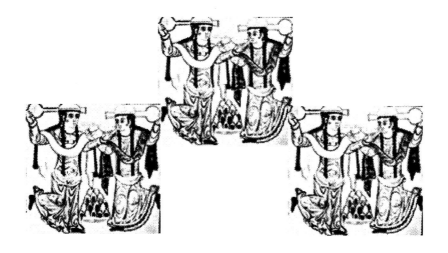

The following are recipes for some of the refreshing and delicious drinks the Iraqi cuisine offers:

Yogurt Drink
(Shineena)

To make one glass of this drink, dilute yogurt, any kind will do, with cold water, in the ratio of 1 part yogurt to 3 parts water. Add a pinch of salt if using plain yogurt. Whisk to create foam. Serve with a few cubes of ice, and garnish with a sprig of mint. Serve immediately, otherwise water will separate from yogurt. If this happens, give it a stir or a whisk before serving.

Fruity Drinks

Cold fruit drinks are made in a variety of ways. They may be made from *Fresh Juices,* **or** *Fresh Fruit Syrups,* **or** *Preserved Fruit syrups.*

1. Fresh Juices
(Aseer)

The most popular juices are orange and carrot in the wintertime, and cantaloupe and pomegranate in the summer. In making pomegranate juice, only the seeds are used since the rind and membranes would make the drink rather bitter if crushed with the seeds. A regular juicer is used to extract juice from seeds.

Cantaloupe Drink:

3 pounds cantaloupe (honeydew melon can be substituted)
1 cup sugar, or to taste

3 cups cold water
1/2 cup fresh lemon or lime juice

Crushed ice, or cubed ice
1 tablespoon rose water
Sprigs of mint for garnish

1. Remove skin and seeds from cantaloupe and cut it into 1-inch pieces to measure 6 cups. Puree with sugar in blender or food processor, in batches, until completely smooth.

2. Pour mixture into a container and stir in cold water, and lemon juice, and refrigerate. To serve, stir in ice and rose water, pour into glasses, and garnish with mint sprigs.

2. Fresh Fruit Syrups

Homemade quick and delicious drinks are far more superior to commercially prepared powders or solutions since they partially contain fresh juices that are not spoiled by boiling. However, these drinks are for the same day's consumption. The possibilities for garnishing them are endless. Here are a few suggestions:

* Give serving glasse an attractively festive look by dipping the rim in shallow water then dipping it immediately in colored sugar. Set aside to dry. You can make your own collection of colored sugar. Simply put some granulated sugar in a small plastic bag, add a few drops of food coloring, and shake the bag. Put sugar in a dish to dry.
* Put a few drops of food coloring to the water you intend to freeze, and use as ice cubes with the drink. This needs planning ahead of time so that color of ice cubes may match color of drink.
* Add some of the juice to the ice before freezing it.
* Before freezing the ice add to it chunks of the fruit you are going to serve as a drink.

Lemon Drink (Sharab al-Leymoun):

1/2 cup sugar
1/2 cup water
A few strips of the lemon rind, only the yellow part

1 cup fresh lemon or lime juice
A few drops green food coloring and rose water or orange blossom water

1. In a small pot make simple syrup by mixing sugar, water and rind. Bring mixture to a quick boil, then let cook for 5 minutes. Cool completely. Add fresh juice and food coloring and rose water.

2. To serve dilute solution with cold water, to taste, with cubes of ice.

Variations:

Lemon Soda Drink: Make your own soda drink. Simply dilute drink not with water but with plain soda water. Serve immediately with colored ice cubes.

Orange Drink: Substitute 2 cups orange juice for lemon juice, and use orange rind, and orange food coloring.

The First Drinking "Straw" in History

Due to the way beer was fermented in ancient Mesopotamian, it came with sediments which were removed by strainers and funnels. The most elaborate examples of such devices were found in the royal tombs of Ur. In order to get rid of the remaining sediments, they used to drink beer through filtering tubes. Thus, driven by necessity, they invented the first drinking "straw" in history.

Red Mulberry Drink (Sharab Tuki'l Sham):

Although this drink is traditionally made with red mulberries, any other kind of juicy berries may be substituted.

3/4 cup sugar
3/4 cup water
2 cups red mulberry juice
1/2 cup lemon juice

Make simple syrup by boiling water and sugar in a small pot, for 5 minutes. Cool completely. Add mulberry juice and lemon juice. To serve, dilute with cold water, to taste, with red-colored cubes of ice.

Beet Drink (Sharaab al-Shuwander):

This drink might sound unusual, but on the land of Mesopotamia it is a very common homemade drink, delicious, healthy, and easy to prepare.

3 cups liquid reserved from boiling beets that are *peeled and washed before boiling*
1/2 cup sugar, or to taste
1/4 cup lemon juice
1 teaspoon rose wate

Dissolve sugar in beet juice while it is still hot. Cool completely. Add lemon juice, and rose water, and serve cold.

Medieval Thirst-quenching Drinks

In al-Warraq's tenth-century Baghdadi cookbook several chapters are allotted to drinks of different types, that help quench the thirst and refresh the body in the heat of summer. Some of them are made from fresh fruits such as apple, lemon, quince, pomegranate, plum, apricot, and unripe grapes. All these drinks are sweetened with honey and flavored with spices such as cloves, cinnamon, mastic, and saffron (314-315).

There are also recipes for syrups made from fruits such as apples and quince, that are diluted with chilled water when ready to serve, exactly as we still do today. An interesting cocktail is made of 20 *ratls* (20 pounds) sugar, and 100 *dirham* (about 300 grams) juice of *jummar* (date palm hearts), and 2 *ratls* (2 pounds) poppy seeds. Bring these to a boil, then add 5 *ratls* (5 pounds) grape juice, 2 *ratls* (2 pounds) mulberry juice, and 1/2 *dirham* (1 1/2 grams) camphor. They are boiled until reduced to syrup, then kept in bottles until needed (307).

شَرِابْت

3. Preserved Fruit Syrups (Cordials) (Sherbet)

Sherbet is preserved syrup made from fruits, and is usually kept in sealed bottles. When served it is diluted with cold water to taste, with a few cubes of ice. It is an elaboration on the medieval *julab*, made of simple syrup scented with rose water, that was either diluted with water and served as a refreshing drink, or added to pastries instead of honey (see p. 467, for more details).

Because these concentrated syrups keep very well, a bit of summer delights can always be preserved for year-round enjoyment. They are usually purchased in sealed bottles, and a bottle or two of these syrups would make an acceptable present when visiting a friend at a hospital or as a simple graduation gift, for instance. However, homemade syrups are far more economical and tastier than the commercial variety. Here are recipes for some of the unusual flavors that are not readily available in the markets:

Syrup for Red Mulberry Sherbet:

For each cup of strained mulberry juice, use 1 cup sugar. Dissolve sugar completely in juice. Heat up mixture. Put pot away from heat before syrup starts to boil. Cool, then keep in sterilized bottles and seal with melted wax. To serve, dilute required amount with cold water, to taste, with ice cubes or crushed ice.

The same can be done with berries like strawberries, blackberries and raspberries.

Syrup for Tamarind Sherbet:

Tamarind drink is very delicious and healthy. The vendors make it doubly attractive by filling the glass with finely crushed ice scooped from a mound of crushed ice kept in a glass container. The following recipe calls for dried compressed tamarind, available in Middle-Eastern or Indian grocery stores. **Tamarind concentrate** may be substituted. For a glass of this refreshing drink use 1 teaspoon tamarind concentrate and 1 1/2 teaspoons sugar, or to taste. Dilute with cold water and serve with crushed or cubed ice.

8 ounces dried tamarind, broken to small pieces
4 cups sugar
1/4 cup lemon juice

1. Soak tamarind in enough water to cover it. Set it aside overnight.

2. Boil tamarind with the water in which it was soaked until mushy. Strain, pressing with back of a spoon against the sieve to squeeze down all juice.

3. Measure strained liquid to see how much plain water you need to add to make a total of 6 cups. Do not mix yet.

4. Add sugar to measured water and dissolve and boil until medium syrup is formed.

5. Add tamarind juice to syrup and let mixture boil for 5 minutes.

6. Add lemon juice and boil for 5 more minutes. Cool, bottle, and seal with wax. To serve dilute required amount with cold water, to taste, with ice cubes or crushed ice.

Syrup for Almond Sherbet (Sherbet al-Lowz):

I got hooked on this milky refreshing drink at quite an early age when I used to accompany my mother on her monthly visitations to a pleasant, well-to-do distant relative, to pay the house rent, and to have a chat with her. I always looked forward to these visitations for the house she lived in was huge and traditionally built with an open yard in the middle, at the center of which there was a small garden and a basin with a fountain. One of her daughters was my age, and there in the orchard we used to play with a doll's house her father made for her, and sweep around it with tiny charming sweeps made from date palm fronds. Every time we were there, we were offered delicious and milky almond drink, flavored with a little rose water.

8 ounces almonds (about 1 /12 cups)
3 cups sugar
1/4 cup lemon juice
1/2 teaspoon almond extract
1 tablespoon rose water

1. In a medium pot cover almonds with water and cook for five minutes. Remove skins and wash in cold water. Dry almonds well then grind.

2. Add 2 1/2 cups boiling water to ground almonds, let steep for 5 minutes, stirring occasionally. Strain in a sieve fitted on a big bowl.

3. Add 2 1/2 cups boiling water to the strained ground almonds, and repeat procedure in step 2.

4. Repeat same procedure described in step 2, but this time add 3 cups boiling water to get a total of 8 cups of strained liquid.

5. Add sugar to strained liquid and dissolve by stirring. Add lemon juice, almond extract, and rose water. Cool, bottle, and seal with wax. To serve dilute required amount with cold water, to taste, with ice cubes or crushed ice.

Syrup for Pomegranate Sherbet (Sherbet al-Rumman):

Fresh pomegranate yields an exotic drink that unfortunately cannot be enjoyed fresh for long, since its season is relatively short. Preserving it this way will enable you to have it whenever you feel like it.

2 cups pomegranate juice
3 cups sugar
1/4 cup lemon juice

1. Use juicer to extract juice from pomegranate seeds (discard rind and membranes before juicing to prevent the drink from getting bitter).

2. Gradually add sugar, and dissolve completely by stirring.

3. Add lemon juice and mix well. Bottle and seal with wax. To serve dilute required amount with cold water, to taste, with ice cubes or crushed ice.

Sit at dinner tables and socialize as long as you can for these are the bonus times of your lives. (Al-Hasan bin Ali bin Abi-Talib, one of the prophet's grandsons)

SUGGESTED MENUS

Food: that's the thing! Drink: that's the thing!

(A Sumerian saying, ca 3500 BC, Gordon, 142)

In preparing a meal from a foreign cuisine, it is essential to know what combination of dishes will make an authentic lunch or dinner. The following are suggested menus for different meals and seasons. Recipes of dishes mentioned below are given in their respective chapters.

Breakfast

Sweet hot tea is always served with breakfast, and some people prefer to have it mixed with a little milk. Canned condensed sweetened milk might sometimes replace fresh milk.

Typical Summer Breakfasts:
*White cheese, warm bread, slices of cucumber, fresh mint, and olives.
*White cheese, warm bread, and cubed watermelon.

Typical Winter Breakfasts:
Bastirma (Iraqi sausages) with eggs, warm bread, and sliced salad vegetables.
Geymer (thick cream), or butter, warm bread, with date syrup or jam.
*Fried eggs, sunny side up, sliced tomatoes browned in a little oil, and warm bread
*White cheese or canned cheddar cheese (Kraft) sandwich, with hot sweet tea.

Weekend Brunch

Late breakfasts are normally reserved for Fridays, the one-day weekend of the week. They can be vegetarian or with meat.

Kahi (baked or fried thin layers of dough drenched in light syrup, and served with a slab of *geymer*), bought from special bakeries. Hot tea.

Tashreeb Bagilla (dried fava beans with flat bread), slices of salad vegetables, pickles, and sweet hot tea.

Hareesa (porridge of shelled wheat, cooked with or without meat), and tea.

Chilifry (cubed meat simmered in vegetable sauce), warm bread, sliced salad vegetables, and tea.

Makhlama (egg omelet) in any of its varieties, with warm bread, slices of salad vegetables, and lots of herbs and greens. Hot sweet tea.

"Fast Food Restaurants" of The Arabian Nights

In an *Arabian Nights* story, a young man, called Judar, was given magic saddlebags that provided whatever dishes one asked for. He went to his mother and asked her to wish for a dish. She wished to have hot bread and a slice of cheese, a simple meal that befitted her social status as a poor old woman. The son, however, had a surprise feast for her, more luxurious and more expensive. "O my mother, what suit thine estate are **browned meat** and **roast chicken** and **peppered rice** [*ruz mufalfal*]. And it becometh thy rank to eat of **sausages** and **stuffed cucumbers** [actually stuffed gourds] and **stuffed lamb** and **stuffed ribs of mutton** and **vermicelli with broken almonds and nuts and honey and sugar** [*kunafa*], and **fritters** [qata'if] and **almond cakes** [baklawa]" (Burton, vol. 6, 235-6).

The way the saddle worked was that after the eater had satisfied his or her appetite, the only thing to do was to empty leftovers into other dishes, (a doggy bag!) and return dirty platters to the saddlebags. It was as easy as that, no waiters to be tipped nor bills to be paid.

An illustration of the hand washing machine in al-Jazari's Book of Ingenious Devices, 1206, AD (Upper Mesopotamia.)
Library of Topqapu Serai, Istanbul.

Table Manners and the Custom of Washing the Hands Before and After Having a Meal

Although nowadays it is more customary among city-dwellers to use forks and spoons when having food, eating from communal dishes with the hand (actually with three fingers of the right hand) is still practiced in rural and Bedouin regions. To the novice it is not an easy task at all. Here is a description of the clumsy first attempts of an English man eating rice and stew with a group of marsh-dwellers, in southern Iraq:

> Eating the Arab manner requires to be learnt, and at the beginning I found it humiliatingly impossible...the fingers enclose the rice, and when the hand reaches the mouth the thumb pushed the rice up into it--if, that is to say, there is any rice left to push. The first evening, I found, there rarely was. The mere fact of being cross-legged made the rice a disconcertingly long way off, and no matter how large a handful I set out with, so to speak, it had dwindled to a few grains by the time the hand reached the mouth (Maxwell, 24-5).

Besides, eating from a communal dish using the hands necessitates the act of washing the hands before and after eating. In *The Arabian Nights* there is so much feasting, eating, drinking and carousing going on. However, with all these gastronomical activities, washing the hands before and after the meals is like a ritual that *Shehrezad*, our story teller, never fails to make mention of, albeit in passing, whenever her characters have some food. The following story of a reeve, tells of what happened when the guy neglected this ritual:

On the wedding night of a reeve to a beautiful damsel, he was presented with a pungent dish for his dinner. It was *zirbajah*, marinated meat dressed with vinegar, hot spices and lots of cumin seeds. The reeve said, "they set before me a tray of food whereon were various meats and among those dishes, which were enough to daze the wits, was a bowl of cumin-ragout containing chickens' breasts, fricandoed (*muhammarah*) and flavored with sugar, pistachios, musk and rose-water." He ate of it and wiped his hands, but forgot to wash them. Then, he continues, "When I found myself alone with her on the bed I embraced her, hardly believing in our union; but she smelt the strong odors of the ragout [stew] upon my hands and forthwith cried out with exceeding loud cry, at which the slave-girls came running to her from all sides." To give him an unforgettable lesson, he had his thumbs and great toes cut off. The punishment definitely sounds cruel to us but it does show how essential washing the hands was to these people (Burton, vol. 1, 278-80).

The tenth century Baghdadi cookbook dedicates two chapters on table manners that stem from the custom of eating from communal dishes. Hand washing is strongly stressed, and perfuming them with rose water, mask or ambergris after the meal was recommended. While eating, one is required to talk as little as possible, lest some food particles should splatter while one is talking. On the other hand there are those who encourage conversations at dinner tables, and consider them an integral part of a hospitable meal.

One should not covet what is not in front of him. Chicken should be cut into parts using a knife and not pulled apart with the hands. Dipping a piece of bread again into the sauce after biting it was severely criticized. It is not good manners to look at a person while eating. It is said of the Ummayad Caliph Mu'awiya that once he was having dinner with a Bedouin. When the latter lifted a morsel of food up to his mouth, the caliph told him to remove a hair that was in his food. The Bedouin was offended and left abruptly saying that the caliph has no business, in the first place, looking at the food he was eating.

Protocols of Treating Dining Guests

One of the traditional protocols of dining is that the host and hostess should wait on the dining guests, and are to eat only when all their guests' needs are satisfied. It is the custom, too, that the host and hostess should urge their guests to eat more of the food, and should not accept, "no" for an answer.

Traditionally the host's generosity and hospitality is, quite often than not, measured by the variety of the foods offered and its quantity. That is why, for instance, it is not comely to serve the crunchy crust of the rice, delicious as it is, because it would be an indication that what you see of the rice on the table is all that there is, and this is not supposed to be.

Our Sumerian mothers have long ago set the rules of hospitality, as stated in the following Sumerian proverb:

Let it be plentiful -- lest there be too little!
Let it be more than enough -- lest it have to be added to!
Let it be boiling hot -- lest it get cold!
(Gordon, 465)

Lunch

In Iraq the main meal of the day is lunch, normally served around one o'clock. The meal is basically rice and stew, and variety is brought about by preparing a different stew for each day. Lunch comes with lots of greens and herbs, salad, and sometimes pickles. Supper is a lighter meal and is served around 8 o'clock. *Nawashif* (dry dishes) are the dishes usually served for this meal. However, for convenience sake, I'm suggesting some light lunch menus mostly soups and *nawashif* to fit in with the Western eating patterns, and will reserve the more serious stuff for dinner. (You can replace the suggested prepared desserts with seasonal fruits)

Summertime Lunch Menus:
*Rice with Fava Beans served with Yogurt sauce, *sanbousa* (pastries filled with meat or vegetables), a bowl of colorful tossed salad
Chilled cream-filled baklawa, with tea or coffee

Kebab (grilled ground meat), or *guss* (gyro) or falafel sandwich, with a glass of *shinina* (diluted yogurt), a small bowl of *taboula*
Chilled *mahallabi* (milk pudding), fresh fruits, tea or coffee

*Hummus with warm bread, a dish of dolma with yogurt sauce
Knafa (shredded dough filled with nuts or sweet cheese), or fresh fruits, tea or coffee

Misaka'a (fried eggplant slices drenched in yogurt sauce), with warm bread, lentil patties, or zucchini squares or pancakes
Pistachio ice cream, Arabic coffee

Wintertime Lunch Menus:
*Lentil soup with warm bread
Boureg (stuffed fillo dough) any of its varieties, with salad, any variety
Warm rice pudding, with tea or coffee

*Cream of Turnip and Swiss Chard soup, with warm bread
Iraqi Burgers sandwich, with a bowl of salad
A slice of cake with tea or coffee

*Spinach soup with warm bread
Cheese and macaroni casserole, or chicken and macaroni casserole
Stuffed dates or prunes, with Arabic coffee

*Tomato soup with rice
Kubbat Halab or any other variety of *kubba* (dough made from rice, potatoes, or bulgar, stuffed with meat mixture), a bowl of salad, any kind
Zlabia (fried fritters) or stuffed *qata'if* (Arabian pancakes) with Arabic coffee

Dinner
Simple menus for the family

For summer:

*Okra Stew with white rice, wedges of raw onion, lots of herbs and greens, and pickles.
Shinina (yogurt drink)
Simmered *loubya* (fresh black-eye beans, or string beans)
Water melon, and tea

*Sheikh Mahshi (stuffed eggplant), served with rice, or dolma. Salad, and pickles
Simmered fresh fava beans
Yogurt drink, with fresh dates
Tea

*Zucchini stew with rice. Salad and pickles
Kubba (dough stuffed with meat mixture), or *booreg* (stuffed fillo dough)
Yogurt drink
Any kind of *halawa* (candies and confections), or seasonal fresh fruits.
Tea

*Timman tacheena (rice cooked with vegetables and meat) in any of its varieties, with yogurt sauce.
Any kind of salad
Simmered *loubya* (fresh black-eye beans, or string beans)
Lemon drink
Cake, chilled cream-filled baklawa, or fresh fruits
Tea

*Mutabbag Samak (layered fish with spicy rice), with greens and herbs
Simmered *loubya* (fresh black-eye beans, or string beans)
Lemon drink
Water melon, and tea

For winter:

*White beans stew or spinach stew, with rice. Salad and pickles
Bourag (stuffed fillo dough)
Date sweetmeat, or any other kind of *halawa* (candy)
Tea

**Kubbat hamudh shalgham* (stuffed bulgar dough with turnip soup), with warm bread, and greens and herbs
Any of the syrupy desserts with tea or Arabic coffee

*Chicken simmered in tomato sauce with rice or bulgar of your choice
Salad and pickles
Potata chap (potato dough stuffed with meat mixture)
Halawa of golden vermicelli noodles, seasonal fruits, and tea
*Eggplant casserole with stuffed bulgar dough discs, served with rice or bread. Greens and herbs

Fresh green beans simmered in olive oil
Fruit, or any of the syrupy desserts.

A Menu from the Arabian Nights

In one of *The Arabian Nights* stories, a table was set for dinner. In the middle of a big tray there was a china dish containing four chickens reddened with roasting and seasoned with spices. Around this center piece four saucers were arranged: one containing sweetmeats, another conserve of pomegranate-seeds, a third almond pastry (*baklawa*), and a fourth honey fritters (*zlabia*), and pudding yellowed with saffron (*zarda*, Burton, vol.2, 311).

Dinner Menus for More Formal Occasions

As is the custom with people in the Arab world, a variety of dishes are prepared for the guests. With the exception of dessert, all the major dishes would be spread on the table for guests to make their pick. If you wish, bring food to the table course by course, after the medieval Baghdadi fashion, beginning with the appetizers and *bawarid* and *nawashif* dishes (cold and sauceless), followed by the main hot dishes, and ending with dessert and coffee.

*Drained yogurt rolled in nuts and za'atar and served with warm bread
Hummus or *baba ghanouj* (baked puréed eggplant with tahini), served with warm bread
Biryani or *parda palaw* (rice pies), served with stew of your choice
Colorful tossed salad
Breaded cauliflower or zucchini pancakes
Baklawa, tea or coffee

*Zucchini soup
Taboula, and *misaqa'a* (fried slices of eggplant drenched in yogurt sauce), served with warm bread
Aromatic shanks braised in vegetable sauce, served with rice of your choice
Chicken shish kebab on a bed of greens and herbs and onion relish. Serve with warm bread
Cake of your choice
Tea or coffee

*Lentil or mung bean soup
Beet salad, and eggplant simmered in olive oil, with warm bread
Grilled fish on a sea of amber (aromatic yellow rice), served with greens and herbs
Any variety of *boureg* (stuffed fillo dough)
Any variety of syrupy desserts
Tea or coffee

*Chicken soup with vegetables
Taboula and hummus with warm bread
Different kinds of *grilled* dishes, such as *kebab* (grilled ground meat), and *tikka* (grilled lamb cubes), served with warm bread, and lots of greens and herbs

Vermicelli and zucchini pancakes, lentil patties
Shinina (yogurt drink)
Znoud al-sit (cream-filled rolls, fried and dipped in syrup
Tea or coffee

*Drained yogurt with warm bread
Taboula and *misaqa'a* (fried slices of eggplant drenched in yogurt sauce), with bread
Leg of lamb in sweet and sour sauce, served with rice of your choice
Colorful tossed salad
Sindibad's seven-layered cake, with tea or coffee

A Representative Menu for Dinner during the Month of Ramadhan

*Fresh or dried dates with yogurt drink
*Lentil soup
*Stew (determined by the season), and rice, with fresh greens and herbs
Kebab (grilled ground meat), or *urug* (ground meat with chopped vegetables, made into patties and fried)
Kubba (dough made from rice, burgul or potatoes, filled with meat mixture, and fried)
Quamar al-deen sherbet (drink made from dried apricot), or tamarind drink. (These drinks are believed to be the best thirst quenchers)
*Tea
*Later in the night baklawa, and *zlabia* (fried fritters dipped in syrup)

Preparing a Big Meal for the Feast After Ramadhan

The place is al-Nuhra, a small village in southern Iraq; time is late 19-fifties; and the occasion is celebrating the end of *Ramadhan*, the month of fasting, by cooking a big feast for the sheik of the village, his guests and his tribesmen. As is the case anywhere else, at any given point in history, it is always the elite that enjoy the gourmet food, whereas the rest have to be content with simpler and more basic foods:

The women had been at work since five o'clock, but now at ten, instead of losing heart at the prospect of the 300 lunches to be served hot at noon, they were gayer than ever… For the feast, a cow and five full-grown sheep had been killed…The kidneys, liver, heart and brains were set aside for special dishes; the head, stomach and feet of three of the sheep were turned over to the skeik's daughter Samira, who would clean them and make them *patcha*, a local delicacy. The other two sheep were to be roasted whole over a charcoal spit and the eyes and ears offered as treats to the most honored guests.

The piles of slippery meat were washed and washed under the water tap, then went into salted water to be boiled until tender over fires of dried palm fronds that were blazing all over the eastern corner of the court. This boiled meat and its broth, together with bowls of vegetable stew, mounds of rice and piles of wheat bread, formed the meal, which would be served to the tribesmen.

The sun climbed higher, and the heat from the fires added to the general discomfort; the women were sweating profusely through their black garments. In one corner the sheik's daughters and their cousins were peeling squash, chopping spinach and cutting up onions and tomatoes for the vegetable stew, to be flavored with a bit of fat meat, garlic, salt, celery leaves and raw ground turmeric. Three women were mixing and patting barley dough into flat loaves; a small girl sat brushing the flies away from rows of plates of cornstarch pudding.

"What are you cooking?" I asked Alwiya, and she showed me into the kitchen, a long mud-brick room without smoke holes, where six or eight women were stirring and tending enormous pots cooking on open fires. The smoke hung in the room like dense fog, and the women would stir for a few moments, then walk to the door to wipe their streaming eyes and mop their sweat-streaked faces. Yet they laughed as they did so.

"These are the dishes for the sheik and the special guests," Alwiya said. This explained the women's good nature despite the heat and smoke. They had been chosen as the best cooks, to prepare food for Haji's tray.

"Don't stay in here, Beeja [Elizabeth]- it's too hot," warned Alwiya with a hand on my shoulder. But I wanted to see the food, so the pots were uncovered one by one: ground liver stewed with tomatoes, kubba, fried eggplant, patcha, saffron rice. Four chickens were being grilled over charcoal in the bank of round brick ovens along one side of the kitchen" (Fernea, 118 ff.).

615

Dinner Buffet

The following suggested dishes are ideal for buffet presentations for they will look good on the table, and will require the minimum of eating utensils. **Choice and number of dishes is determined by the occasion, number of guests, and your time:**

Hummus or *baba ghanouj* (mashed baked eggplant with tahini), served with bread
Drained yogurt, rolled in toasted nuts and za'atar, served with crackers or bread
Taboula, or lentil salad
Falafel, with a side of tahini sauce
Dolma
Sanbousa
Bourag (stuffed fillo dough rolls), or *fatayer* (stuffed triangles)
Kubbat Halab (rice dough stuffed with meat mixture) or *potata chap* (stuffed potato)
Casserole of green beans with cubed potatoes, served with rice of your choice
Casserole of cauliflower with meatballs, served with rice of your choice
Eggplant casserole with discs of stuffed bulgar dough, served with bread or white rice
Stuffed zucchini simmered in yogurt sauce
Kufta simmered in dill sauce, served with yellow rice, almonds and raisins
Sheikh mahshi (stuffed vegetables simmered in tomato sauce), with white rice
Biryani (spicy rice with meat), served with zucchini stew
Maqlouba (eggplant upside down) , served with yogurt sauce
Chicken drumsticks simmered in cumin sauce, served with white rice
Sweet and sour salmon simmered in almond-prune sauce. Serve with white rice
Cake, such as golden apple squares, prune cake, or pumpkin cake
Assortment of baklawa and *knafa*
Luqmat al-qadhi (the judge's morsel or fritters), stuffed *qata'if* (Arabian pancakes)
Tea and coffee

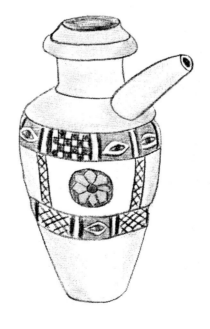

The Legendary Banquet of Ashurnasırpal II

The following banquet menu was found inscribed on a mud brick placed near the doorway to the throne-room of the palace of the Assyrian king Ashurnasirpal II (ninth century BC) in Kalhu near Nineva (also known as Nimrud). The cuneiform inscriptions tell of a huge feast thrown in celebration of the opening of the royal palace. Put exactly, he invited 69,574 guests from the surrounding countries as well as the people of Kalhu. The basic features of the banquet menu include the following:

*Meat dishes cooked from 1,000 fattened head cattle, 1,000 calves, 10,000 stable sheep, 15,000 lambs, and for the goddess Ishtar alone 200 head of cattle and 1,000 *sihhu*-sheep. 1,000 spring lambs, 500 stags, 500 gazelles, 1,000 ducks, 500 geese, 500 *kurku*-geese, 1,000 *mesuku*-birds, 1,000 *qaribu*-birds, 10,000 doves, 10,000 *sukanunu*-doves, 10,000 other assorted small birds, 10,000 assorted fish, 10,000 jerboa.

*10,000 assorted eggs.

*10,000 loaves of bread.

*10,00 jars of beer, 10,00 skins with wine.

*Side dishes such as pickles and spiced condiments made from a variety of seeds, sesame oil, vegetables, fruits, salted seeds, parched barley, garlic, turnip, spices, onion, nuts and olives.

*Desserts such as sweet fruits of pomegranates, grapes, dates, honey, rendered butter, milk, cheese, and shelled pistachio nuts.

* Perfumed oil, and sweet smelling matters.

We are also told that the guests wined and dined for ten days, and that they were provided with the means to clean and anoint themselves. Last but not least, the king declared that he did his guests due honors, and sent them back to their own countries, healthy and happy.

(Cited in Pritchard,102-4)

A modern impression of a Sumerian cylinder seal (3rd millennium BC).
It depicts a party scene in which the participants are women only. In the upper register, the attendant to the left is fanning her lady while the others are serving drinks.
In the lower register, some attendants are playing music, and others are serving food and drinks. The table is laden with bread, and fruit and meat (?). University of Pennsylvania Museum of Archaeology and Anthropology.

Suggestions for Tea Parties

Up until the early sixties, when society was still, relatively speaking, gender segregated, women used to hold their own tea parties, called *qaboul*. They were a kind of get-together parties usually held in the afternoons. Males in the family were kicked out of the house while the party was on. Thus women would feel free to discard their *abayas* (black cloaks covering the body from head to feet), and other head dresses. Some would sing or belly dance, whilst others would be cracking toasted water melon and pumpkin seeds. *Ka'ak* and *baqsam* (dunking sesame cookies) and *kleicha* (Iraqi traditional cookies) were the usual pastries offered and were washed down with hot sweet tea. In high-class *qabouls* an array of other food items is offered.

The following list includes both savory and sweet dishes, some are finger food and others might require a fork. **Number and kind of dishes chosen will be determined by the occasion, number of guests, and your time**.

618

Taboula
Baba ghanouj served in ridges of 1-inch long celery stalks
Lentil patties
Zucchini squares
Urug Musiliyya (baked mixture of meat and bulgar dough, cut into squares or wedges)
Dolma of grape leaves, simmered in olive oil
Spinach rolls
Sanbousa
Boureg (stuffed fillo dough rolls)
Olive bars
Dill weed balls
Kleicha (Iraqi cookies)
Any variety of the sweet cookies
Apricot balls (chapter on desserts)
Any variety of the cakes
Tea, coffee, or other beverages

Suggested Mezza Dishes

For drinking parties-- which are, by the way, exclusively men's parties-- a number of savory dishes are prepared. The word *mezza*, itself, is derived from the verb *mazza* (take in small dozes), or from the adjective *mazz* (sour). In their drinking parties, the medieval Baghdadis used to nibble on salted nuts such as almonds, pistachio, and hazelnuts, as well as raisins, sugar cane, sugar crystals, fruits such as jujube, quince, sour pomegranate, apples, and pears, and jerked meat. They called it *naql*, because while drinking they switched from wine to those goodies, and from those, back to wine.

Today's *mezza* dishes are similar to the *kawamikh* (condiments) and *bawarid* (cold) dishes the medieval diners used to have as a preliminary course, to whet the appetite. They were brought to the table in small bowls and consisted of a variety of dishes, seasoned with vinegar or juices of sour fruits. They could be pickles, dried fish, vegetables cooked in oil and vinegar, grilled meats served with sour-based *sawabigh* (sauces), or yogurt salads such as *jajiq* (for more information, see Introduction).

Mezza, as served today, might consist of any collection of the following:

Lablabi (chickpeas simmered to tenderness)
Bagilla (dried fava beans simmered to tenderness)
*Slices of pickled cucumber
*Leaves of romaine lettuce, and sliced cucumber
*Nuts such as pistachio, hazelnut, almonds, and peanuts
Taboula
*Hummus and *baba ghanouj*
*Sometimes grilled meat and lamb liver are also offered. Grilled sparrows when in season

A Ninth-Century AD Banquet Menu

This is a poem by Kushajim, a poet, astrologer, and culinary expert. It describes a banquet in which *bawarid* (cold) dishes were presented. It must have been a huge feast, judging from the number of the items served:

When to banquet we are eager
Well the table floweth o'er,
And the ready cook doth fill it
With the choicest foods in store

First a **roasted kid**, a yearling,
With its inwards firmly strung,
And upon it, well to season,
Tarragon and mint are hung.

Next a **chicken**, full and tender,
Fattened many moons agone,
And a **partridge**, with a **fledgling**,

Roast with care, and nicely done.

After **pastry of *tardina*** [ground meat, pressed thin and fried, like hamburgers]
Follows ***sanbusaj,*** *well* fried:
Eggs vermilioned after boiling
Lie with **olives** side by side.

Strips of tender meat in slices, [sandwiches]
Dipped [brushed] in oil of finest make,
Tempt anew the flagging palate,
And the appetite awakes;

Lemons, too, with *nadd* [a mixture of perfume] besprinkled,
Scented well with ambergris,
And, for garnishing the slices,
Shreds of appetizing **cheese**.

Vinegar that smarts the nostrils
Till they snuffle and they run;
Little **dates** like pearls that glisten
On a necklace one by one.

Sauce of *buran* served with **eggplant**,
That will tempt thy very heart,
And **asparagus**-- enchanted
With asparagus thou art!

Lastly, **Lozenge** [baklawa], soaked in butter,
Buried deep in sugar sweet.
(Arberry, 22-3)

RSVP

"I am going to have a house-warming," so goes the invitation, "come yourself to eat and drink with me. Twenty-five women and twenty-five men shall be in attendance."

This invitation was written by Kadasman-Enlil, king of Babylon about 3500 years ago, and sent to Akhenaten (Amenhotep IV) pharaoh of Egypt. It was written in the Akkadian, which at the time was an international language used by many countries with whom the Babylonians and Assyrians had relations (Hunter, 45)

GLOSSARY

The whole country is scented with them,
and exhales an odor marvelously sweet.

(Herodotus, 484-425 BC, writing on Near Eastern spices)

As far back as the Sumerian times the Iraqi cuisine had the tendency to use combinations of spices to add rich flavors to the food. From the culinary Sumerian records we learn that the "naga" was a seasoning for the poor, and the "gazi" was for the well-to-do families. According to a Sumerian proverb, "the poor man is the one who does not have the gazi when he has meat, nor does he have meat when he has gazi." Mills to grind spices and seeds reached a high degree of specialization in ancient Mesopotamia. The cumin mill, for instance, was different from the one used for crushing mustard seeds.

Today, if you stroll along *Souq al-Shorja,* a crowded roofed one-street spice bazaar in Baghdad, you'll fill your senses probably with the same aromas that Herodotus inhaled some 2500 years ago. They are the aromas of the *baharat* (mixed spices), cardamom, cinnamon, rose water, and mastic gum, to mention but a few.

Shopping. A painting by Badi'a Ameen. Permission, Altoma.

The following is a list of the most commonly used spices and ingredients, the majority of which are available at regular grocery stores. For ingredients unique to the Iraqi cuisine, more readily available substitutes are given, whenever possible.

Allspice (*kababa*) is a tropical spice that grows mainly in Jamaica and was introduced to the Old World by Columbus. The reddish-brown berries were mistaken for peppers at first and hence the Spanish name "pimiento," later Anglicized to pimento. Allspice has a pleasantly fragrant aroma that resembles a peppery compound of cloves, cinnamon, and nutmeg, and hence the name allspice. It is nice with meat dishes and used whole in pickles. It is better to buy the allspice berries whole and crush or grind them as needed.

Ambergris. See **Anber**

Anber. Waxy, grayish substance located in the intestines of sperm whales, and found floating at sea, or washed ashore. It is valued for its scent, and is added to perfumes to slow down evaporation.

Anise or Aniseed (*habbat hilwa* =sweet seeds). Botanically, this plant is related to caraway, cumin, dill, and fennel. It is one of the oldest spices known and is native to the Middle East. The ancient Mesopotamians valued it for its medicinal digestive property and the ancient Romans were accustomed to serve anise-spiced cakes after a rich meal. In Iraq it is sold at confectioneries as comfits in the shape of seeds coated with colored sugar, playfully called "mice droppings." The aniseeds are brownish-yellowish green. They are oval in shape but a little shorter and plumper than cumin seeds, and tend to have bits of tiny stalks attached to them. Anise tastes and smells rather sweet, and licorice-like. It is widely used in savory and sweet dishes, and in flavoring drinks and liqueurs. The anise oil is sometimes used instead of licorice root to give food a licorice flavor. Anise loses its aroma very quickly so it is better to buy it in small quantities and grind it as needed.

Apricot leather. See *quamar al-deen*.

Arrowroot is a starchy powder obtained from the dried cassava plant. It has no gluten and is mainly used in cooking as a thickener instead of cornstarch. The European settlers discovered it in the New World. The Arawak people who lived in the Caribbean Islands named the plant aru-aru, "meal of meals," because they thought highly of the starchy nutritious meal made from it. It was also used as a medicine to draw poison from wounds inflicted by poison arrows, and hence its name. It has almost no taste, and has more thickening power than flour or cornstarch. (1/2 teaspoon arrowroot=1 teaspoon cornstarch). Since it thickens at lower temperatures it can be used in delicate sauces without leaving that starchy taste characteristic of undercooked cornstarch. Arrowroot is used mostly as a thickener in making ice creams, which helps reduce amount of whipping cream used, and gives the ice cream a delightful chewiness. To use, dissolve amount required in a little cold water before adding it to hot mixtures. See also *sahlep*.

Baharat (from the old name of India, Bahar). It is all-purpose blend of spices, somewhat similar to the Indian **Garam Masala** (=mixture of spice). The medieval Baghdad cooks used a mixture of spices similar to what we are using nowadays. It was called *atraf al-teeb* (collection of aromatic spices) made of spikenard, bay leaves, nutmeg, mace, cardamom, cloves, rose hips, pepper, ginger, and other spices. You can buy *baharat* ground from gourmet shops, or make your own freshly ground blend. If you make a big amount, keep it in the freezer in a well-sealed plastic bag.

1/2 cup black pepper corns
1/3 cup cumin seeds
1/3 cup coriander seeds
1/3 cup cardamom pods
1/4 cup whole cloves
1/4 cup allspice berries
4 nutmegs, whole or 1/4 cup ground
1/4 to 1/2 cup ground chili, to taste
3 cinnamon sticks, 3 inches long, each
1/4 cup dried rose petals, optional
2 tablespoons ground ginger
1 tablespoon turmeric, optional

1. Dry toast pepper corns, cumin seeds, coriander seeds, cardamom pods, cloves, and allspice berries. Let cool. Grind in batches
2. Grate nutmeg separately and add it to the blend.
4. Mix all ingredients very well and store in an airtight container. It would stay fresher if stored in the freezer.

   If you are in a hurry and have no need for a big amount of the blend, just mix the already ground spices in the following proportions: (Makes about 1/2 cup)

2 tablespoons black pepper
1 1/2 tablespoon cumin
1 tablespoon coriander
1 tablespoon allspice
1tablespoon cinnamon
2 teaspoons cardamom
1 teaspoon cloves
1 teaspoon nutmeg
1/2 teaspoon chili
1/2 teaspoon ginger
1/2 teaspoon turmeric

Bulgar (*burgbul*) is a wheat product like cracked wheat but processed differently. Cracked wheat is made by crushing raw whole kernels, whereas bulgar is made from whole-wheat berries steamed first, dried and then crushed. It is available in 3 grinds: grind #1 is suitable for making *kubba* and *taboula*, and the coarser grinds #2 and #3 are suitable for making pilafs and soups.

Cardamom (*hayl*) is a key spice to the entire Middle Eastern cuisine. The Baghdadis like it so much they call it *teen al-Janna* (mud of Paradise). It is used in both savory and sweet dishes such as rice, meat dishes, desserts, as well as beverages such as tea and coffee. It is also used for medicinal purposes as a digestive agent and as a breath freshener. Among Bedouins the lavish use of cardamom in coffee offered to guests is an indication of generosity on the part of the host. Green cardamom is the best; the white variety is simply bleached green cardamom. It is agreeably aromatic and slightly camphorous, and when chewed its aroma lingers for a while. It is better to slightly dry toast the pods and cool before grinding them to bring out their flavor. If kept in sealed plastic bags and stored in the freezer, cardamoms will stay fresh for a very long time.

625

Cardamom and Nordic Breads

Have you ever wondered how cardamom, a typically Middle-Eastern spice, became one of the main spices used in the Scandinavian cuisine particularly in breads and pastries? Following is the story how such spices traveled to northern Europe as told by Judith Gabriel (*Aramco World*, Nov./ Dec., 1999):

More than a millenium ago, as fleets of Viking raiders were striking fear into the hearts of coast- and river-dwellers throughout western Europe, other Norsemen of more
mercantile inclination were making their way east. With no less boldness and stamina, bearing luxurious furs and enticing nodules of amber, they penetrated the vast steppes of what is today Ukraine, Belarus and Russia and entered Central Asia. There they met Muslim traders who paid for Norse wares with silver coins, which the Vikings themselves did not mint, and which they coveted.

Their routes were various, and by the ninth and tenth centuries, a regular trade network had grown up. Some Norsemen traveled overland and by river, while others sailed over both the black and Caspian Seas, joined caravans and rode camelback as far as Baghdad, which was then under Abbasid rule and populated by nearly a million souls. There, the Scandinavian traders found an emporium beyond their wildest dreams (37).

Carob was used in the Mesopotamian region ever since ancient times. In the Assyrian cuneiform tablets it is referred to as "harubu" (cf. the Arabic *kharoub*, or *Kharnoub*). It is also called Saint John's bread because of the legend that John the Baptist ate in the wilderness only the sweet carob pods and honey. The pulp from the carob-pods somewhat resembles the manna. Nowadays, carob powder is made from the dried pulp of carob beans, and is used sometimes in recipes as a substitute for cocoa and chocolate. The Arabs used to call the hard small seeds of the carob, cock's eyes, and it is believed that the seeds known as carats were the origin for the carat (= 4 grains), used in weighing precious stones.

Cassia is sometimes known as Chinese cinnamon. It is used interchangeably with cinnamon in Iraq, or simply sold as cinnamon. In appearance it is thicker and coarser than cinnamon, and its taste is less delicate. It is better suited to savory dishes like *Hareesa*, curried dishes or whenever savory dishes call for cinnamon.

How Cinnamon and Cloves Came into Being

Legend has it that when Adam was driven out of Paradise he landed on the Indian mountain, and there he remorsefully wept for a hundred years until his tears flew in Sarnadeeb valley. Out of his tears there grew cinnamon and cloves, and the valley's birds turned into peacocks. Then Gabriel came down and said unto Adam, "Raise your head for God has forgiven thee".

(Ibn al-Jawzi's *The Book of Anecdotes and Spiritual Medicine*, 15)

Chickpeas also known as **garbanzo beans**. They can be used whole or skinned and split (yellow or green). Whole chickpeas need to be soaked overnight. I always keep a bag or two of already soaked chickpeas in the freezer. They come in handy when preparing an unplanned recipe that calls for whole chickpeas. In fact you can do the same thing with all beans that require long hours of soaking. It is also a good idea to have a few cans of cooked chickpeas in the pantry for emergencies. You can make delicious hummus at five minutes' notice.

Chili (*filfil ahmer*). Columbus found it in the Caribbean, called it "aji", and brought it to Spain in 1514. It reached India in 1611 through the Portuguese, and from there it spread to southern and western Asia. The date of its arrival to the Middle East is unknown. In Iraq food is generally mild but people in the southern region tend to like their food spicier and hotter. The so called Hungarian **paprika,** and referred to as Turkish pepper in Hungarian cookbooks, was in fact originally brought to Hungary by the Muslim Turks during the Ottoman rule. Use paprika whenever you want to add less heat but more flavor and color to your dish.

Cilantro (*kizbara Kdadhra*) also referred to as **green coriander** or **fresh coriander**, almost looks like Italian flat-leafed parsley, but it has a different, more pungent flavor. Use it sparingly, otherwise it will overpower the rest of the seasonings in the dish. It can be substituted with parsley, if wished.

Citric Acid (*lemon doozy*) is used sometimes as a substitute for lemon juice, mainly because fresh lemon juice in Iraq is mostly available in wintertime. However, at a place where lemon juice is available year round, by all means use lemon juice except where the recipe specifically calls for citric acid. **Unsweetened lemonade powder,** such as Kool-Aid can be used as a substitute for citric acid and lemon juice especially when added liquid to the dish is not desirable.

Clarified Butter: see **Ghee**

Coriander (*kizbara*) comes in two forms: green leaves and seeds, and they have a completely different aroma and appearance. The green leaves are also called **cilantro**. The seeds can be used whole or ground according to recipe directions. The ancients used coriander extensively in their cooking and in the Akkadian it was known as "kisibaru," (cf. the Arabic *kizbara)*.

Cumin (*kammoun*) is a strong aromatic spice whose pungent flavor persists for some time, and is used in seed form or crushed. In the ancient Akkadian it was known as "kamunu" (cf. Arabic *kammoun).*

Curry Powder (*kari*) is a blend of many spices including curry leaves. Madras Curry blend is recommended. However, you can make your own blend. Make it as mild or as hot as you wish it to be. Here is a homemade blend for curry powder:

> Dry toast cumin, pepper corns, coriander, cinnamon, cloves, cardamom, mustard and fenugreek until fragrant, stirring and shaking to prevent them from burning. Cool and grind. Mix them with chilies, turmeric, and ginger.

Dried Lime: see **Noomi Basra**

Farina (or **cream of wheat**) is the meal prepared from nondurum wheat, and is used as a cooked cereal pudding in the West. However, in the Iraqi cuisine, it is an important binding substitute ingredient in making the stuffed bulgar dough known as *Kubba*. The ingredient actually used in Iraq is *jareash*, which is crushed grain or grits of grain. Farina is the best substitute.

Fava Beans (also called **broad beans**) is known as *bagilla* in the Iraqi dialect, and is called *fool* in other Arab countries. Fava beans available in Iraq are much bigger than the ones consumed in the rest of the Arab countries. The fresh young pods are cooked either whole or cut into smaller pieces and used in appetizers and stews. As the outer skin toughens towards the end of summer, only the beans are used, the outer skin is discarded. Some of the recipes will sometimes require removing the bean skin. In this case, when buying these beans look for big pods that have a soft and leathery texture, which are signs of full growth. When out of season frozen or dried fava beans are used. Dried skinned beans are also available at gourmet shops. Dry beans require about 24 hours of soaking. 1/2 cup dry beans yields 1 cup cooked beans.

Fenugreek (*Halba*) are seeds used as seasoning, the strong aroma of which is similar to that of celery. In form they are fawn-colored three-sided seeds. Uncooked and untoasted, they rather taste bitter, and astringent. Toasting will bring out their aroma. Fresh green fenugreek is sold as an herb in bunches. Use only the small green leaves and discard the stalks because they impart bitterness to the dish. The Arabs valued it for its medicinal qualities. Ancient doctors used to say, if people knew its benefits, they would have bought its weight with gold.

Feta cheese is used as a substitute for the local Iraqi white cheese, and the *halloum* cheese. It is a semi soft salty white cheese usually made from goats', or sheep's milk. It will stay fresh longer if stored in salted water (1 tablespoon salt for each quart water), to which may be added a few seeds of **nigella seeds** for freshness.

Fillo or **phyllo** dough are paper-thin sheets of dough used instead of homemade dough to make sweet and savory pastries.

Garbanzo beans (*Hummus*). See **chickpeas**.

Ghee (*dihin hur*) is clarified butter used a lot in traditional general cooking, but especially pastries like baklawa. It is pure butter fat, i.e. without any of the traces of water, milk, and sugars that fresh butter contains. The practice of clarifying butter goes back to ancient Mesopotamian times. It prevented their butter from getting rancid quickly especially in hot weather. To make it heat butter gently until it melts and foams. Reduce heat to low and let it simmer, until foam subsides and sediments brown a little and sink to the bottom of the pot. You need to watch it at this stage to prevent sediments from burning. The clarified butter will have a lovely nutty flavor. Strain using a fine sieve. I do not throw away the sediments but add them to cookie dough or cake batters to add some buttery nutty taste to my pastries. One cup of butter will yield 3/4 cup clarified butter.

The Magical powers of Olive Oil and Beer

Besides animal fat, vegetarian oils were quite common in ancient Mesopotamia. Olive oil in particular was deemed valuable due to its healing powers. Edward Chiera in his amusing book *They wrote on Clay* proclaims that "it is a fact that olive oil mixed with

beer was the ancient predecessor of our oil shampoos and alcoholic massage as a remedy for baldness. And few are aware that our prescription of warm oil for earache was anticipated twenty-five hundred years ago by the Assyrians" (151).

Beer also was valued for its medicinal powers. Back in the Sumerian times a preparation was given to cure some ailment. The instructions were to pulverize pears and roots of the manna plant, and to mix them with beer and let the sick person drink it.

Ginger (*zanjabeel*) is an ancient spice that has a warm aroma and taste. The Arabs transmitted it to Spain during the medieval times. In Iraq it is available in its dried form only, and is usually used in blends of spices and curry powders. The whole dried roots may be used in pickling.

Grape leaves are used in the famous *dolma* dish. In countries or regions where grapes grow, grape leaves are used fresh. The best way to prepare fresh leaves is to wash the leaves and stack them in a rather deep metal or glass dish. Pour boiling water to cover them and set aside for about 30 minutes. The leaves will change color. Strain and use as directed, or freeze for future use. To thaw immerse in hot water, until all ice melts, and strain. Canned grape leaves kept in brine can also be used. However, make sure to get rid of salt by immersing the leaves for a while in water. Repeat until you get rid of all the salt. Drape leaves on the sides of a colander to drain.

Hummus: see **chickpeas**

Juniper Berries (*'ar'ar*) are the size of small peas, and have a pleasant bitter-sweet aroma. They leave a slight burning sensation in the mouth. It was one of the spices used in ancient Mesopotamian cooking, and it is also included in some of the meat dishes given in the medieval Baghdadi cookbooks.

Kishk is dough made of bulgar and yogurt, cut into pieces and dried. It is then used as needed, for the preparation of some healthy dishes such as soups mostly cooked in northern Iraq.

Knafa is shredded dough usually bought ready made like fillo dough. The packages available in the markets might sometimes carry the name "kataifi" but in fact it is what is more commonly known in the Arab world as *kunafa*.

Lemon Douzy: see **citric acid**

Lemon Omani: see *noomi Basrah*

Lemonade Powder: see **citric acid**

Lentils (*adas*) is a legume widely used in the entire Middle-Eastern region ever since ancient times, and was brought to the Americas by the Spanish missionaries. The Arabic word for lentils gave its name to the word meaning lenses in Arabic, which is *adasa* (the Latin form of "lense" was also derived from "lentils"). It is a delicious source of protein, high in fiber, complex carbohydrates and nutrients, and low in calories and fat. Lentils come in different colors. There are brown whole lentils (with the shell on), green whole lentils (with the shell on), and a smaller variety of green lentils referred to as French lentils. The **red lentils** are shelled, and are frequently used in soups, for they cook faster and disintegrate more easily. The red lentils actually come in different hues: orange, yellowish orange, and lemony yellow, but they all taste the same. It is better to soak whole lentils before cooking them, whereas red lentils can be used unsoaked. Soaking them for 30 minutes; however, will cut down cooking time considerably.

Liquorice in the Akkadian was called "susu" (cf. Arabic *soos*). It was eaten by the kings of Assyria, and used as an herbal medicine. Historians tell us that Cleopatra used it to enhance her beauty. Nowadays it is sold as a refreshing drink believed to have rejuvenating properties. It also makes a very delicious tea.

Mahleb is the aromatic kernel of the black cherry pits. The scientific name is "prunus mahaleb" It is a small beige-colored oval seed, used ground mainly to flavor breads and pastries. The seeds are soft and have a nutty chewy texture to them. They taste a little bitter and sour when tried by themselves.

Mastic (*mastaki*) is a resin from a Mediterranean evergreen tree, also known as "gum Arabic." It is widely used in making chewing gum, incense, varnish, and for flavoring liquors, pastries and desserts. In the medieval times it was used in meat dishes and stews, as well. Since mastic tends to melt rather than dissolve into the food, it is advisable to pulverize the translucent light-yellow lumps before adding them. It also comes in the form of cream much like marshmallow cream, and this variety is good for dessert only because it has sugar in it.

Mint (*ni'na'*) is an ancient herb known as "ninu" in the ancient Akkadian. Its cool refreshing flavor is a staple in the Middle-Eastern cooking in general. Other herbs belonging to the mint family are also used, such as *rihaan*, which is like basil but more fragrant, and is eaten as a salad green. The other kind is *butnij*. The herb under this very name was mentioned al-Warraq's tenth century AD cookbook (119). It is also known as *habak* in some Arab countries. In Iraq *butnij* is dried and crushed, and is rarely eaten raw. In the United States I have seen it grows along creeks and river banks, and hence the name "wild mint" or "river mint." Folklore has it if you want to drive away snakes, grow this herb around the house. Indeed so legendary is the enmity between the snake and this herb is that if the chemistry between two persons does not work at all, people would say they are *mithil al-hayya wal butnij* (like the snake and *butnij*). If *butnij* is hard to find, it might be substituted with regular mint.

Mung beans (*mash*) are small, olive-green, rounded legume. In the Iraqi cuisine they are used whole and unshelled. The Chinese use them for sprouting because they grow fast. Mung beans have an exceptionally high vitamin A content for a legume, and vitamin B and a little C. These beans are to be soaked overnight before cooking. One cup unsoaked mung beans will yield 2 1/2 cups soaked beans.

Nigella seeds (*habbat soda*) are sometimes referred to as "black cumin." The seeds are black, and are the size of sesame. They do not have a strong aroma, but they are valued for their nutty and rather sharp taste especially in breads. They are also believed to be good for the digestion. It is a good idea to dry toast them to bring out their aroma.

Noomi Basrah **(dried lime, or lemon Omani)** is used to give a pleasant tang to some of the dishes and to make delicious tea. It may be substituted with lime juice (**1 tablespoon lime juice and 1 teaspoon grated lime rind for each dried lime**). However, the genuine dried limes will give the dish a distinguished aroma and taste. They are naturally dried on trees, and are imported from India and Oman through the port city of Basrah in southern Iraq, and hence the name *noomi Basrah*. Some of the recipes call for whole ones. In this case they should be pricked with a pointed knife to allow cooking juices to penetrate. They can also be used crushed or ground (**referred to in the recipes as prepared n*oomi Basrah***). Remember to remove the seeds before grinding since they tend to add a bitter aftertaste to it. Dried limes are available in Middle-Eastern shops and the International isles in some of the major supermarkets. However, you can make your own dried limes by bringing the small round variety of limes to a full boil in some salted water for 5 minutes. Then dry them in a ventilated container such as a wicker basket, in a sunny or warm dry place for a few weeks. They should turn brown and sound hollow.

Nutmeg (*joz al-teab*, or *joz bawwa*) is the kernel of the seed of a large evergreen tree native to Indonesia. The lacy growth on the seed is called mace. Indians and Arabs valued the spice as a medicine for digestive disorders, and to treat liver and skin complaints. Mace and nutmeg are similar in aroma and taste. The aroma they give is rich, fresh and warm. Nutmeg is basically added to meat dishes and some pastries.

Orange-blossom water (*ma' al-zahar*) is distilled liquid from orange blossoms used mainly to flavor desserts and pastries.

Pomegranate syrup (*dibs al-rumman*) also called pomegranate molasses or concentrate. A recipe for making this syrup is included in al-Warraq's tenth-century Baghdadi cookbook. It calls for reducing the pomegranate juice by boiling it down, until of syrupy consistency). The finished product is fruity and tangy, and is used in cooking for the pleasant acidity it gives to the dish. It is available at Middle-Eastern shops, and a bottle would go a long way, since it is used sparingly. Keep bottle refrigerated after opening it.

A substitute for pomegranate syrup:

1/2 cup tomato juice
Juice of one lemon or lime
1 tablespoon brown sugar

Mix and use as directed in the recipes.

Poppy Seeds (*khishkhash*) have a slightly sweet, pleasant, and nutty taste. Roasting the seeds would extenuate their aroma. They come from the opium poppy plant known and used ever since antiquity. The plant contains compounds from which morphine and codeine are extracted, but these compounds are not present in the ripe dried seeds used for cooking. It is believed to have a valuable medicinal value. In a-Warraq's tenth-century cookbook, a recipe is given for curing chest pain and coughs. It is prepared by boiling poppy seeds, then straining them. The resulting liquid, mixed with some honey, is boiled down to syrup (312).

Quamar al-deen is apricot pureed, dried and then made into thin sheets that are folded or rolled up. It is sweet and sour and chewy in texture, similar to what is known in the West as **apricot leather**. It is eaten by itself as a snack, or made into delicious drink or ice cream.

Rashi: see **tahini paste**.

Rice Flour is ground rice, white or brown, available at supermarkets, and used as a thickening agent in cooking, or for making dessert and *kubba*.

Rihaan is sweet basil. In the Iraqi cuisine it is consumed uncooked as a salad green.

Rose Water (*may warid*) is one of the earliest distilled liquids made from the petals of what is known as "Damask roses." Although roses grew in the ancient Mesopotamian gardens, it is believed that the dried flowers used to be imported from Persia, and were made into rose water in the ancient temples. Like the orange-blossom water, rose water is nowadays mainly used to flavor desserts and pastries.

Saffron (*za'faran*) is the dried, thread-like, red-orange and sometimes yellow stigmas of the blue-violet, lily-shaped flowers. The deeper the color of the stigmas is the better quality saffron is. It was known ever since antiquity in Mesopotamia as well as the surrounding areas. It was used in food, wines, as a dye, in perfumes, and as a medicinal drug. In the Akkadian it was called "azupiranu" from which the Arabic *za'faran* was borrowed. Around the eighth century AD, the Arabs transported it to Spain. It is one of the most expensive spices in the world, almost ten times as much as vanilla, because its stigmas are very light and are handpicked. About 20,000 stigmas will produce only 4 ounces of saffron.

Saffron can be used ground, but it should be mixed well with other liquid ingredients to distribute its flavor evenly. However it is better to buy whole saffron threads and grind them yourself, since ground saffron could be adulterated very easily by mixing it with turmeric or other additives. Saffron should not be confused with safflower, which is sometimes referred to as bastard saffron. Safflower is cultivated in China, the Middle East and Mexico. Its color is more regularly orange than saffron, and it is much cheaper. It will make the food yellow but it has no flavor. Spanish saffron is of excellent quality and is widely available. However, the deep-red Kashmiri saffron is the best.

Saffron has a very distinctive flavor and should be used sparingly. A small amount goes a long way. It was used more often in the past than nowadays. For even coloring and economic use soak the stigmas briefly in a little hot water and add to the dish. Avoid adding it to hot oil for it will lose its color, and will not impart its flavor to the food. **Turmeric** can be conveniently used as a substitute for saffron in meat and rice dishes, potatoes and chickpeas.

Salep (*sahlep*) is a starchy stone-colored powder ground from the dried roots of various species of Old World orchids called orchis mascula. It is also called the "fox's testicles" or 'the brother killer," because it grows out of two tubercles, one of which will live at the expenss of the other. Like cornstarch, it is used as a thickening agent especially for making ice cream. But it is more powerful than cornstarch, and unlike the latter it does not have a starchy after taste when undercooked. About 50% of it is a gluey substance. See also "**arrowroot.**"

The Salt of Life

As evident from the ancient Mesopotamian economic texts, salt was one of the staples of their diet. In the Akkadian it was called "tabti" which means "good". In their food-lists it was sometimes referred to as a "brick of salt", but apparently it also came in other forms such as a "mass of salt", "crystal of salt", "salt stone", and there is also "me tabti" which could be salt water or brine. It must have been an essential item for normal human maintenance for it always made an important item in the food allowances that the government used to give out to its subjects. It was very cheap, and was sold by special salt dealers. While traveling it was kept in "salt bags", and at home it was kept in "salt cellars", or in a special "box for salt and mustard" and used as a condiment. Salt was also used for preservation. A letter written around the first millenium BC declared that "the meat which has been sent to you, was put in salt."

In their religious incantations salt was repeatedly mentioned, such as, "May her tongue be salt." Another incantation incidentally stresses its importance, "You, salt, who are born in a bright spot…, without you no meal in the temple is prepared. Without you, god, king, lord, and noble do not enjoy a sacrifice."

Salt also acquired an ethically symbolic significance. If an Assyrian said about a person "he is the man of my salt," he meant, "he is my friend."
(Levey, 170-1)

Semolina (*samead*). The word "semolina" is derived from the Latin "simila," which means fine flour. Ultimately the word goes back in origin to the Akkadian "samidu," which was a type of groats. Nowadays semolina is granular flour made from durum wheat, a variety of hard wheat with the bran and germ removed. It is rather yellowish in color, and its texture is similar to that of finely ground cornmeal. Like cornmeal, it can be sprinkled on the work surface to keep rising dough from sticking. Various grades are available, ranging from fine to coarse. Fine semolina is used to make puddings and pastas, while the coarser grades are good for giving crumbly texture to cake mixtures.

Sesame Seeds (*simsim*). Etymologically, the word "sesame" is related to the Akkadian "samassammu", from which the Arabic *simsim* was derived. In ancient Mesopotamia, sesame was an important source of oil, and this became a staple of their diet to the extent that in the Old Babylonian period commercialized production of sesame was one of the economic mainstays of the palace administration. Sesame was immortalized in the *Arabian Nights* story of "Ali Baba and the Forty Thieves." Interestingly, the gang's command "open sesame" may suggest the way sesame pods suddenly burst open when they ripen, scattering the seeds all around the place. Throughout the world sesame seeds are used with breads and pastries. In the Arab world it is also used in making the popular candy, *simsimiyya*. Ever since ancient times the Mesopotamians have exploited the possibilities of sesame seeds to the full. The seeds were used with pastries, and sesame oil was used for general cooking purposes, especially frying. It is also ground to make what is known in the rest of the Arab countries as *tahini*, derived from the Arabic source verb "to grind." In Iraq ground sesame is called *rashi*, and there are many references to it in the thirteenth century Baghdadi cookbook.

Sumac is the red, tart berry of a bush that has been growing wild, and has been used in the Middle East ever since ancient times. It should not be confused with the poisonous sumac trees of North America. The berries are dried and used whole or ground as a seasoning or a souring agent. Only the husk is used, though, for the seed are too hard to eat. *Sumac* is not prized for its aroma as much as for the fruity and pleasantly sour taste, believed to have the power to enhance and excite the appetite. It is not well known in the West, and is only available in Middle Eastern shops. Ground *sumac* husk is tossed with raw sliced onions, and is especially good in meat dishes like *Kebab* and *Kufta*. When *sumac* is used as a souring agent instead of lemon juice, whole berries are used. They are cracked and soaked in hot water for about 30 minutes, then strained very well. The resulting reddish juice will be added to the dish, and strained berries are discarded. *Sumac* is also an important ingredient in **Za'tar**.

Tahini Paste (*rashi*) is a smooth thin paste made from toasted ground sesame seeds. It is an important ingredient in the well-known dip "Humus." It is also used in sauces for sandwiches, and in making the "tahini halva." In Iraq, the best tahini can be purchased freshly ground from *Tell Keif* (the hill of merriment) in northern Iraq, about seven miles north of Mosul (Ancient Nineveh). There you can see tahini oozing out of the pressing machine, and the delightful aroma of toasted sesame is everywhere. The area is also a very nice picnic spot, where the grain fields stretch as far as the eyes can see, and colorful wild flowers cover the hills like precious carpets.

Tamarind (*tamur Hindi* =Indian dates) is the dark brown, bean-shaped pod of the tamarind tree, which has been growing in India for centuries, hence the name *tamur Hindi*. It was popular among the Muslims of the Middle Ages, and was valued for its thirst quenching qualities. The Spanish transmitted it to the West Indies. It is sold either in sticky partially dried brown blocks of broken pods and pulp, or as a concentrate or syrup. The whole pods are sometimes available in major grocery supermarkets. Tamarind is used as a souring agent like lime or lemon. It has a slightly molassy aroma, and a pleasantly sour and fruity taste. To use the fibrous blocks of tamarind, soak amount needed in hot water for about 30 minutes then rub it between the fingers and strain it to get rid of the fibers.

Tamarind has a strong flavor so it should be used sparingly. It is especially good in curry dishes, and is particularly tasty in fish and meat dishes. It can also be served as a delicious and healthy drink. Medicinally it works as a very gentle, natural laxative. It is said to be rich in vitamins, and is good for the liver and kidneys. In the West it is mostly used commercially in condiments like Worcestershire sauce. If you cannot find tamarind use Worcestershire sauce as a substitute.

Turmeric (*kurkum*) is a bright yellow spice made from the ground dried root-like part of a plant in the ginger family. It has been used in Mesopotamia ever since ancient times, and was recognized as a spice and medicine. In the Akkadian it was called "kurkanu." Modern research shows that the active ingredient in turmeric, curcumine, has anti-inflammatory and anti-cancer properties. Animals given large doses of curcumine developed significantly fewer colon tumors than animals in a control group (*Food and Wine*, June, 1997). Moreover, that same substance has been found to help "ward off Alzheimer's" (*Boston Globe*, "Health and Science, March, 12, 2002).

Marco Polo's comment when he saw it on his travels to China was that it is "a fruit that resembles saffron; though it is actually nothing of the sort, it is quite as good as saffron for practical purposes" (Norman, 35). Apparently it was he who set the tone for its use as a cheap substitute for saffron. It is lightly aromatic and smells fresh of orange and ginger. In taste it is pungent and a little peppery, musky, and bitter, so it is to be used sparingly. Like curry powder, it is traditionally cooked in a little oil with onion or meat, for instance, before mixing it with other ingredients. Thus it becomes more aromatic and loses its bitter taste.

Za'tar is an ancient herb. It was known in the Ancient Akkadian language as "zateru" from which the Arabic word was derived. *Za'tar* is thyme, but it is also a blend the components of which are dried thyme, sumac, toasted sesame seeds, and salt. This blend is often sprinkled on drained yogurt, meat dishes, vegetables, or used as a dip. It is sometimes mixed with olive oil and spread on bread before baking. I especially like to sprinkle it on my tossed salad. The proportions for making it vary from place to place or even from family to family. The following is an acceptable standard:

> **Two parts sesame seeds**
> **One part ground dried thyme**
> **One part ground sumac**
> **A dash of salt**

Dry toast sesame seeds in a skillet or in the oven. Stir frequently since sesame tends to burn quickly. Allow it to cool completely, then mix it with the rest of the ingredients. Keep mixture in an airtight container. It stays fresh longer if kept in the freezer.

The Assyrian Herbal: an Ancient Book of Medicine

The Assyrian Herbal is a hand-stenciled publication, dealing with 660 Assyrian cuneiform tablets that discuss vegetable drugs used to cure the known ailments at the time. Apparently so many herbs and plant extracts were used to the extent that herbs became synonymous with medicine. Campbell Thompson translated these cuneiform tablets into English in 1924. The text includes around 250 species of vegetables, occurring around 4600 times; 120 species of minerals occurring 650 times; and around 180 other unidentified species, to which must be added alcohol, fats, oil, honey, wax and milk. By going through such a rare text, one gets glimpses of what was available at the time in the Mesopotamian "grocery stores." Nearly all the identified objects still grow in the region, and to this day many of the herbs mentioned in the book are still valued for their medicinal properties.

Interesting Tidbits from the Book:
1. Fennel was used as a stomach comforter.
2. Sumac was used to excite the appetite before the meals.
3. Chamomile was used as a stomach medicine.
4. Green juice of licorice was used for "feet that cannot walk", applied to swellings, and the roots were used as a drink for jaundice. Licorice powder was sprinkled on ulcers of the mouth.
5. Thyme was used as a drug for the lungs, to be chewed and drunk for hardness of breathing. It was taken alone or in oil and beer for coughs and for the intestines. Oil of thyme was used for sprains and for decayed teeth. Its smell was said to have the power to revive an epileptic.
6. Pomegranate rind was used to "bind the stomach." It was also ground and mixed with water and used as a dye.
7. A cake of compressed figs was used as an application to a boil. The fig juice was used to wash the stomach.
8. Bitter almonds were recognized as a powerful poison. Confections were flavored with "spirit of almond" or "almond flavor." One of the medicinal values of almond oil was laxative.
9. It was advised that prunes, plums, cherries and quince were to be eaten alone, or with honey and butter. The reason for this was not supplied.
10. Lentil cooked as soup was recommended as a "vegetable for lungs," and was given as a remedy for colds.
11. Turmeric was used as an ointment for eyes, mouth, hands and feet, and was also used for insect bites. As a drink it was recommended for jaundice, and was fumigated for ears and nose.
12. Binj was used as a drug for depression. The Assyrian botanists also knew the narcotic properties of the poppies.
13. Cardamom was prescribed for hollow teeth. Cavities were filled with gum Arabic.
14. Garlic was used as a chew and fumigator for hard and painful breathing.

BIBLIOGRAPHY

An Anonymous Andalusian Cookbook of the 13th Century. Trans. Charles Perry. (Website: davidfriedman.com/Medieval/Medieval.html)

Adeeb, Nazeeha, and Firdos al-Mukhtar. *A Guide to Cooking and Nutrition.* (Arabic) Baghdad, 1971.

Arberry, A.J. "A Baghdad Cookery-book." *Islamic Culture* 13.1 (Jan. 1939): 21-47.

---. "A Baghdad Cookery-book." *Islamic Culture* 13.2 (Apr. 1939): 189-214.

Arndt, Alice. "The Flavors of Arabia." *Aramco World* 39.2 M-A 1988: 33-35.

Al-Baghdadi, Ibn al-Khateeb. *Wasf al-At'ima al-Mu'tada* (description of familiar foods, augmented fourteenth-century manuscript), trans. and Introduction by Charles Perry, 275-465. In *Medieval Arab Cookery.* Prospect Books, 2001.

Basmachi, Faraj. *Treasures of the Iraqi Museum. Baghdad, 1975*

Bottèro, Jean. "The Culinary Tablets at Yale." *Journal of the American Oriental Society*, 107,1 1987: 11-19.

---. "The cuisine of Ancient Mesopotamia." *Biblical Archaeologist.* 48. 1 March 1985: 36-47.

---. *Mesopotamia, Writing, Reasoning and the Gods.* Chicago, 1992.

---. *Mesopotamian Culinary Texts.* Indiana, 1995

Brothwell, Don and Patricia. *Food in Antiquity.* New York, 1969.

Burton, Richard, trans. *The Book of the Thousand Nights and a Night.* London, 1886.

Buren, E. Douglas. "Fish Offerings in Ancient Mesopotamia." *Iraq* 1948-1949: 101-121.

Chiera, Edward. *They Wrote on Clay: The Babylonia Tablets Speak Today.* Chicago, 1932.

Contenau, George. *Everyday Life in Babylon and Assyria.* London, 1954.

Crawford, H. E. W. "Mesopotamia's Invisible Exports in the Third Millenium BC." *World Archaeology* 5, 2 Oct 1973: 232- 41.

Draudt, Susan. *Sourdough Baking.* Tucson, 1994.

Eigeland, Tor. "The Cuisine of Al-Andalus." *Aramco World* 40, 5, S-O. 1989: 28-35.

Ebla to Damascus: Art and Archaeology of Ancient Syria. Smisthonian Institution Traveling Exhibition Service. Washington D.C., 1985.

Ellison, Rosemary. "Diet in Mesopotamia: The Evidence of the Early Barley Ration Texts (c.3000-1400 BC)." *Iraq* 43 1981: 35-45.

---. "Some Food Offerings from Ur, Excavated by Sir Leonard Woolley, and Previously Unpublished." *Journal of Archaeological Science* 1978 5: 167-177.

Fagan, Brian. *Return to Babylon.* Boston, 1976

Fernea, E. W. *Guests of the Sheik.* New York, 1964.

Fisher, M. F. K. *With Bold Knife and Fork.* New York, 1968

Gabriel, Judith. "Among the Norse Tribes." *Aramco World*, Nov./ Dec. 1999: 36- 42.

Gilgamish: Epic of Ancient Babylonia. A rendering in free verse by William E. Leonard. New York, 1934.

Gelder, Geert Jan van. *God's Banquet: Food in Classical Arabic Literature.* New York, 2000

Goodman, Naomi. *The Good Book Cookbook.* Michigan, 1986.

Gordon, Edmund. *Sumerian Proverbs.* Museum of Philadelphia Museum, 1959.

Guthrie, Shirley. *Arab Women in the Middle Ages: Private Lives and Public Roles.* London, 2001.

Al-Hamadani. *Maqamat* (the assemblies, Arabic). Cairo, 1962.

Al-Hariri. *Maqamat* (the assemblies, Arabic) Cairo, 1888.

Al-Hasan, Ahmed, Donald Hill. *Islamic Technology: An Illustrated History.* Cambridge, 1986.

Heffman, Ruth and Helen. *Our Arabian Nights.* New York, 1940.

The History of Herodotus. Trans. George Rowlinson. New York, 1956.

Hunter, Erica. *Cultural Atlas for Young People: First Civilizations*. New York, 1994.

Ingram, Christine, and Shapter, Jennie. *The Cook's Guide to Bread*. London, 1999.

Al-Jahiz. *Al-Bukhala'*. (the misers, Arabic). Introduction by Taha al-Hajiri (editor) Cairo, 1963.

Al-Jawzi. *The Book of Anecdotes and Spiritual Medicine*. (Arabic) Cairo, nd.

Joannes, Francis. "The Social Function of Banquets in the Earliest Civilizations," 33-7. In Albert Sonnenfeld, *Food: A Culinary History from Antiquity to the Present*. (English edition) New ork, 1999.

Kramer, S. Noah. *The Sumerians, their History, Culture, and Character*. Chicago, 1963.

---. *History Begins at Sumer*. Philadelphia, 1956.

Kramer, S. Noah, and the editors of Time-Life Books. *Cradle of Civilization*. New York, 1967.

Lehner, Ernest and Johanna. *Folklore and Odysseys of Food and Medicinal plants*. New York, 1962.

---. *Folklore and Symbolism of Flowers, Plants and Trees*. New York, 1960.

Leonard, J. Norton, and editors of Time-Life books. *The First Farmers*. New York, 1973.

Levey, Martin. *Chemistry and Chemical Technology in Ancient Mesopotamia*. Amsterdam, 1959

Limet, Henri. "The Cuisine of Ancient Sumer." *Biblical Archaeologist* 50, 3 Sept. 1987: 132-140.

Lloyd, Seton. *Ruined Cities of Iraq*. Chicago, 1980

Lowton, John. "Mesopotamian Menus." *Aramco World*. 39, 2 M-A 1988: 4-9

Lunde, Paul, "New World Foods, Old World Diet: Questionable Origins." *Aramco World*. 43, 3 M-J 1992: 48-55.

Mahdi, Muhsen, ed. *Kitab Alf Leila wa Leila* (the book of one thousand and one nights, Arabic). Leiden, 1984.

Marin, Manuela. "Beyond Taste: the Compliments of Color and Smell in the Medieval Arab Culinary Tradition." In *Culinary Cultures of the Middle East*, ed. by Sami Zubeida and Richard Tapper. London, 1994.

Maxwell, Gevin. *People of the Reeds*. New York, 1957.

McIntire, Anne. *Flower Power*. New York, 1996.

Mieroop, De Marc Van. *The Ancient Mesopotamian City*. Oxford, 1997

Moor, Janny. "Eating Out in the Ancient Near East." *Oxford Symposium of Food and Cookery*, 1991: 213-219.

Al-Mousawi, Muhsen. *Mujtama' Alf Layla wa Layla* (society in the book of *The Arabian Nights*, Arabic). Tunis, 2000

Nemet-Nejat, Karen Rhea. *Daily Life in Ancient Mesopotamia*. Forte Wayne, 1998

Nickles, Henry, and the editors of Time-Life Books. *Middle Eastern Cooking*. New York, 1969.

Norman, Jill. *The Complete Book of Spices: A Practical Guide to Spices and Aromatic Seeds*. New York, 1990.

Oppenheim, A. Leo. *Ancient Mesopotamia: Portrait of a Dead Civilization*. Chicago, 1964.

---. *Letters from Mesopotamia*. Chicago, 1967.

Perry, Charles. "Buran: Eleven Hundred Years in the History of A Dish," 241-50. In *Medieval Cookery*. Prospect Books, 2001.

---. "*Kitab al-Tibakhah*: A 15th-century cookbook." *PPC*. 21, Nov. 1985: 17-22.

---. "Notes on Persian Pasta," 253-5. In *Medieval Arab Cookery*. Prospect Books, 2001.

---. "The Sals of the Infidels," 499-502. In *Medieval Arab Cookery*. Prospect Books, 2001

---. "A Thousand and One 'Fritters': The Food of The Arabian Nights," 489-96. In *Medieval Arab Cookery*. Prospect Books, 2001.

---. "What to Order in Ninth Century Baghdad." *Oxford Symposium of Food and Cookery*, 1991: 231-233.

Postage, J. N. *Early Mesopotamia: Society and Economy at the Dawn of History*. New York, 1992.

Pritchard, James, ed. *The Ancient Near East: An Anthology of Texts and Pictures.* Princeton, 1954.

Al-Qurawi, Ibrahim. *Social Classes in Baghdad during the Early Abbasid Period.* (Arabic) Alexandria, 1989.

Roden, Claudia. "Middle Eastern Cooking: The Legacy". *Aramco World.* 39, 2 M-A 1988: 2-3.

Rodinson, Maxime, "Ma'muniya East and West," tans.by Barbara Inskip, 185-97. In *Medieval Arab Cookery.* Prospect Books, 2001.

---. "Romania and Other Arabic Words in Italian," trans. by Barbara Inskip, 165-82. In *Medieval Arab Cookery.* Prospect Books, 2001.

---. "Studies in ArabicManuscripts Relating to Cookery," trans. by Barbara Inskip, 91-163. In *Medieval Arab Cookery.* Prospect Books, 2001.

---. "Venice, the Spice Trade and Eastern Influences in European Cooking," trans by Paul James, 199-215. In *Medieval Arab Cookery.* Prospect Books, 2001

Rosenberger, Bernard. "Arab Cuisine and its Contribution to European Culture," 207-23. In Albert Sonnenfeld, *Food: A Culinary History from Antiquity to the Present.* (English edition) New York, 1999.

Rosi, Pierre. *The Land of the New River.* Paris, 1980.

Roux, Georges. *Ancient Iraq.* New York, 1964.

Rowland, Joan. *Good Food from the Near East.* New York, 1950.

Saggs, H. W. *The Greatness that was Babylon.* New York, 1962.

---. *The Might that was Assyria.* London, 1984

Severy, Merle. "Iraq: Crucible of Civilization." *National Geographic.* 179, 5 May 1991: 102-115.

Tannahill, Reay. *Food in History.* New York, 1973.

Al-Tanukhi. *The Table-Talk of a Mesopotamian Judge.* Trans. D. Margolouth. London, 1922.

Al-Tawheedi, Abu-Hayyan. *Al-Risala al Baghdadiyya* (the Baghdadi tract, Arabic), ed. Abboud al-Shalchi. Beirut, 1997.

Teta, Jon A. *Iraq in Pictures.* New York, 1971.

Thompson, Campbell. *The Assyrian Herbal.* London, 1924.

Trager, James. *The Food Chronology.* New York, 1995

Al-Tujibi, Ibn Razin. *Fidalat al-Khiwan fi Tayyibat al-Ta'am wal-Alwan* (the superfluity of food). Published in *La cuisine andalou-marocaine au xiii-e siècle* by Muhammed Benchekroun.

Al-Warraq, Ibn Sayyar. *Kitab Al-Tabikh.* Ed. Kaj Ohrnberg and Sahban Mroueh. *Studia Orientalia.* The Finnish Oriental Society 60, Helsinki, 1987.

Waines, David, *In a Caliph's Kitchen.* London, 1989.

Wason, Betty. *Cooks, Gluttons and Gourmets: A History of Cookery.* New York, 1962.

Wellard, James. *By the Waters of Babylon.* London, 1972.

Wood, Michael. *Legacy: The Search for Ancient Cultures.* New York, 1992.

Wright, Clifford. *A Mediterranean Feast.* New York, 1999.

Zalzala, Muhammad. *Qusas al-Amthal al-'Ammiya* (Proverbial Anecdotes in the Iraqi Vernacular, Arabic) 3 vols. Beirut, 1986. English Translation by Nawal Nasrallah

Zettler, Richard, Lee Horne. *Treasures from the Royal Tombs of Ur.* University of Pennsylvania Museum, 1998

Al-Zubeidi, M. Hussein. *Economic and Social Life in Kufa in the First Century Hijri.* (Arabic) Cairo, 1970.

Index

(Note: In addition to the following INDEX a list of recipes is also provided at the beginning of each chapter)

About the Book

"A monument to energy, knowledge and enthusiasm. It is an account of origins and development as well as of the complex ethnic make-up of present-day Iraq."

-Tom Jaine, *Petits Propos Culinaires*

****

"This book is not just an introduction, but a thorough overview of a diverse, delicious and enduring cuisine."

-Alice Arndt, *Saudi Aramco World*

****

"*Delights from the Garden of Eden* is a project of meticulous and thorough research. Not only Iraqis will be proud of Nawal's achievement in presenting information, known in the main only to specialized Assyriologists and anthropologists, in such an accessible and easy-to-read volume.

Thank you Nawal, for introducing this rich cuisine to anglophone readers. The dishes we've cooked so far have tasted delicious."

-Margaret Obank, *Banipal*

****

"A culinary odyssey through 8,000 years of Mesopotamian culture and some of the world's oldest recipes, preserved on 3,700-year old cuneiform tablets."

-Ralph Blumenthal, *New York Times*

****

"There are over 400 recipes, and the ones I have tried are wonderful. But although the recipes are in a way the main point of a cookbook, in another way they are here a mere vehicle for the stories, the food lore, the proverbs, the poetry, the word play and the sociological tidbits that Nasrallah has to share."

-Christine Barbour, *Herald Times* of Bloomington, IN

******

About the Author

Nawal Nasrallah, a native of Iraq, was a university professor at Baghdad and Mosul universities, teaching English and American Literature, 1977-90.

The author is a member of the Culinary Historians of Boston, and gave lectures, presentations and demonstrations on the ancient Mesopotamian and medieval Baghdadi cuisine, as well as modern Iraqi cooking in Indiana, Boston and New York.

Nasrallah produced a television program entitled "Baking with the Ancient Mesopotamians and Much more" on the ancient Sumerian flat *tannour* bread which is still cooking today.

Nasrallah won second-place prize for "Milk on the Menu" cooking contest arranged by *Gourmet Magazine*, February 1997, and won first prize of the 1998 annual Holiday Cookie Bake-off in Bloomington, Indiana.

Delights from the Garden of Eden earned Honorable Mention in the Writer's Digest 11th Annual International Self-Published Book Award. One of the recipes in the book was chosen to be included in *The Best American Recipes* 2004-2005 (Houghton Mifflin), which showcases the outstanding recipes of the year.

To contact author:
E-mail: nnasrallah@iraqicookbook.com

About the Front and Back cover

Front cover painting by Ismail al-Sheikly, 1924-2001. Permission, Altomas.
Back cover dishes clockwise from top left: (photographs, Nawal Nasrallah)

1. *Kubbat Halab*, 321
2. *Churek*, 88
3. *Khubuz al-Tannour*, 63
4. *Kubbat Mosul*, 327
5. *Masgoug*, 385
6. *Margat Bamya*, 210
7. *Tea and Ka'ak, 536*
8. *Kleicha,*526
9. *Znoud al-Sit*, 489
10. *Parda Palau*, 254

Arabic Calligraphy on spine by Shakir Mustafa. It is a saying traditionally attributed to al-Hasan bin Ali bin Abi-Talib, one of the prophet Muhammad's grandsons:

Sit at dinner tables and socialize as long as you can for these are the bonus times of your lives

Printed in the United States
31030LVS00001B/38

9 781403 347930